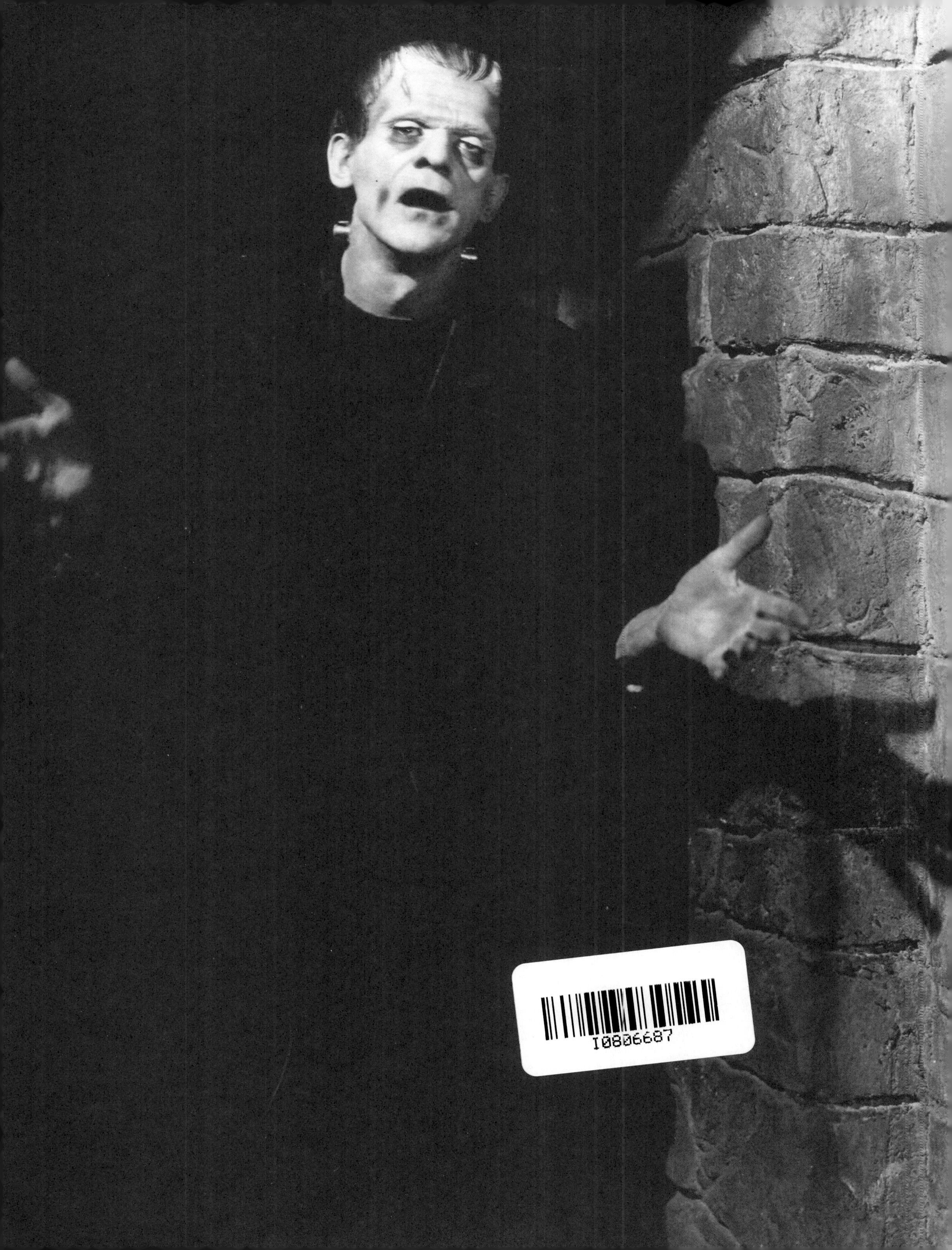

0040826

Graphic Horror
MOVIE MONSTER
MEMORIES

Schiffer Publishing Ltd

4880 Lower Valley Road • Atglen, PA 19310

Graphic

MOVIE

MEM

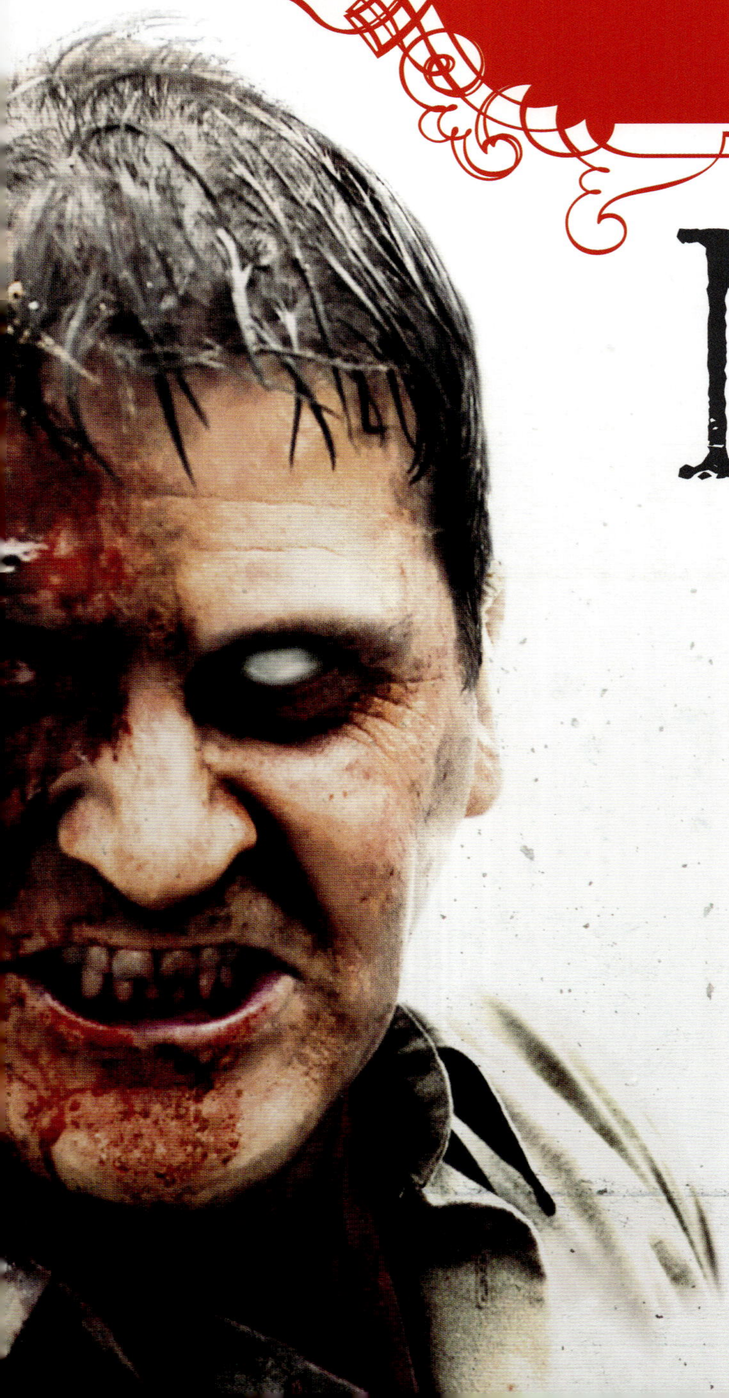

EDITED BY
JOHN EDGAR BROWNING

FOREWORD BY
David J. Skal

AFTERWORD BY
Chelsea Quinn Yarbro

Horror

MONSTER

ORIES

COMMENTARY BY (ALPHABETICALLY)

Glennis Byron
Ramsey Campbell
Mort Castle
L. Andrew Cooper
Pete Crowther
David Drake
Donald Glut
Rosemary Ellen Guiley
Richard J. Hand
Steffen Hantke
Maurice Hindle
Peter Hutchings
Marvin Kaye
Nancy Kilpatrick
(a.k.a. Amarantha Knight)
Leslie Klinger
Elizabeth Miller
Robert Morrish
Cemetery Dance Magazine, Editor
John Kenneth Muir
Kim Paffenroth
Caroline Joan (Kay) Picart
Katherine Ramsland
Philip J. Riley
Carol A. Senf
David J. Skal
Brian Stableford
Dacre Stoker
Jesse Stommel
Tony Timpone
Fangoria, Editor Emeritus
[1987-2010]
Bev Vincent
Gregory A. Waller
F. Paul Wilson
Jeanne Keyes Youngson
The Vampire Empire,
President and Founder [1965-]

Library of Congress Control Number: 2012932400

Designed by Justin Watkinson
Cover by Bruce Waters
Type set in Viner Hand ITC/Trebuchet MS

ISBN: 978-0-7643-4082-6
Printed in China

Schiffer Books are available at special discounts for bulk purchases for sales promotions or premiums. Special editions, including personalized covers, corporate imprints, and excerpts can be created in large quantities for special needs. For more information contact the publisher:

Published by Schiffer Publishing Ltd.
4880 Lower Valley Road
Atglen, PA 19310
Phone: (610) 593-1777; Fax: (610) 593-2002
E-mail: Info@schifferbooks.com

For the largest selection of fine reference books on this and related subjects, please visit our website at
www.schifferbooks.com
We are always looking for people to write books on new and related subjects. If you have an idea for a book, please contact us at
proposals@schifferbooks.com

This book may be purchased
from the publisher.
Please try your bookstore first.
You may write for a free catalog.

In Europe, Schiffer books
are distributed by
Bushwood Books
6 Marksbury Ave.
Kew Gardens
Surrey TW9 4JF England
Phone: 44 (0) 20 8392 8585; Fax: 44 (0) 20 8392 9876
E-mail: info@bushwoodbooks.co.uk
Website: www.bushwoodbooks.co.uk

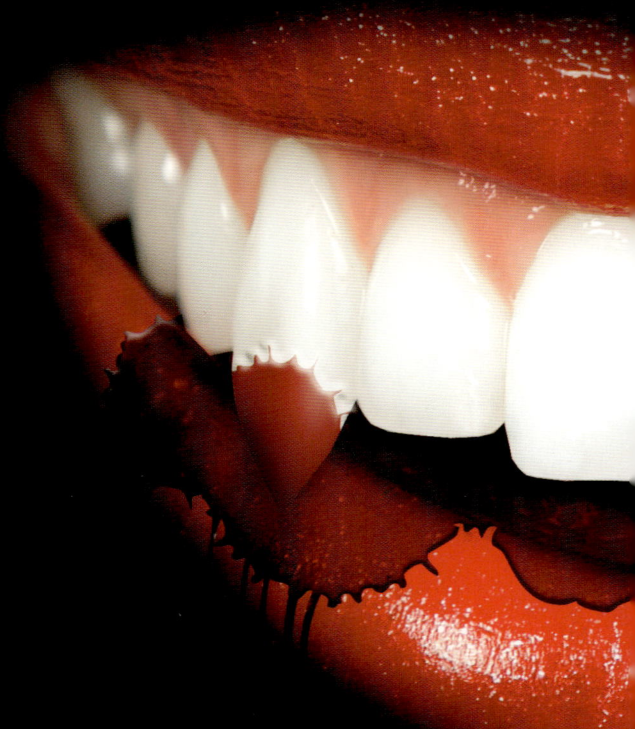

IN MEMORY OF

Martin H. Greenberg

(1941-2011)

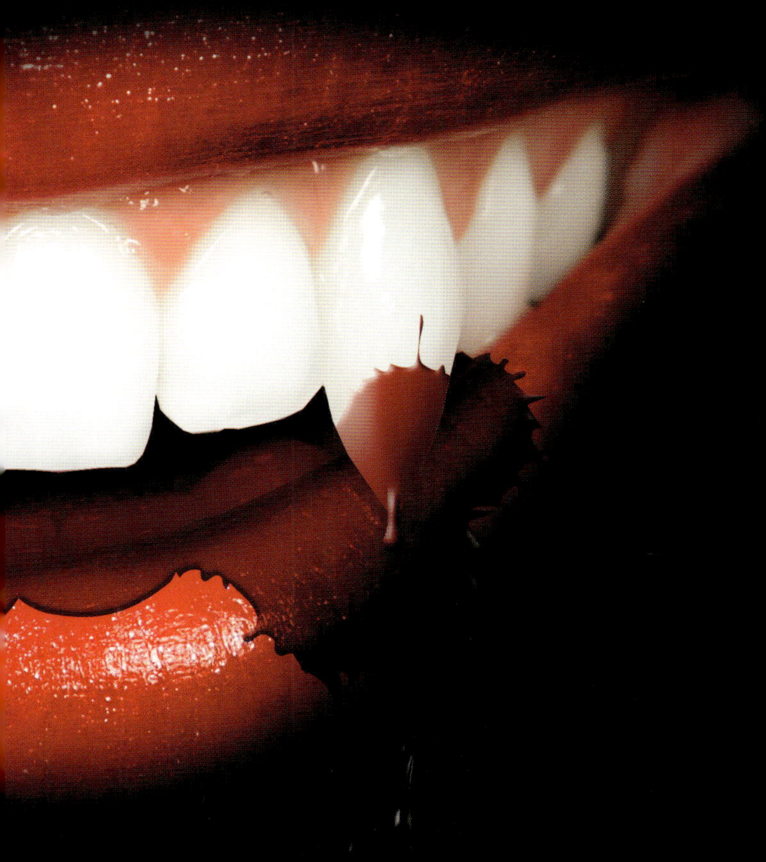

ACKNOWLEDGMENTS

My initial outline for this book called for concisely written histories to accompany the illustrations, providing what I hoped would be a sort of introductory guide to the meaning and importance of these films as cultural artifacts by emphasizing their historical background and international currency. In lieu of this approach, however, I have chosen instead to commission seasoned, as well as aspiring horror fiction writers, editors, and anthologists of horror and fantasy, and academic scholars who treat the subject of horror. They include (alphabetically) along with their website information:

Glennis Byron (http://www.english.stir.ac.uk/staff/glennis-byron/index.php)
Ramsey Campbell (http://www.ramseycampbell.com/)
Mort Castle (http://mortwrites.freeservers.com/)
L. Andrew Cooper (http://www.lcc.gatech.edu/cooper/)
Pete Crowther (http://www.pspublishing.co.uk/)
David Drake (http://david-drake.com/)
Donald Glut (http://www.donaldfglut.com/)
Rosemary Ellen Guiley (http://www.visionaryliving.com/)
Richard J. Hand (http://drama.research.glam.ac.uk/rhand/
Steffen Hantke (http://hompi.sogang.ac.kr/america/menu_a/05_pf3.htm)
Maurice Hindle (http://www.mauricehindle.com/)
Peter Hutchings (http://www.northumbria.ac.uk/sd/academic/sass/about/arts/staff/p_hutchings/)
Marvin Kaye (http://www.marvinkaye.com/; http://spaceandtimemagazine.com/wp/marvin-kayes-nth-dimension/)
Nancy Kilpatrick (http://www.sff.net/people/nancyk/)
Leslie Klinger (http://www.lesliesklinger.com/index.html)
Elizabeth Miller (http://www.ucs.mun.ca/emiller/)
Robert Morrish (http://www.cemeterydance.com/)
John Kenneth Muir (http://www.johnkennethmuir.com/)
Kim Paffenroth (http://gotld.blogspot.com/; http://www.iona.edu/academic/artsscience/departments/religion/faculty/kpaffenroth.cfm)
Caroline Joan (Kay) Picart (http://www.carolinekaypicart.com/)
Katherine Ramsland (http://www.katherineramsland.com/)
Philip J. Riley (http://www.amazon.com/Philip-J.-Riley/e/B0032F140U)
Carol A. Senf (http://www.iac.gatech.edu/faculty-and-staff/faculty/bio/senf)
Brian Stableford (http://www.isfdb.org/cgi-bin/ea.cgi?Brian_Stableford)
Dacre Stoker (http://www.draculatheun-dead.com/)
Jesse Stommel (http://www.jessestommel.com/Home/Home.html)
Tony Timpone (http://fangoria.com/index.php?option=com_content&view=article&id=3187&Itemid=236)
Bev Vincent (http://www.bevvincent.com/)
Gregory A. Waller (http://www.indiana.edu/cmcl/faculty/waller.shtml)
F. Paul Wilson (http://www.repairmanjack.com/)
Jeanne Keyes Youngson (http://www.benecke.com/stoker.html)

These fine people have generously supplied the commentary included herein, and their doing so has made the present volume a thousand times more enjoyable and valuable for readers. Also deserving of thanks are my esteemed friend David J. Skal and the truly great Chelsea Quinn Yarbro, who supplied the Foreword and Afterword, respectively. Finally, this volume would be entirely impossible without the fine studios and distributors whose films and images are chronicled in these pages.

CONTENTS

F FOREWORD

THANKS FOR THE MAMMARIES; OR, THE MERCHANTS OF MENACE

David J. Skal

Strange as it may seem in today's world of ubiquitous on-demand video, movie fans didn't always have easy access to movies. For most of Hollywood's golden age, films inhabited our consciousness within the confines of darkened theatres for a week or two; the rest was blindness and silence. Outside of major cities, revivals and retrospectives were virtually unknown before the 1960s, and unless you had your own 16mm Bell and Howell Filmosound projector and knew an eccentric film collector willing to lend some of his stash, the occasional television broadcast, mutilated with commercials, was the best chance you had to enjoy the company of your most cherished movies. Silent 8mm reductions of the Universal horror classics were available for home use, but they ran only about ten minutes and, like bad Chinese food, left you feeling even more famished. The film I wanted to see most in the early 1960s was *Dracula* with Bela Lugosi, but for whatever reason, Cleveland's television stations weren't showing any of the Universals. Once, upon learning that the film was being shown in Erie, Pennsylvania, I constructed an add-on to my family's rooftop TV antenna that made it resemble one of the electrical kites from *Bride of Frankenstein*, but the experiment was a failure.

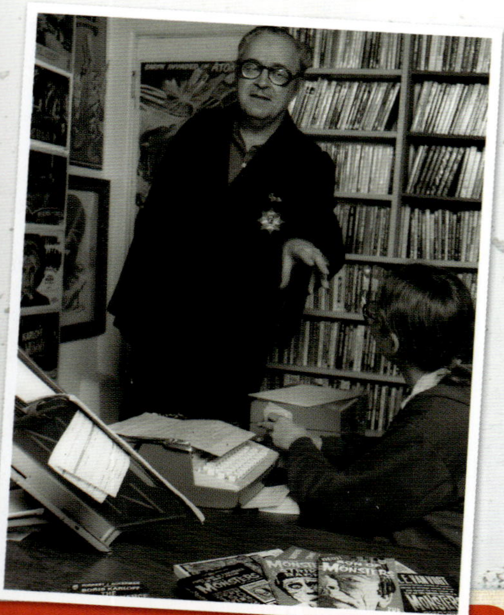

Forrest J Ackerman

My own professional life has been divided fairly equally between movies and the stage. Like Prospero's fictional revels in "The Masque of the Red Death," live performance always ends on a note of existential emptiness — the settings are struck and the company disbands, leaving the auditorium "untenanted by any tangible form." Torn ticket stubs and souvenir programs and posters are about all one retains in the way of Proustian madeleines. The staged event itself is truly *perdu*. Motion pictures get lost, too (actually, half the films ever made are gone forever), but there is always at least the possibility of revival, or, at the very least, ongoing reverential homage.

One stubborn subset of cinephiles resisted the '50s/'60s access embargo with special gusto. Horror, fantasy, and science fiction aficionados were (and are) among the most obsessive and tenacious people in the world. The culture that grew up around monsters drew its energy from promotional ephemera — publicity photos, posters, and advertisements — that formed the backbone of publications like Forrest J Ackerman's *Famous Monsters of Filmland*. The overhead for magazines like *Famous Monsters* was negligible, since most of the content derived from public domain photos, pressbooks, and posters. These all combined to create a powerful mystique for films that were for the most part missing-in-action (and frequently mystiques that the films themselves didn't really deserve).

Given all the ritual fetishization, it's no wonder that fantastic film memorabilia have consistently held their own, commanding record sales at auction. Prestige golden-age films like *Citizen Kane, Casablanca*, and *Gone with the Wind* all have their cult followings, but no one has ever spent $453,500 on a poster from one of them — as someone actually did for a one-sheet display from Boris Karloff's *The Mummy* (1933). In fact, the top-grossing poster auctions of all time are overwhelmingly artifacts from the cinema of mystery and imagination: *Metropolis* (1927; $690,000); *Frankenstein* (1931; $198,000): *Bride of Frankenstein* (1935; $334,600), *King Kong* (1933; $244,500), *The Black Cat* (1934; $286,800), and *Dracula* (1931) are just a sampling from the top dozen or so sold since the 1990s. It's hard to think of a safer investment in our current apocalyptic economy. I've known people who have moved dwindling 401K assets into horror memorabilia (something like storing precious metals in Dracula's crypt for supernatural safekeeping). And so it shouldn't be surprising that in 2010, federal charges were brought against a Georgia poster dealer alleged to have defrauded eBay customers to the tune of a million dollars with clever forgeries of vintage posters and lobby cards from Universal horror classics like *Son of Frankenstein* (1939), and *The Mummy's Hand* (1940), and *The Wolf Man* (1941).

The monetary value placed on horror says much about our cultural priorities and preoccupations, as well as the stories we like to tell about ourselves. Throughout the twentieth century, the stories were anxious and strange, befitting the most mind-bogglingly macabre century in human history. Science fiction and horror posters provided freeze-frames of our most deeply felt anxiety dreams: narrative tableaux depicting various forms of predation and dehumanization (feasting vampires, zombies starved for human brains, aliens taking over the world — or at least our minds — people metamorphosed into animals, or machines). It all looked like an alien world, but in point of fact, it was our very own.

Posters from the 1920s and 1930s benefited from the stylish design sensibility popularized by European artists and lithographers, many of whom resettled in America between the wars. Their work in Hollywood was energized by the conventions of pulp magazine illustrators. The fact that poster work was considered ephemeral led directly to their scarcity, and their collector's market value. Some of the most spectacular, large-scale work took the form of 24-sheet billboards, which of course were routinely papered over from week to week. Virtually none survive, except in photographs.

Posters of the 1950s — the decade in which I first became aware of movies, and their magic — are especially notable for their celebration of postwar abundance, which, for the first time in the history of Hollywood ballyhoo, focused on the iconography of the female breast as an all-purpose tool for celebrating and promoting the good life. The visual delirium wasn't limited to Hollywood; even automotive styling became suggestive of the female form. Howard Hughes's *The Outlaw* (produced during World War II, but not widely released until 1946, and then with a celebratory flourish — "The Movie that Couldn't Be Stopped!" — as if some enforced rationing of the female form had finally come to an end). *The Outlaw* was the first film to spotlight the headlights of its full-figured star (Jane Russell), and both the picture and its advertisements caused no small share of moral outrage. Soon, breasts were boomeranging everywhere in '50s visual culture, especially in genre film promotion, where bug-eyed monsters (known affectionately to fans as BEMs) pursued the bugging breasts of space-age women strapped into nose-cone brassieres. The graphic results were less a Rorschach test than a great collective mammogram of the popular imagination.

Breasts have never appeared as anxious or strange as the ones sported by Bela Lugosi's unconscious victim on the one-sheet from *Bride of the Monster* (1955). I bought mine mail-order from the legendary memorabilia emporium Movie Star News in New York City for a just few dollars. (Had I not lost it in an apartment move, it would be worth several thousand today. But that's another horror story.) Movie Star News was an offshoot of, or perhaps just a front for, proprietor Irving Klaw's major interest: hawking fetish pinups of mid-century cheesecake cuties (like the "notorious" Bettie Page) striking poses of dominance and submission for select and discriminating customers.

As a poster, *Bride of the Monster* was a collector's compromise, at least for the time. The words "Dracula" and "Frankenstein" (as in "More Terrifying Than") were evoked, but not very convincingly. *Bride of the Monster*, which I did manage to finally see on late-night Cleveland television, was a terrible movie. It had not yet been reclaimed as "camp"; Susan Sontag had only just published her famous essay on the subject in 1964, and at the age of twelve I wasn't reading the *Partisan Review*. I was reading *Famous Monsters of Filmland*.

I do not know exactly how many times I opened and closed the folded poster over the years, but toward the end of my custody, the creases were coming apart. Obviously, I looked at it a lot. Obsessively. Like some kind of treasure map whose secret information could only be

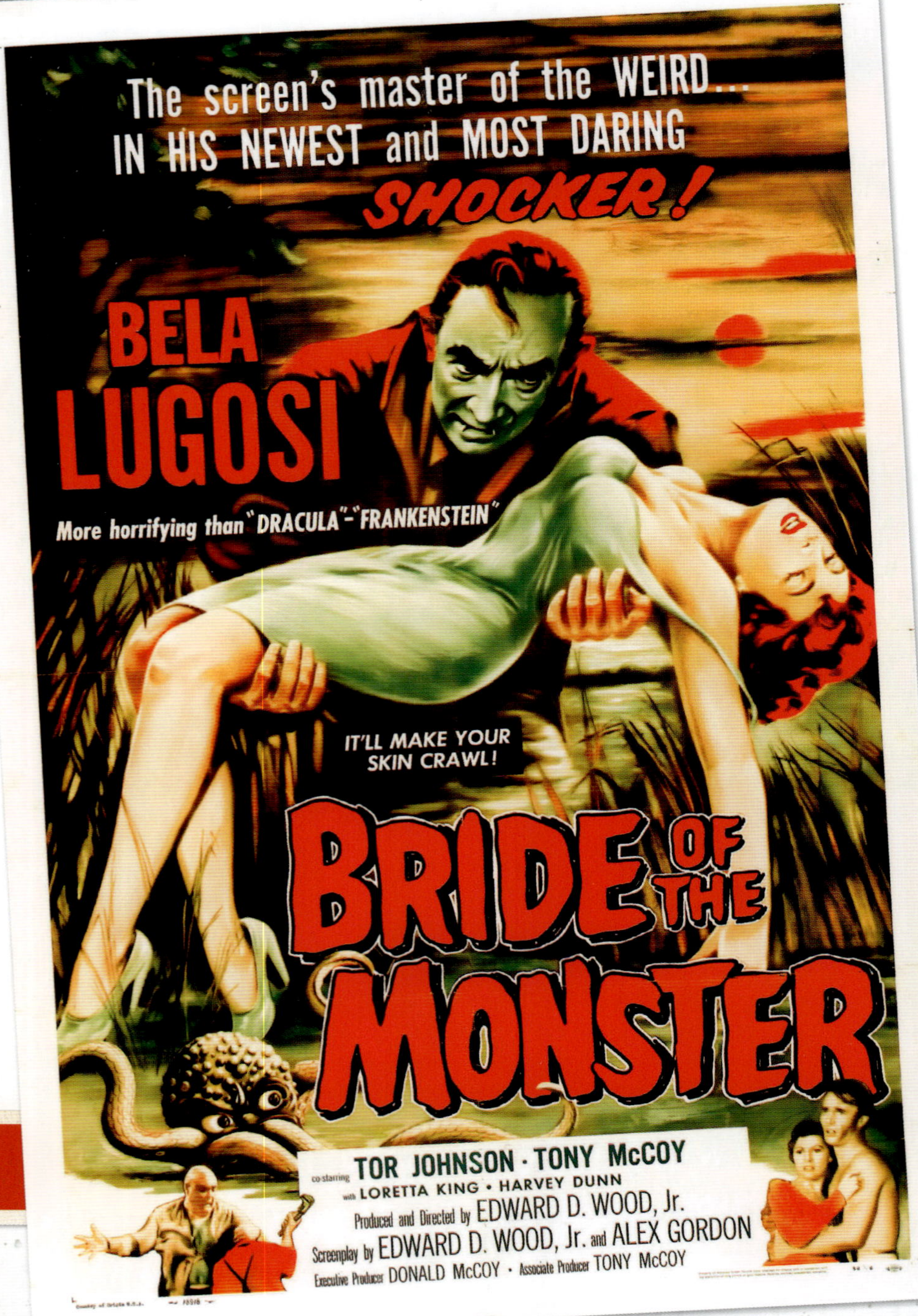

Bride of the Monster.
Rolling M. Productions (1955).

divined through intentional eye strain. The mad scientist Dr. Eric Vornoff (Lugosi) was carrying a girl with high heels and a clingy dress either into or out of a swamp; it wasn't clear which. There was an actual swamp in the film, but for iconographic purposes, the wetness might as well have been Lugosi's own lascivious drool. It's doubtful the artist even saw the movie; Lugosi's image seemed to be based on a photo taken much earlier in his career. Everything was orange and green, the color of 3-D comic books, but without the 3-D.

But back to the breasts. I also wondered if the illustrator had ever actually looked at a real woman, because both the woman's breasts were on the left side of her torso, while her throat angled off insanely toward her right shoulder. As a gay teenager just beginning to come to grips with my own sexuality, I already knew that female flesh in magazines and posters wasn't particularly arousing. But in this case, what about straight guys? Did they even know what they were *looking* at? Were wildly asymmetrical mammaries genuinely erection-producing? Better than regular ones?

Had there been a corresponding level of beefcake in the horror posters and monster magazines, no doubt I would have been reading *Famous Monsters* exclusively with one hand. However, one place I did find a sexy nexus for cold-war horror, a place where atomic blasts and orgasms truly overlapped, was in a family medical guide my parents kept in the back of the linen closet. The straight sex information was pretty tepid — there was an evocative line in an otherwise dreary chapter called "Facts for the Barren Woman" that mentioned, only in passing, *the insertion of the penis*, but the steamiest discovery was a fully illustrated appendix on surviving a nuclear attack. After the blast, the reader was told in no uncertain terms to find the nearest public restroom, strip off all your clothes ("Do *not* let a sense of false modesty prevent you from taking these life-saving steps!") and wash off the fallout with whatever soap and water was available. And there was an illustration of a naked man doing exactly that, lathering up in front of other frantic naked strangers, his crotch hidden by the suit and fedora he had draped over a chair.

Now this was pretty *hot*, and certainly more evocative to me than the queasy admixture of nuclear terror and sexual panic evidently intended by the straight-themed sci-fi posters. I pulled out that book many times for what I realize now was the biggest visual turn-on in my life in the years before I managed to get a glimpse of actual pornography.

I was careless with the *Bride of the Monster* one-sheet, and ultimately lost it during a move. I acquired other random posters over the years, but none engaged and fascinated me as much. Posters generally have gotten a great deal less interesting as photography has almost completely replaced illustration. Posters no longer serve the function of standing in for an elusive experience; indeed, if the poster's out, the film itself is probably showing on thousands of screens, and might even be available soon for downloading directly to your smart phone. The kind of top-notch talent that used to design movie posters has long been chased away to the realm of dust jackets and CD covers — quite a shaky realm these days, as our personal libraries and music shelves increasingly evaporate into digital clouds. As much as I enjoy accessing almost any movie released on DVD through Netflix, it's always with a distinct twinge of loss that I pop a naked disc into the player with no clamshell art or liner notes to peruse. Those low-resolution, matchbook-sized jpegs that pop up as thumbnails aren't anything I can hang on my wall.

Those classic Universal posters remained forever out of my financial reach, but my frustrated collector instincts stayed strong. I worked in the professional theatre for many years, and it was there that I was first exposed to the poster work of macabre Polish masters like Franciszek Starowieyski and Wieslaw Walkuski, both of whom can transform anything in the standard theatrical or operatic repertoire into something evocative of a horror movie. They're artistically superior to anything ever produced in Hollywood, yet share the same morbid sexuality and sense of impending apocalypse that riveted my attention during the Cold War (Starowieyski's work in particular emphasizes breasts and nightmarishly mutating women). Fortunately, during the 1980s, several book-research trips to Europe allowed me to amass a moderately impressive collection of those strange Polish graphics, which I obtained for a song in Left Bank bookstalls and elsewhere. And, when that time comes (as it seems it inexorably must), when I am faced with an embargo on physical access to my favorite books and films, I will simply employ a good picture framer to exteriorize my interior world of terrors and wonders, making it tenanted, and tangible, once more.

David J. Skal is the author of the seminal works *Hollywood Gothic: The Tangled Web of Dracula from Novel to Stage to Screen* and *The Monster Show*, in addition to many other books on horror and monsters in popular culture, including *Dracula: The Ultimate, Illustrated Edition of the World-Famous Vampire Play*, *Dark Carnival: The Secret World of Tod Browning*, *V Is for Vampire: The A-Z Guide to Everything Undead*, *Screams of Reason: Mad Science and Modern Culture*, *Dracula* (Norton Critical Editions), *Vampires: Encounters With the Undead*, *Death Makes a Holiday: A Cultural History of Halloween*, and *Romancing the Vampire: Collectors Vault*. He is presently completing a new "cultural biography," *Bram Stoker: The Final Curtain*, and is a visiting lecturer in popular literature at Trinity College, Dublin.

I INTRODUCTION

MOVIE MONSTERS AND THE PRINTED PAGE

Dave Kehr, in his introduction to *Art of the Modern Movie Poster: International Postwar Style and Design* (Chronicle Books, 2008), writes that "film posters retain an appeal and mystique that no advertisement for fruit-flavored vodka or cell phone services will ever be able to capture.... More than just marketing, these posters are invitations to the imagination, forever beckoning us to join new worlds."[1] It is perhaps fortuitous then that horror cinema's increasing acceptance in academe has provided a unique and rewarding opportunity to re-visit these valuable works. The movie posters in this volume provide a colorful visual history of "movie monsters," recording the classic icons of the early black and white "talkies" (like Dracula and Frankenstein) to the more contemporary zombie and slasher figures of the last thirty years, while chronicling also the decline of hand-painted posters, to the rise of photomontage posters that follow.

Posters perform much in the same manner as the films they advertise, demonstrating stylistic developments in response to shifting social and political needs and fears. Other similar works to the present volume, like Bruce Hershenson and Richard Allen's *Attack of the 'B' Movie Posters (The Illustrated History of Movies Through Posters Series)* (Bruce Hershenson, 2001), *Horror Movie Posters (The Illustrated History of Movies Through Posters Series)* (Bruce Hershenson, 1998), and *Horror, Sci-Fi & Fantasy Movie Posters* (Bruce Hershenson, 1999), offer sweeping explications of these stylistic intricacies in their general introductions, while other works like James A. Gresham, Diane Andrews, and Joelle Gresham's *Children of the Night: A Comprehensive Guide to Horror Posters* (Jim Gresham, 2008) and Graham Marsh and Tony Nourmand's *Film Posters Horror* (Evergreen, 2006) provide sectional overviews or synopses that relay information mostly concerning production history and the current value of the posters themselves. Finally, Graham Marsh and Tony Nourmand's *Horror Poster Art* (Aurum Press, 2004) provides absolutely stunning imagery and draws from production notes to offer concise historical and biographical discussions throughout the text. However, the loose organizational schemata it employs offers readers little guidance in tracing horror's and the monster's evolutionary progression in the cinema.

Without taking away the value of these notable precursors to the present work, it is important to observe that texts dealing with horror posters thus far (with the exception perhaps of the Marsh and Nourmand text) have remained predominantly Anglo-centric in their attempts to catalogue and elucidate horror's and the monster's visual appeal by relying too heavily on Western advertisements, in lieu of a more globalized, multicultural sample. Thus, they offer little to readers in terms of scope and international appeal. The present volume aims to rectify this neglect by offering readers a collectible illustrated reference of the most thrilling "movie monsters," from major as well as minor horror films, through the medium of international posters, as well as the more conventional domestic variety, with the addition of specially selected and strategically placed movie stills and publicity shots. I've employed a chronological organization to help show both cultural as well as technological developments in the cinema in order to reveal the history of the indelible "movie monster." While this book is comfortably situated to provide to the nostalgic, knowledgeable connoisseur of horror an invaluable visual reference, it is also equally suited, if not recommended for the burgeoning enthusiast as well.

Editing a book of this sort, of which there were many similar volumes in my youth, is for me both nostalgic and fulfilling. For, with its writing comes the realization of a dream of mine, to take part in the process of choosing films, images, and posters that best display, in all their beautiful, macabre form and crimson splendor, our most beloved monsters. I make no claim that those chronicled here are "the best." My selection of films for this volume is a rather eclectic assemblage of the monstrous, one that will gratify some and displease others, as horror films tend to instill in the hearts of viewers a most unusual, tenacious loyalty that is upheld and defended vehemently. Be that is it may, there is something here in this volume for everyone, and all manner of reader — from scholar to general enthusiast, from the 12-year-old backseat reader to the nostalgic 40-year-old father — will delight in its phantasmagoria of colors, knives, bloodstains, and terror-stricken faces.

1. Dave Kehr, Introduction to *Art of the Modern Movie Poster: International Postwar Style and Design*, ed. Judith Salavetz, Spencer Drate, and Sam Sarowitz (San Francisco: Chronicle Books, 2008), 9.

1

THE 1920s

THE TWENTIES: AN EMERGENCE OF HORROR

Horror film iconography after World War I was particularly stylish, owing to the genre's roots in the intensely visual style of German expressionism. Unforgettable compositions of light and shadow were a hallmark of films like *The Cabinet of Dr. Caligari* (1920) as well as their promotional graphics. Like *Caligari, Der Golem* (1920), and *Nosferatu* (1922), silent American horror pictures were intended as prestige efforts rather than genre programmers. They differed from their European prototypes in resisting frankly fantastic themes—American "monsters" in the 1920s—often played by Lon Chaney, "The Man of a Thousand Faces," were always revealed to be human agents, either disfigured or disguised. It would take the coming of sound, and Universal's *Dracula* (1931) in particular, to convince Hollywood to openly embrace supernaturalism.

~David J. Skal

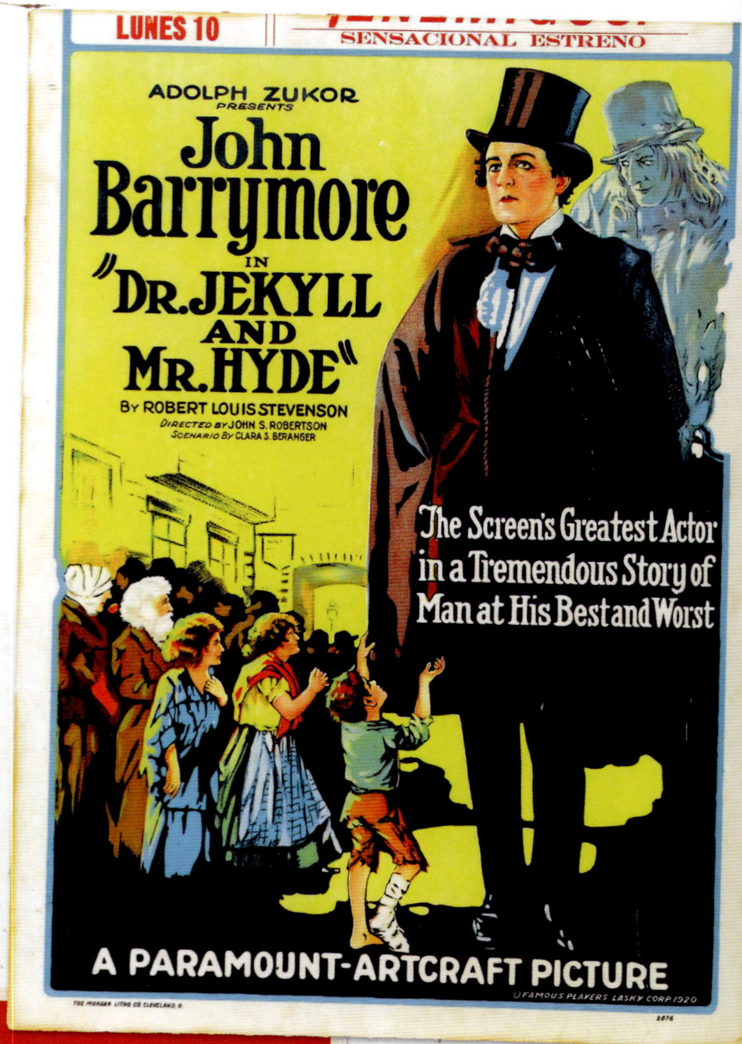

Dr. Jekyll and Mr. Hyde.
Famous Players-Lasky Corporation (1920).

As an actor John Barrymore would model his performances on tarantulas in the zoo as much as the grand tradition of nineteenth-century stage melodrama and this film demonstrates both. His astonishing performance as he transforms before our eyes or haunts himself in nightmare visions is at the heart of this powerful adaptation which portrays a society that is divided – and syphilitic.

Richard J. Hand

The Golem.
Projektions-AG Union (1920).

I have, for years, been fascinated by the Golem, who, unfortunately, has never received as much publicity or recognition as his great, great grandson Frankenstein's Monster.

The bizarre sets, the shock of seeing the Golem come to life, the hideous, explosive rage of the huge creature running wild through the streets – and then the climax, where a small child innocently obliterates the magic word, causing the Golem to crash lifelessly to the ground.

Obviously our friend the Golem has had far more influence on monsters through the years than most people realize. For what is considered by many to be a minor personage, the Golem is very much in evidence in numerous shapes, forms and guises.

Jeanne Keyes Youngson

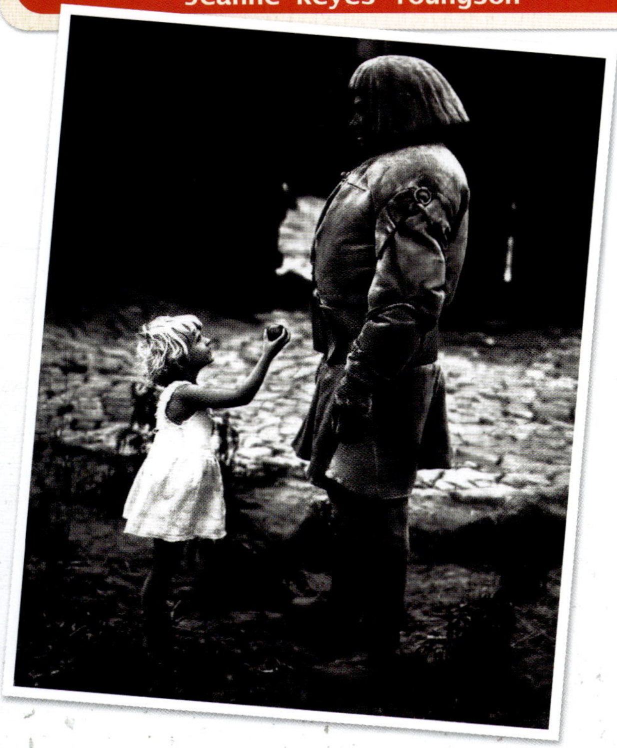

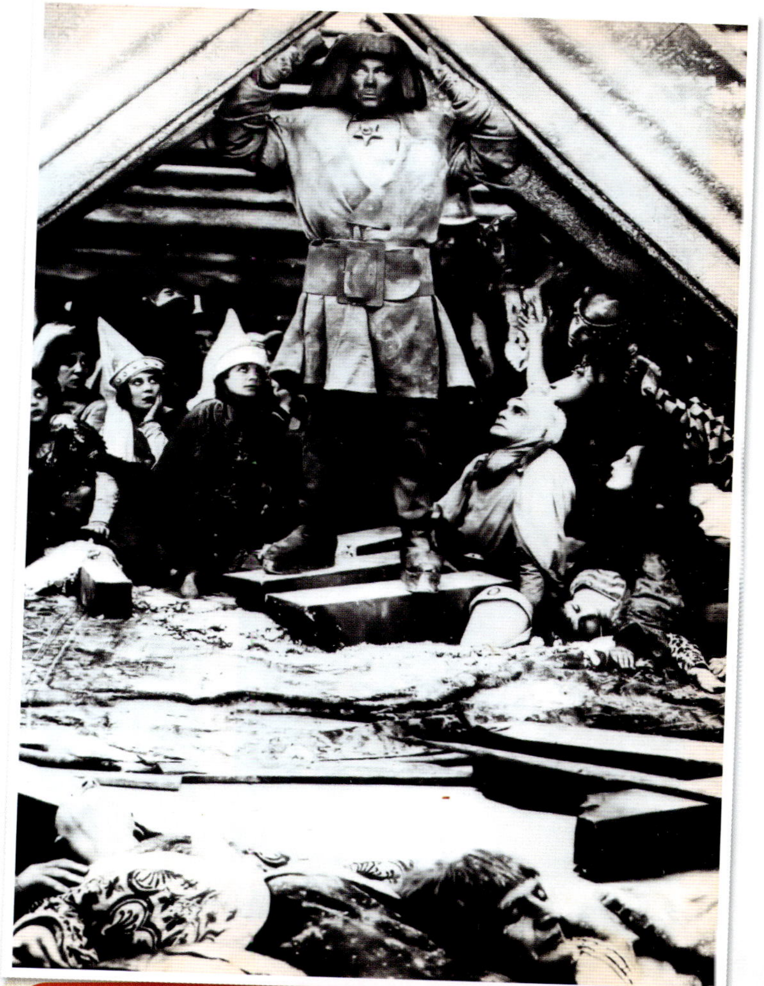

The Golem.
Projektions-AG Union (1920).

As a faithful 13-year-old reader of Famous Monsters of Filmland, *seeing stills from this film, I had to say, "Nah, the Golem looks silly, not scary," an awful lot like something you make up with mud and sand and water and a pail and shovel. But I so trusted the word of "Uncle Forry" that I was sure if I could only see this silent film, yeah, it would be terrifying ... Not that there was much chance of that. When I was 13, color television had yet to catch on, and DVD was either Denmark's secret police or a really nasty upper respiratory infection.*

Then comes college and silent films are presented (more or less) as they were meant to be presented: Big(ger than TV) screen, sound (albeit on a track on the film itself and not emanating from a pit orchestra), and at last, I am seeing THE GOLEM.

Mort Castle

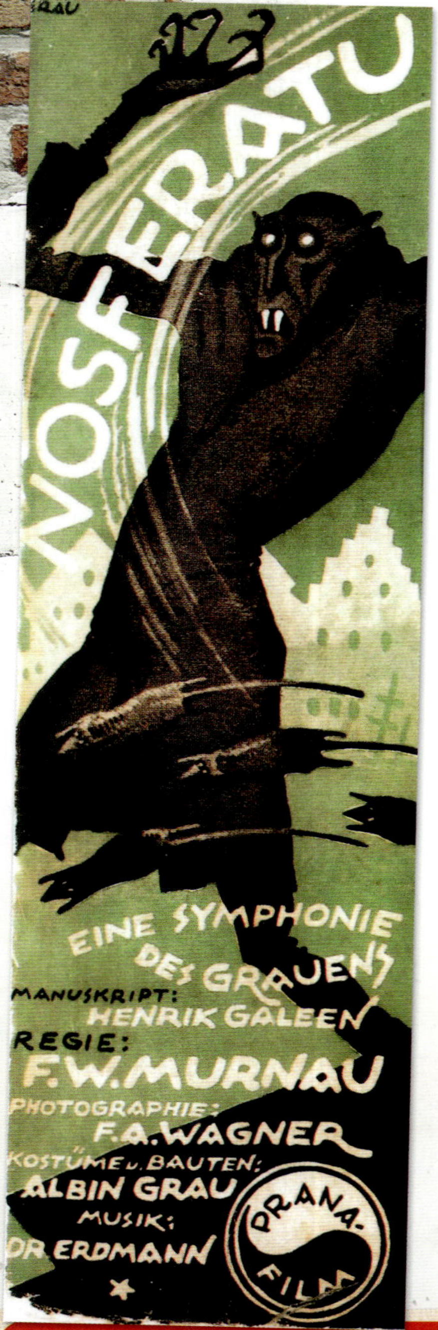

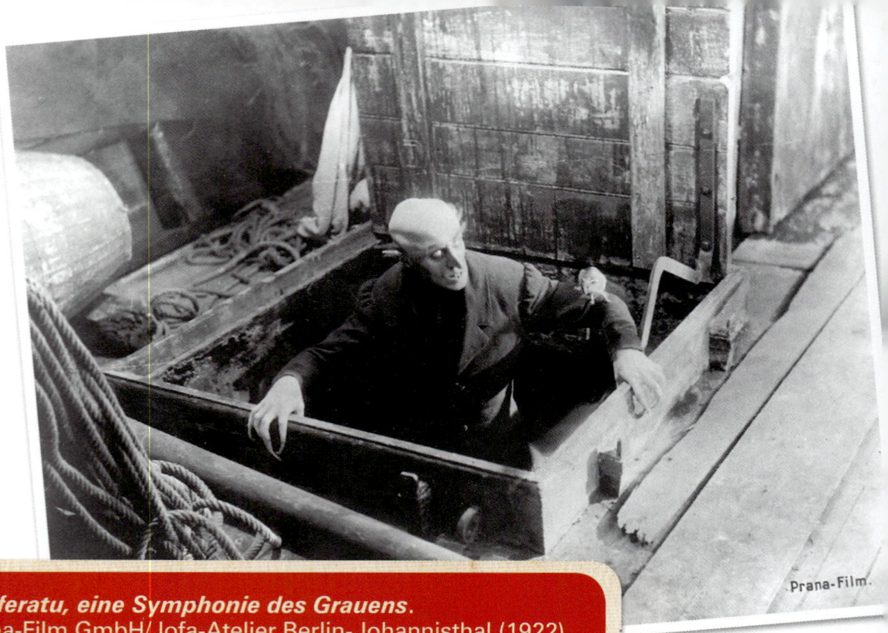

***Nosferatu, eine Symphonie des Grauens*.**
Prana-Film GmbH/Jofa-Atelier Berlin-Johannisthal (1922).

Still the creepiest vampire film ever made. Its psychological terror is evoked by shadow and suggestion rather than special effects. Max Schreck literally embodies the unholy undead, looking more like the horror known to our ancestors instead of the antiseptic, glamorized creatures found in many vampire films today. I sympathize with Florence Stoker in her fight against the blatant plagiarism of Prana Film, but on the other hand, I am grateful that not all copies of the film were destroyed in accordance with court order. We would have lost a great classic!

Rosemary Ellen Guiley

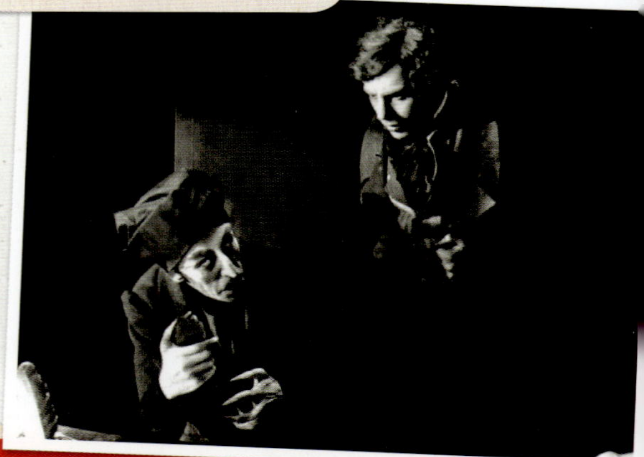

***Nosferatu, eine Symphonie des Grauens*.** Prana-Film GmbH/Jofa-Atelier Berlin-Johannisthal (1922) Germany.

Nosferatu *(1922) is for me the quintessential vampire film. I like my vampires to be SCARY-looking, and Max Shreck is really convincing in the title role (so convincing that* Shadow of the Vampire *[2000], in which he's revealed to be a real vampire, seems true to me!) We have F. W. Murnau and Albin Grau to blame for the revelation that vampires are destroyed by sunlight, actually a new idea that has since become firmly implanted in the world mind.*

Leslie Klinger

***Nosferatu, eine Symphonie des Grauens*.**
Prana-Film GmbH/Jofa-Atelier Berlin-Johannisthal (1922).

It's been hard for subsequent vampires to match the astonishing bizarrerie of Max Schreck in Nosferatu*, although the more conscientiously Byronic representations of Dracula by Bela Lugosi and Christopher Lee have a different kind of charisma.*

Brian Stableford

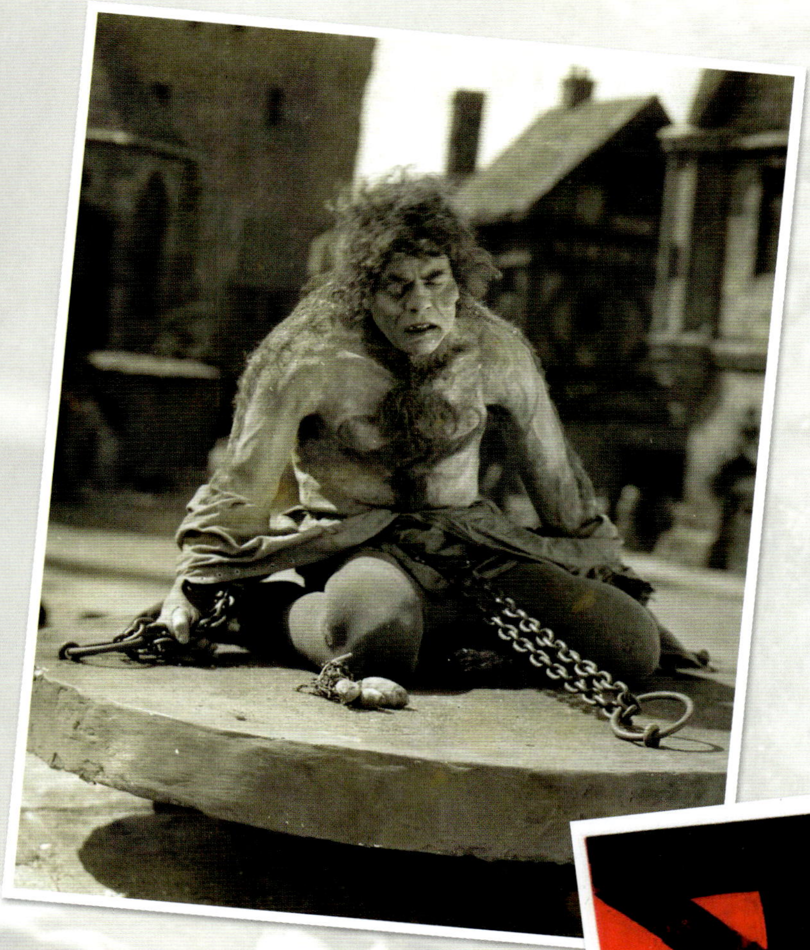

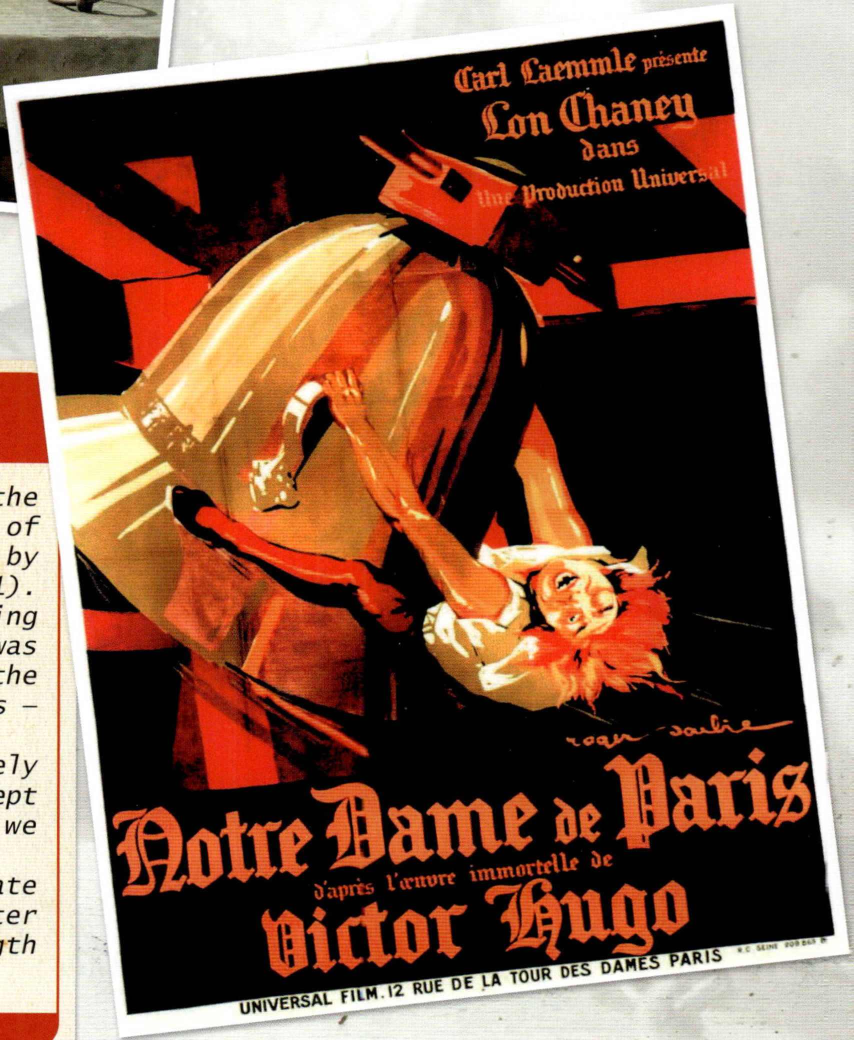

The Hunchback of Notre Dame.
Universal Pictures (1923). France.

I think I recall first seeing the condensed (half hour) presentation of this one on the ABC TV show hosted by Ernie Kovacs Silents Please (1960-1961). The physicality of Lon Chaney swinging and jumping gave me the sensation I was watching something truly not human, the product of human and orangutan perhaps – ugly human and ugly orangutan.

We don't want it to be so, but genuinely ugly scares us, no matter how many "accept diversity/embrace ugly" workshops we attend.

Once more because of Illinois State University's film program, years later I had a chance to see the full length Chaney Hunchback. Terrific.

Mort Castle

The Phantom of the Opera.
Universal Pictures (1925). Sweden.

When I was 11, I saw pictures of Lon Chaney as "The Phantom" in Famous Monsters of Filmland. *I took a job as a paperboy to earn enough to buy a hand-cranked 8mm projector and a full feature 8mm copy of the film. That got me "hooked" on Horror Films for the rest of my life. Chaney's unmasking scene still horrifies even after 86 years.*

Philip J. Riley

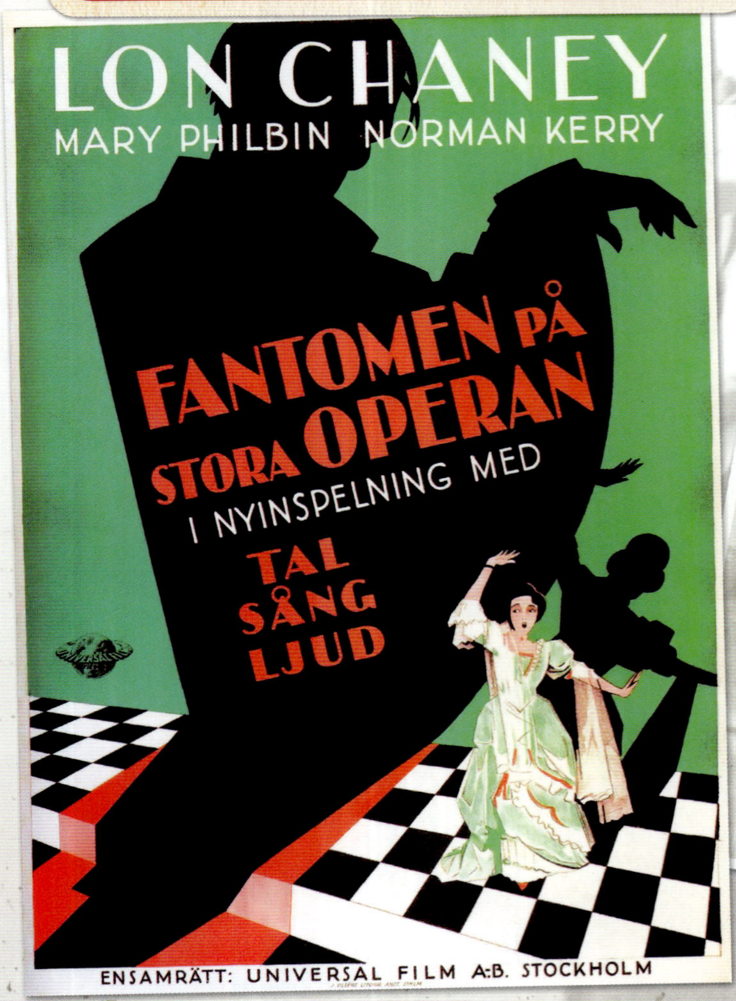

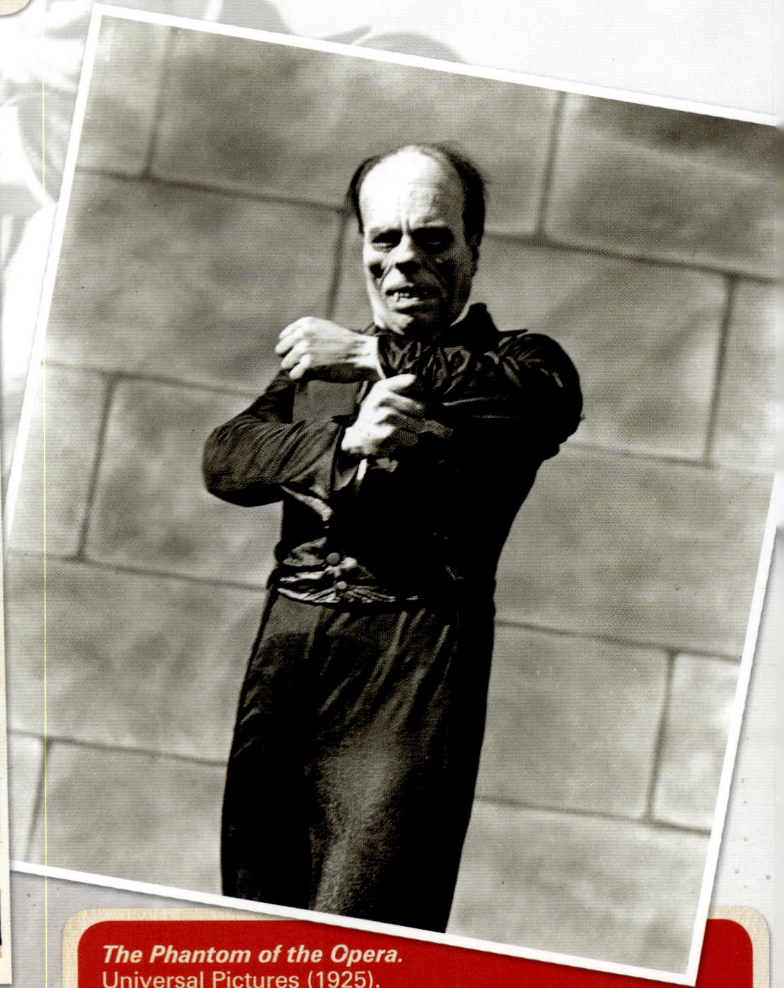

The Phantom of the Opera.
Universal Pictures (1925).

In terms of more humanoid monsters, it's been difficult for many of the talkie versions to reproduce the sheer eeriness of silent portrayals by Lon Chaney, who was aided by the relatively poor quality of the cinema image in his day and the artificiality of silent film – however inappropriate that might seem, at first glance, to such productions as The Phantom of the Opera.

Brian Stableford

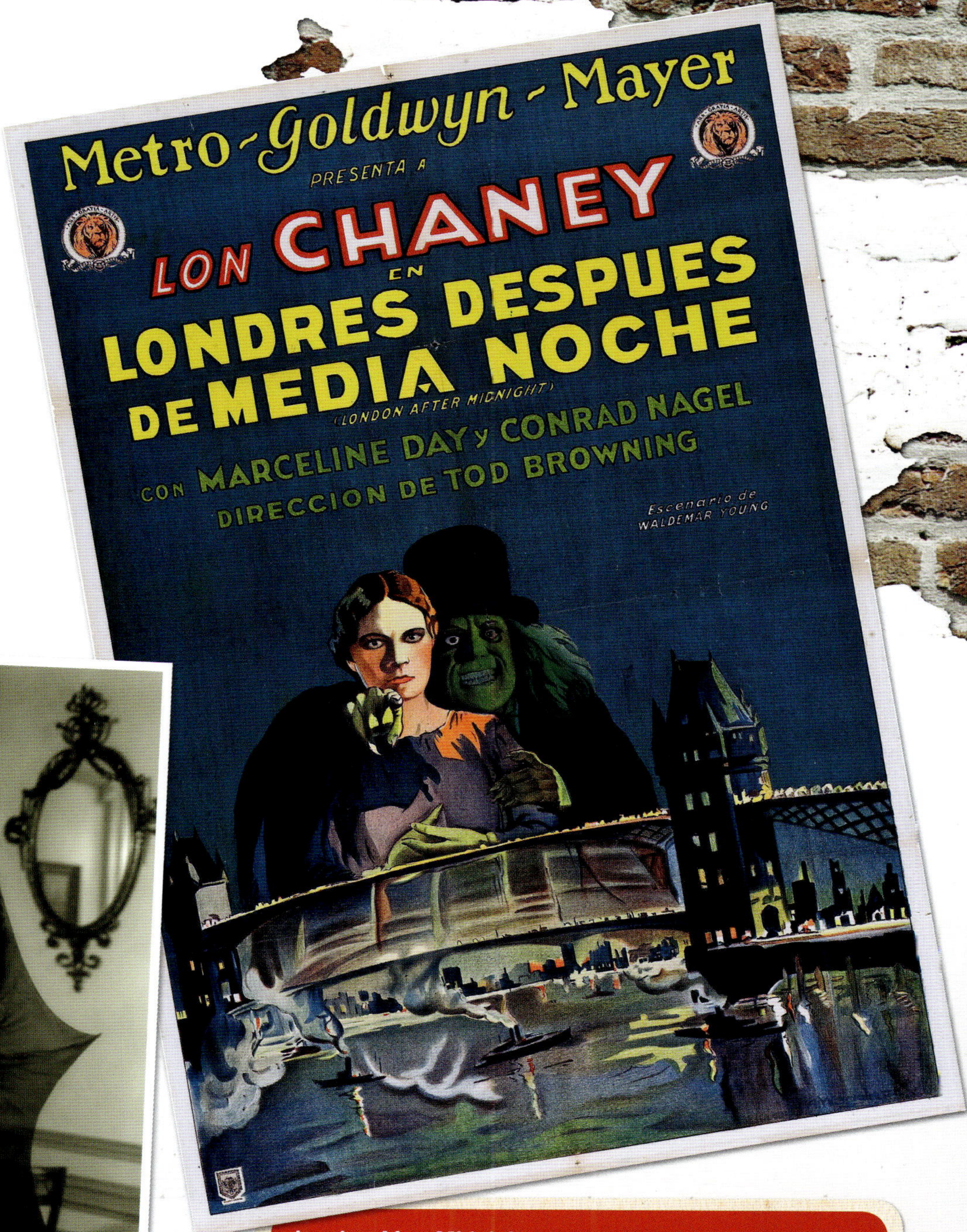

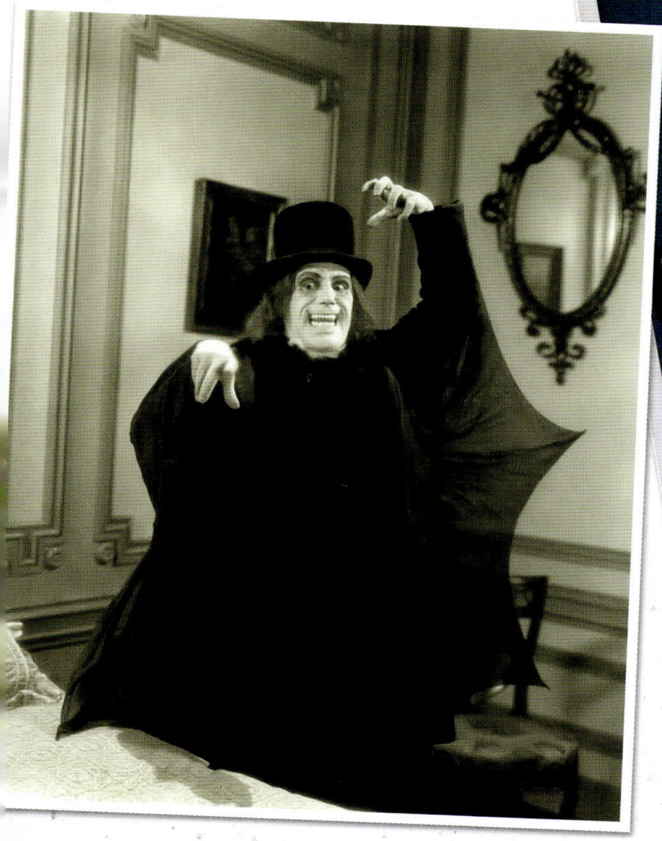

London After Midnight.
Metro-Goldwyn-Mayer (1927). Argentina.

While working for Forrest J Ackerman in the 70s, I found out that the film itself was considered "lost." After months of work, I reconstructed the film using stills and silent film titles in book form, but nothing could compare to seeing Lon Chaney's vampire in the actual film.

Philip J. Riley

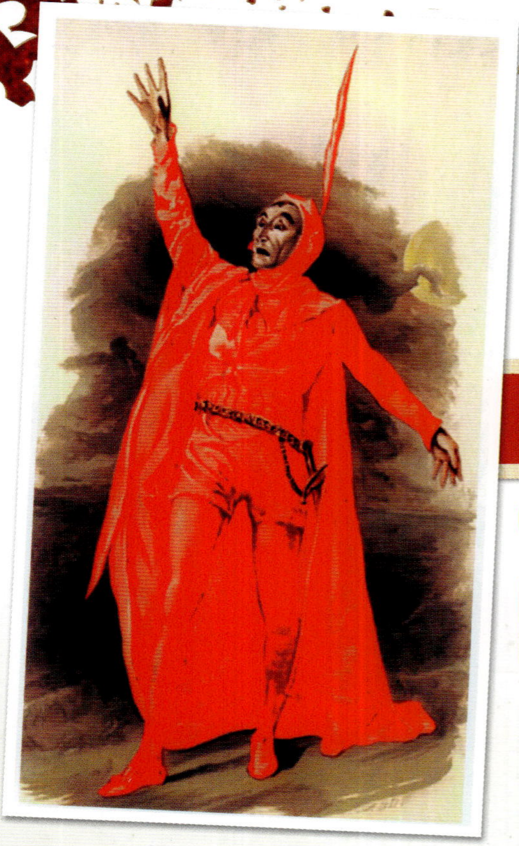

Sir Henry Irving (as Mephistopheles). c. 1885.

ON THE PROTOTYPE OF **COUNT DRACULA**

From the very first brief notes he made in March 1890 for his novel *Dracula* (1897), Bram Stoker shows how a relationship of power, possession, and control was at the frenzied heart of his defining vampire tale. This was a relationship paralleled in life by Stoker and the long-term employer he served and hero-worshipped at London's Lyceum Theatre, the demonic Shakespearean actor Henry Irving. The notes tell of an encounter between a "young man" and an "old dead man" who roams his "old Styria Castle" in a "waking trance." This is not a bad description of the compulsive acting style adopted by Irving when playing such roles as Mephistopheles in Goethe's *Faust*, his most successful and startling role, as depicted here. The Devil competes with Divinity to have Mastery over vulnerable souls which, once "bitten," loyally follow his commanding and possessive power. In Stoker's condensed notes, the young man "goes out sees girls one tries to kiss him not on lips but throat" when suddenly the "Old Count interferes" and with "rage & fury diabolical" admonishes them: "this man belongs to me I want him." The Romantic Irishman, Stoker was seduced into serving Mephisto-like Irving from his first encounter in 1876, not to be released from his Master until 1903, when Irving collapsed on stage and died. Stoker's only son, Noel, thought the demonic Irving had "worn out" Bram — it seems so — one man's life-energy drained so that vampire icon Count Dracula could be created and live forever.

~Maurice Hindle

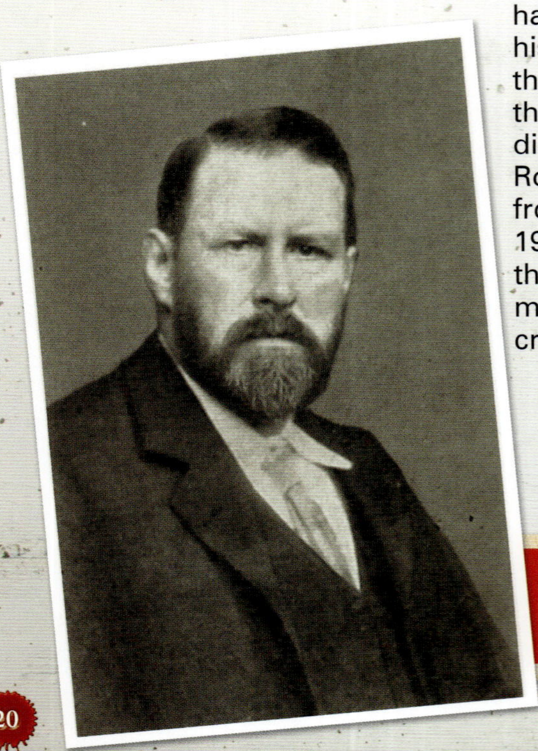

Bram Stoker (1847-1912). Virtual Museum, Royal Borough of Kensington and Chelsea, from the Illustrated London News.

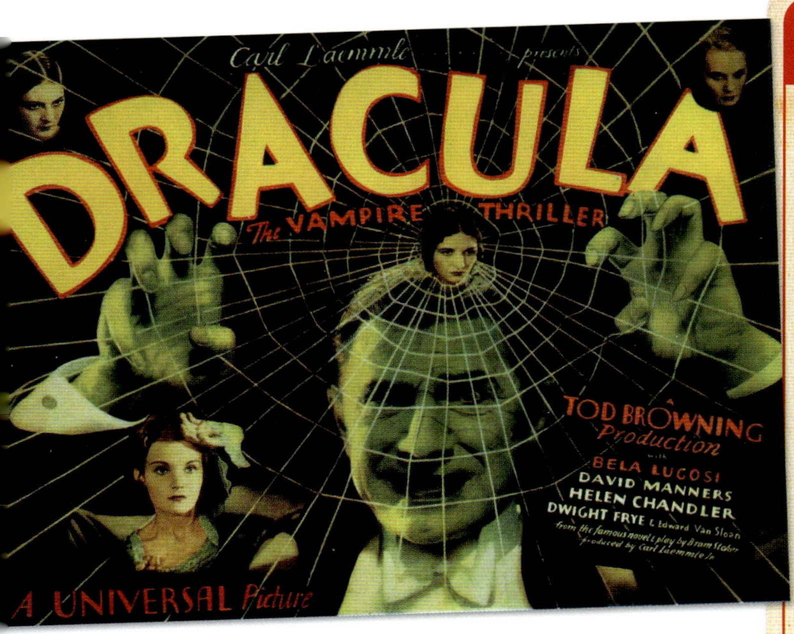

Dracula.
Universal Pictures (1931).

Dracula (1931) by Tod Browning, based on the highly successful stage play that also starred Lugosi, is a milestone of monster movies. It forever changed the image of the vampire (for the worse, IMHO) from the monstrous creature of Nosferatu to the "lounge-lizard" foreign romantic adventurer. It's ironic that Carl Laemmle, Jr. desperately wanted to cast anyone but Lugosi in the title role (he conducted a national talent search), because of course Lugosi will always be remembered for this iconic portrayal. The script played fast and loose with Stoker's original tale, conflating characters and eliminating the great action in Whitby and Transylvania, but the scenes of seduction are true to the underlying sexual elements of the book.

Leslie Klinger

Dracula.
Universal Pictures (1931).

Despite all challenges, Dracula retains his status as the most powerful and complex of all vampires, bar none, because as a literary figure he entwined the darkly sexualized subconscious of a deeply repressed culture. Bela Lugosi produced a subtle malevolence that successfully transmitted a larger-than-life, blacker-than-death aura. He was as attractive in that Kierkegaardian sense of dread as he was repellent. He left you unsettled but wanting more.

Katherine Ramsland

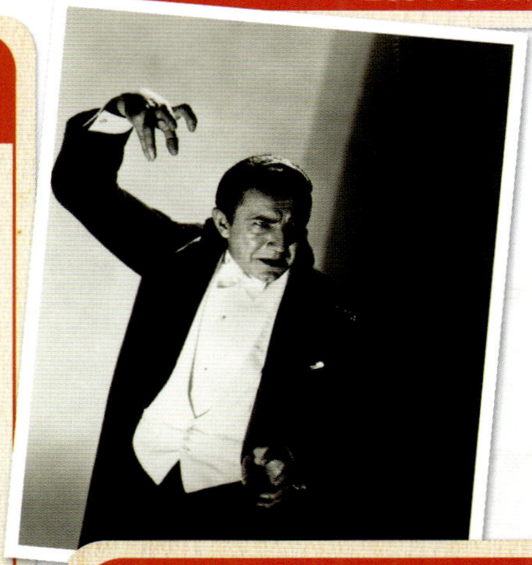

Drácula (Spanish Dracula).
Universal Pictures (1931).

A fascinating film, to be watched by every fan of the Tod Browning English-language version. Shot on the same sets as the popular film, the crew worked at night, following almost literally in the footsteps of the Browning crew. Not only are the actors better (and sexier) than those in the English-language version (with the exception of Lugosi, of course – I always find that Carlos Villarias reminds me of a dentist), the script is a significant improvement! The puzzle of Lucy's fate is resolved, and the added length of the film (almost 30 minutes longer than Browning's) allows for deeper character development.

Leslie Klinger

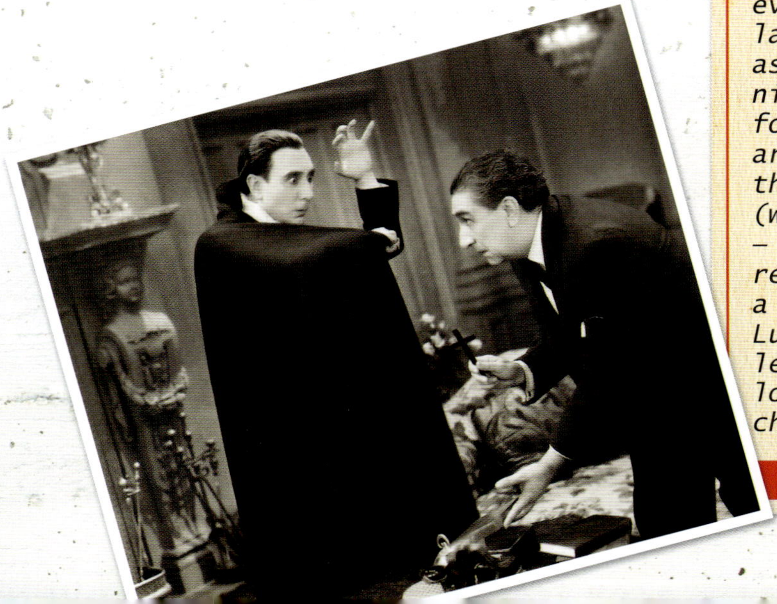

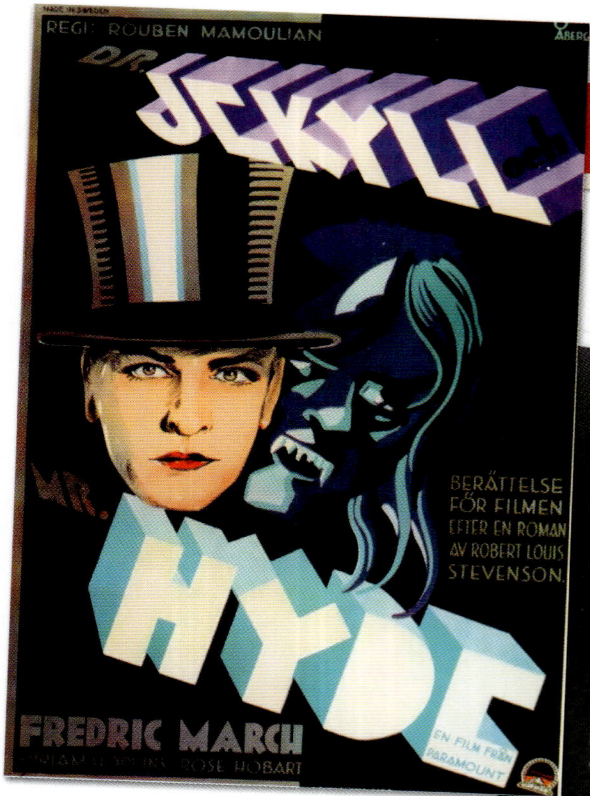

Dr. Jekyll and Mr. Hyde.
Paramount Pictures (1931). Sweden.

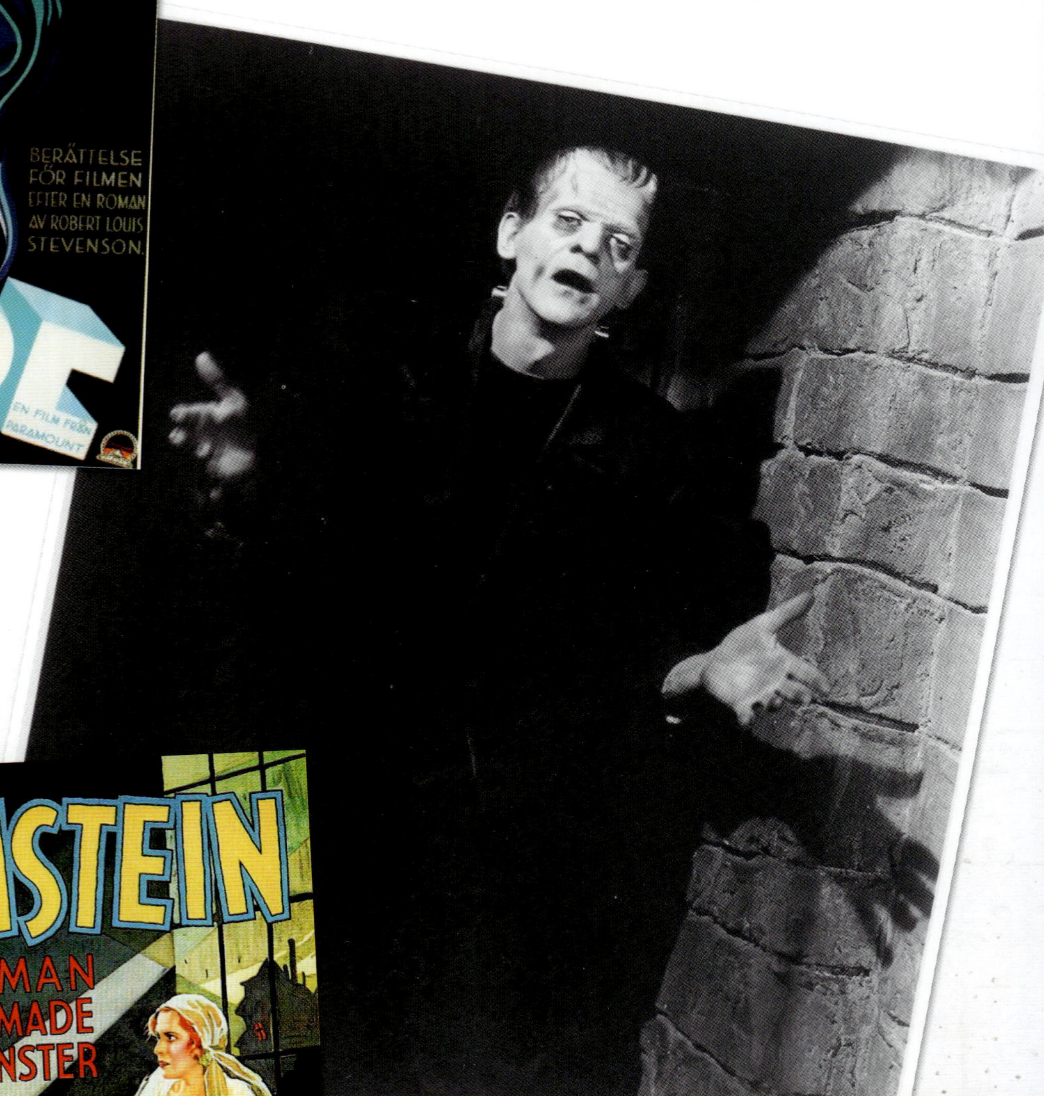

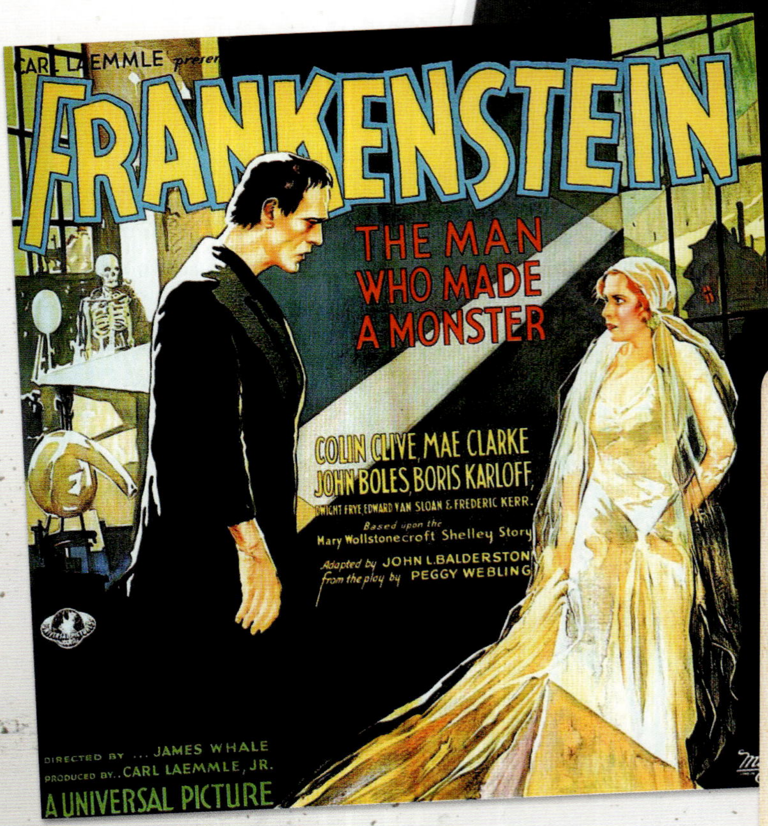

Frankenstein.
Universal Pictures (1931).

Bela Lugosi, after the success of Dracula, actually had been originally cast and done test footage, as the creature in Frankenstein. *But it was a then unknown actor, Boris Karloff, who turned what was a radical handicap for the actor who played the nameless creature – the inability to speak–into an eloquent testimony of the creature's childlike innocence and humanity.*

Caroline Joan (Kay) Picart

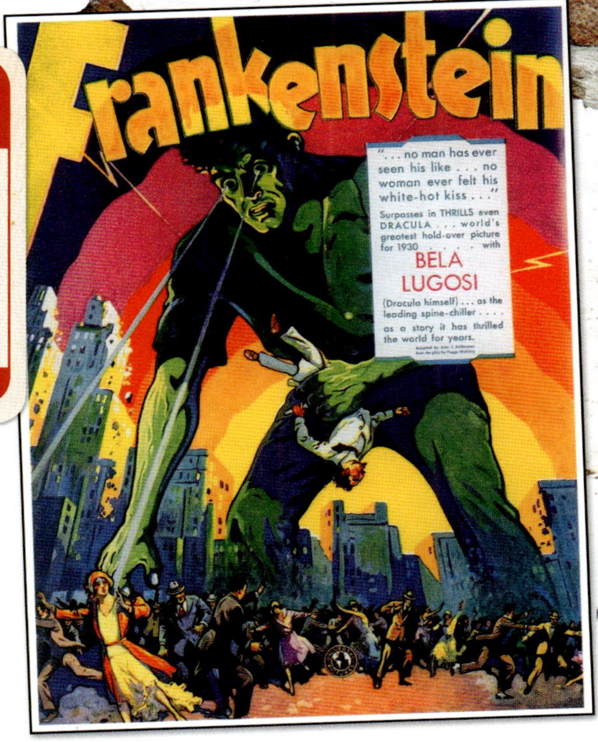

***Frankenstein*.**
Universal Pictures (1931).

Boris Karloff, who had endured the grueling make-up sessions and the physical stress of acting the part of the creature, later suffered from severe health problems. Thus, he became one of the strongest advocates of actors' rights.

Caroline Joan (Kay) Picart

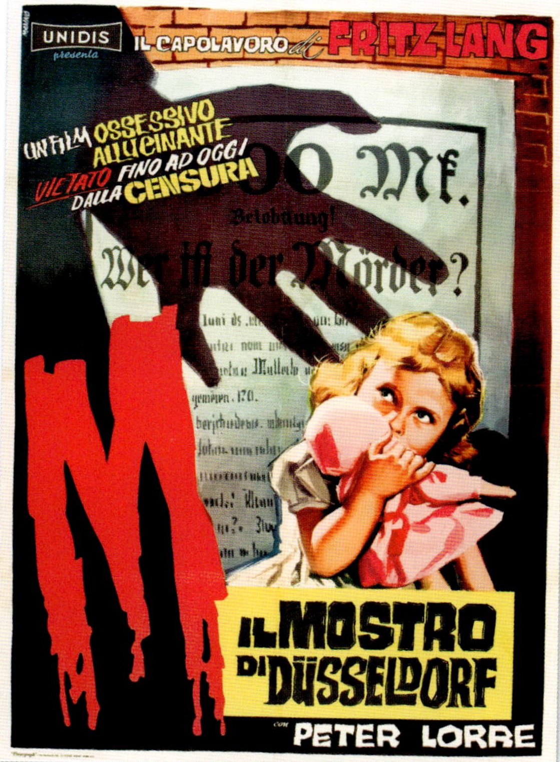

***M*.**
Nero-Film AG (1931) Italy.

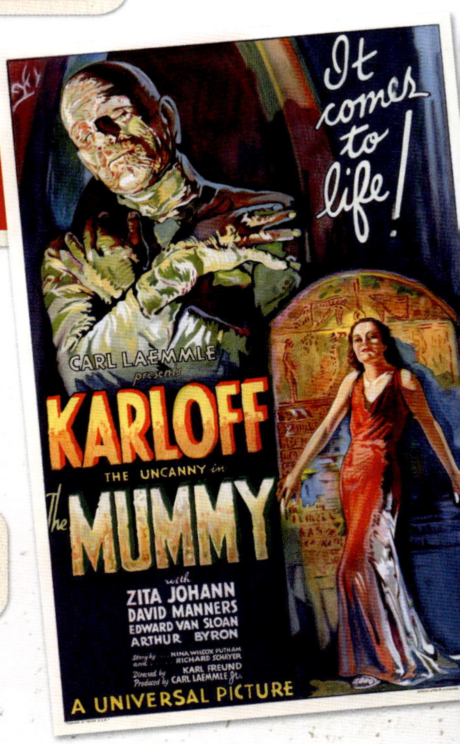

***The Mummy*.**
Universal Pictures (1932).

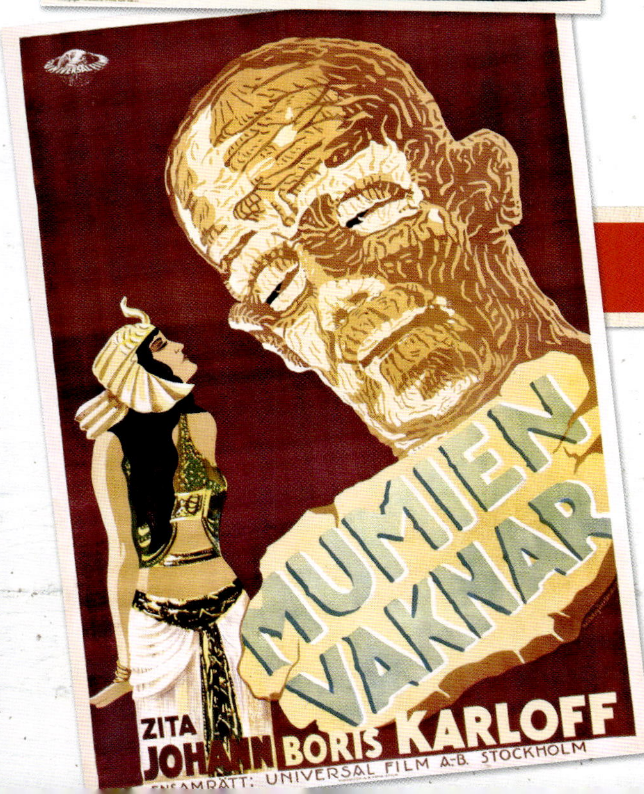

***The Mummy*.**
Universal Pictures (1932). Sweden.

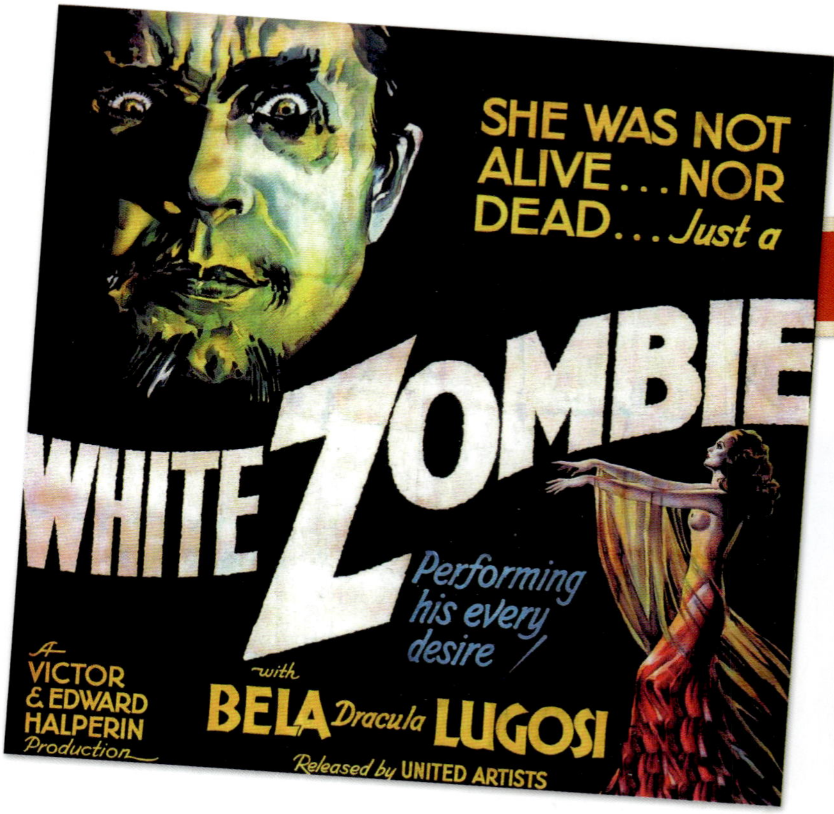

White Zombie. Edward Halperin Productions/ Victor Halperin Productions (1932). UK.

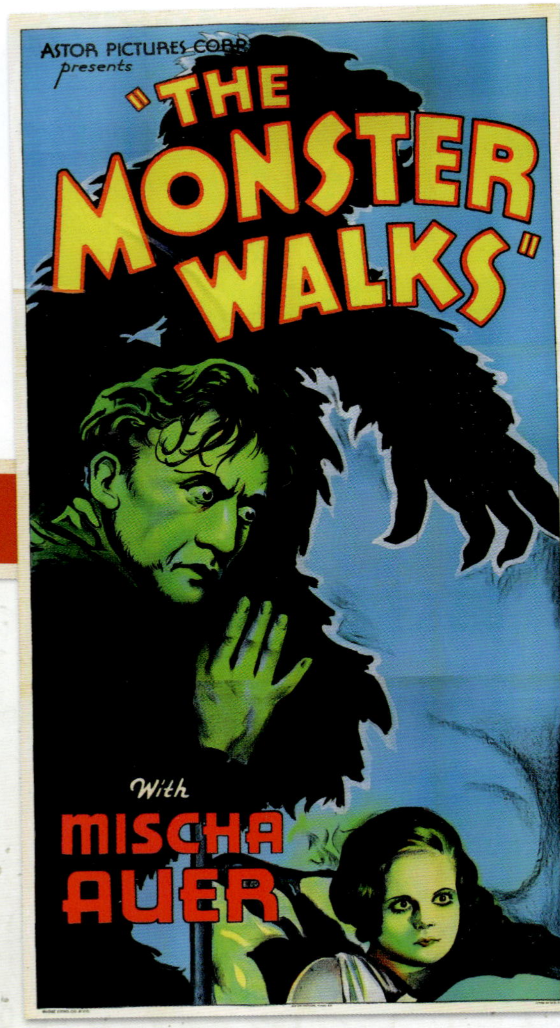

The Monster Walks. Ralph M. Like Productions (1932).

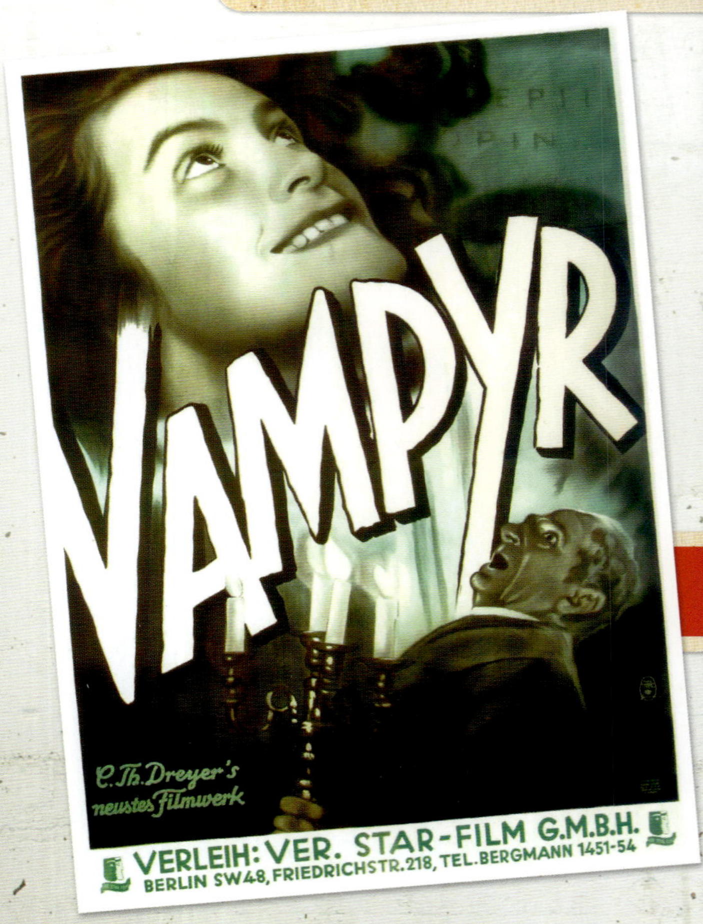

Vampyr. Tobis Filmkunst (1932) Germany.

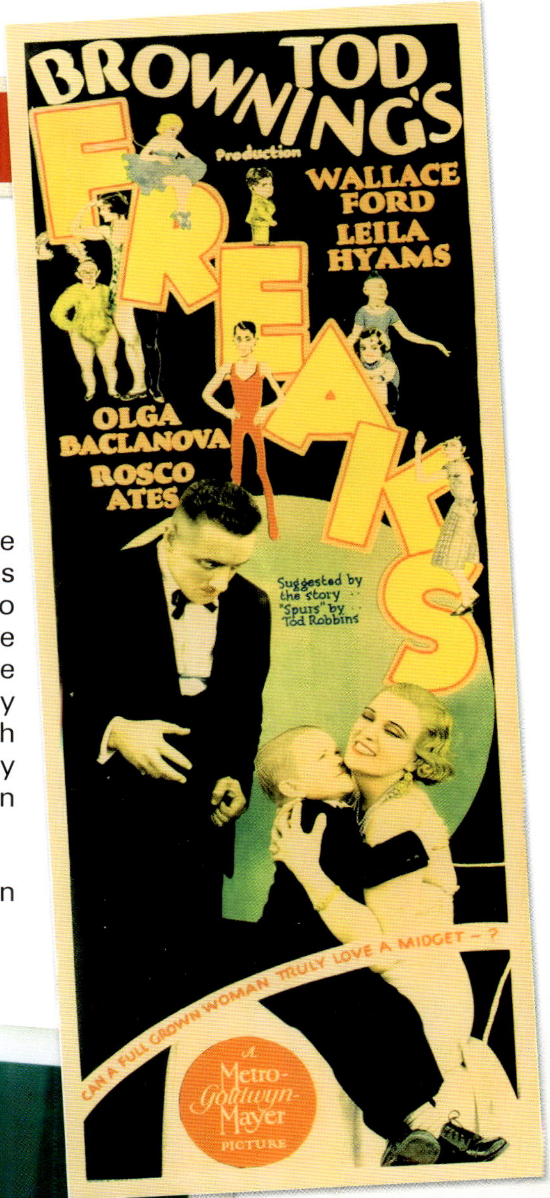

Freaks.
Metro-Goldwyn-Mayer (1932).

ON *FREAKS* (1932)

I'd have to say Tod Browning is my favorite, and how I would love to have known him. We had a lot of things in common. When I was little and living with my mom and grandmother, we used to go to Gibsonton, Florida, in the winter, which is where the freaks went in the winter. I saw the giant, and remember seeing little people in the post office and on the street. I have been fascinated by freaks ever since. Later my best friend, Nini Finkelstein, was a publicist for Barnum & Bailey which had (another coincidence) winter quarters in Venice, Florida, where my mother and stepfather had retired to. I was even a "clown for a day" in Madison Square Garden once, through her.

~Jeanne Keyes Youngson

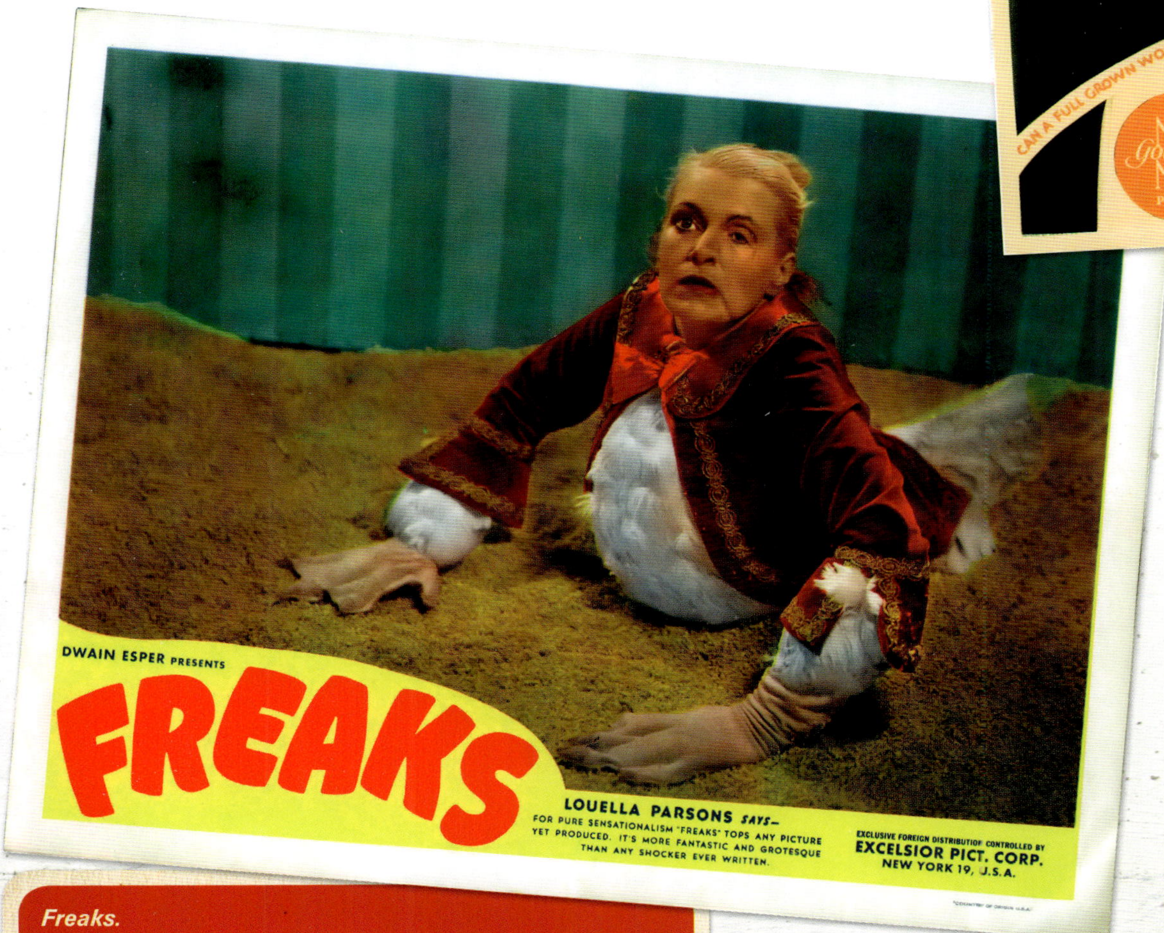

Freaks.
Metro-Goldwyn-Mayer (1932).

Freaks.
Metro-Goldwyn-Mayer (1932).

Freaks still has the power to horrify and fascinate. When I interviewed dwarf actor Angelo Rossitto in 1985, he said director Tod Browning loved his cast and felt one with them.

Tony Timpone

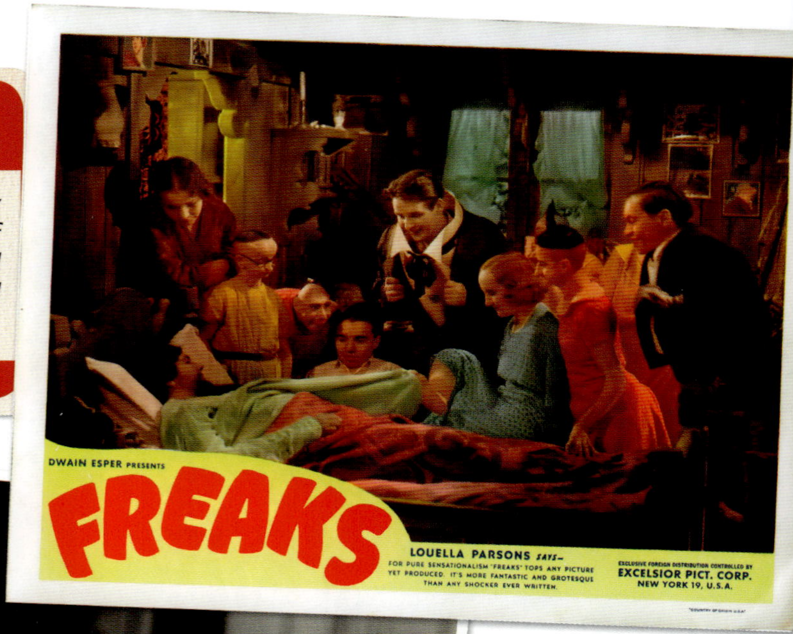

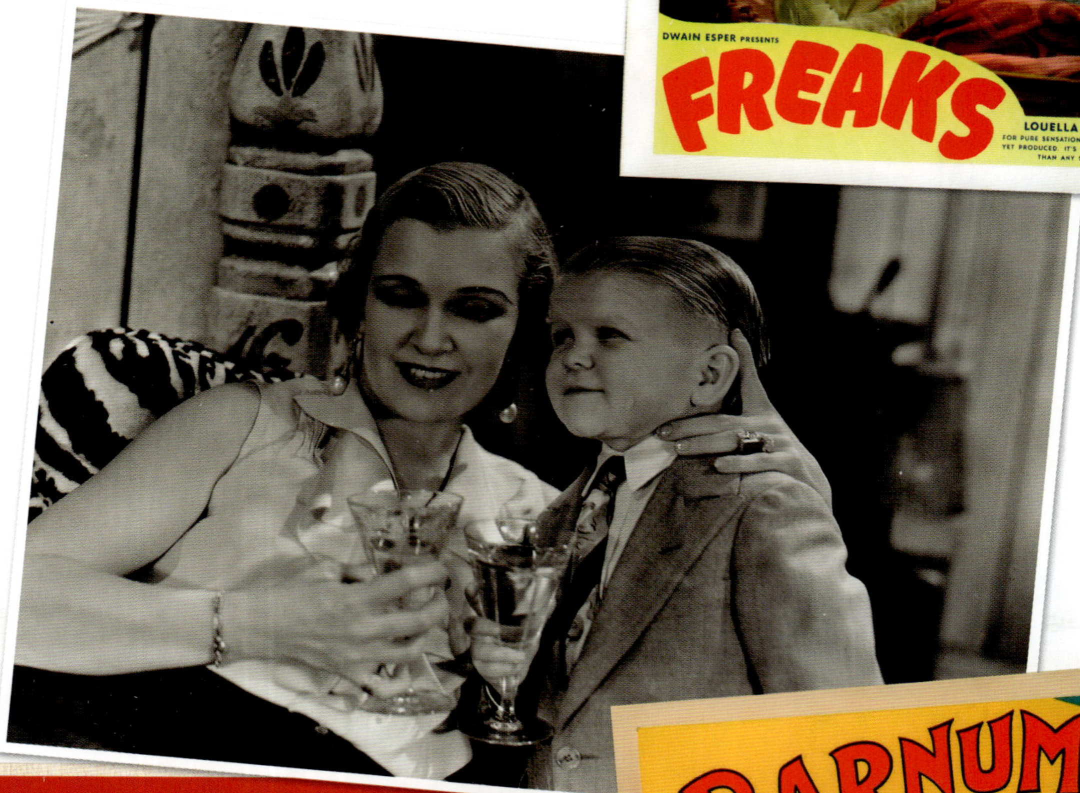

Freaks.
Metro-Goldwyn-Mayer (1932). Belgium.

Too many of our social get-togethers wind up with everyone banging on the table and chanting "Gooble-gobble, Gooble-gobble, one of us..."

Mort Castle

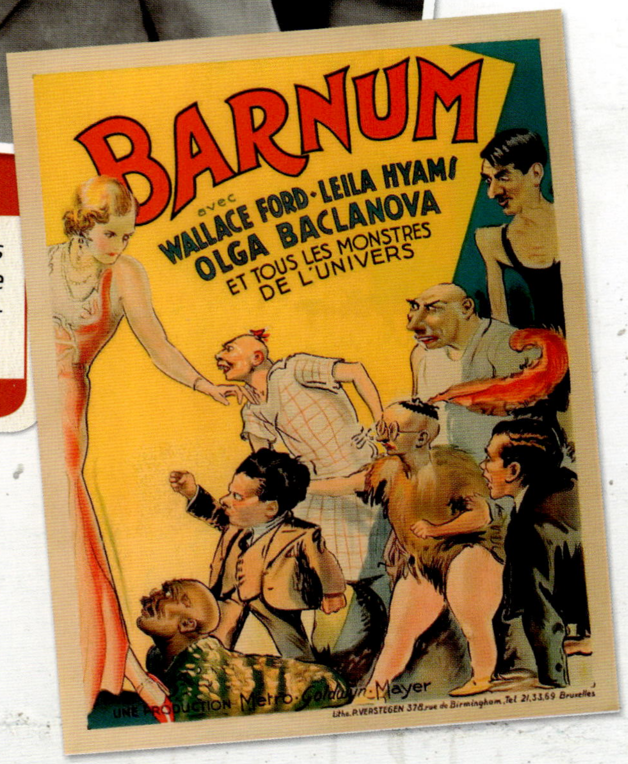

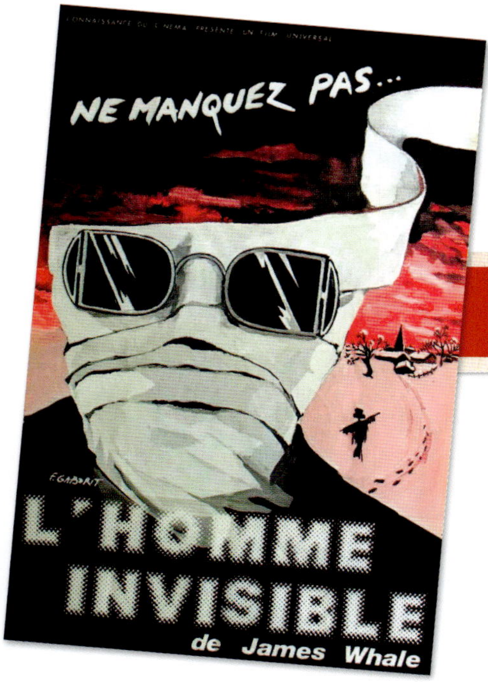

The Invisible Man.
Universal Pictures (1933). France.

The Vampire Bat.
Majestic Pictures (1933).

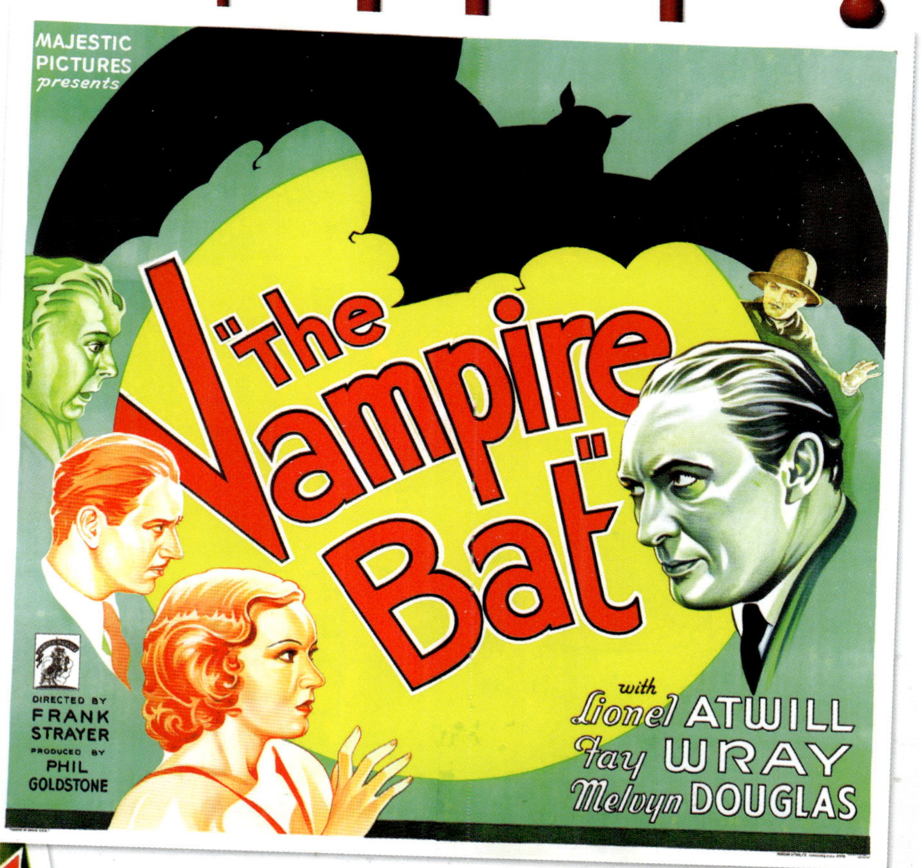

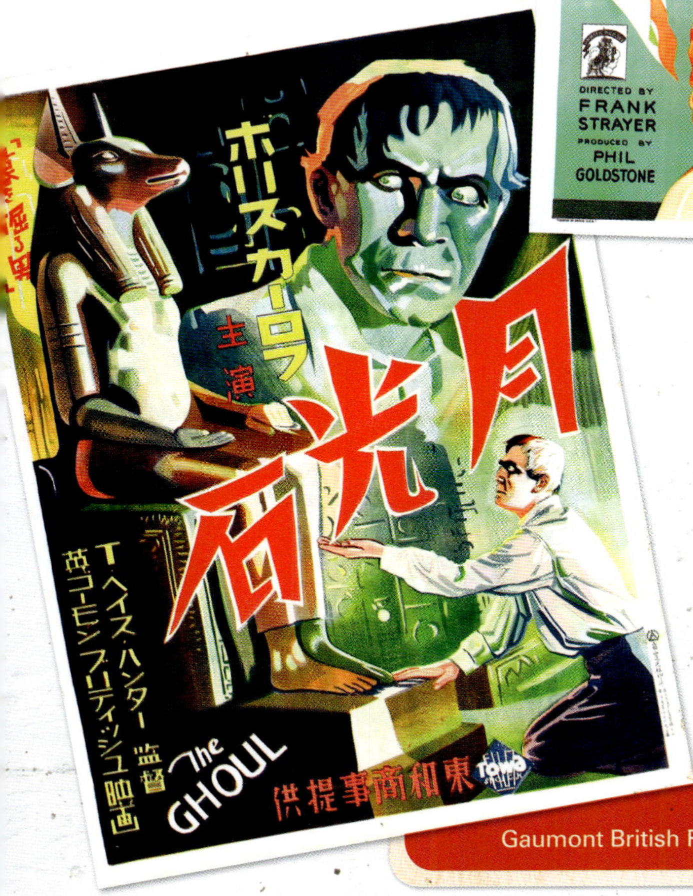

The Ghoul.
Gaumont British Picture Corporation (1933) Japan.

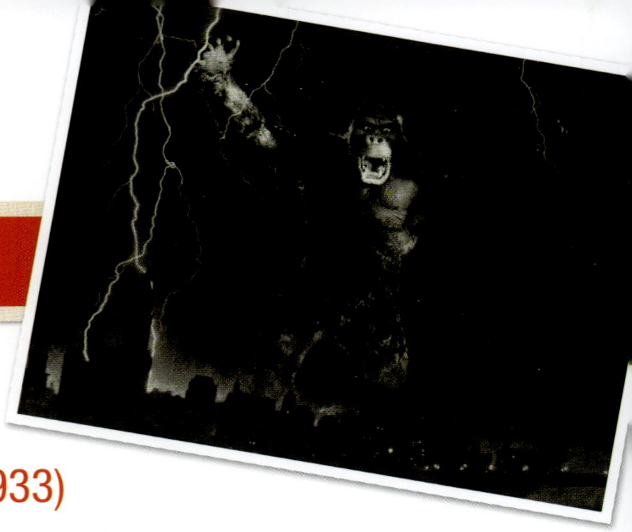

King Kong.
RKO Radio Pictures (1933).

ON *KING KONG* (1933)

The most outstanding "classic" movie monster, in my view, is *King Kong*, mainly because he's by far and away the most important one to have originated in the movie medium rather than being adapted from another, as Dracula and Frankenstein's monster — and, admittedly to a less extent, the Wolf Man — were. The others already had a measure of mythic status, which was merely transfigured by the further mythic status provided by the movie imagery, but King Kong is a modern myth entirely created by the movies and entirely defined by movie imagery. Other movie monsters gleaned sympathy in their visual representations, but none in quite the same seemingly-paradoxical fashion as King Kong, whose iconic stand against the biplanes on top of the Empire State Building is unmatched in movie history (and unrepeatable, as the two remakes have demonstrated); of all monster movies, the 1933 *King Kong* comes closest to being a work of genius — and is, of course, the seed of the entire Japanese monster movie tradition as well as numerous American follow-ups.

~Brian Stableford

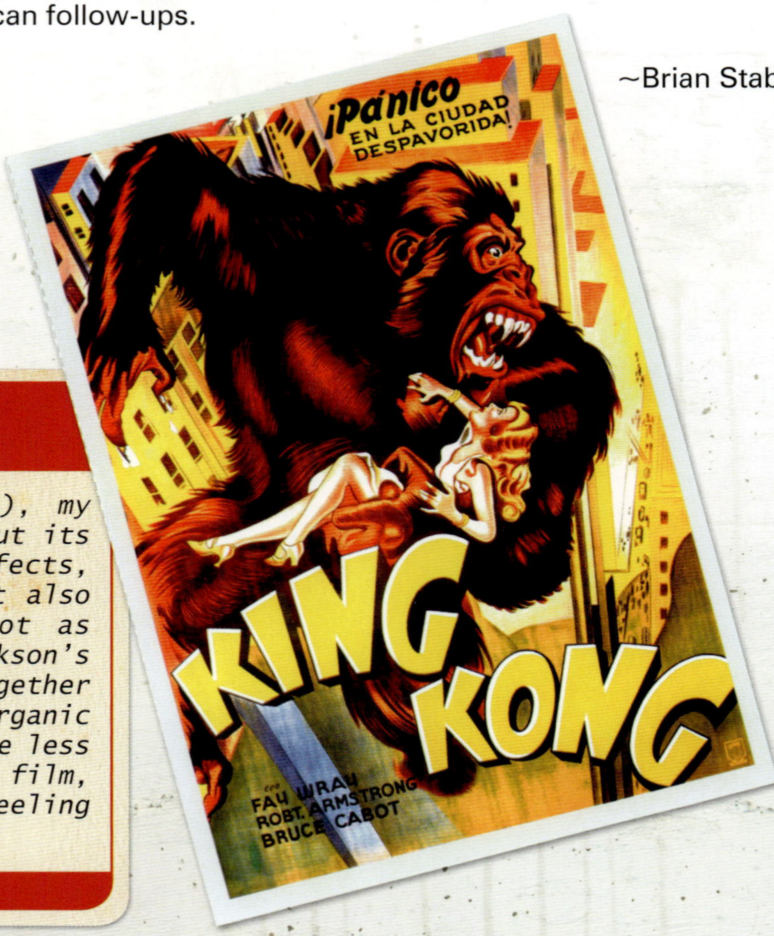

King Kong.
RKO Radio Pictures (1933). Spain.

When I teach King Kong *(1933), my students often talk at length about its archaic stop motion special effects, usually finding them wondrous but also distracting. While certainly not as realistic as the CGI in Peter Jackson's remake, I find the 1933 Kong altogether more frightening. There is an organic quality to his movements, which are less fluid, more syncopated. In this film, what looks less real ends up feeling more real.*

Jesse Stommel

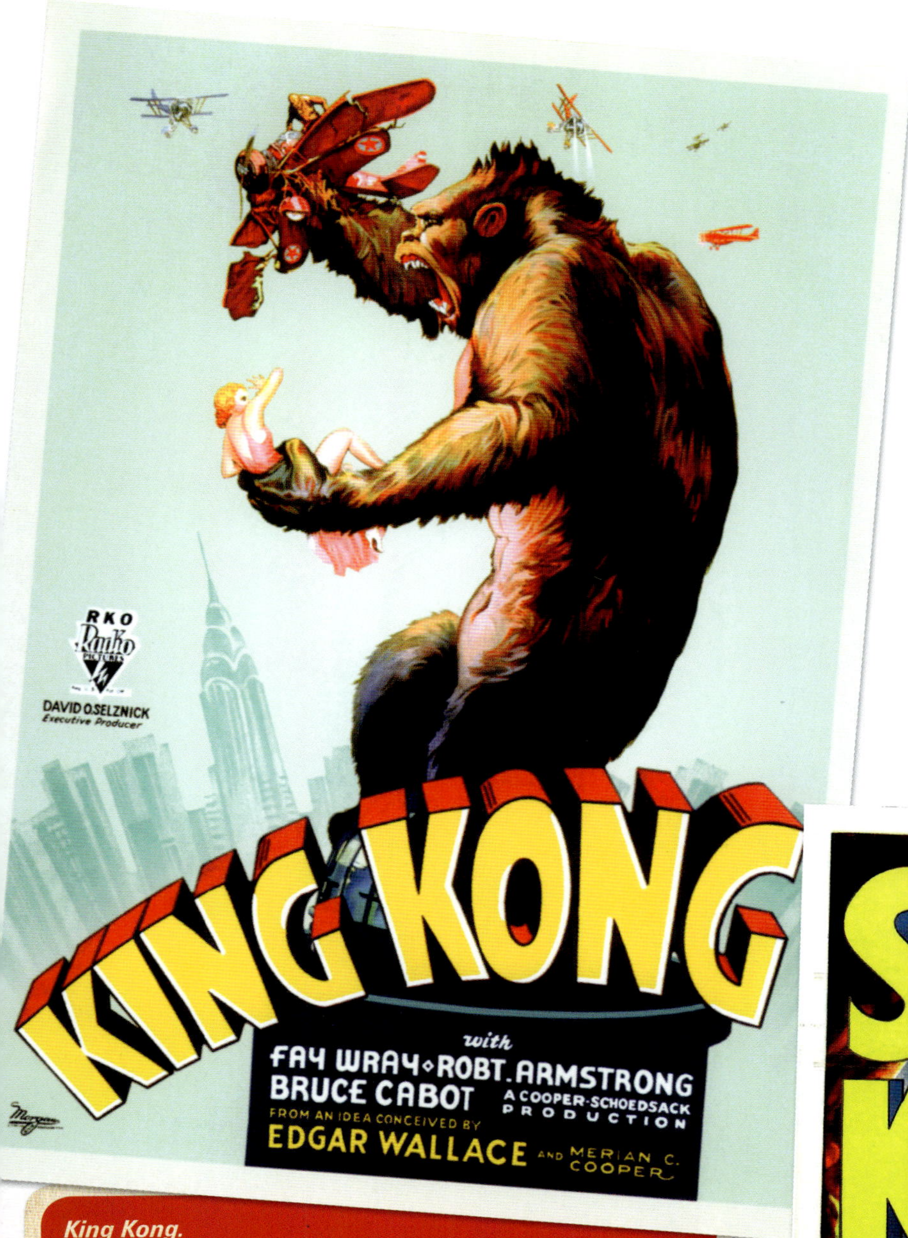

King Kong.
RKO Radio Pictures (1933).

NYC Monster Kids like me fondly recall the time WWOR Channel 9 aired this movie for a whole week on their MILLION DOLLAR MOVIE. By Friday night, I knew the movie by heart!

Tony Timpone

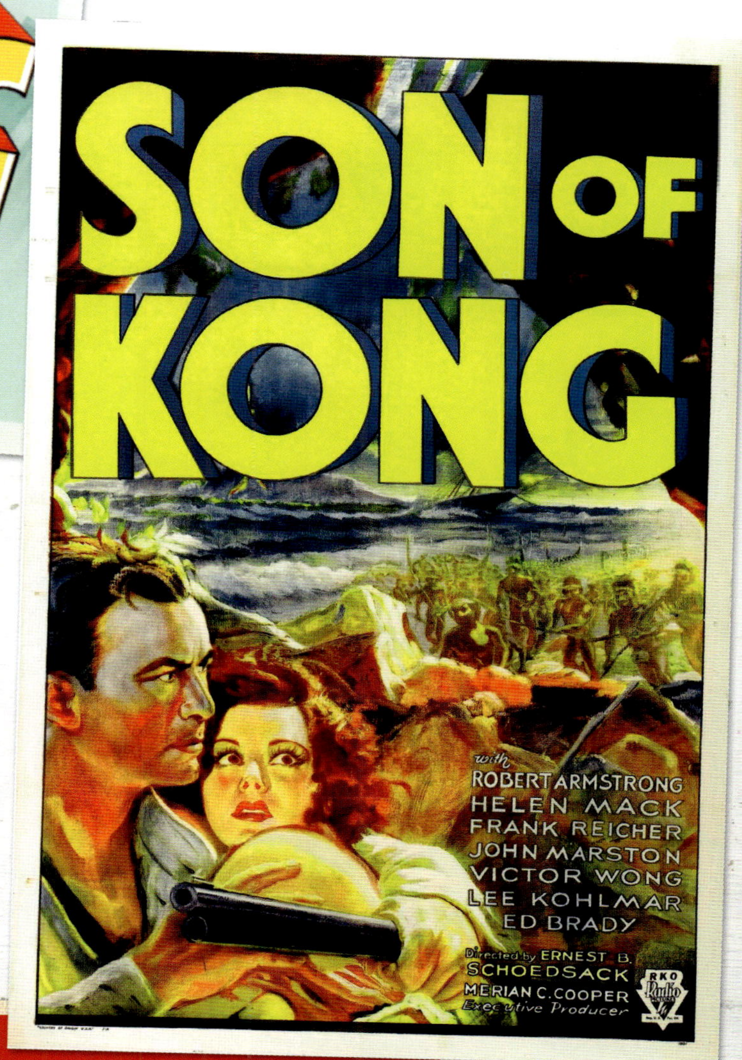

Son of Kong.
RKO Radio Pictures (1933).

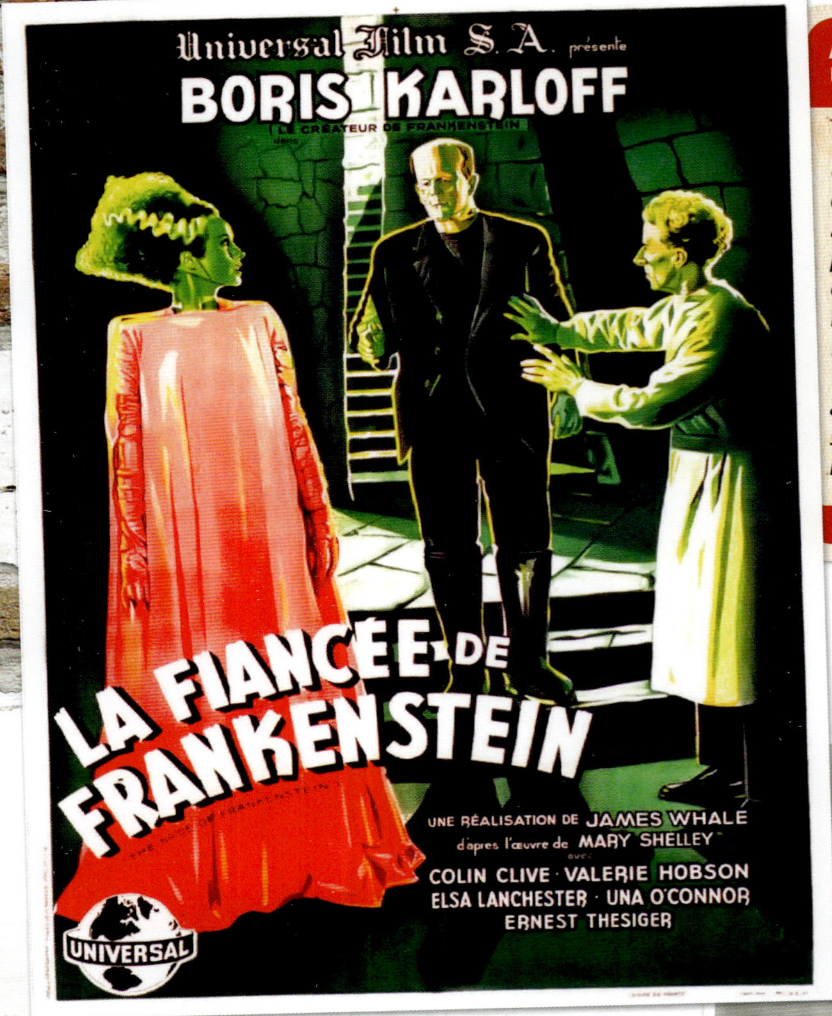

Bride of Frankenstein.
Universal Pictures (1935). France.

Bride of Frankenstein *is best experienced back to back with the original 1931* Frankenstein *since they are essentially one film – the second picks up right at the moment the first ends (although Dwight Frye, the murdered Fritz of the first film, is somehow resurrected as Karl in the second).* Bride *is unquestionably the better of the two, a visually stunning film with a stirring score by Franz Waxman and the inimitable Ernest Thesiger as Dr. Pretorius.*

F. Paul Wilson

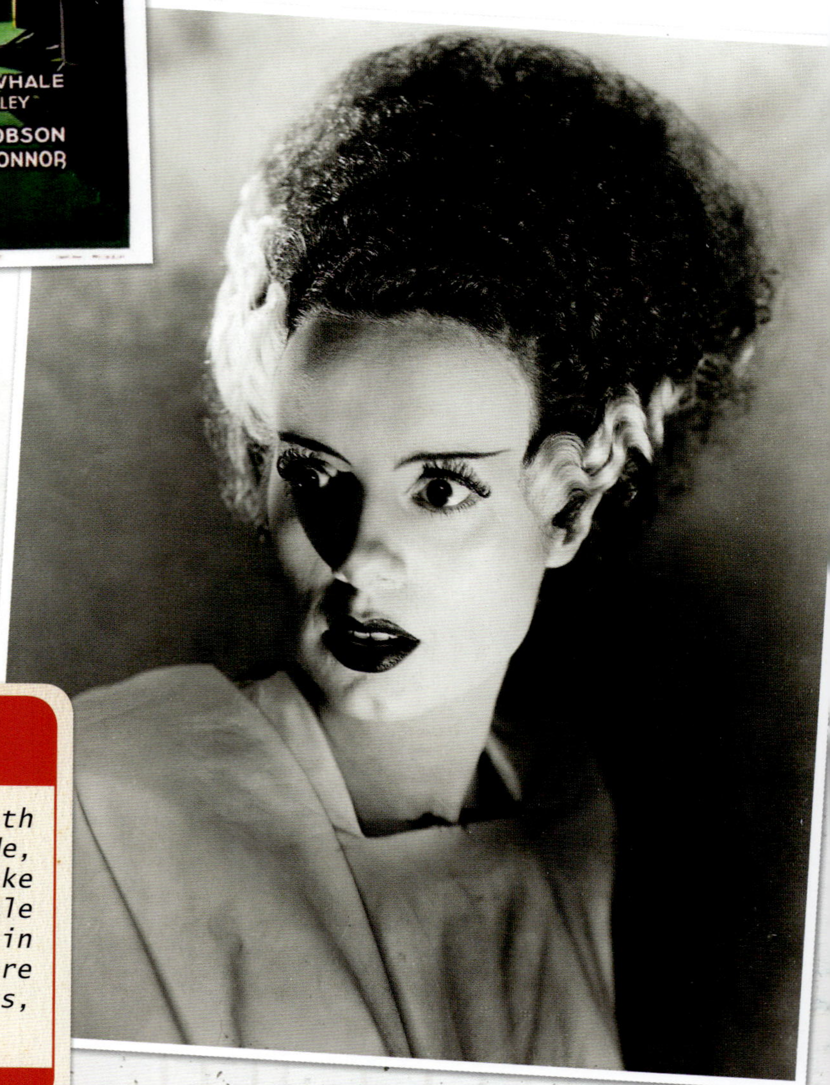

Bride of Frankenstein.
Universal Pictures (1935).

Elsa Lanchester, who played both Mary Shelley and the creature's bride, is reputed to have learned how to make the sounds she produced as the female monster from watching swans at a park in London. In her view, because swans were as beautiful as they could be vicious, they were a fitting exemplar.

Caroline Joan (Kay) Picart

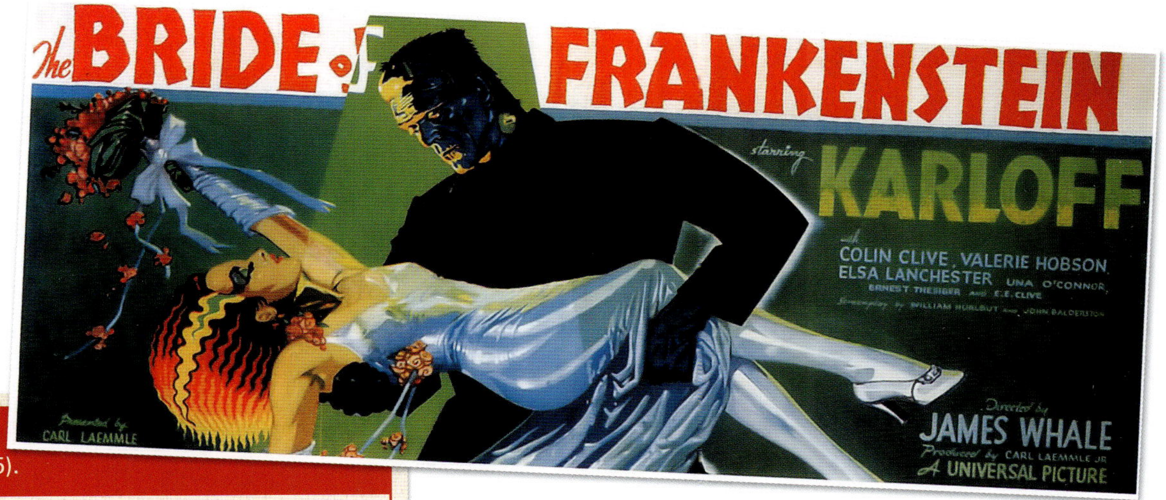

Bride of Frankenstein.
Universal Pictures (1935).

One of the funniest production history footnotes I have read about Bride of Frankenstein *is how James Whale had intended it to be a parody of the first; unfortunately, some horror fans did not catch the humor. At the premiere of the film, Whale was laughing at the jokes he thought would be obvious to everyone, when one of the viewers turned around, rebuked him, and told him he could leave, if he did not like the film. Humor did not return to the depiction of the creature until 1946, with* Abbott and Costello Meet Frankenstein, *where the creature is a mindless prop, but even more strikingly, Mel Brooks's loving parody,* Young Frankenstein *(1974).*

Caroline Joan (Kay) Picart

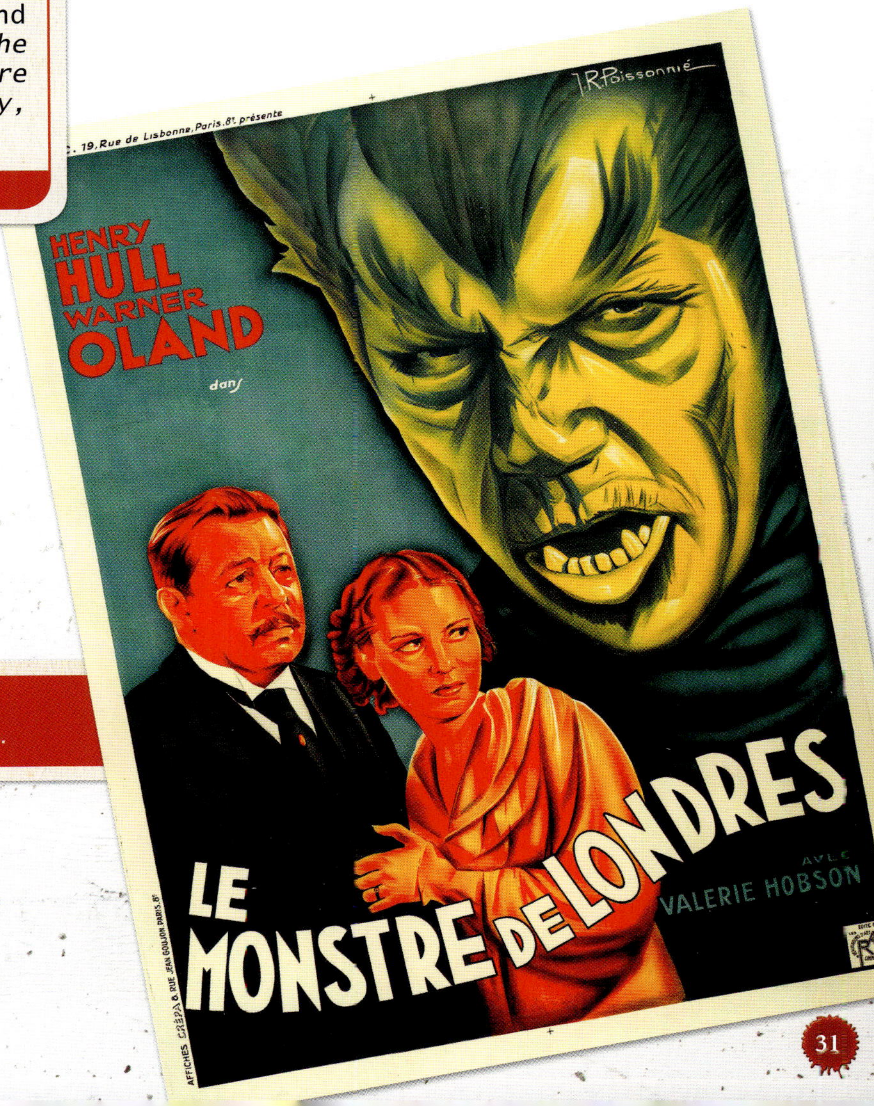

Werewolf of London.
Universal Pictures (1935) France.

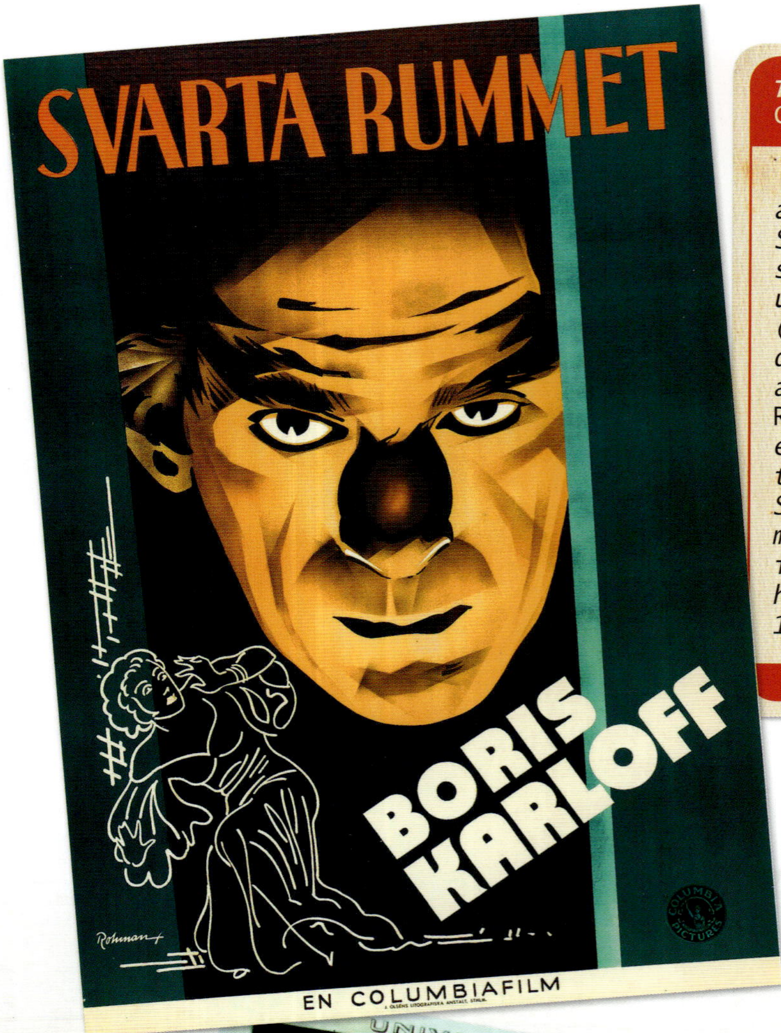

The Black Room.
Columbia Pictures Corporation (1935). Sweden.

My mom and I (aged about 12) went to a Saturday afternoon double feature in Sussex, NJ, where I grew up. Even though she had played the piano for silent movies upstate, she was not a real movie fan. (Odd, huh?) This one Saturday afternoon the double feature was an Eddie Cantor comedy and a Boris Karloff film called The Black Room *(1935). After the Eddie Cantor movie ended, Mom had had enough, so she left me there to see the other film. It scared the SH*T out of me. I had nightmares about that movie for years and years. Later I saw it on TV and found it hard to believe it had so terrified me. Still, when you are 12 years old ...*

Jeanne Keyes Youngson

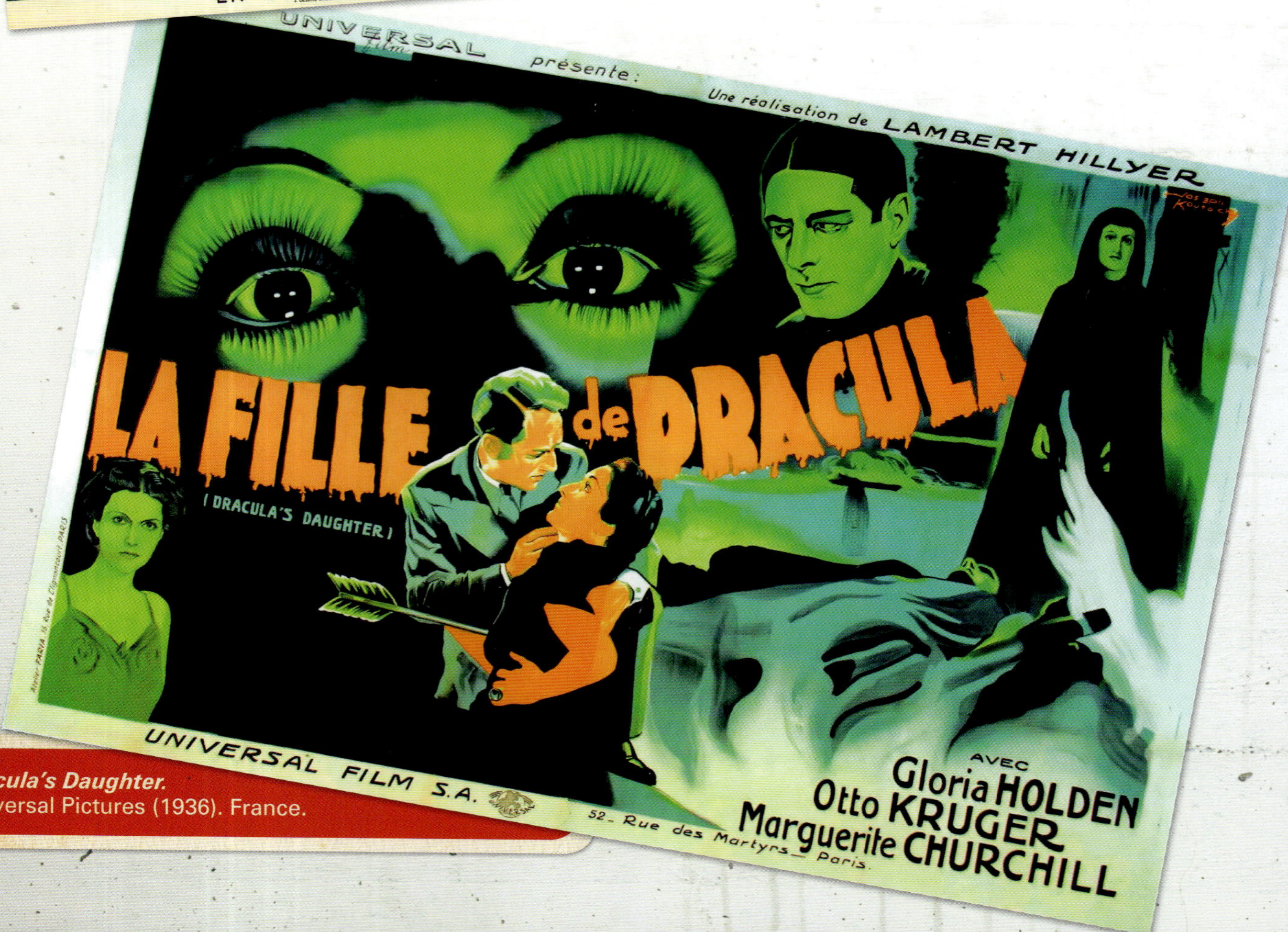

Dracula's Daughter.
Universal Pictures (1936). France.

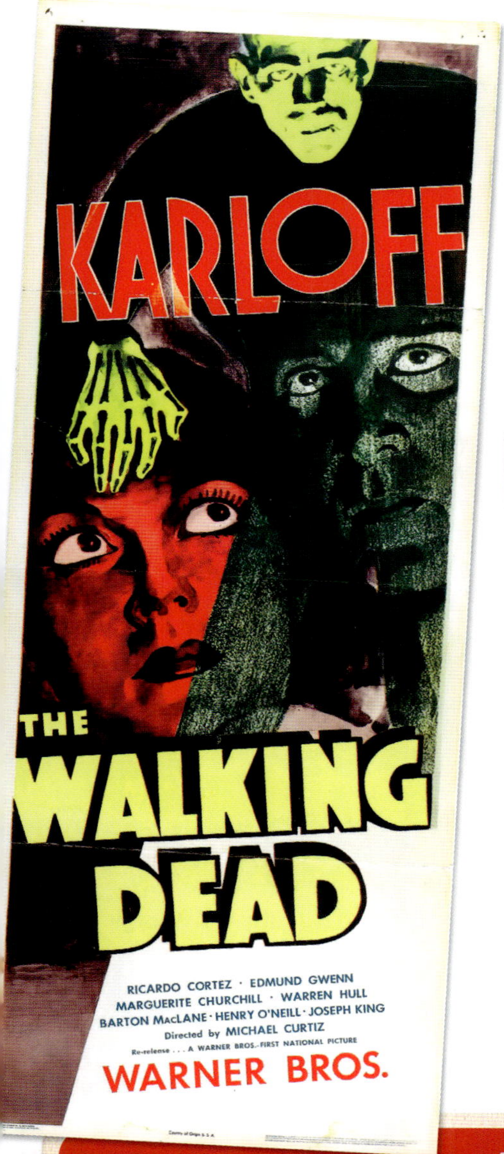

The Walking Dead. Warner Bros. Pictures (1936).

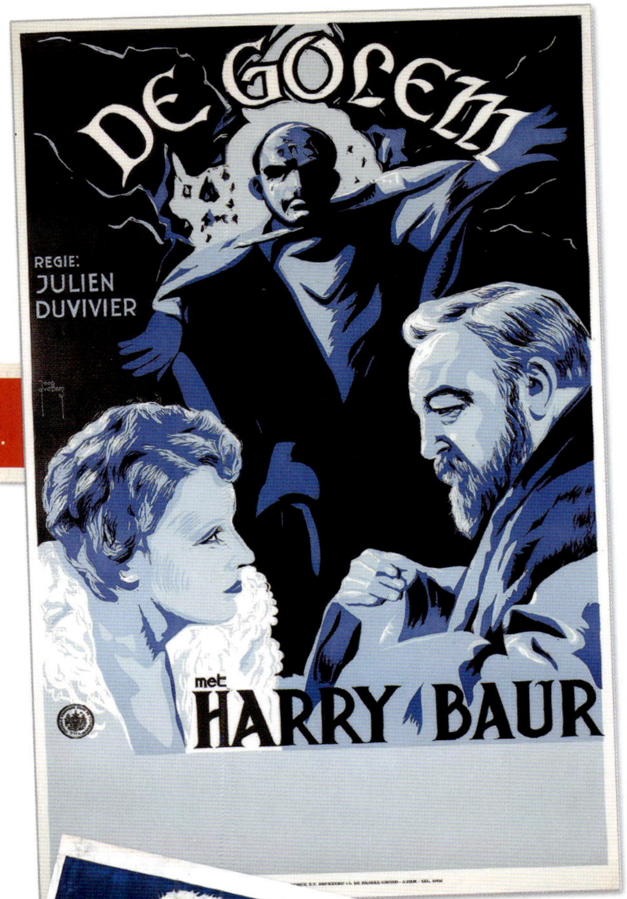

The Golem. AB (1936). Netherlands.

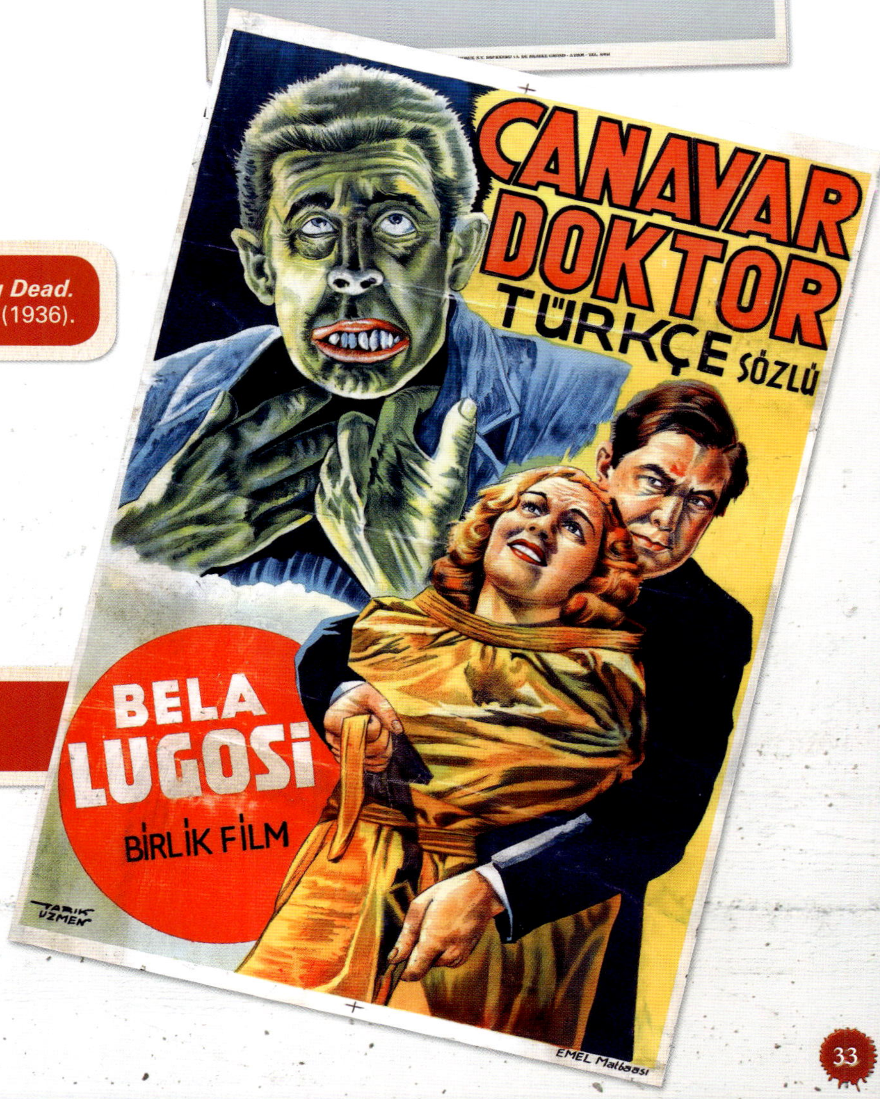

The Human Monster. Associated British-Pathé/ John Argyle Productions (1939). Turkey.

3 THE 1940s

THE FEARSOME FORTIES

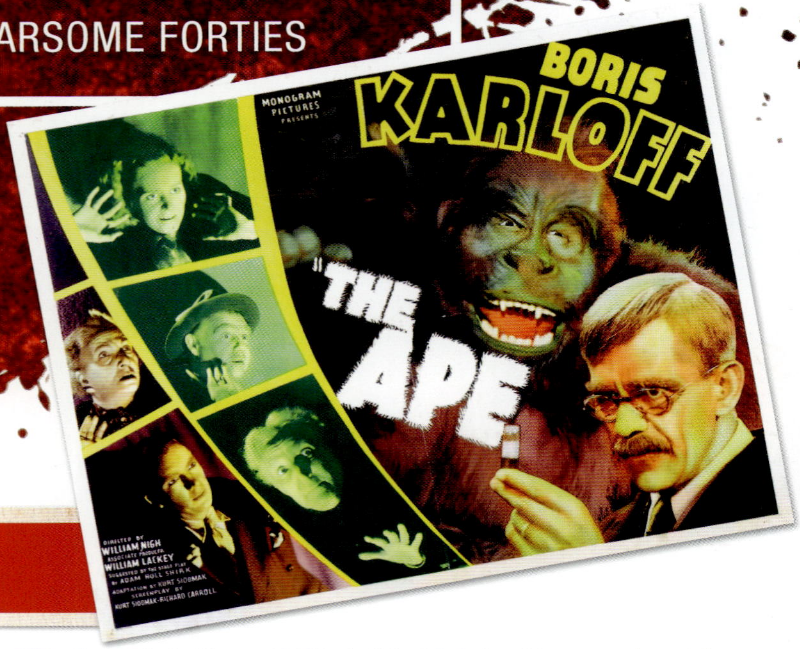

The Ape.
Monogram Pictures (1940).

After a brief late-1930s lull (which had less to do with an overestimated resistance by British censors, and more to do with the end of the Laemmle regime at Universal), war drumbeats in Europe gave a new purpose to pulse-pounding entertainment, and sequels and spinoffs based on the horror classics became a cinematic staple of World War II. An unconscious, but especially popular, war parable was found in *The Wolf Man* (1940) and the implied "battle" of *Frankenstein Meets the Wolf Man* (1943) provided an effective tie-in promotion for war bonds. The real-life atrocities of Nazi doctors were darkly echoed by a plethora of mad scientist movies, with Bela Lugosi and Boris Karloff occupying the laboratory the way the Germans occupied France. The immediate postwar period saw some important developments in psychological horror by director Val Lewton, as well as horror comedy, best exemplified by *Abbott and Costello Meet Frankenstein* (1948).

~David J. Skal

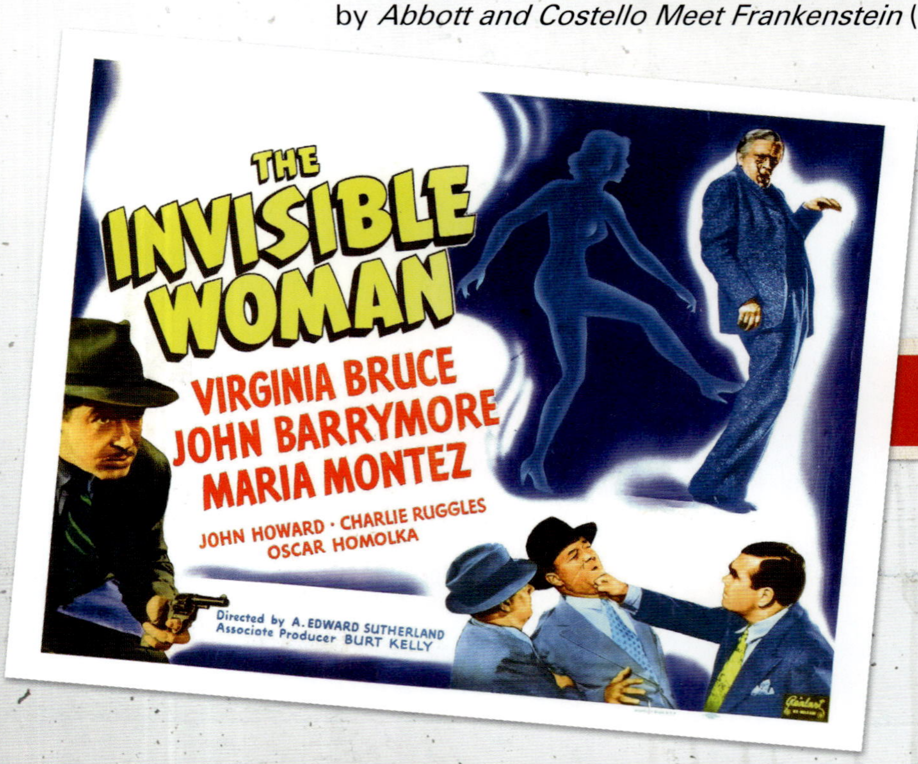

The Invisible Woman.
Universal Pictures (1940).

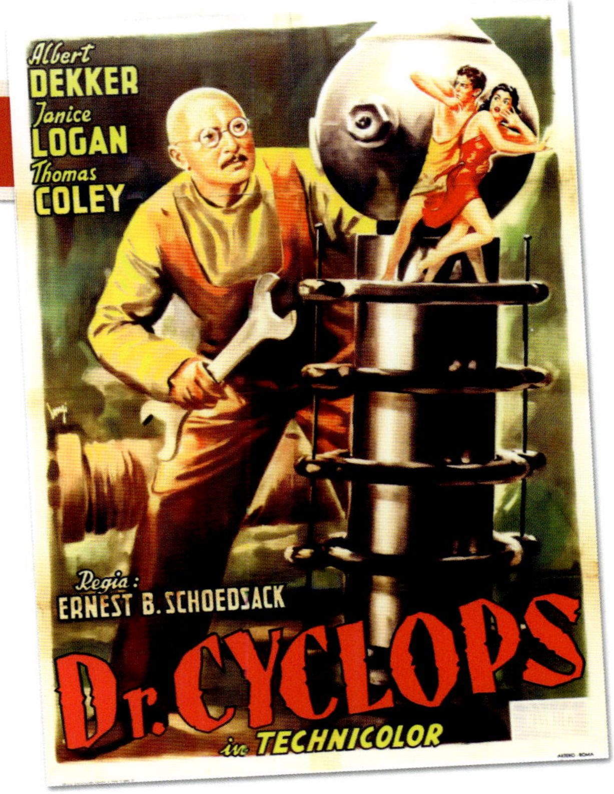

Dr. Cyclops.
Paramount Pictures (1940) Italy.

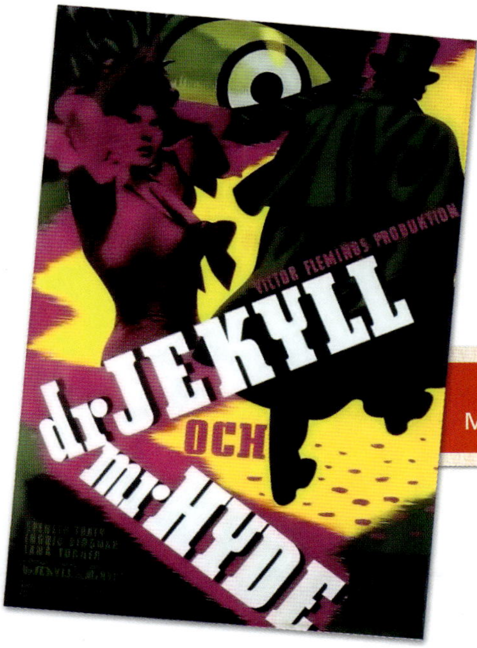

Dr. Jekyll and Mr. Hyde.
Metro-Goldwyn-Mayer/Loew's (1941). Sweden.

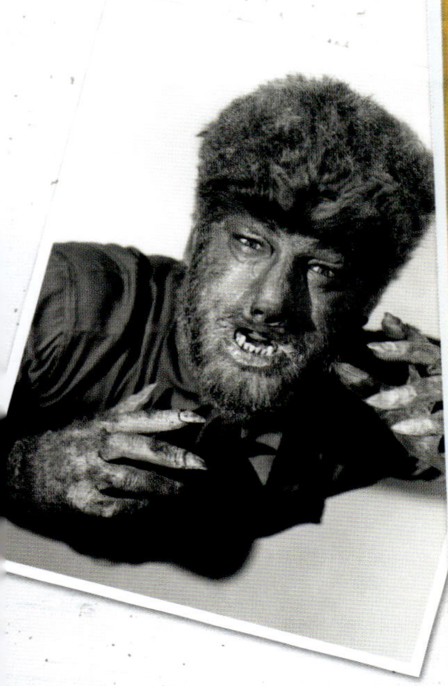

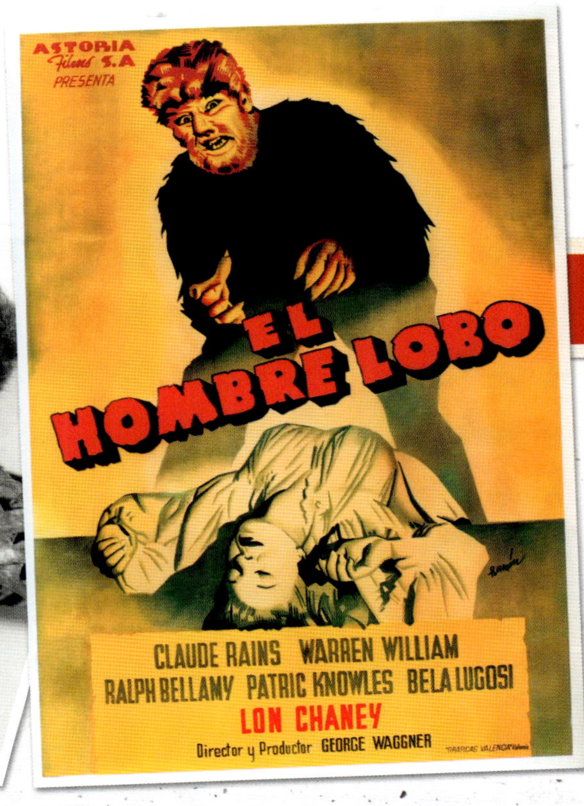

The Wolf Man.
Universal Pictures (1941). Spain.

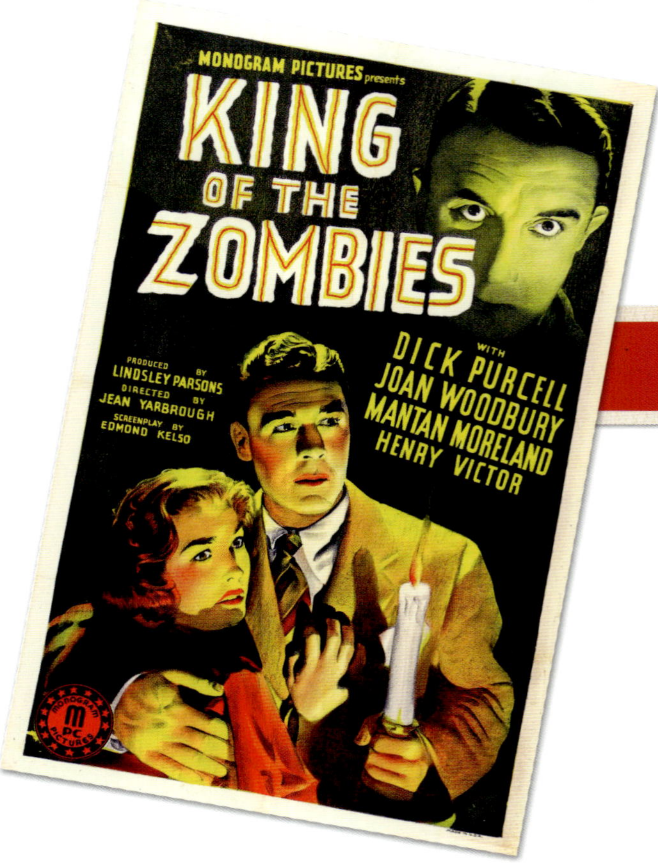

King of the Zombies.
Monogram Pictures (1941).

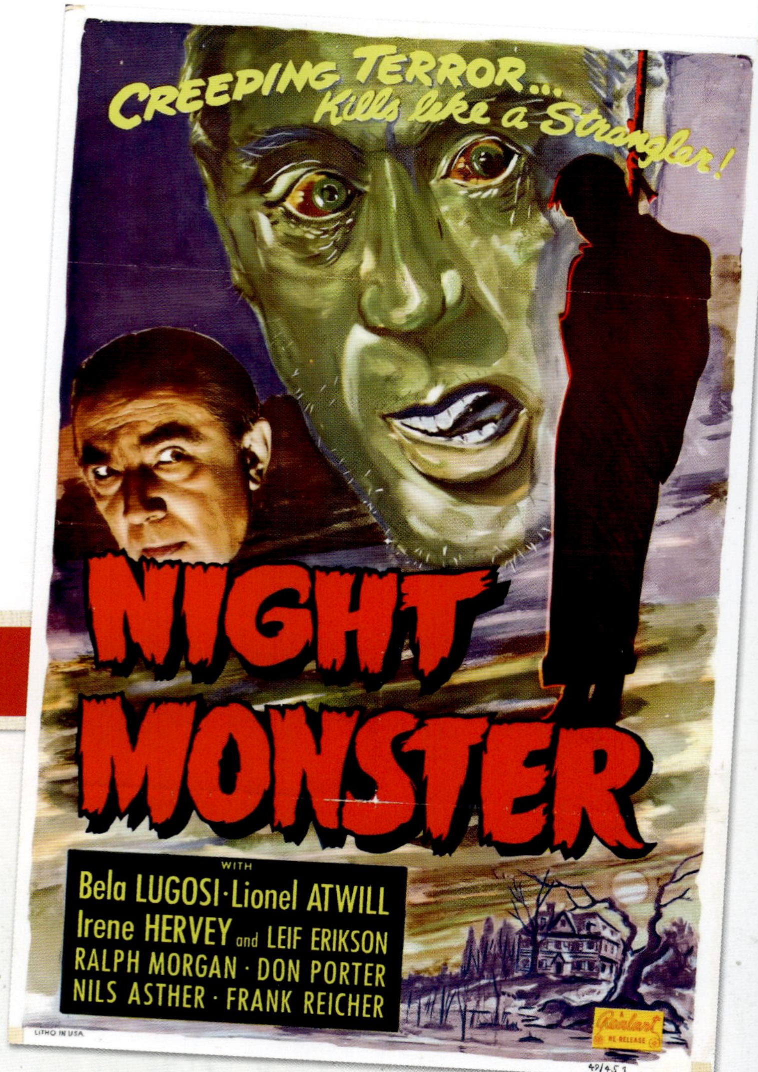

Night Monster.
Universal Pictures (1942).

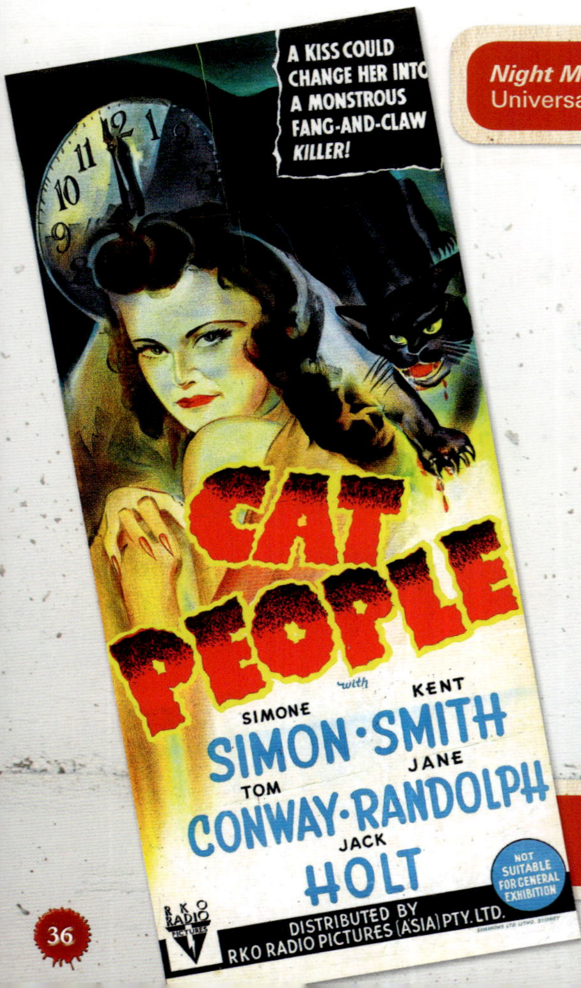

Cat People.
RKO Radio Pictures (1942). UK.

The Ghost of Frankenstein.
Universal Pictures (1942).

In Bride of Frankenstein *(1935), the creature is given a criminal brain but he seems to act more like an abandoned child, reacting against a hostile world. In* Ghost of Frankenstein *(1943), the ghost reasons that because of the criminal brain, the creature has turned destructive, but it could easily be saved by giving it a new brain. Unfortunately, that, too, turns to be a false hope, as it is Ygor's maniacal brain that becomes transplanted into the creature's powerful body.*

Caroline Joan (Kay) Picart

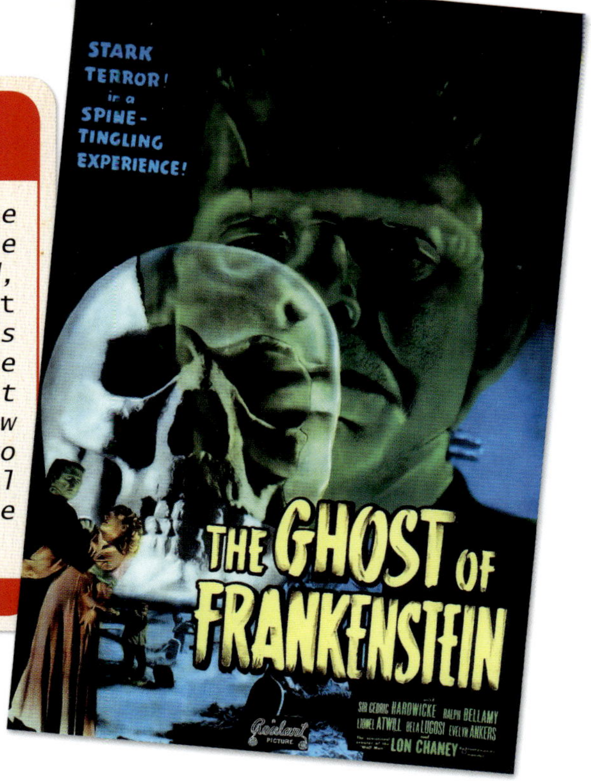

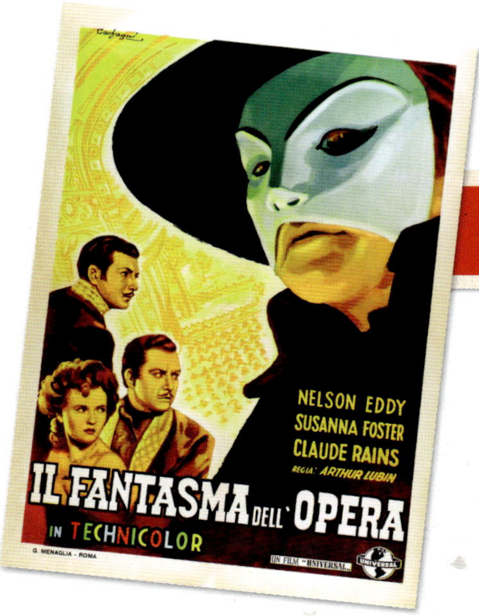

The Phantom of the Opera.
Universal Pictures (1943). Italy.

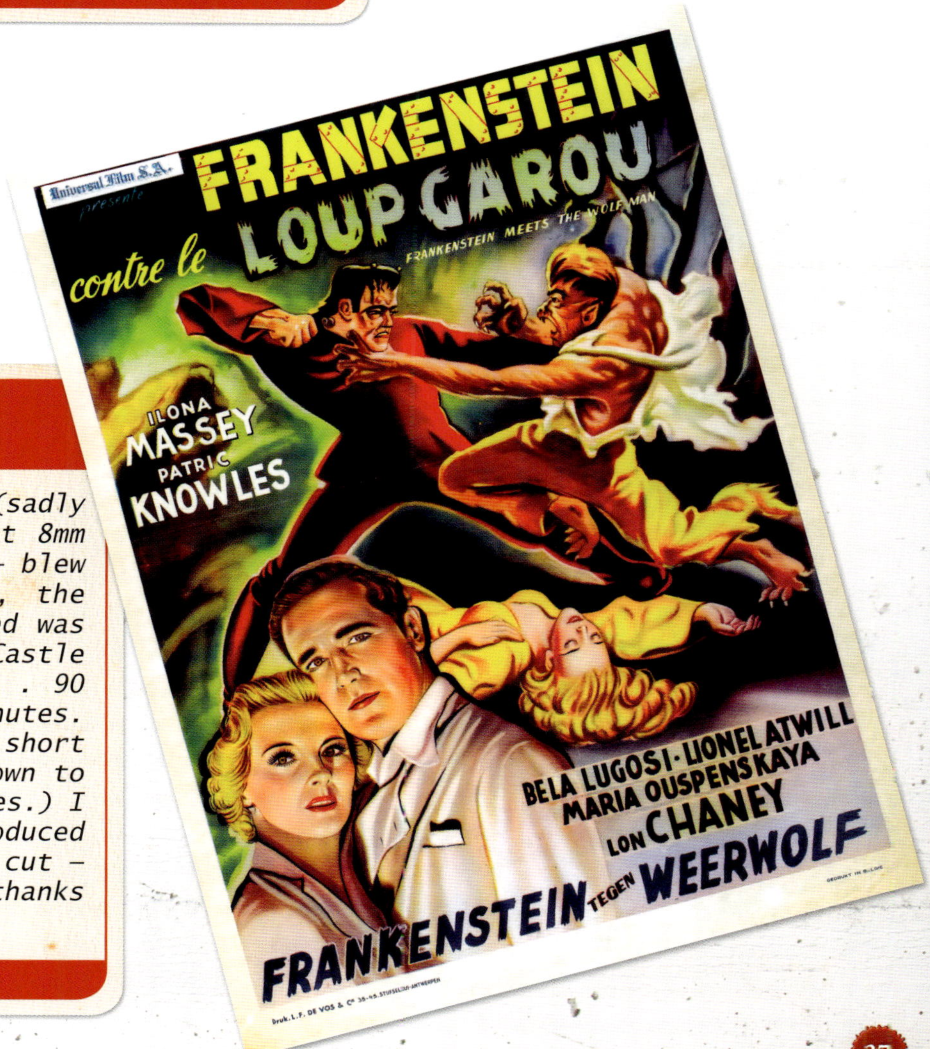

Frankenstein Meets the Wolf Man.
Universal Pictures (1943). Belgium.

Back to the days of Castle films (sadly no relation): When I got my first 8mm movie projector (Bell and Howell – blew a bulb about every 15 seconds), the very first Castle film I purchased was Frankenstein Meets the Wolf Man. *Castle films were somewhat condensed . . . 90 to 120 minutes became 7 to 9 minutes. (Those were Castle features. The short subjects were features squished down to 50 feet of film: about three minutes.) I think even before Hemingway introduced me to the prime rules – cut, cut, cut – I started to understand editing thanks to this film.*

Mort Castle

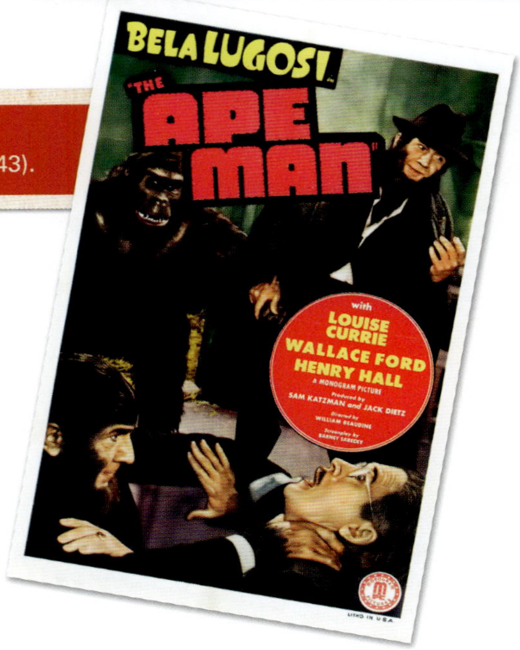

The Ape Man.
Banner Productions/Monogram Pictures (1943).

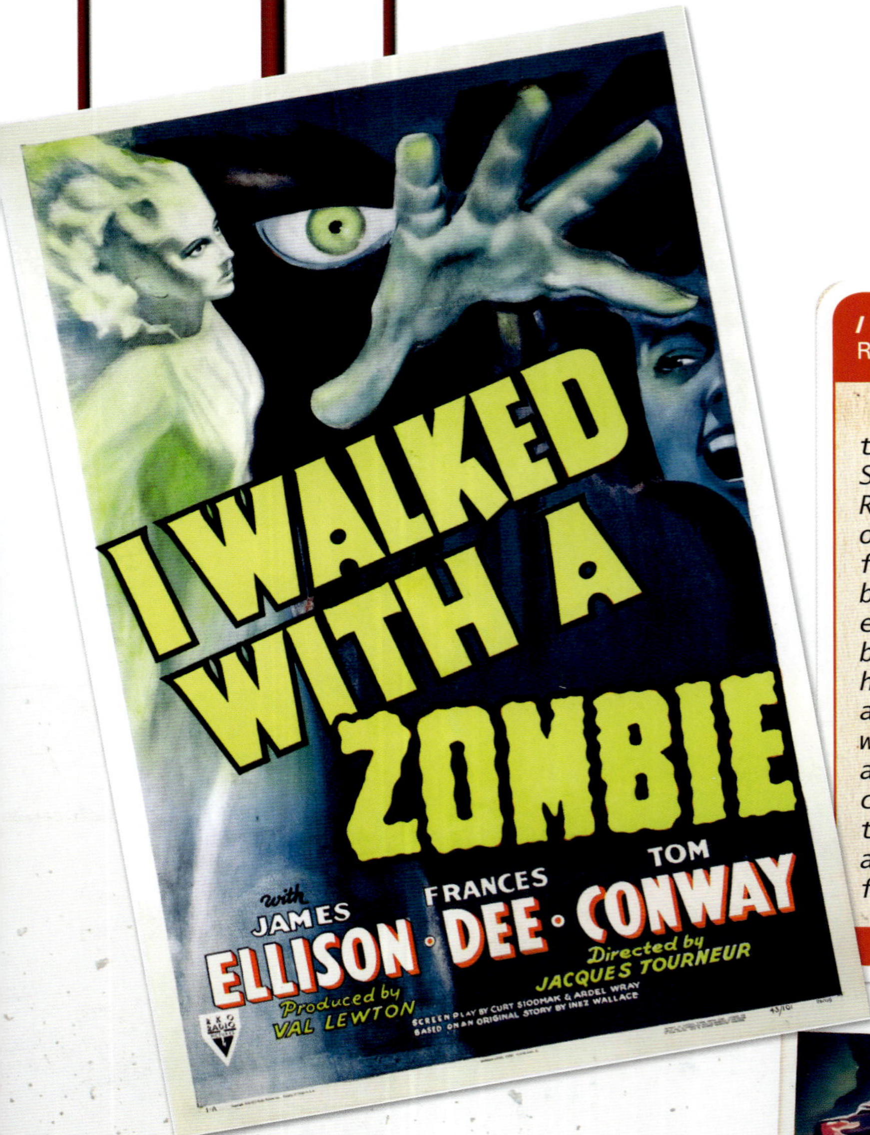

I Walked with a Zombie.
RKO Radio Pictures (1943).

I Walked with a Zombie, *Lewton's worst title and finest film (not to mention Curt Siodmak's). The title was preordained by RKO and dismissed in the opening voice-over. While the basic concept of the film is* Jane Eyre *in the tropics, this becomes as elusive and ambiguous as the entire narrative. Far too delicate to be contained by even my definition of horror,* I Walked with a Zombie *shares an unemphatic sense of the supernatural with a very few other films (*Vampyr *and* Ugetsu Monogatari *among them). Its contradictions and subtleties resonate in the mind, leaving echoes of an experience almost impossible to define and aching for repetition.*

Ramsey Campbell

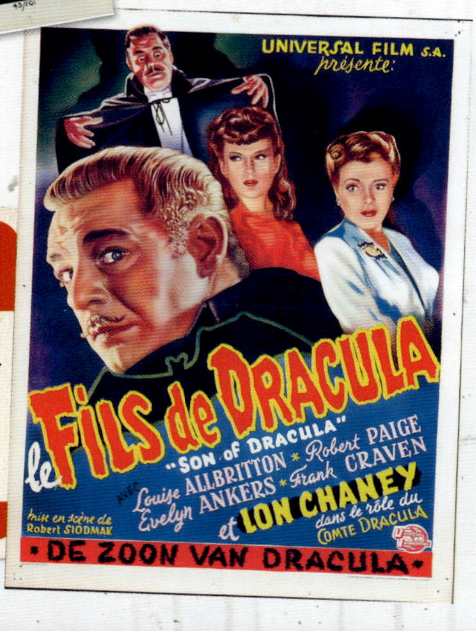

Son of Dracula.
Universal (1943). Belgium.

Lon Chaney Jr. had been "Lenny" in the splendid stage and screen adaptations of Steinbeck's Of Mice and Men. *Now, showing his range, he became Count Alucard; he played it as Lenny in a cape.*

Mort Castle

Curse of the Cat People.
RKO Radio Pictures (1944).

1944 brought Curse of the Cat People, originally to be called Amy and her Friend, a line that survives into the film. The normal couple who survived Cat People return, now with a daughter, Amy. The husband is more thumpingly – indeed, spankingly – conventional than ever, while his wife is ineffectually protective. No wonder Amy seeks companionship from a ghostly Simone Simon, whose first shadowy singing manifestation has a quiet eeriness that pervades the film's best spectral scenes. The film's solitary shock, involving the Headless Horseman, is witty and also relevant insofar as Amy has borrowed the image from the imagination of a local recluse, a surprisingly sharp portrait of schizophrenia. Just as this lady's daughter is driven to the edge by her mother's behavior, so is Amy by her father's dogged inconsistency.

Ramsey Campbell

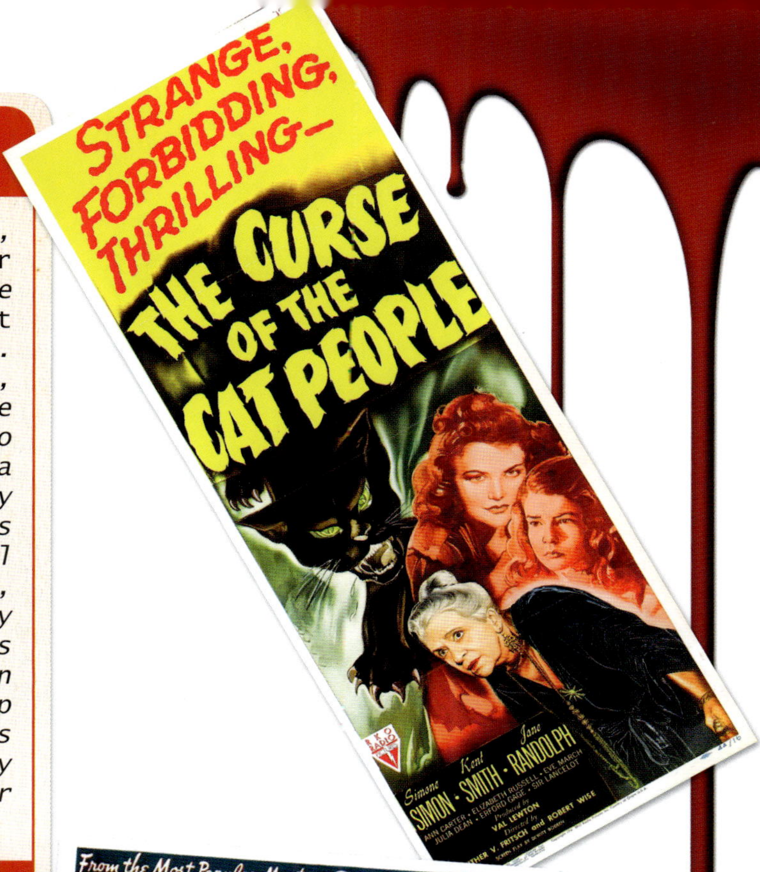

The Uninvited.
Paramount Pictures (1944).

The Uninvited *(1944) is a movie I tried to catch up with for years. It was released when I was about six years old; I remember being in the movie house across the street from where I lived in West Philadelphia, and when the "Coming Attractions" for* The Uninvited *came on the screen, my mother made me put my hands over my eyes. Well, of course I peeked – and saw that shivery moment when two siblings enter a room in the seacoast house where they are staying and do not notice the flowers they brought with them start to wither! It is perhaps America's first great haunted house film.*

Marvin Kaye

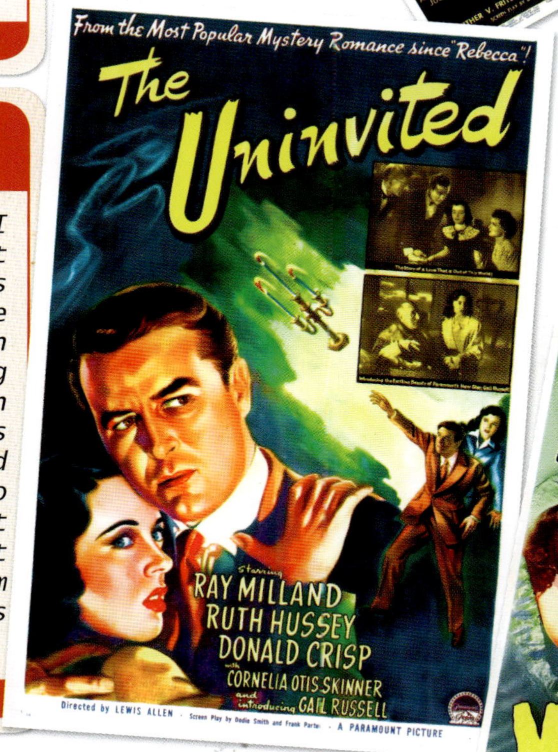

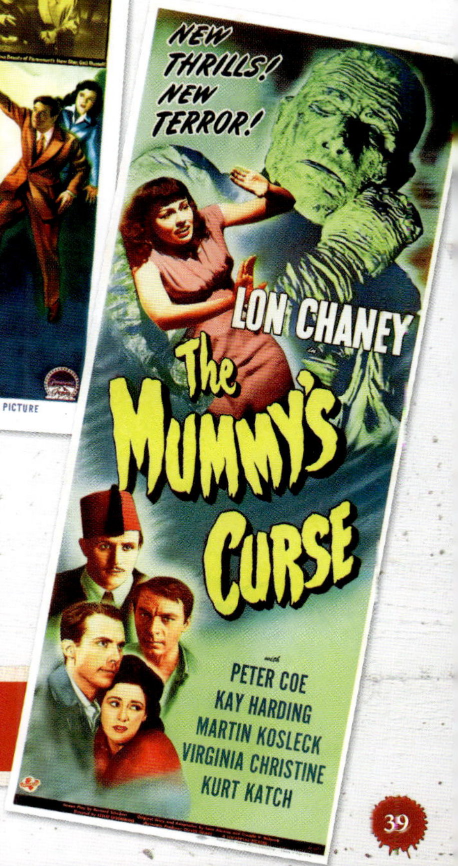

The Mummy's Curse.
Universal Pictures (1944).

House of Frankenstein.
Universal Pictures (1944). Sweden.

House of Frankenstein *was (on a triple bill with follow-up movie* House of Dracula *and* The Mummy*) the first movie I ever saw in Universal's Frankenstein/Dracula/Wolf Man series. Until then, I'd been truly afraid to see one of those movies, fearing the Monster might be the horrible creature drawn by Dick Briefer in the artist's early 1950s comic-book series. Instead of being scared, I found myself captivated by the Universal "mood" and the continuity that existed from one movie in the series to the next, which I'd later carry over into my own motion picture career.*

Donald Glut

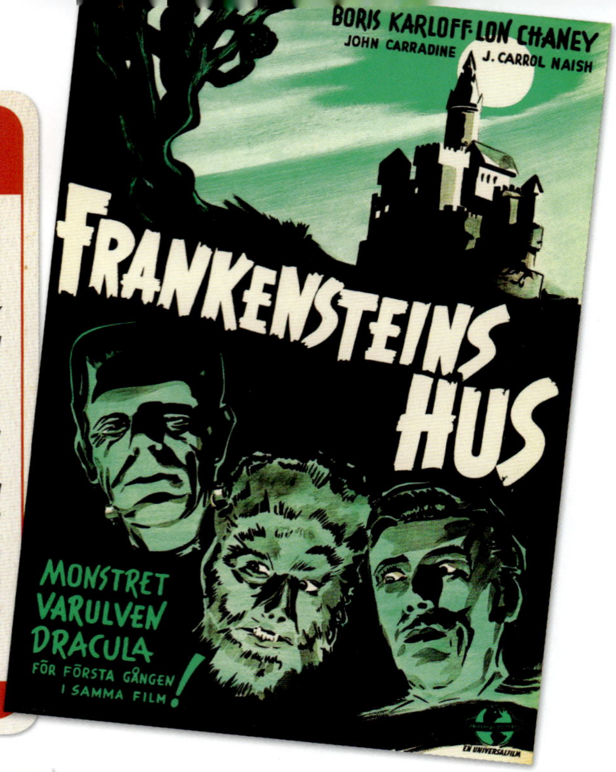

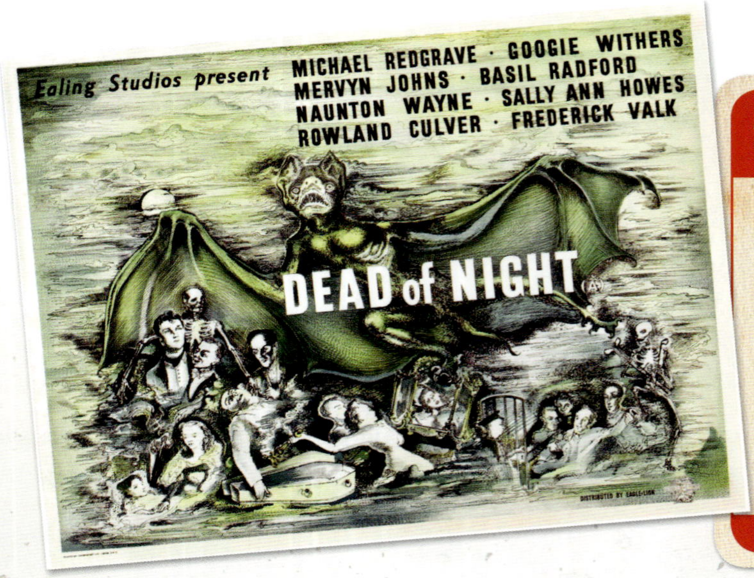

Dead of Night.
Ealing Studios (1945).

British portmanteau horror at its best: A sequence of very British nightmares playfully mingling the trite with the genuinely disturbing that can still astonish. Some exemplary and influential performances from actors such as Mervyn Johns and Michael Redgrave reflect a post-traumatic world of horror: World War 2 may be just over, but angst and paranoia and disruption seem interminable...

Richard J. Hand

Zombies on Broadway.
RKO Radio Pictures (1945).

Wally Brown and Alan Carney, a low budget Abbot and Costello, were really funny in this one. Darby Jones did that unique zombie thing: dislocating his eyes. Freakish. A damned good funny scary film that more so than any other provided the template for the film that revived Abbot and Costello's career and the classic Universal monsters, Bud Abbott and Lou Costello Meet Frankenstein. *And if you're asking whatever happened to Brown and Carney...nothing much.*

Mort Castle

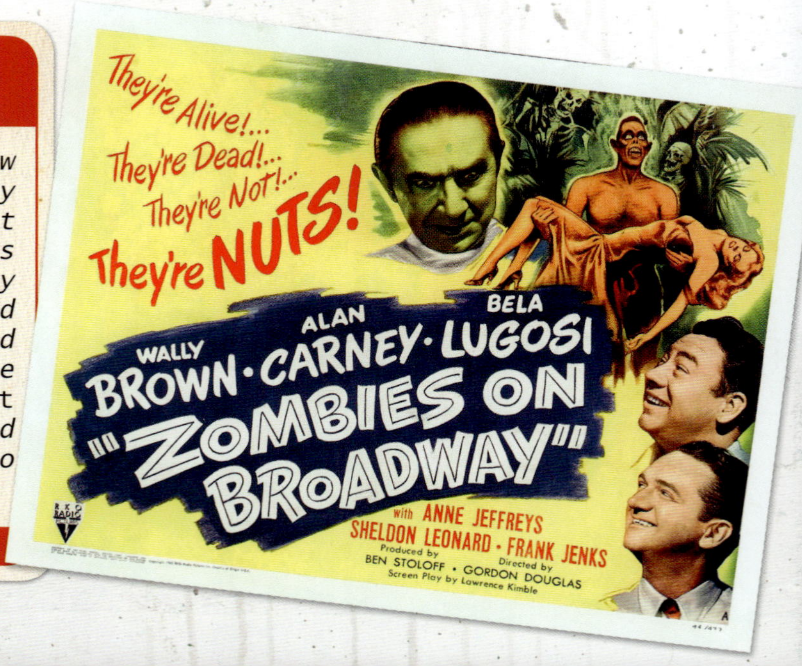

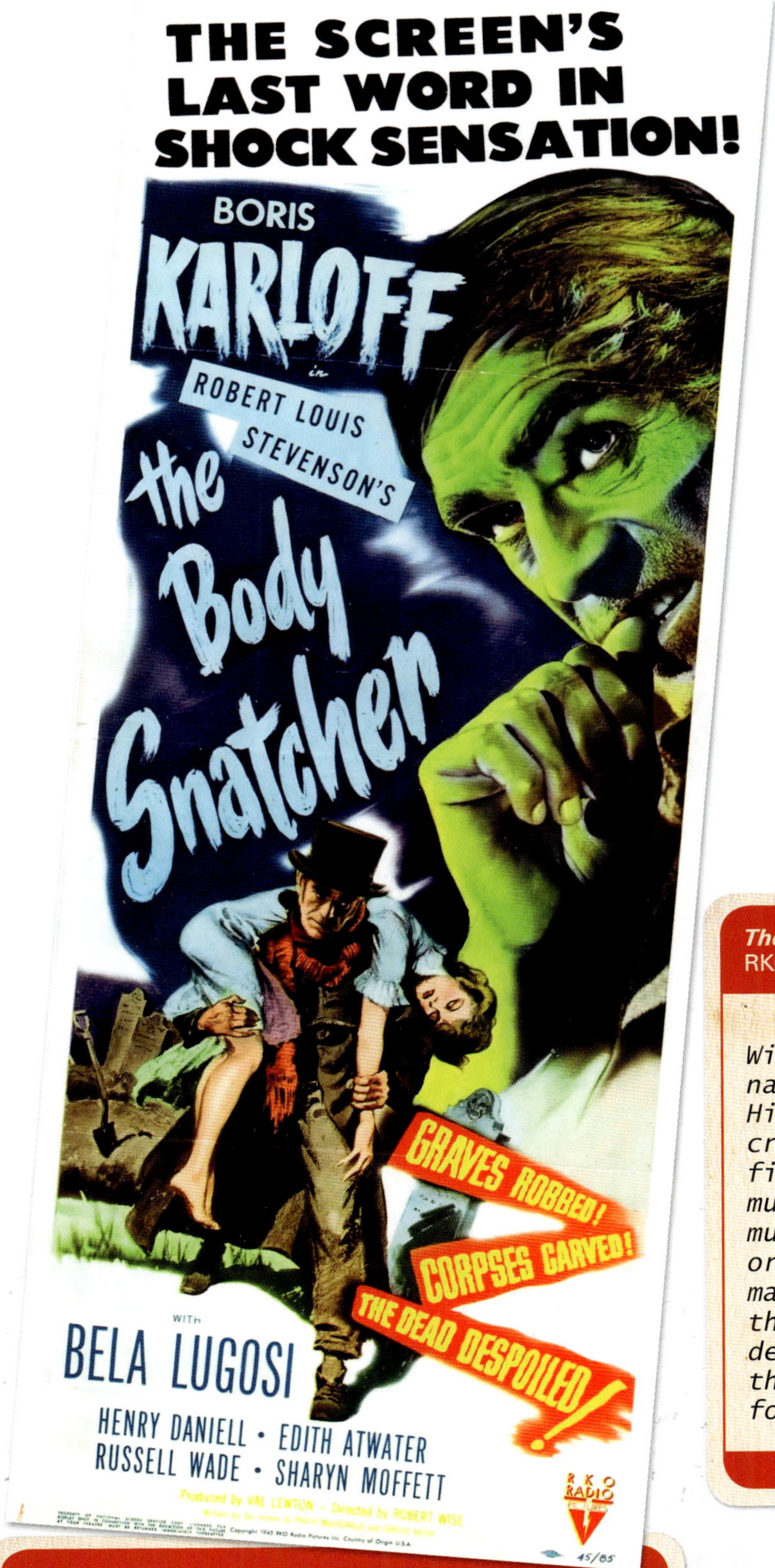

The Body Snatcher.
RKO Radio Pictures (1945).

I think the final ghostly sequence in The Body Snatcher *is one of the most chilling scenes in cinematic history.*

Marvin Kaye

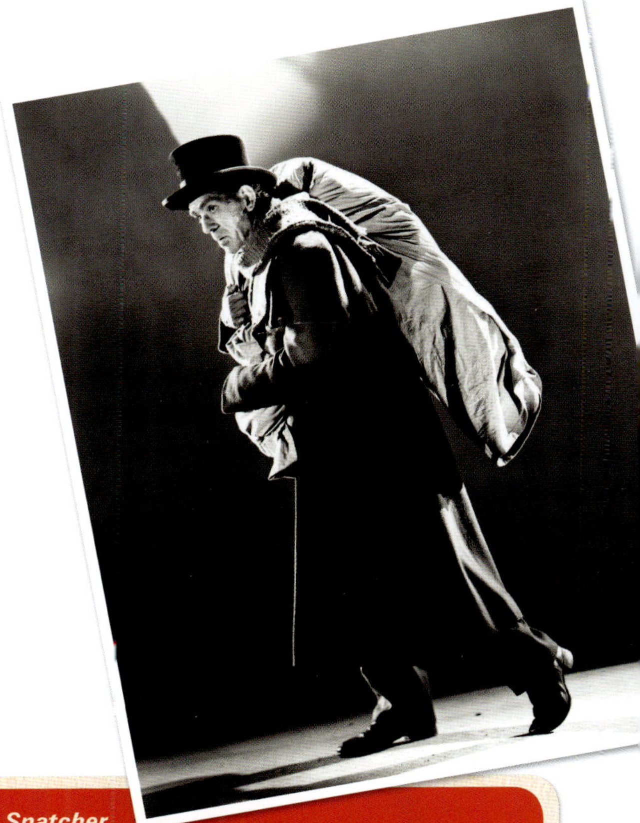

The Body Snatcher.
RKO Radio Pictures (1945).

The Body Snatcher *(1945) is Robert Wise's first solo horror. Karloff has his name above the title, and quite rightly: His performance (one of his finest) is crucial to the moral complexity of the film. Wise's filming of the offscreen murder of a street singer may be a little muffled by comparison with Tourneur's or even Robson's handling of similar material – it's a literal transcription of the screenplay without extra imaginative detail – but the final apparition is a thing of true horror, and proved too much for the British censor.*

Ramsey Campbell

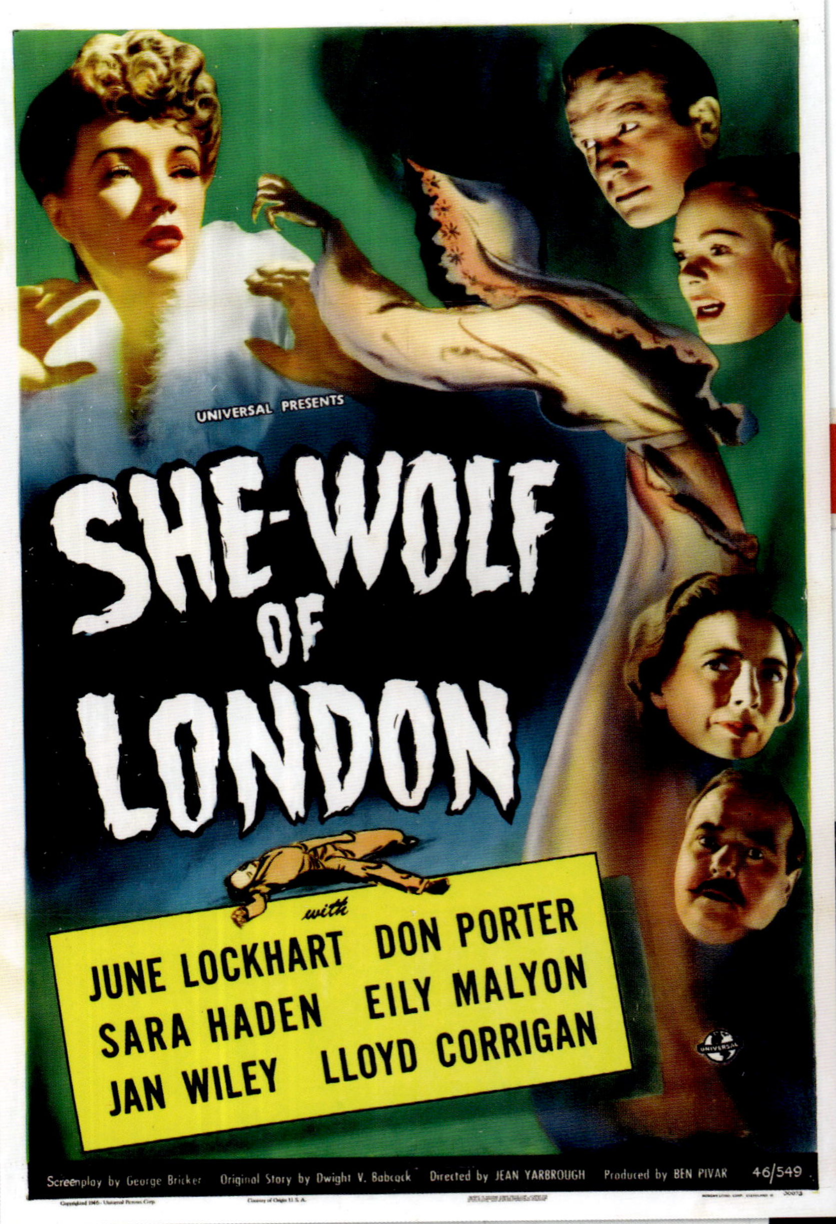

She-wolf of London.
Universal Pictures (1946).

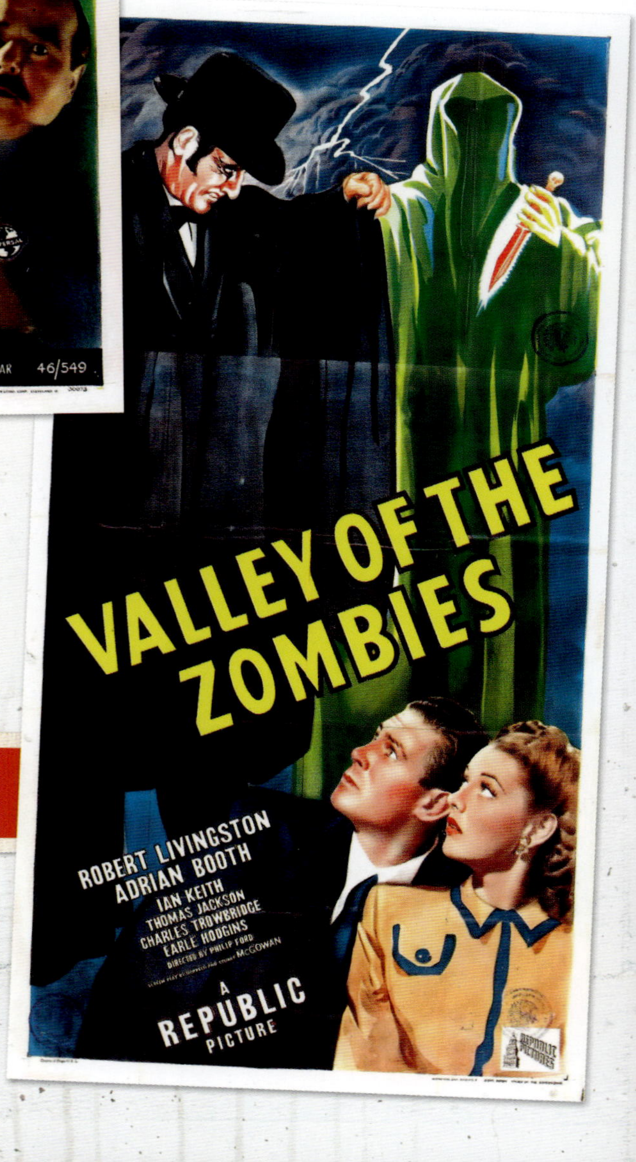

Valley of the Zombies.
Republic Pictures (1946).

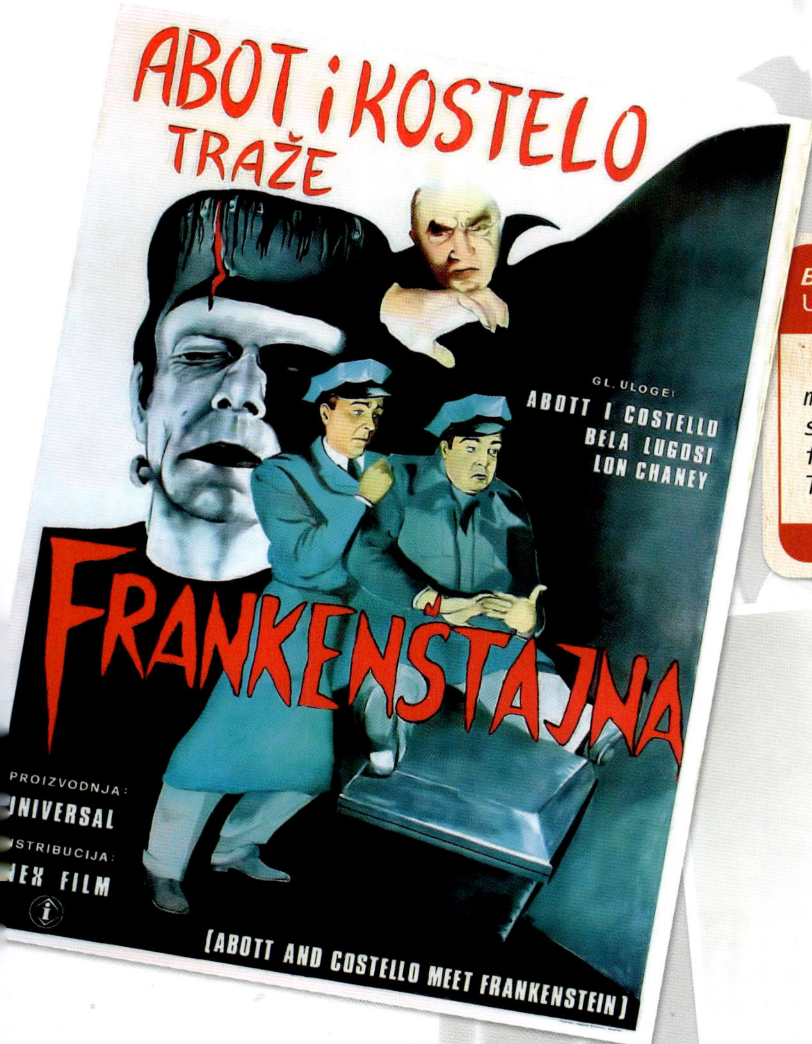

Bud Abbott and Lou Costello Meet Frankenstein.
Universal International Pictures (1948). Yugoslavia.

As a boy, I loved Universal monster movies and Bud Abbott and Lou Costello slapstick, so imagine my joy seeing all my favorites assembled in one fabulous movie! The quintessential horror comedy!

Tony Timpone

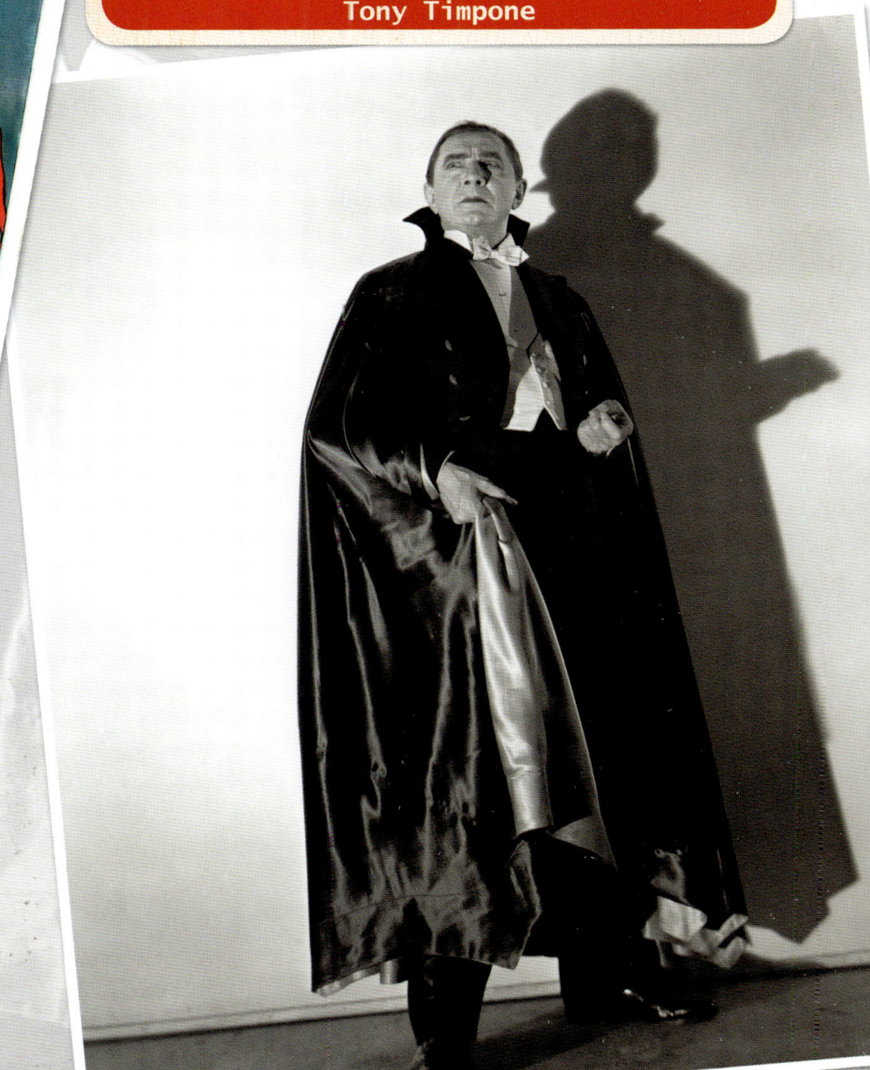

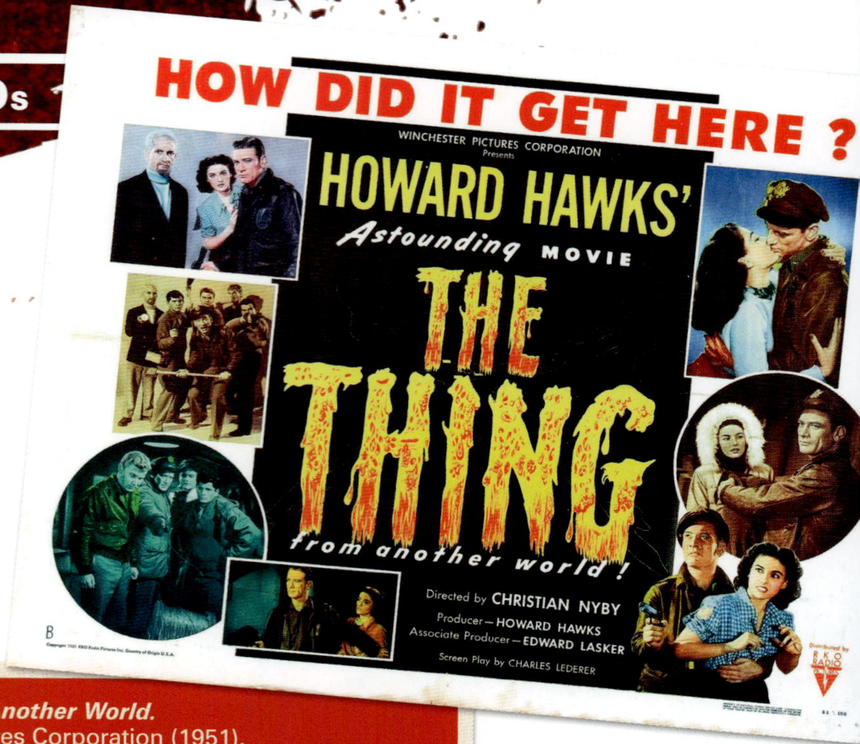

The Thing from Another World.
Winchester Pictures Corporation (1951).

Bud Abbott and Lou Costello Meet the Invisible Man.
Universal International Pictures (1951).

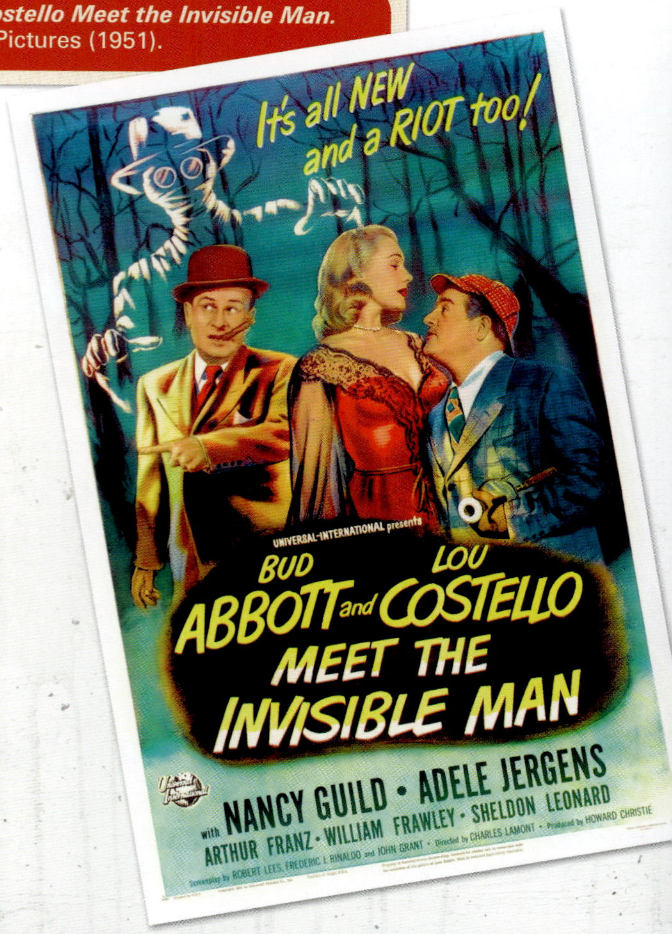

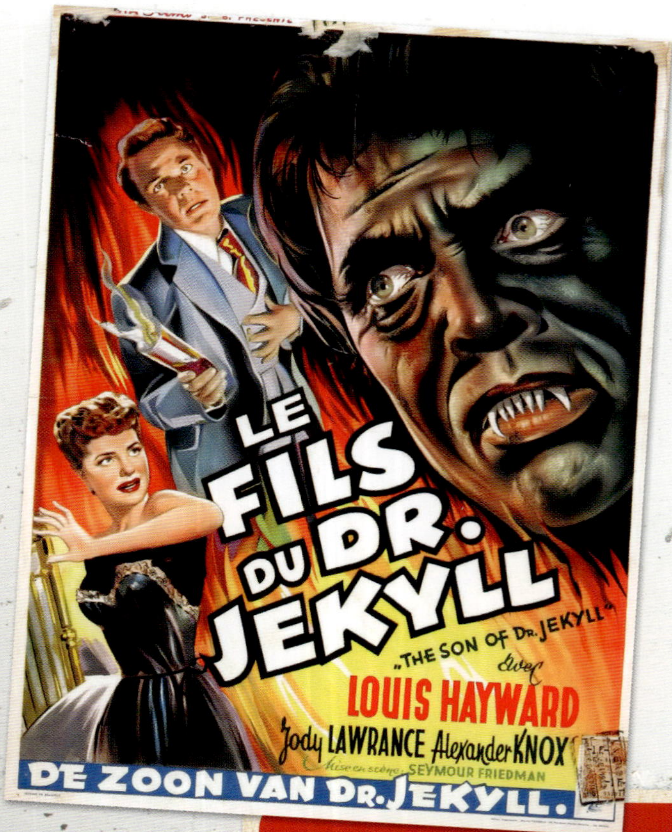

The Son of Dr. Jekyll.
Columbia Pictures Corporation (1951). Belgium.

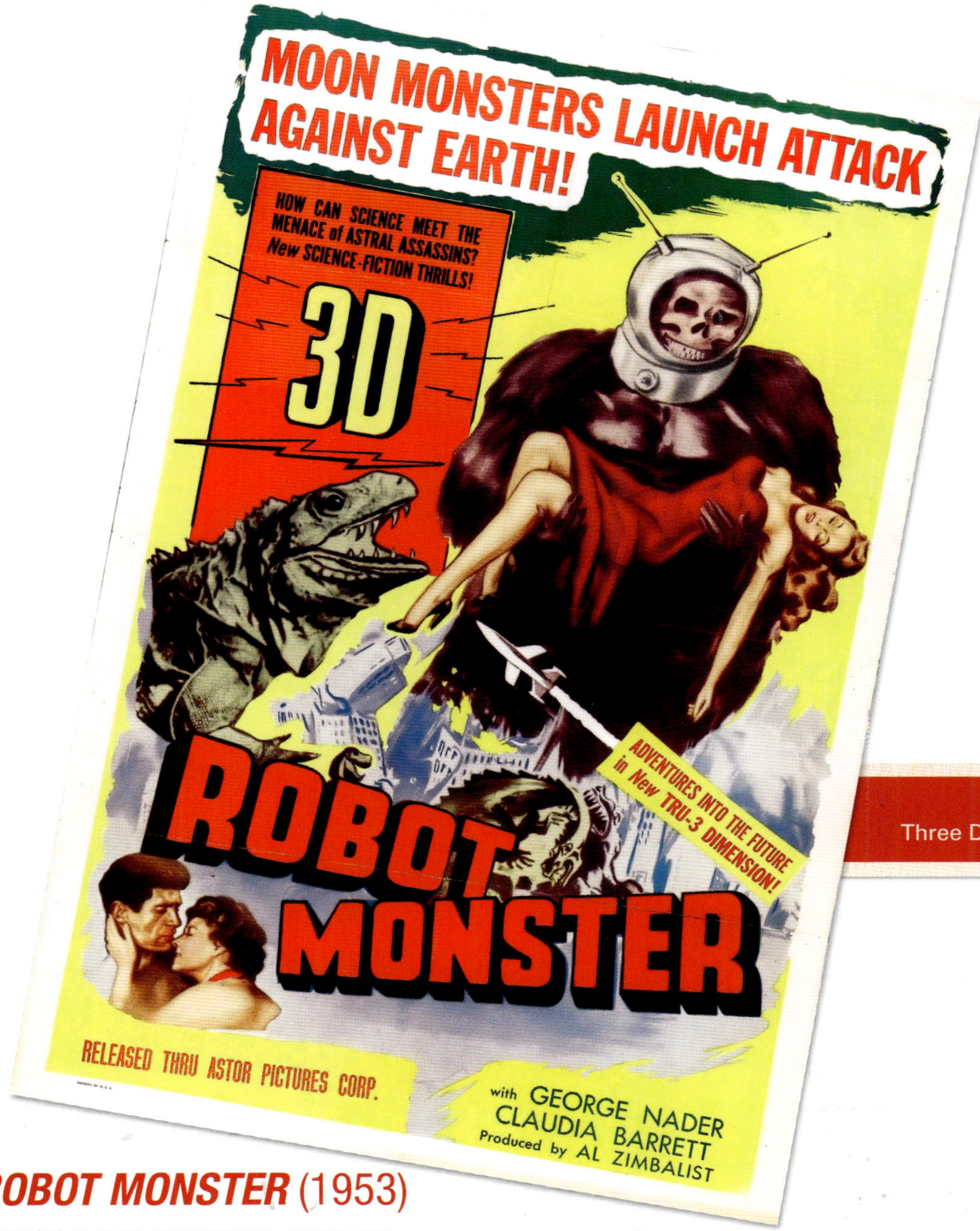

Robot Monster.
Three Dimension Pictures (1953).

ON *ROBOT MONSTER* (1953) AND THE AGE OF THE BOMB

This one is supposedly in contention with *Plan Nine* on the "worst" list. But let's say you're an eight-year-old kid, seeing this one at the slightly sinister and not so slightly smelly Alex Theatre, seeing it not with your parents, but with your pal Darren Carlson . . . And there on the screen you have the titles superimposed on images of all the comic books you're always reading — the creepy s-f/horror/monster weirdo comics. And then, you're into the premise...which is that there's a family of five still living in a basement of a bombed out house, and this is, of course, exactly a scenario you've thought of plenty and dreamed about more, because this is the atomic age of scaring the hell out of kids with "Dive under those desks and drop and roll because the Ruskies are gonna blow us up" and much of Saturday morning TV is about Civil Defense drills and what to do when we are attacked by hydrogen and atom and cosmic ray bombs. This film follows the illogical logic of a kid's dream (every kid is a Kafka!) and it does it all in ... 3D! Scared me royally.

~Mort Castle

Bud Abbott and Lou Costello Meet Dr. Jekyll and Mr. Hyde. Universal International Pictures (1953). Belgium.

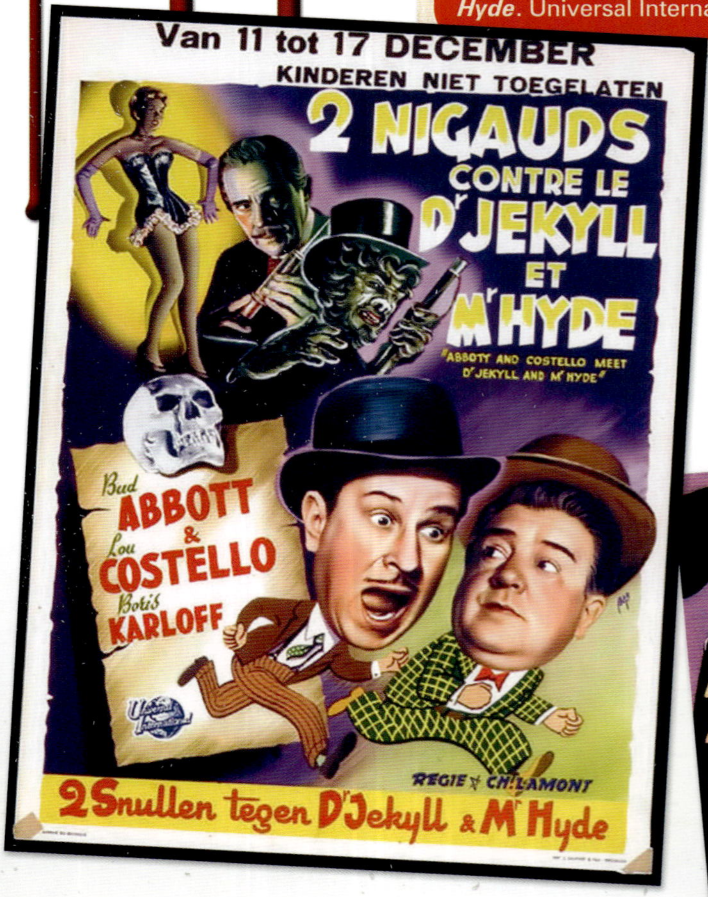

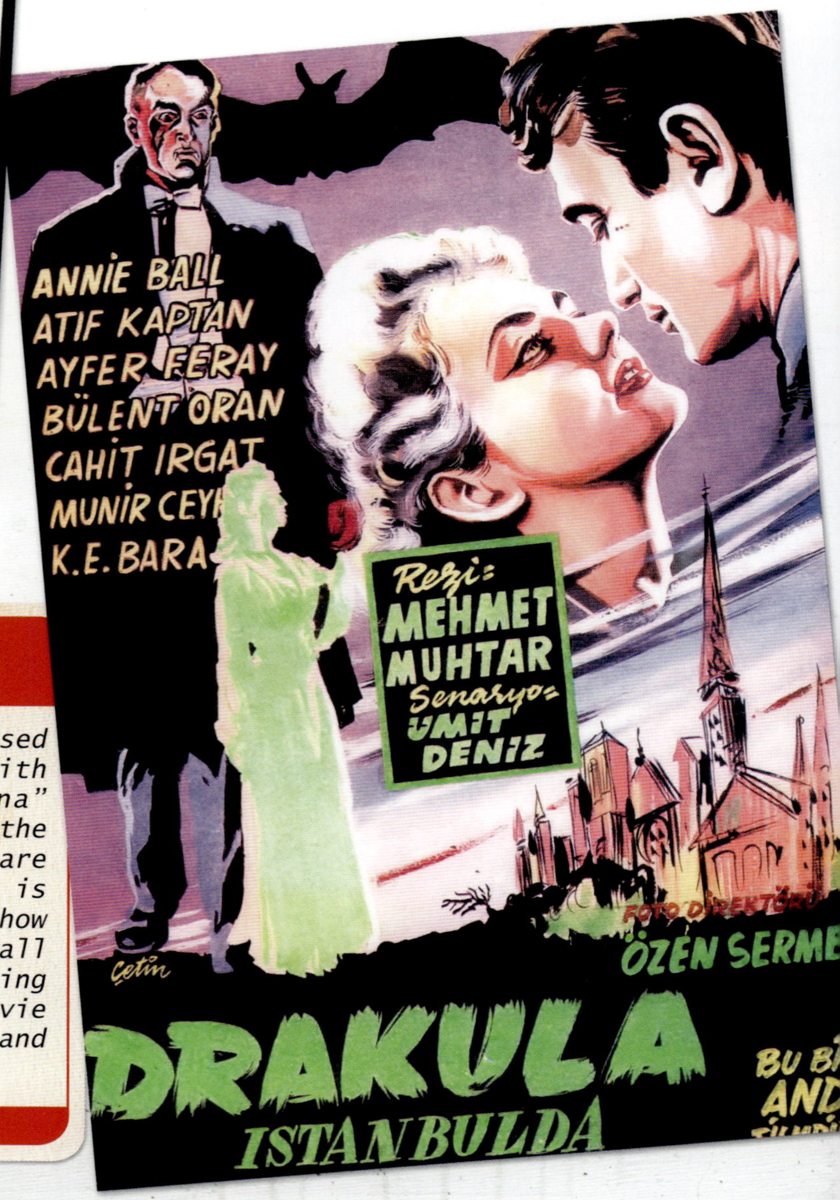

Dracula in Istanbul.
And Film (1953). Turkey.

The screenplay is recognizably based on Bram Stoker's novel, though with significant variations: the "Mina" character is a belly-dancer, much of the story is set in Turkey, and there are no Christian symbols used. The film is unique in that it was the first to show the Count crawling down the castle wall and the first to show Dracula sporting canine fangs. It was also the first movie to mention a link between Dracula and Vlad the Impaler.

Elizabeth Miller

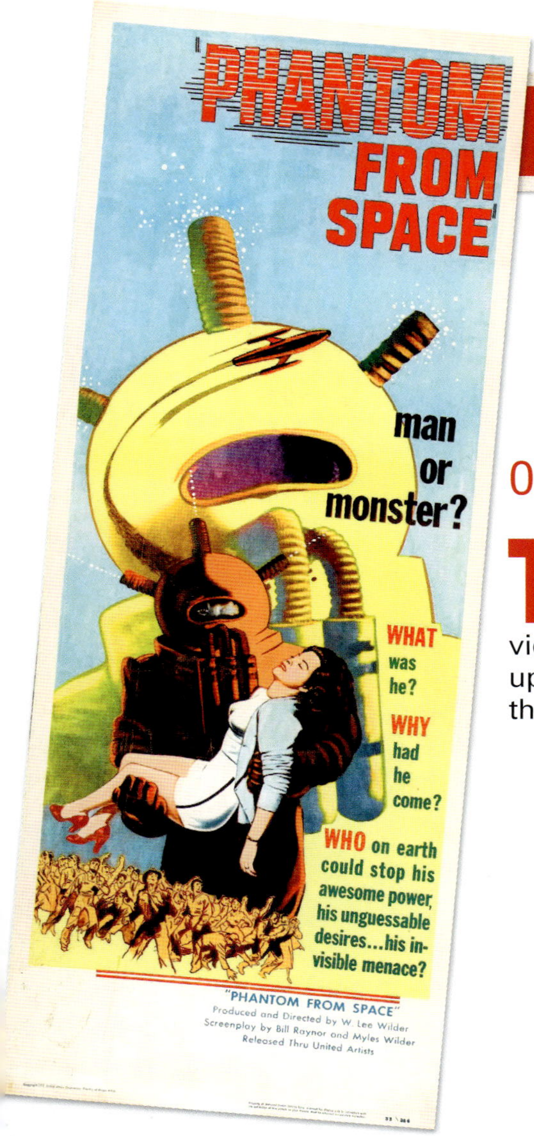

***Phantom from Space*.** Planet Filmplays (1953).

ON **TECHNOHORROR** AND THE 1950s

Technohorror has thrived at times when technology felt particularly overwhelming: The Bomb spawned as many nightmares in the 1950s as genetic engineering does now. But taking the bird's eye view, all these periods begin to blend into each other; even with each up and down, science and technology are THE central theme of horror throughout the last two centuries.

~Steffen Hantke

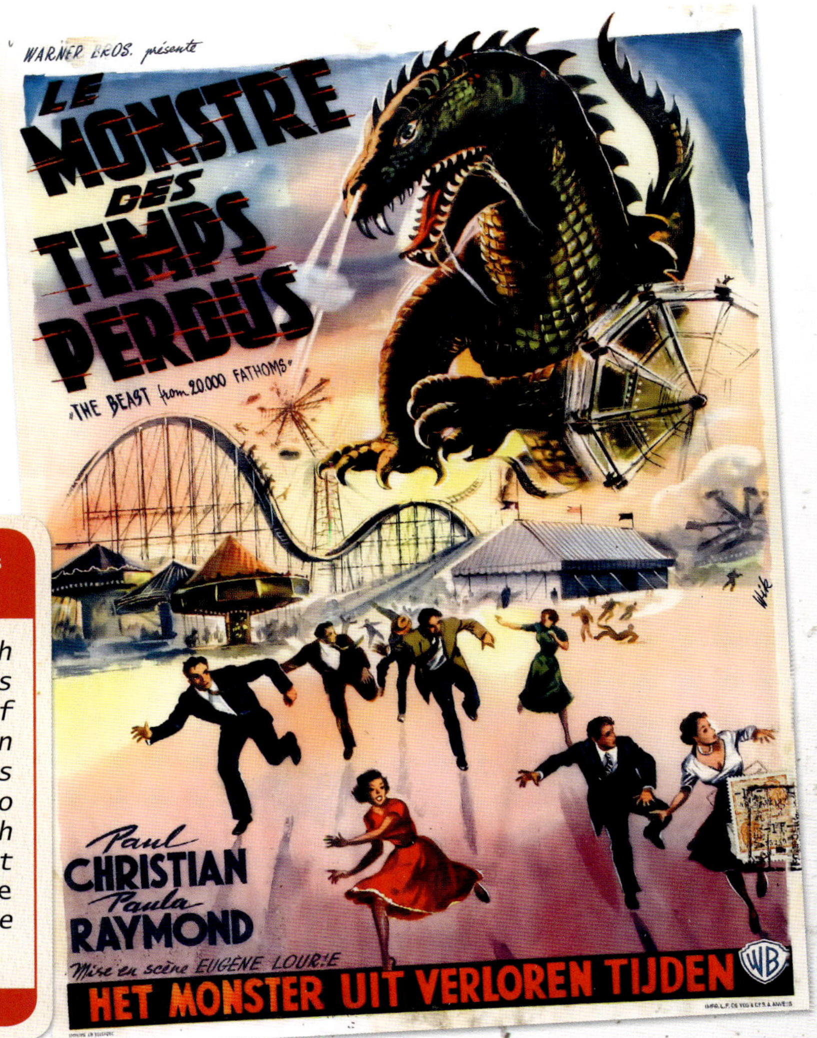

***The Beast from 20,000 Fathoms*.** Jack Dietz Productions (as Mutual Pictures of California) (1953). Belgium.

"The Beast" From 20,000 Fathoms, *with those great stop-motion special effects created by Ray Harryhausen, was one of several things that "jump-started" my keen interest in prehistoric creatures. Its scene, where the scientists are trying to identify the "beast" by shuffling through batches of illustrations of extinct animals, led directly to* Dinosaurs: The Encyclopedia, *the series of books I've authored since the late 1990s.*

Donald Glut

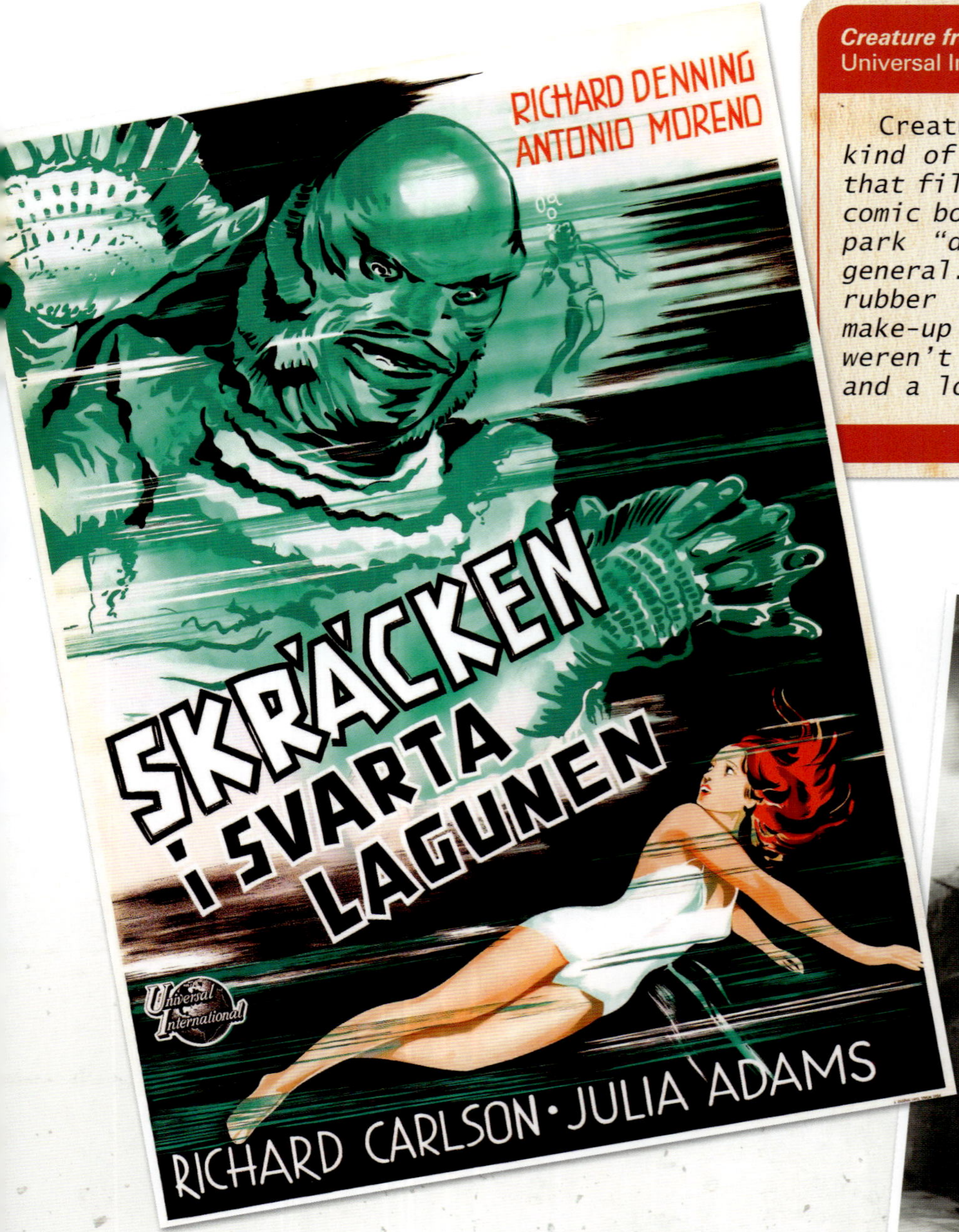

Creature from the Black Lagoon.
Universal International Pictures (1954). Sweden.

Creature from the Black Lagoon *was a kind of "epiphany" for me. Until I saw that film, I was scared of horror movies, comic books, imaginary demons, amusement park "dark rides" and "the dark" in general.* Creature, *with that incredible rubber suit created by Bud Westmore's make-up team, showed me that these films weren't really scary, but "really neat" and a lot of "fun."*

Donald Glut

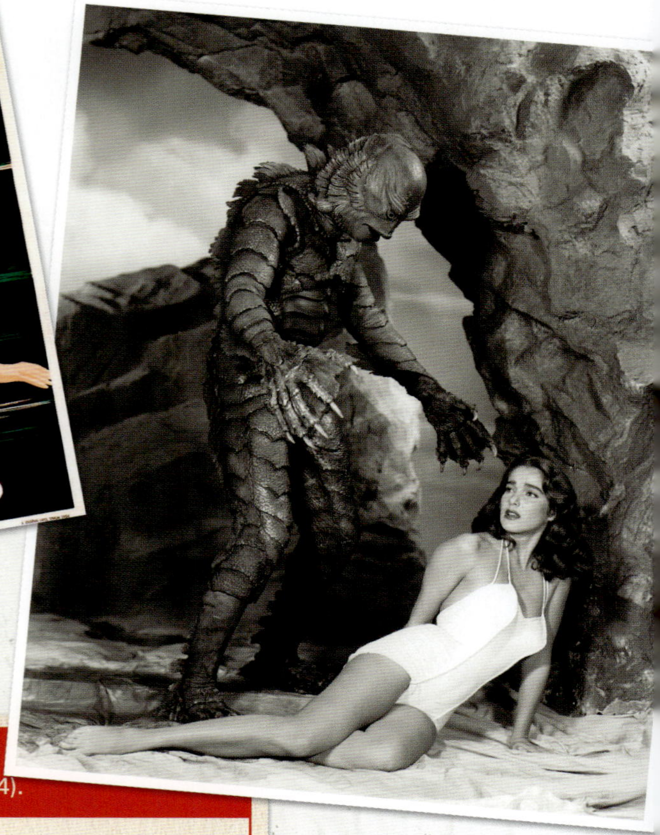

Creature from the Black Lagoon.
Universal International Pictures (1954).

Despite his reptilian features, the Creature was a sympathetic figure for anyone who felt victimized during the 1950s by the dominant white male establishment. It represented the "ugly" side of male lust and aggression, showing the male characters who they really were (which they of course failed to recognize), while also just being a creature in a natural habitat that should have been left alone.

Katherine Ramsland

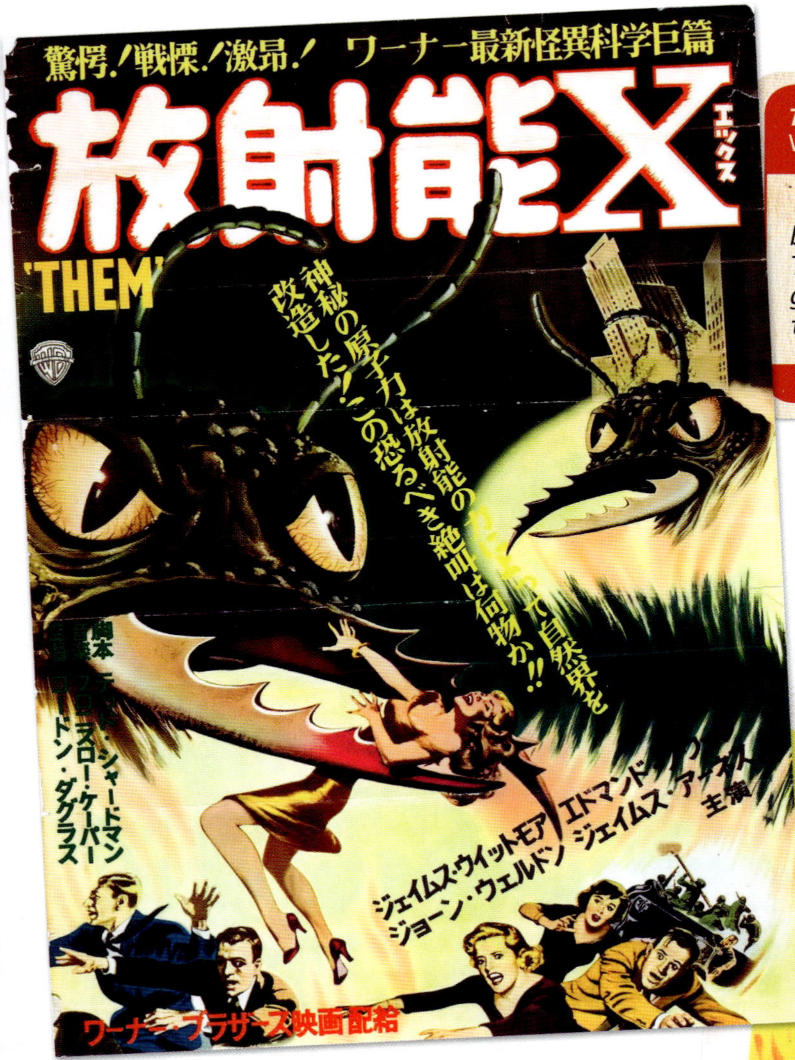

Them!
Warner Bros. Pictures (1954). Japan.

I went into this classic big monster movie blind, and the opening reels terrified me! Those sound FX of the ants and the little girl's terrorized face and scream give me the creeps till this day.

Tony Timpone

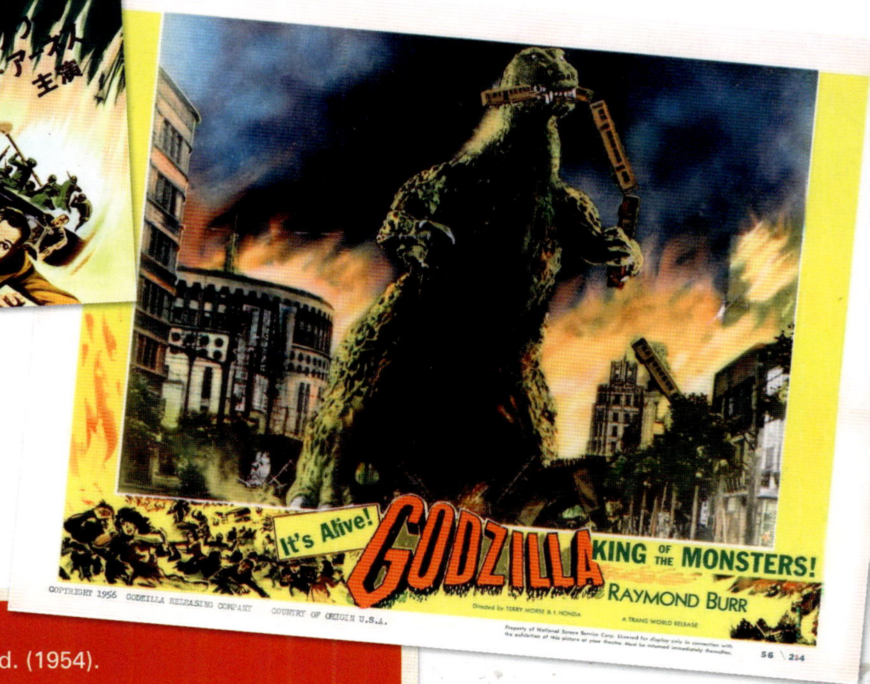

Godzilla.
Toho Film (Eiga) Co. Ltd. (1954).

Godzilla was a cautionary tale about the human propensity to act without appropriate consideration of the possible consequences. The monster was the released contents of Pandora's Box in the form of a fire-breathing dinosaur. Yet despite his propensity to destroy, it was easy to root for him and to despise the men who were trying to trap and kill him. In fact, he became a protector in later films. He was more like a big pet than a scary monster. I think a lot of kids in that generation loved more than feared him.

Katherine Ramsland

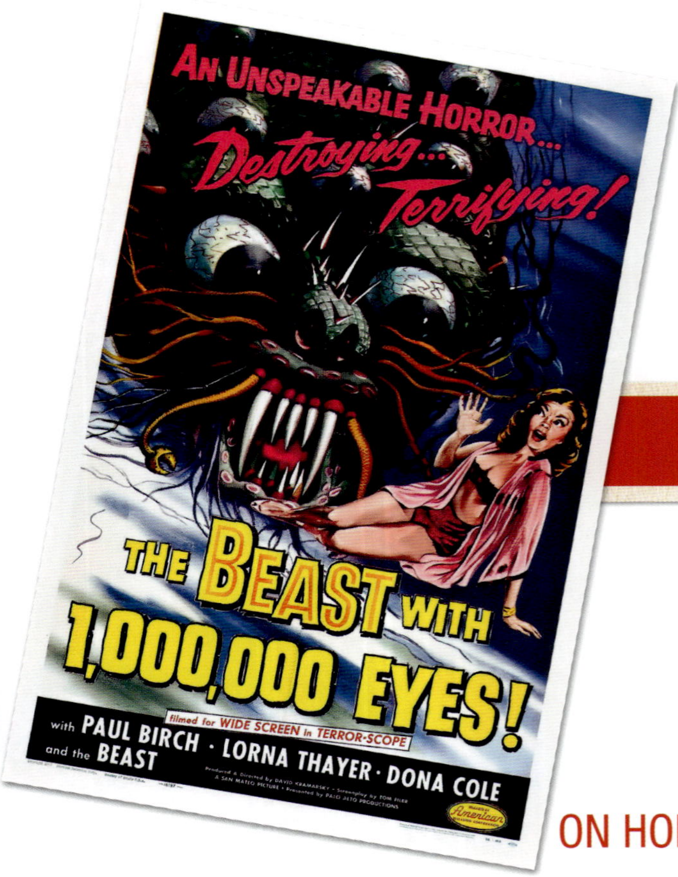

The Beast with a Million Eyes.
San Mateo Productions (1955).

ON HORROR IN **THE 1950s AND 1960s**

The 1950s to 1960s — we saw huge changes in horror cinema in these two decades, which brought us *Night of the Living Dead, The Last Man on Earth, Them!, Horror of Dracula,* and so much more. It was a time of change, post-war, post-Depression, and a sense of creative freedom prevailed. In the literary world, perhaps the 19th century reflects this same innovative spirit, especially in the horror genre, bringing us works by Mary Shelley, Edgar Allan Poe, Oscar Wilde, Bram Stoker, Robert Louis Stevenson, and others.

~Nancy Kilpatrick

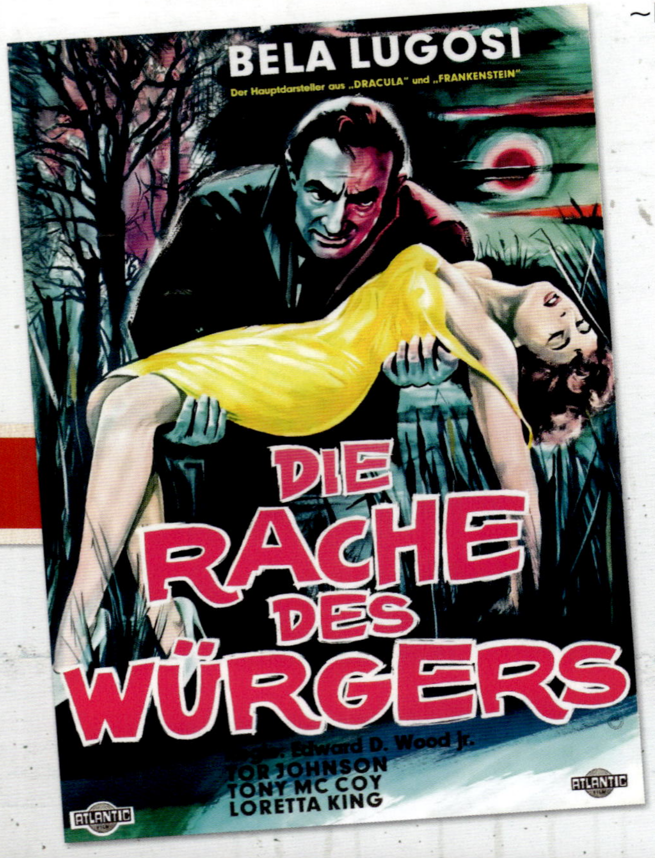

Bride of the Monster.
Rolling M. Productions (1955). Germany.

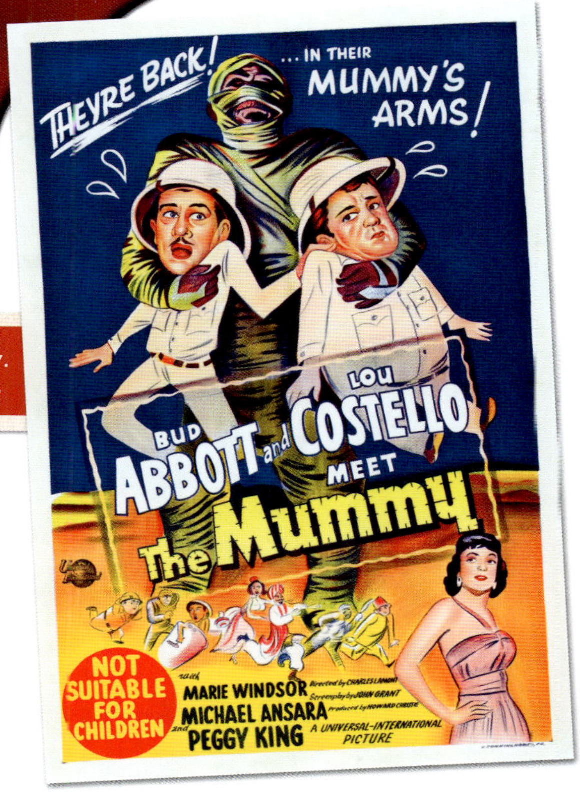

***Bud Abbott and Lou Costello Meet the Mummy*.**
Universal International Pictures (1955). Australia.

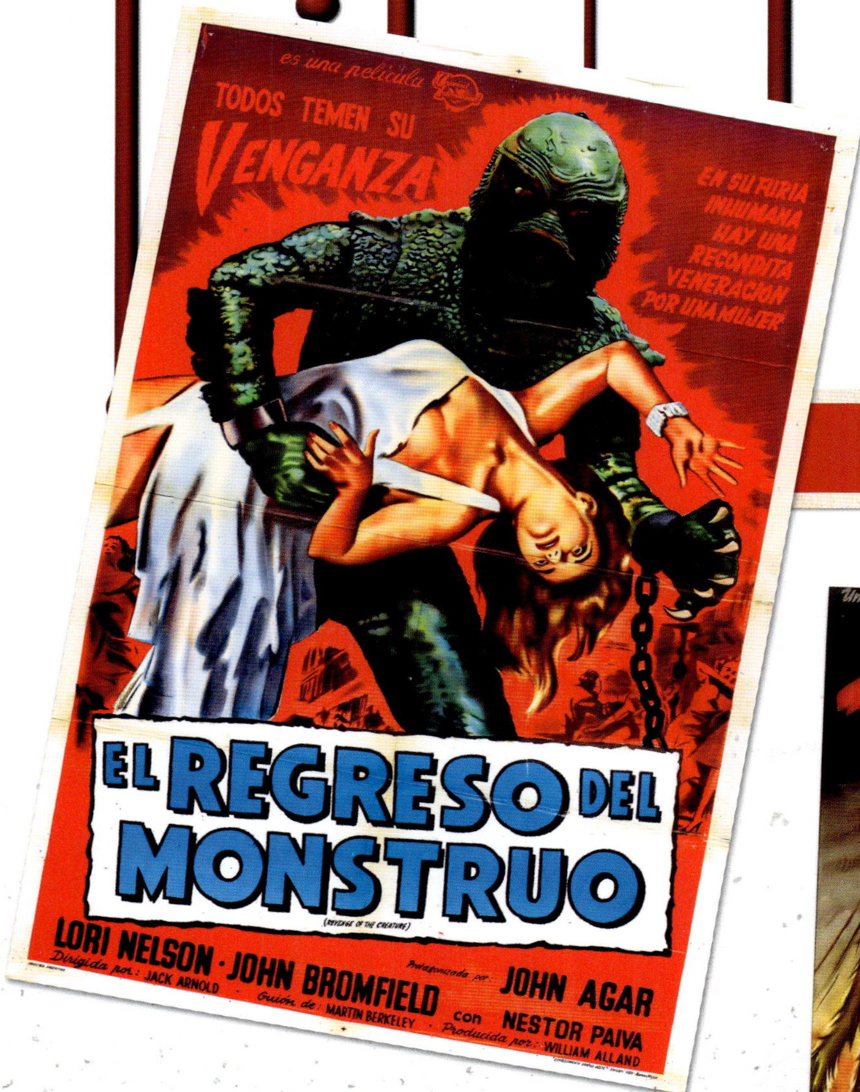

***Revenge of the Creature*.**
Universal International Pictures (1955). Spain.

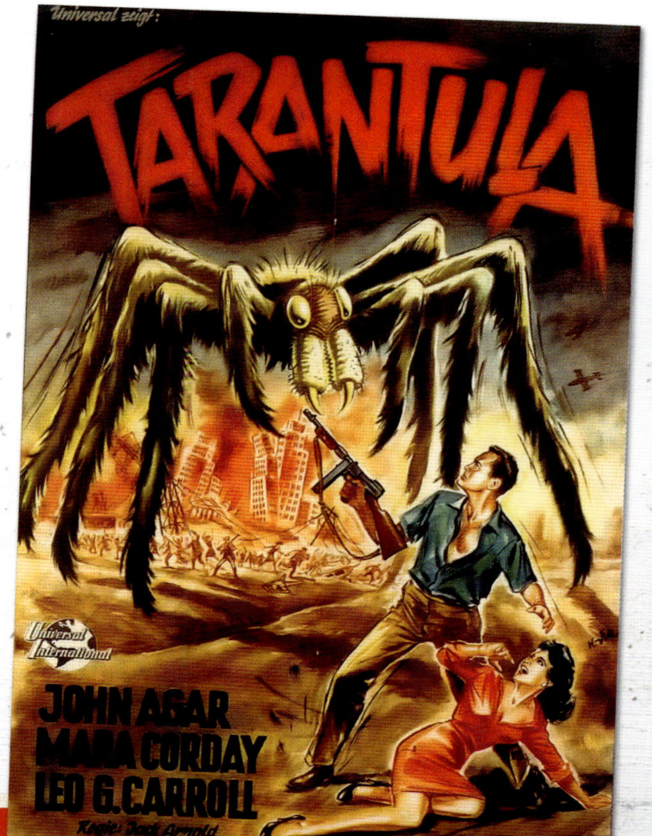

***Tarantula*.**
Universal International Pictures (1955). Germany.

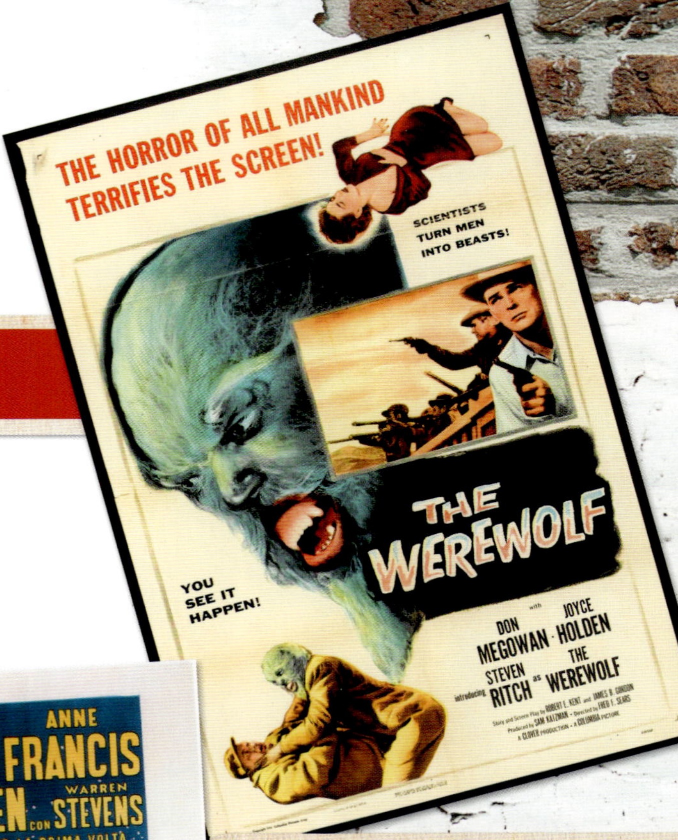

The Werewolf.
Clover Productions (1956).

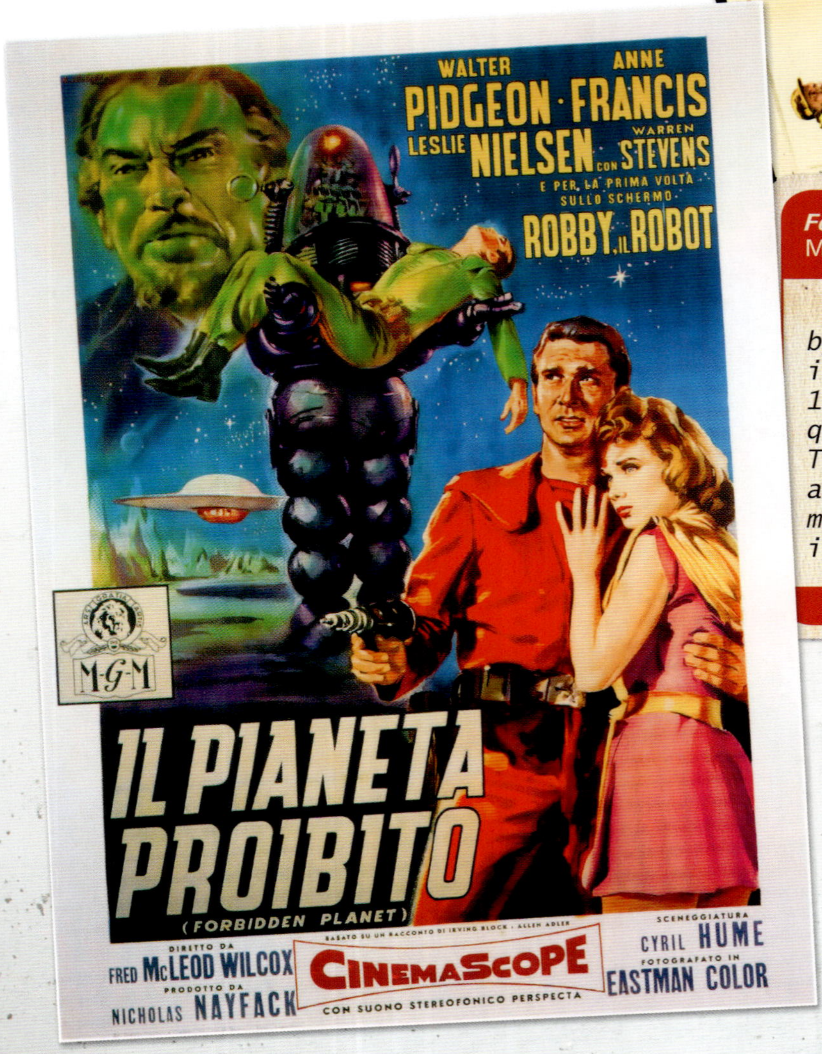

Forbidden Planet.
Metro-Goldwyn-Mayer (1956). Italy.

I remember being absolutely riveted by Forbidden Planet *when I somehow got into a cinema to see it at the age of 11 or 12, although the movie now seems quite ordinary, especially if viewed on TV; that id-creature, invisibly running amok, still has a special place in my memory in consequence of having viewed it at the fright time and place.*

Brian Stableford

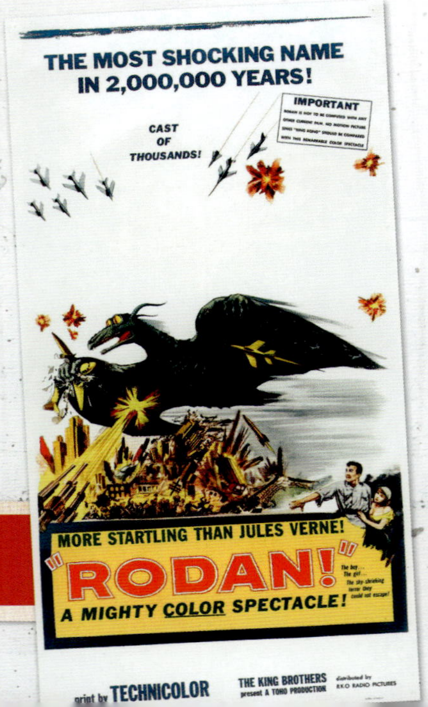

Rodan.
Toho Film (Eiga) Co. Ltd. (1956).

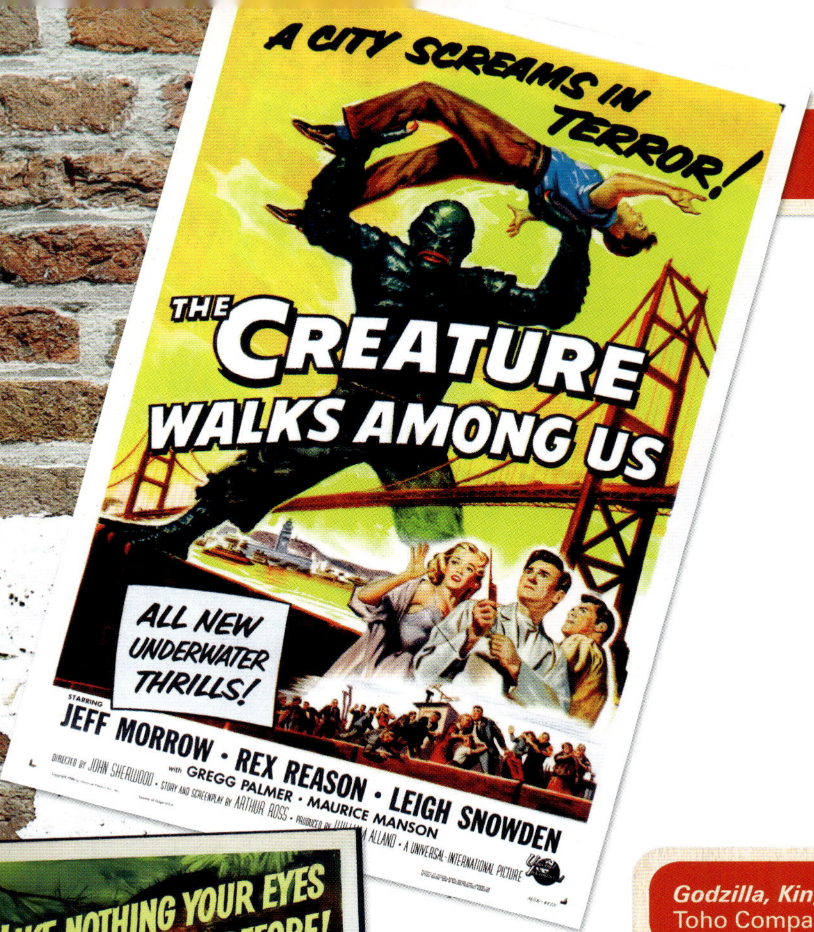

The Creature Walks Among Us.
Universal International Pictures (1956).

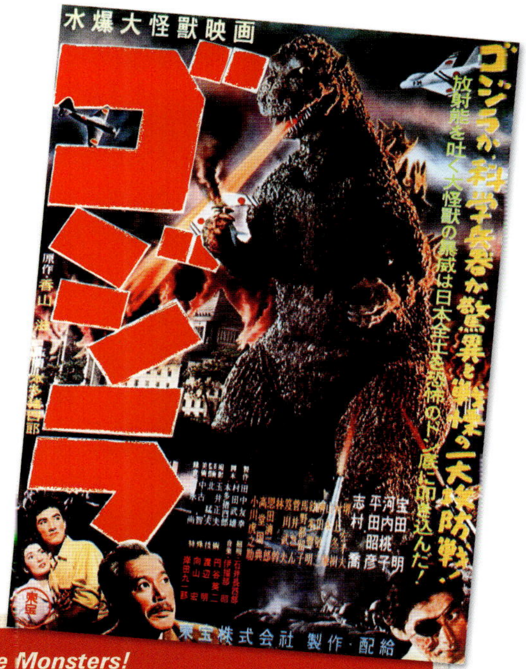

Godzilla, King of the Monsters!
Toho Company/Jewell Enterprises Inc. (1956) Japan.

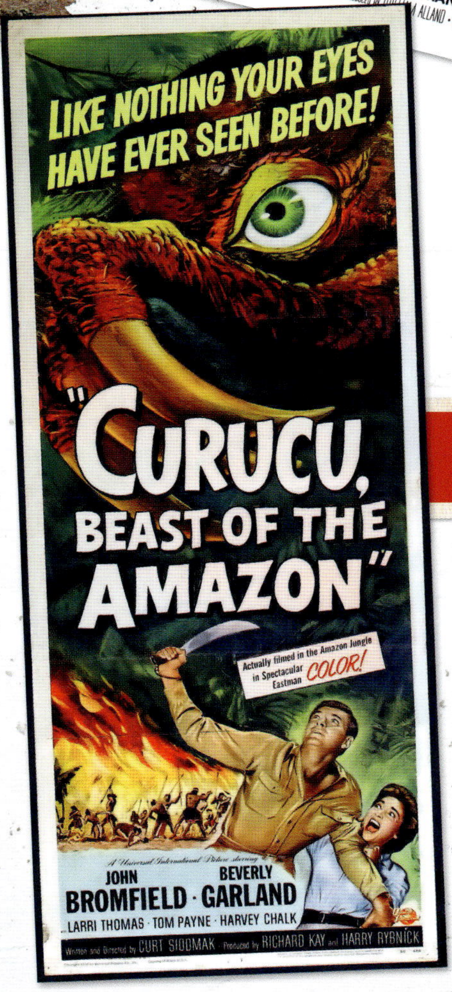

Curucu, Beast of the Amazon.
Jewel Productions (1956).

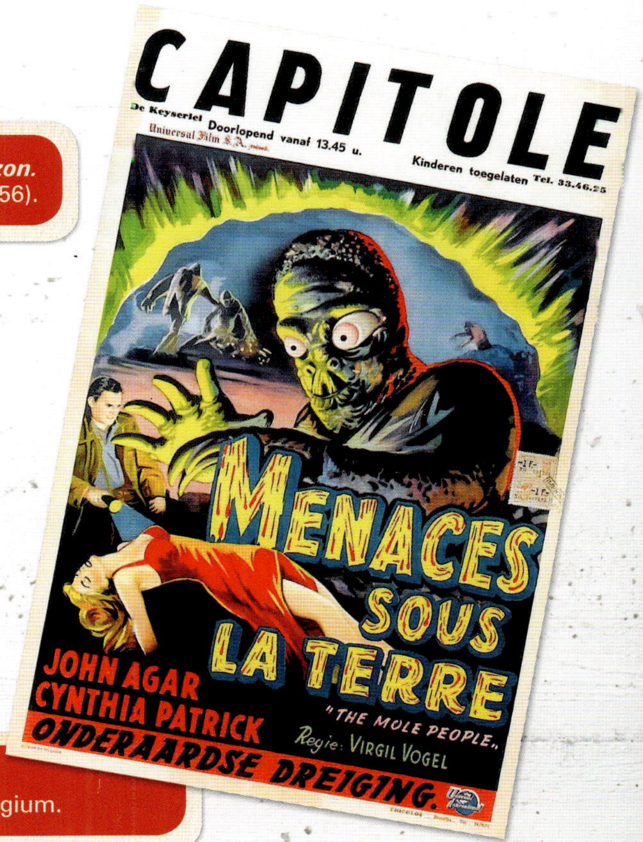

The Mole People.
Universal International Pictures (1956). Belgium.

***Invasion of the Body Snatchers*.** Allied Artists Pictures/ Walter Wanger Productions (1956).

Forget about the Red Scare and McCarthyism, this film – the best version of this classic story of identity loss and paranoia – speaks most directly to the terrors of small-town Americana.

Gregory A. Waller

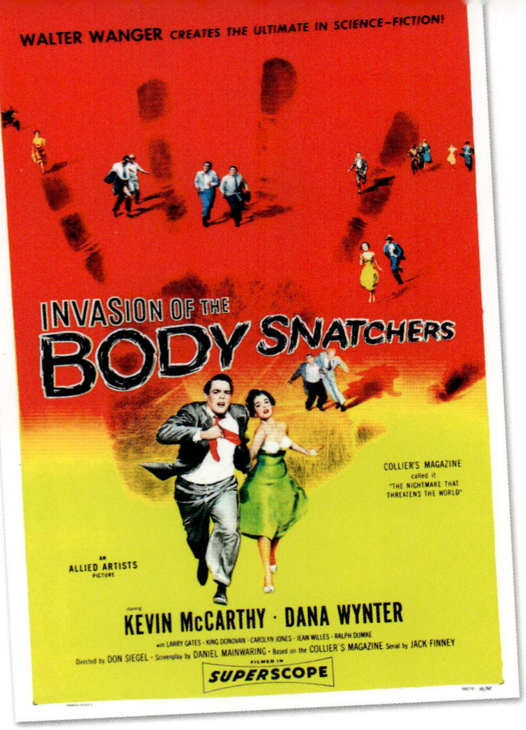

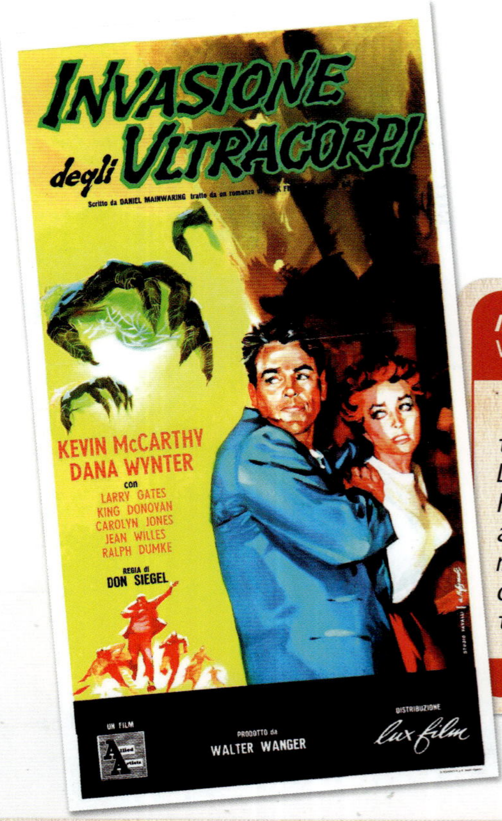

Invasion of the Body Snatchers. Allied Artists Pictures/ Walter Wanger Productions (1956). Italy.

A spirit of overwhelming paranoia in the cosy banality of the 50s American Dream. There is the iconic performance of Kevin McCarthy hysterical in the streets, and the prolifetrating pods, but even more chilling are the moments of sheer ordinariness: Uncle Ira mowing the lawn; the blank-eyed kiss...

Richard J. Hand

***Invasion of the Body Snatchers*.** Allied Artists Pictures/ Walter Wanger Productions (1956). UK.

The original Invasion of the Body Snatchers *(1956) didn't come alive for me until I watched it as an adult after reading Jack Finney's novel. Finney writes, "Sometimes I think we're refining all humanity out of our lives." It's a line that Don Siegel's version of the film captures more clearly than any of its remakes. While I would say that I feel dirty after watching a film like Tobe Hooper's* The Texas Chainsaw Massacre *(1974),* Invasion of the Body Snatchers *is so neat and tidy (narratively, photographically, and aurally) that I leave the film feeling entirely too "clean."*

Jesse Stommel

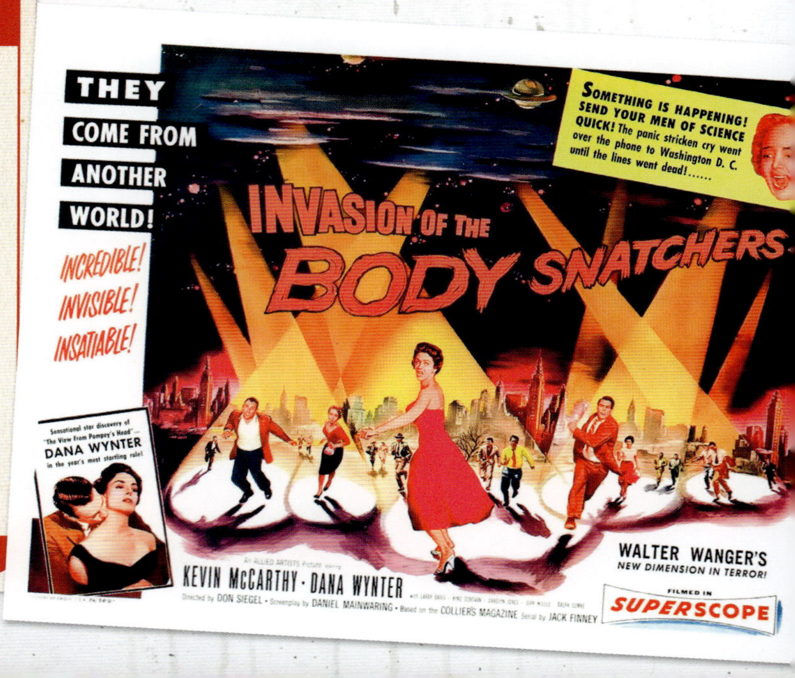

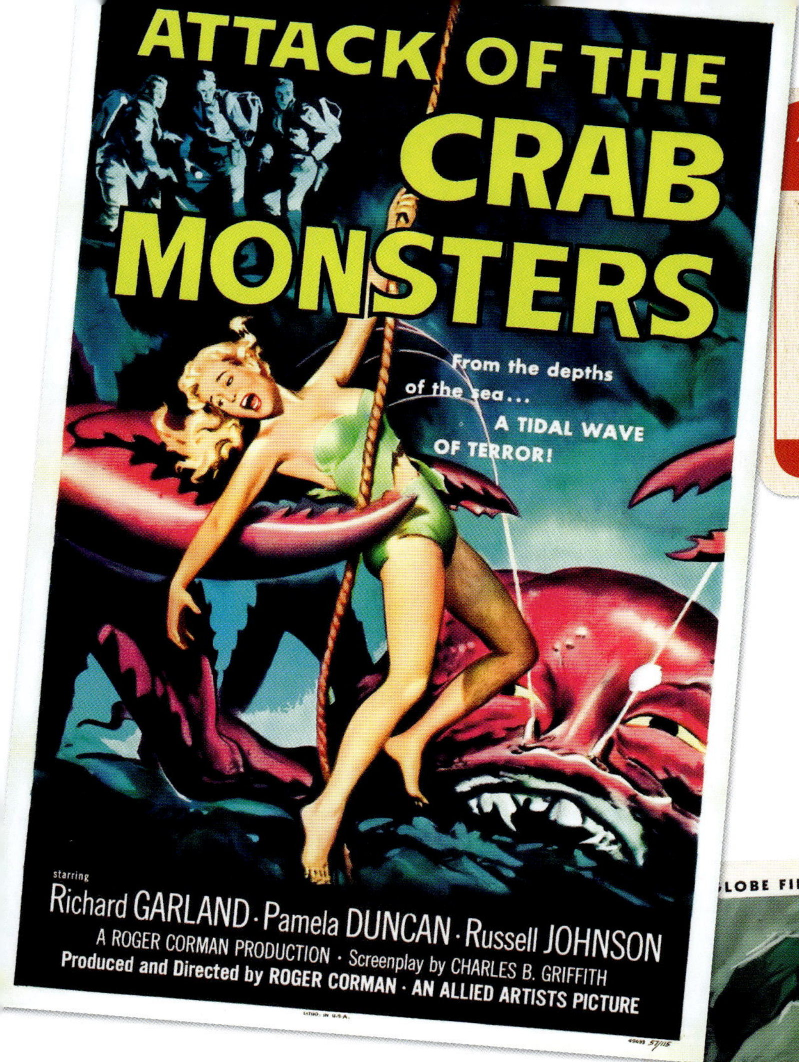

Attack of the Crab Monsters. Los Altos Productions (1957).

This Roger Corman quickie offered up this young viewer his first taste of gore; in one scene, a rock falls on the hand of actor Mel Welles and severs his appendage at the wrist. He then holds up the bloody stump and screams! What a shock, even in B&W!

Tony Timpone

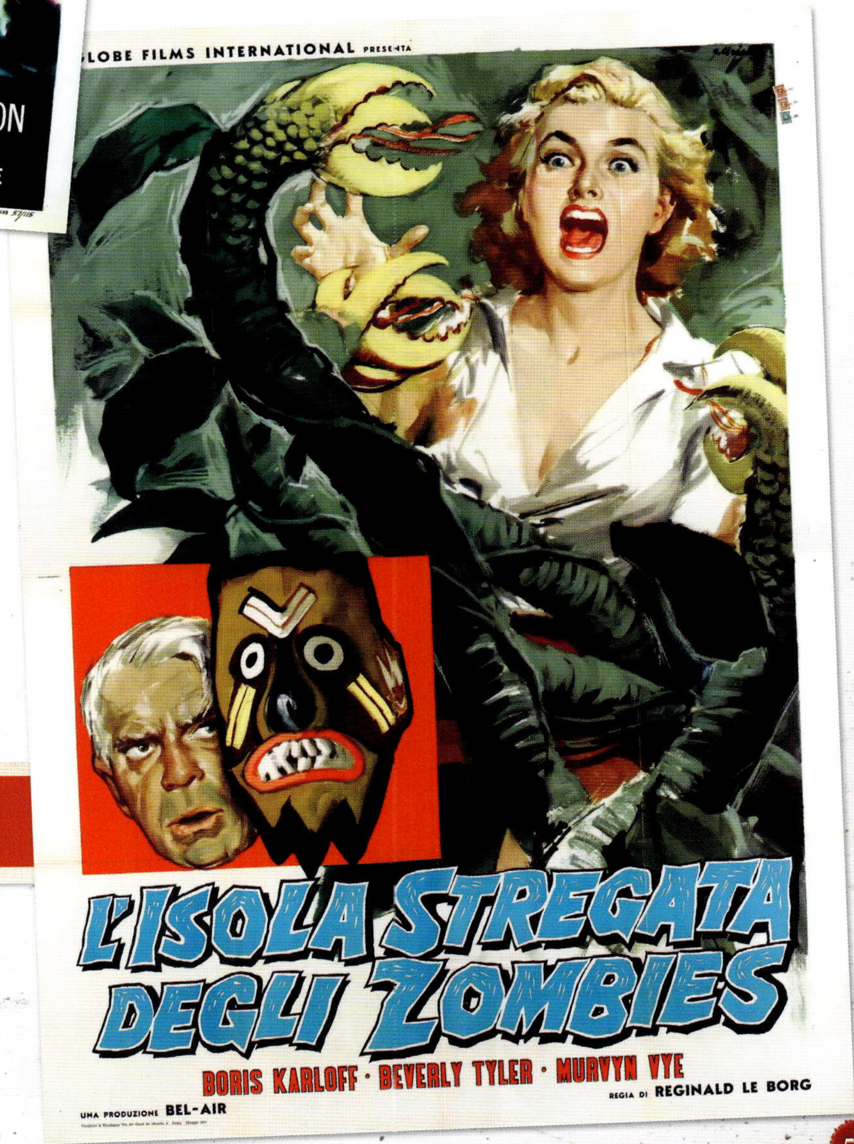

Voodoo Island. Aubrey Schenck Productions (as Oak Pictures Inc.)/Bel-Air Productions (1957). Italy.

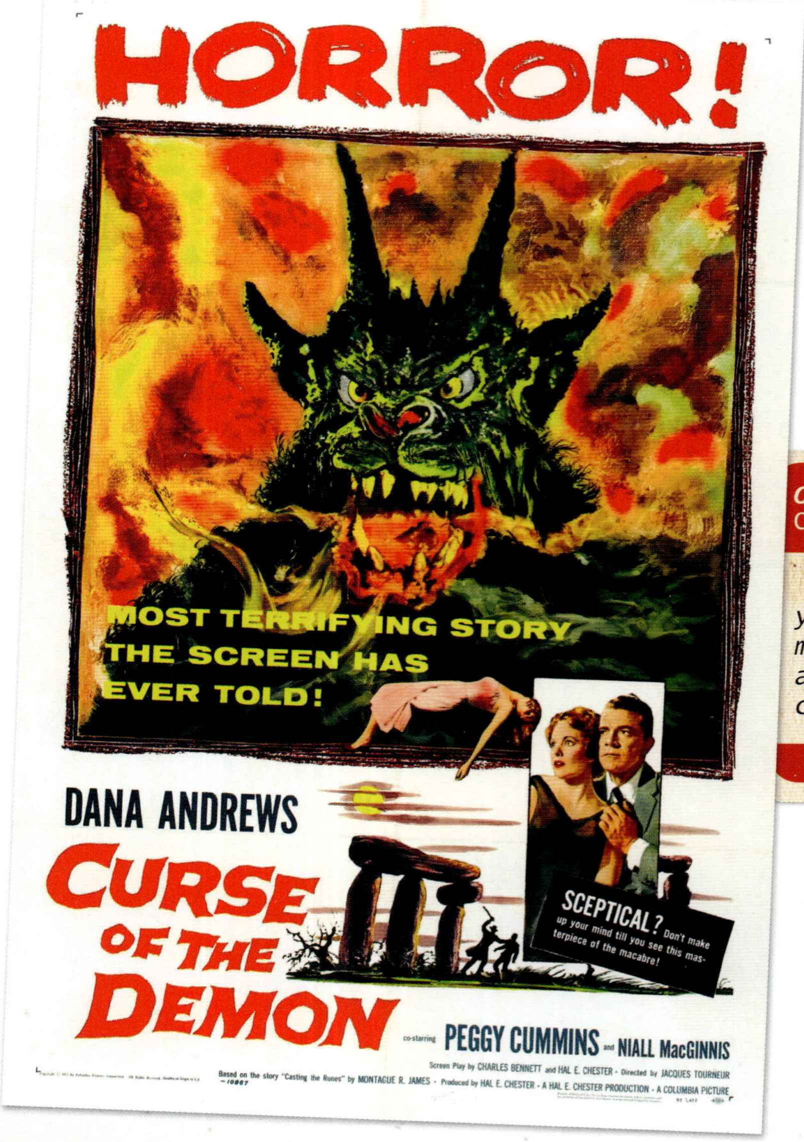

Curse of the Demon. Sabre Film Production/ Columbia Pictures Corporation (1957).

In many respects so ordinary a film, yet there are set pieces and virtuoso moments which make this M. R. James adaptation a masterful journey into cinematic terror.

Richard J. Hand

ON **FRANKENSTEIN** AND '50s TEEN CULTURE

Its title repeating the common mistake of attributing the name of his Creator to the Creature, this film nevertheless brings the audacity of the Mad Scientist's ambitions to new and memorably crazy heights. It persuades us because Whit Bissell plays this seriously insane Frankenstein with such terrifyingly urbane calm. When his fiancée, Margaret, pushes him too hard toward marriage, he sets the grotesquely disfigured and angry teenage creature he has reanimated from a car wreck on to the "interfering" woman, who is then dumped in his laboratory's secret subterranean pool to be consumed by an ever-hungry alligator. Professor Frankenstein then drives his Teen Creature to a drive-in movie telling him he can "pick the face that pleases you" from the car-bound couples making out, the handsome male victim he chooses and wrenches away from his girl having literally to lose his head so that the Teen Creature can become a James Dean look-a-like. The newly endowed narcissistic hunk cannot last long however. In a film essentially about an ageing scientist maniacally striving to revive his own youth by literally re-creating it in Fifties Teen culture (this is 1957), the most spectacular moment comes when the Teen Creature is accidentally electrocuted in the lab, and the black and white film stock turns into color. Wow!

~Maurice Hindle

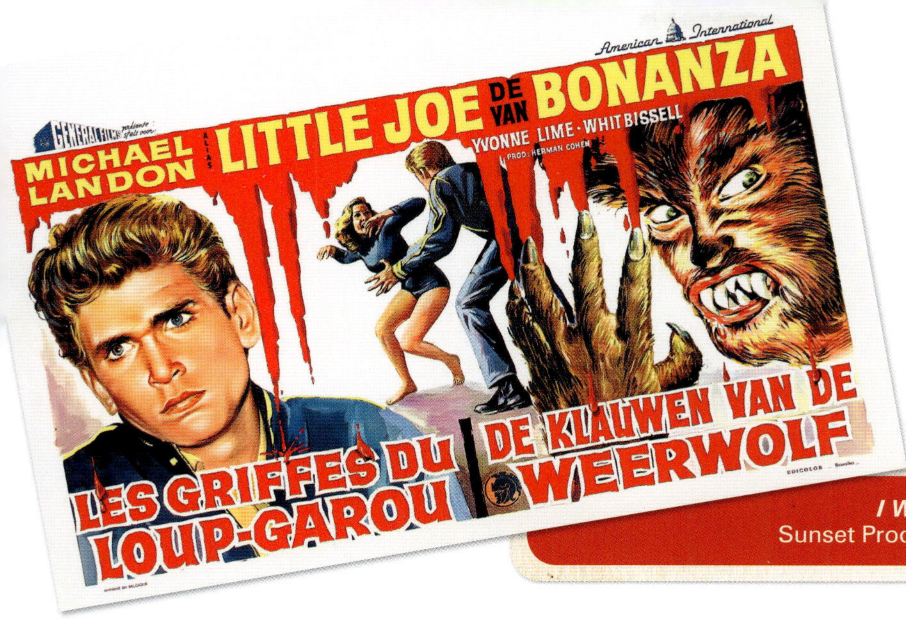

I Was a Teenage Werewolf.
Sunset Productions (1957). Belgium.

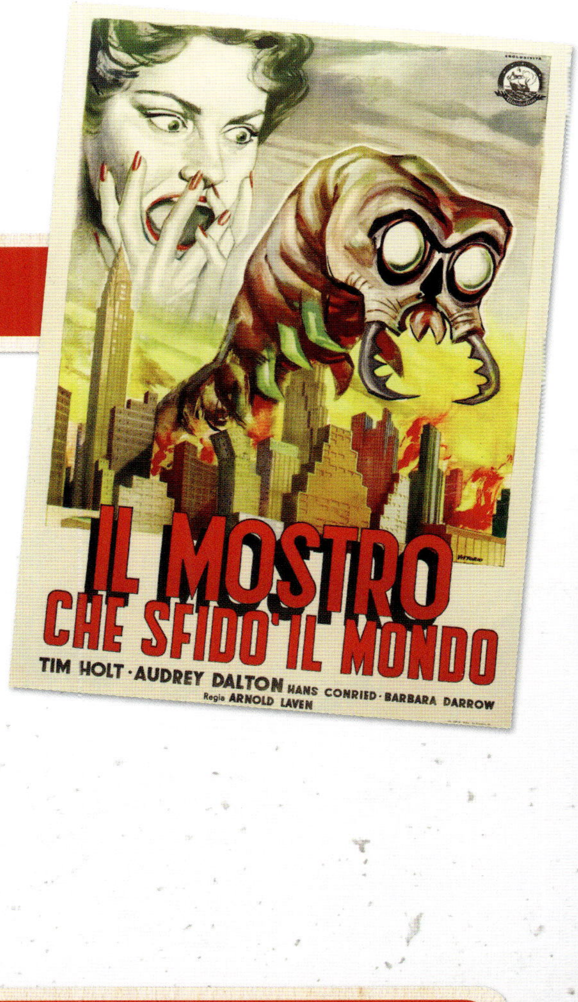

The Monster That Challenged the World.
Gramercy Pictures (1957). Italy.

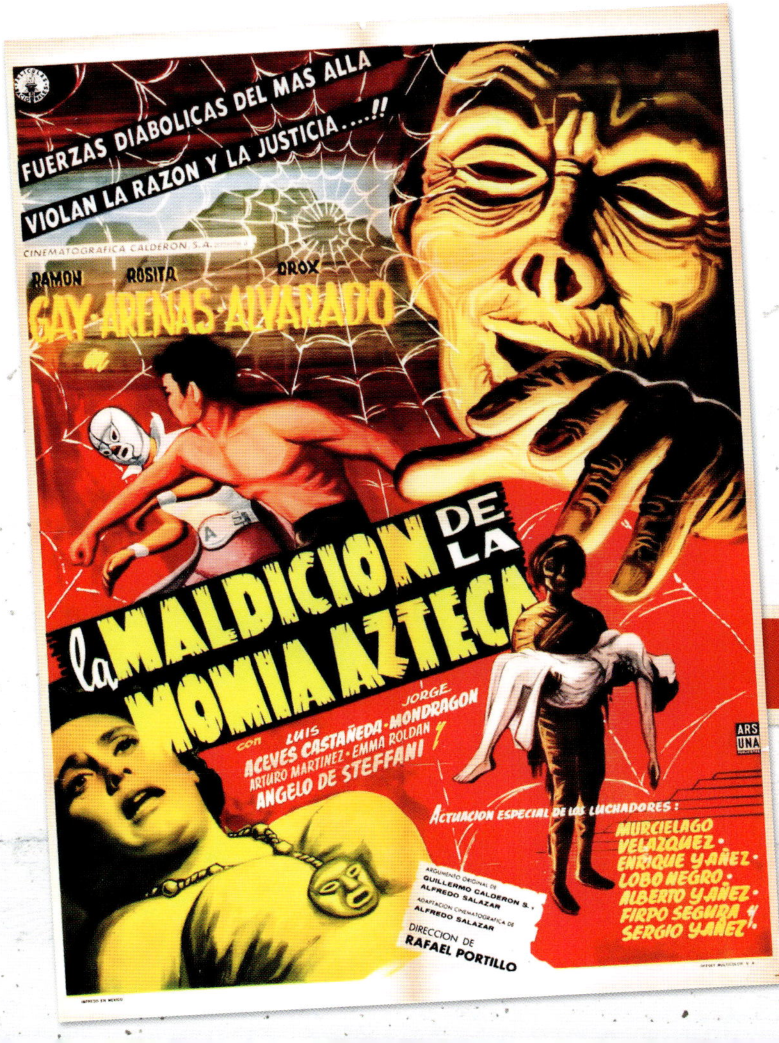

The Curse of the Aztec Mummy.
Cinematográfica Calderón S.A. (1957). Mexico.

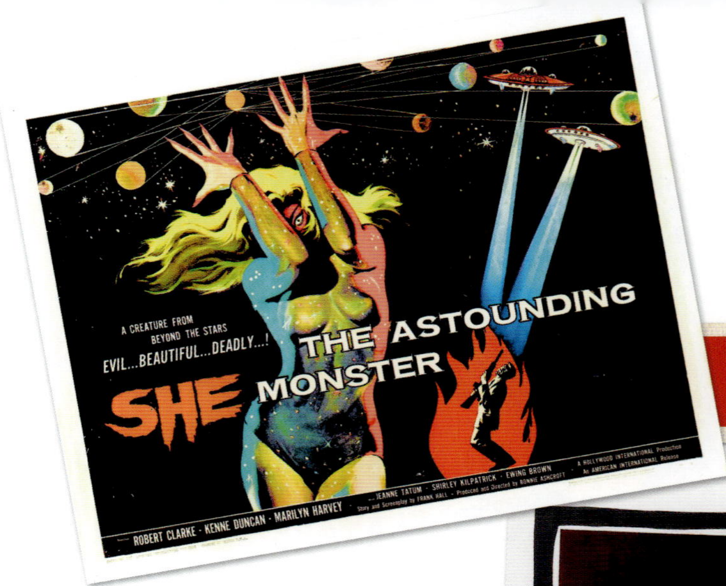

The Astounding She-Monster.
Hollywood International Pictures (1957).

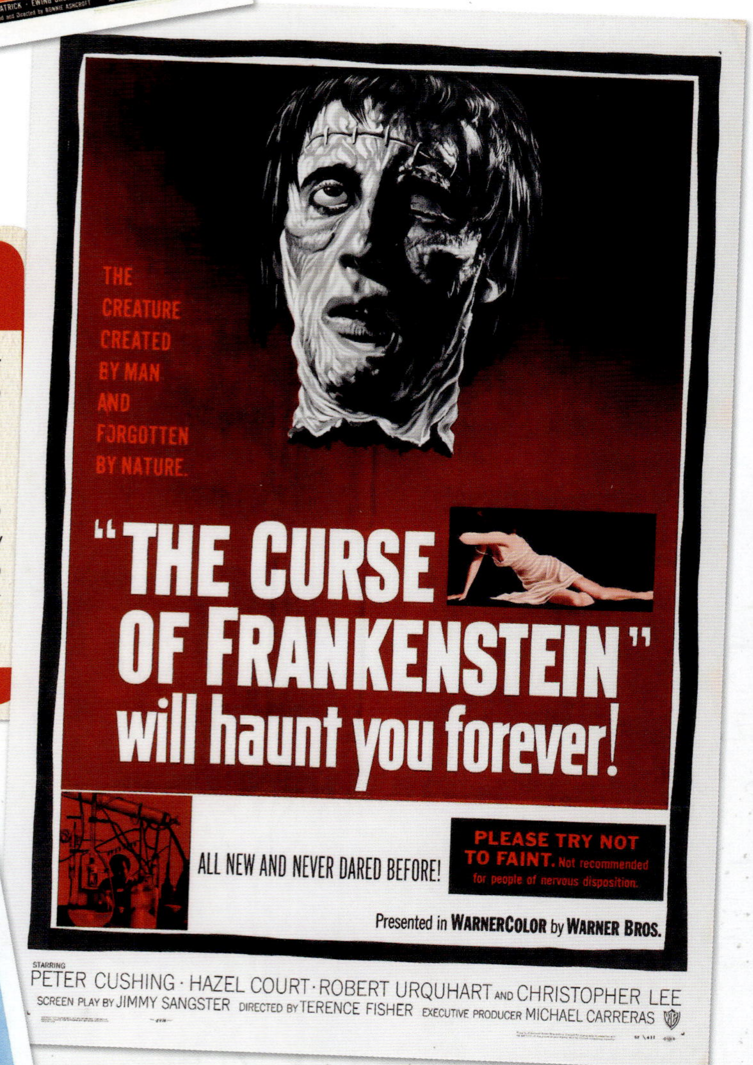

The Curse of Frankenstein.
Hammer Film Productions (1957).

Some of Hammer Studio's cinematic innovations in the recreation of the creature in The Curse of Frankenstein *(1957) were actually legal compunctions. Fearing trademark and copyright violations, the "Frankensteinian Monster" now became called "The Creature" and a whole new look, shot in vivid color, as opposed to Universal Studio's Gothic look of black and white, was created.*

~Caroline Joan (Kay) Picart

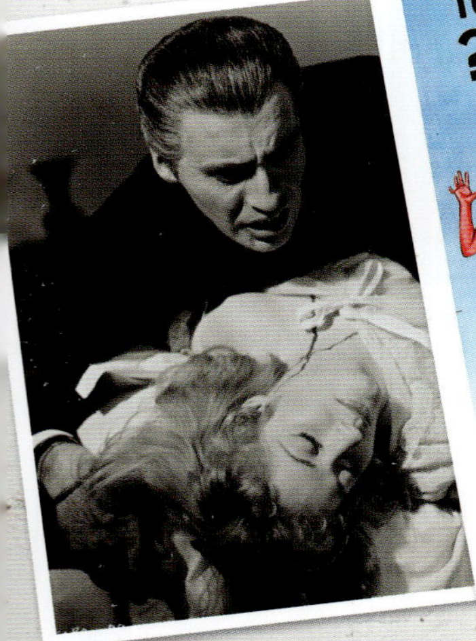

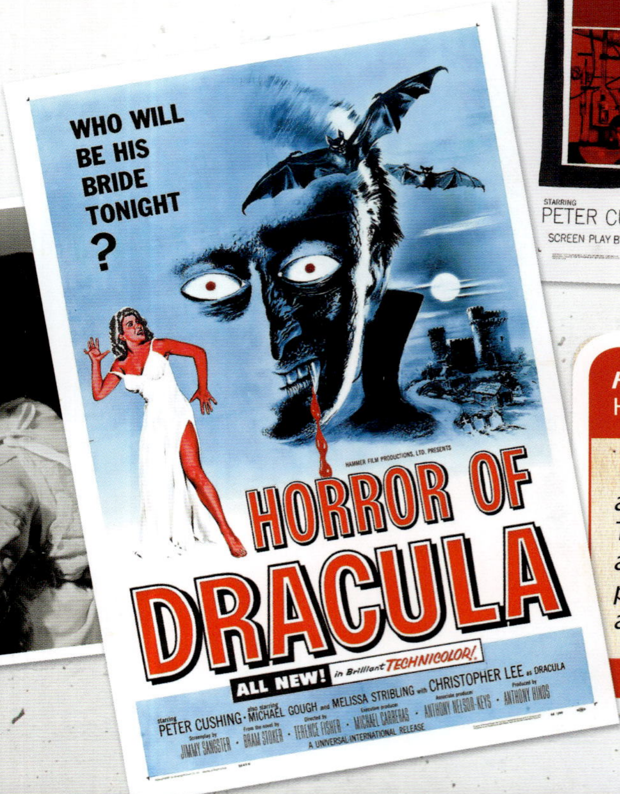

Horror of Dracula.
Hammer Film Productions (1958).

Lee surpassed Lugosi, in my opinion, as the most stately Dracula on screen. This film affected me profoundly and in my adulthood, led to the archetypal vampire playing an enormous role in my writing and editing work.

Nancy Kilpatrick

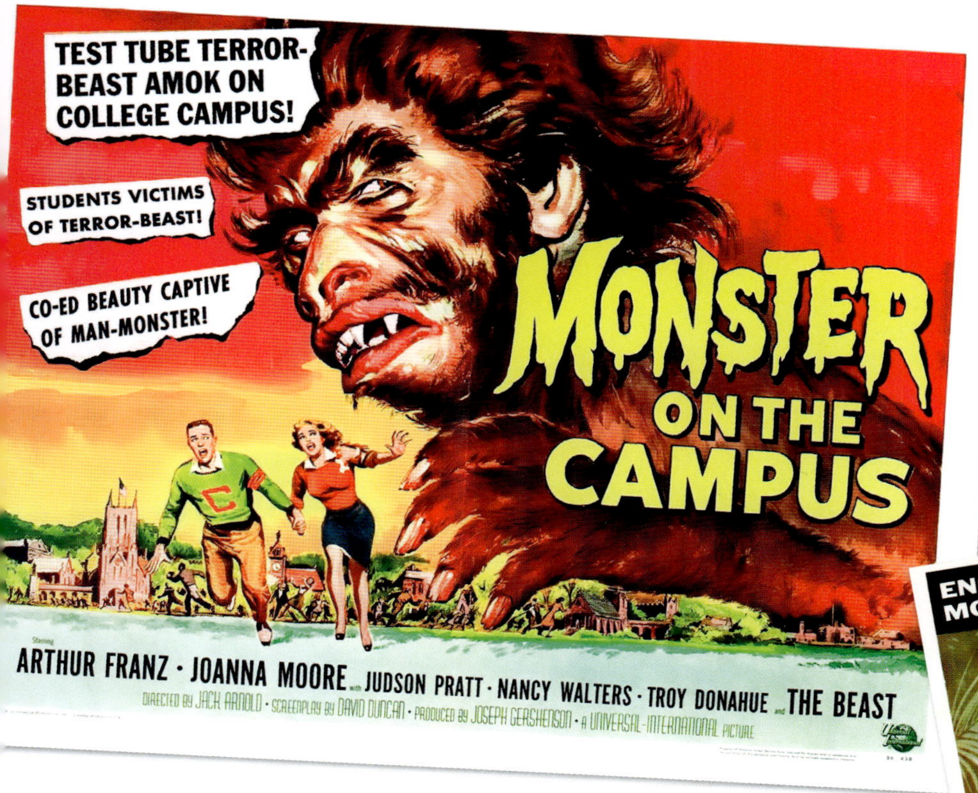

Monster on the Campus.
Universal International Pictures (1958).

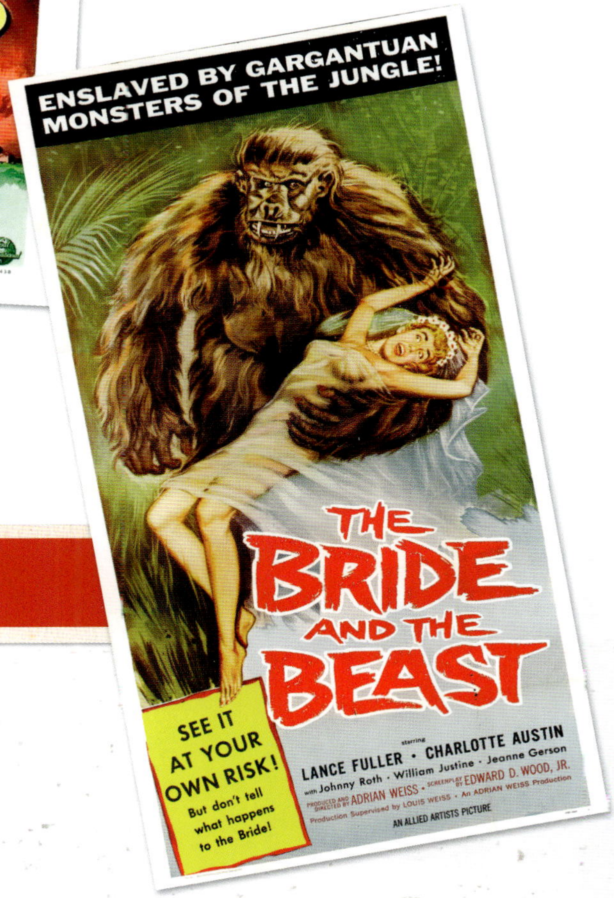

The Bride and the Beast.
Allied Artists (1958).

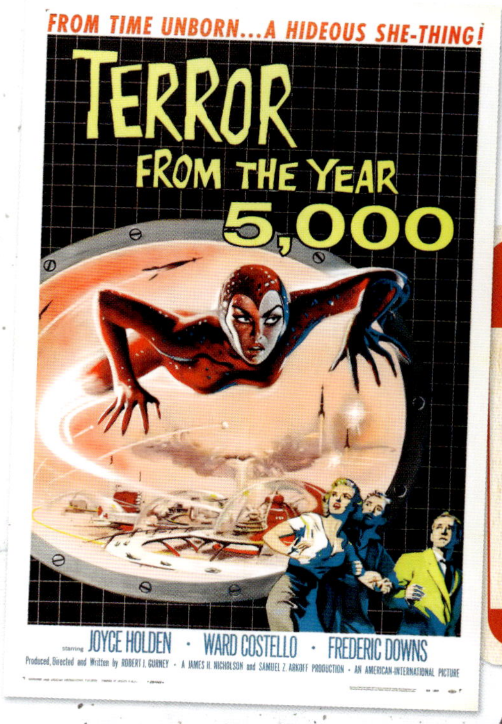

Terror from the Year 5000.
La Jolla Pictures (1958).

For me, Terror from the Year 5000 captures the real horror hovering over me and other bright kids who read science fiction in the '50s. The film has no aliens or giant insects. Instead, the future is a radioactive wasteland whose inhabitants try hopelessly to keep human civilization alive.

David Drake

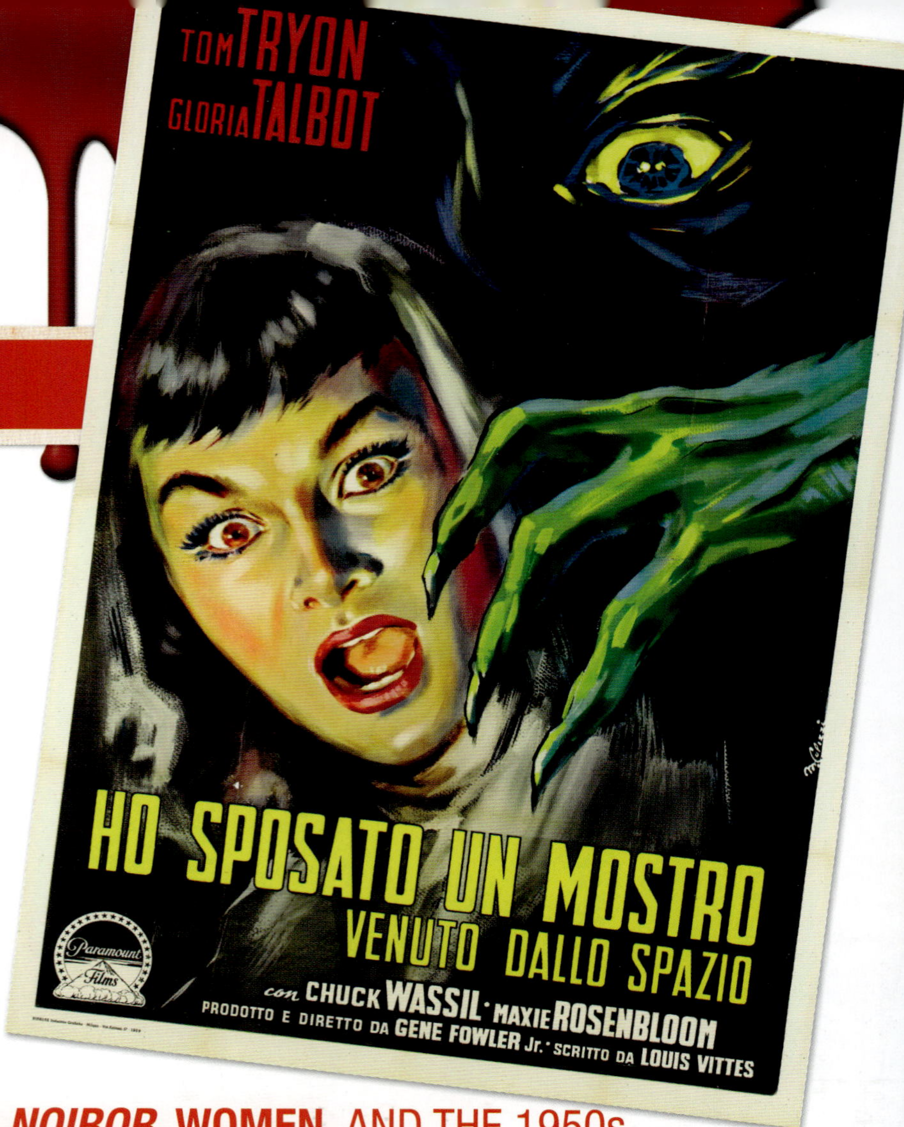

I Married a Monster from Outer Space.
Paramount Pictures (1958). Italy.

ON *NOIROR*, WOMEN, AND THE 1950s

In Gene Fowler Jr.'s noir-styled nightmare of marital emotional alienation, aliens from Andromeda have arrived to impregnate unlucky, Eisenhower-era Earth women. The most unsettling scene in the picture is one directly related to the patriarchal view of a woman's "proper" role in American society of the 1950s. The scene involves a hooker, Francine, as she approaches a prospective John on a street corner. The camera only reveals her target of opportunity from behind. His face and head are sheathed beneath a hood, and the stranger ignores Francine's approach for an object in a storefront display: a baby doll. When confronted by Francine, the John pivots to reveal that he is a hideous alien beast. The monster shoots the frightened Francine in the back without mercy, and then returns to gaze at the baby doll, the object of his fascination.

In terms of theme, *I Married a Monster from Outer Space* serves as a warning to women not to step out of their traditional role as child-bearers, lest they be destroyed. This viewpoint is evident as well in the film's treatment of the lead character, Marge (Gloria Talbott). She finds herself in a marriage (to an alien) that feels more like a prison sentence, but she has little opportunity to escape. In fact, the only such opportunity at Marge's disposal is to convince her family doctor — a man, naturally — to believe her "crazy" story that her husband is a monster from another world. Without a man's help to vouch for her, Marge has no say over her own future.

~John Kenneth Muir

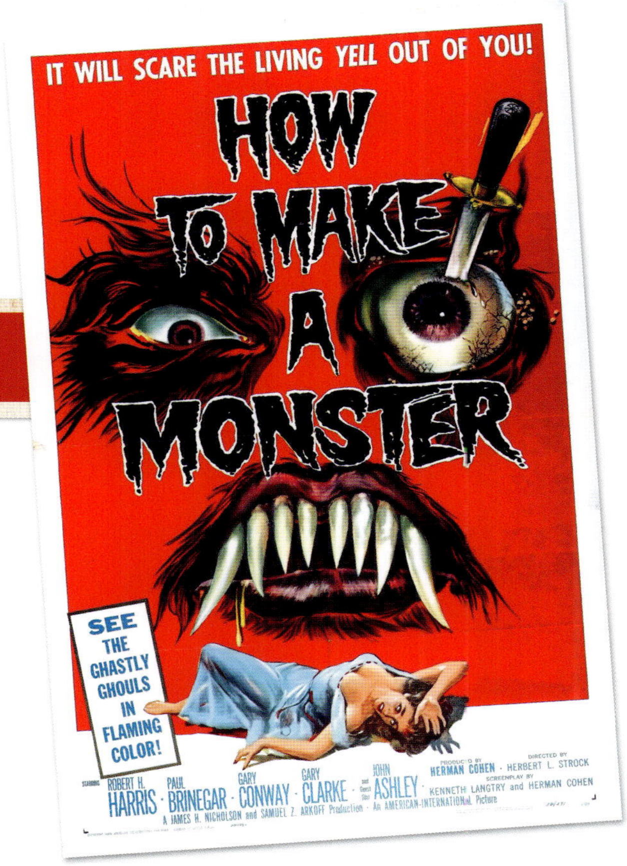

How to Make a Monster.
American International Pictures (1958)

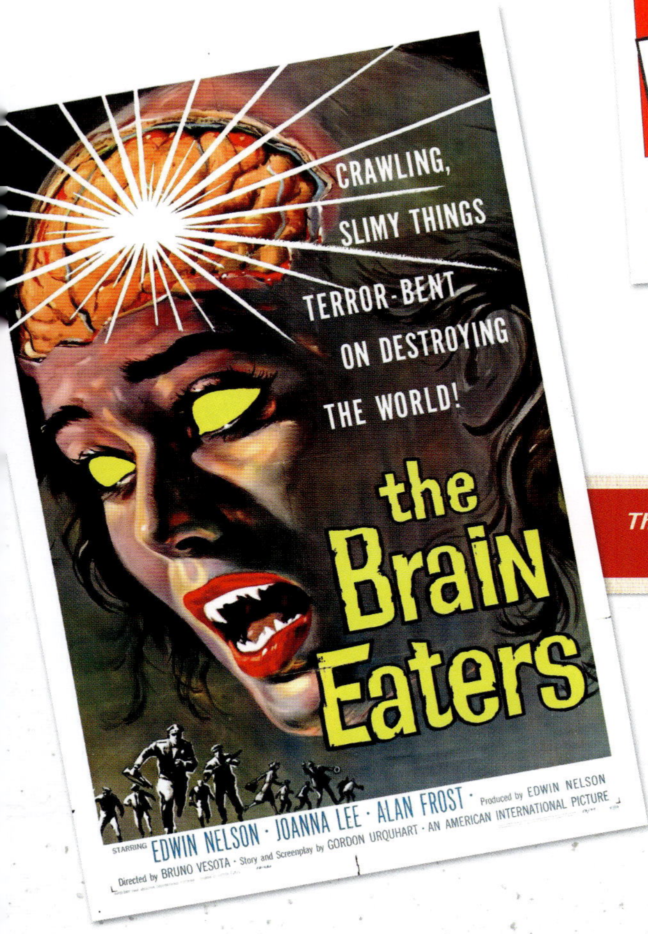

The Brain Eaters. American International Pictures/ Corinthian Productions (1958).

The Return of Dracula.
Gramercy Pictures (1958).

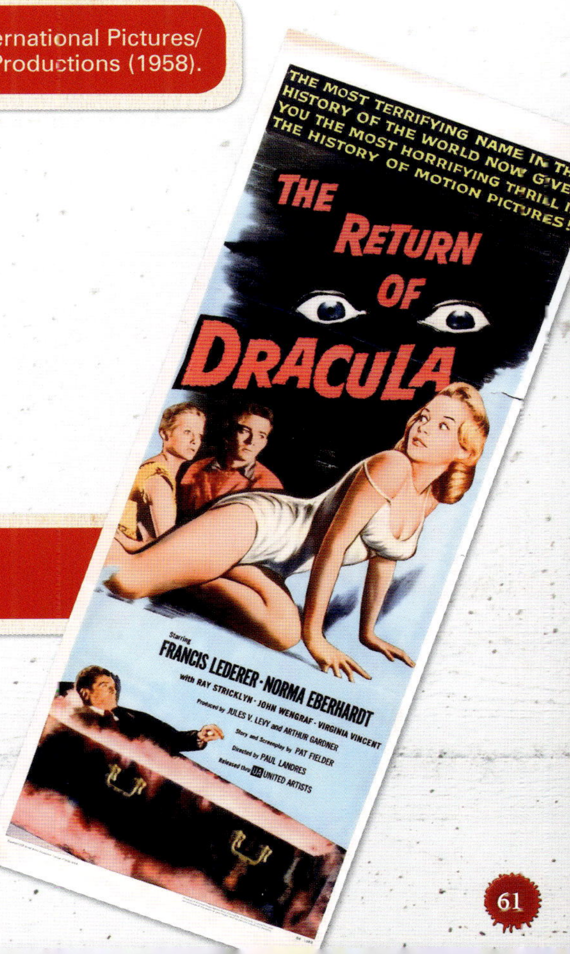

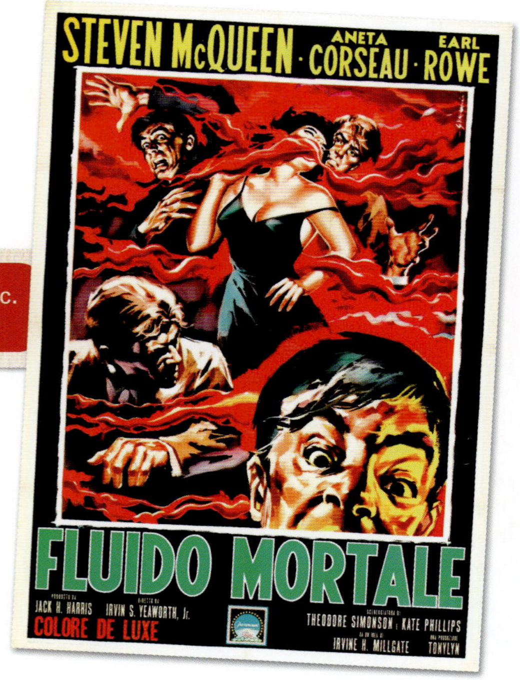

The Blob. Fairview Productions/Tonylyn Productions Inc. (1958). Italy.

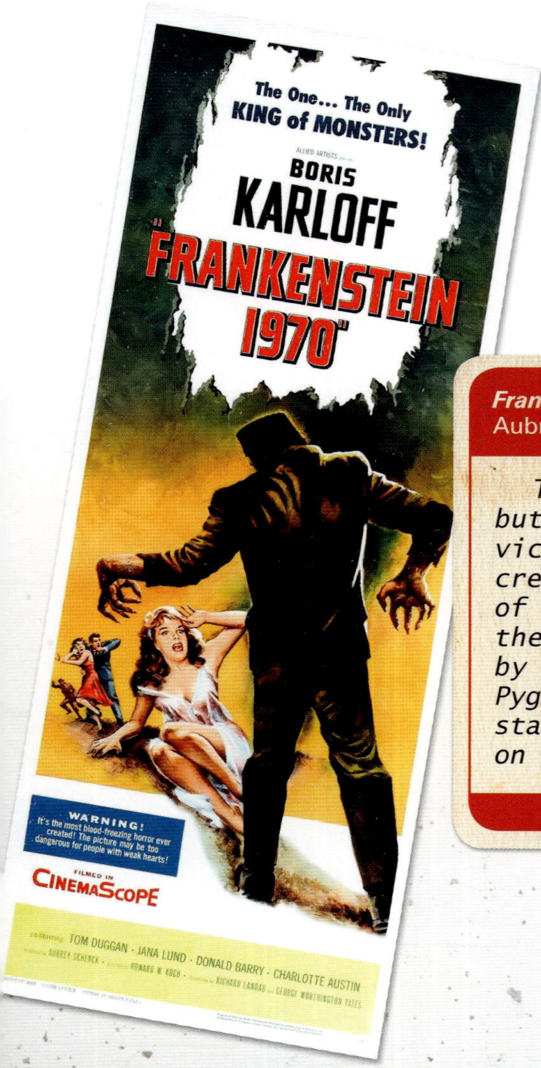

Frankenstein 1970.
Aubrey Schenck Productions (1958).

This film features Boris Karloff again, but this time, as the mad scientist victimized by Nazis, rather than the creature. The film references the horror of Nazism as much as it caricaturizes the commercialization of real horror by Hollywood, and its production of Pygmalion-like directors and narcissistic starlets, willing to sacrifice themselves on a celluloid altar.

Caroline Joan (Kay) Picart

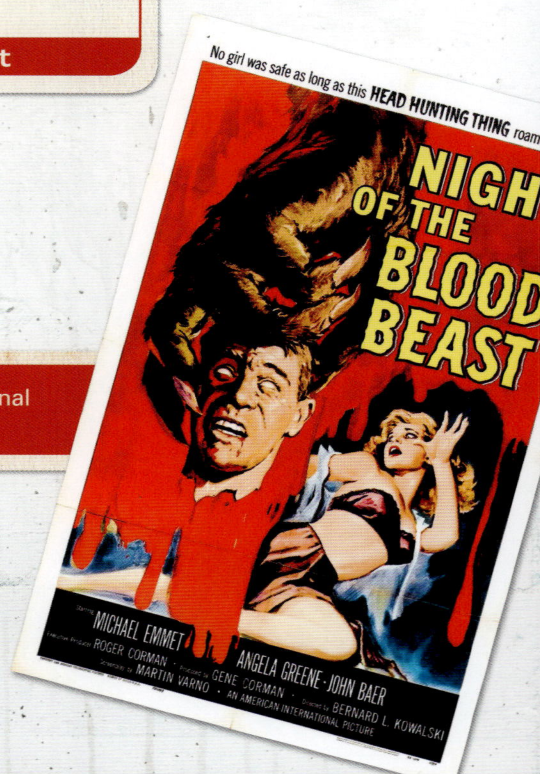

Night of the Blood Beast. American International Pictures/Balboa Productions (1958).

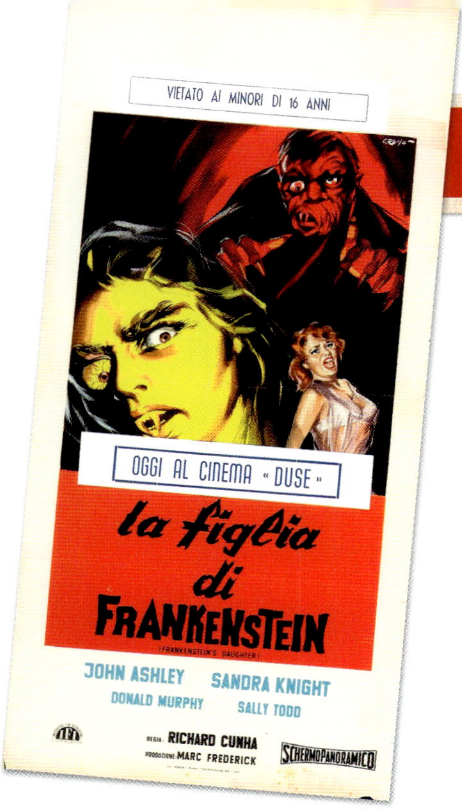

Frankenstein's Daughter.
Layton Film Productions Inc. (1958). Italy.

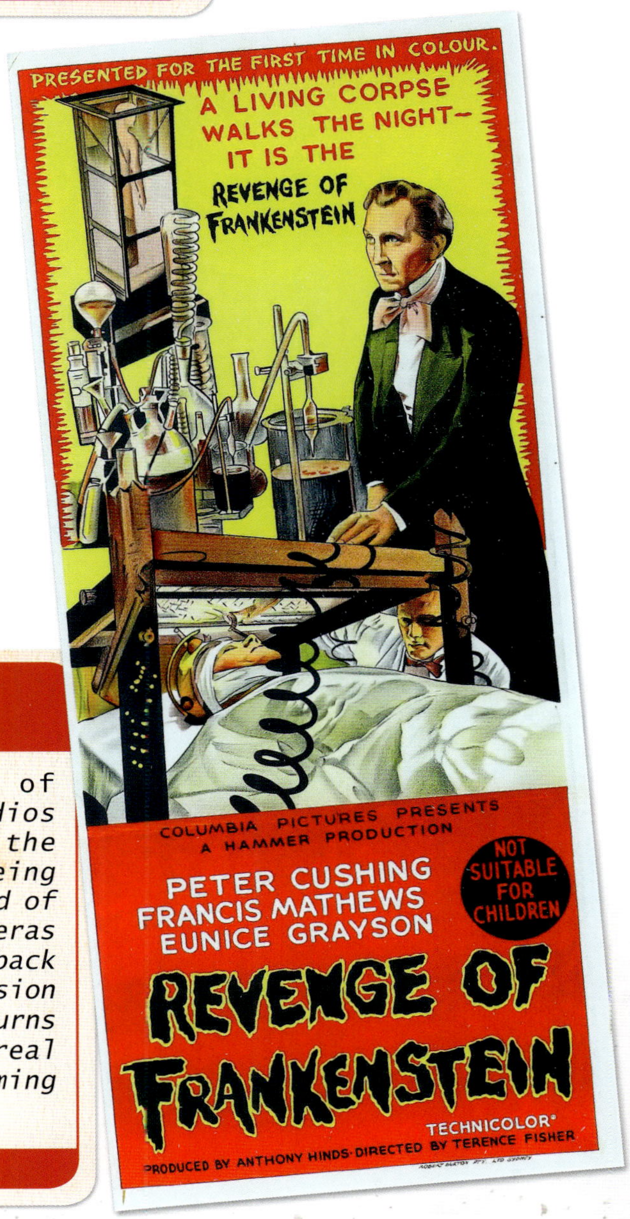

The Revenge of Frankenstein.
Cadogan Films/Hammer Film Productions (1958).

Given the success of Curse of Frankenstein *(1957), Hammer Studios could not resist a sequel. To the narrative glitch of the baron being destined to be guillotined at the end of* Curse of Frankenstein, *producer Carreras remarked: "Oh we just sew his head back on. It's fascinating!" The Hammer version of the Frankensteinian mytheme thus turns the Baron Frankenstein into the real Monster, with the creatures becoming increasingly disposable.*

Caroline Joan (Kay) Picart

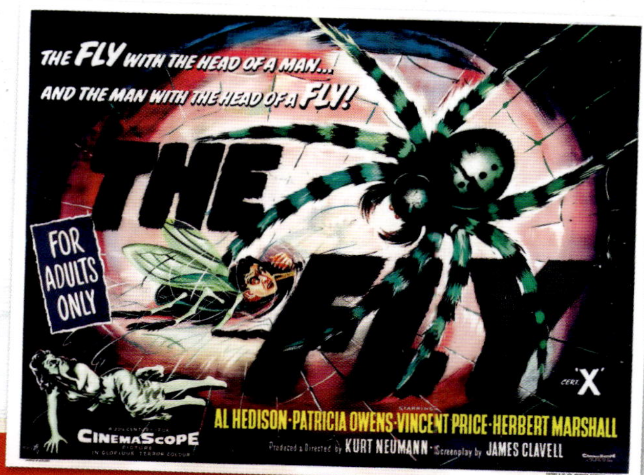

The Fly.
Twentieth Century Fox Film Corporation (1958).

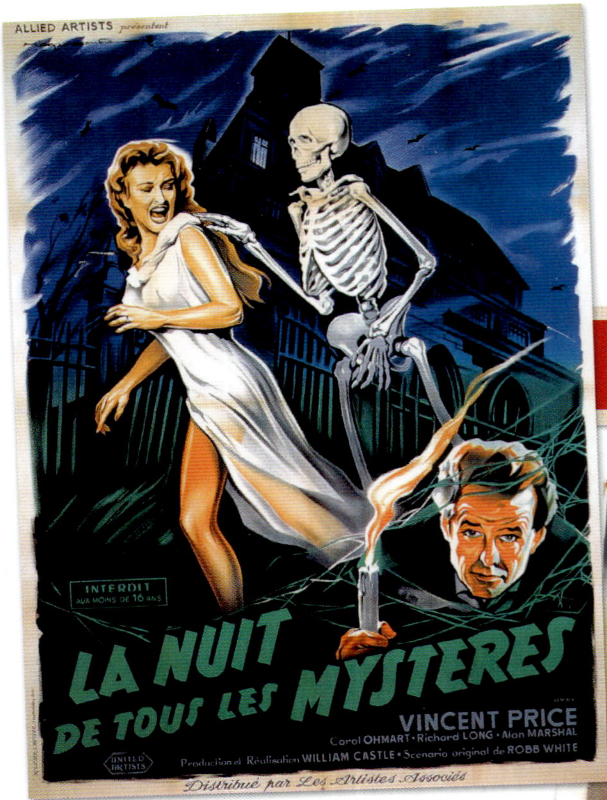

House on Haunted Hill. William Castle Productions/ Legend Films (1959). France.

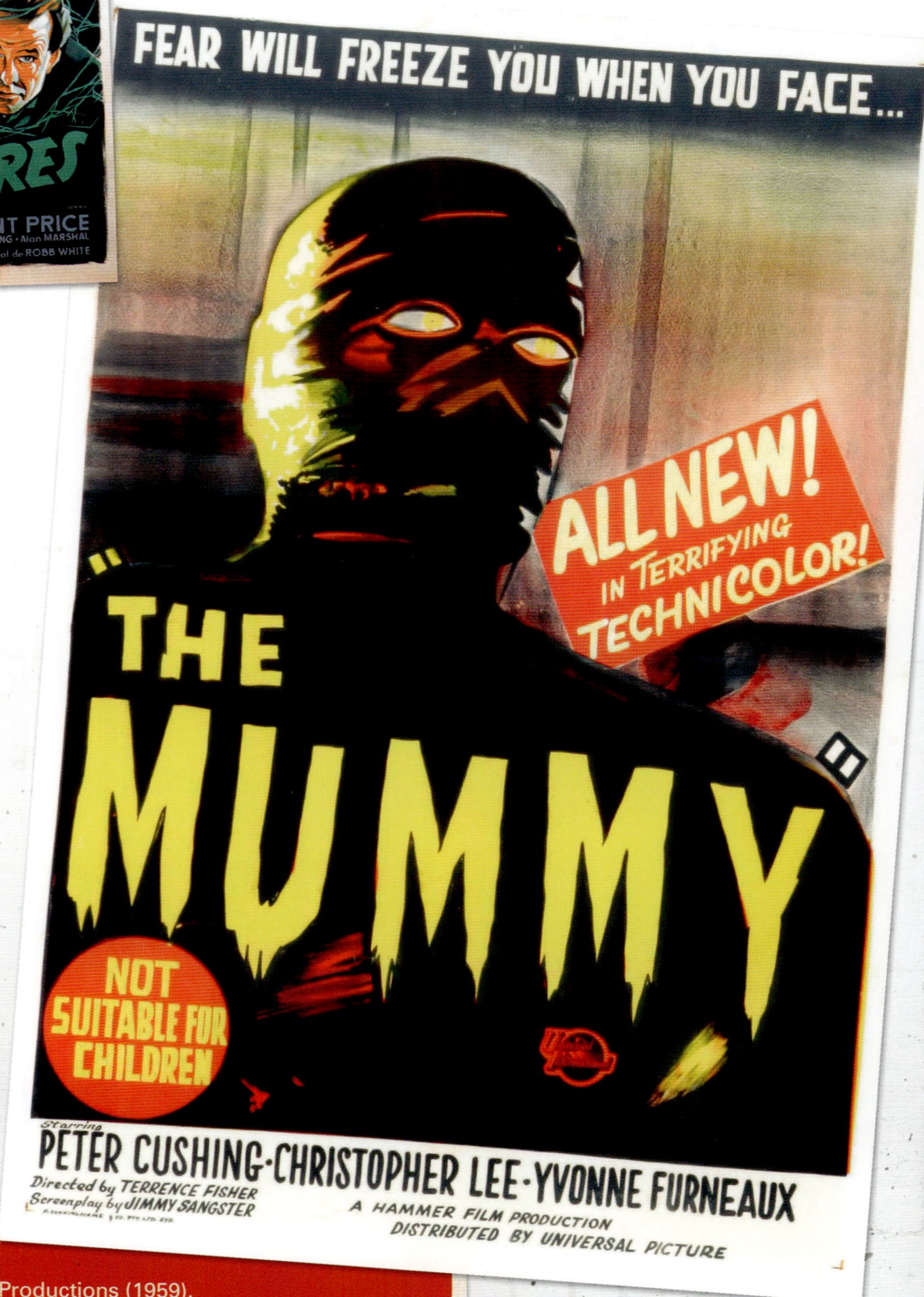

The Mummy.
Hammer Film Productions (1959).

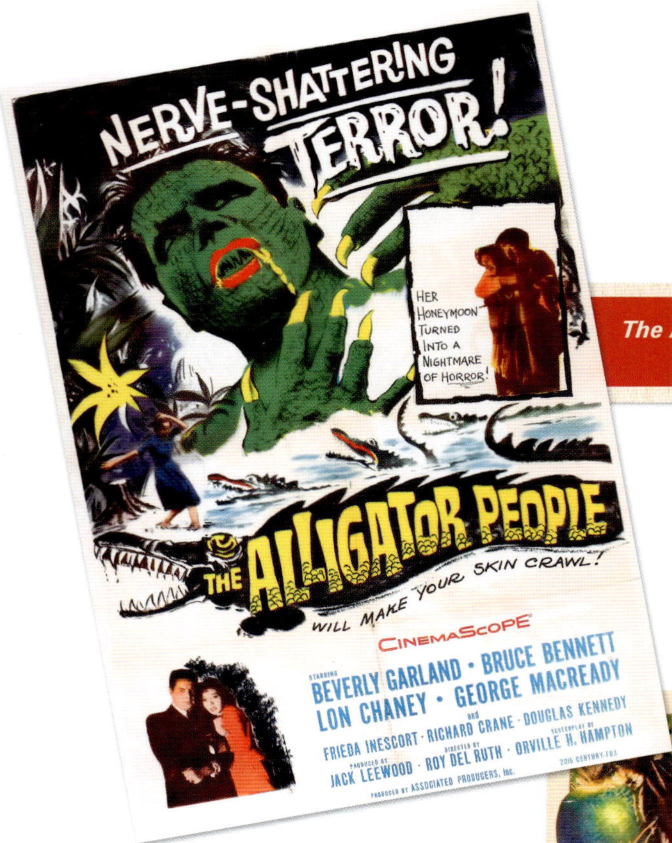

The Alligator People. Twentieth Century Fox Film Corporation/Associated Producers (1959).

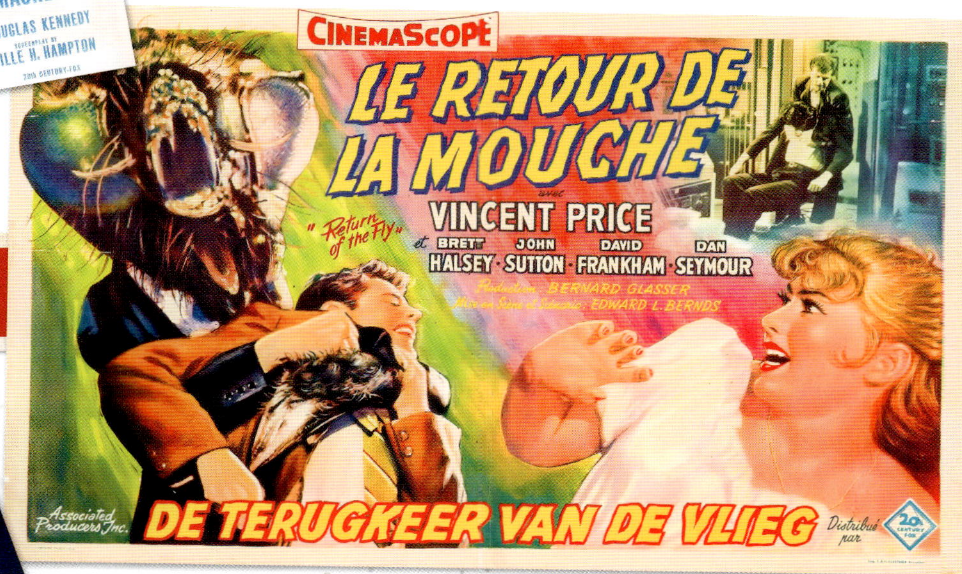

Return of the Fly.
Associated Producers (1959). Belgium.

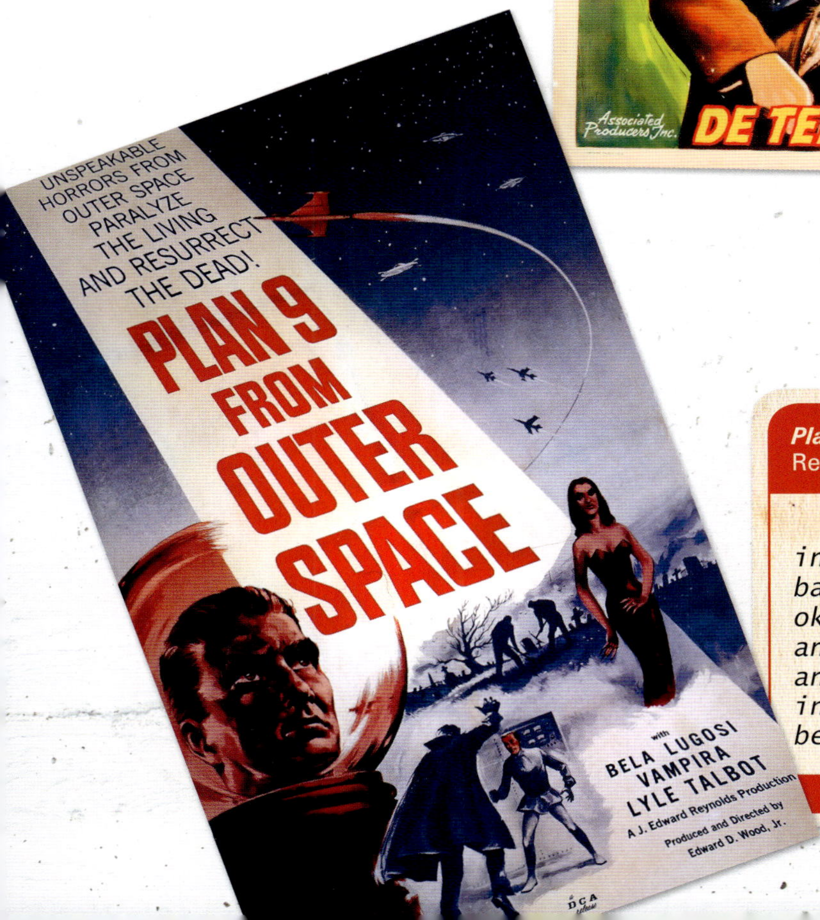

Plan Nine from Outer Space.
Reynolds Pictures (1959).

After midnight, when viewed on a 12-inch Emerson console by this not yet bar-mitzvahed youth... It was creepy, okay. Later, you learn about Ed Wood, and transvestites, and Bela the Junky, and Criswell and ... Creepy living can indeed produce creepy movie moments, you betcha, Sarah Palin.

Mort Castle

5 THE 1960s

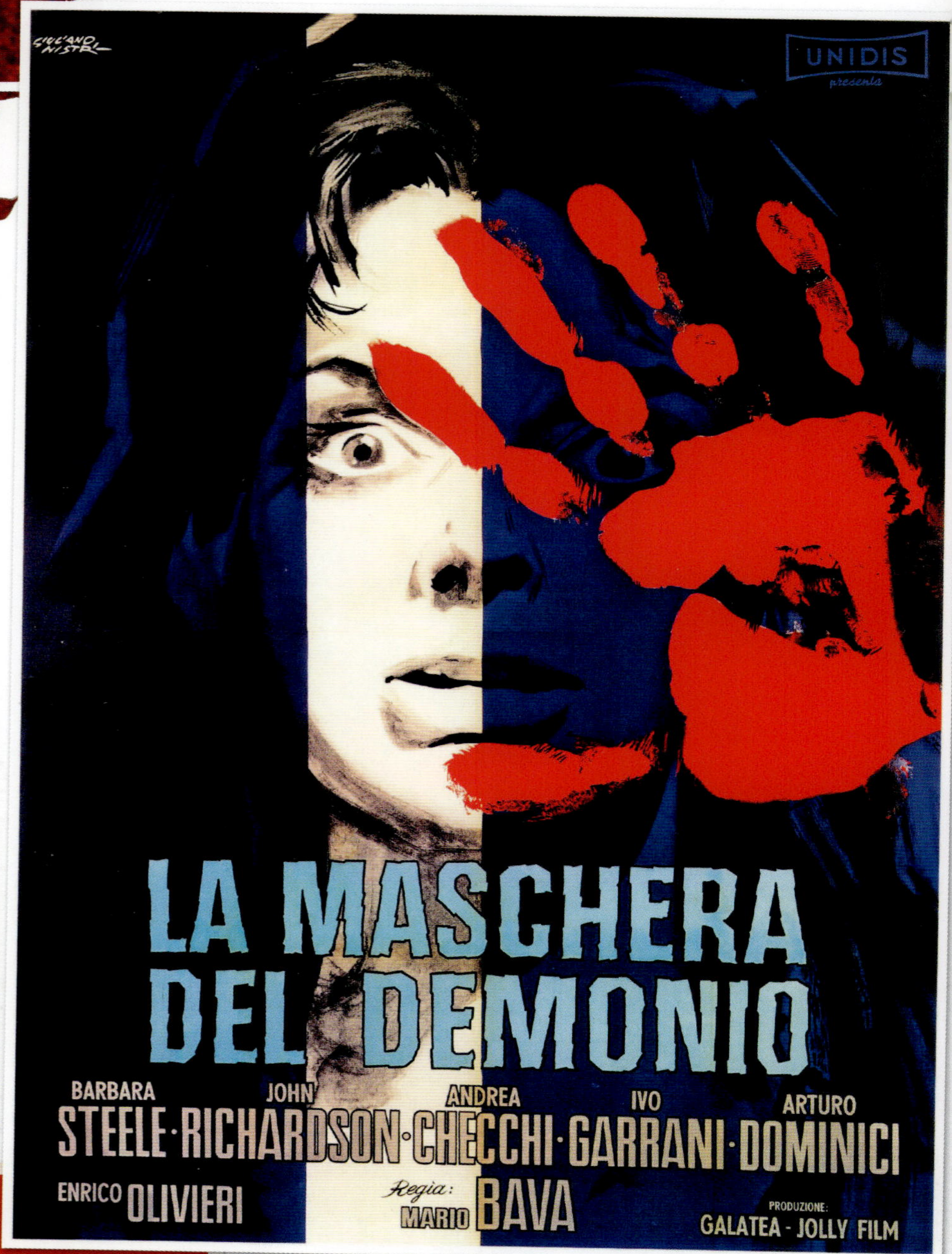

Black Sunday. Alta Vista Productions/ Galatea Film/Jolly Film (1960). Italy.

I first encountered Mario Bava's Italian horror classic in London's legendary Scala cinema at some point in the 1980s. The run-down, slightly seedy theatre provided the perfect atmospheric setting for this most haunting, dream-like and beautiful of all horror films. I have seen Black Sunday *many times since but my vivid memory of that first viewing supports my firm belief that it is not just the films you see that count, it's where you see them.*

Peter Hutchings

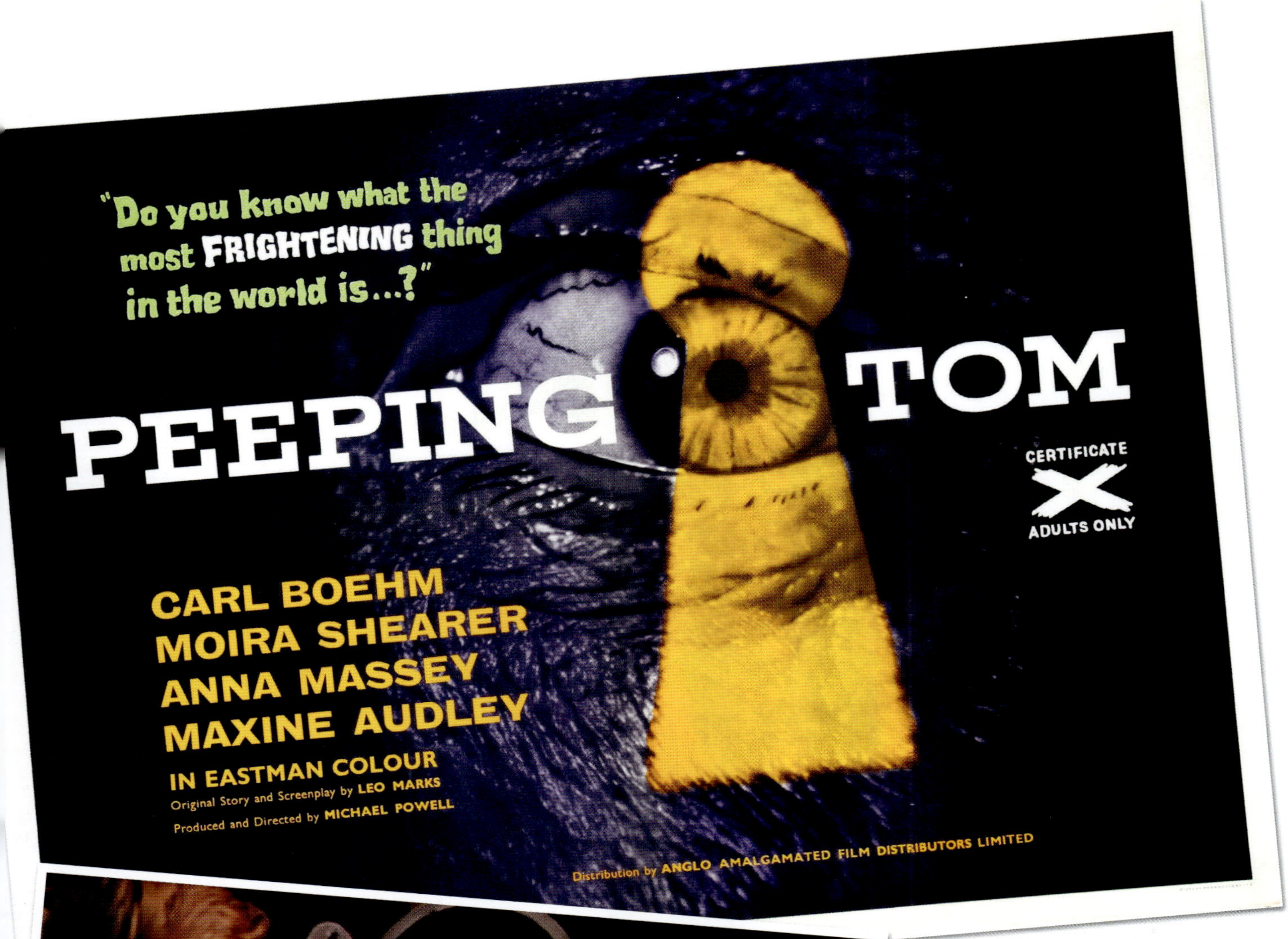

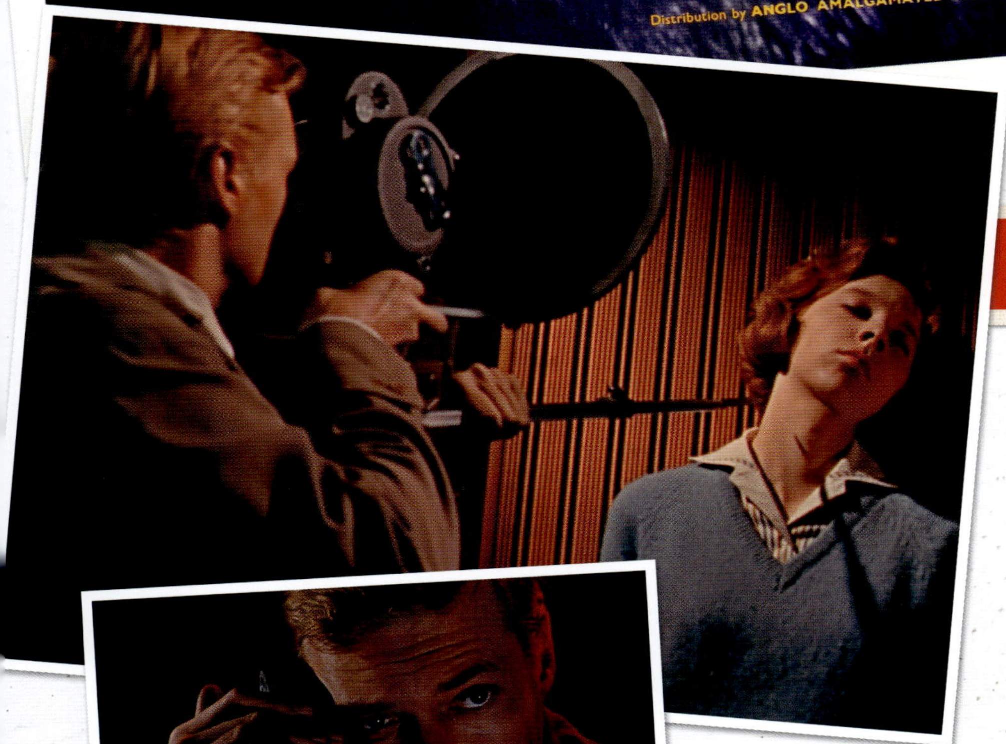

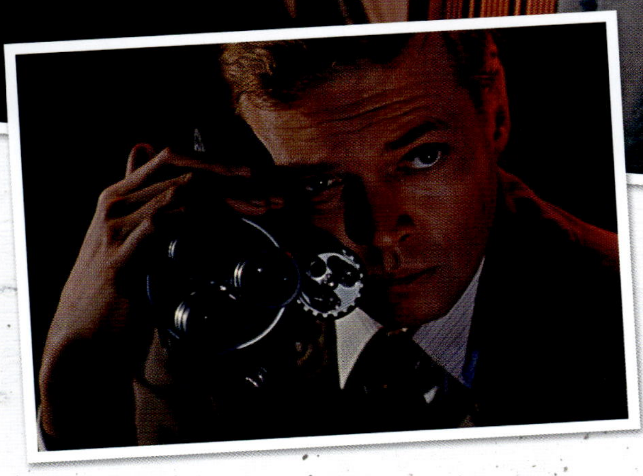

Peeping Tom.
Michael Powell (Theatre) (1960). UK.

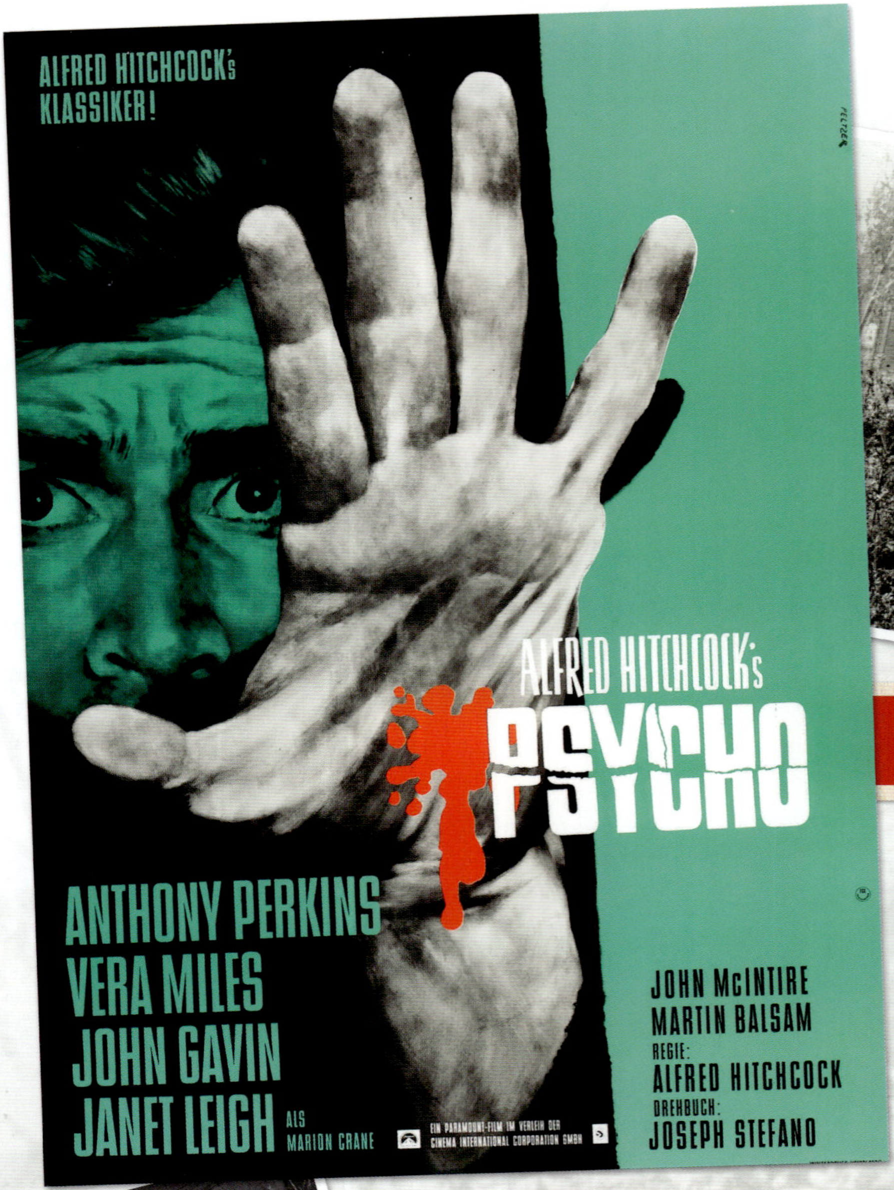

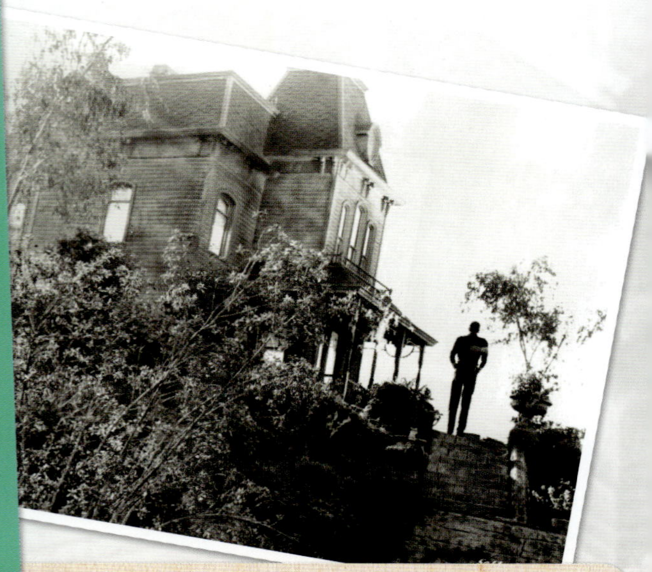

Psycho.
Shamley Productions (1960). Germany.

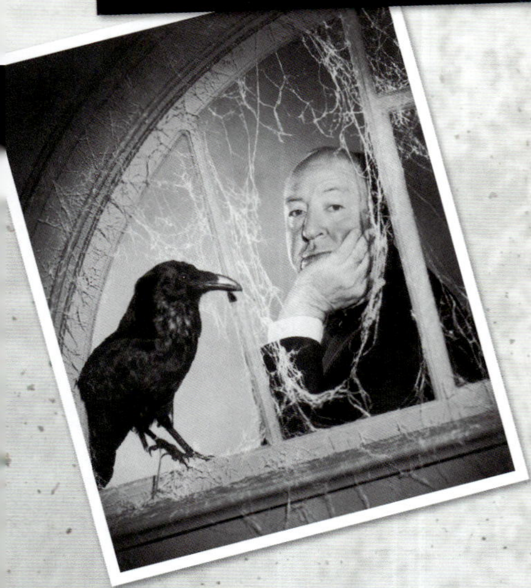

ON *PSYCHO* (1960) AND MODERN HORROR

Hitchcock's extraordinary mordant joke with tremendous, paradigmatic performances and music. It presents a fissured and split world, whether in the psyche of the killer at its heart or the overarching structure of the banal modern world versus the Bates's neo-gothic mansion. The starkness of the divisions should not work, but they do. The fullest horrors hang or stagger or swing or sink between: hanging onto a shower curtain, staggering backwards down the stairs, a lightbulb swings to and fro, a car sinks into a swamp. The modern world is born in this cultural product as radically as it is in the Beatles' first LP or the Lady Chatterley's Lover obscenity trial...

~Richard J. Hand

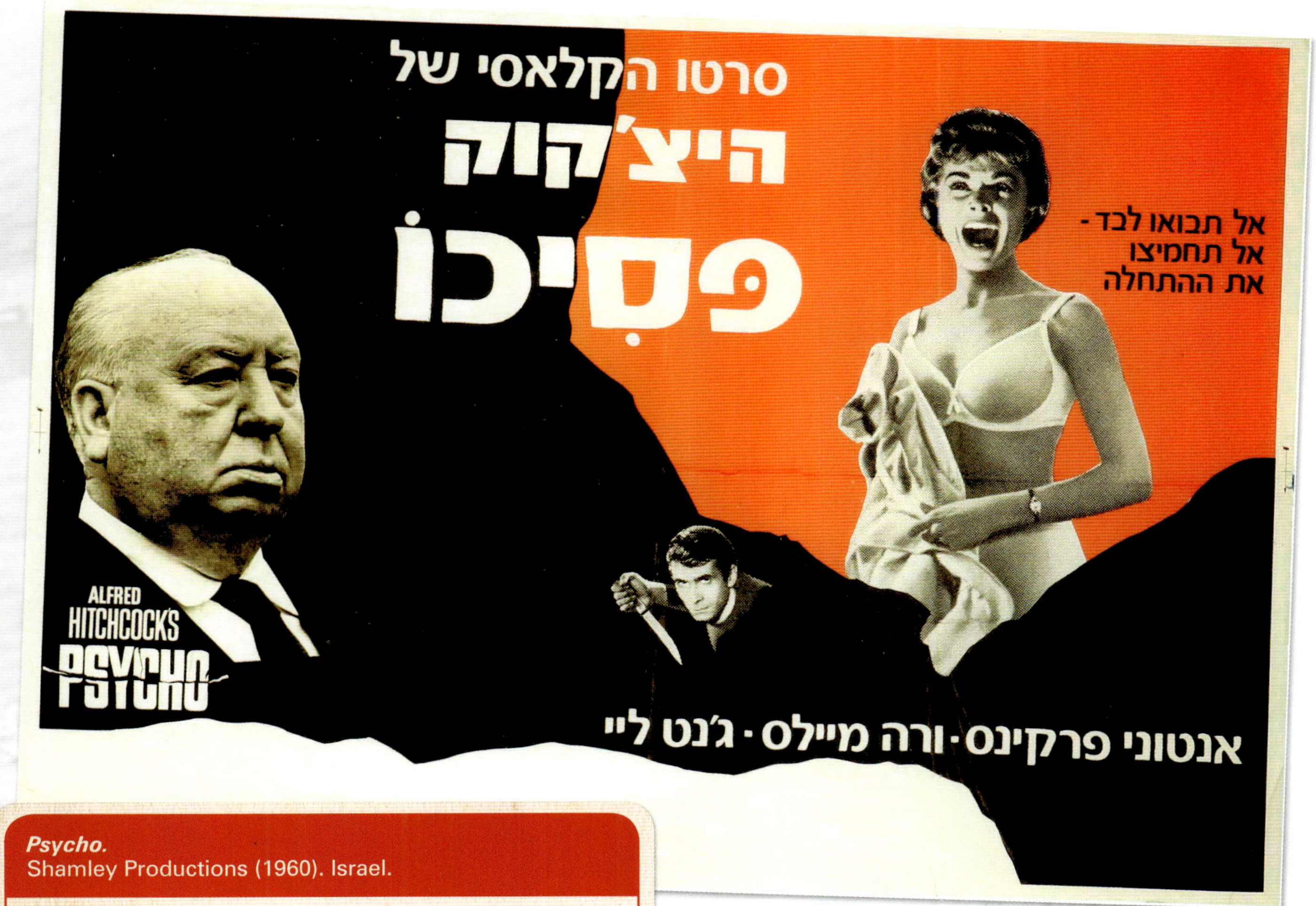

Psycho.
Shamley Productions (1960). Israel.

My all-time favorite horror film, granddaddy of the modern slasher. A spine-tingly delight from start to finish. Never gets old. Pure Hitchcock genius. And, oh, that Bernard Herrmann score!

Tony Timpone

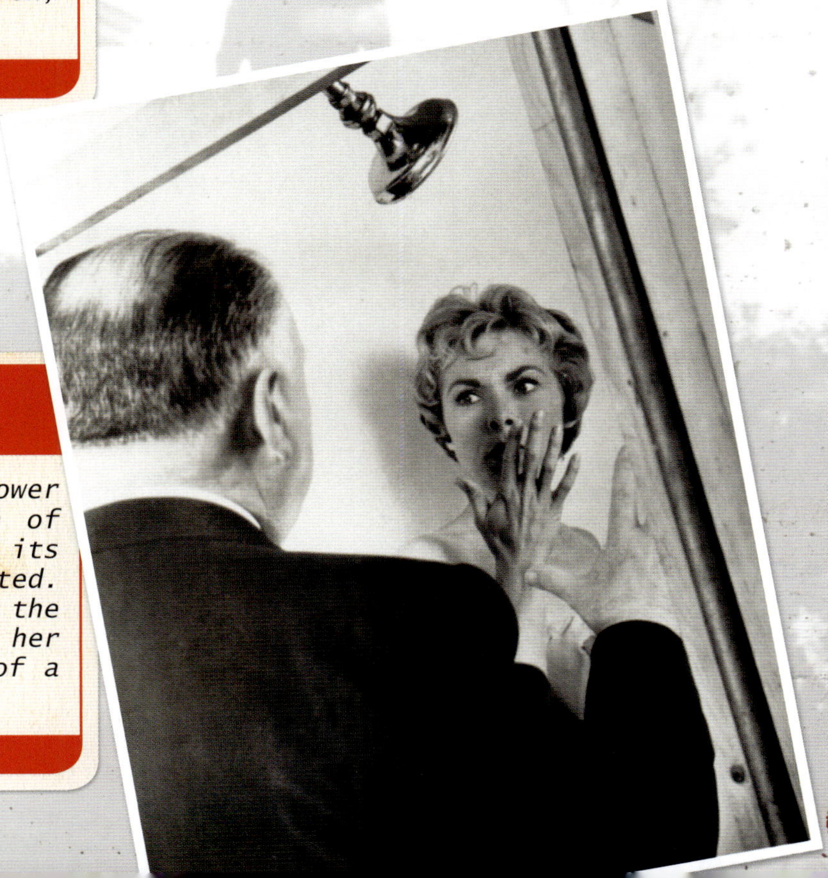

Psycho.
Shamley Productions (1960).

Shower scene, shower scene, shower scene. Not only is the execution of this graphic murder brilliant, but its location in the story is unprecedented. We've been with Marion Crane since the beginning of the movie, and to have her dispatched so unceremoniously all of a sudden is beyond disorienting.

Bev Vincent

The Innocents. Achilles/Twentieth Century Fox Film Corporation (1960). Australia.

The Innocents heads my list. It is the cinematic version of William Archibald's play of that title, which was based on the Henry James classic, The Turn of the Screw. Its cast is perfect: Deborah Kerr, Peter Wyngarde, Megs Jenkins, Pamela Franklin, Martin Stephens, and a cameo appearance by Michael Redgrave. Effectively photographed in black and white by Freddie Francis, it features two ghosts – or does it? – who may be trying to possess two children. The maddening ambiguity of the James original is brilliantly captured by the director Jack Clayton and Truman Capote, who did the screen adaptation.

Marvin Kaye

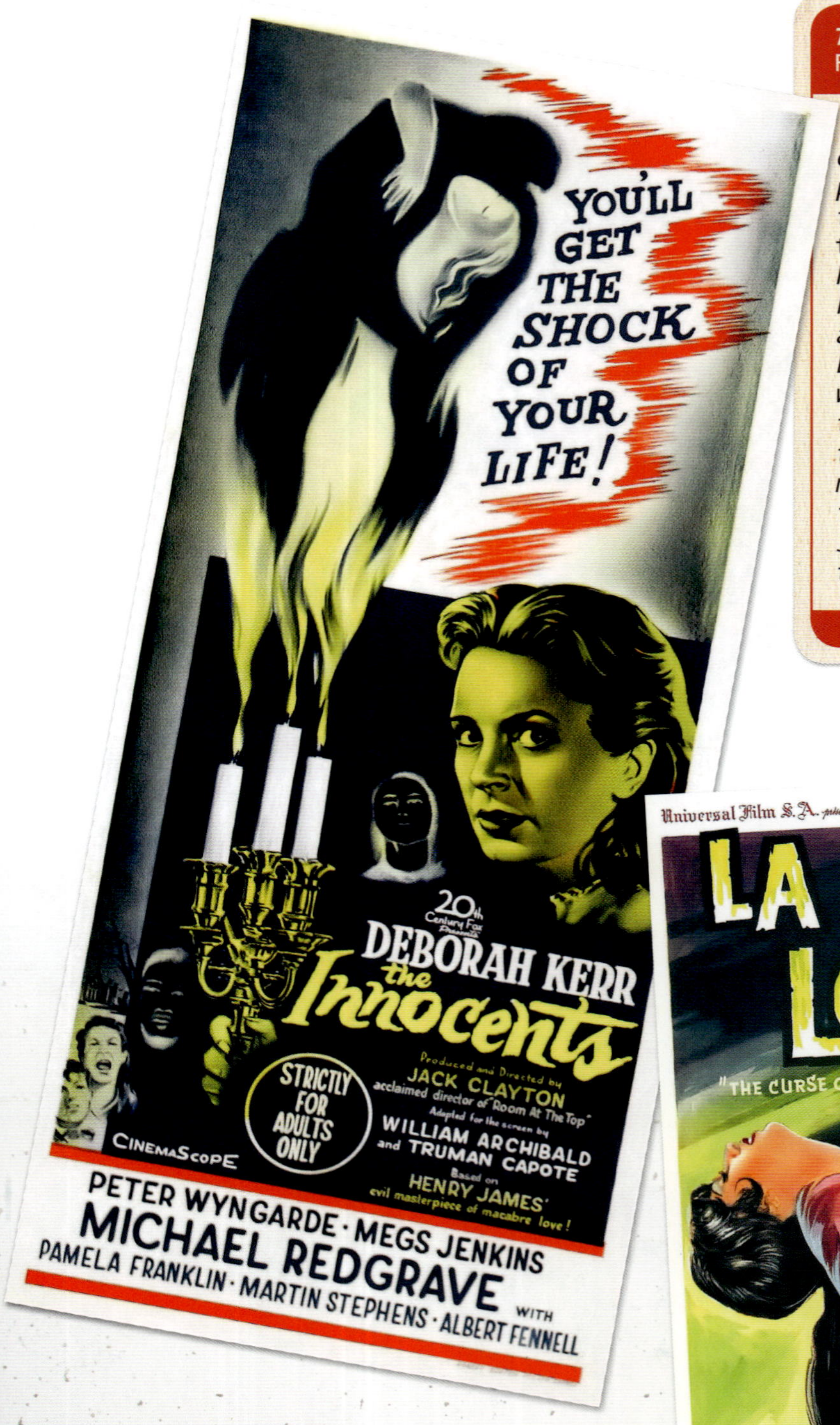

The Curse of the Werewolf. Hammer Film Productions (1961). France.

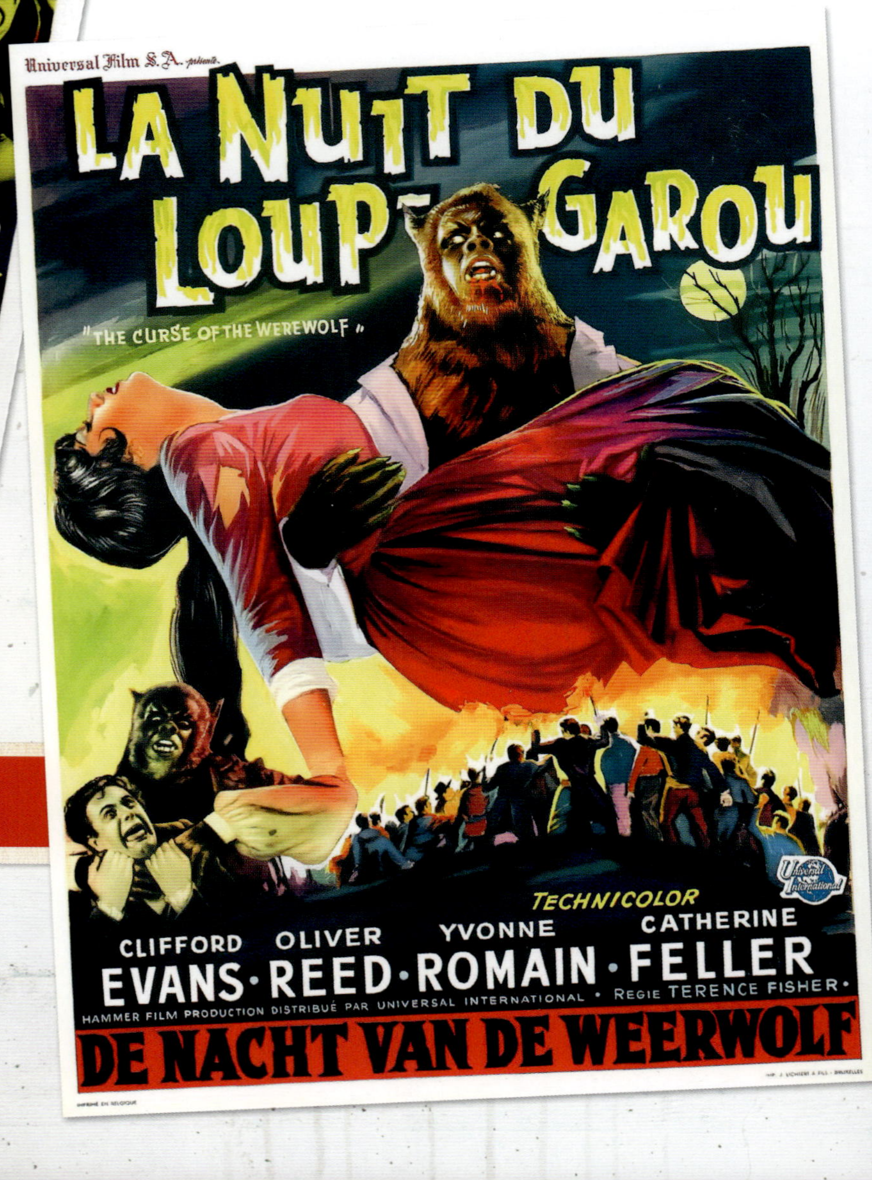

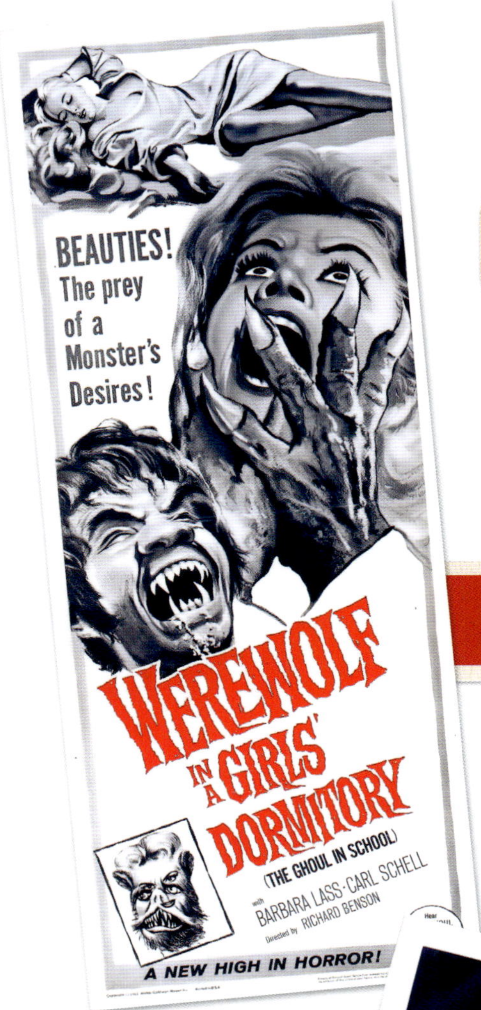

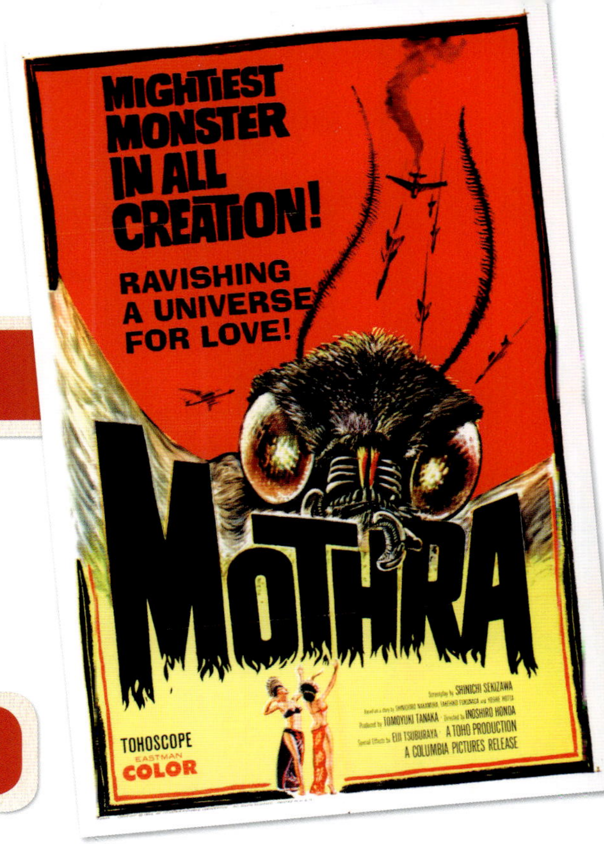

Mothra.
Toho Company (1961).

Werewolf in a Girls' Dormitory.
Royal Film (1961).

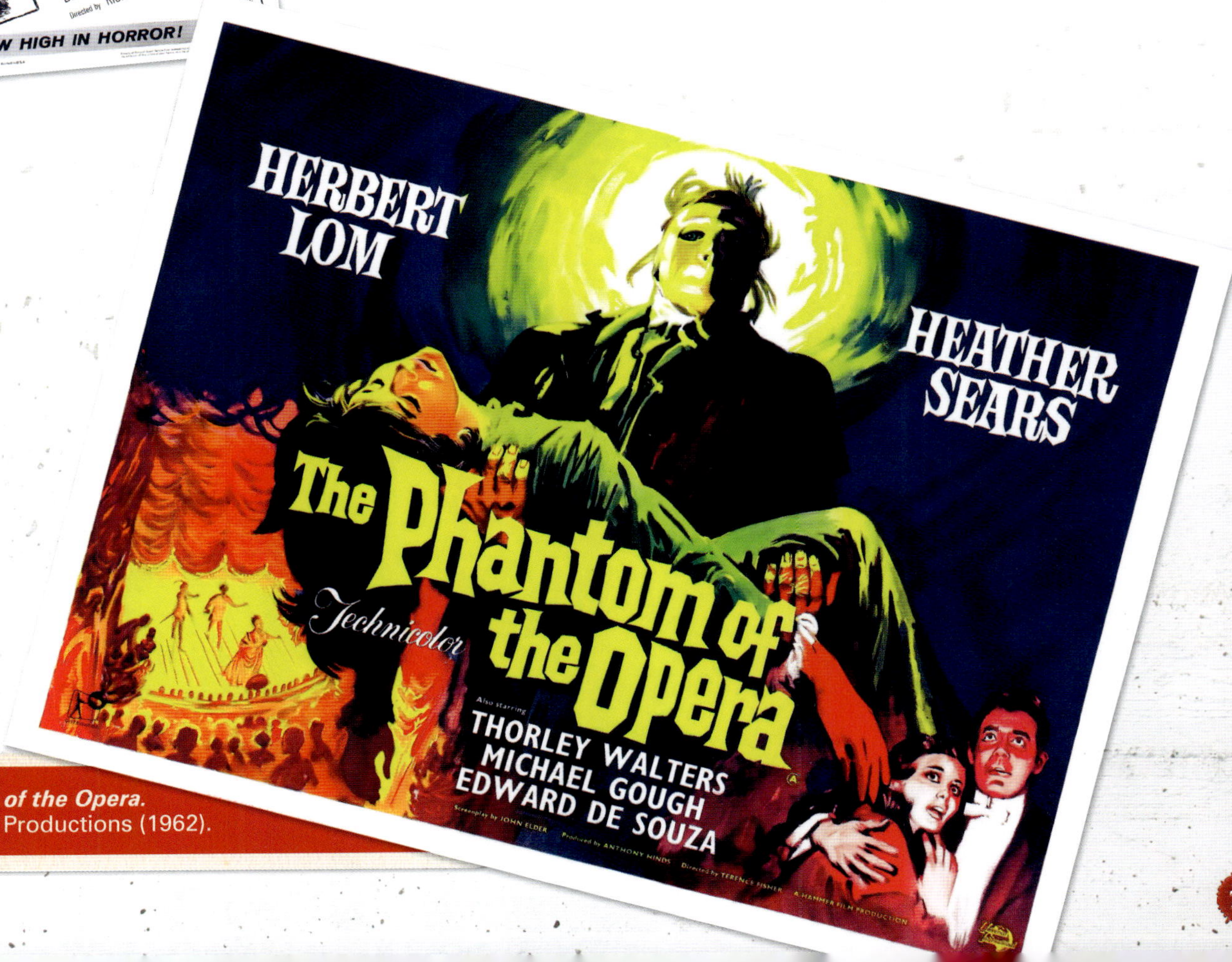

The Phantom of the Opera.
Hammer Film Productions (1962).

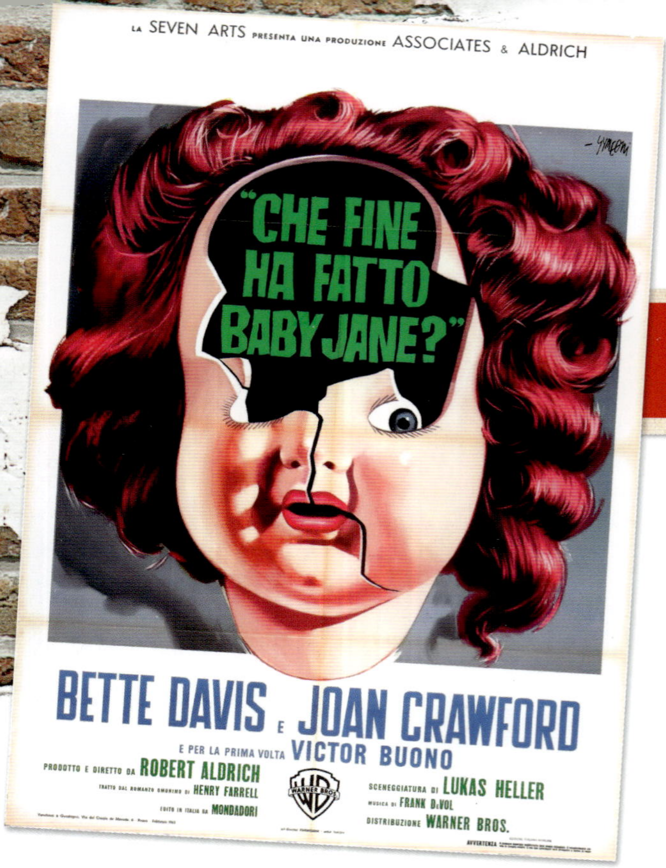

Whatever Happened to Baby Jane.
The Associates & Aldrich Company/Seven Arts Productions/Warner Bros. Pictures (1962). Italy.

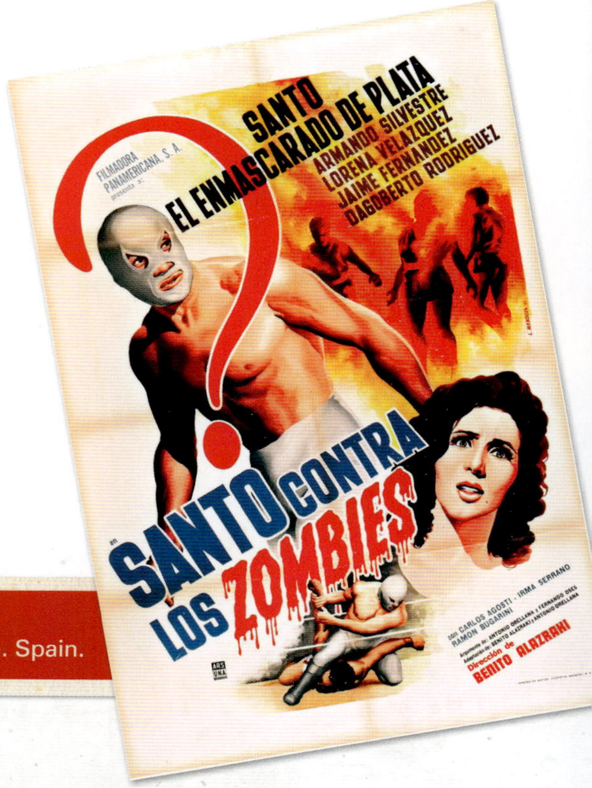

Santo Contra Los Zombies.
Filmadora Panamericana (1962). Spain.

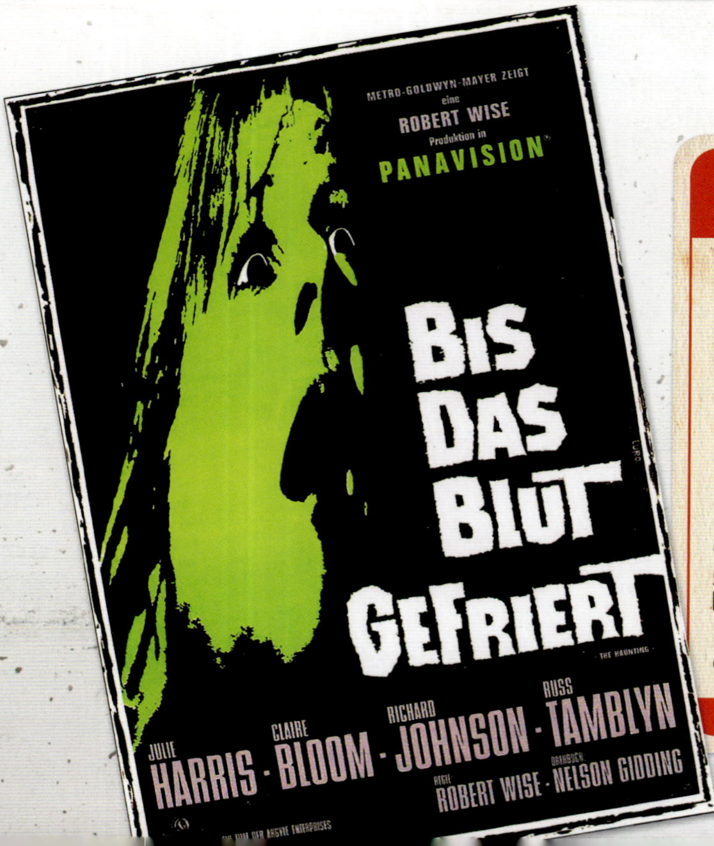

The Haunting.
Argyle Enterprises (1963). Germany.

The Haunting *(1963) is Robert Wise's superb cinematic adaptation of Shirley Jackson's novel,* The Haunting of Hill House, *starring Julie Harris, Claire Bloom, Richard Johnson, Russ Tamblyn, Lois Maxwell, and Fay Compton. True, the novel's ending strongly suggests that the haunting is entirely in the mind of its protagonist, whereas the screenplay by Nicholas Gidding objectifies the ghostliness, but one cannot fault* The Haunting *for pure nerve-wracking chills. To echo Leonard Maltin, "Don't see this one alone!"*

Marvin Kaye

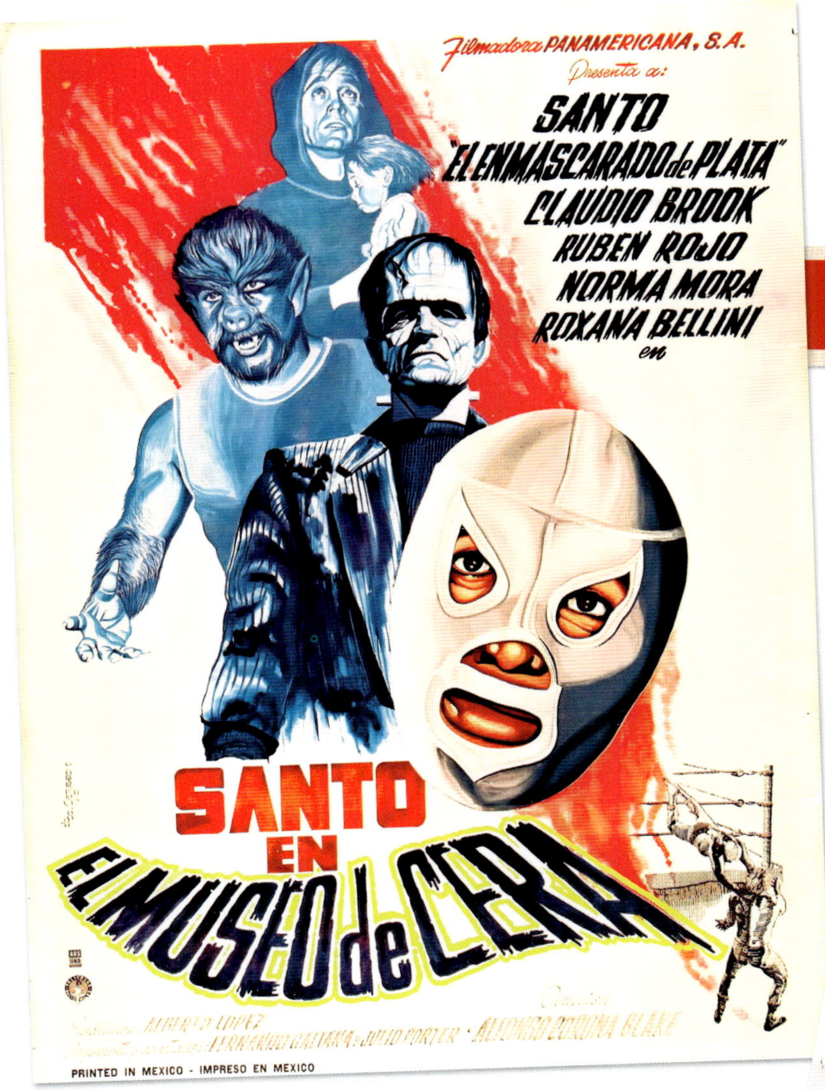

Santo in the Wax Museum. Filmadora Panamericana (1963). Mexico.

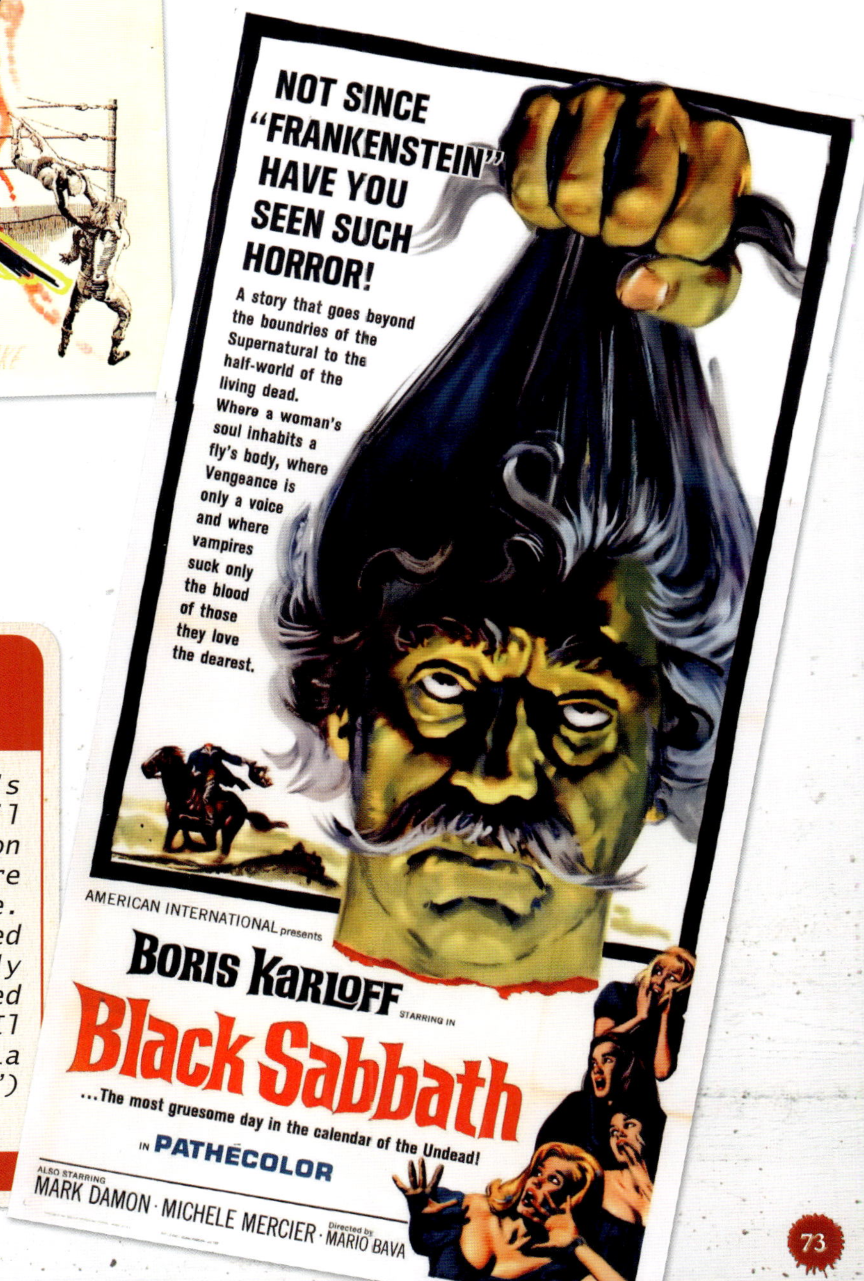

Black Sabbath. Alta Vista Film Production/ Emmepi Cinematografica/Galatea Film/ Societé Cinématographique Lyre (1963).

Although I didn't see Mario Bava's Black Sabbath *in its entirety until much later, I watched the third section "The Wurdulak" on a late-night creature feature while I was home from college. Seeing the father-turned-vampire (played by Boris Karloff) return to his family and beg to be let into the home haunted me for days. The other two stories ("Il telefono" or "The Telephone" and "La goccia d'acqua" or "The Drop of Water") are nothing by comparison.*

Carol A. Senf

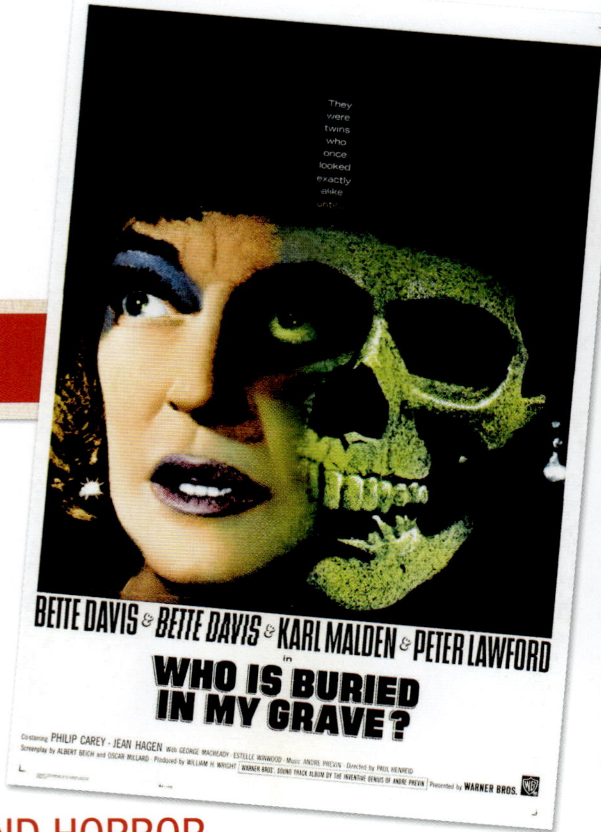

Dead Ringer.
Warner Bros. Pictures (1964).

ON **BETTE DAVIS** AND HORROR

Late in her career, when whatever little physical beauty she used to have had evaporated, Bette Davis turned against Hollywood convention and presented herself defiantly as a crone, a hag, a monster. In three films — *Whatever Happened to Baby Jane, Dead Ringer, and Hush, Hush, Sweet Charlotte* — she went against all the Garbos and Dietrichs who had taken themselves out of the public eye before age could catch up with them. After all, she was the author of that gritty bon mot that "Growing old is not for sissies." Especially under the merciless, unsentimental gaze of Robert Aldrich, Davis reinvents herself courageously in *Hush, Hush, Sweet Charlotte*, a film replaying her earlier work in Jezebel with a meat cleaver and a decapitation thrown in for good measure. All aspects of her performance style are there — the brittleness in the voice, the body language on the verge of histrionics, the introverted sulk masking latent violence — recast in the vernacular of Gothic extremity. Southern Gothic at its finest!

~Steffen Hantke

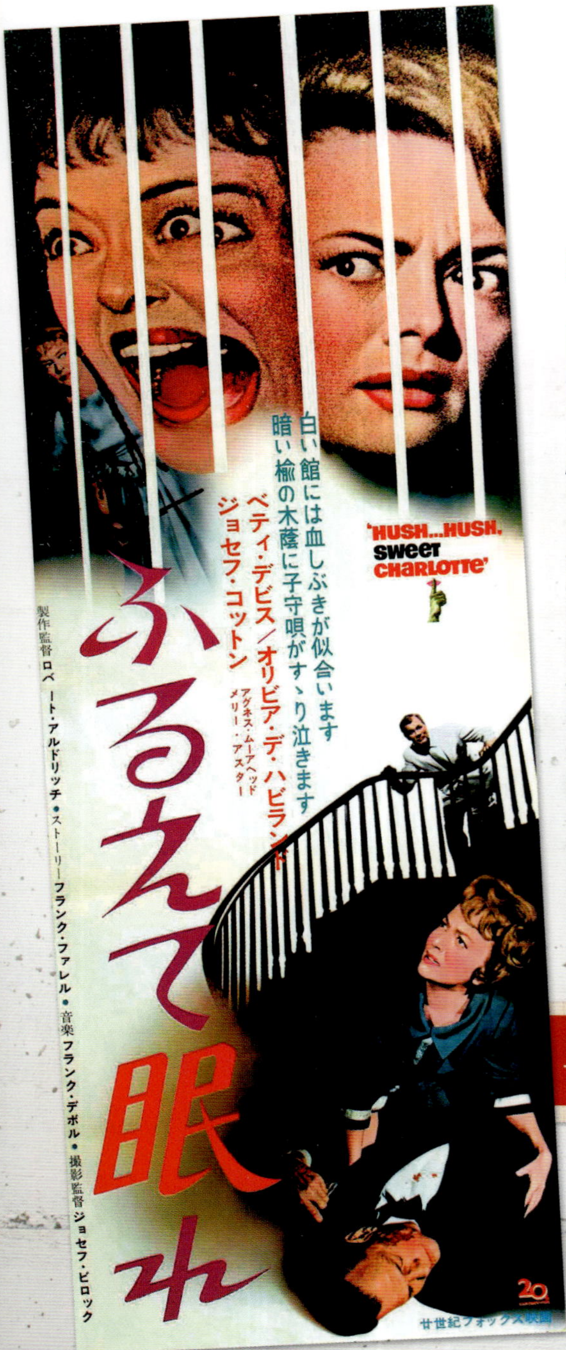

Hush...Hush, Sweet Charlotte.
The Associates & Aldrich Company (1964). Japan.

The Evil of Frankenstein. Hammer Film Productions/ Universal International Picture (1964).

The Evil of Frankenstein *(1964) is often decried as the least skillfully crafted of the Hammer versions of the Frankenstein narrative. Freddie Francis was given this directorial assignment because Terence Fisher, who had directed* Curse of Frankenstein *(1957) and* Revenge of Frankenstein *(1958) had failed at producing another commercial success with* Phantom of the Opera *(1962). The result was a film less fascinated physical sensation and the stern morality of confronting evil with good (characteristic of Terence Fisher's Frankenstein films), than one rooted in the creation of mood and atmosphere. Glimmers of Francis's talent at creating mood and atmosphere may be seen in the film's Gothic opening sequence.*

Caroline Joan (Kay) Picart

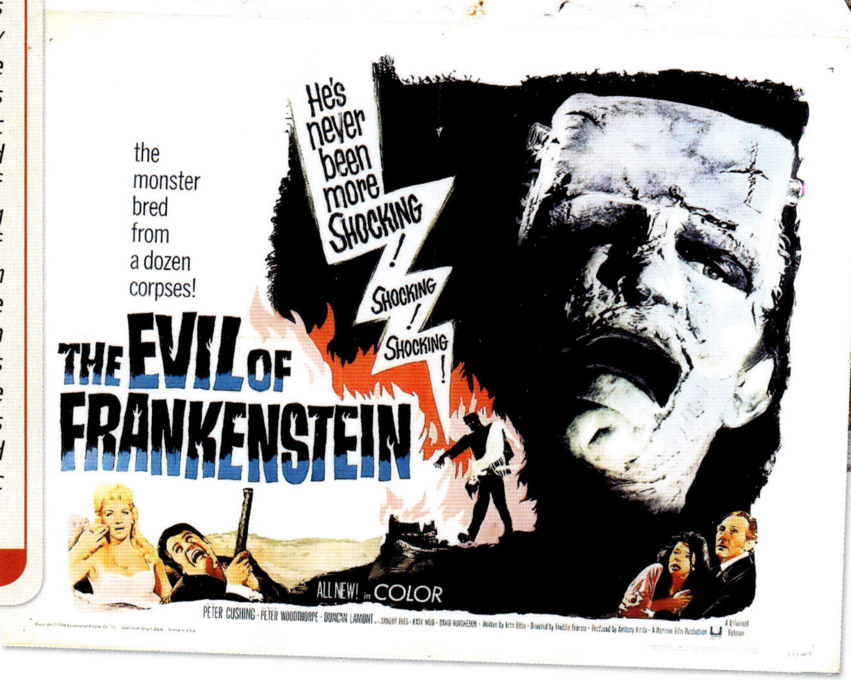

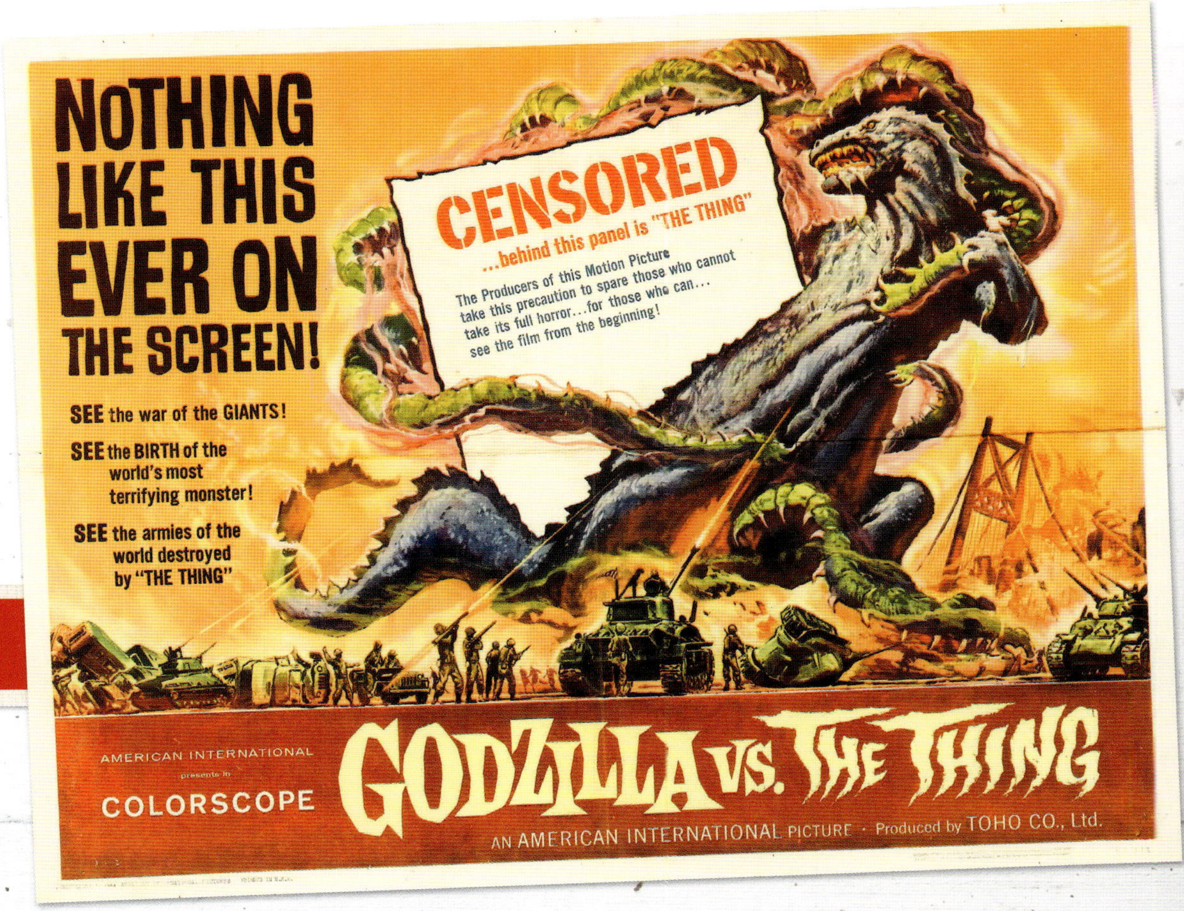

Mothra vs. Godzilla. Toho Company (1964). UK.

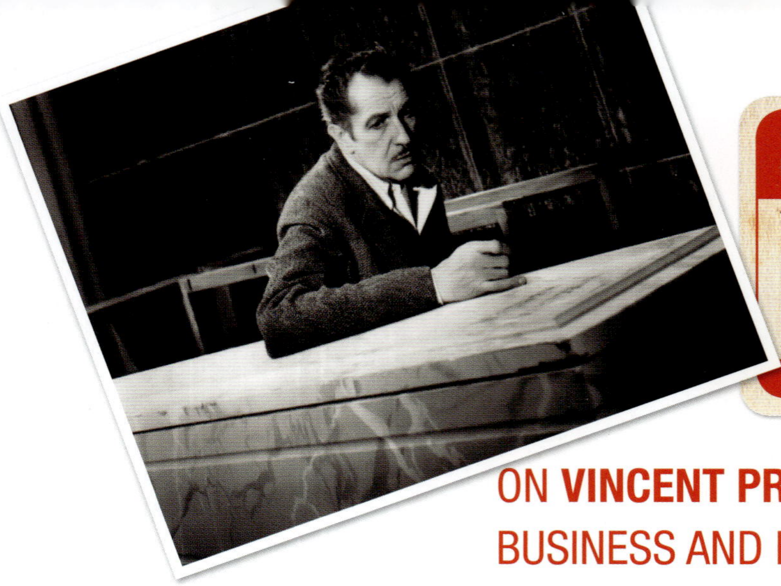

The Last Man on Earth.
Produzioni La Regina/Associated Producers (1964).

The first 15 minutes of this film ... better than Omega Man *by plenty, far better than any minutes of* I Am Legend. *(No, Will Smith, you're not.)*

Mort Castle

ON **VINCENT PRICE** AND THE BUSINESS AND HORROR OF MONOTONY

The early portions of *The Last Man on Earth* play out almost as a grotesque commentary on the modern "rat race" as audiences follow Vincent Price on the "day of the life" of the last man on Earth. After early views of a ruined, largely unpopulated metropolis, the film targets Price's character: his dilemma and his modus operandi. As the film proper starts, the camera glides through a suburban house's bedroom window as Robert sleeps fitfully... and then his alarm clock goes off. He rouses himself and walks past a wall of hand-drawn calendars and then gets down to grim business. Robert sharpens his stakes, replaces the garlic on the front door of his home, cleans up the corpses sprawled in his front yard and then realizes he needs supplies (gasoline and fresh garlic) to survive the day. Robert sits down and tallies up the stops he'll need to make that day on "the job" before the sun sets, from shopping at an eerily lifeless grocery store to going about the ghoulish business of disposing of vampire bodies in a huge, fiery pit.

These moments expose how deeply human beings cling to the idea of routine, especially in times of stress, in order to impose a sense of control, order and comfort over our chaotic lives. The result of such moments is an intimate film that captures the horror of the apocalypse more successfully than many a special effects extravaganza because audiences feel connected to the man and his daily life. "Another day to start over" for Robert Neville*, is actually another day of Hell on Earth.*

~John Kenneth Muir

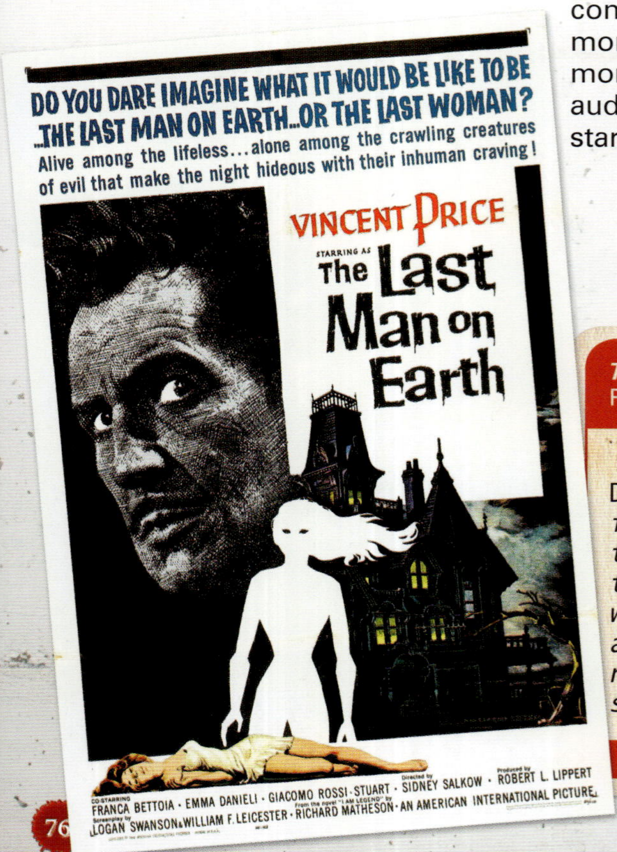

The Last Man on Earth.
Produzioni La Regina/Associated Producers (1964).

I suppose I was lucky enough to read Dracula *when I was still young enough to fear the undead, but it's been a long time since vampires have "worked" for me; the last author who did anything unusual with the theme was Richard Matheson in a few short stories and, of course, his novel,* I Am Legend, *which is, however, science fiction.*

Marvin Kaye

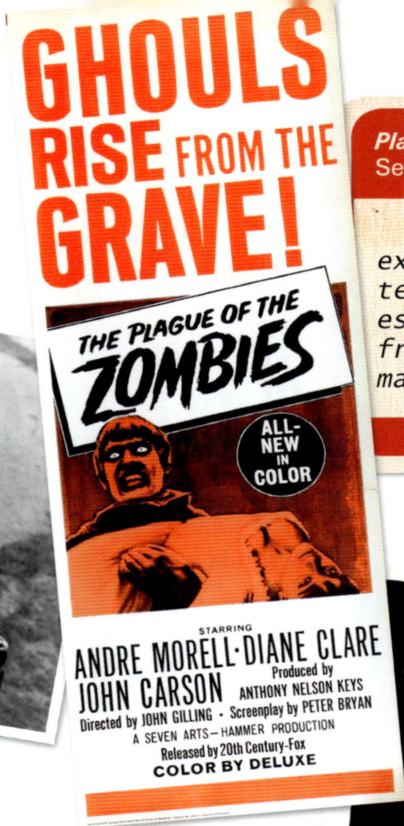

Plague of the Zombies. Hammer Film Productions/ Seven Arts Productions (1964).

In many respects an unexceptional example of its era of cinema, but the terrifying spectacle of the zombies, especially in the scene when they rise from the earth, is a creation of complete mastery.

Richard J. Hand

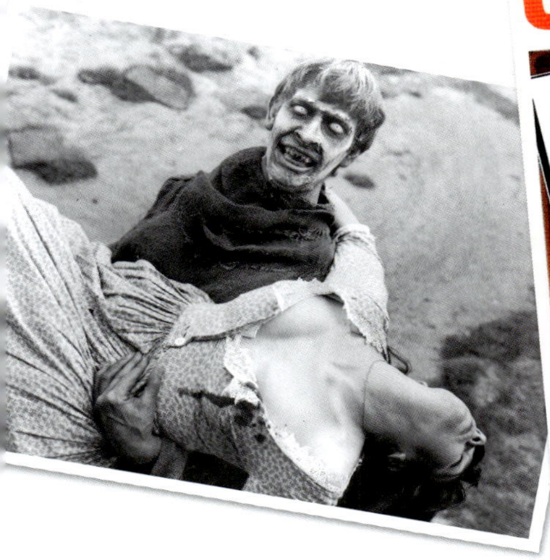

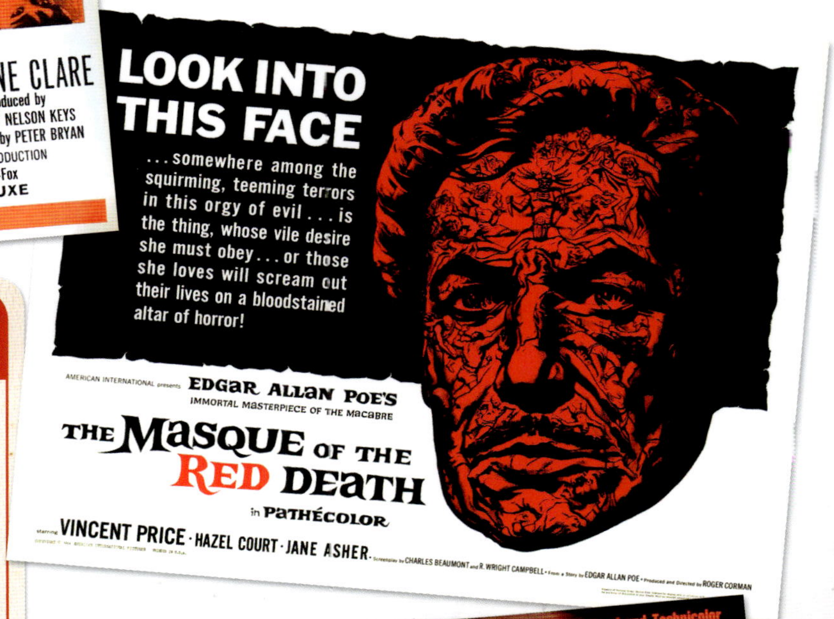

Masque of the Red Death. Alta Vista Productions (1964).

This is the first horror film that made me jump. I must have been 10 or 11, watching the film on British television. Jane Asher ventures into a creepy dungeon and a prisoner suddenly leaps out at her; you know the routine. I probably screamed; I certainly travelled up the back of the chair in which I was sitting. It is the sort of experience that might put people off horror. For me, it was the moment when I realized that I had found my genre. I have been following horror ever since (and that's now coming up to 4 decades). Thank you, Roger Corman.

Peter Hutchings

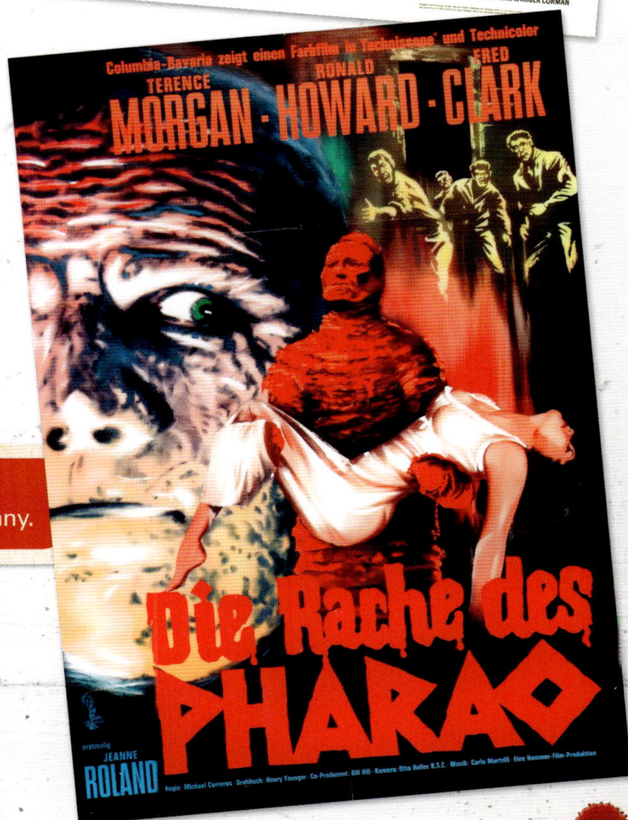

The Curse of the Mummy's Tomb. Hammer Film Productions/Swallow Productions Ltd. (1964). Germany.

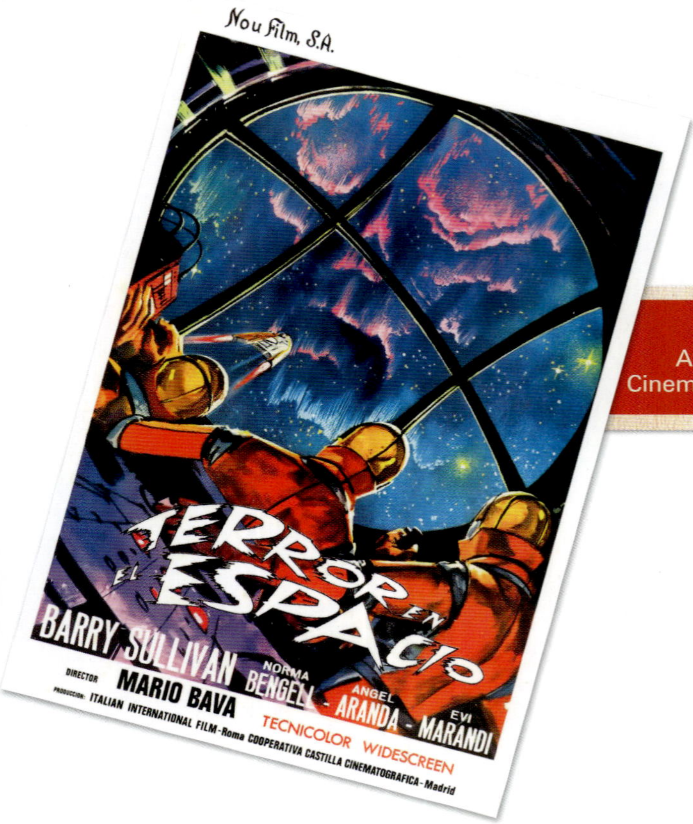

Planet of the Vampires. America-International Pictures/Castilla Cooperativa Cinematográfica/Italian International Film (1965). Spain.

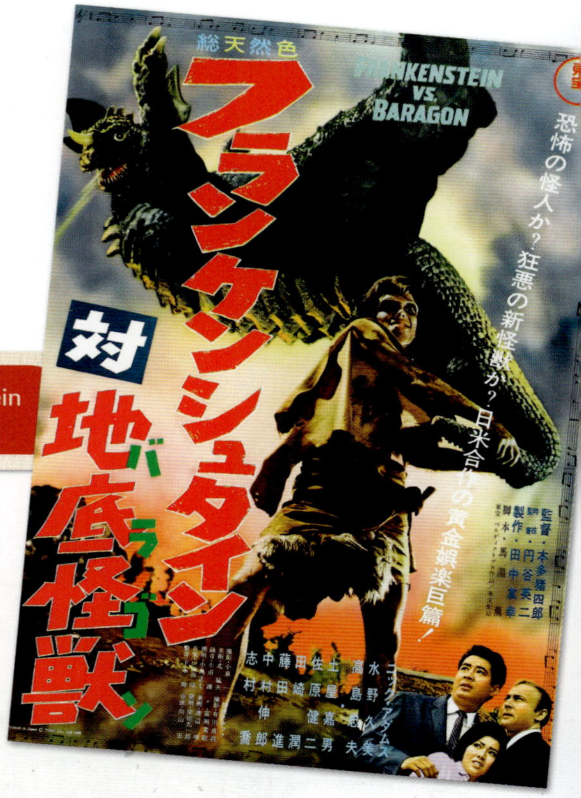

Frankenstein Conquers the World. Henry G. Saperstein Enterprises Inc., Toho Company (1965). Japan.

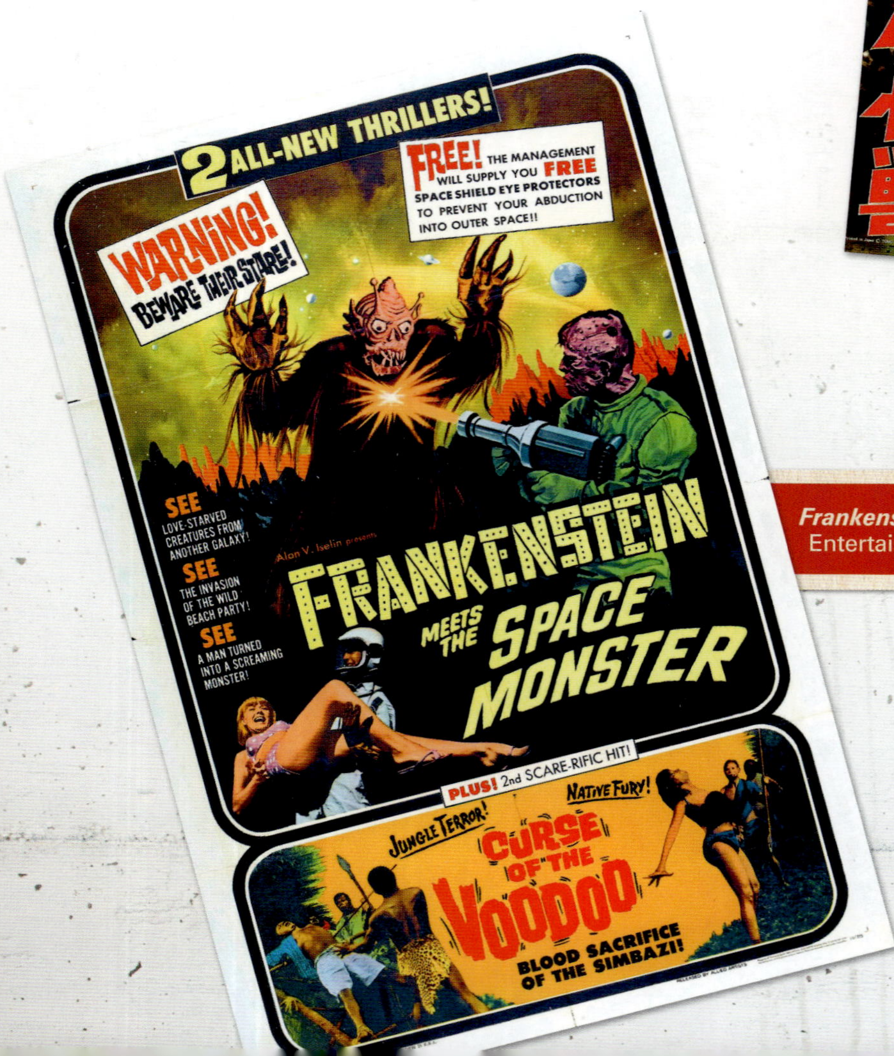

Frankenstein Meets the Space Monster. Futurama Entertainment Corp., Vernon-Seneca Films (1965).

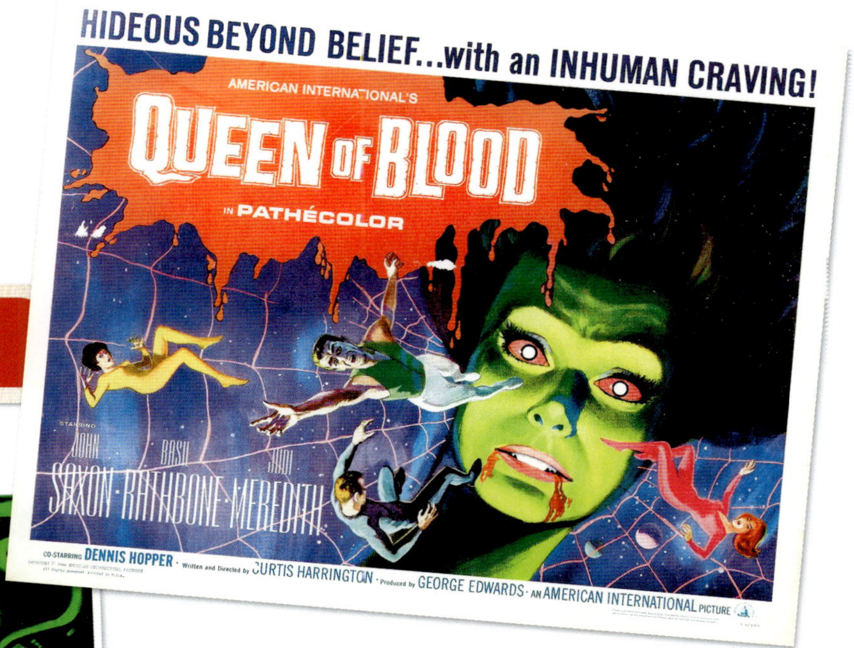

Queen of Blood.
Cinema West Productions (1966).

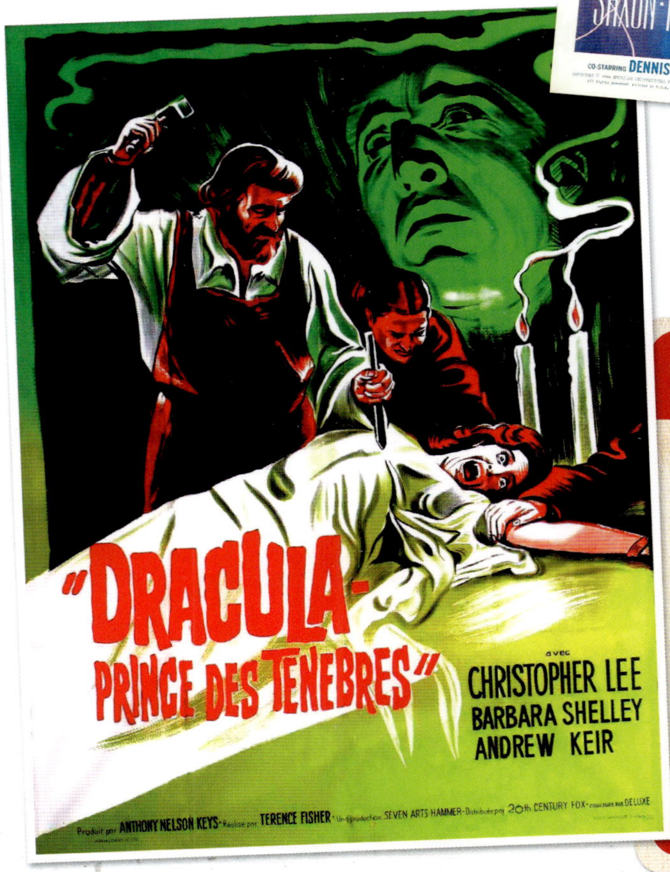

Dracula: Prince of Darkness. Seven Arts Productions, Hammer Film Productions (1966). France.

I cannot remember when or where I first saw Dracula: Prince of Darkness. *It was probably on television back in the 1970s, but the film possesses an aura of familiarity that makes pinning down that first encounter difficult. For me, it is the quintessential Hammer horror, the one in which the Hammer formula of the 1950s and 1960s is reduced down to its essence. It is spare, elegant, and stern, and it feels as if it has always been inside my head.*

Peter Hutchings

Dark Shadows.
Dan Curtis Productions (1966-1971).

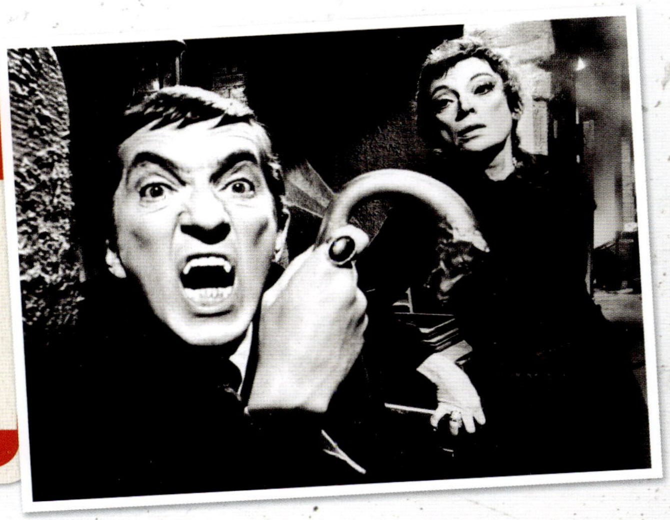

Barnabas opened the door to the complex vampire who felt trapped by his monstrosity, who wanted to be loved, and who tried to contain – even cure – his bloodlust. His visibility to millions of TV fans humanized the vampire genre in both subtle and dramatic ways.

Katherine Ramsland

Frankenstein Created Woman.
Hammer Film Productions (1967). Japan.

Hammer's Frankenstein Created Woman *(1967) is based on Anthony Hinds' script, written in 1958, "And Frankenstein Created Woman," in parodic mimicry of the then popular* And God Created Woman, *starring Brigitte Bardot. But Hammer's reiteration of the script was far from parodic, and the young woman who played the female creature, Susan Denberg, was a twenty-two-year-old Austrian* Playboy *"playmate," whose constant appearances in mini-skirts were much-heralded by the press.*

Caroline Joan (Kay) Picart

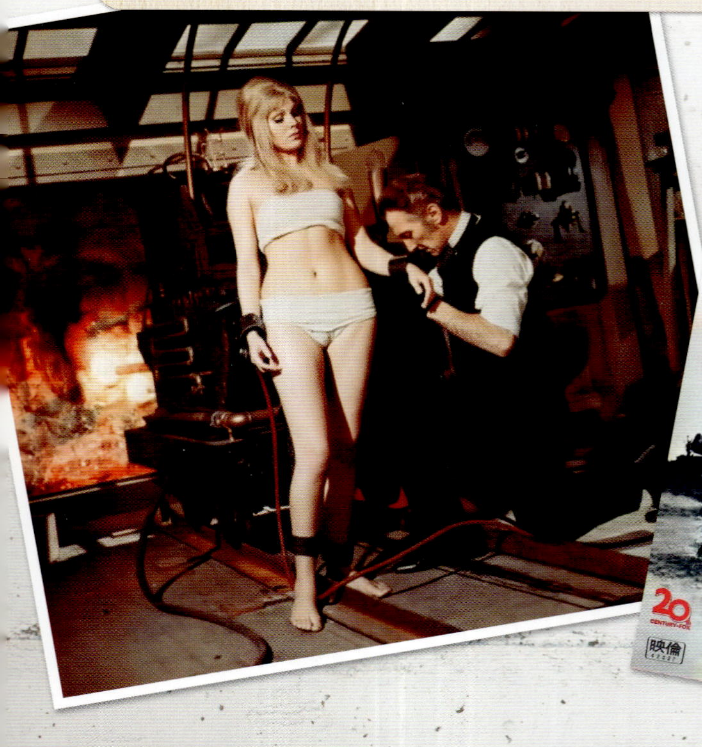

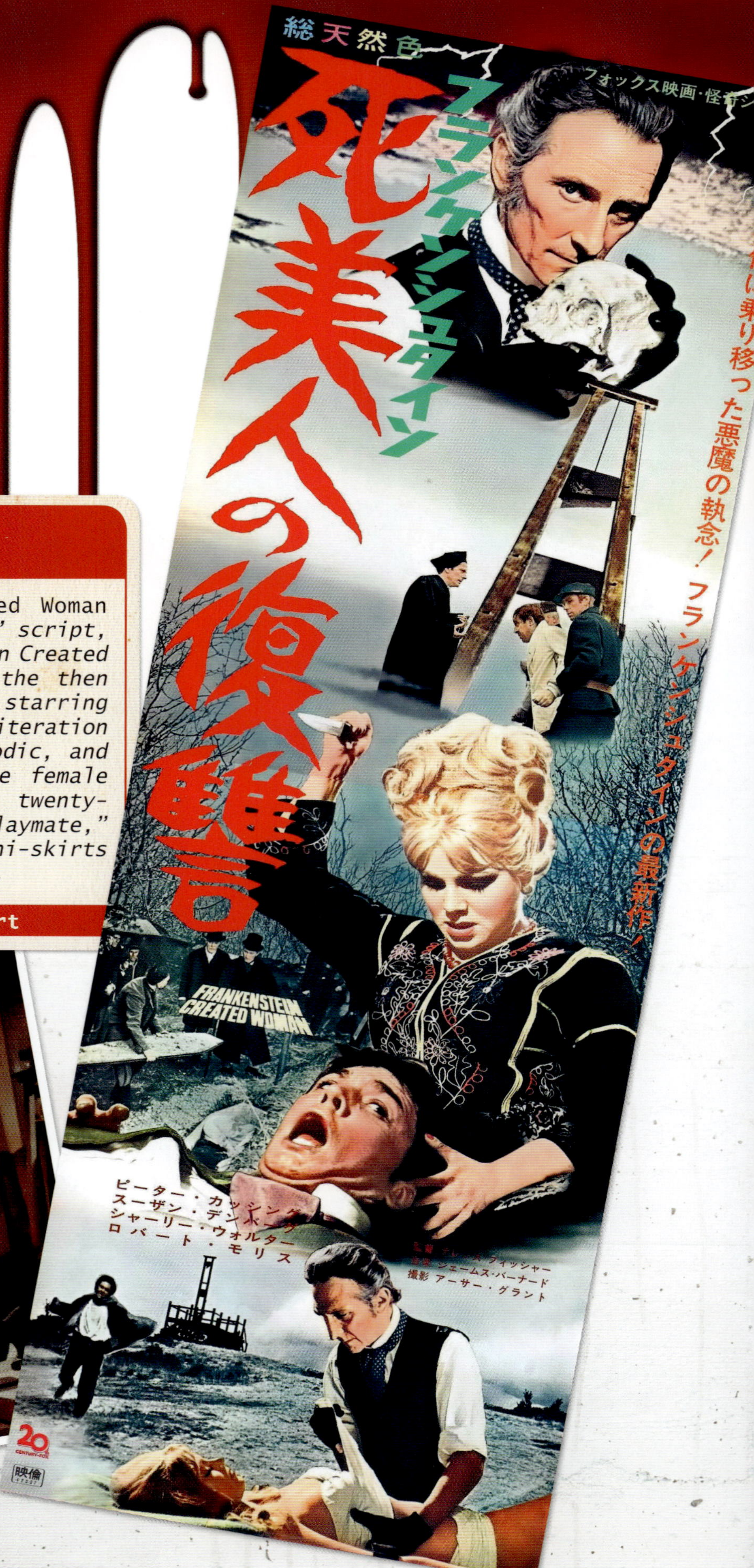

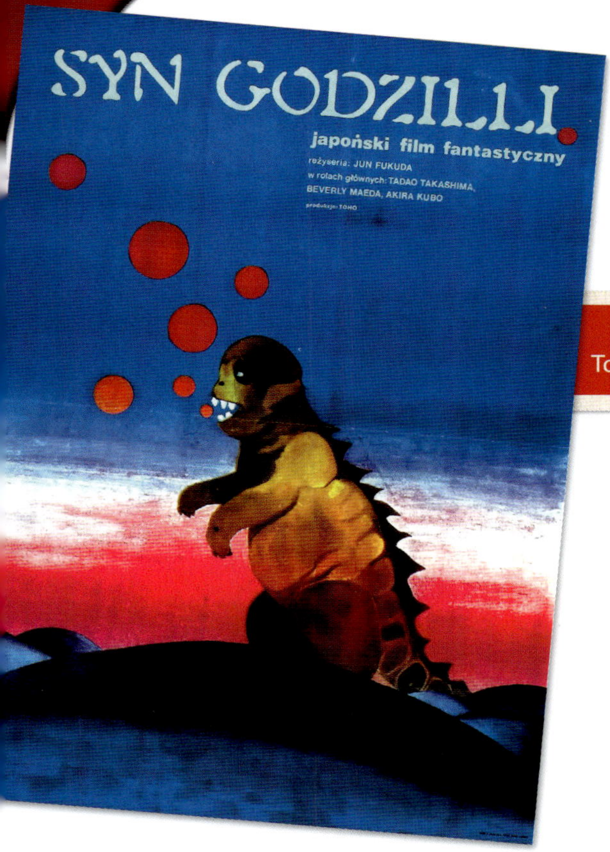

Son of Godzilla.
Toho Company (1967). Poland.

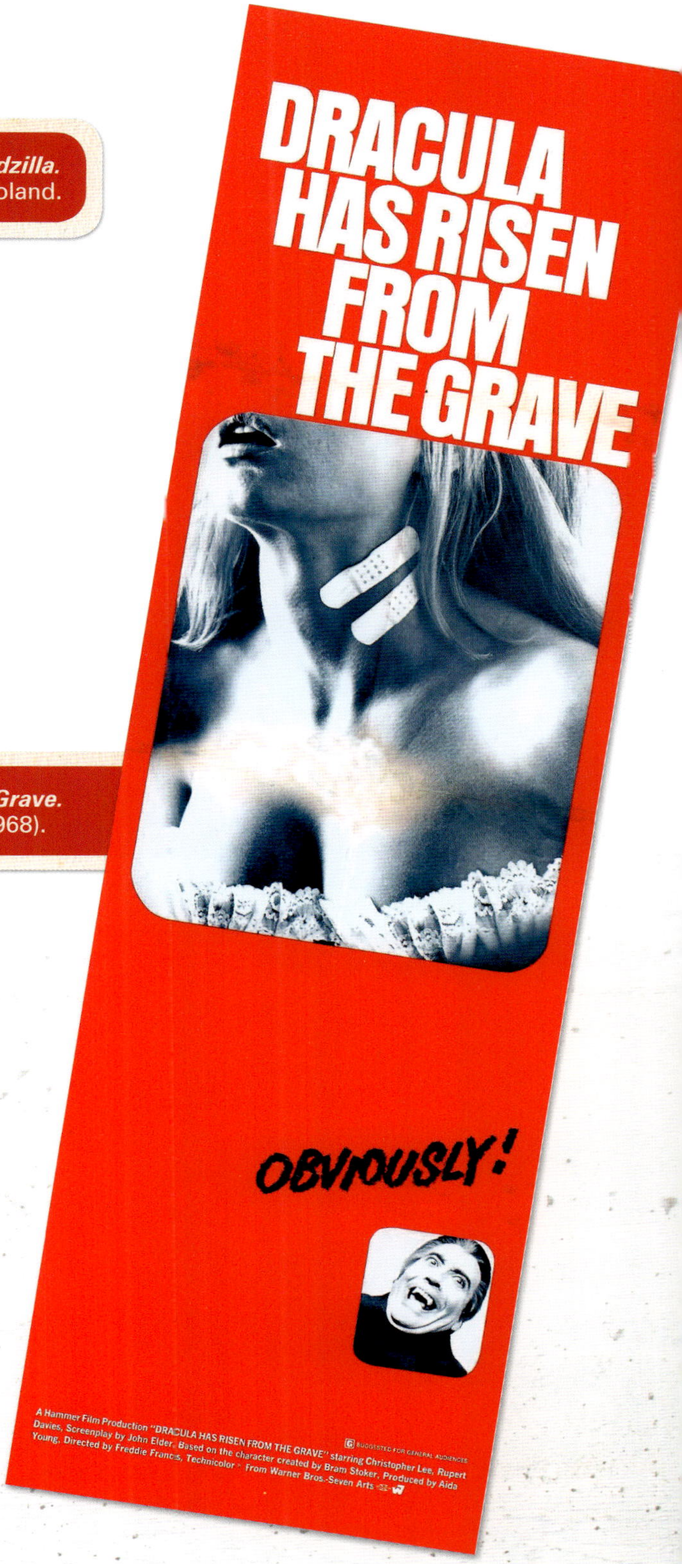

Dracula Has Risen from the Grave.
Hammer Film Productions (1968).

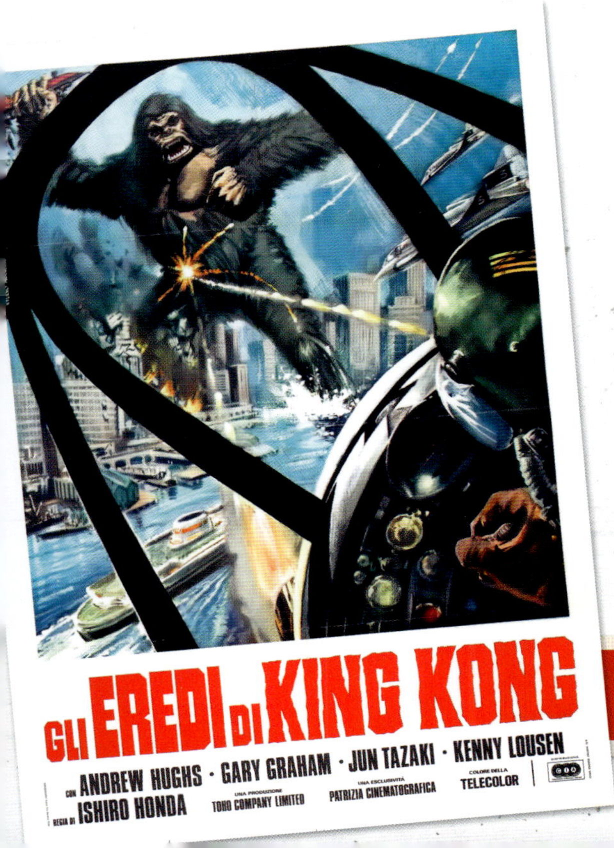

Destroy All Monsters.
Toho Company (1968). Italy.

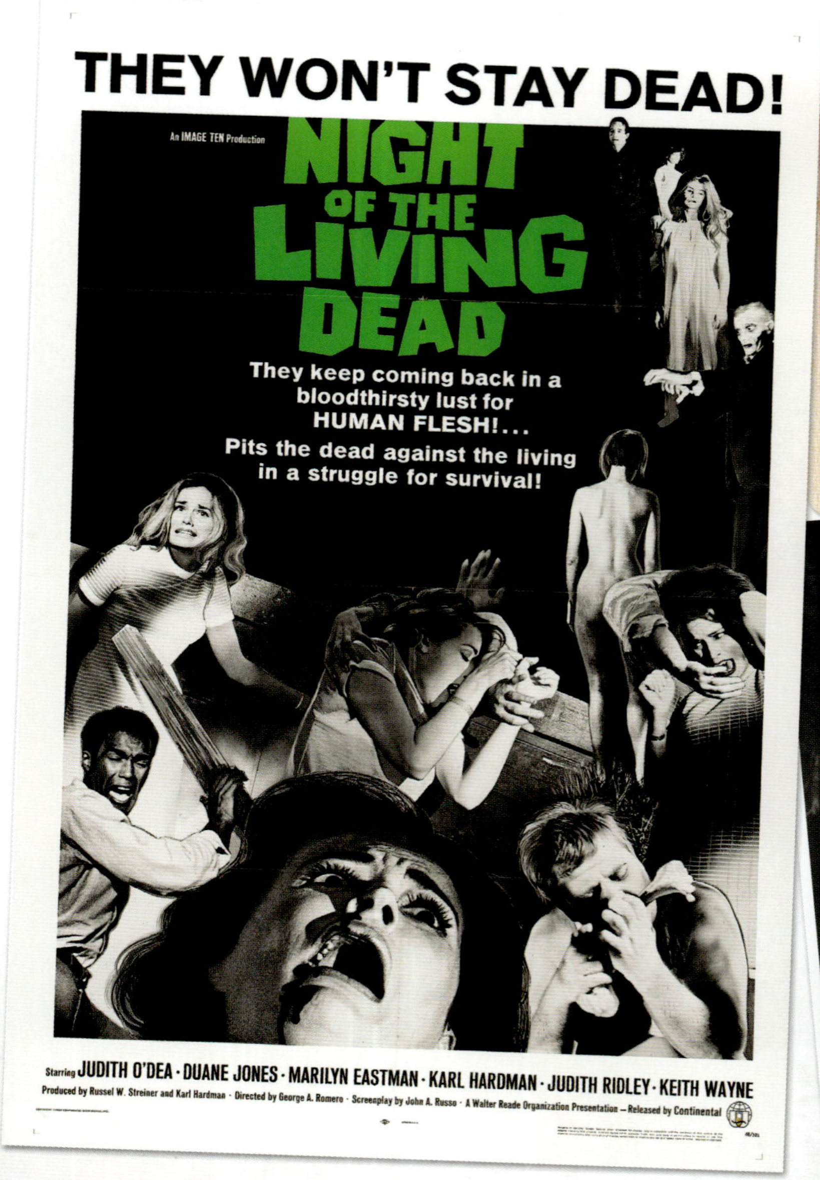

Night of the Living Dead. Image Ten/Laurel Group/Market Square Productions/Off Color Films (1968).

Were there zombie movies before this? It's hard to imagine now, as it seems like the avatar of all such films. It starts out scary and shocking and then it turns bleak, dismal and terrifying. Certainly there are other films of its kind where everyone dies in the end, but that last bullet is supremely devastating.

Bev Vincent

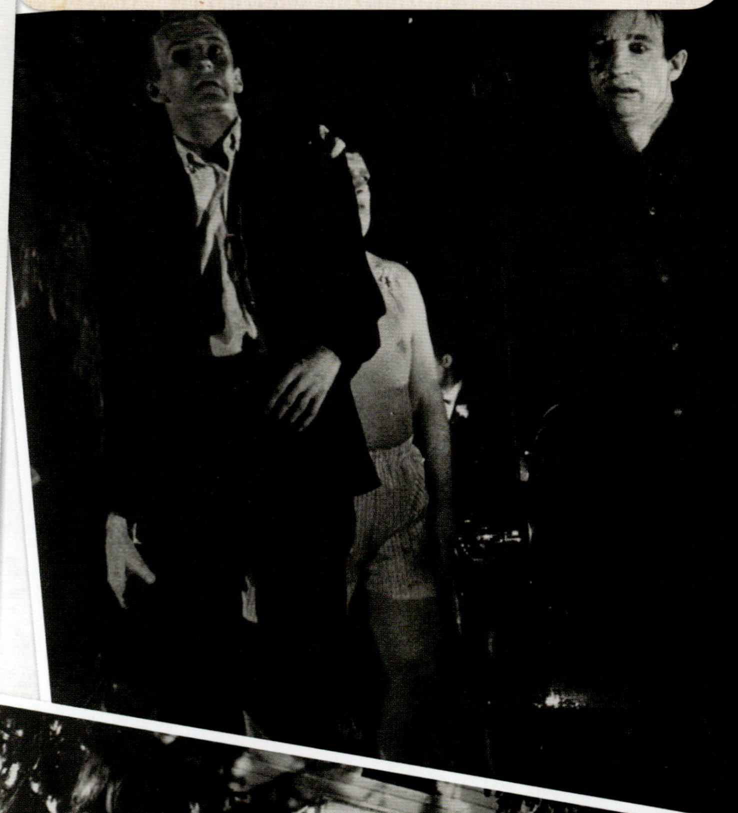

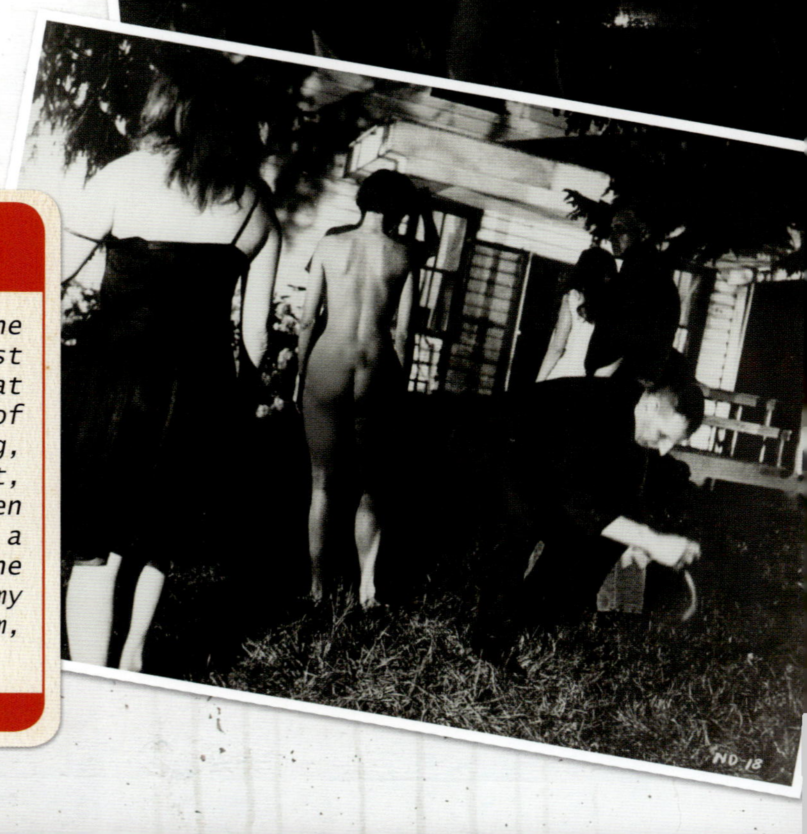

Night of the Living Dead. Image Ten/Laurel Group/Market Square Productions/Off Color Films (1968).

Night of the Living Dead *(1968) is the horror film that produces in me the most visceral reaction. The film demands that the audience bring its body into the act of viewing. I find myself, in turn, gasping, groaning, laughing, and screaming. But, at its most powerful moments, like when the little girl stabs her mother with a trowel, I find myself staring mutely, the horror moving out of my mouth and into my flesh as my skin tingles, my feet squirm, and my stomach buckles.*

Jesse Stommel

Night of the Living Dead. Image Ten/Laurel Group/ Market Square Productions/Off Color Films (1968).

I first saw this late one night on a 5-inch black and white television, and I've been fascinated by zombies ever since. Few movies convey claustrophobia and hopelessness with such numbing, overwhelming power.

Kim Paffenroth

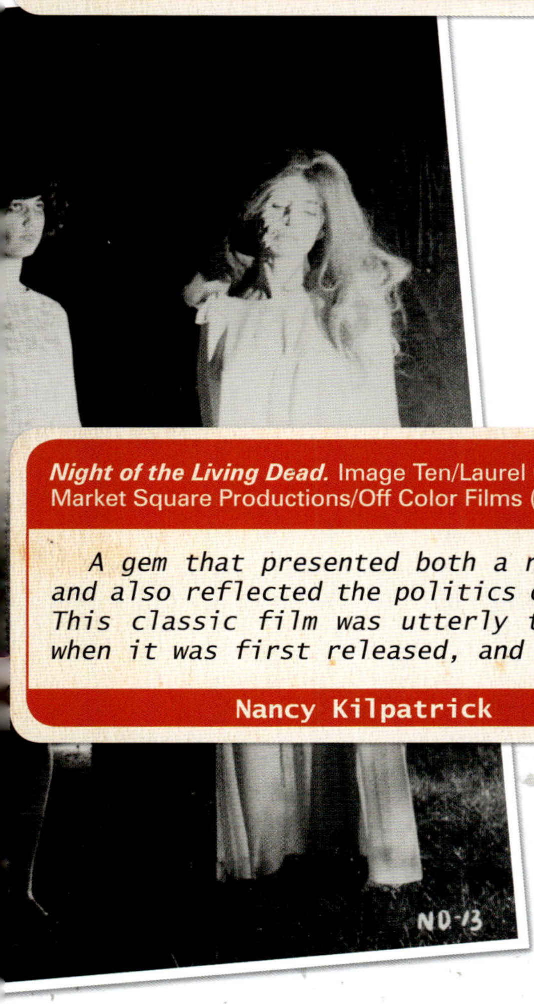

Night of the Living Dead. Image Ten/Laurel Group/ Market Square Productions/Off Color Films (1968).

A gem that presented both a new zombie and also reflected the politics of an era. This classic film was utterly terrifying when it was first released, and still is!

Nancy Kilpatrick

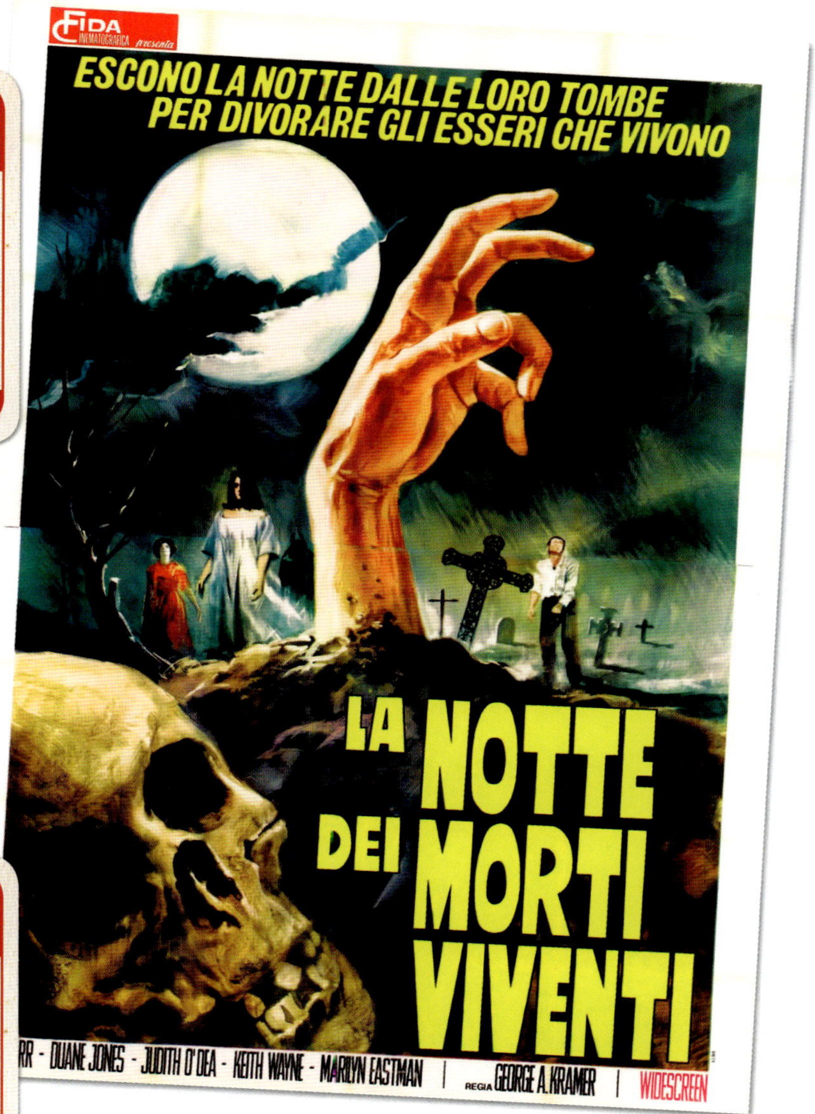

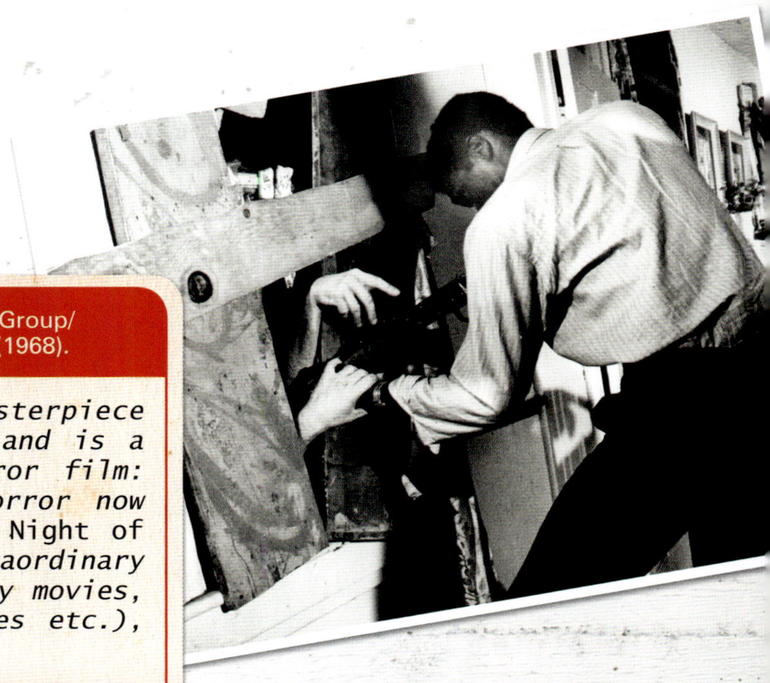

Night of the Living Dead. Image Ten/Laurel Group/ Market Square Productions/Off Color Films (1968).

Romero's site-specific masterpiece that has grown in greatness and is a watershed point for the horror film: everything in post-modern horror now seems either before or after Night of the Living Dead *(1968). Extraordinary levels of influence on so many movies, games (video, RPG, board games etc.), radio, comics...*

Richard J. Hand

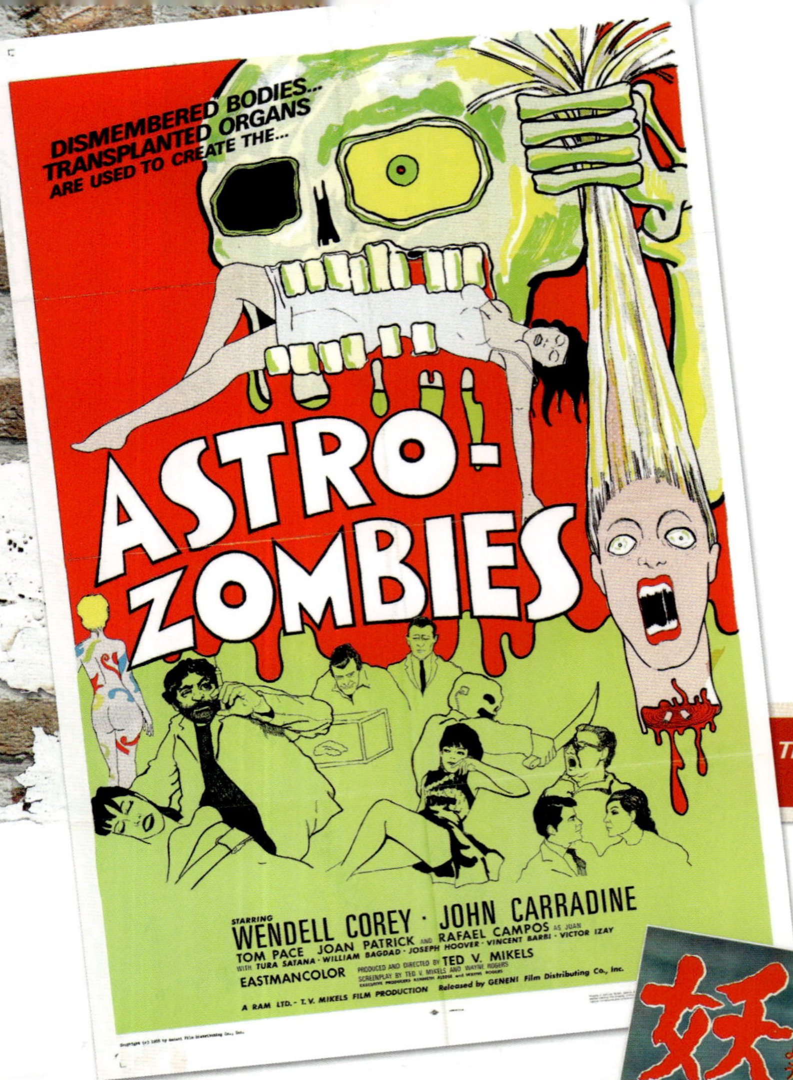

The Astro-Zombies.
Ram Ltd. (1968).

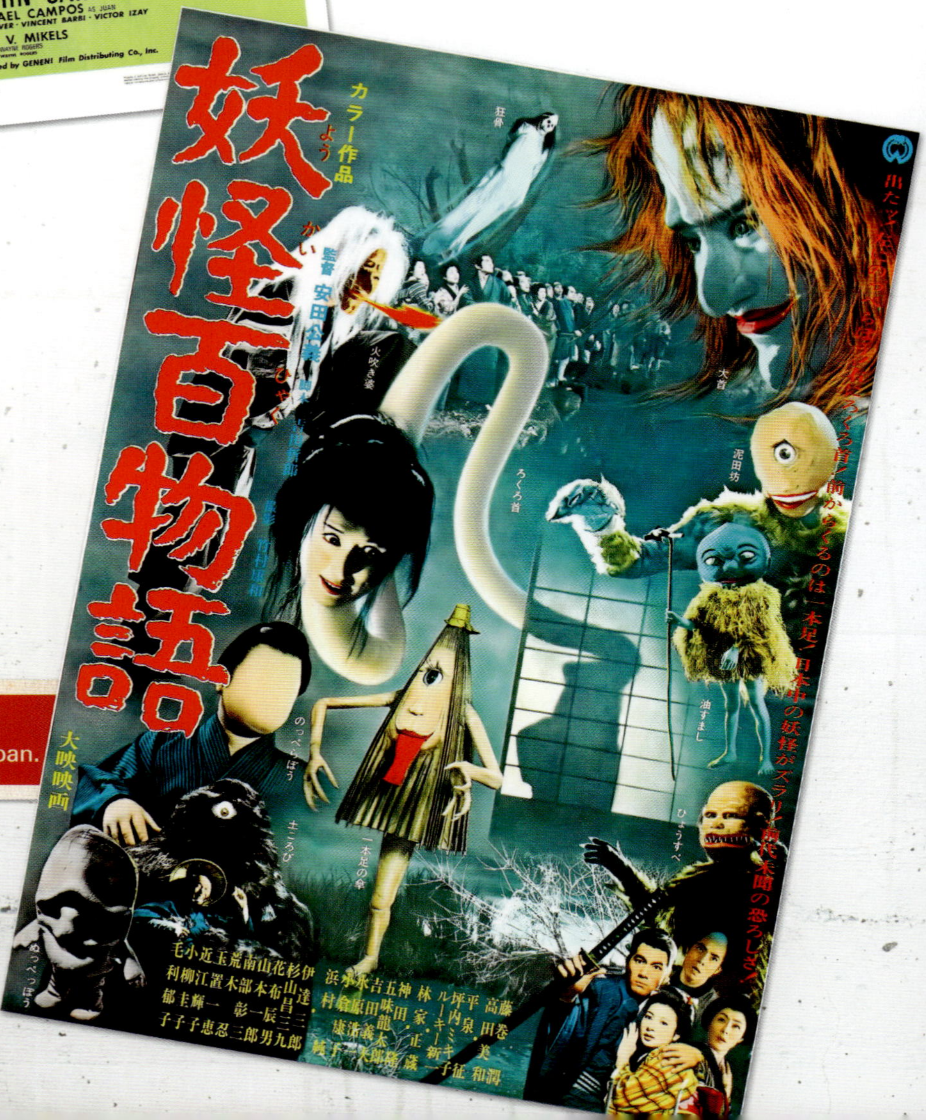

100 Monsters.
Daiei Motion Picture Company (1968). Japan.

The Devil Rides Out. Associated British-Pathé, Hammer Film Productions, Seven Arts Productions (1968).

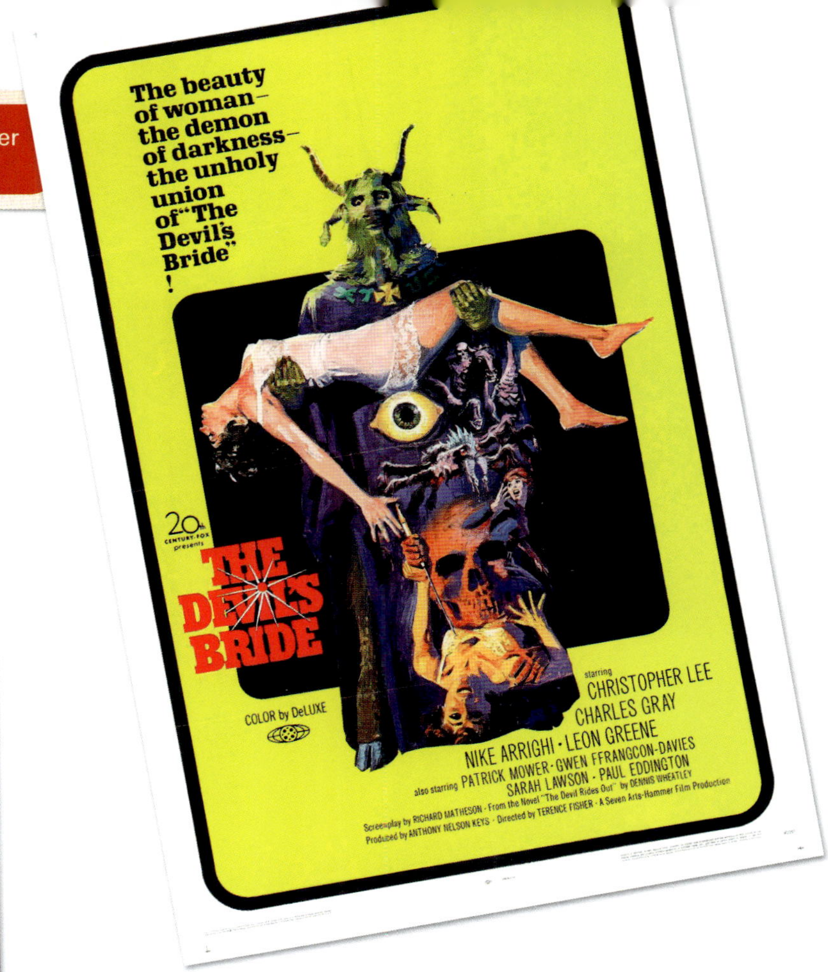

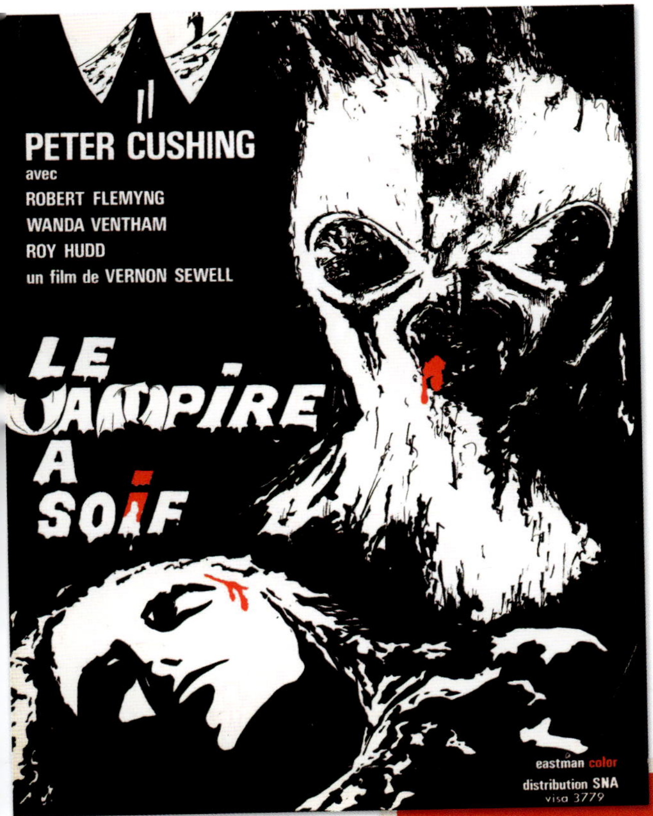

The Vampire-Beast Craves Blood. Tigon British Film Productions (1968). France.

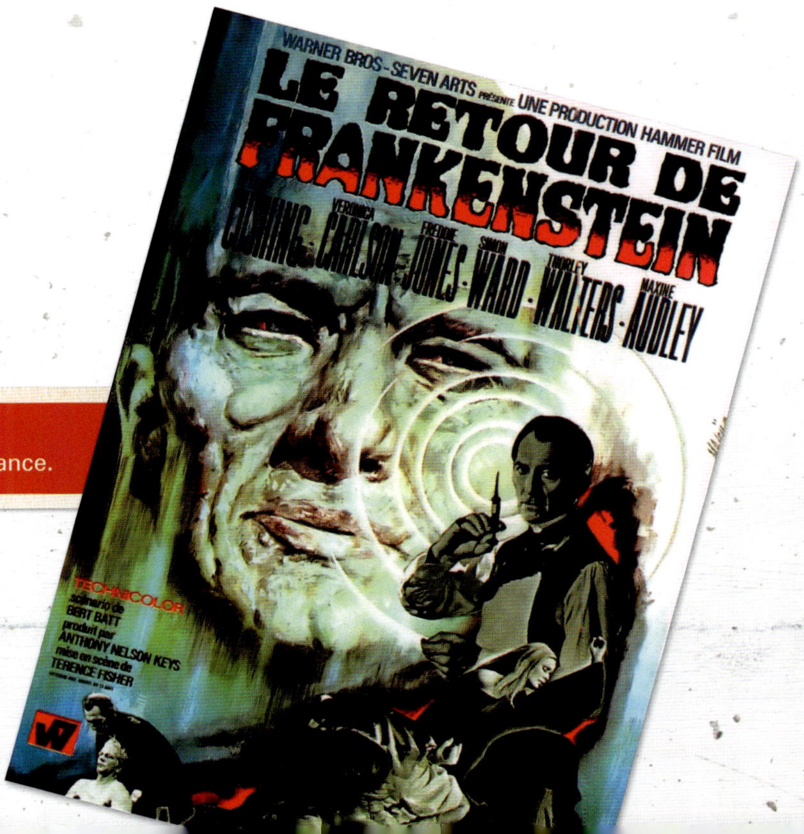

Frankenstein Must Be Destroyed. Hammer Film Productions (1969). France.

6 THE 1970s

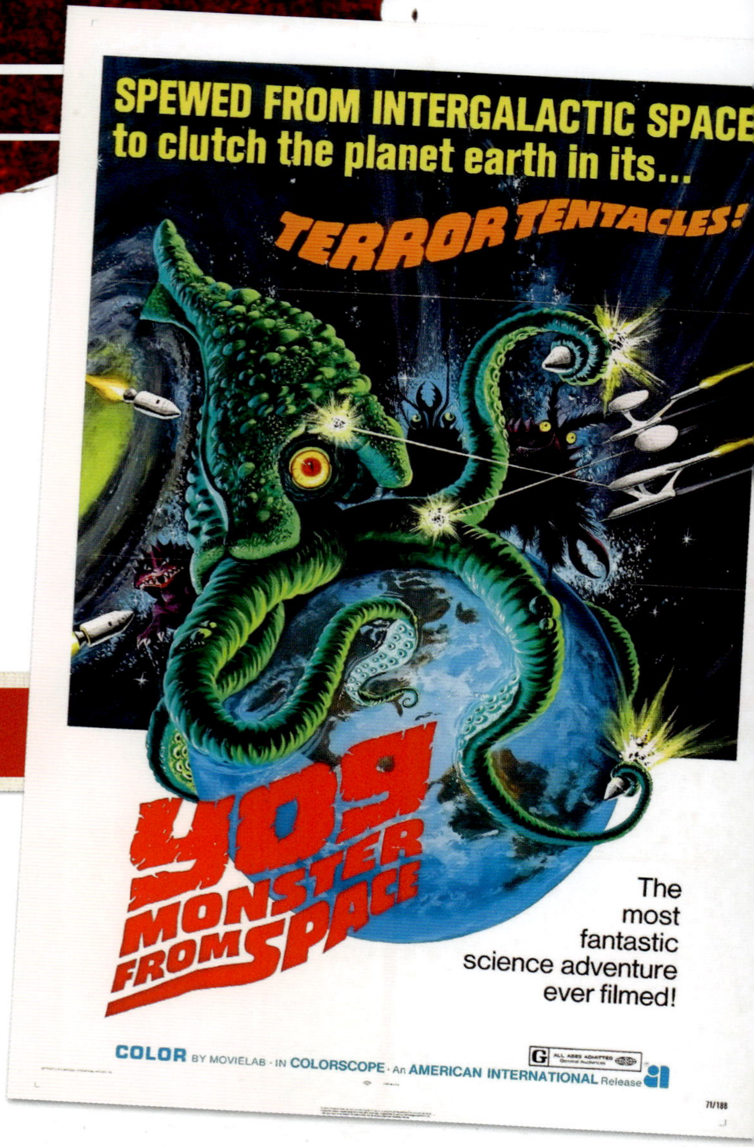

Yog, Monster from Space. Toho Company (1970).

ON THE "BODY HORROR" GENRE AND THE 1970s

The early films of David Cronenberg, and *The Texas Chainsaw Massacre* (1974) all played important roles in developing the body horror genre, but for me the genre hit its peak during a very short period between October of 1978 and May of 1979, which saw the release of *Halloween, Dawn of the Dead*, *Alien* and *The Brood*. After seeing these four films, my body will never be whole, right-side-out, or singularly inhabited again.

~Jesse Stommel

The Dunwich Horror.
American International Pictures (1970).

I saw The Dunwich Horror *in 1970 at the base camp of my unit in Di An, South Vietnam. I had just been pulled in from the field. I found the opening title sequence as effective (of course in a very different fashion) as that of* Touch of Evil. *The film itself, however, didn't strike me as particularly horrible. That was probably inevitable, given where I had spent the previous five months.*

David Drake

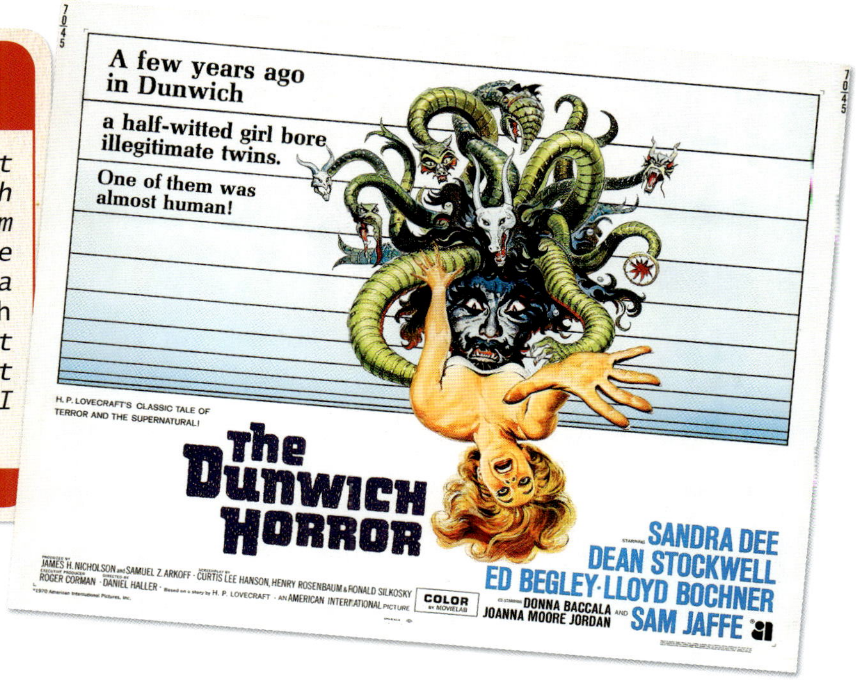

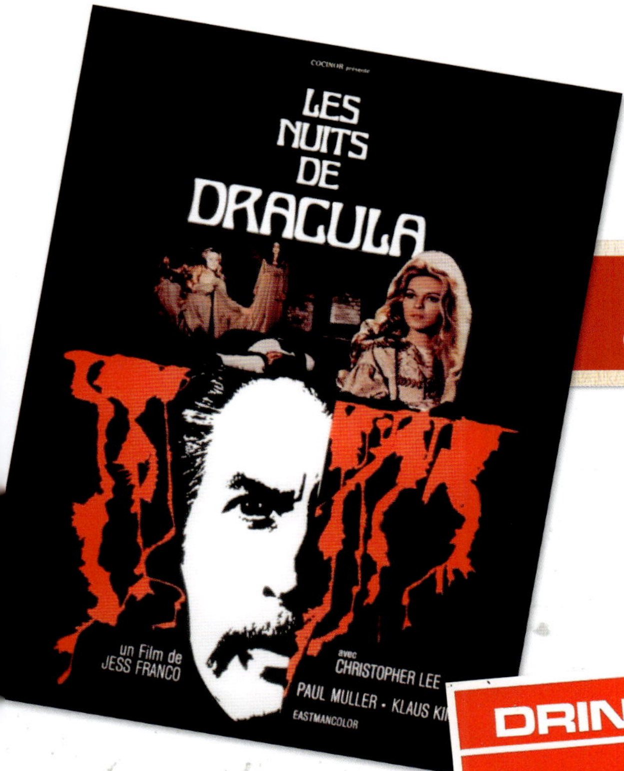

Count Dracula. Corona Filmproduktion/Filmar Compagnia Cinematografica/Fénix Cooperativa Cinematográfica/Towers of London (1970). France.

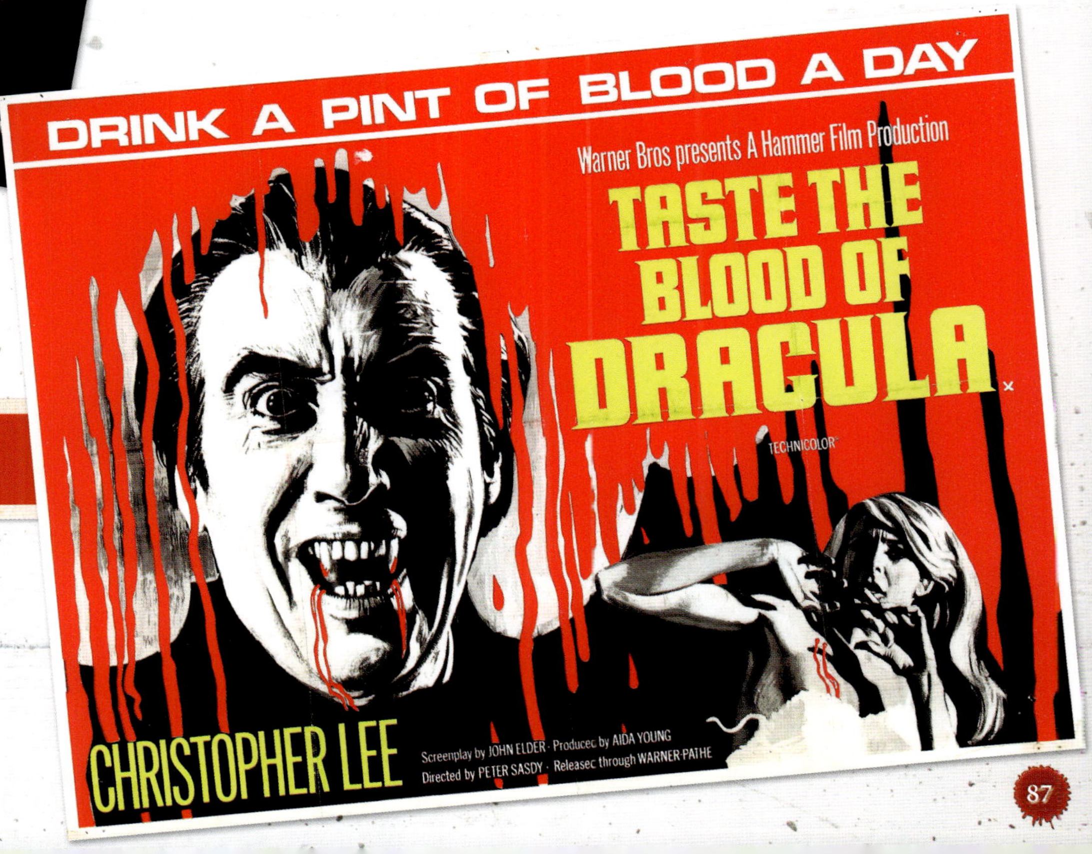

Taste the Blood of Dracula.
Hammer Film Productions (1970).

Count Yorga, Vampire.
Erica Productions Inc. (1970).

Underrated US horror: highly derivative and cliché yet has a vigor, passion and panache that marks it out as an unsettling and special example of '70s horror. Childhood memories of this one – loved every minute and immediately wrote my own homage in the cold light of day (I was 10!)

Richard J. Hand

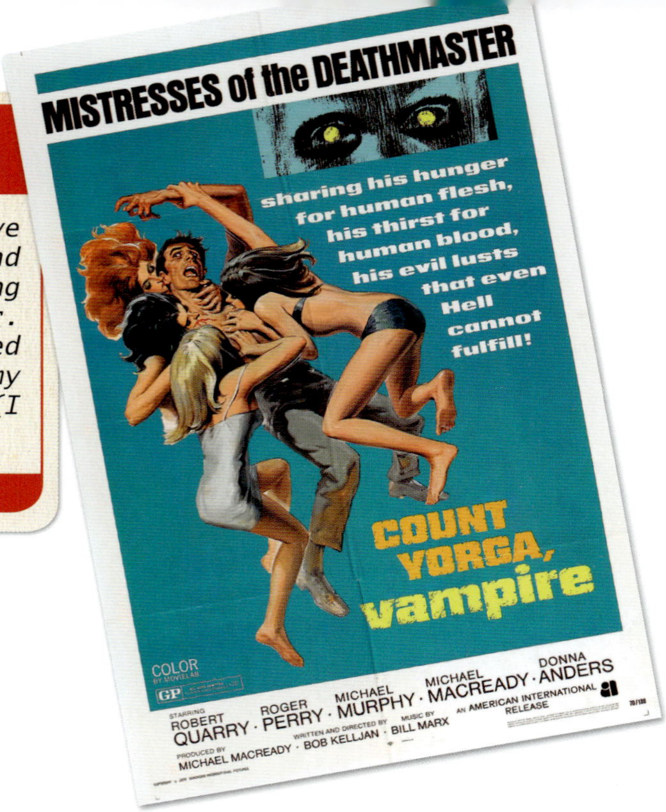

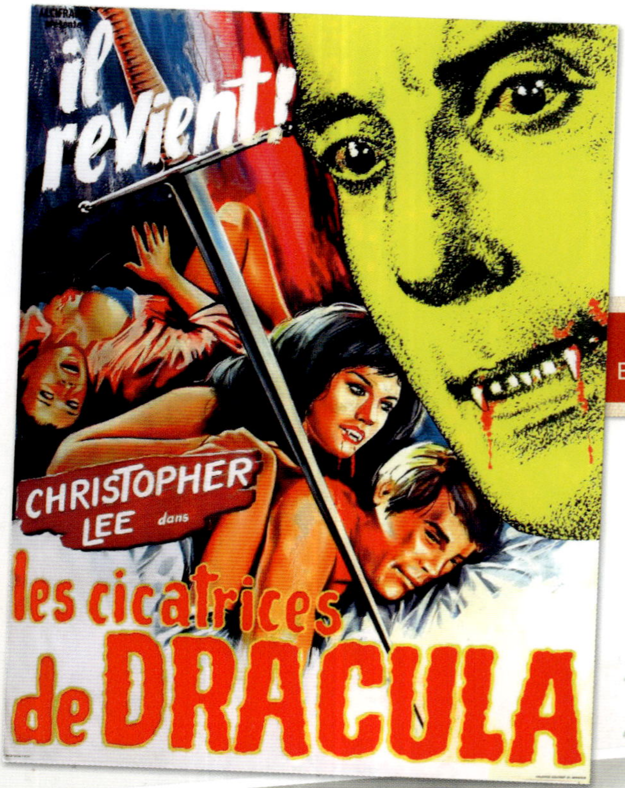

The Scars of Dracula.
EMI Films/Hammer Film Productions (1970). France.

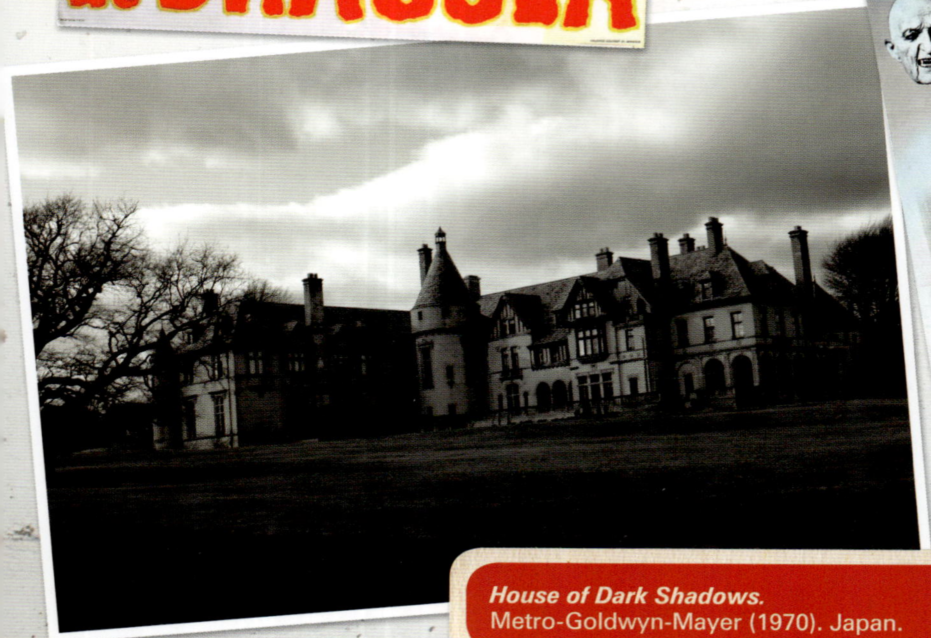

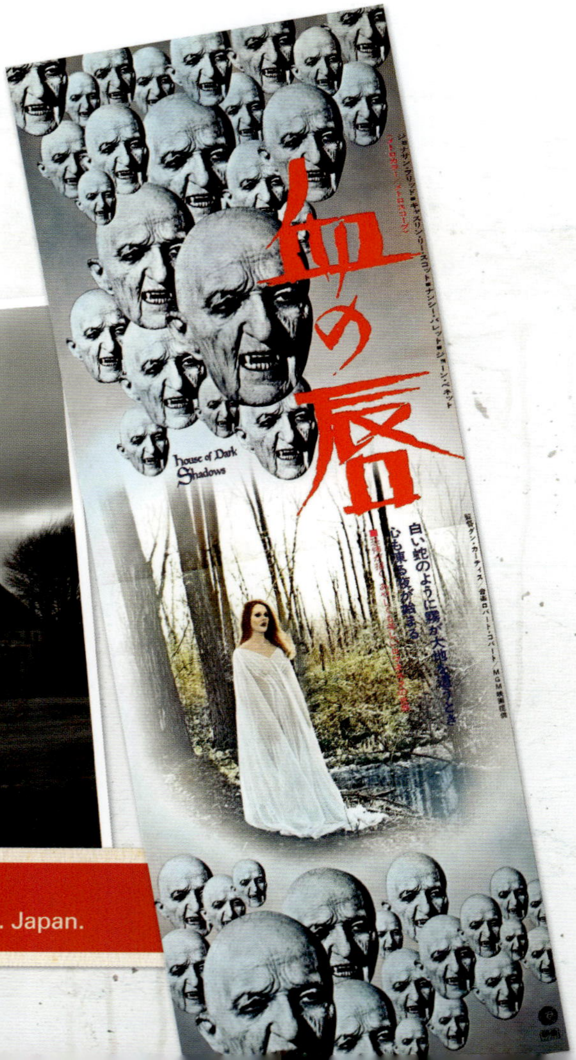

House of Dark Shadows.
Metro-Goldwyn-Mayer (1970). Japan.

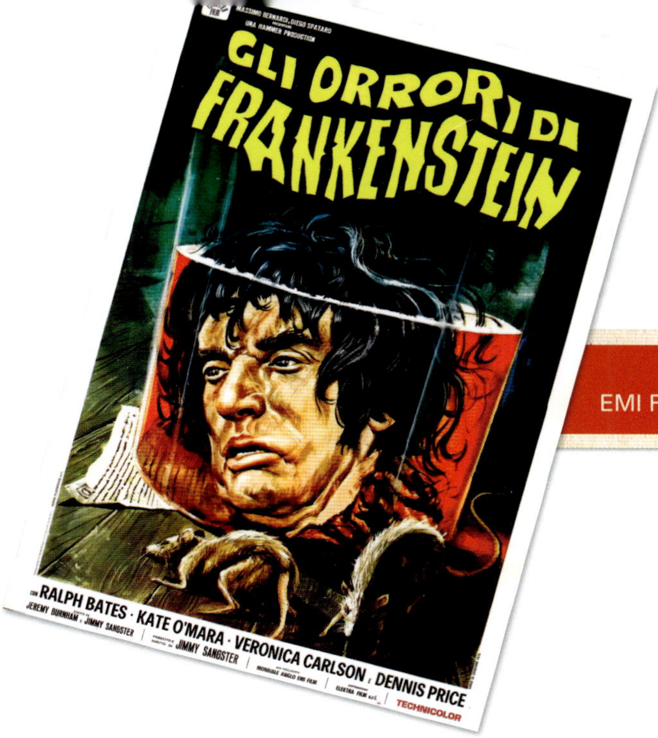

The Horror of Frankenstein.
EMI Films/Hammer Film Productions (1970). Italy.

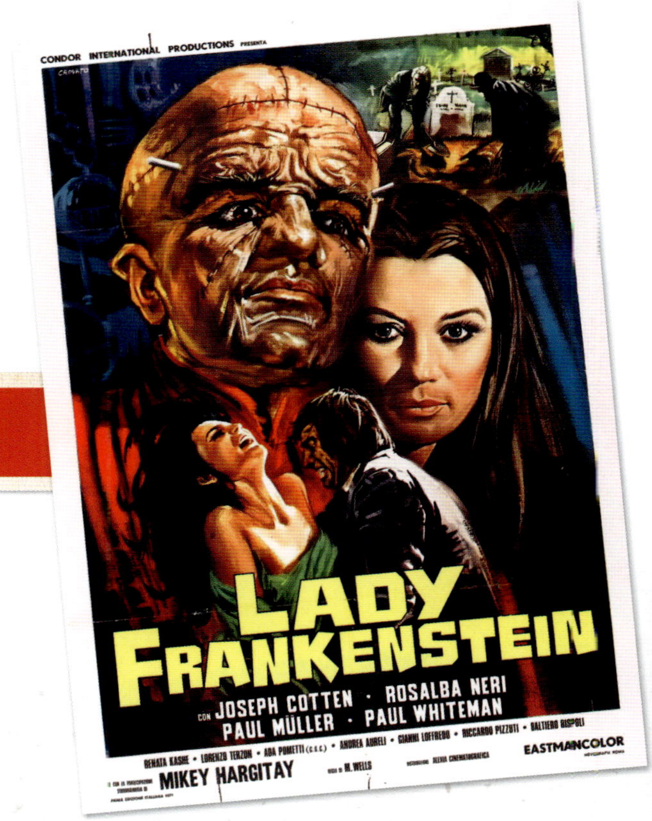

Lady Frankenstein.
Condor International Productions (1971).

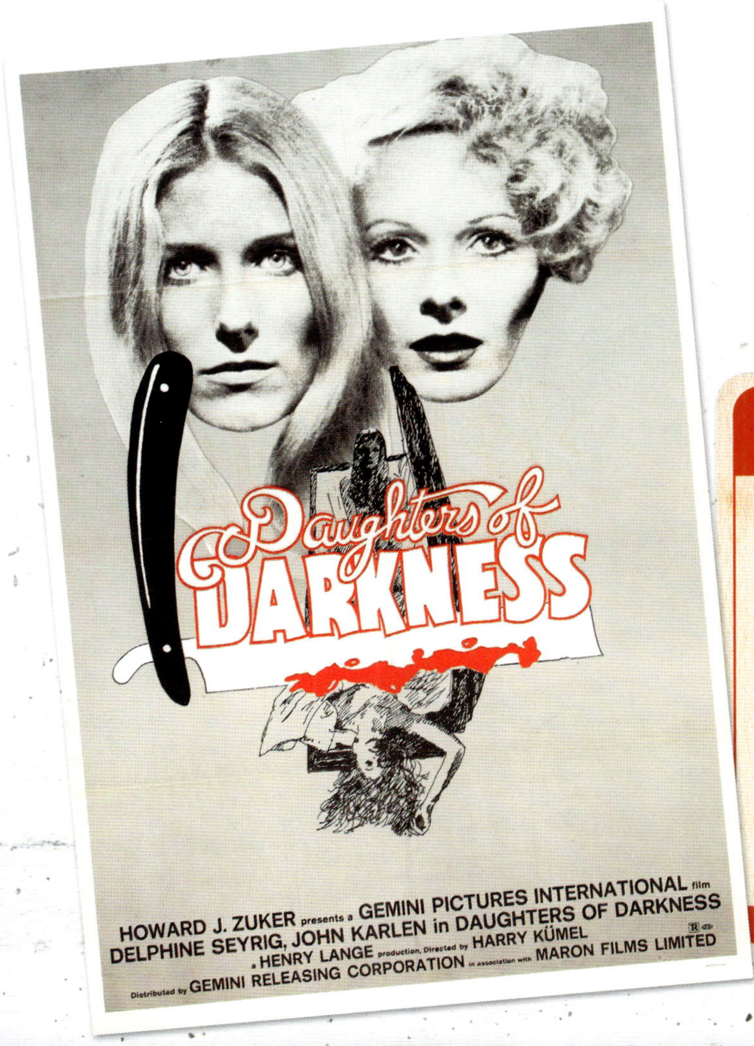

Daughters of Darkness. Showking Films/Maya Films/Ciné Vog Films/Roxy Film (1971).

This 1971 film took an idea from *Dracula's Daughter*, which created an elegant offspring, blending Carmilla and Dracula. *Daughters of Darkness* is well known to aficionados of vampire films but not so much outside that realm. Delphine Seyrig played the role of Countess Bathory with panache, a style and grace that reflects former eras (look at her hairstyle!) and pits them against the changes brought about in the 1960s. Flawed but still an exquisite film, not to be missed.

Nancy Kilpatrick

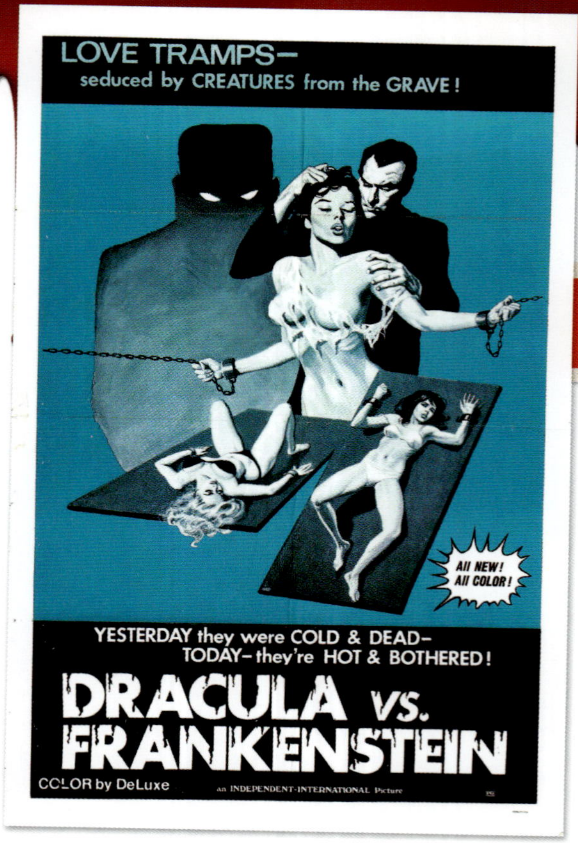

Dracula vs. Frankenstein. Independent International Pictures (1971)

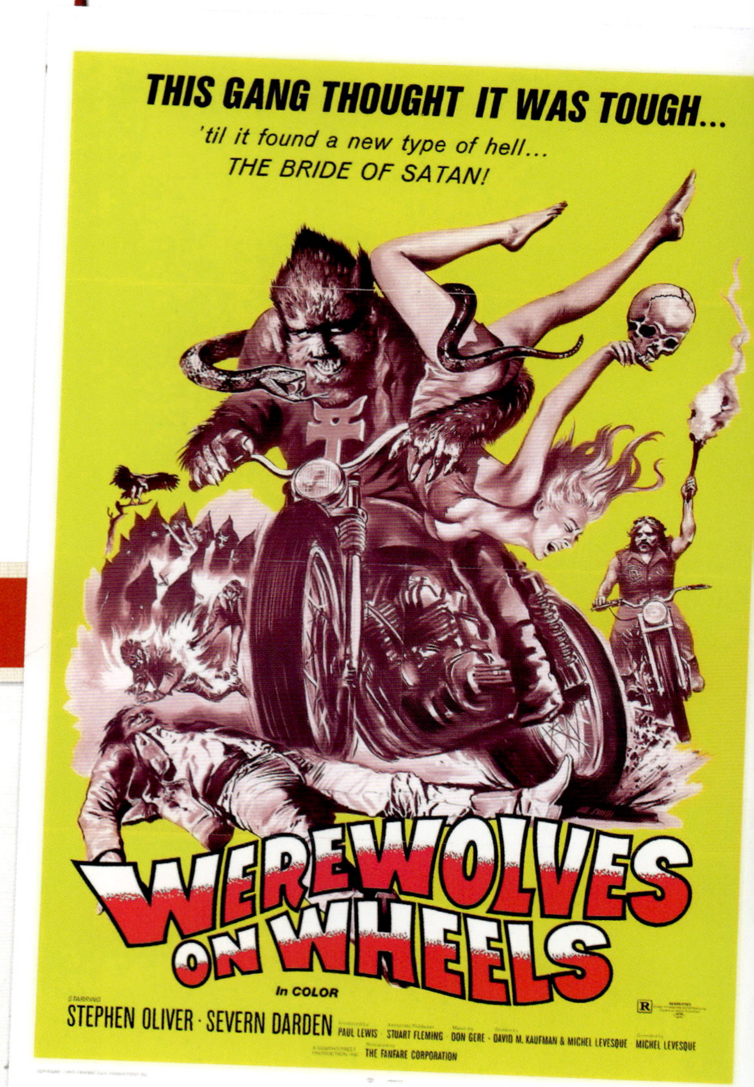

Werewolves on Wheels. South Street Films (1971).

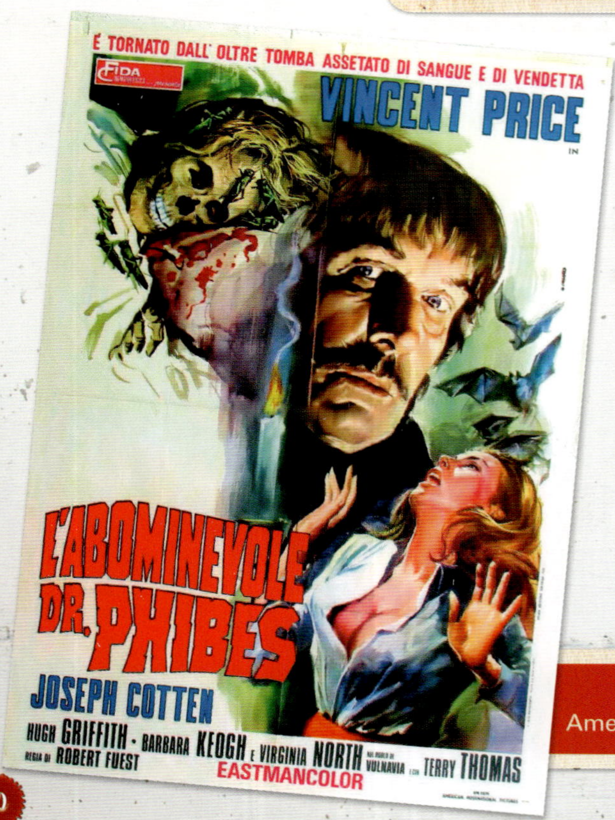

The Abominable Dr. Phibes. American International Pictures (1971). Italy.

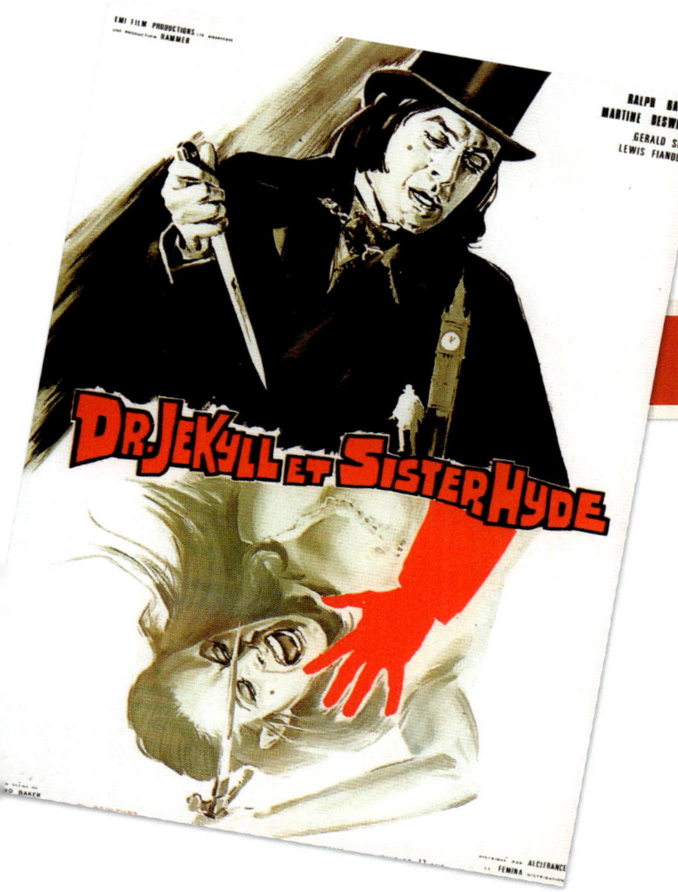

Dr. Jekyll & Sister Hyde.
Hammer Film Productions (1971).

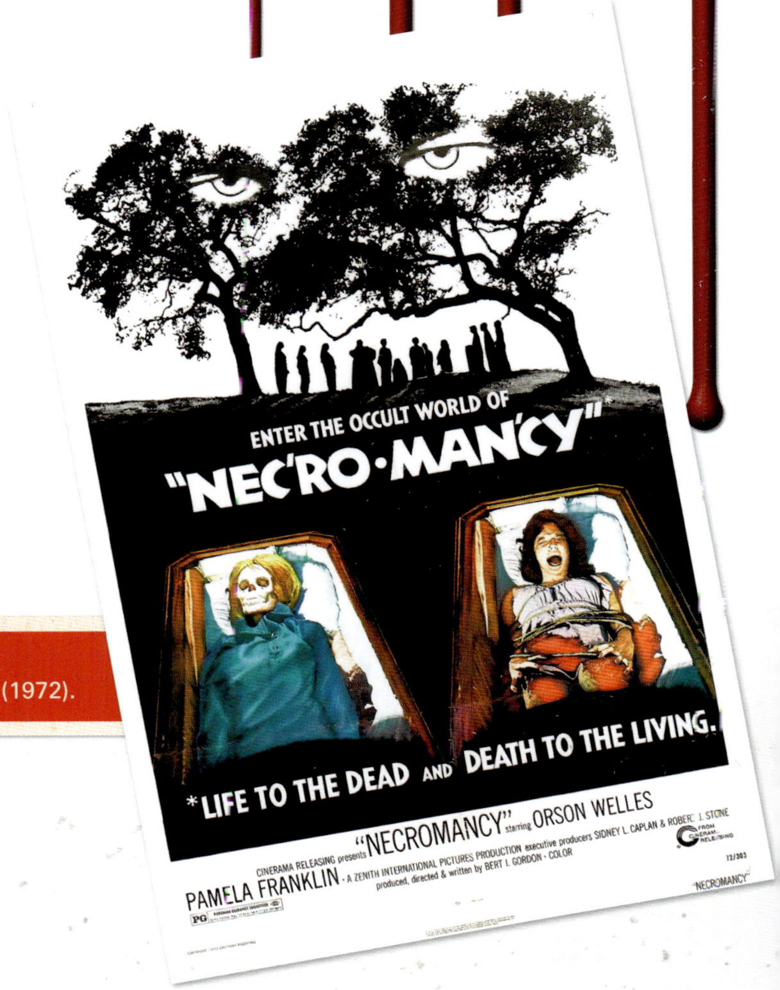

Necromancy.
Compass/Zenith International (1972).

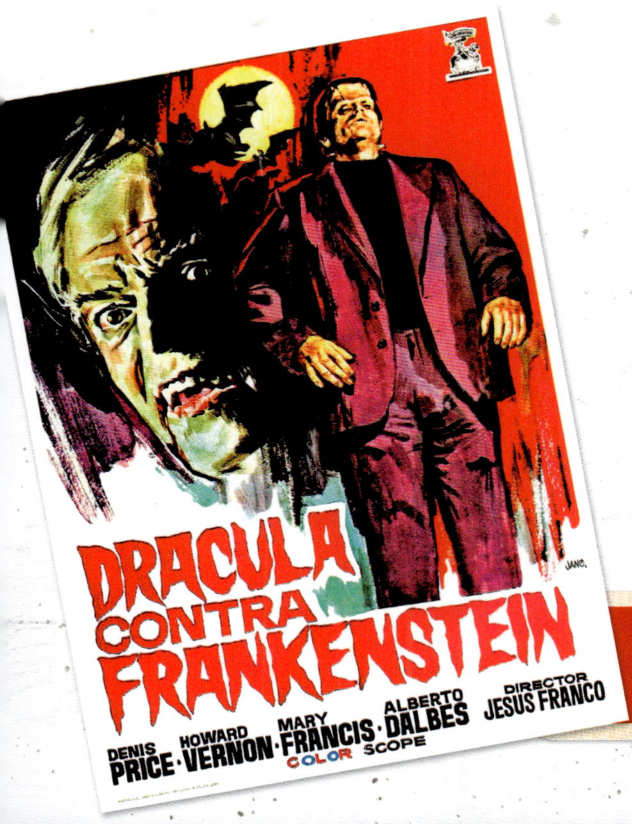

Dracula, Prisoner of Frankenstein.
Prodif Ets./Comptoir Français du Film Production/
Fénix Cooperativa Cinematográfica (1972). Spain.

The Last House on the Left. Lobster Enterprises, Sean S. Cunningham Films, The Night Co. (1972). Japan.

This one came out and, hoo – I knew there was a new take on not just film horror but ALL the horror genre. There's a coldness here, a surface of ice and detached affect, and we suddenly had in "pop lit/pop film/pop horror" the monotone of Mersault explaining his killing of the Arab: It was because of the sun. Call this one a harbinger and trendsetter, and whole lots of other things, and forget the remake.

Mort Castle

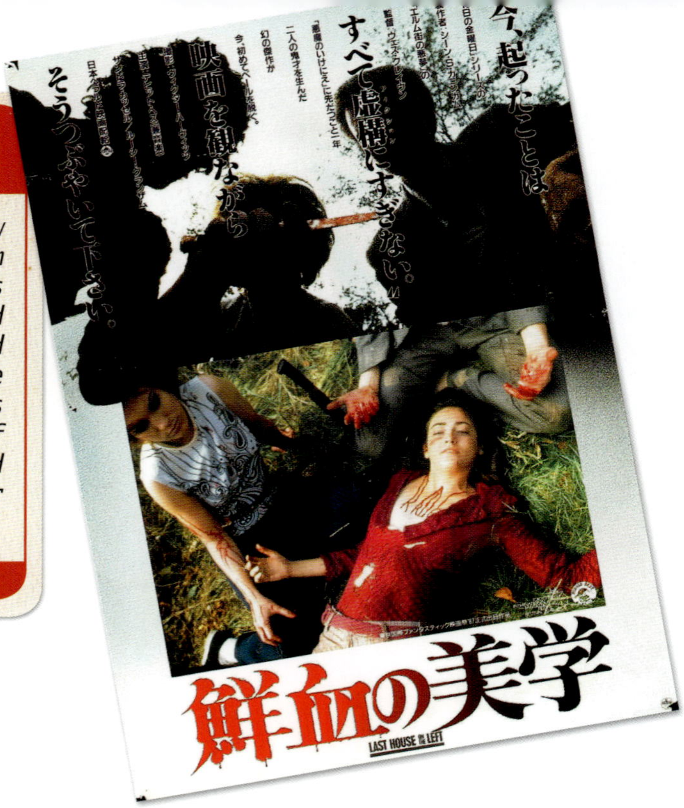

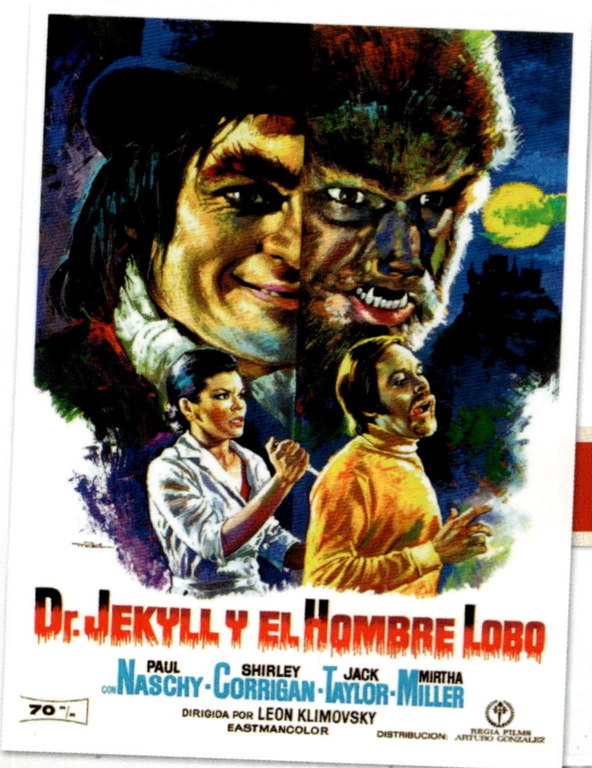

Dr. Jekyll vs. the Werewolf. Arturo González Producciones Cinematográficas (1972). Spain.

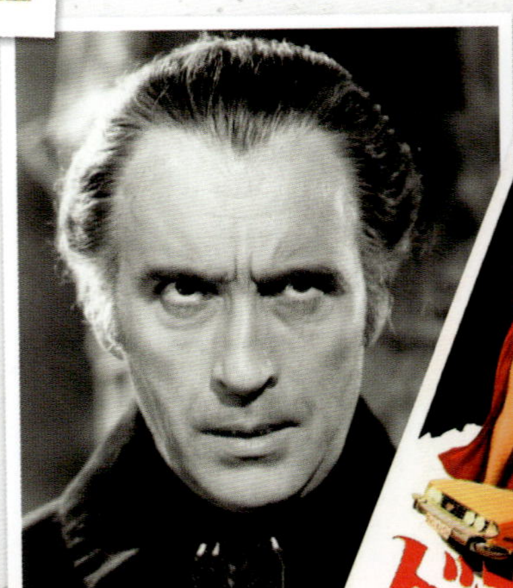

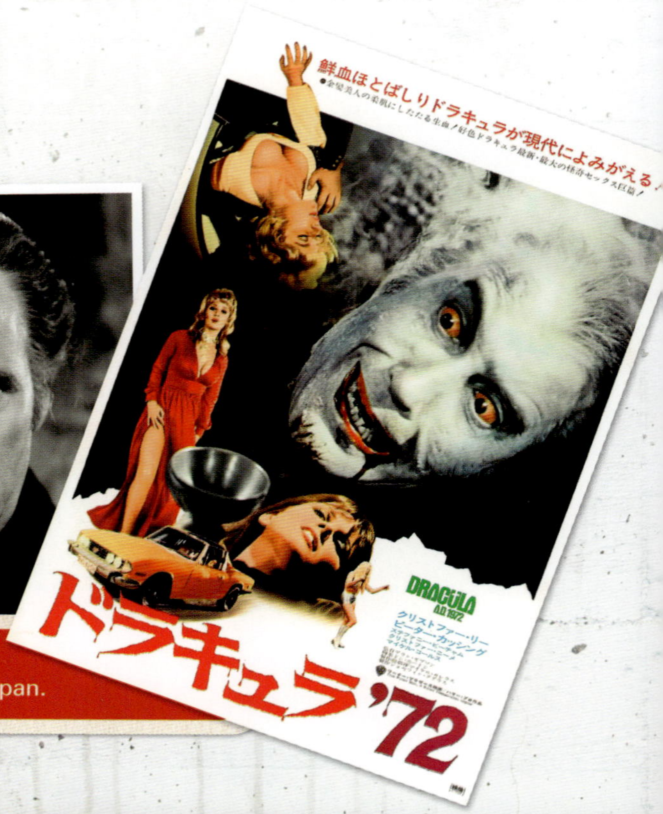

Dracula A.D. 1972. Hammer Film Productions (1972). Japan.

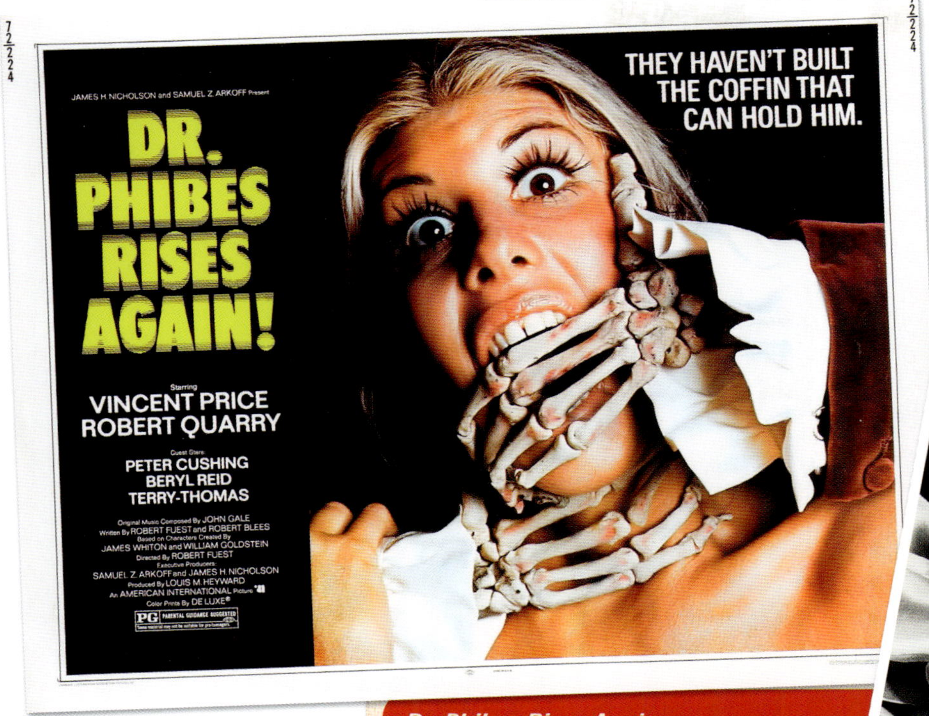

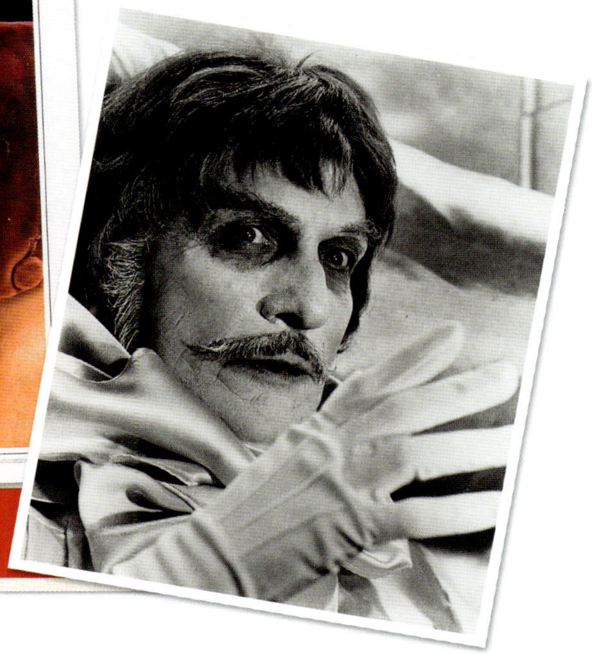

Dr. Phibes Rises Again.
American International Pictures (1972).

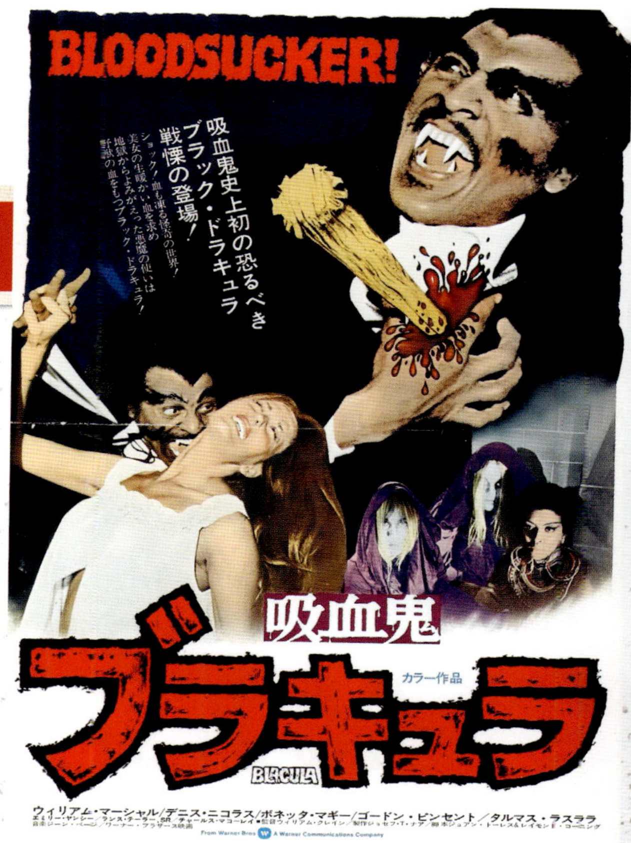

Blacula. American International Pictures, Power Productions (1972). Japan.

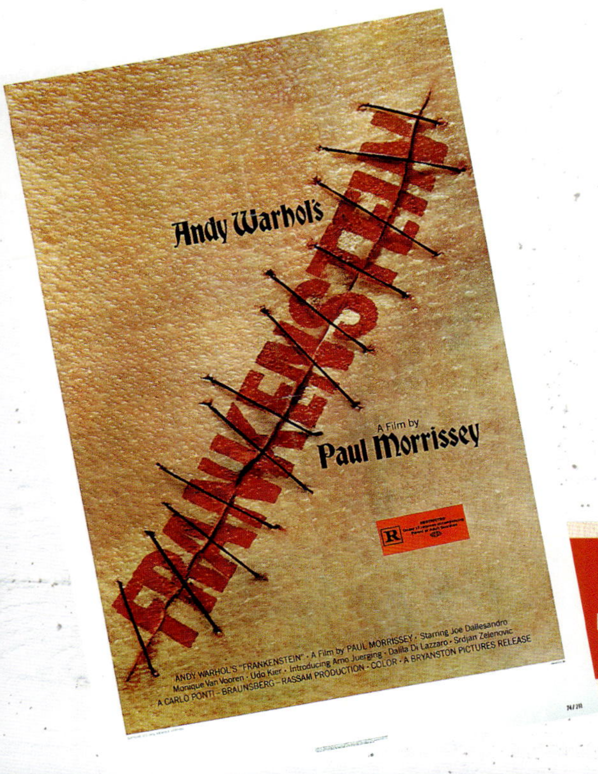

Andy Warhol's Frankenstein.
Compagnia Cinematografica Champion/ Braunsberg Productions/Carlo Ponti Cinematografica/ Rassam Productions/Yanne et Rassam (1973).

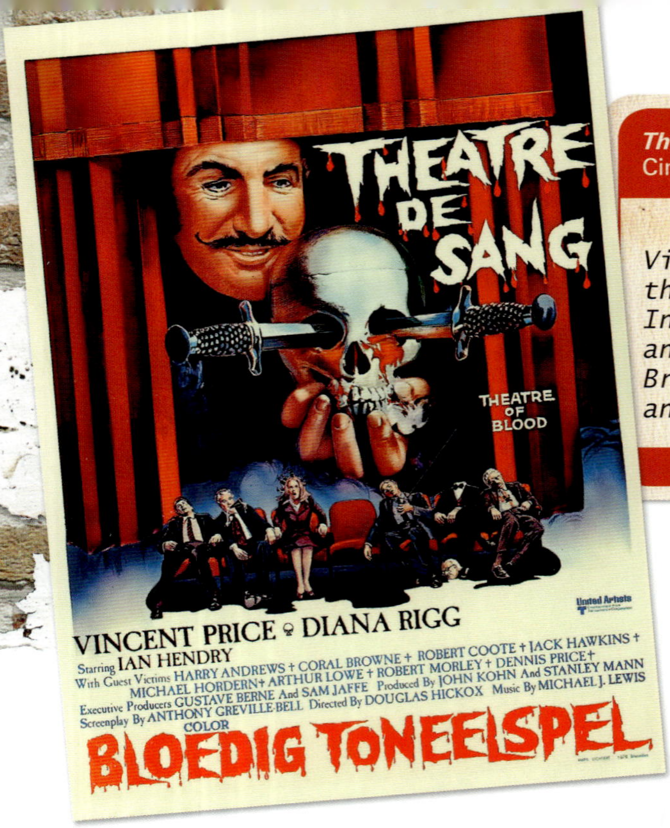

Theatre of Blood.
Cineman Productions (1973). Belgium.

Masterpiece of theatrical horror. Vincent Price at his best, not to mention the other stalwarts and great thespians. Ingenious relationship with Shakespeare and as funny and terrifying a picture of British horror and social division as any ever made.

Richard J. Hand

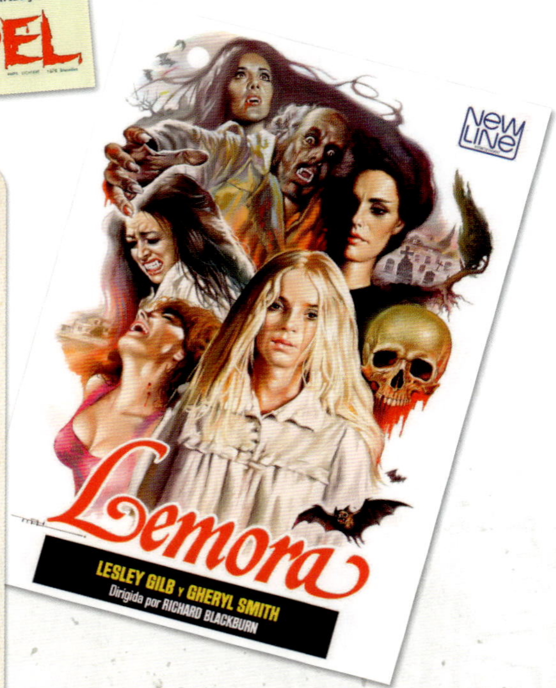

Lemora, A Child's Tale of the Supernatural.
Blackfern (1973). Spain.

Forget the last quarter of the film, which almost makes sense if you don't or can't think. The first three quarters is your non-forgettable childhood nightmare, gauzy visions when it should be, and a bus ride though HPLand that Dracula's coachman could have mapped out. Add a singing old crone, stone walls, a somewhat lovely lady, gibber-laughing... Lemora: A Child's Tale of the Supernatural *terrified the adult in me – and even when I'm studying it now, learning from it, it bypasses my analytical mind and totally engages my fear zones.*

Mort Castle

Dracula.
Canadian Broadcasting Company (1973).

CBC's Dracula *is more faithful to Stoker's original than any of its predecessors, and certainly more so than some of its successors (I am thinking specifically of Coppola's* Bram Stoker's Dracula.*) In fact, I'd place this one in the same league as the BBC production of 1978 with Louis Jourdan (though the latter, a three-hour production, with larger budget is a superior film). Not once did I scream "How dare you do that!" at the monitor in front of me.*

Elizabeth Miller

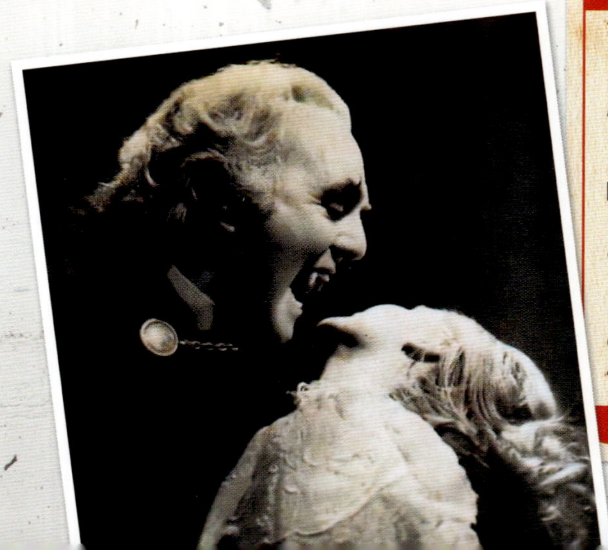

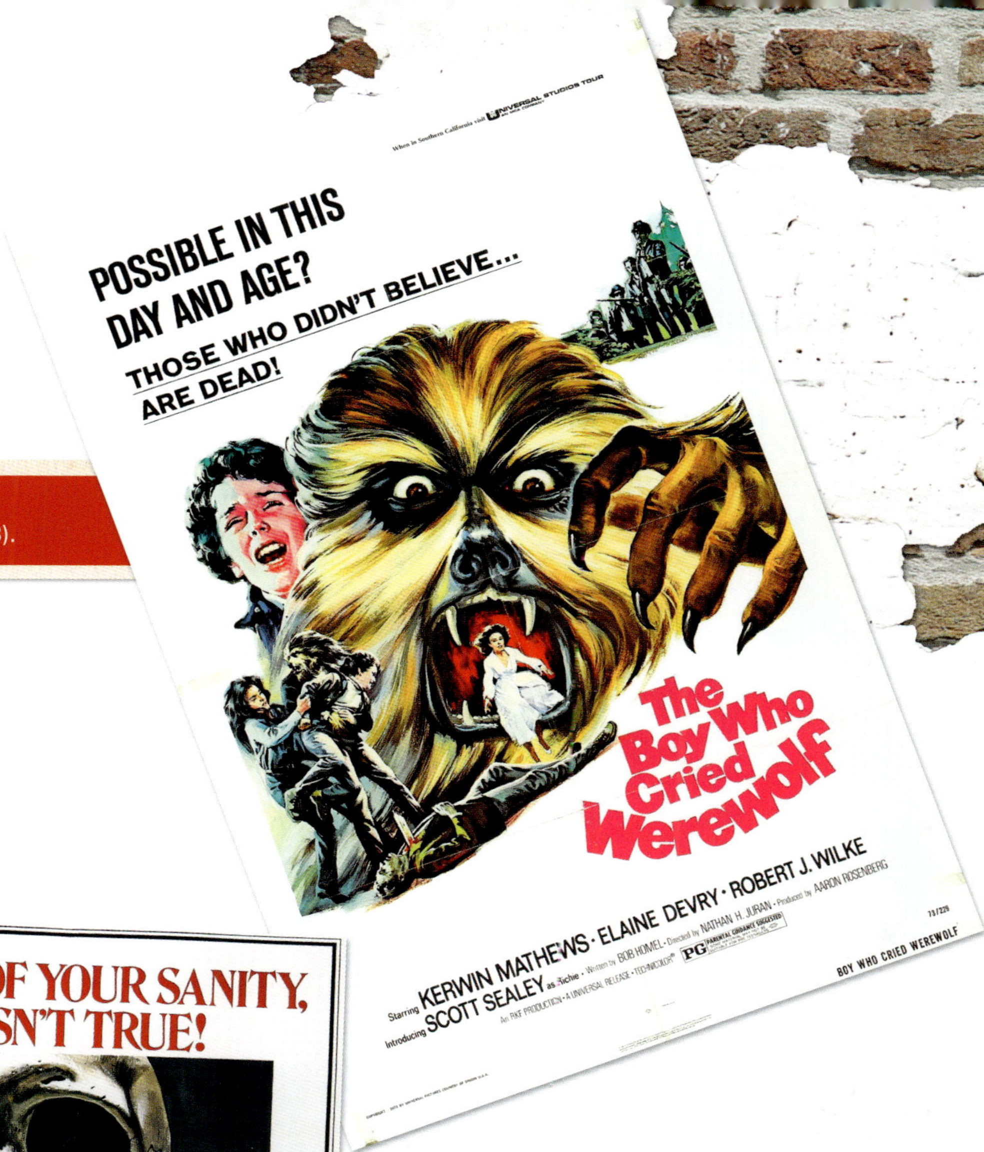

The Boy Who Cried Werewolf.
Pacific Bay Entertainment/RKF (1973).

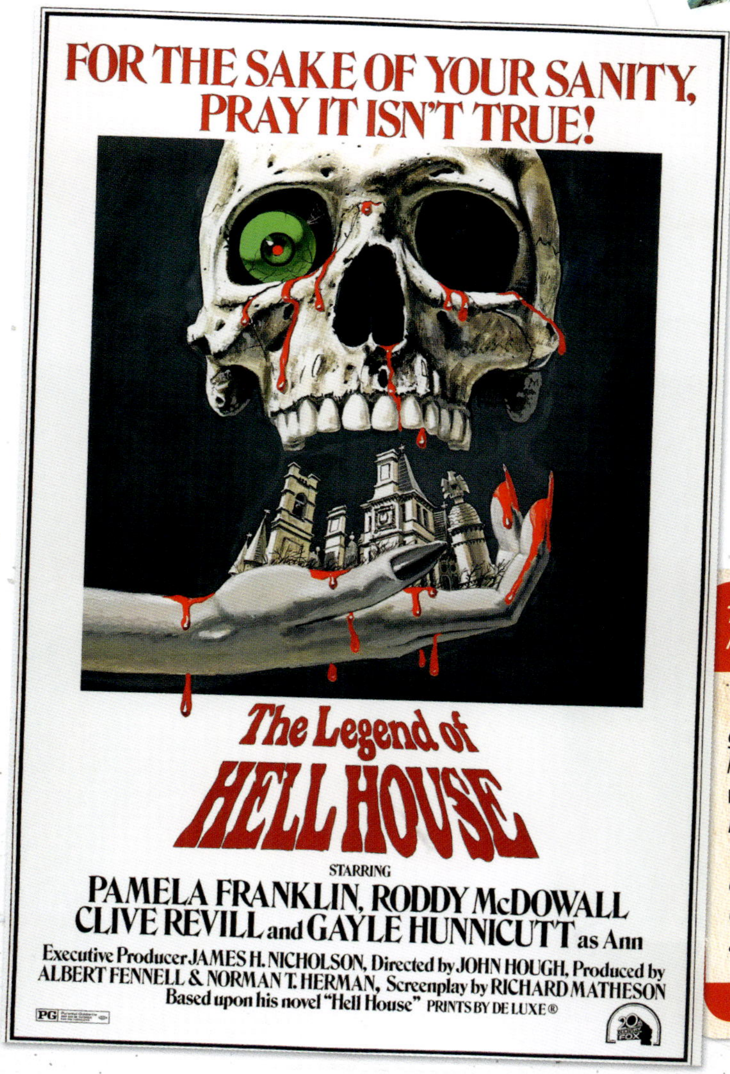

The Legend of Hell House.
Academy Pictures Corporation (1973).

This is a truly harrowing tale, with a grim cameo near the end by the estimable Michael Gough. The only one thing wrong with the film is that the book is even better; Hell House is my nominee for the most terrifying haunted house novel ever written; compared to it, said one critic, "Rosemary's Baby is like a night at the Nixons!"

Marvin Kaye

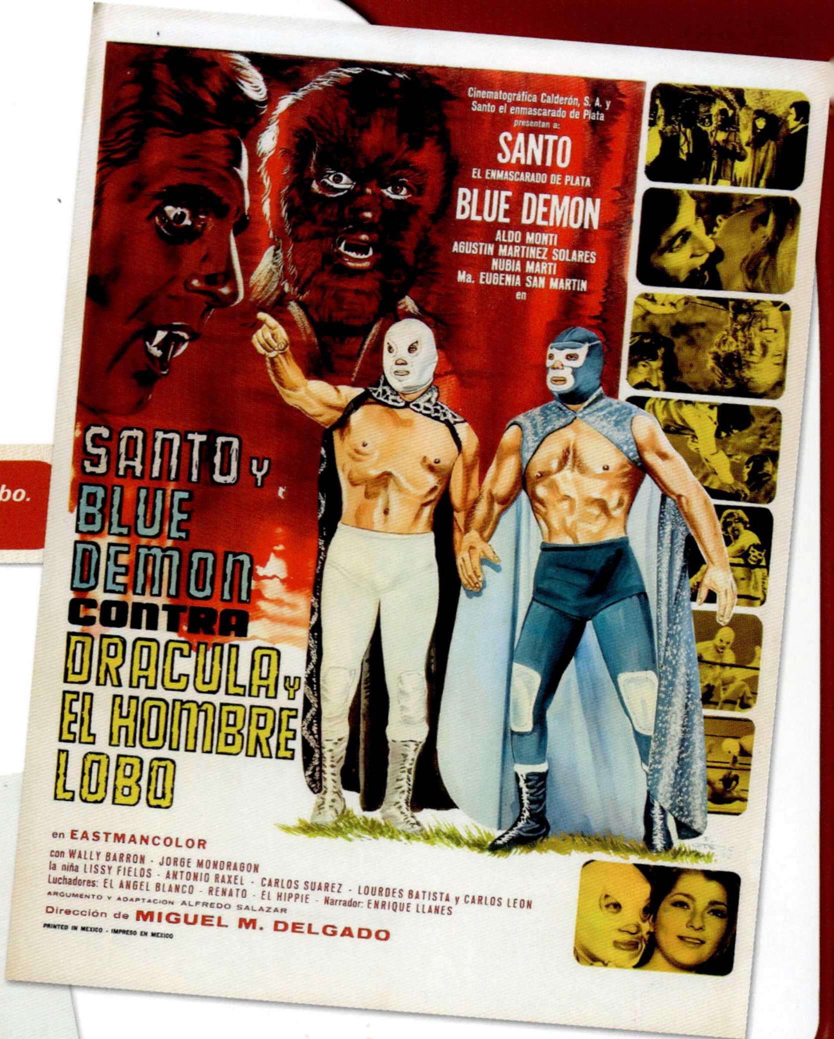

Santo y Blue Demon Contra Drácula y el Hombre Lobo. Cinematográfica Calderón S.A. (1973). Mexico.

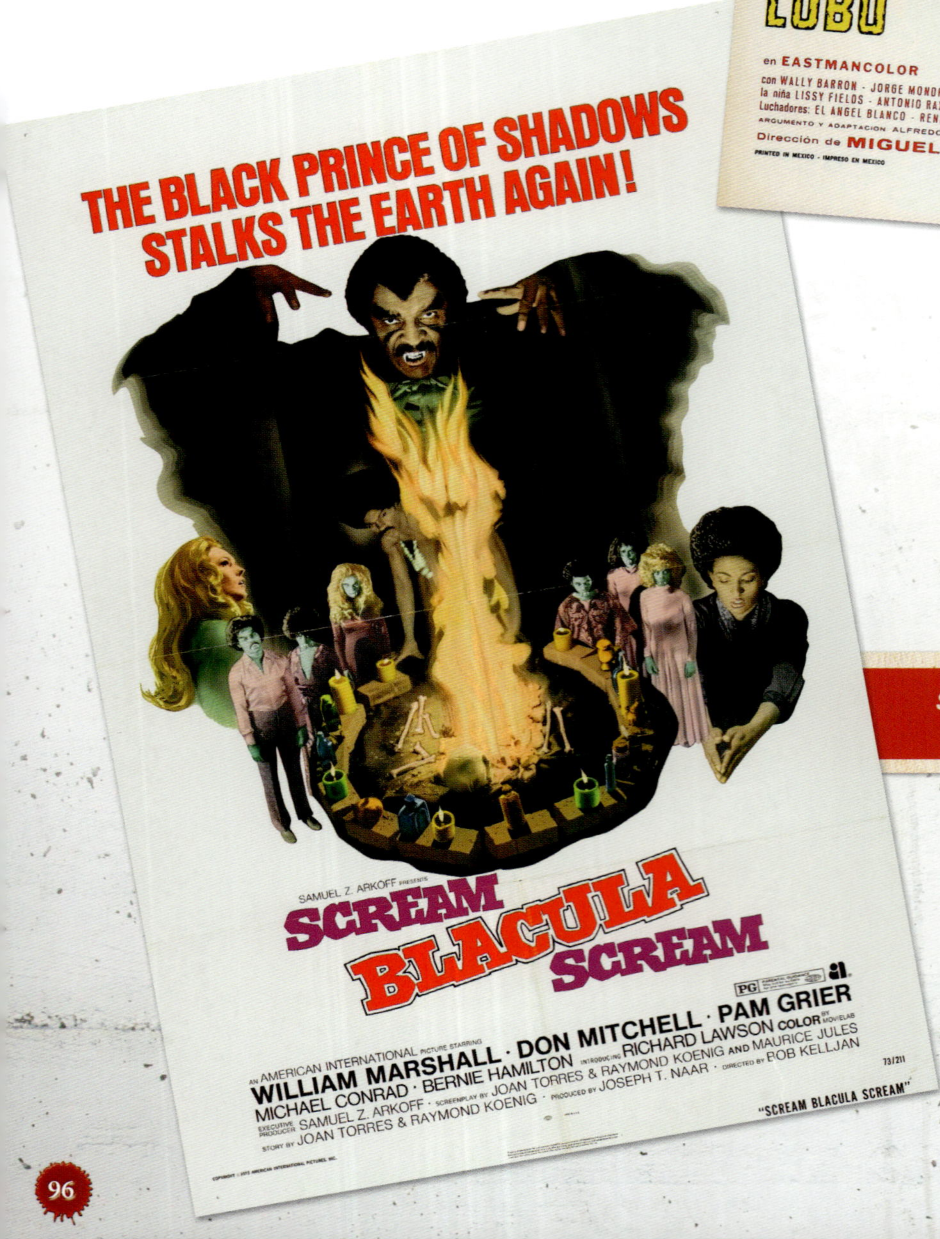

Scream, Blacula, Scream. American International Pictures/Power Productions (1973).

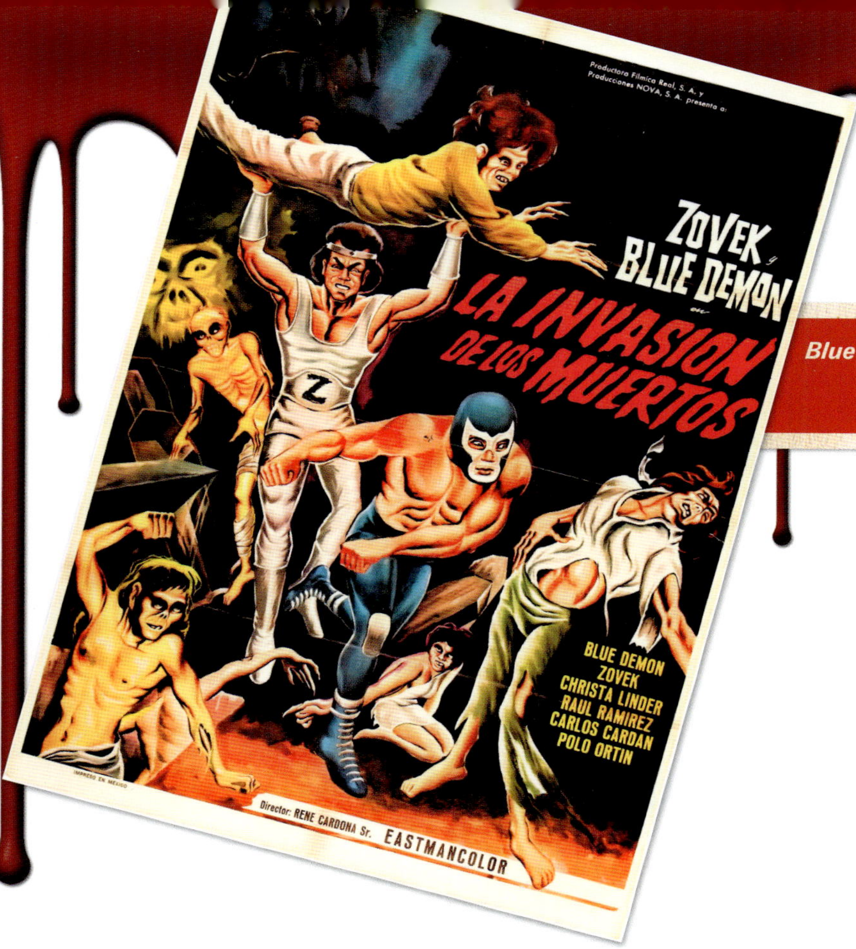

Blue Demon y Zovek en La Invasión de los Muertos. Azteca Films, Producciones Nova, Productora Fílmica Real (1973). Mexico.

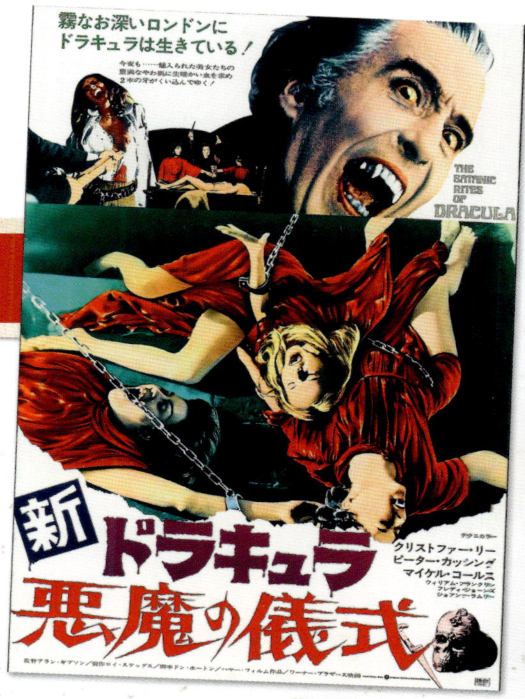

The Satanic Rites of Dracula. Warner Bros. Pictures, Hammer Film Productions (1973). Japan.

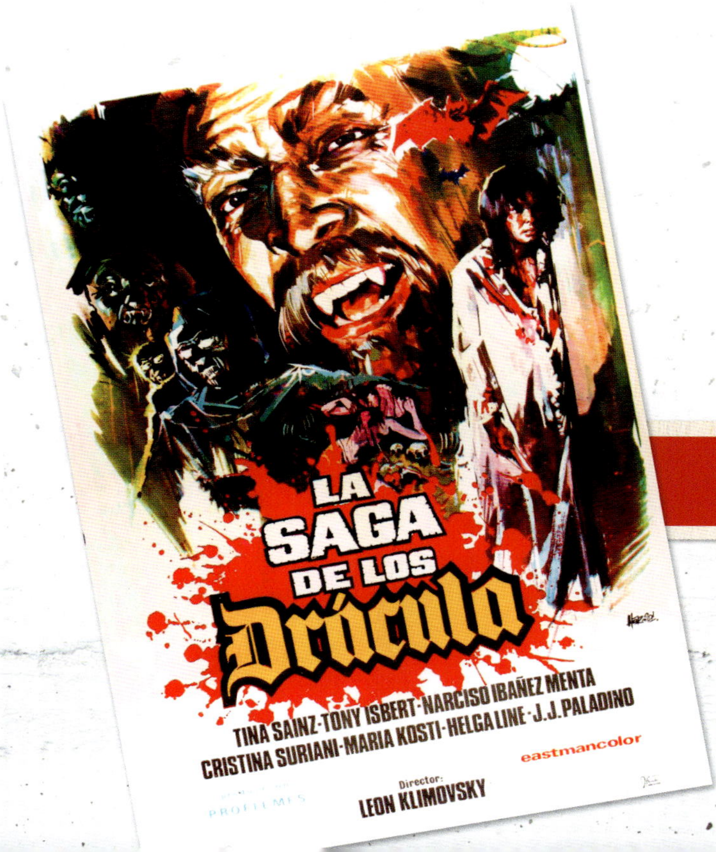

La Saga de los Drácula. Profilmes (1973). Spain.

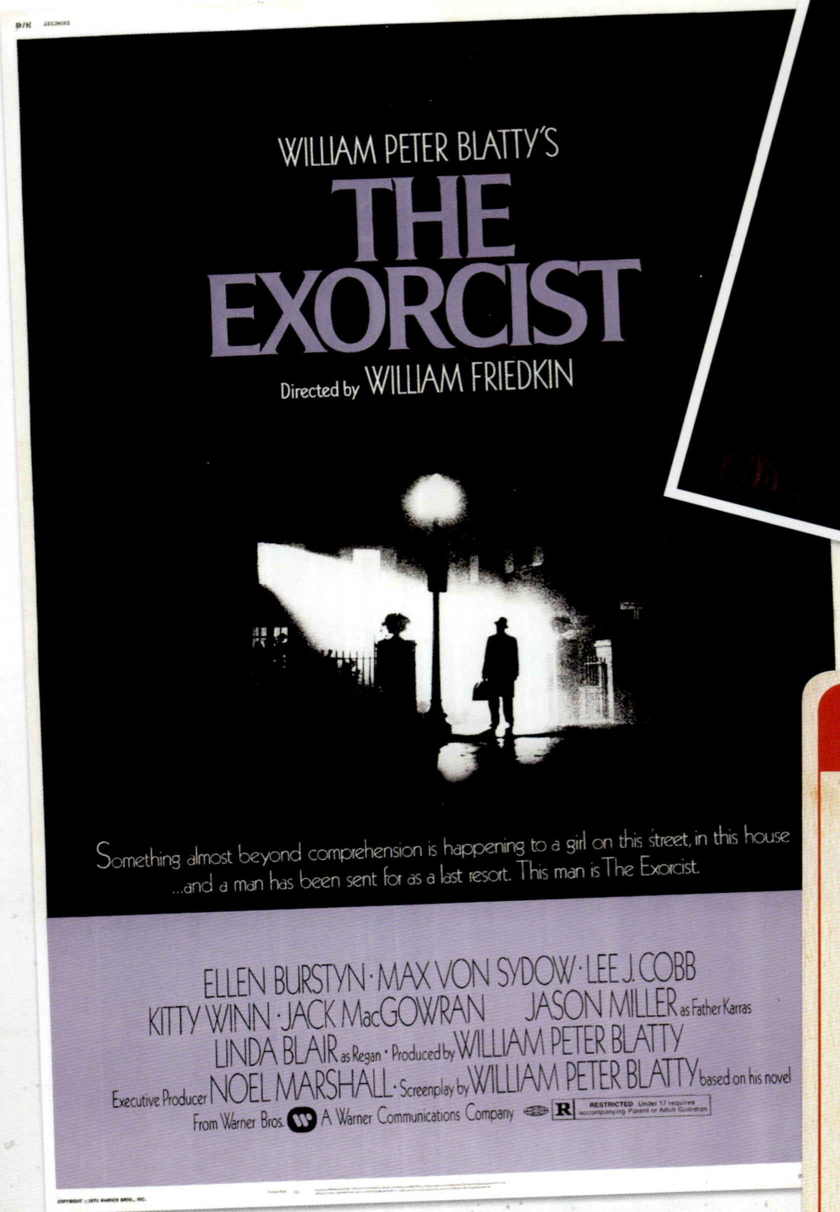

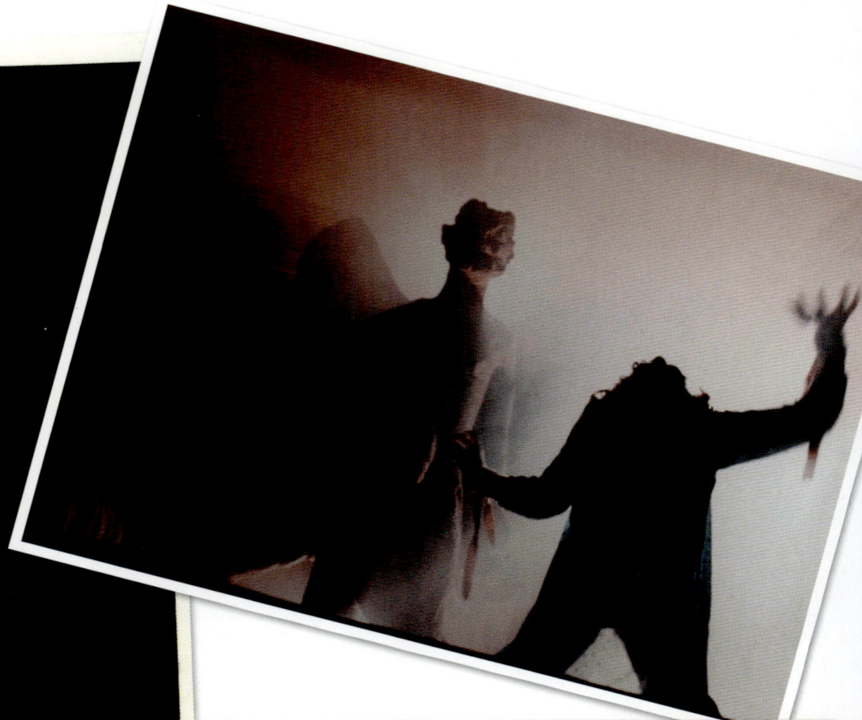

The Exorcist.
Hoya Productions/Warner Bros. Pictures (1973).

Despite what now look like rather clunky special effects, The Exorcist *remains for me one of the most frightening films ever made: I still can't hear Mike Oldfield's "Tubular Bells" without a shiver. And Friedkin's stark encapsulation of good and evil in those images of Father Merrin – facing the statue of Pazuzu in the opening sequence or standing in the light streaming from Regan's window in that Georgetown street – have surely attained the kind of iconic stature we associate with Lugosi's Dracula or Karloff's monster.*

Glennis Byron

The Exorcist.
Hoya Productions/Warner Bros. Pictures (1973).

This film broke the mold on demonic possession films, and none have come close to it ever since. It brought the potential for demonic possession into mainstream living, and sent untold numbers of people who were suddenly plunged into fear of demons to shrinks, counselors, priests, and ministers. It left me looking uneasily into shadows and mirrors for some time, and the "Tubular Bells" theme music still gives me the shivers.

Rosemary Ellen Guiley

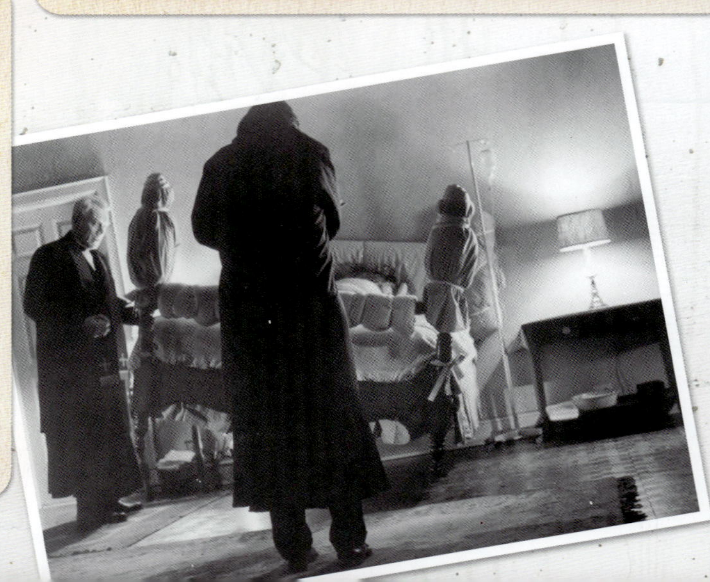

The Exorcist.
Hoya Productions/Warner Bros. Pictures (1973). Mexico.

I was not old enough to see The Exorcist *on its first release, although I do recall the furore it generated. I finally caught up with it in the late 1970s, during one of its many re-releases. I had to choose between seeing the film and revising for a difficult school test. Of course, I made the right choice (and also got an A for the test). It is one of those films that really does live up to its formidable reputation. It is an engulfing experience, a roller-coaster ride, a brilliant example of cinematic technique; there is nothing else quite like it in horror history.*

Peter Hutchings

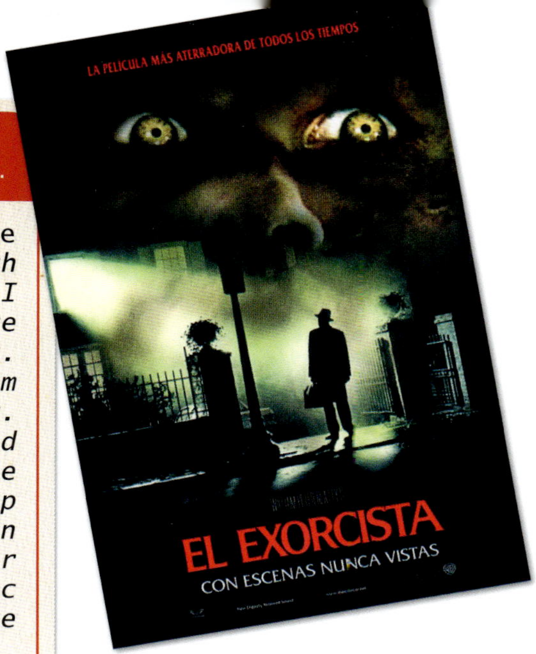

The Exorcist.
Hoya Productions/Warner Bros. Pictures (1973).

Still stands tall as one of the top 5 greatest horror films of all time. No other devil possession movie can hold a candle to it. The Exorcist *set the template that is still being copied till this day.*

Tony Timpone

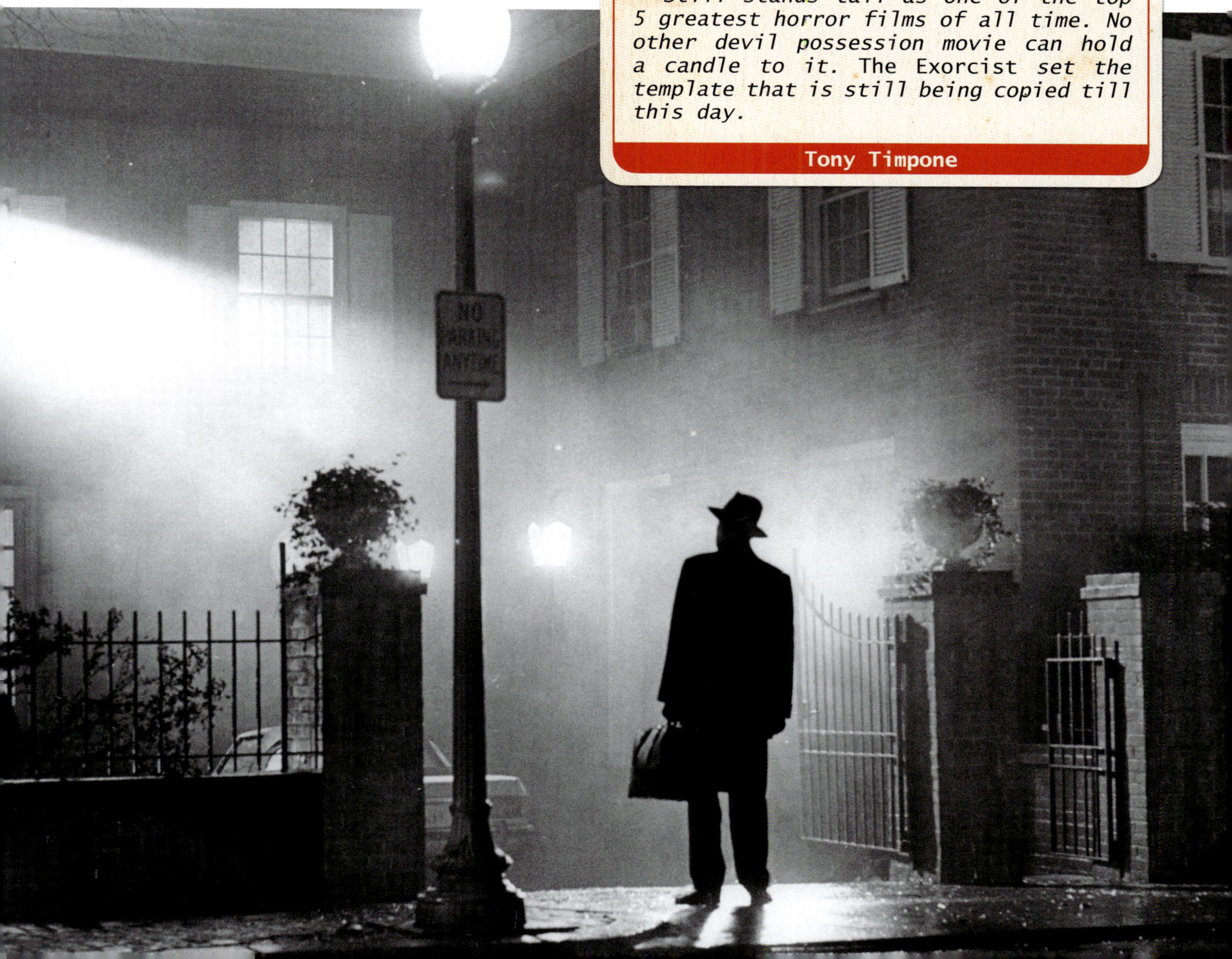

Dan Curtis' Dracula.
Latglen Ltd. (1974).

Is made-for-television horror – Dan Curtis's territory in the 1970s – a contradiction in terms? This intriguing adaptation of Dracula *might be seen as a way of keeping alive the Count on television during the pre-cable era, tailoring the king-vampire to fit the aesthetics and politics of the small screen.*

Gregory A. Waller

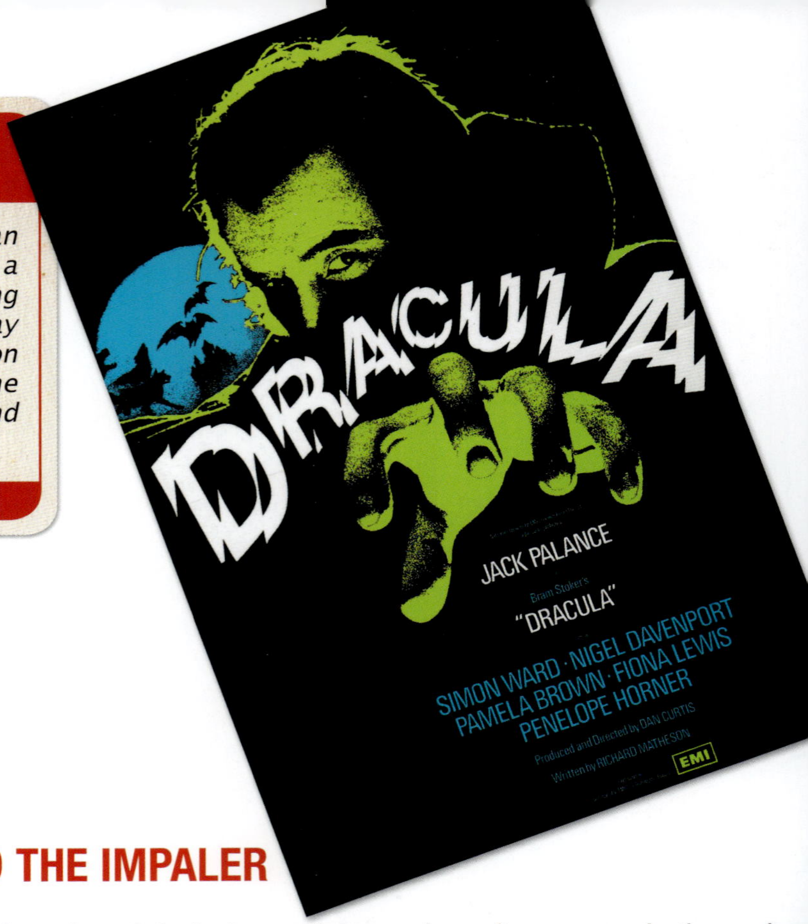

ON **VLAD THE IMPALER**

Vlad the Impaler exploded onto the popular culture scene in the early 1970s with the publication of *In Search of Dracula* by Raymond McNally and Radu Florescu. While they were not the first to note the connection, their book brought the fifteenth-century Wallachian *voivode* to centre stage. Their exaggerated claims concerning the nature of the link between Count Dracula and Vlad became widely accepted — and still is standard "knowledge" today. Its immediate influence is apparent in Dan Curtis' *Dracula* (1974).

~Elizabeth Miller

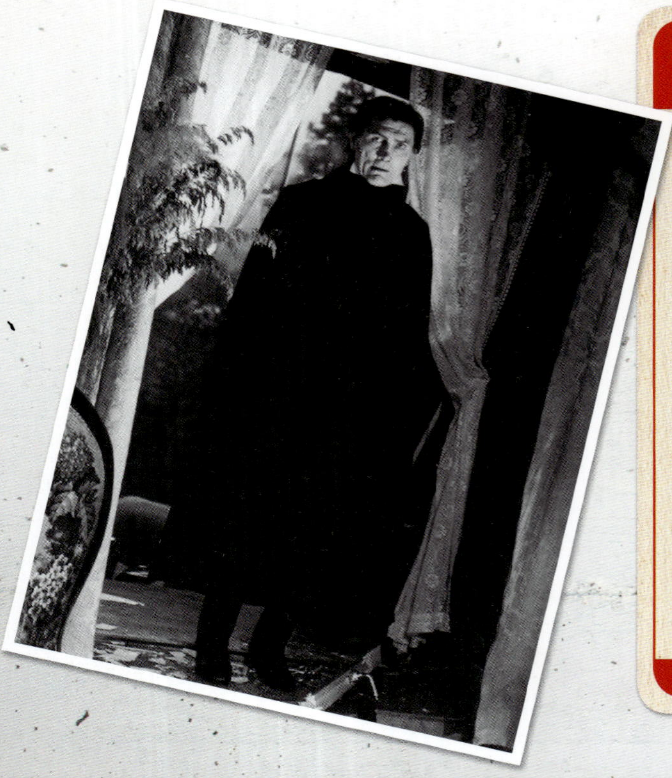

Dan Curtis' Dracula.
Latglen Ltd. (1974).

Jack Palance is stunning as a suave but deeply scary vampire, but more importantly, Curtis arrived at what I believe to be a satisfying resolution of the problem of why Dracula came to England and why he was attracted to Lucy Westenra and Mina Harker. Curtis proposes that Lucy is the reincarnation of Dracula's mortal wife, and when Dracula discovers her, he naturally seeks her out (with fatal results). Francis Ford Coppola tried out a similar solution (Mina as the reincarnation), but it's difficult to watch that film after its fine beginning, as it degrades into a romance with graphic sex and a ridiculously pretty "youthened" version of Dracula.

Leslie Klinger

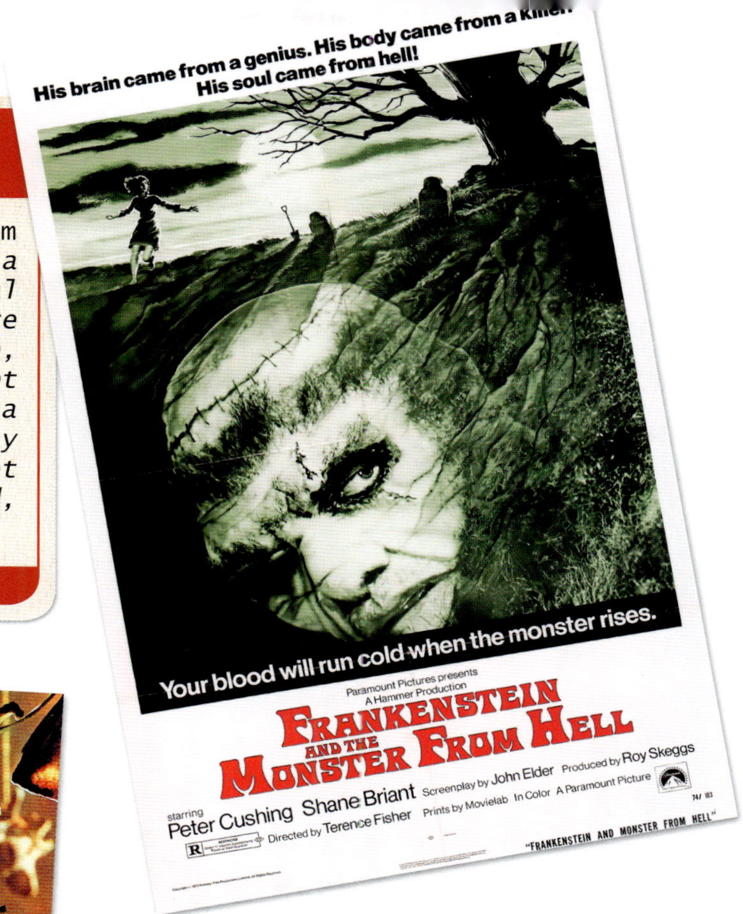

Frankenstein and the Monster from Hell.
Hammer Film Productions (1974).

Frankenstein and the Monster from Hell *(1974) paradoxically combines a restraint in color with a vivid portrayal of violence. This is the last of Terence Fisher's* Frankenstein *films, and here, he showed what he usually evoked or kept hidden, such as the processes of sawing a head or extracting a brain. Yet the gray backdrop that seeps into every scene set in the asylum gives the film a distanced, "objective" feel.*

Caroline Joan (Kay) Picart

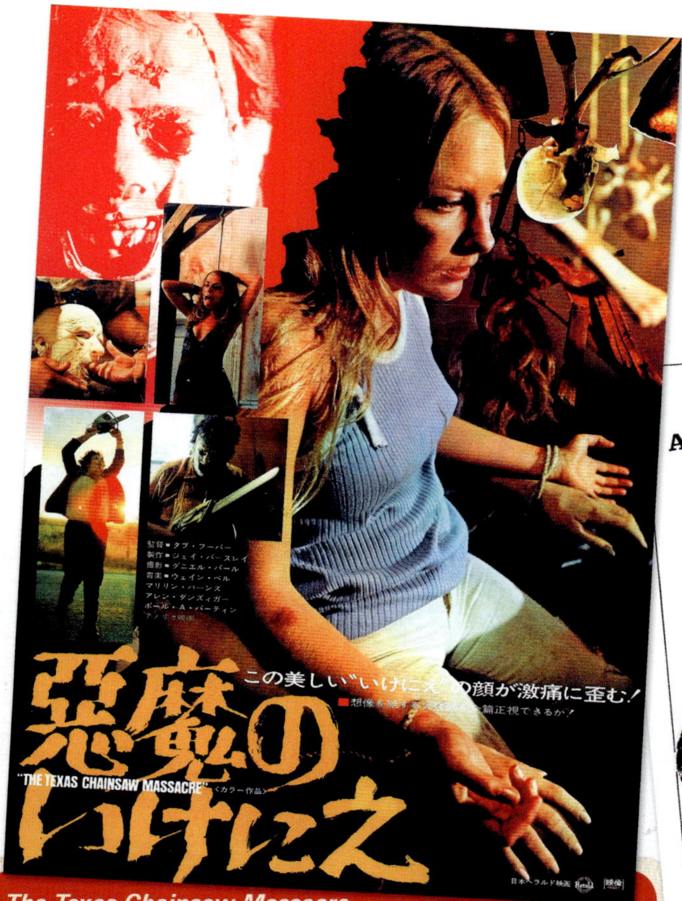

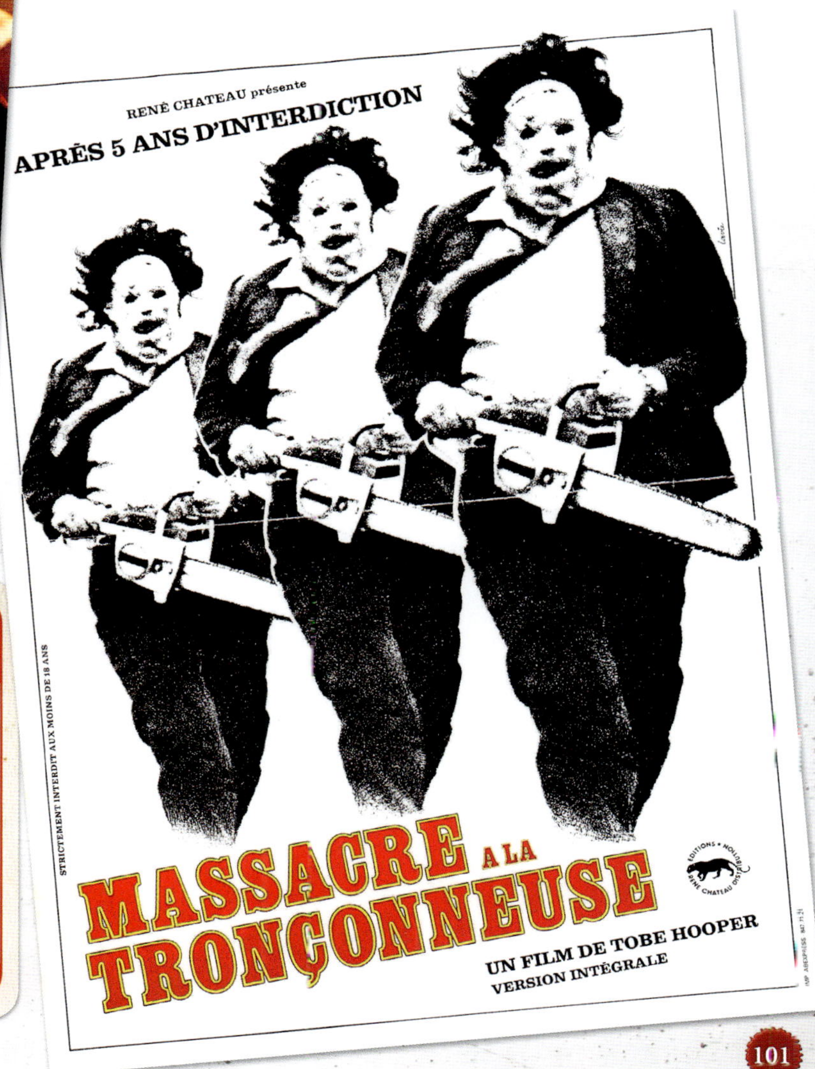

The Texas Chainsaw Massacre.
Vortex (1974). Japan. (above) France. (right)

I wrote the comic book adaptation Leatherface, *supposedly based on* Texas Chainsaw Massacre III. *In its spirit, the comic was truly based on this original's feeling and on the only other splatter horror film of the 1970s to equal it,* The Hills Have Eyes. *Why, we had us a real look at family values, uh-huh.*

Mort Castle

Sugar Hill.
American International Pictures (1974).

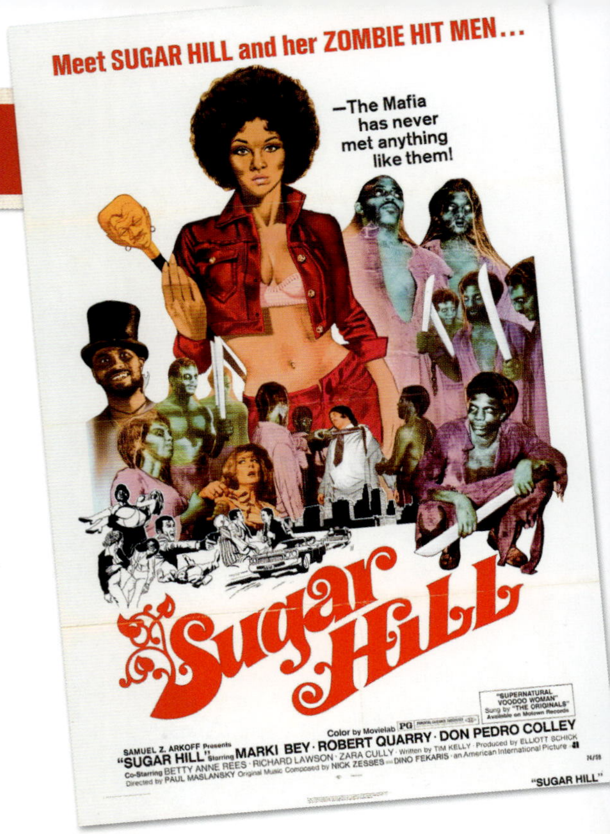

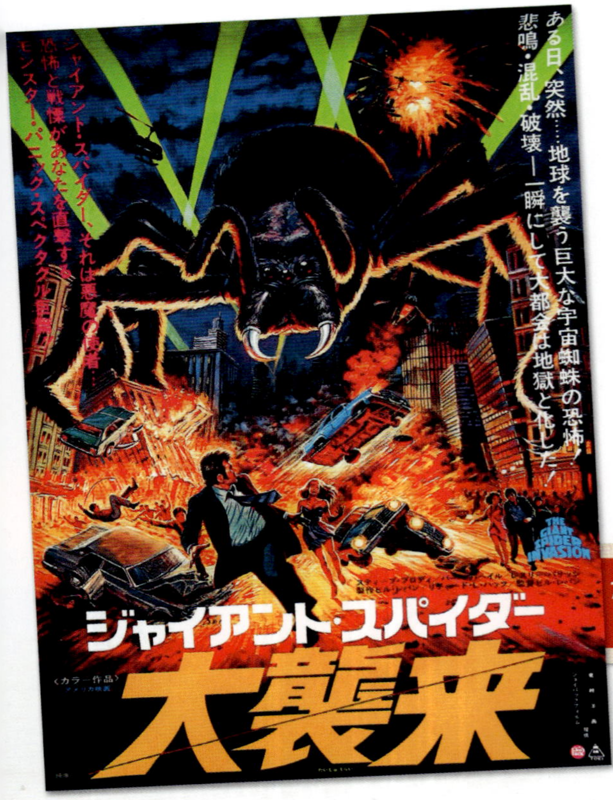

The Giant Spider Invasion. Cinema Group 75/ Transcentury Productions (1975). Japan.

Deep Red.
Rizzoli Film/Seda Spettacoli (1975).

Like most of the monsters in the slasher genre it helped inspire, the monster in this movie is human, but what surprised me about this one is that the "pain" is human, too. As an adult, I watch most stalk-and-kill movies from a comfortable distance. The best of them turn the death scenes into bloody abstract art, and the worst, well, they don't do much of anything. Dario Argento's gloved killer certainly gets the victims to the abstract art stage, but on their way, they get pounded by intimate, familiar kinds of pain. A woman gets her face plunged into boiling bath water. A man gets his teeth knocked out after a fall against a fireplace. Those are the types of pain we can relate to, and when grown-up-me saw those scenes the first time, I was wincing and closing my eyes, just like a kid.

L. Andrew Cooper

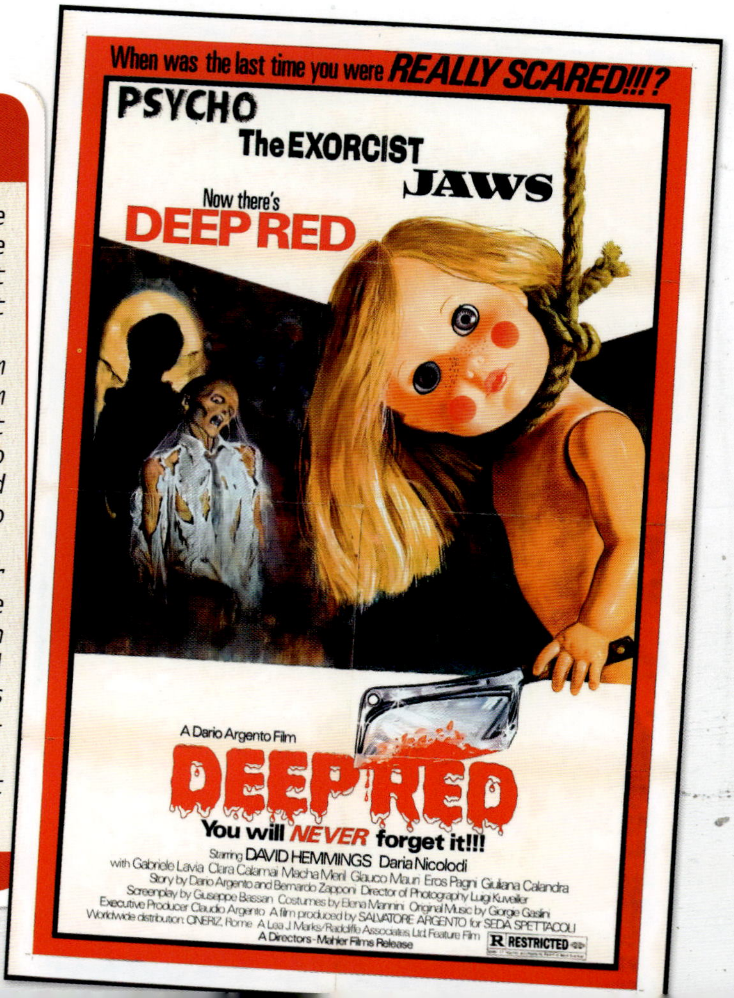

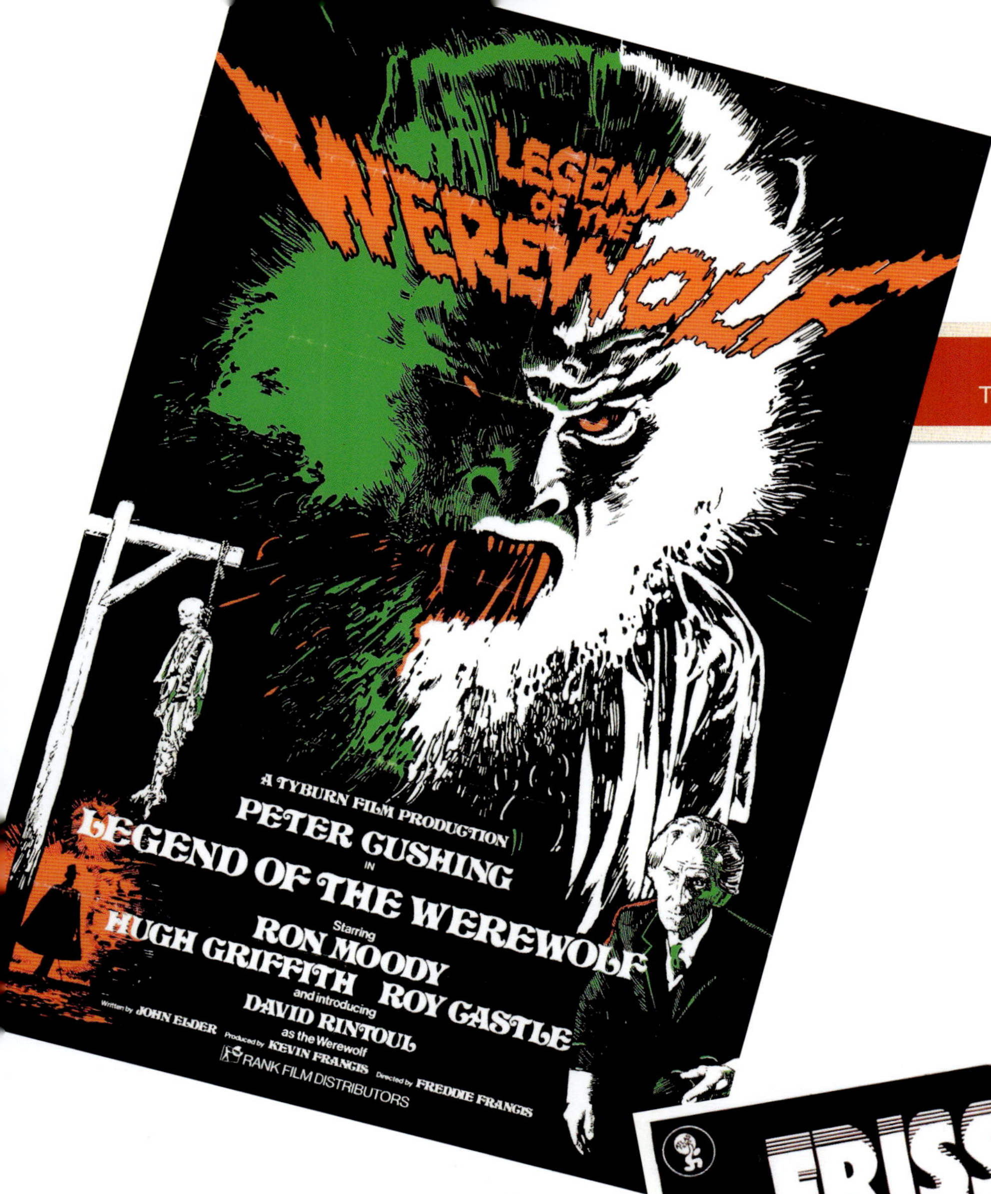

Legend of the Werewolf. Tyburn Film Productions Limited (1975).

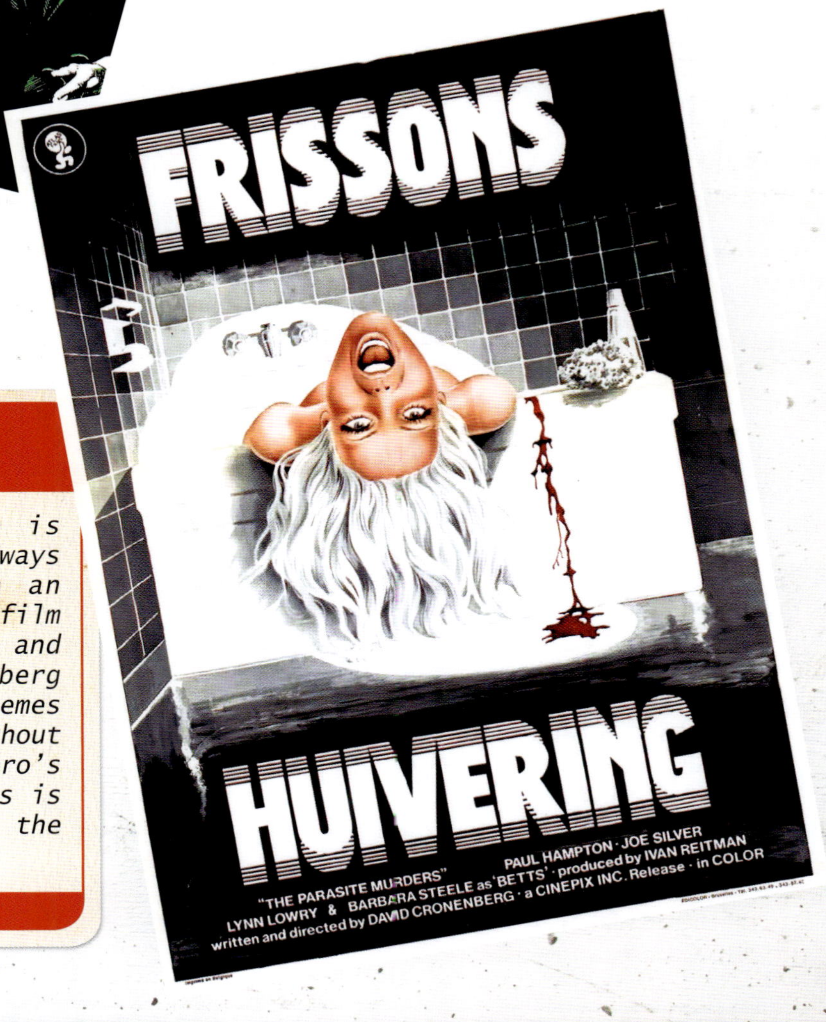

Shivers. Canadian Film Development Corporation/ Cinépix/DAL Productions (1975). Canada.

David Cronenberg's first film is still, in my mind, his best. I've always appreciated Cronenberg's work on an intellectual level, but this is the film I appreciate most on an emotional and physical level. In Shivers, Cronenberg manages to encapsulate many of the themes that he has continued to explore throughout the rest of his career. Along with Romero's Night of the Living Dead (1968), this is the film that helped give birth to the contemporary zombie narrative.

Jesse Stommel

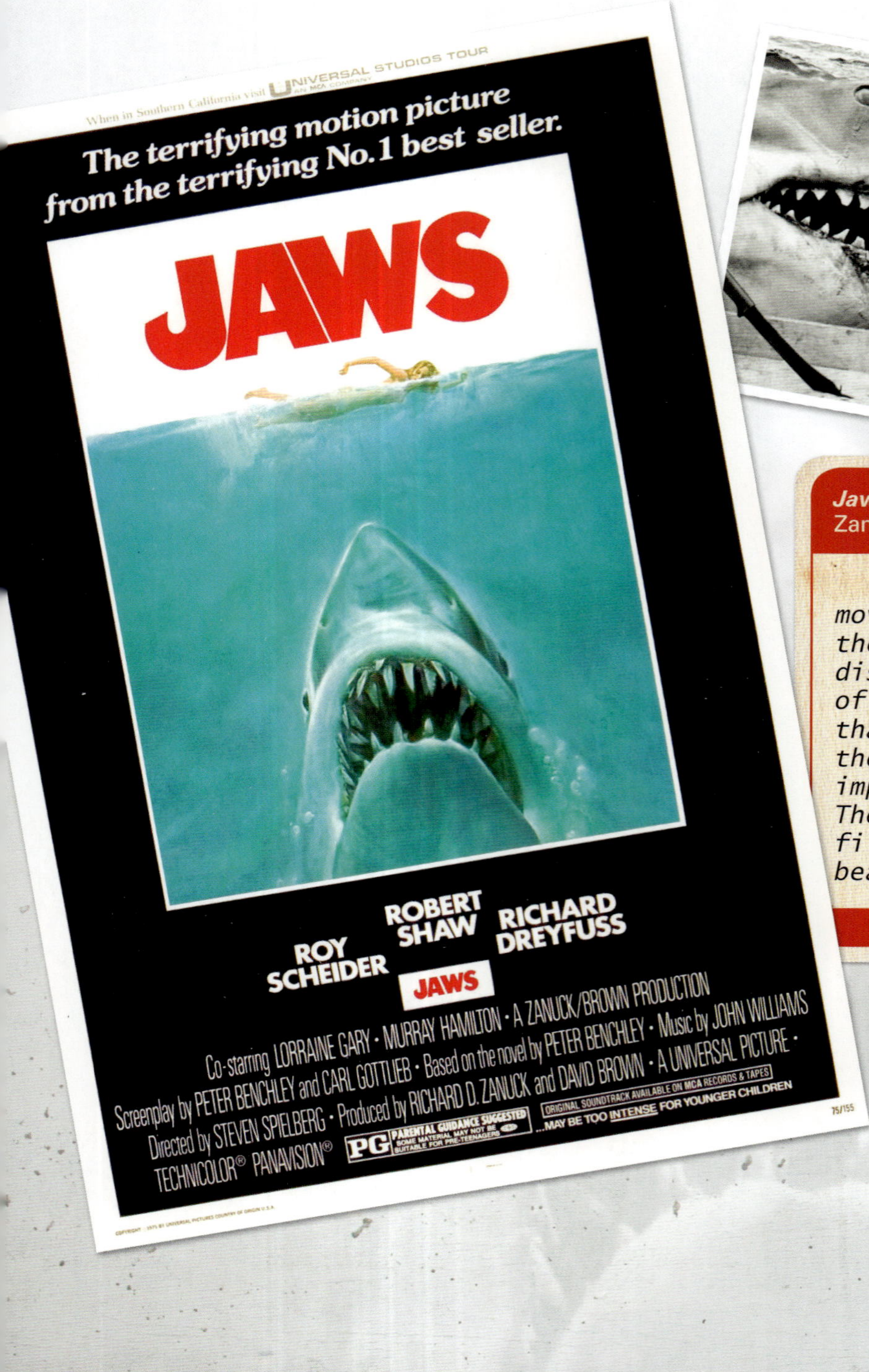

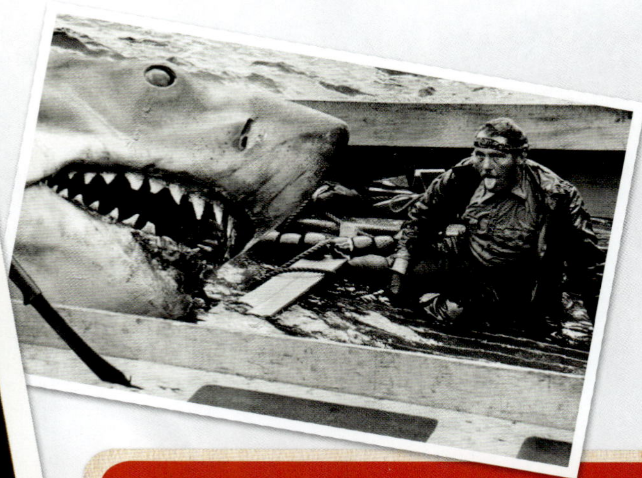

***Jaws*.**
Zanuck/Brown Productions/Universal Pictures (1975).

I was only fifteen when I saw this movie in the theaters after having read the Benchley novel. The scene where the disembodied head falls through the bottom of the sunken boat made me jump. The fact that this story could be true, and that the monster wasn't supernatural, gave it impact that other horror films couldn't. The cinematography is gorgeous and the film holds up nearly 40 years later as a beautifully plotted and executed film.

Bev Vincent

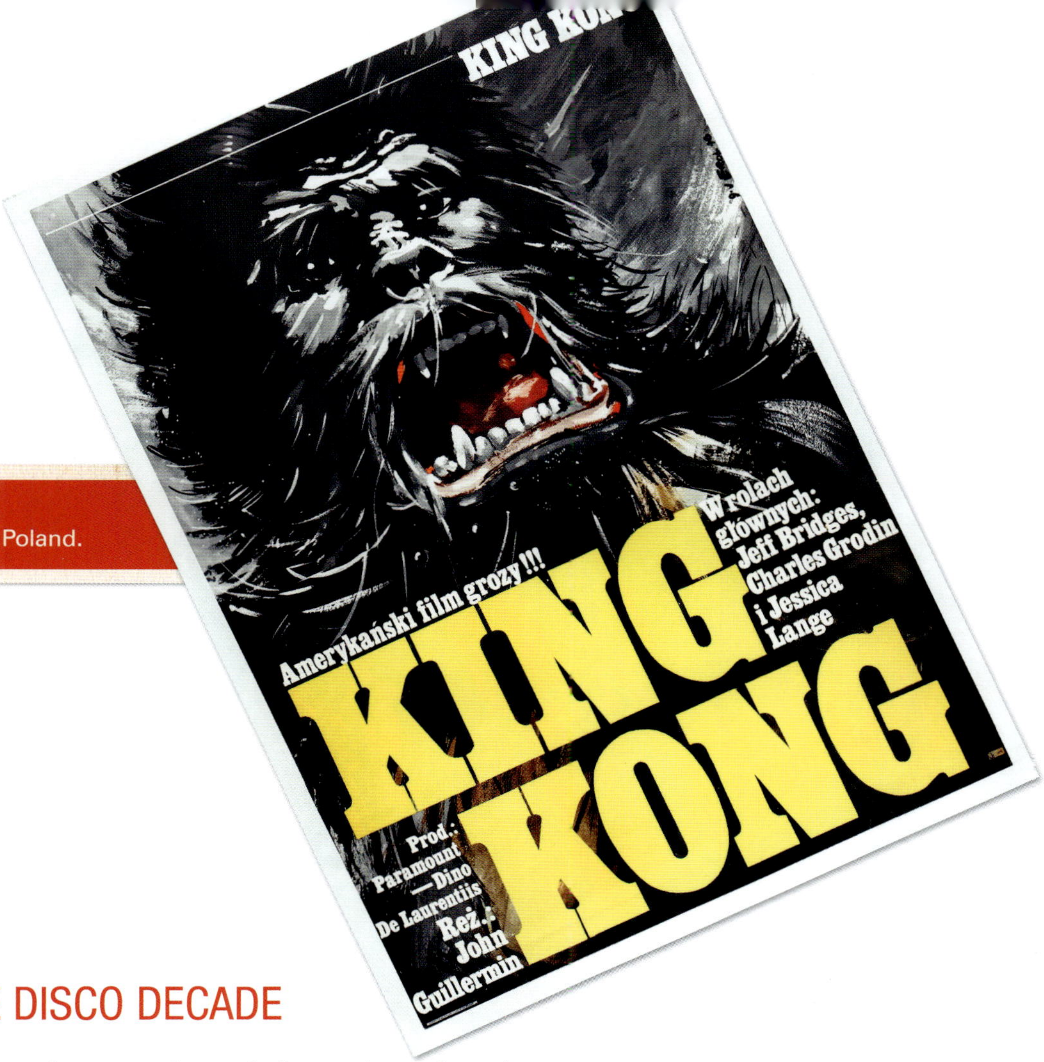

King Kong.
Dino De Laurentiis Company (1976). Poland.

ON **KING KONG** AND THE DISCO DECADE

When Dino De Laurentiis's remake was released, the purists winced at the alterations in established Kong lore, yet the bicentennial remake of *King Kong* proved an ideal reflection of the epoch in which it was produced. If 1933's original concerned American macho men adventurously taming nature with new technology (such as Denham's new gas grenades), the disco decade *King Kong* was colored by the 1970s energy crisis and failed international intervention in Vietnam. The original film's romantic attitude about exploration and American exceptionalism was supplanted by a tale of greed and exploitation, with Kong himself re-positioned as a natural resource to be used up and tossed out by a commercial culture in which everything is disposable. King Kong was no tiger in the tank, however, but rather a proud savage who would not bow to slavery, which in this case involved an oil company's desire to profit from his suffering.

~John Kenneth Muir

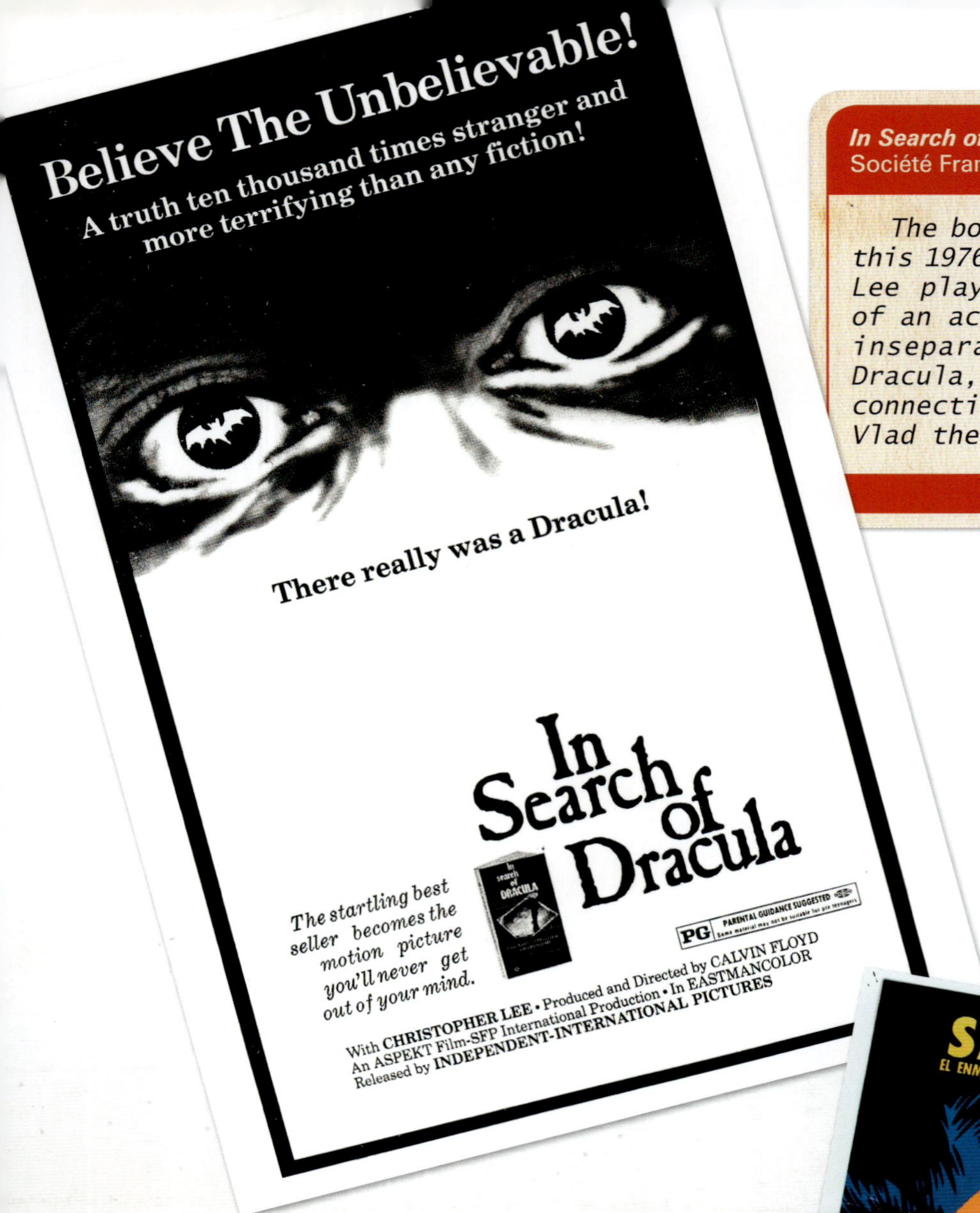

In Search of Dracula. Aspekt Telefilm-Produktion GmbH/ Société Française de Production (1974).

The book In Search of Dracula *inspired this 1976 documentary in which Christopher Lee played the role of Vlad. This use of an actor, who was at the time almost inseparable from the role of Count Dracula, served to cement the tenuous connection between Stoker's Count and Vlad the Impaler.*

Elizabeth Miller

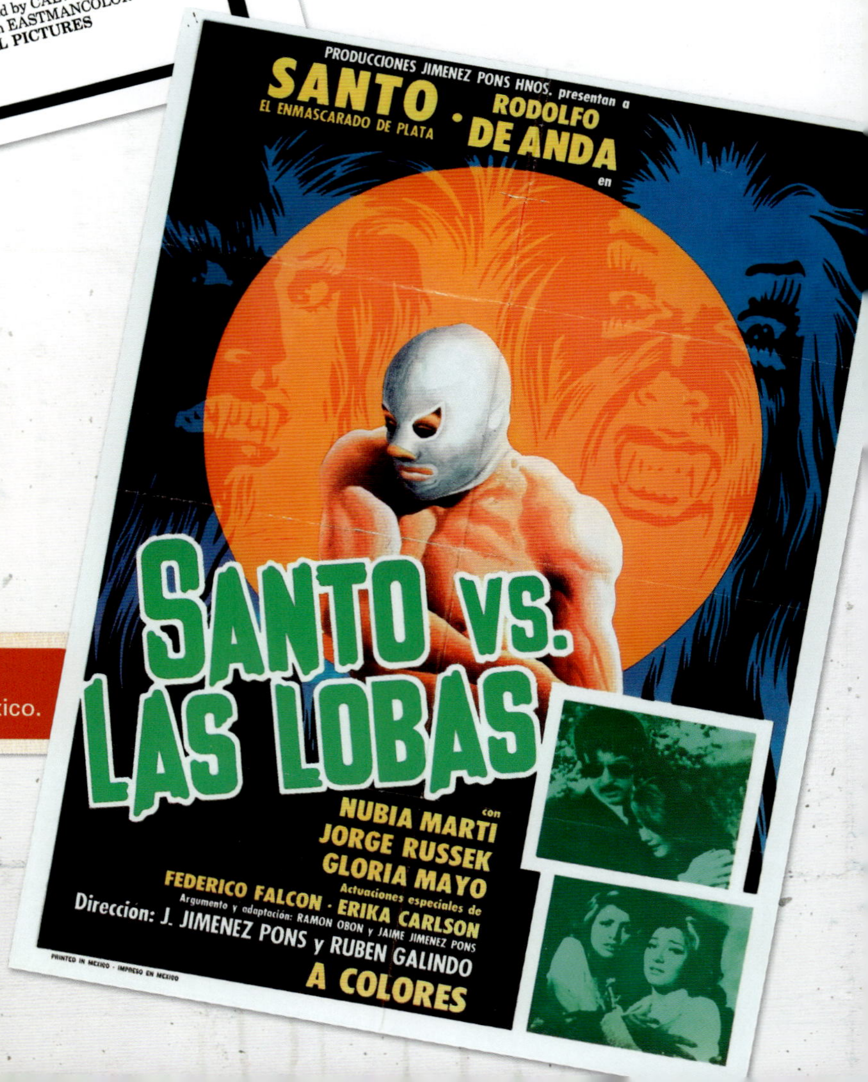

Santo vs. the She-Wolves.
Producciones Jiménez Pons Hermanos (1976). Mexico.

Carrie.
Redbank Films (1976). Spain.

Piper Laurie apparently treated the movie as if it was a comedy, which gives her performance a manic quality. If there's a monster in this movie, it's Margaret White, not Carrie, who is pitiful and pitiable until the moment where she unleashes her full power in retribution against all those who have persecuted her – her mother being the worst offender. The split-screen presentation of certain scenes might have been distracting, but it worked. The casting was all over the map, but De Palma extracted brilliant performances from everyone. "They're all going to laugh at you." How haunting is that? Every schoolgirl's worst nightmare.

Bev Vincent

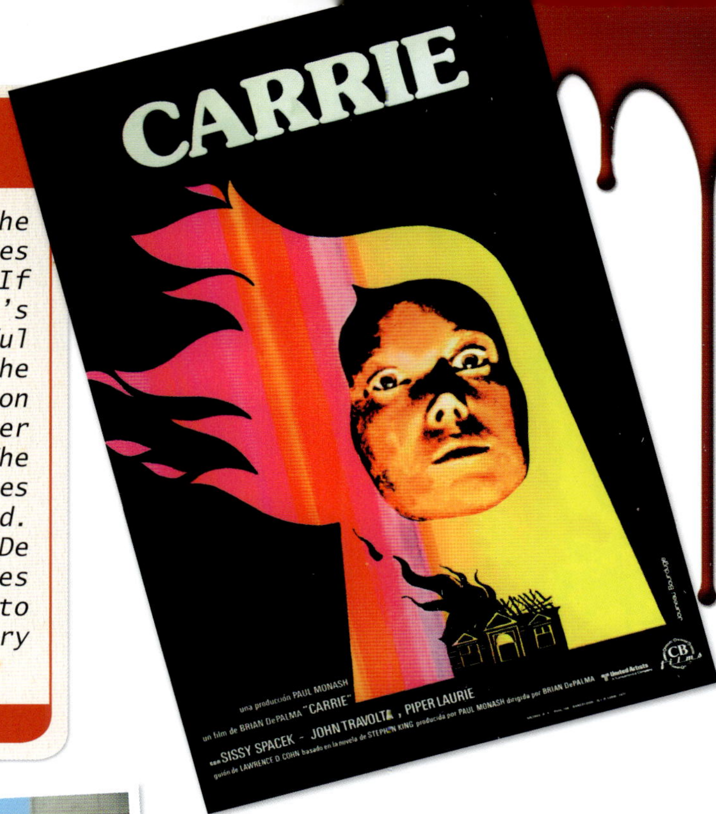

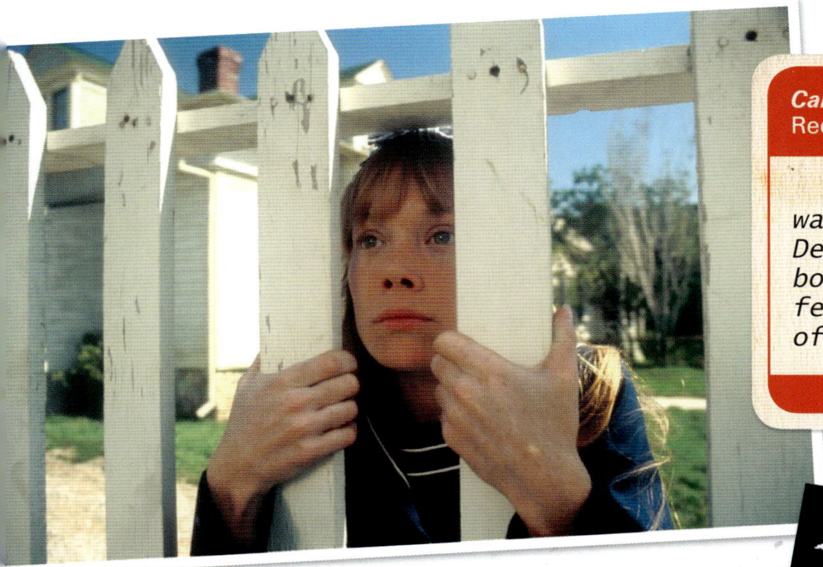

Carrie.
Redbank Films (1976).

One of the best Stephen King adaptations was also the first. And director Brian De Palma even improved on the original book! First time I witnessed full-frontal female nudity in a film. It was the talk of the school yard back in '76!

Tony Timpone

Carrie.
Redbank Films (1976). Japan.

I saw this during the 1970s on a double bill with Piranha. In those pre-video, DVD, and Internet days, it was still possible not to know about the shock ending. It is the only time in my life that I have witnessed an entire audience screaming in unison. But there is so much more to Carrie than its ending or its bravura visual style. Superb performances from Sissy Spacek and Piper Laurie give the film heart and pathos and make its drama as memorable as any of its shock effects.

Peter Hutchings

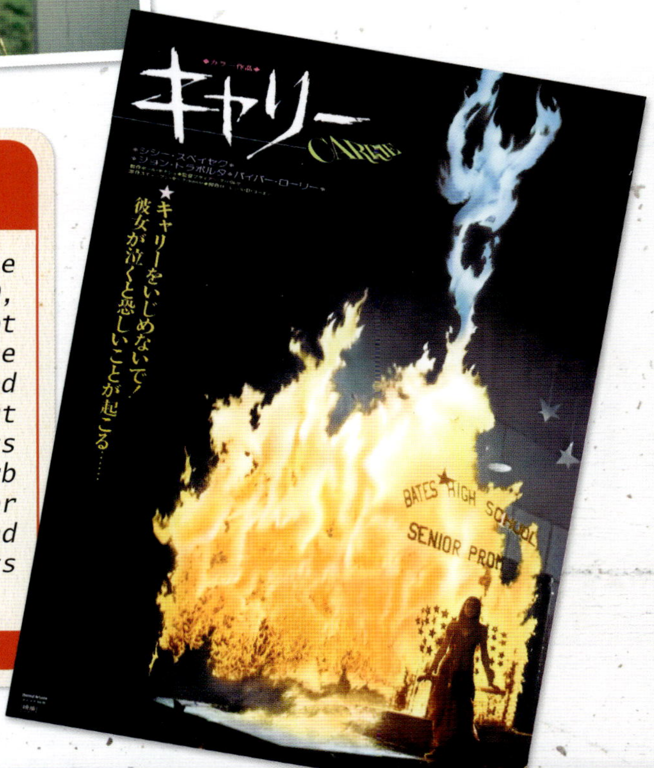

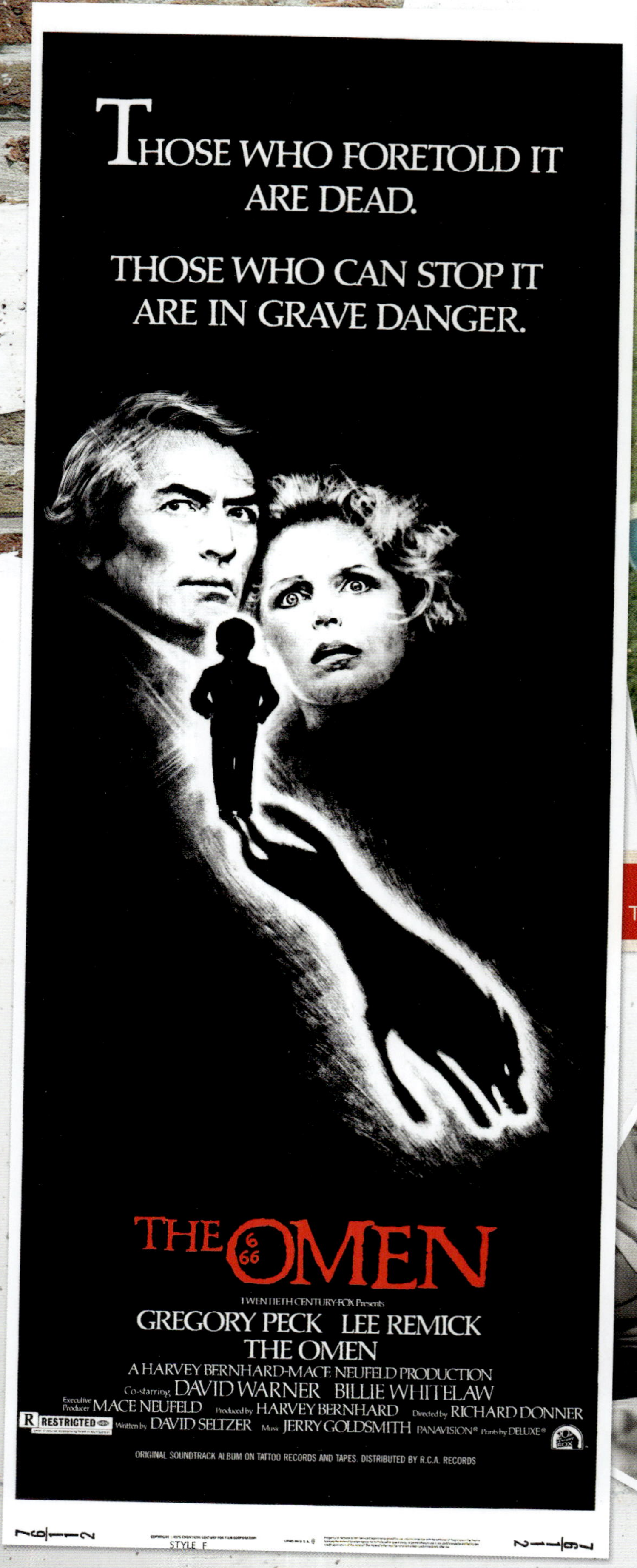

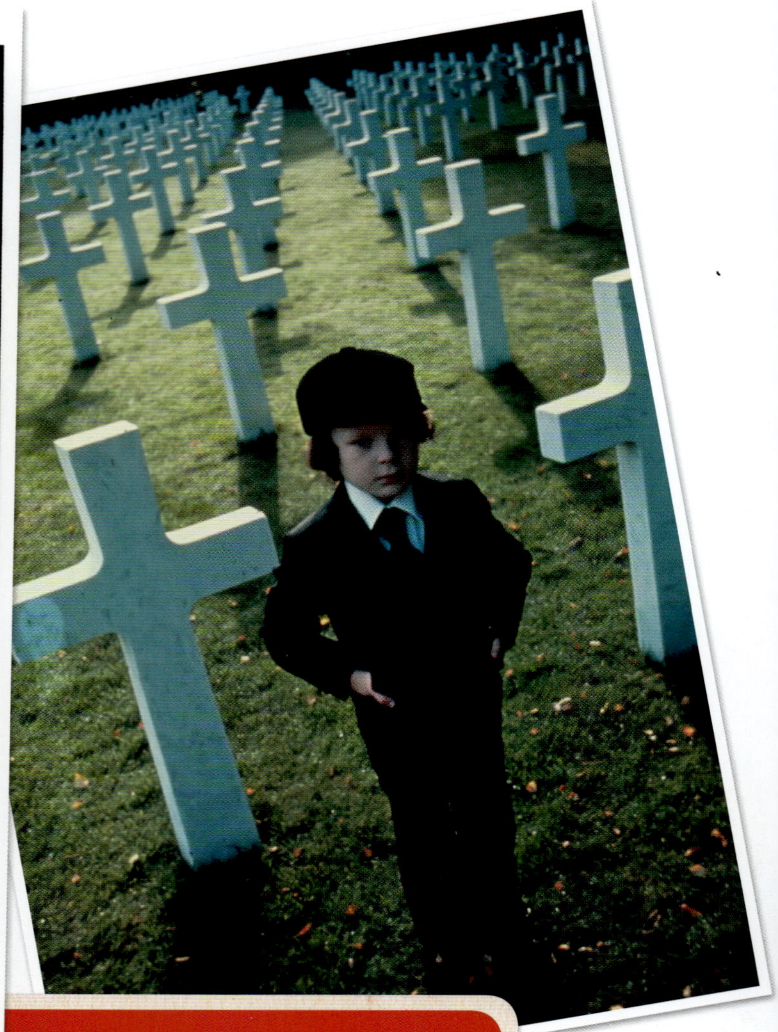

The Omen.
Twentieth Century-Fox Productions (1976).

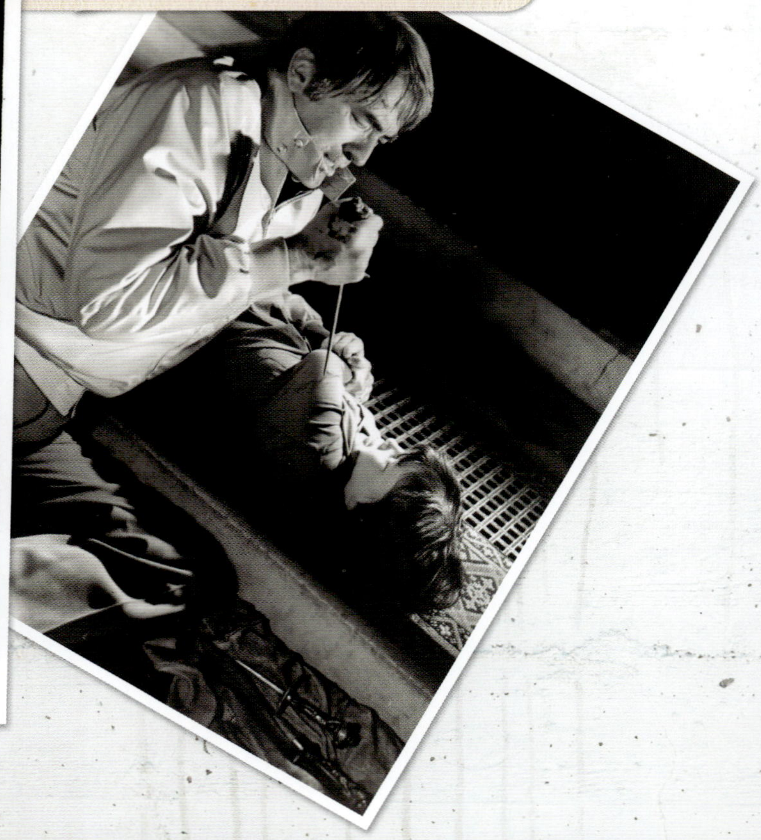

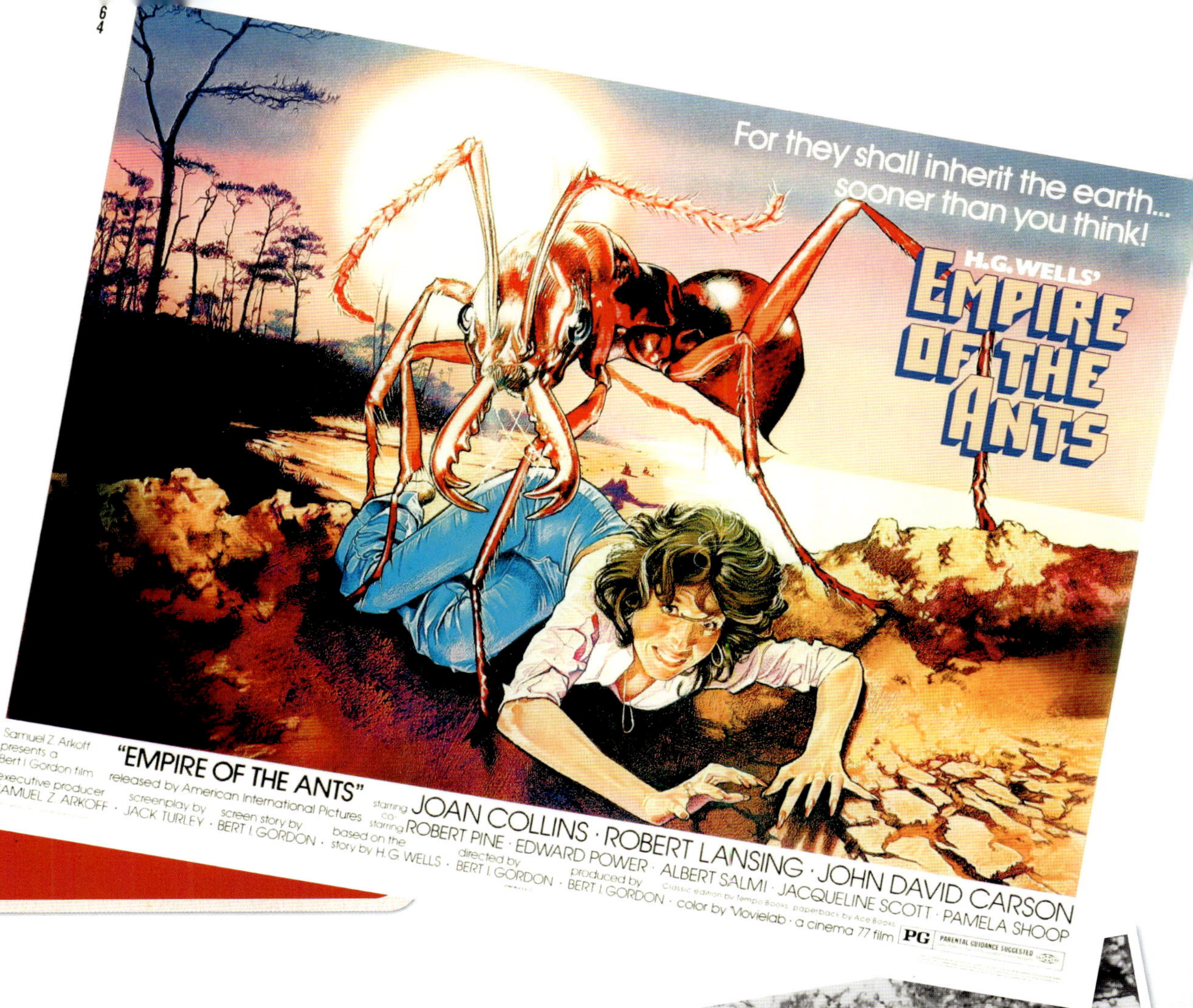

Empire of the Ants.
Cinema 77 (1977).

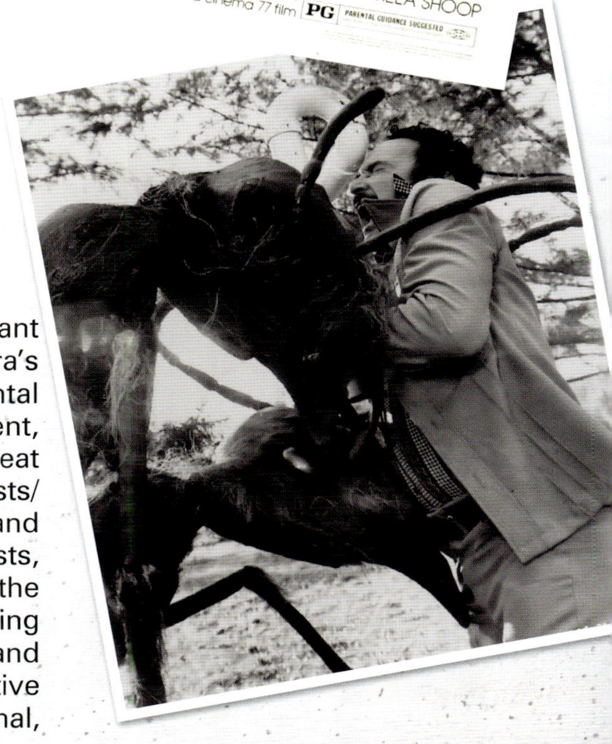

ON GIANT ANTS AND THE "ME GENERATION"

This film serves as a powerful and intriguing contrast to 1951's giant ant movie, *Them!* In *Them!*, atomic science opened up a Pandora's Box and created giant, menacing ants. Here, casual, accidental pollution of the environment is the culprit. In *Them!*, law enforcement, science, and government seamlessly combine forces to defeat the threat of the giant ants. In *Empire of the Ants*, a group of prospective capitalists/investors are imperiled by the insect attackers and it's every man and woman for himself. To put a finer point on the differences, the scientists, G-men, and police of the 1950s have become, in the disco decade of the 1970s, real estate con artists and divorced, dysfunctional people striving to get ahead financially; the common good be damned. Spouses and lovers often get abandoned and killed in *Empire of the Ants*, a negative portrait of the "me generation" when juxtaposed with the communal, cooperative nature of the giant ants.

~John Kenneth Muir

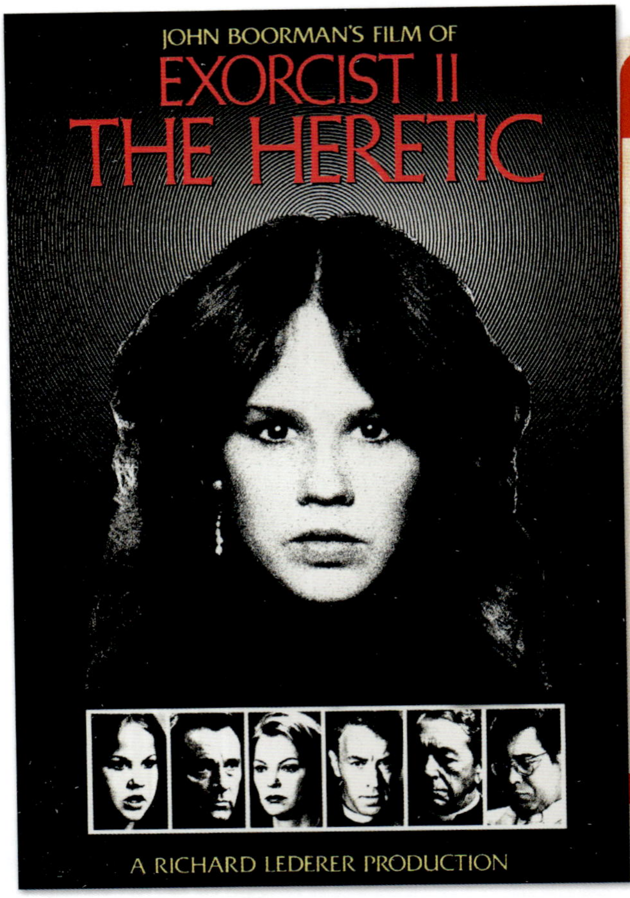

Exorcist II: The Heretic.
Warner Bros. Pictures (1977).

I came to this one as an adult, knowing that it routinely makes people's scariest-of-all-times lists. I was skeptical because it's about witches. Witches show up in movies all the time, but not in "serious" horror movies. Okay, maybe Rosemary's Baby, *but even as a kid, I thought that one was more interesting than scary. In* Suspiria, *an impish creature stabs a woman to death, and we see her beating heart violated by the knife in extreme close-up. A blind man's possessed guide dog rips out his throat. So THAT'S what an evil witch can do! In my early teens, I would rent horror movies so I could watch them at night and then again the next morning, when the viewing could be more objective. After a ten-year hiatus, I saw this movie, and the rental-repeat practice got resurrected.*

L. Andrew Cooper

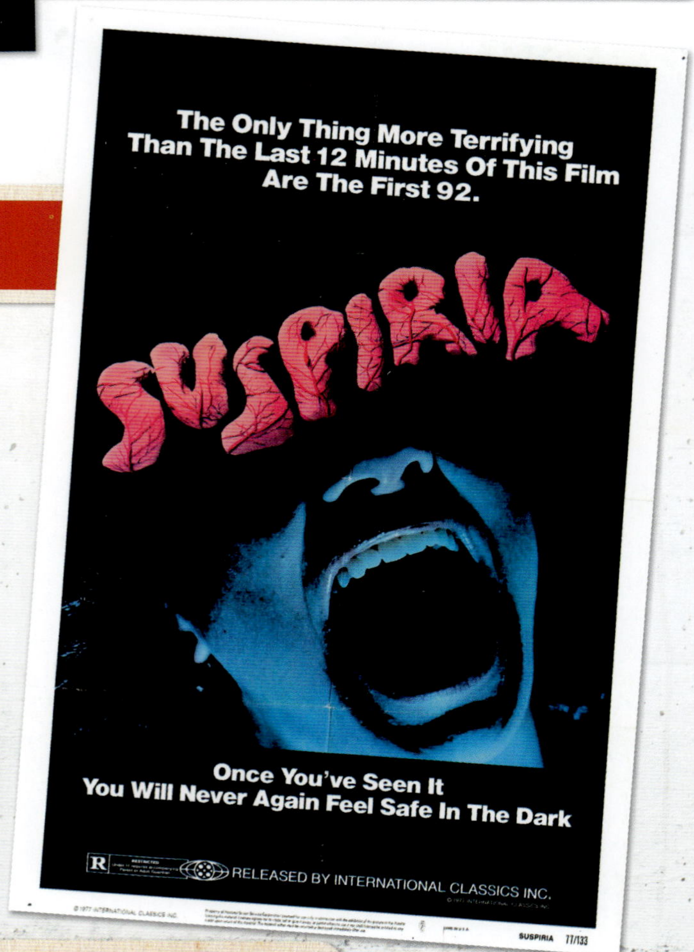

Suspiria.
Seda Spettacoli (1977).

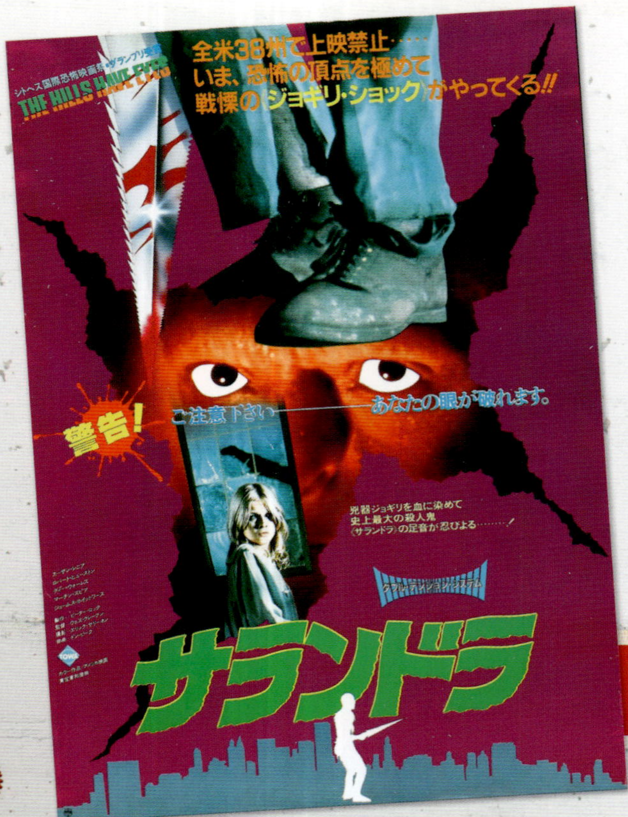

The Hills Have Eyes.
Blood Relations Co. (1977). Japan.

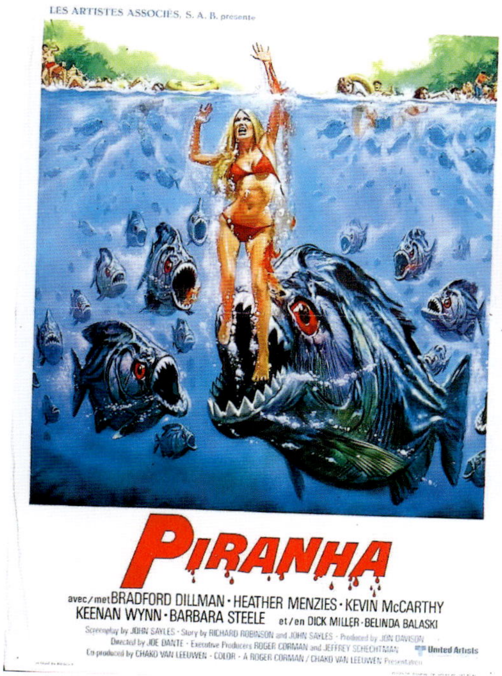

***Piranha*. New World Pictures (1978).**

***The Manitou*. Mid-America Pictures/Simon Productions/ Manitou Productions Ltd. (1978).**

This is not a very good film, at least in the conventional sense of that term, but it is hard for me to dislike it. It was the first horror film that I saw in the cinema, and I remember it being an enjoyable, lively and in places, a very silly introduction to the world of big-screen horror. It had energy and the director William Girdler – a low budget specialist who died in a helicopter crash before the film's release – managed to make the sets look more expansive than they probably were in reality. It is the sort of film that is often overlooked in histories of horror but which lingers in the memories of those who saw it when it first appeared.

Peter Hutchings

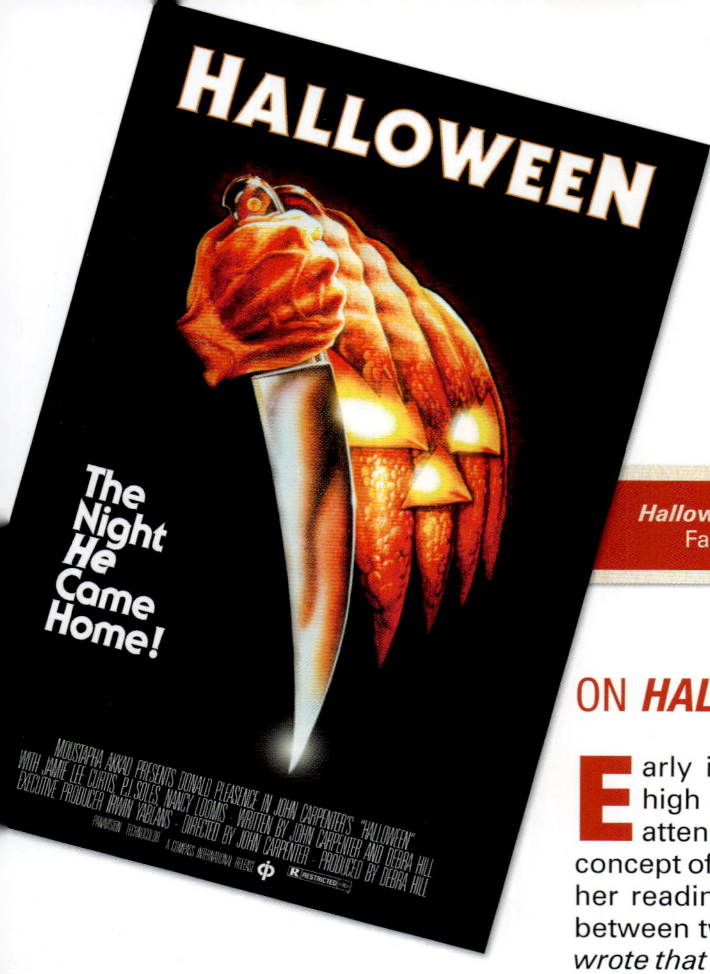

Halloween. Compass International Pictures, Falcon International Productions (1978).

ON *HALLOWEEN* (1978) AND THE ESSENCE OF EVIL

Early in *Halloween*, there is a fascinating if brief scene set in a high school English class. Laurie Strode (Jamie Lee Curtis) is in attendance, listening as an off-screen teacher drones on about the concept of fate in literature. The unseen instructor then asks Laurie about her reading assignment and Laurie answers by making a distinction between two authors, Samuels and Costaine. She notes that *"Costaine wrote that fate was only somehow related to religion, where Samuels felt that fate was like a natural element; like Earth, Air, Fire, and Water."*

The teacher further notes that Laurie is correct, that Samuels definitely *"personified"* fate. *"It [fate] stands"* where a *"man passes away."* Who else stands where a man passes away? *Michael Myers, of course,* a screen monster who survives stabbings and shootings and keeps on coming at you. John Carpenter's "Shape" is actually Fate "Personified" (as Samuels dictated) and you can't kill something like Earth, Air, Fire, or Water, can you? This revelation of Michael Myers as Agent of Fate opens up the whole "Boogeyman" Argument — that perhaps there is actually a fifth element in nature: Earth, Air, Fire, Water ... And *Evil*.

~John Kenneth Muir

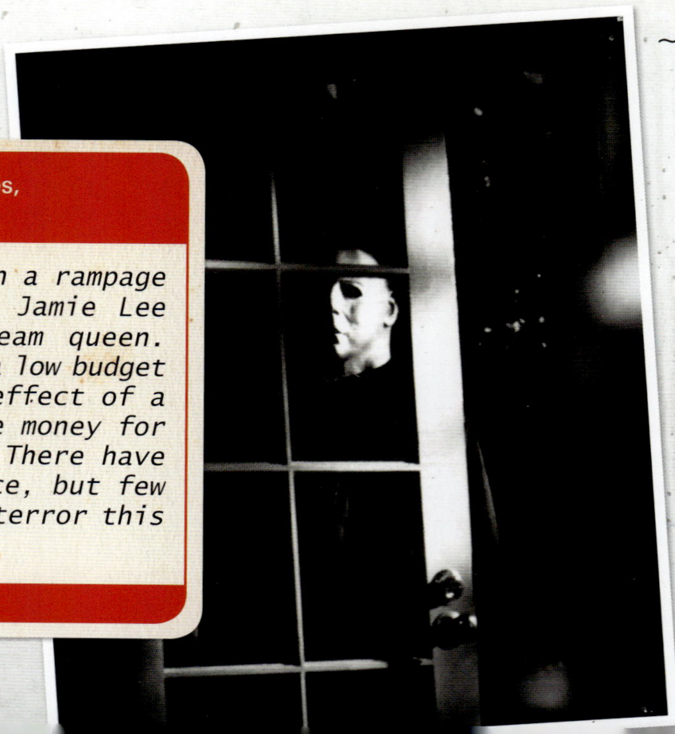

Halloween. Compass International Pictures, Falcon International Productions (1978).

Captain Kirk [mask] goes on a rampage and terrorizes a very young Jamie Lee Curtis as the original scream queen. What's not to love? Sometimes a low budget enhances the claustrophobic effect of a film because they didn't have money for larger, more elaborate sets. There have been many slasher movies since, but few have captured the legitimate terror this movie invokes.

Bev Vincent

Dawn of the Dead.
Laurel Group (1978). Spain.

As soon as I saw the hands coming through the elevator doors on the television commercial, I couldn't stop thinking of this movie. I was like the kid in A Christmas Story bugging his parents for a BB gun. Romero's using the two nauseating bloodbaths in the apartment building and the mall to bracket the central section of ennui and purposelessness is one of the most brilliant works of pacing and suspense I've ever seen.

Kim Paffenroth

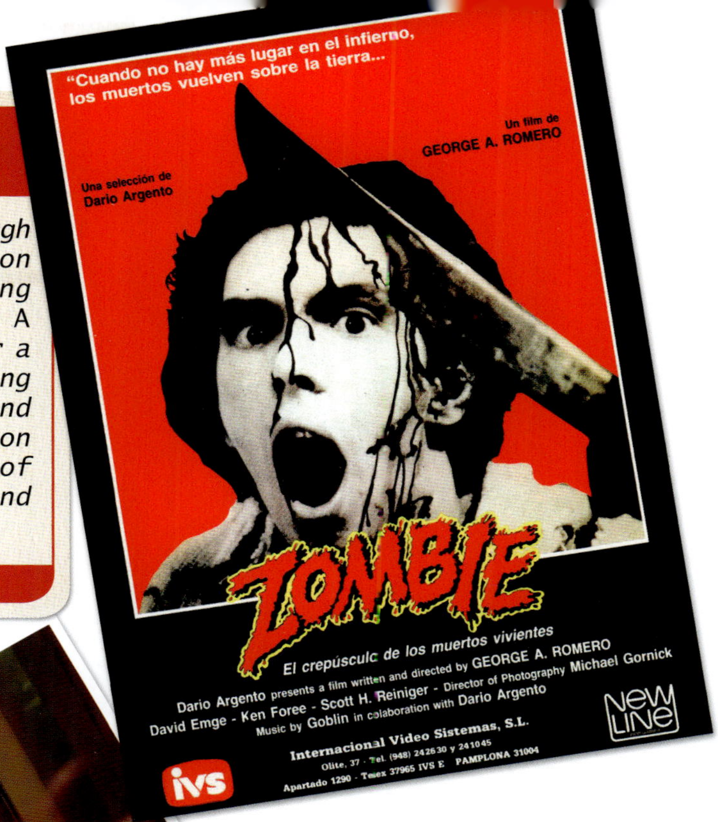

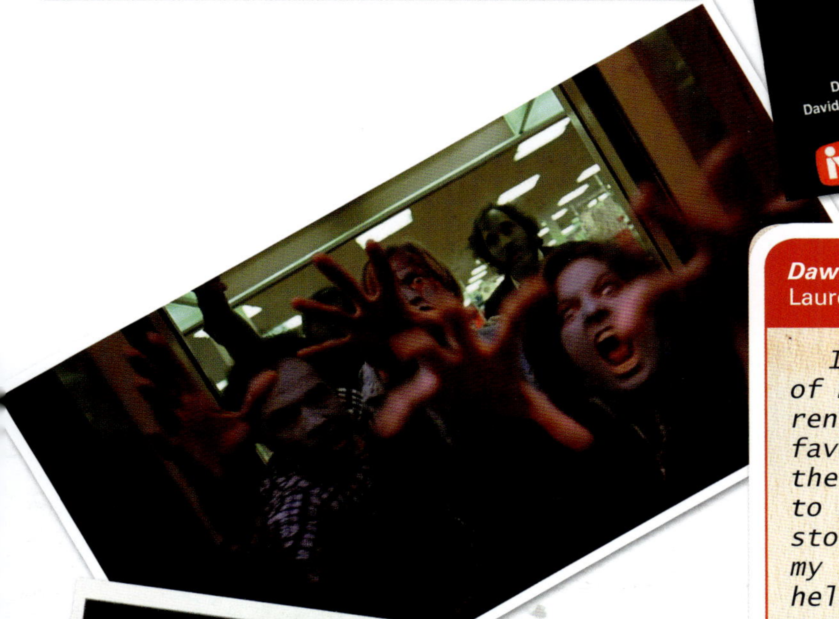

Dawn of the Dead.
Laurel Group (1978).

I didn't see this one until the advent of relatively inexpensive VCRs and movie rental, but it quickly became a personal favorite. Without having read much on the subject, I immediately caught on to what Romero was doing by setting the story in a bland shopping mall. By far my favorite scene is the one where the helicopter blade takes off the top of a zombie's head. I don't know how many times we rewound that tape to watch the scalp rocket out of frame like a Frisbee.

Bev Vincent

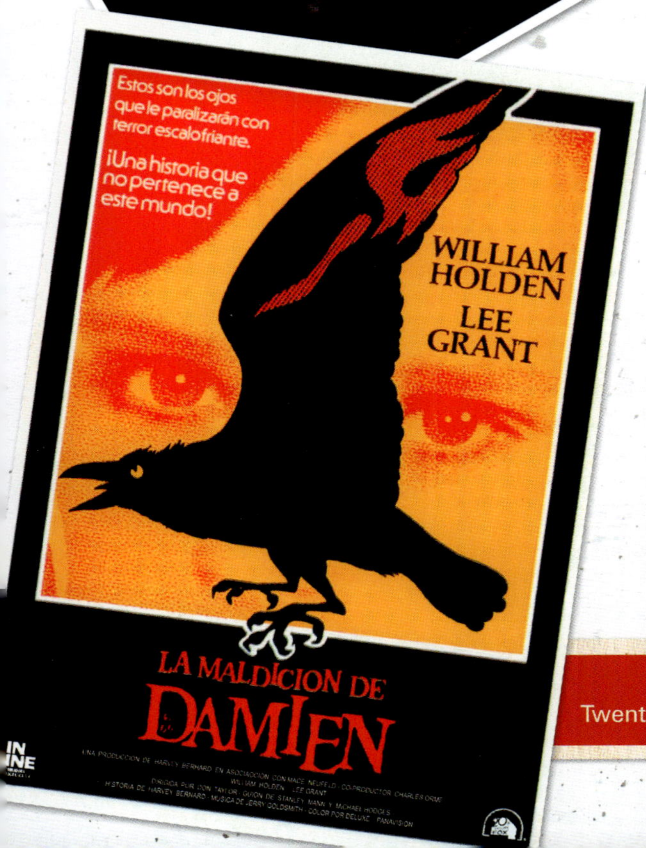

Damien Omen II.
Twentieth Century Fox Film Corporation (1978). Spain.

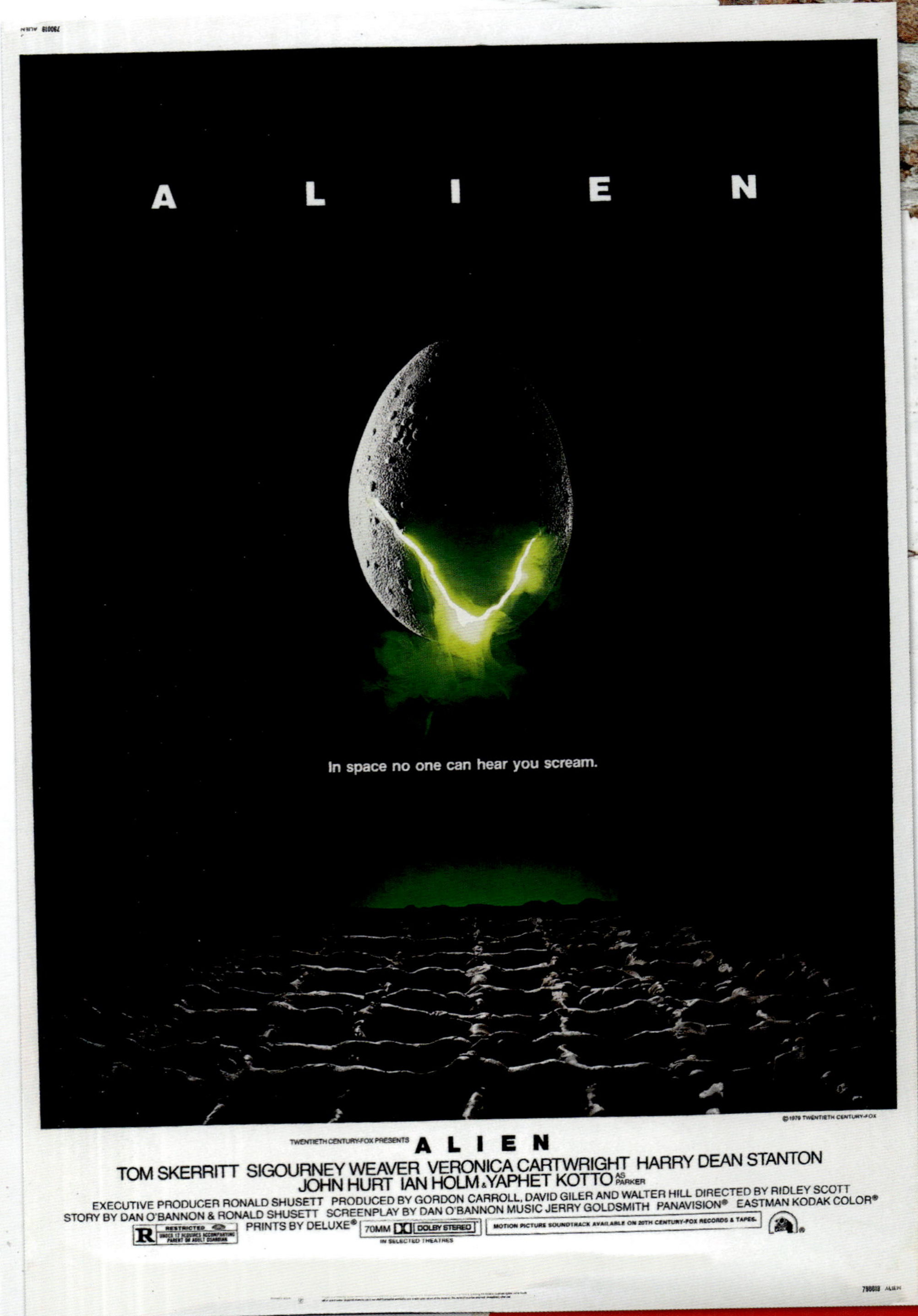

Alien. Brandywine Productions/ Twentieth Century-Fox Productions (1979).

Modern CGI techniques make gruesome monsters far easier to produce, and have put a long distance between post-Alien monster movies and their predecessors, which now have to rely on aesthetic effects like camp and kitsch for much of their appeal, but some of the more understated monsters of earlier cinema could be very effective in context.

Brian Stableford

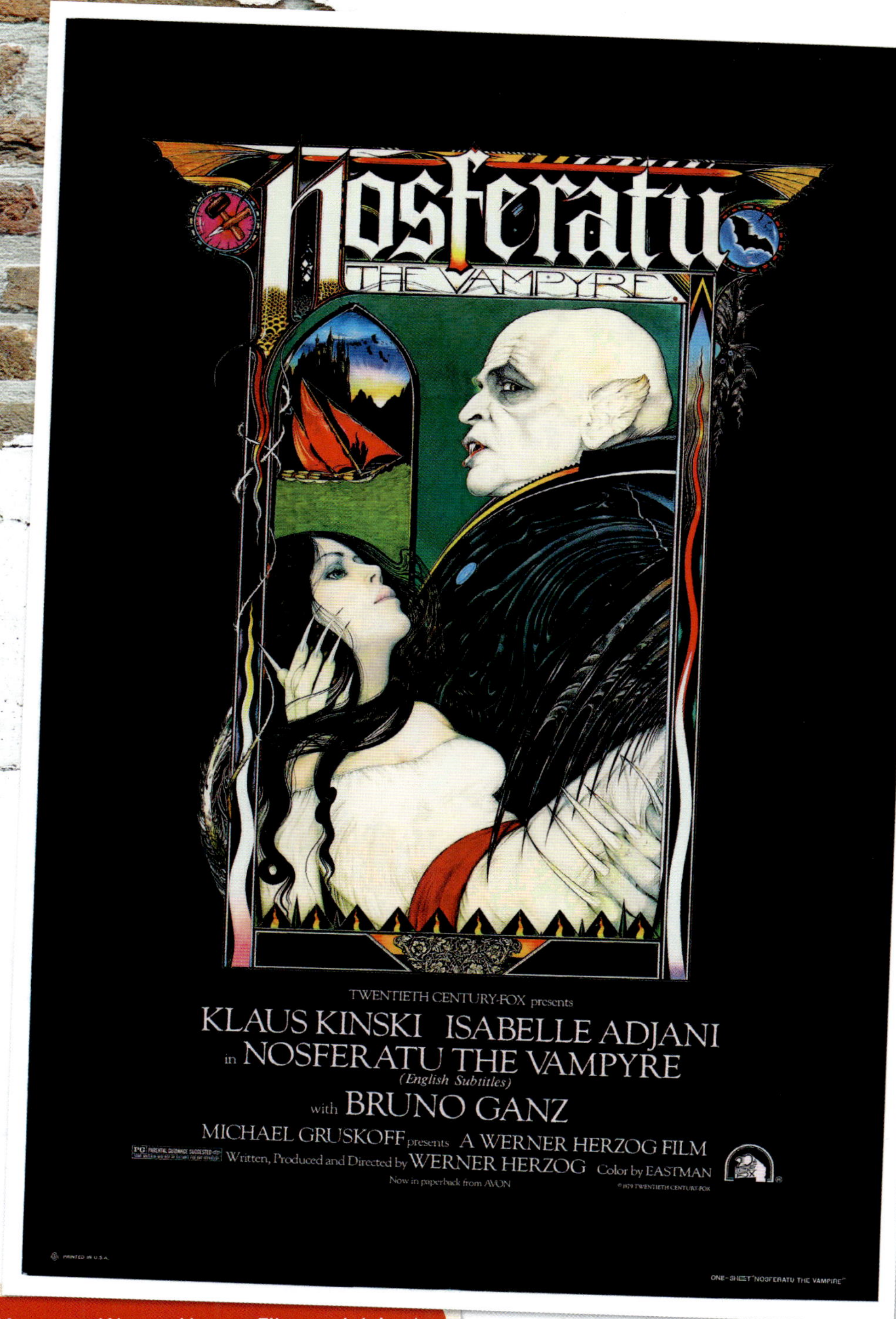

Nosferatu the Vampyre. Werner Herzog Filmproduktion/Gaumont/Zweites Deutsches Fernsehen (1979).

Werner Herzog's remake of the 1922 Prana Film classic is one of the few remakes of horror films that can stand on its own as a gripping experience. Klaus Kinksi looks like a reincarnation of Max Schreck. My favorite scene is when the plague-bearing rats stream out through town, an unholy event juxtaposed against one of the holiest of musical compositions, "Sanctus" from Gounod's "Mass of St. Cecilia." It made me a fan!

Rosemary Ellen Guiley

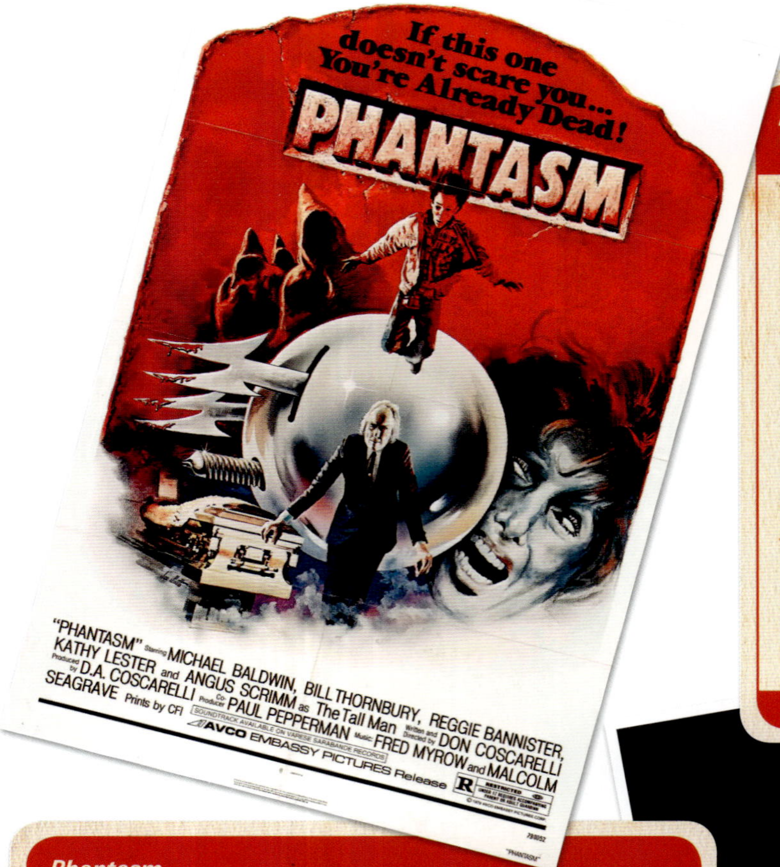

***Phantasm*.**
New Breed Productions Inc. (1979).

This low-budget film functions best if interpreted as the subconscious fantasy of a lonely, adolescent kid attempting to make sense of all the death he sees around him, both in his town and in his immediate family. The Tall Man and his minions symbolize evil, but evil as viewed by a child, both a little scary and a little silly too. As human beings, we construct mythologies and religion around our mortality, and Phantasm *gets at that notion better than just about any horror film ever made. It's the bad dream of a kid who wakes up one day to realize that life is full of death, and that there are no do-overs.*

John Kenneth Muir

***Phantasm*.**
New Breed Productions Inc. (1979).

I saw this on VHS in a dark dormitory room about five years after its release. I don't remember a lot about this movie other than the flying "sneetches," but I recall it as being a terrifically effective horror film despite its obvious low budget.

Bev Vincent

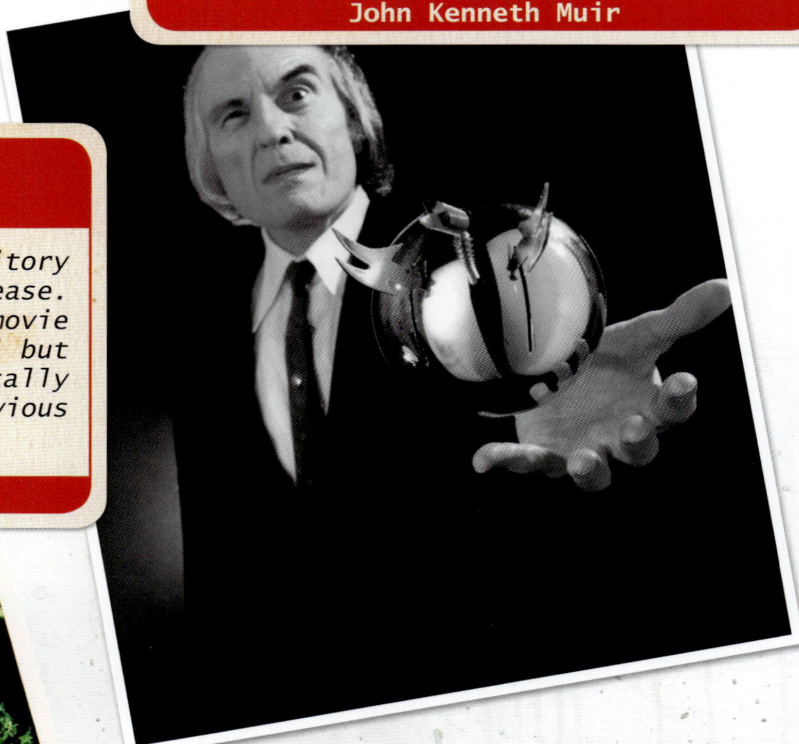

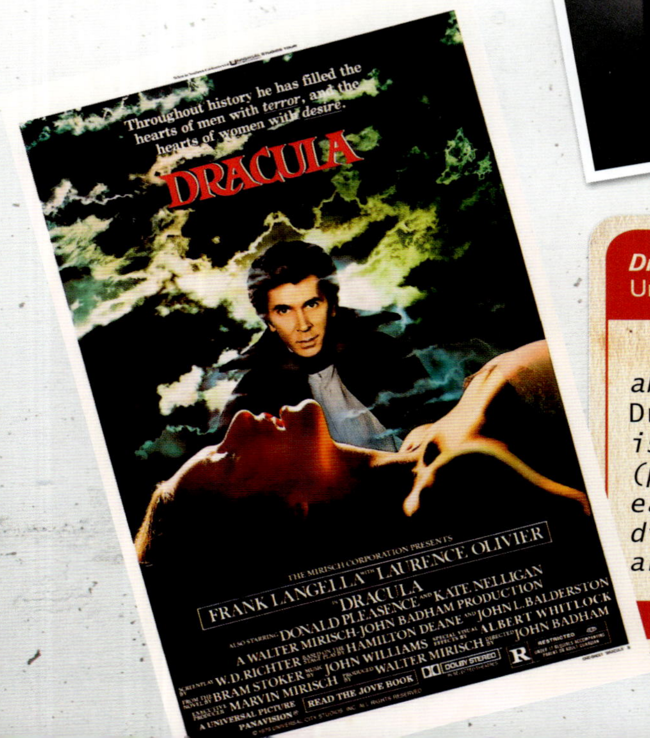

***Dracula*.**
Universal Pictures/The Mirisch Corporation (1979).

One of the most disgusting things about John Badham's interpretation of Dracula *is the film's orality. Not only is Dracula a bloodsucker, but Dr. Seward (played by Donald Pleasance) is always eating something, making it rather difficult to discern who the monsters are in this film.*

Carol A. Senf

The Brood. (left)
Canadian Film Development Corporation/
Elgin International Films Ltd./Mutual Productions Ltd./
Victor Solnicki Productions (1979).

Salem's Lot. (right)
Warner Bros. Television (1979). Spain.

The director who has impressed me most with his genre work is David Cronenberg, whose early movies developed a tremendous sense of creepiness without overmuch reliance on special effects. They Came from Within *is a masterpiece, aptly followed up by* Rabid *and* The Brood, *and* Videodrome *is brilliantly surreal – after which, I think, he lost something of his initial perversity and almost all of his edginess.*

Brian Stableford

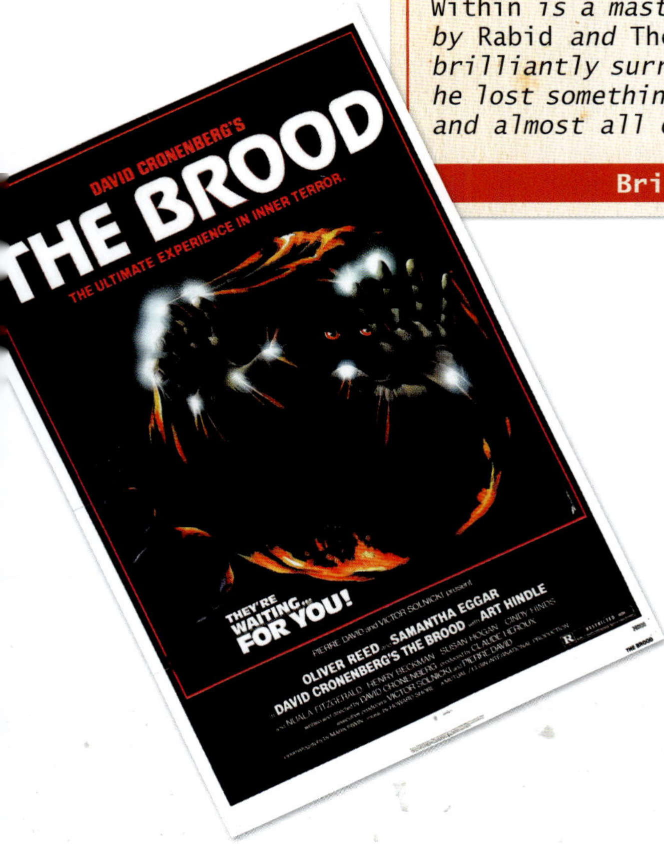

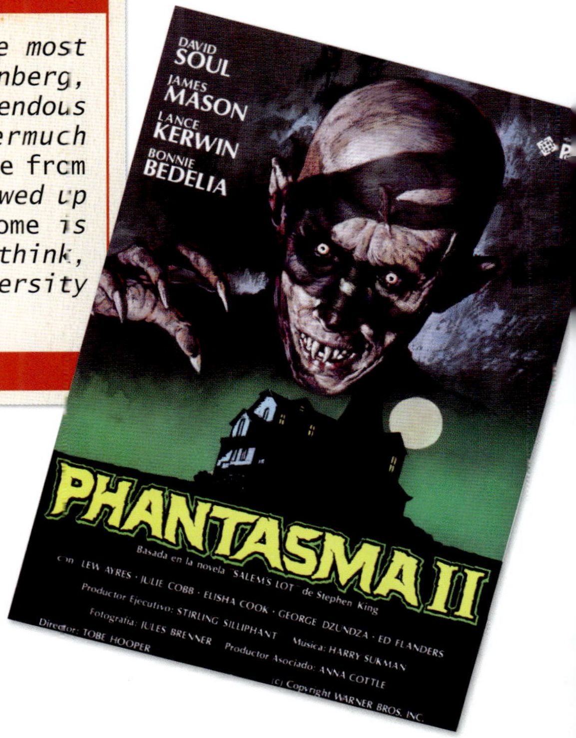

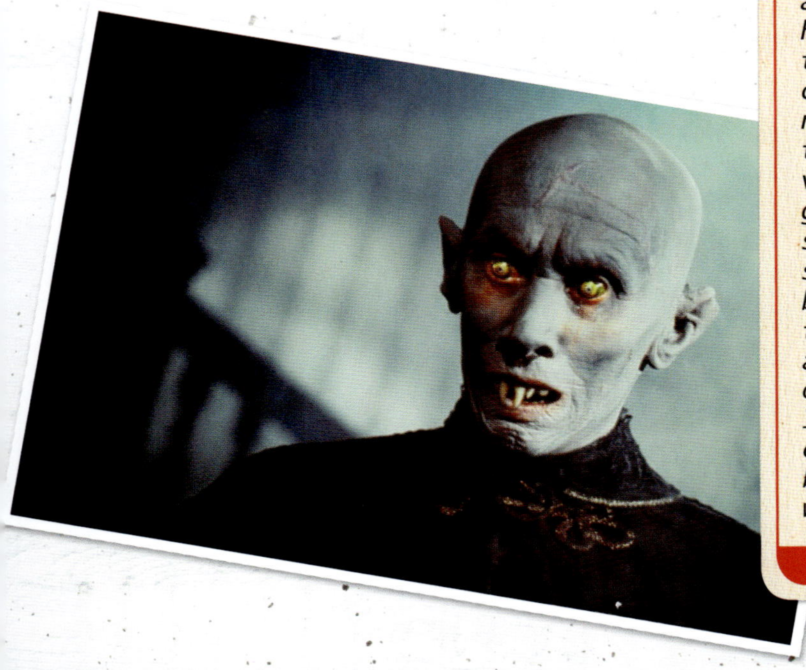

Salem's Lot.
Warner Bros. Television (1979).

The decision to turn Barlow into a mute Nosferatu clone was questioned at the time, but it gave James Mason a bigger role as Barlow's familiar and he was definitely the best thing about this TV miniseries. His dapper, urbane charismatic character and his neater than neat antiques shop is in sharp contrast to the ruined decay of Marsten House. The version now available on DVD has a few gory, explicit scenes that couldn't be shown on TV, most notably the impalement scene. Ralphie Glick hovering outside the bedroom window scratching and tapping on the glass gave me the creeps at the time and it remains the most effective part of this somewhat toothless adaptation. It's definitely representative of its era and it hasn't aged all that well, but for its time and given the medium it wasn't terrible.

Bev Vincent

City of the Living Dead. Dania Film/ Medusa Distribuzione/National Cinematografica (1980).

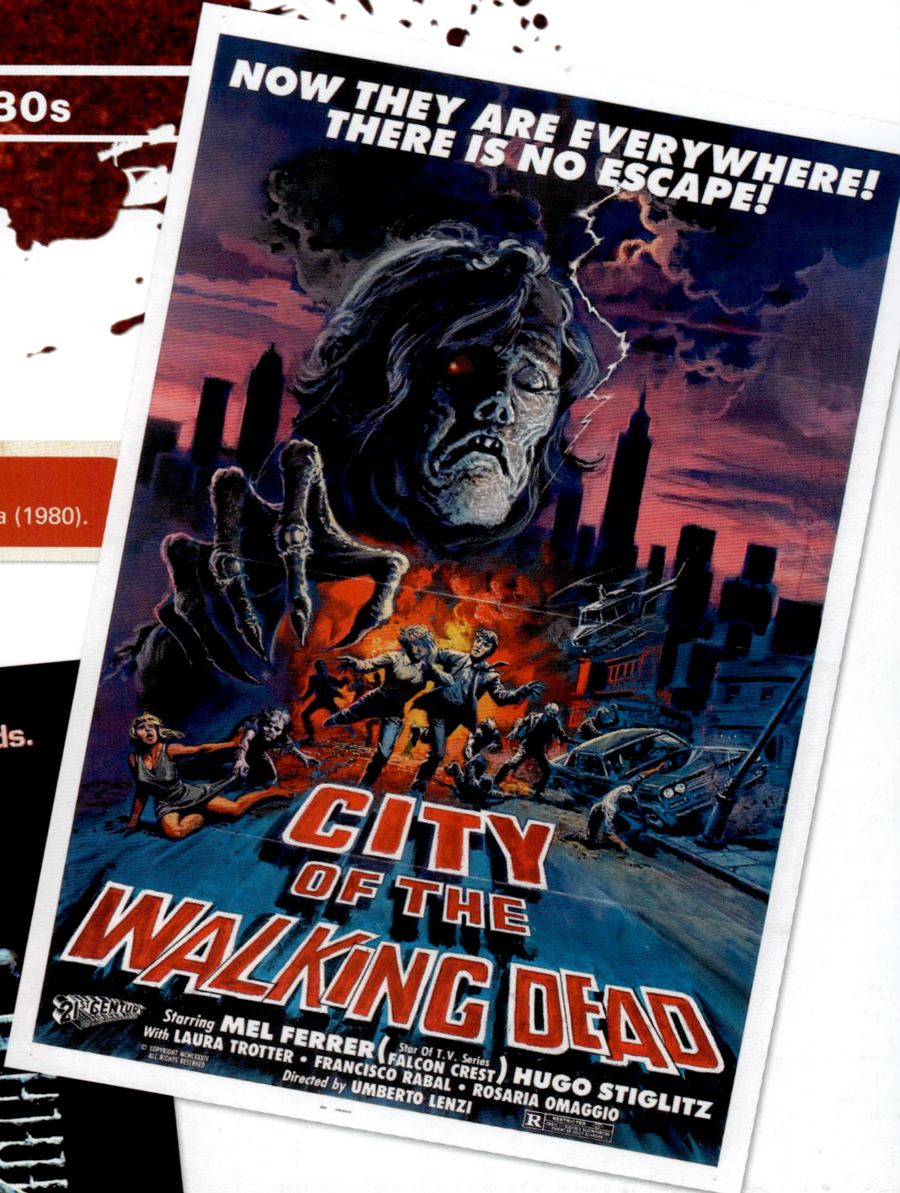

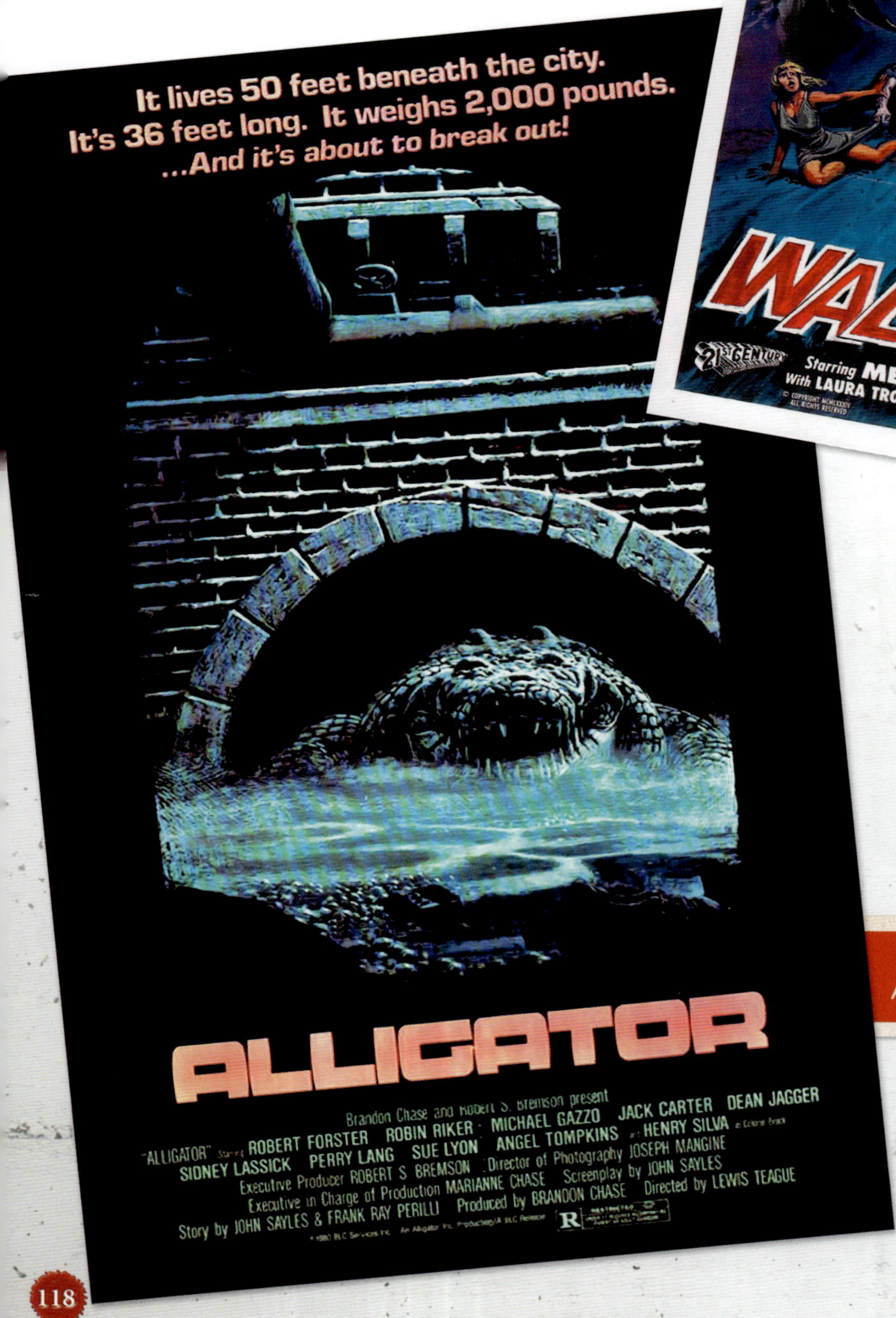

Alligator. Alligator Inc. (1980).

***Friday the 13th*.** Paramount Pictures/Georgetown Productions Inc./Sean S. Cunningham Films (1980). Japan.

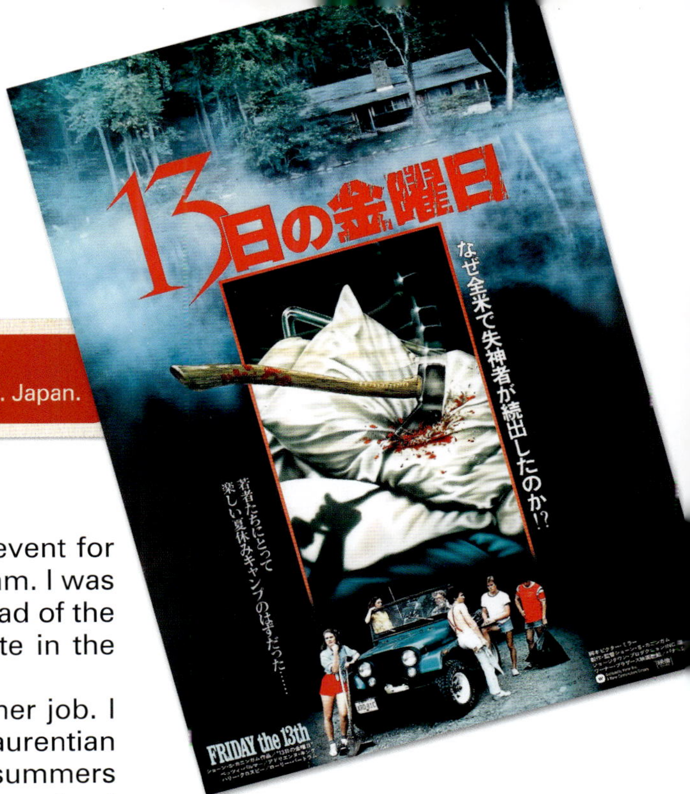

ON CAMP JITTERS AND ***FRIDAY THE 13TH***

In late April of 1980, I finished second in a final selection event for the 1980 Canadian Olympic team and was named to the team. I was elated, but it was very anticlimactic. Canada followed the lead of the US and many other Western nations in refusing to participate in the Olympic Games due to the Russian invasion of Afghanistan.

In early May, I headed home to Montreal seeking a summer job. I found a job as a waterfront Director at a summer camp in the Laurentian Mountains, north of Montreal. Wonderful memories of a few summers spent as a camper were rekindled. To celebrate the new job, I went out to dinner and a movie with a few friends. We chose the newly released *Friday the 13th*. I had no idea what I was in for. Little did I know that the story line was going to coincide so much with the next few weeks of my life! The movie was great; for the next week all I could think about were these hormonally charged counselors sneaking off for some private liaisons during pre-camp, only to be brutally murdered. The remote and rustic nature of the camp where the counselors were killed was very similar to where I would be spending my summer, and this made me feel even more vulnerable. Beyond the normal, natural creatures that went bump in the night, now we had to deal with Jason's mother who could open doors and stalk her victims, I remember thinking. She just seemed to appear when you would least expect it.

When all the counselors arrived at Camp Pine Valley for our own training, we raised during the first night's bonfire that many had also recently seen *Friday the 13th* and were equally as affected by the movie as I was. As we recounted the scary parts of the movie, one of the camp Directors snuck off from the group. At just the right moment he jumped out of the woods completely covered in mud, into the circle next to the Bonfire, and scared us all to death; we all screamed, and a few even wet their pants. Apparently, the camp Director saw the movie, too!

~Dacre Stoker

***Friday the 13th*.** Paramount Pictures/Georgetown Productions Inc./Sean S. Cunningham Films (1980).

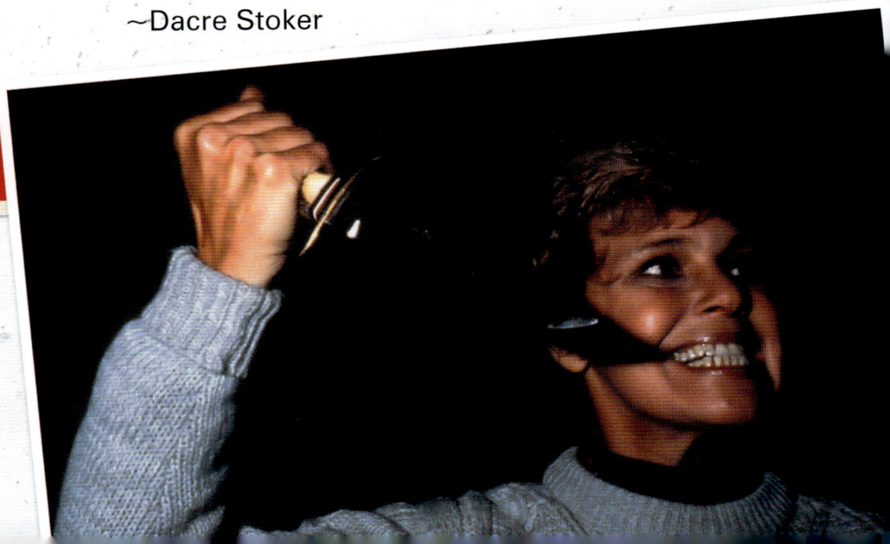

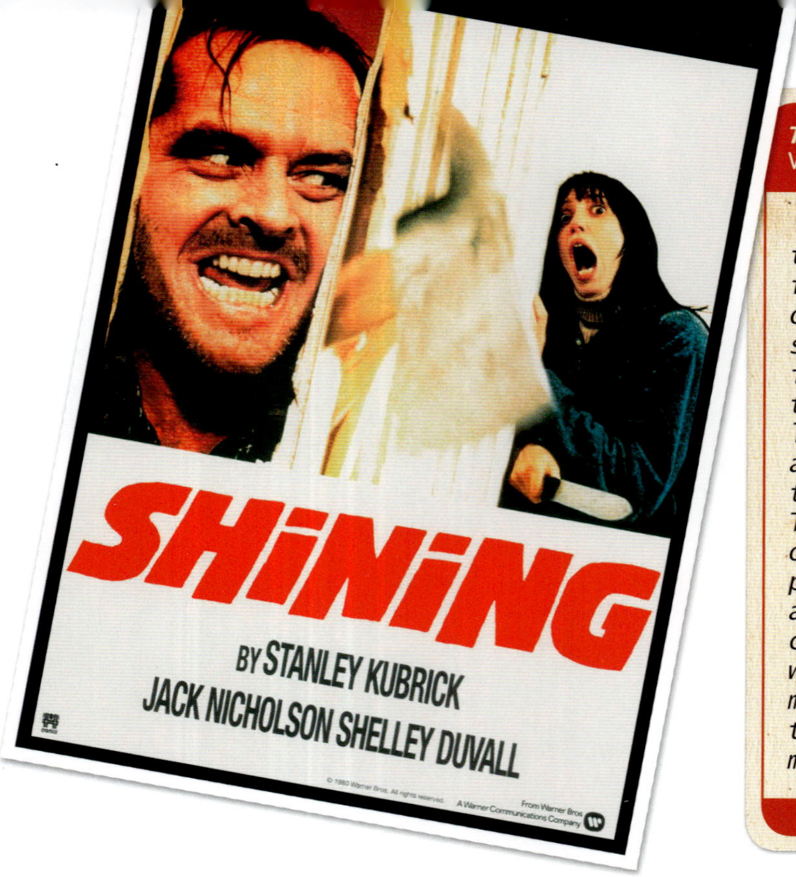

The Shining.
Warner Bros. Pictures/Hawk Films/Peregrine (1980).

I saw Kubrick's horror film in the week that I arrived at university to study film; it became my favorite horror film on the spot and has remained so ever since. From the disorientating thrill of its extraordinary opening shot through to the enigmatic conclusion, it felt like a rich and intense expression of all that was wonderful not just about the horror genre but about cinema itself. The brilliant visual and aural evocation of the haunted hotel, alongside note-perfect performances from Jack Nicholson and Shelley Duvall, are expertly choreographed by one of the few directors who can genuinely be thought of as a master. I have now seen The Shining *many times; it remains as enthralling and as mysterious as ever.*

Peter Hutchings

ON **KING vs. KUBRICK**

A very polarizing film. If you're in the King camp, you might hate the fact that Nicholson's Jack Torrance seems crazy from the very first frame of film. However, if you can separate the movie from the source material, you can appreciate this film for the work of art it is. The cinematography is gorgeous and it is filled with "Easter eggs." Have you noticed the bloody handprint on the woman's rear during the ballroom scene? You have to watch it in slow motion to catch it, but it's there! So many iconic shots: those demonic twin girls. The elevator filled with blood. The cadence of Danny's Big Wheel tricycle going down the long corridor, sometimes on hardwood, sometimes on carpet. The woman in the bathtub, of course. It says a lot about a movie that it can imprint memories on the book that aren't there. Jack's novel, consisting of "All work and no play" over and over again is a construct of the film — it doesn't appear in King's book. "Here's Johnny" — again, purely Kubrick. It has some problems (Why bring Dick Halloran back all that way just to kill him the minute he steps into the hotel?), but it is a great movie. A poor adaptation, but a terrific movie.

~Bev Vincent

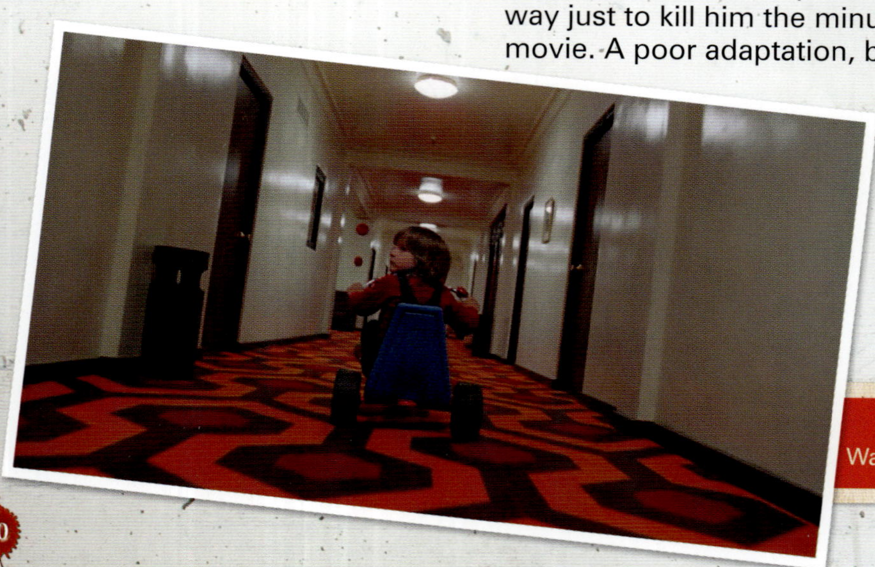

The Shining.
Warner Bros. Pictures/Hawk Films/Peregrine (1980).

The Shining. Warner Bros. Pictures/ Hawk Films/Peregrine (1980). Russia.

There is at least one psychologically frightening moment in Stanley Kubrick's The Shining, *when the camera shows us what its deeply disturbed protagonist has been writing. But* The Shining *does not make my personal list because Jack Nicholson's way-over-the-top hamming scuttled it for me.*

Marvin Kaye

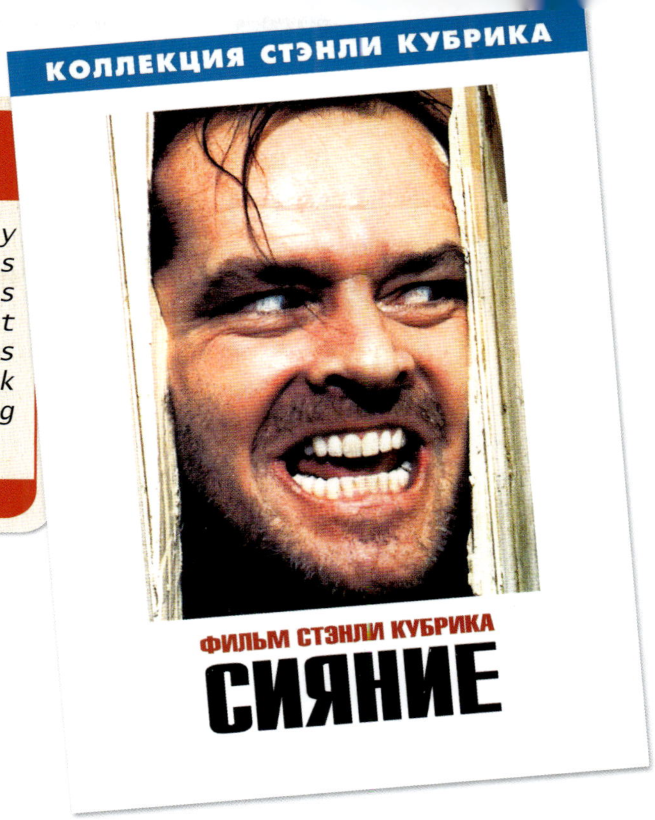

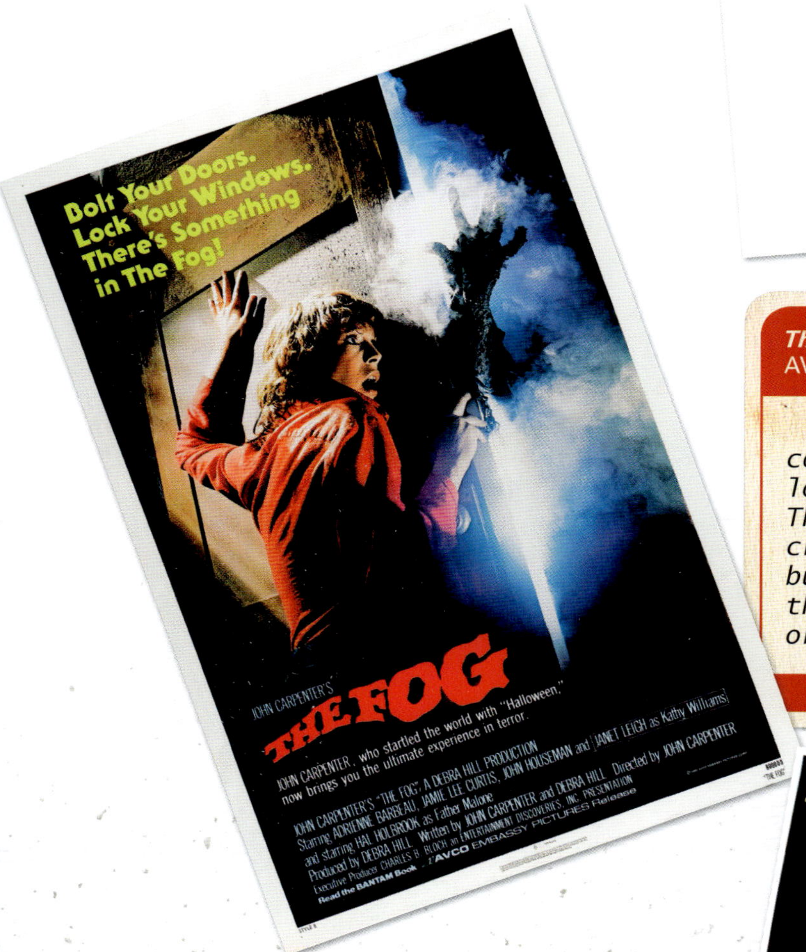

The Fog.
AVCO Embassy Pictures/EDI/Debra Hill Productions (1980).

The past comes back to haunt a coastal community, and it comes in a fog. A lot of people confuse this with King's The Mist, *but they are very different creatures. It's set on the west coast, but it feels like it should have been on the east coast, off the coast of Maine or Massachusetts.*

Bev Vincent

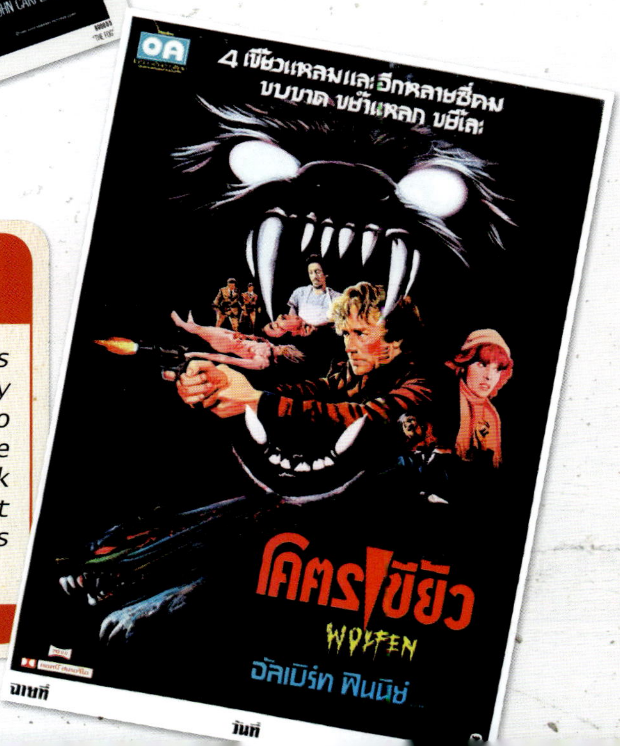

Wolfen. Orion Pictures Corporation/ King-Hitzig Productions (1981). Thailand.

Wolfen *effectively reconfigures the labyrinthine fears conventionally associated with the urban Gothic to articulate the terrors underlying the progressive and modern world of New York City and the anonymity and paranoia that have come to characterize the inhabitants of the contemporary urban space.*

Glennis Byron

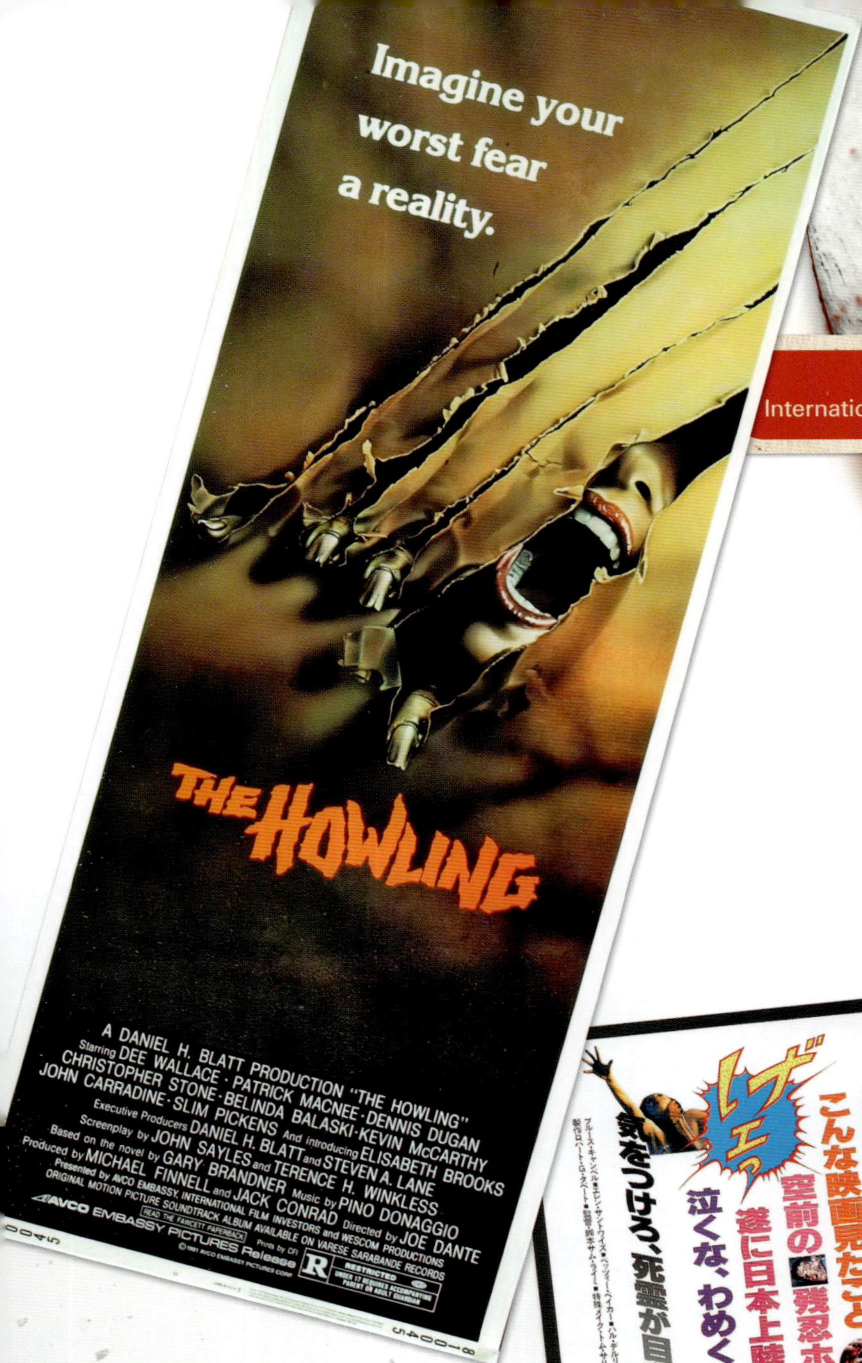

The Howling. AVCO Embassy Pictures/ International Film Investors/Wescom Productions (1981).

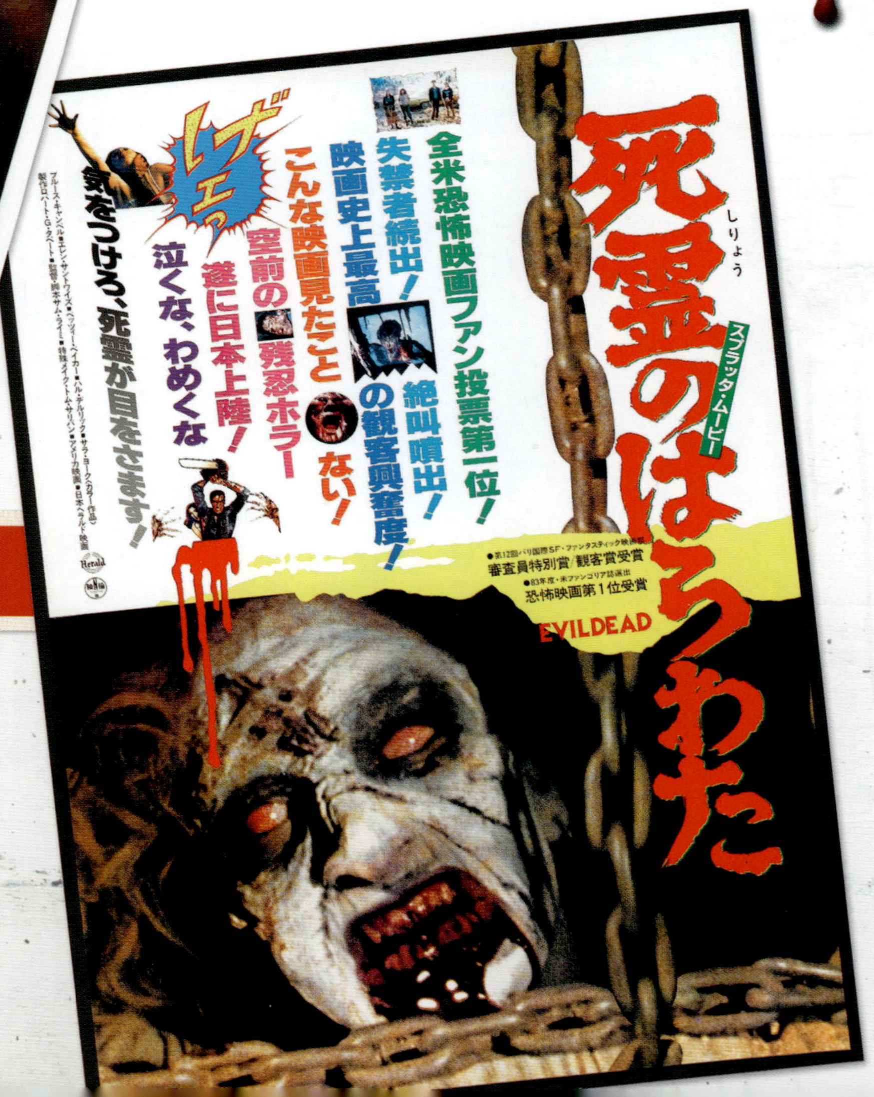

The Evil Dead. Renaissance Pictures (1981). Japan.

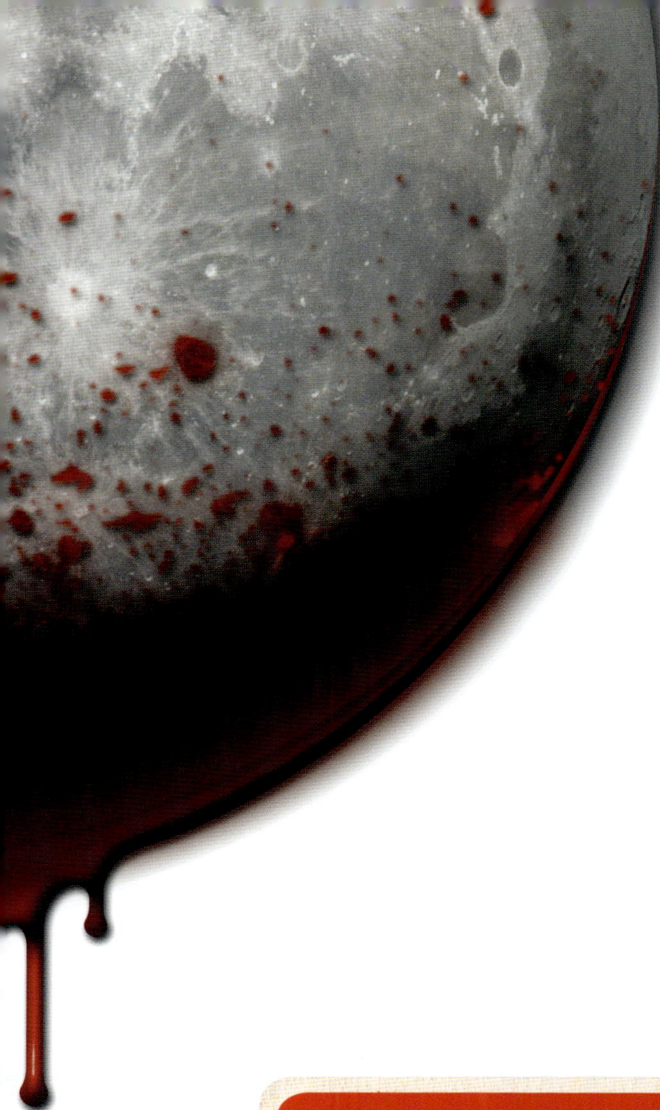

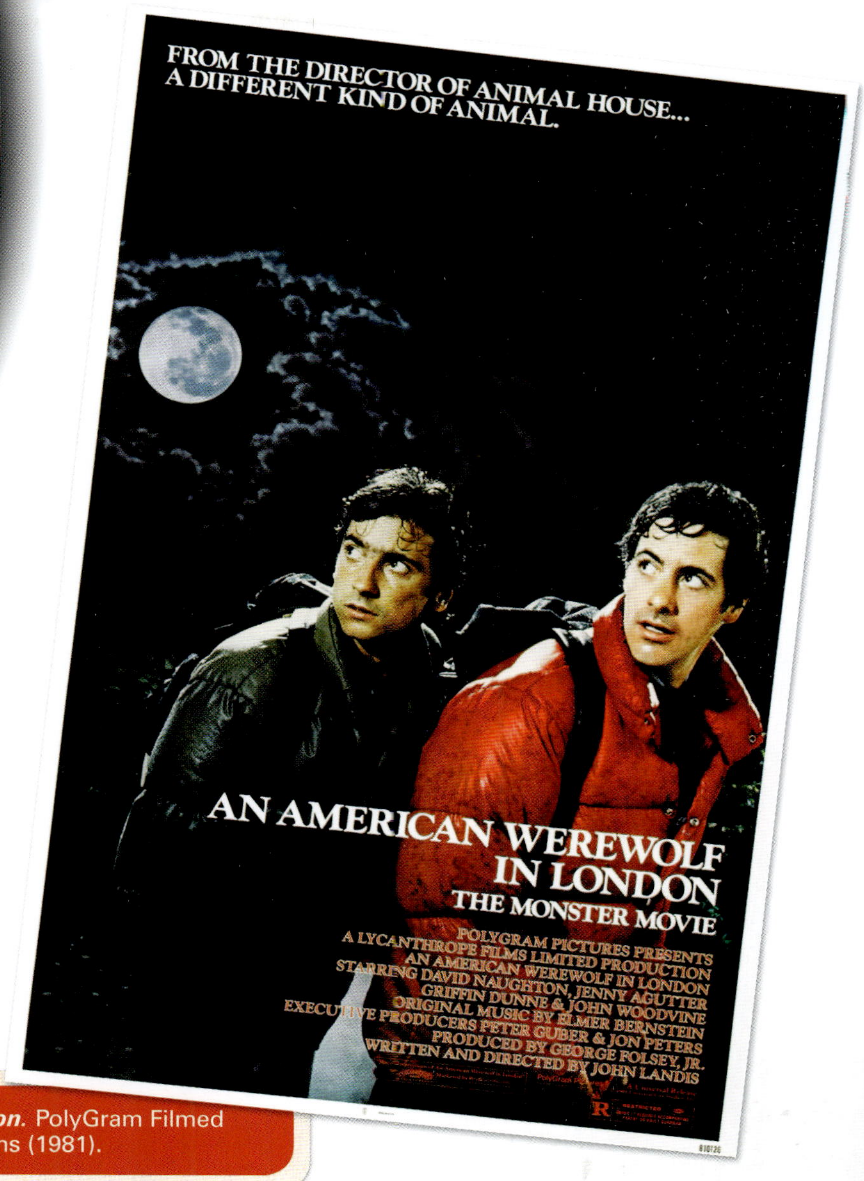

An American Werewolf in London. PolyGram Filmed Entertainment/Lyncanthrope Films (1981).

ON **SPECIAL EFFECTS** AS ART

There was a time — it's almost hard to remember it now — when special effects were considered works of art. The ease with which computers can render virtually anything possible has removed much of the *ooh-aah* factor. However, the transformation scenes in *An American Werewolf in London* were revolutionary, which explains why so much camera time is spent on them. Seeing those hairs pop out of skin, watching facial bones rearrange themselves and a man's body elongate into something lupine — that was astonishing in 1981. A more contemporary version of this movie would probably pay less attention to the transformation because viewers have become more jaded thanks to technology. The entire scene could be constructed on a laptop. A rare movie that finds a balance between horror and humor.

~Bev Vincent

Halloween II.
De Laurentiis, Universal Pictures (1981).

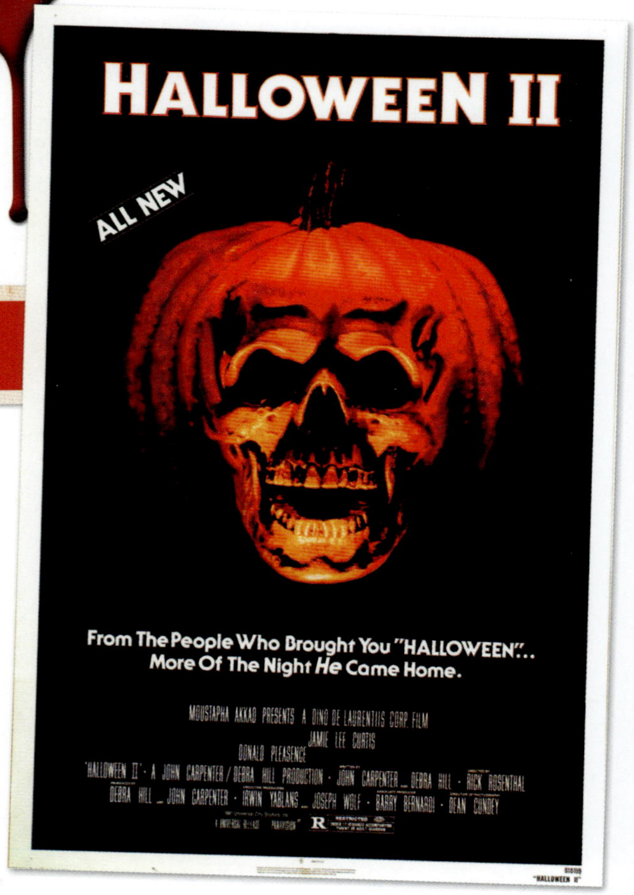

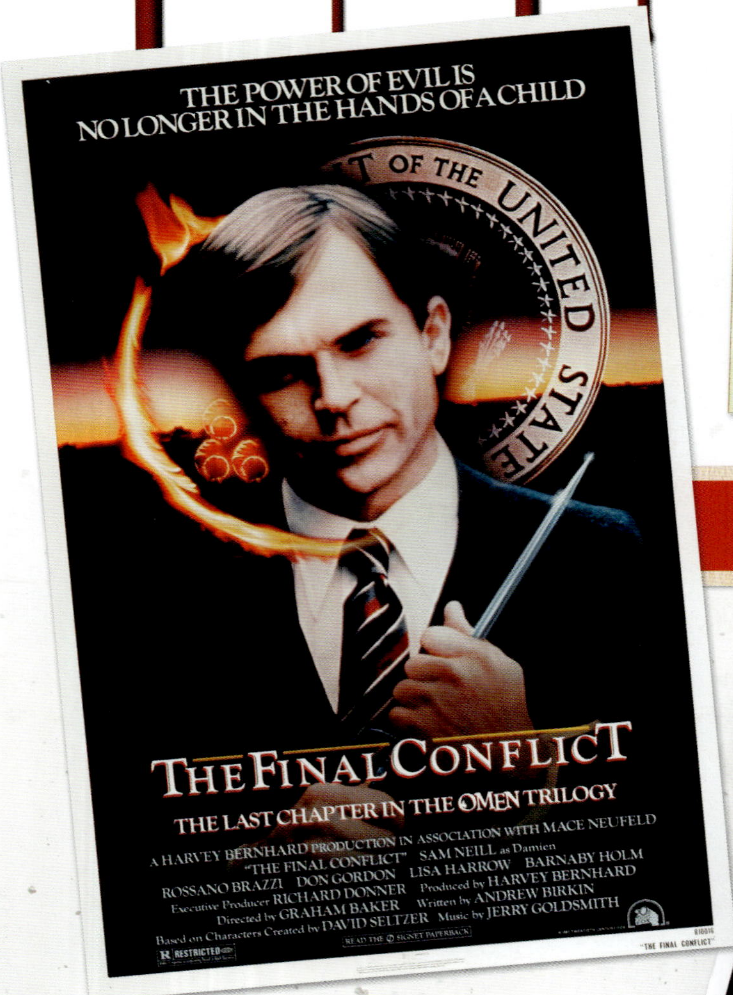

Omen III: The Final Conflict.
Twentieth Century Fox Film Corporation (1981).

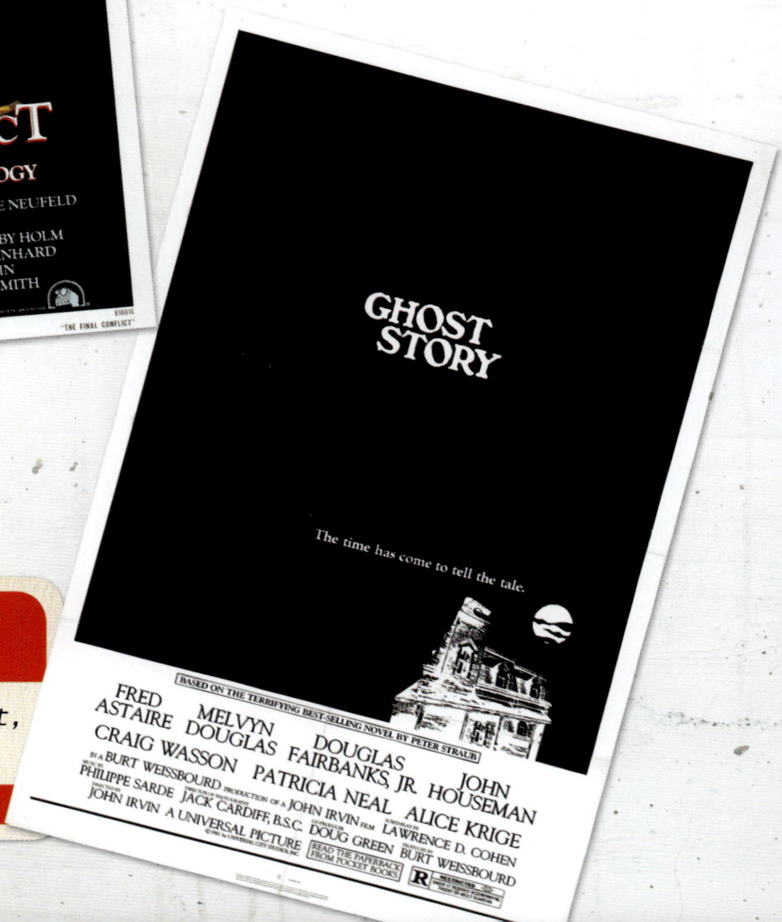

Ghost Story.
Universal Pictures (1981).

Ghost Story, *despite its superb cast, I found tediously unimaginative.*

Marvin Kaye

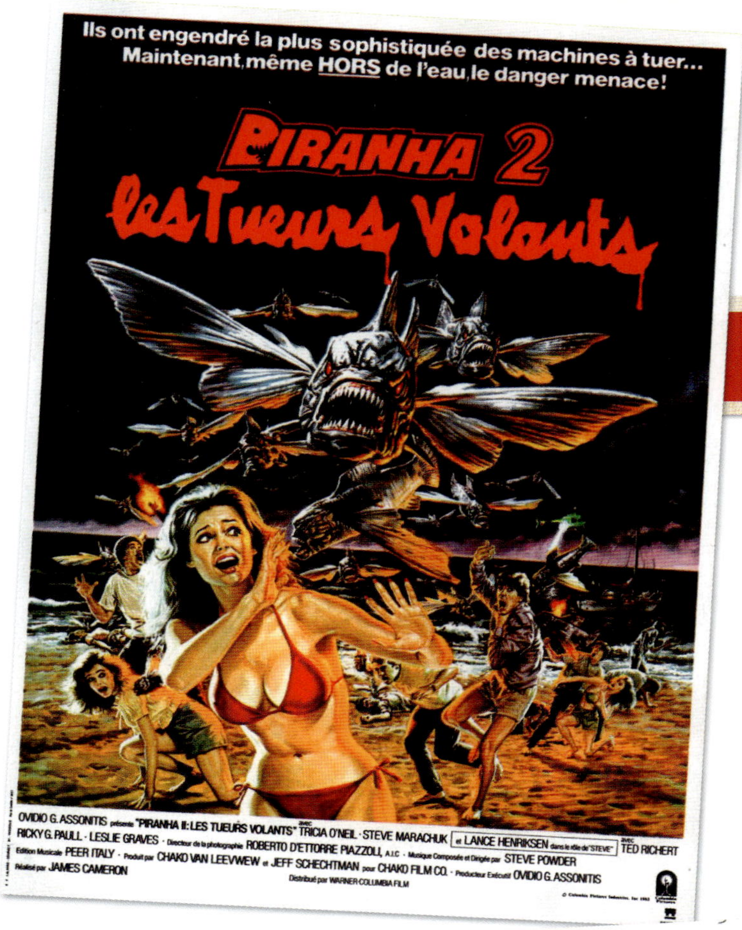

Piranha Part Two: The Spawning. Brouwersgracht Investments/Chako Film Company (1981). France.

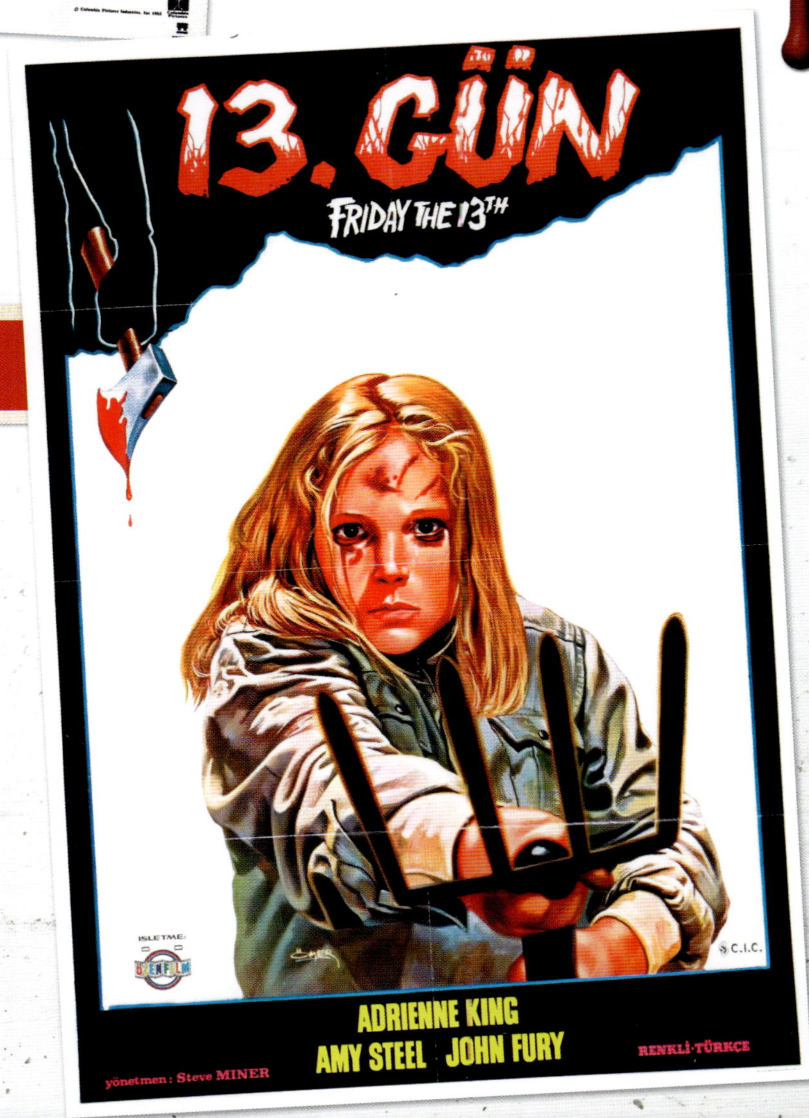

Friday the 13th Part 2. Georgetown Productions Inc. (1981). Turkey.

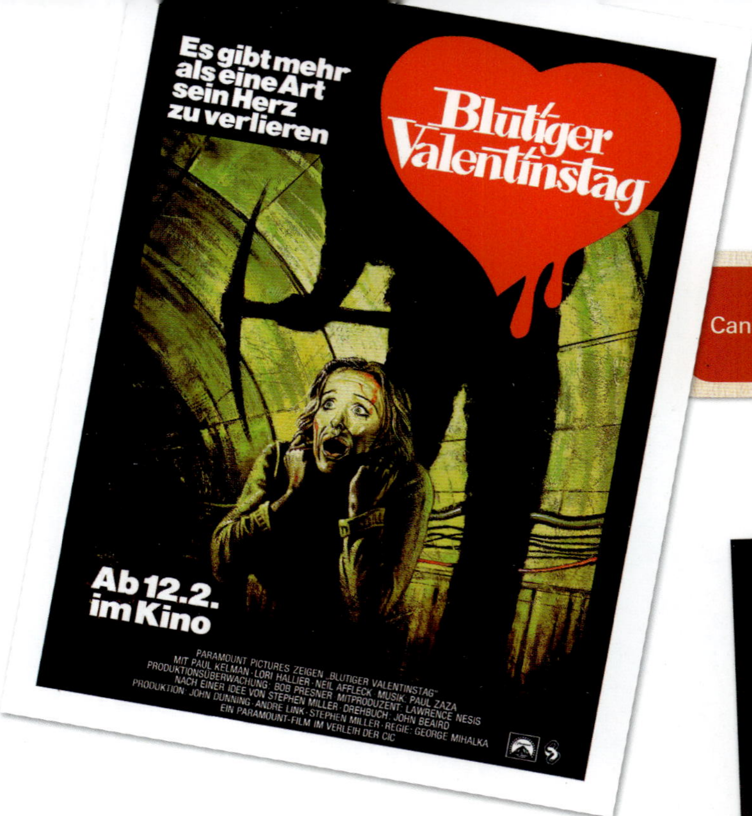

My Bloody Valentine.
Canadian Film Development Corporation/Famous Players/
Paramount Pictures/Secret Films (1981) Germany.

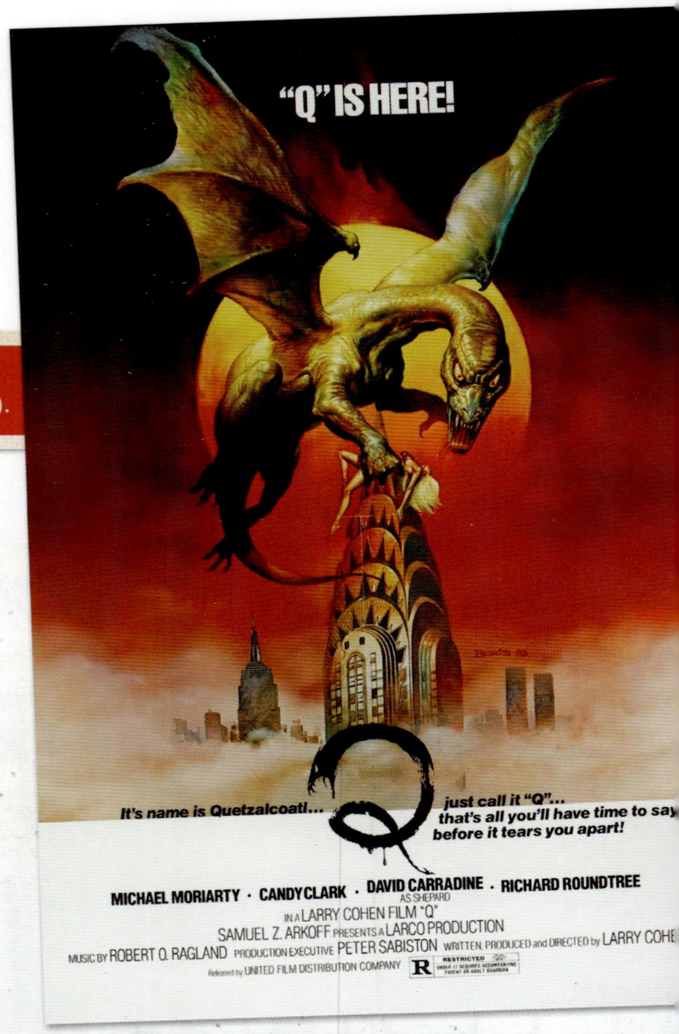

Q: The Winged Serpent.
Arkoff International, Larco Productions (1982).

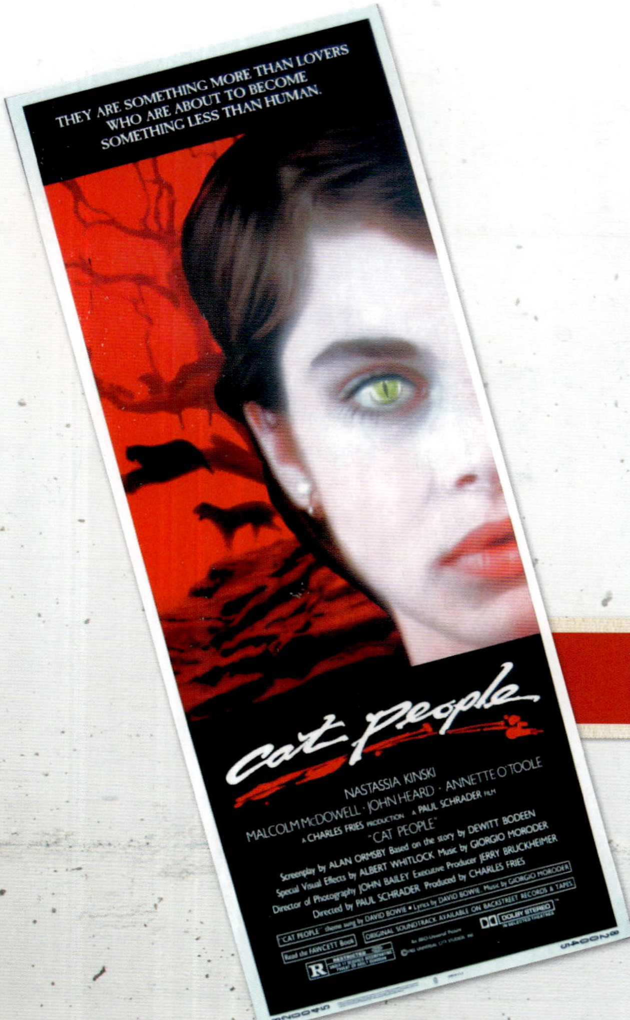

Cat People.
RKO Pictures/Universal Pictures (1982).

John Carpenter's The Thing.
Universal Pictures/Turman-Foster Company (1982).

This movie uses two of the best ways to create unease: a claustrophobic setting and paranoia. There's a monster among us and we can't get away – and that monster is one of us. It's like a classic murder mystery in an isolated setting, except far creepier and scarier. It features one of the most iconic scenes in a horror film, right up there with the alien bursting from John Hurt's chest in Alien: the severed head that sprouts legs like a spider and scuttles away.

Bev Vincent

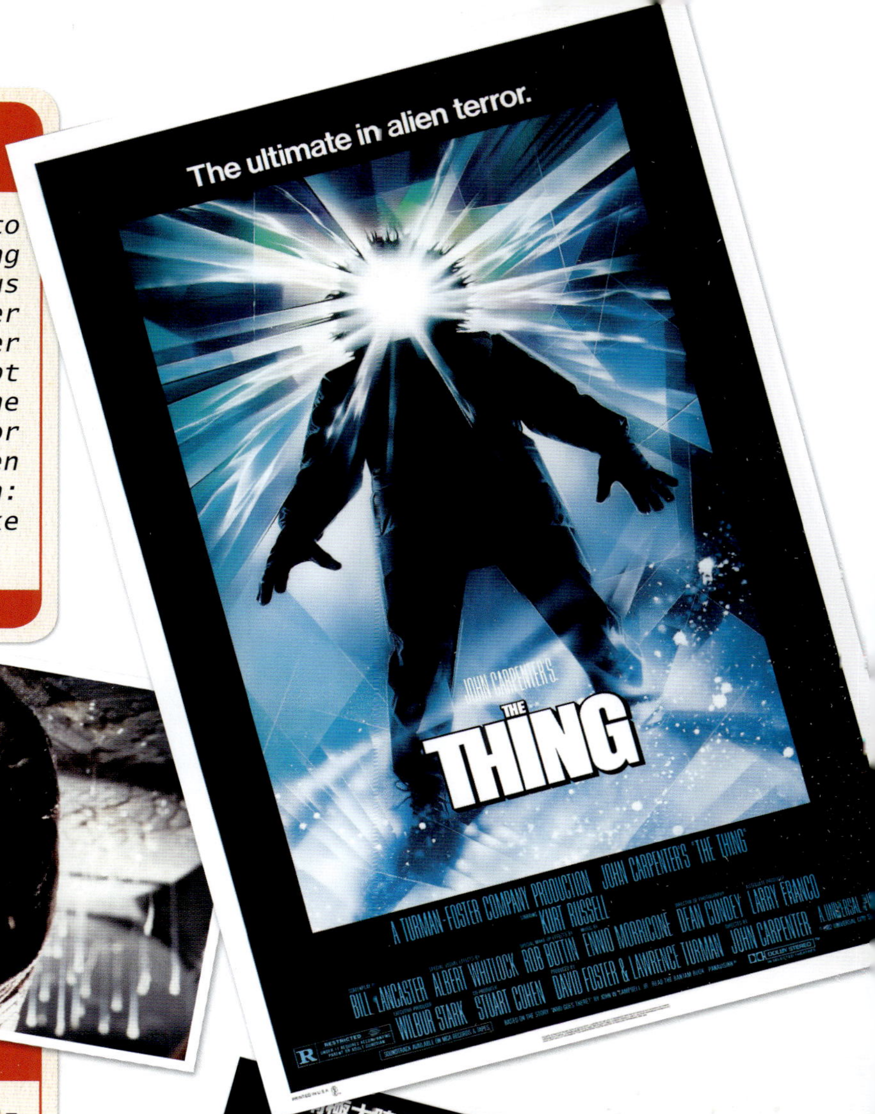

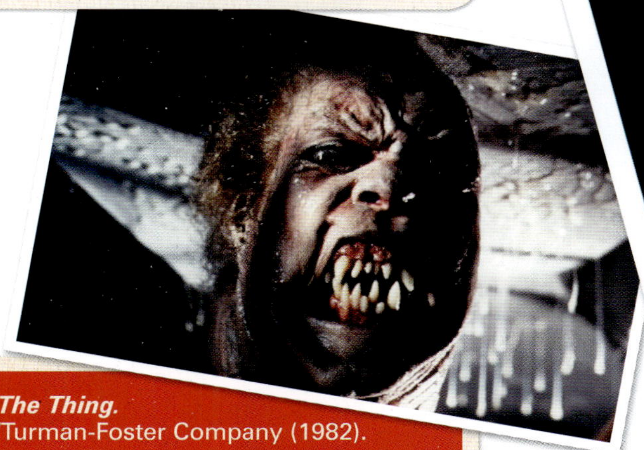

John Carpenter's The Thing.
Universal Pictures/Turman-Foster Company (1982).

A film as compelling and nerve-racking through its music as much as its narrative. There is a deliciously sardonic humor to the dialogue as the "weird and pissed off" alien (evidently female) wipes out the macho team in the snowy wastes.

Richard J. Hand

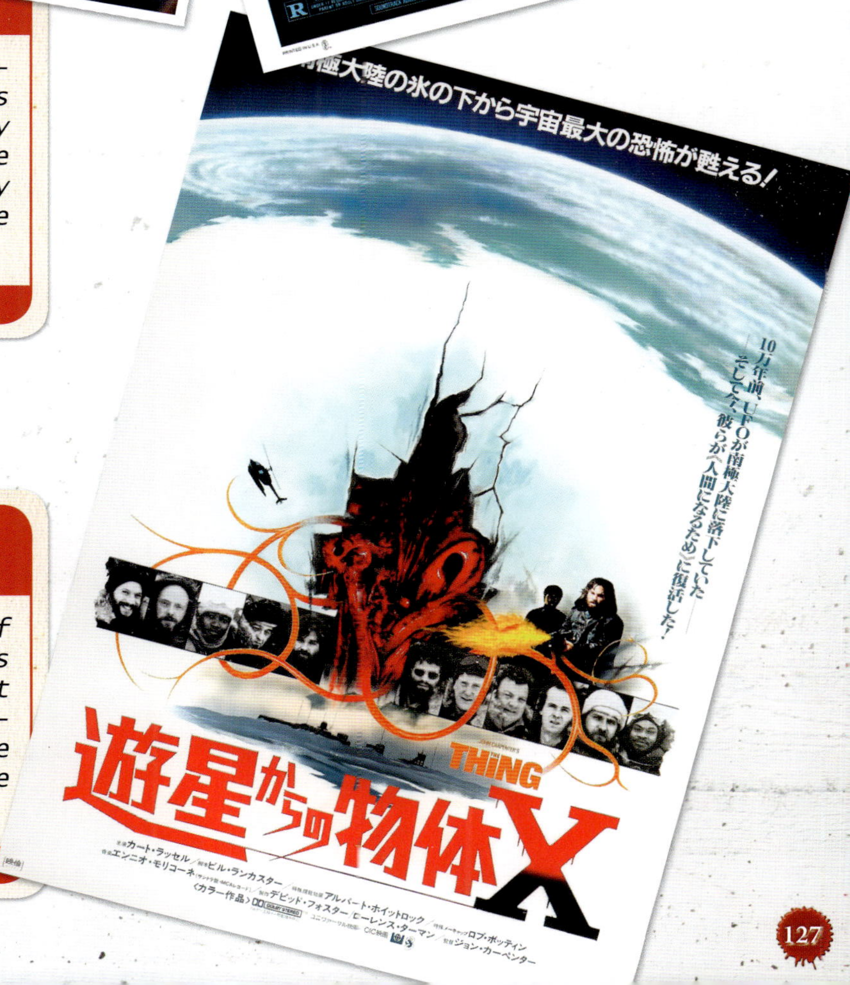

John Carpenter's The Thing. Universal Pictures/Turman-Foster Company (1982). Japan.

Trashed by critics at the time of its post-E.T. debut, John Carpenter's remake has finally earned the respect it deserves decades later. For sheer jaw-dropping audacity, the amazing creature FX have yet to be topped, even in the era of CGI.

Tony Timpone

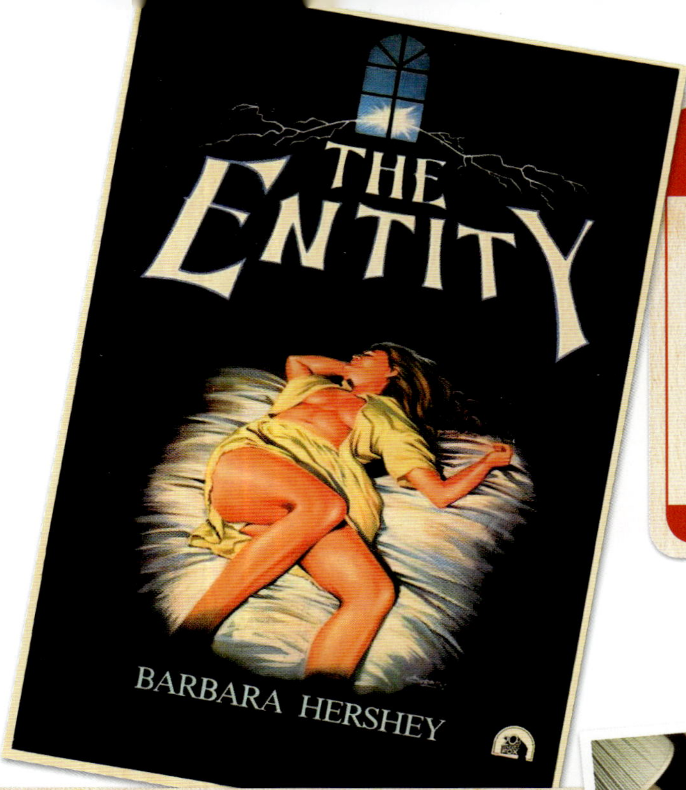

The Entity. American Cinema Productions/ Pelleport Investments (1982).

This film stands as one of the best examples of science vs. the paranormal ever made. The dichotomy of rigid, contained rationality sharing the same space as the invisible, untrappable entity was the perfect metaphor during its day of the materialist regime trying unsuccessfully to eliminate the mystical. It was an in-your-face pre-quel to The X-Files.

Katherine Ramsland

The Entity. American Cinema Productions/ Pelleport Investments (1982).

A disturbing film for its lack of explanation as to why a woman suffers a hellish experience by an invisible, raping presence. Like The Exorcist, *it makes ordinary people feel vulnerable to supernatural horrors that suddenly are convincingly real and not make-believe.*

Rosemary Ellen Guiley

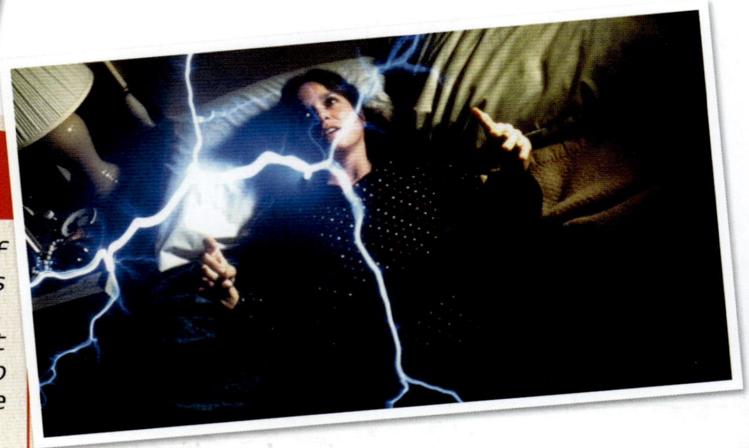

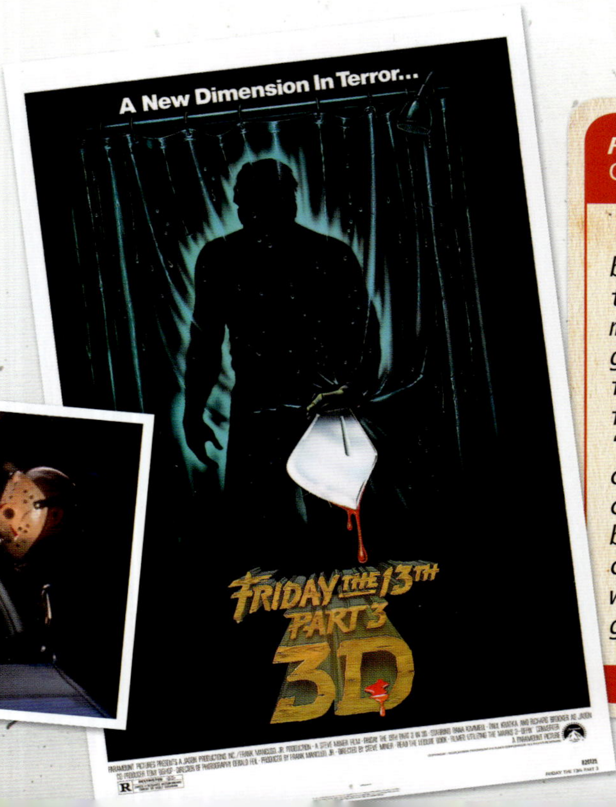

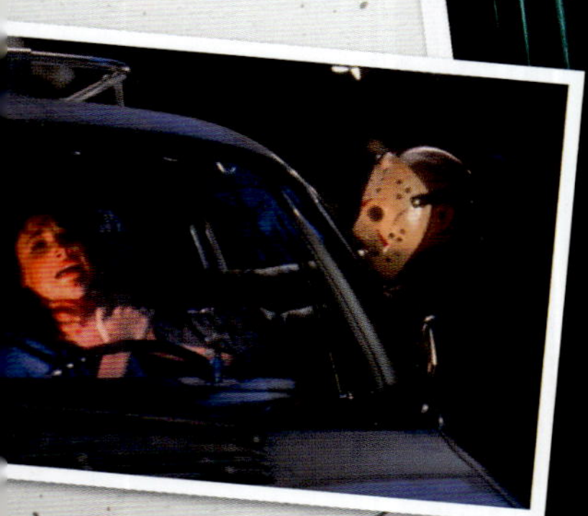

Friday the 13th Part III. Paramount Pictures/ Georgetown Productions Inc./Jason Productions (1982).

It's not considered by many to be the best of the series, but this is the one that made Jason Voorhees one of cinema's most legendary monsters. How? Simple – it gave him the iconic hockey mask. In the fifth grade, I was on a campaign to go from being nerd-boy number one to being "cool," and one of my strategies was to come to school in a badass Halloween costume. I couldn't find a toy machete, but I got a scythe from a grim reaper costume and thought it went pretty well with my fake plastic hockey mask. The girls screamed; I was a god.

L. Andrew Cooper

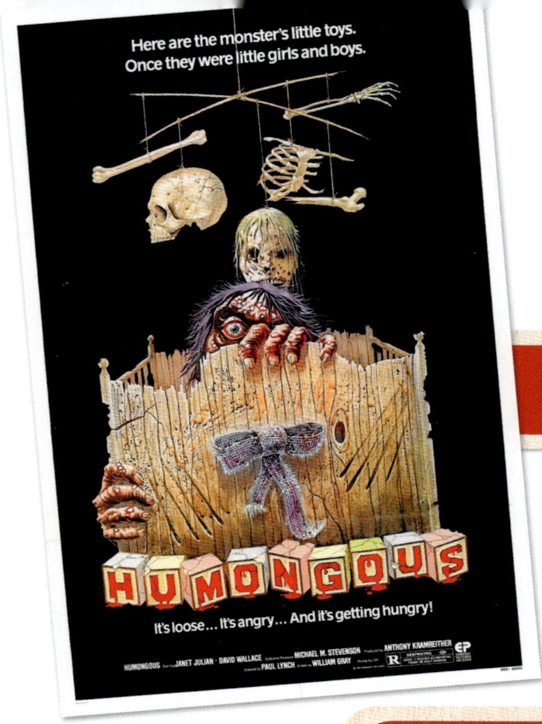

Humongous.
Humongous Films (1982)

Kung Fu Zombie.
The Eternal Film Company (1982). Germany.

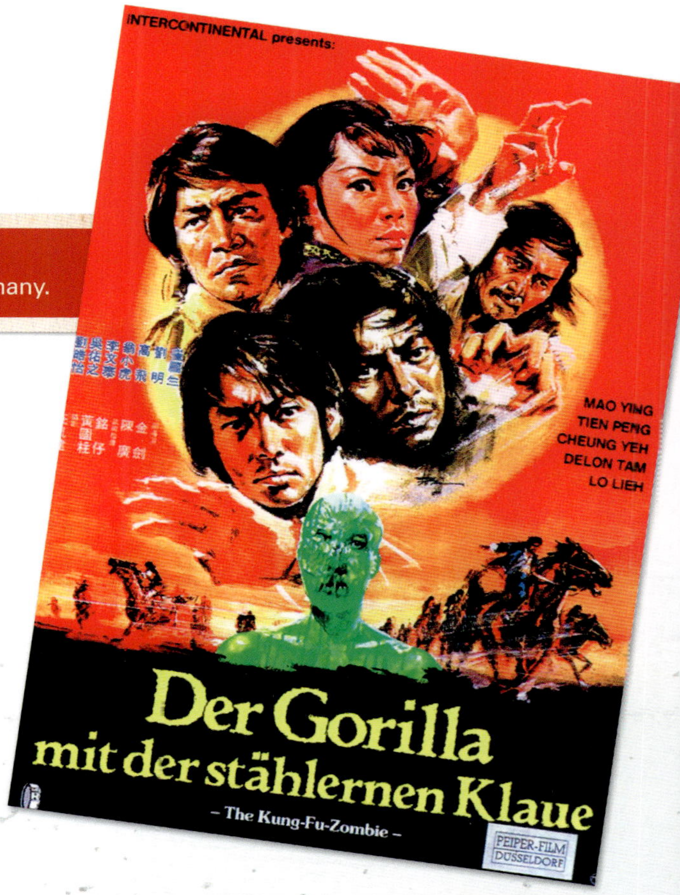

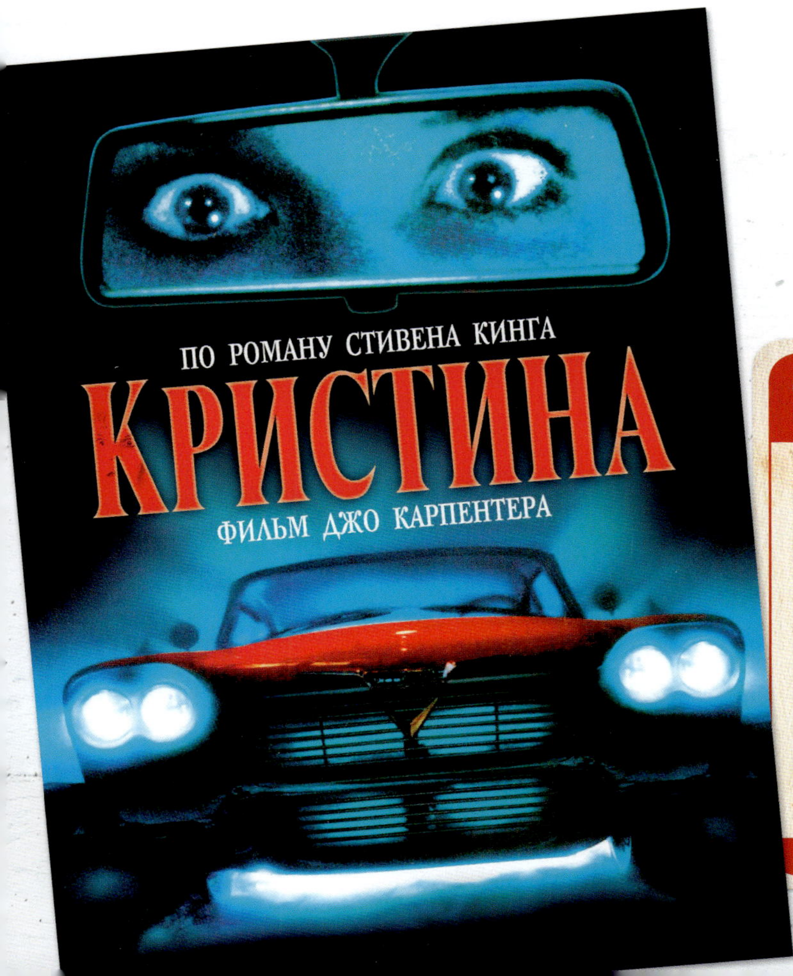

Christine. Columbia Pictures Corporation/
Delphi Premier Productions/Polar Film (1983). Russia.

I saw the John Carpenter film shortly after reading the Stephen King novel of the same name and immediately knew what it was like to be possessed by a car that wanted to kill me, having driven a series of cars over the years that left me stranded in isolated areas or dangerous parts of town. However, it wasn't until I owned an '89 Sterling (complete with unreliable British electronics and an alarm system that went off at will) that I actually named a vehicle "Christine."

Carol A. Senf

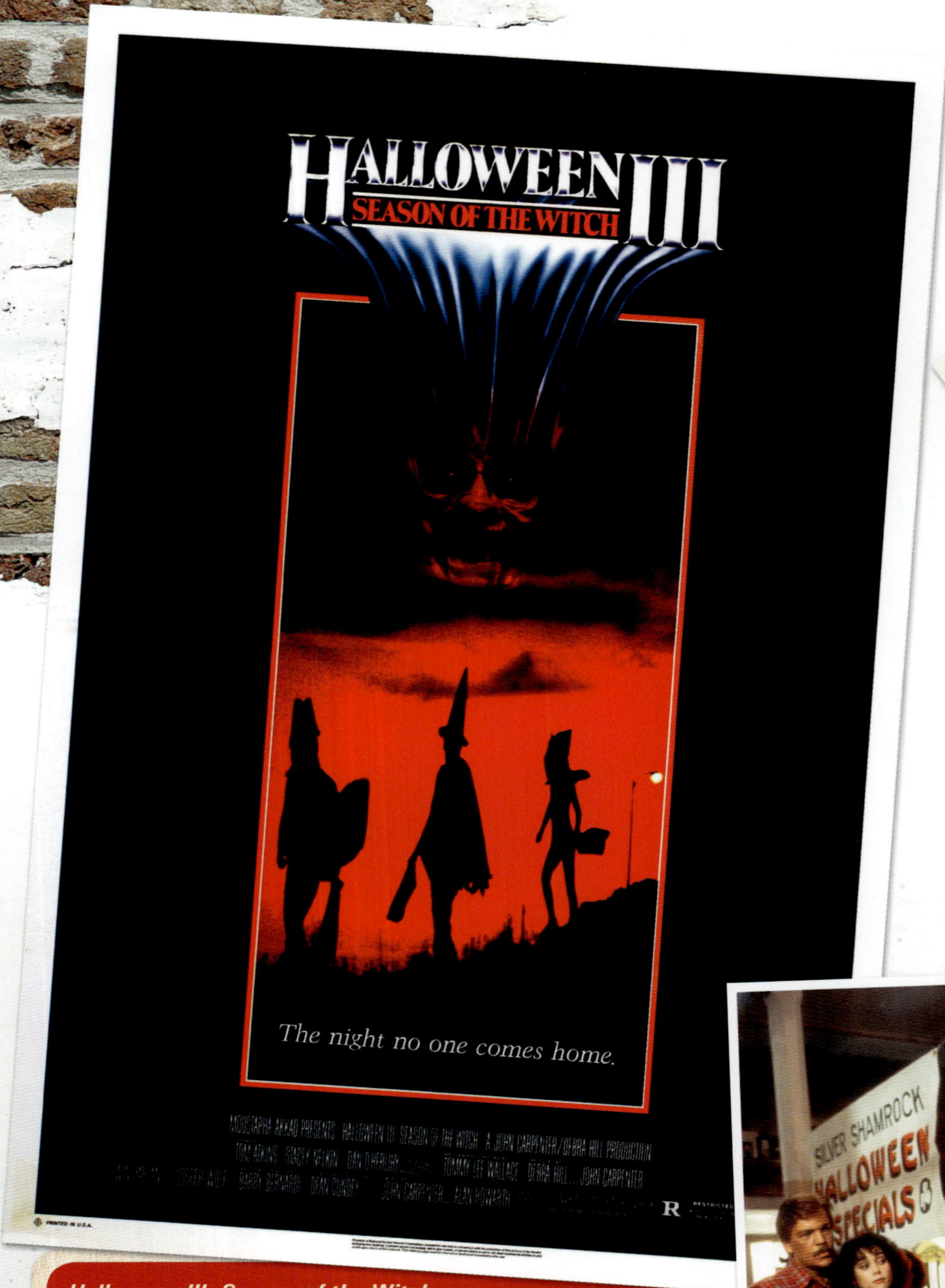

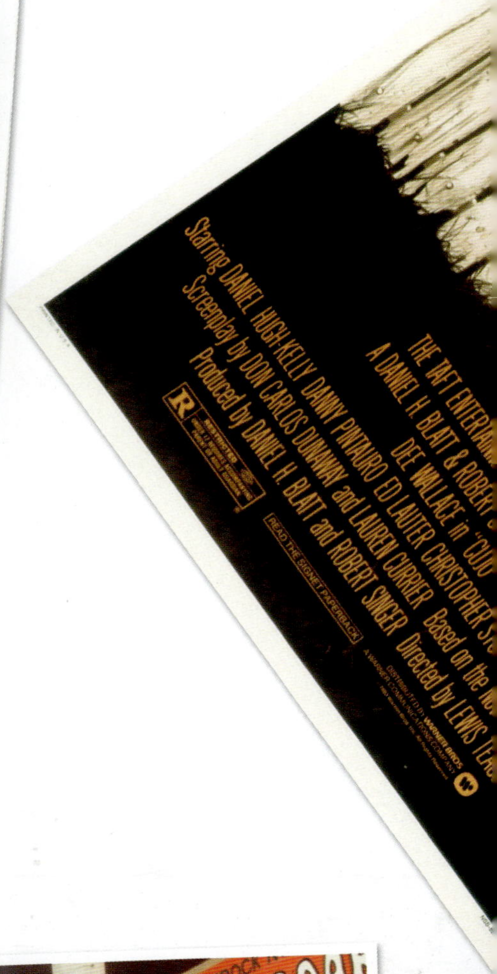

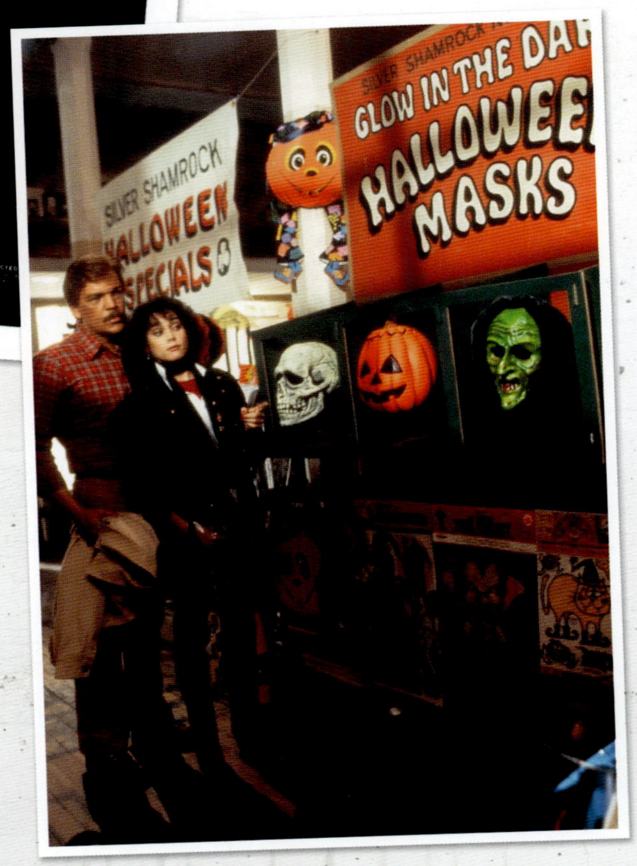

Halloween III: Season of the Witch.
Dino De Laurentiis Company/Universal Pictures (1983).

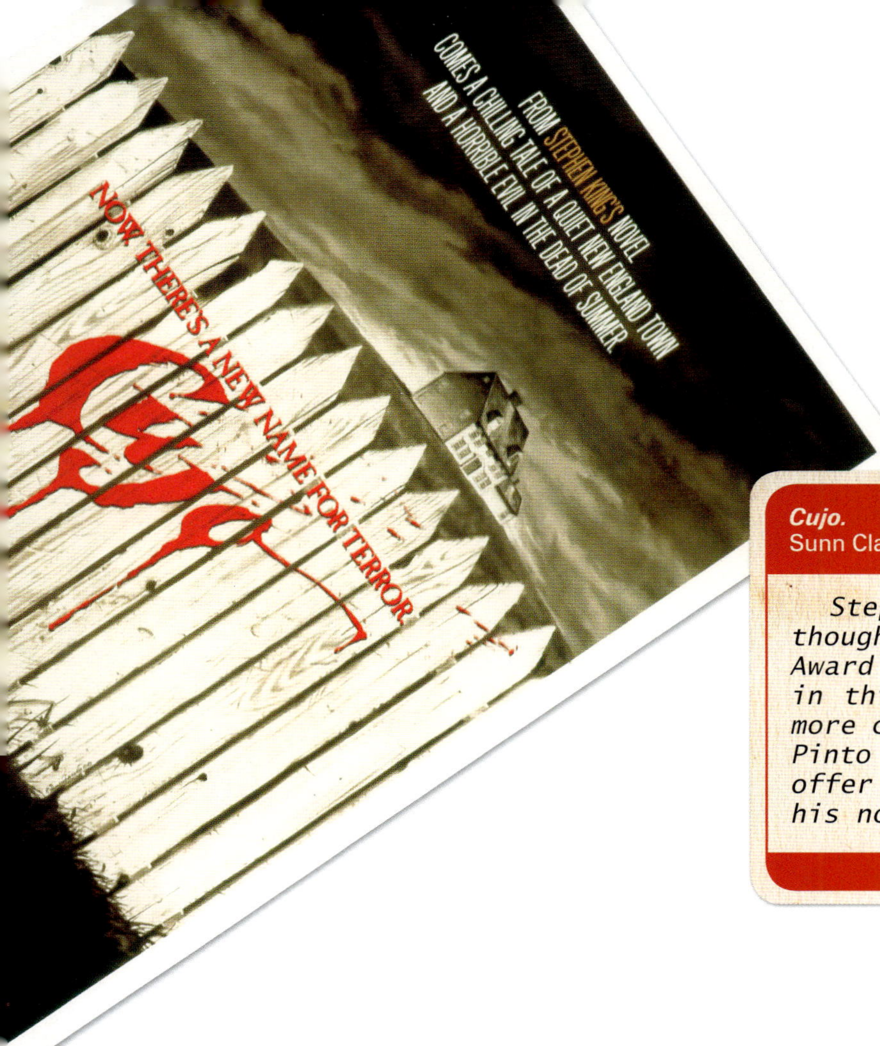

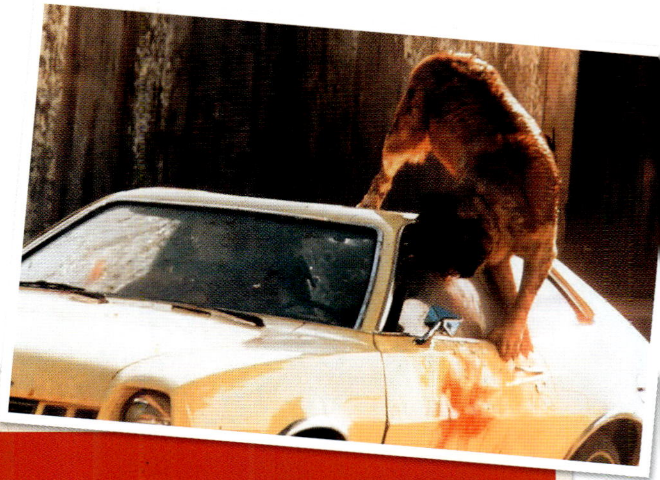

Cujo.
Sunn Classic Pictures/TAFT Entertainment Pictures (1983).

Stephen King has often said that he thought Dee Wallace deserved an Academy Award nomination for her performance in this movie. It's hard to imagine a more claustrophobic setting than a Ford Pinto on a hot summer day. The filmmakers offer a softer ending than King does in his novel.

Bev Vincent

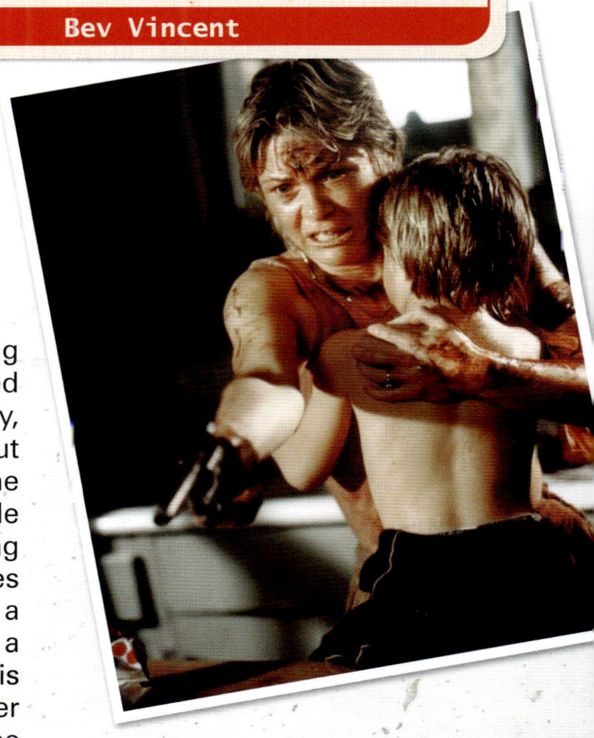

ON *CUJO* (1983) AND PERFORMING TERROR

In even the edgiest American horror film, there's a tacit understanding that children can be menaced, terrified, and chased, but never killed (other national cinemas are less squeamish in this regard). Consequently, child actors can rise to the level of performing terror "convincingly," but even the most "convincing" performance is never to overstep the line separating it from a glimpse of genuine terror in the underage actor. While Hollywood gossip is rife with stories about directors torturing their leading ladies to the point of physical and emotional collapse — Hitchcock comes to mind: just ask Tippi Hedren! — I have yet to find such a story about a director assaulting a child actor in pursuit of a performance. Which is a long-winded way to preface the praise Danny Pintauro deserves for his performance in Lewis Teague's *Cujo*. The film is good but not great; after all, Pintauro's character, who dies in Stephen King's novel, survives to see the end of the film — there's that ironclad rule again! But along the way there are moments, when Pintauro is "performing" terror, as he is being menaced by the film's eponymous killer dog, that are jaw-dropping in their intensity. What, one wonders, did they *do* to this poor kid on the set? How did Teague get *this* performance out of this little kid? Pintauro explodes all categories of acting, especially of child acting, in these moments. A little too much reality, and the film becomes uncomfortable to watch. Any actor in a horror film should be happy to be the cause of such discomfort to the viewer!

~Steffen Hantke

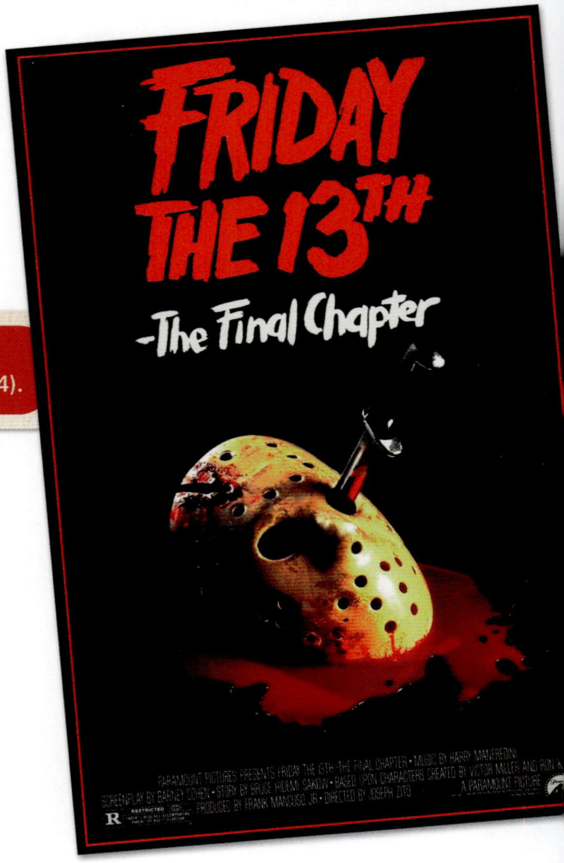

Friday the 13th The Final Chapter. Paramount Pictures/Georgetown Productions Inc. (1984).

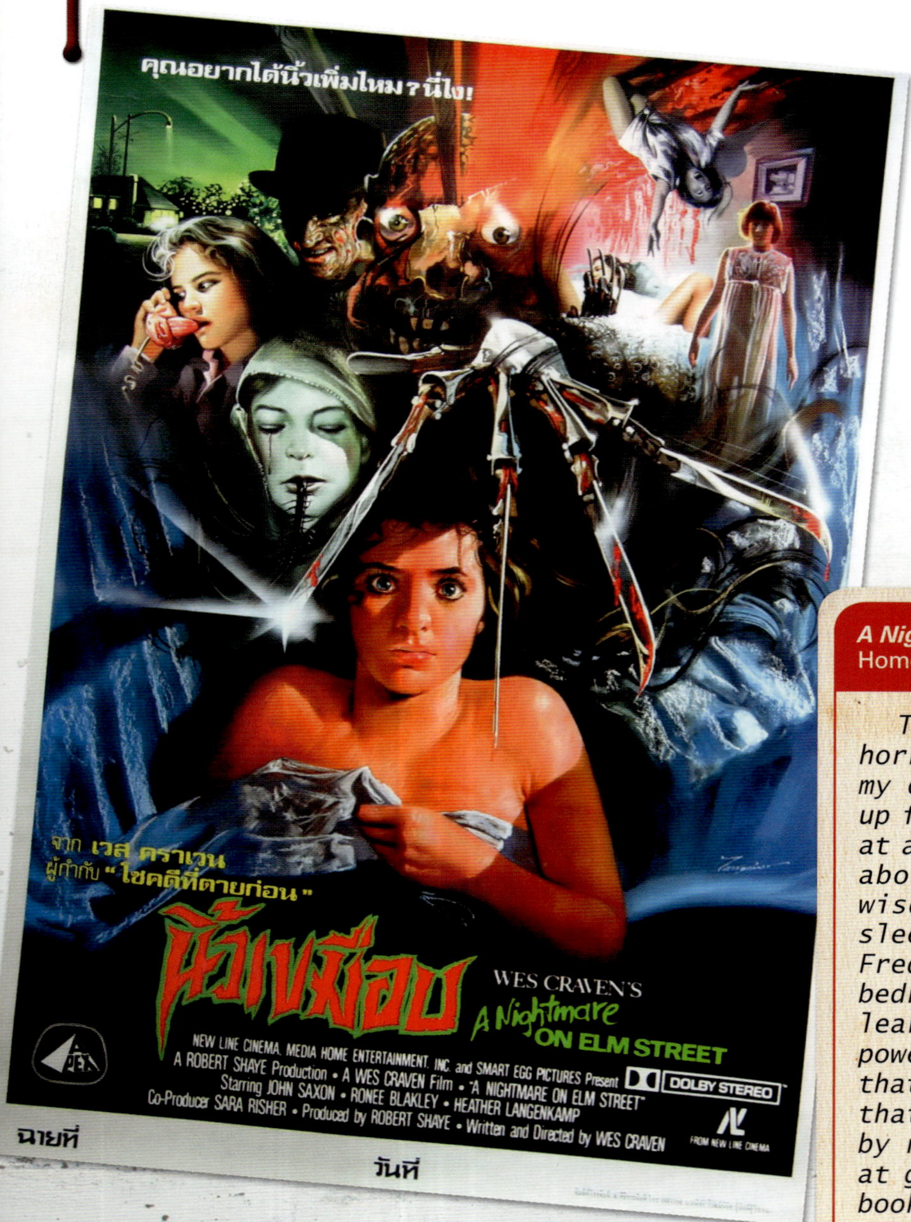

A Nightmare on Elm Street. New Line Cinema/Media Home Entertainment/Smart Egg Pictures (1984). Thailand

This is the one that made me a lifelong horror fan. I wasn't supposed to see it; my own nightmares would keep my parents up for weeks. After I snuck and watched it at a friend's house, I had second thoughts about my decision to defy parental wisdom. I was terrified of going to sleep. When I closed my eyes, I could see Freddy Krueger making his way toward my bedroom. But then I remembered what Nancy learns: We give nightmare monsters their power, and we have the ability to take that power back. I didn't have nightmares that night, and I was never as bothered by nightmares again. (I tell this story at greater length at the beginning of my book Gothic Realities*).*

L. Andrew Cooper

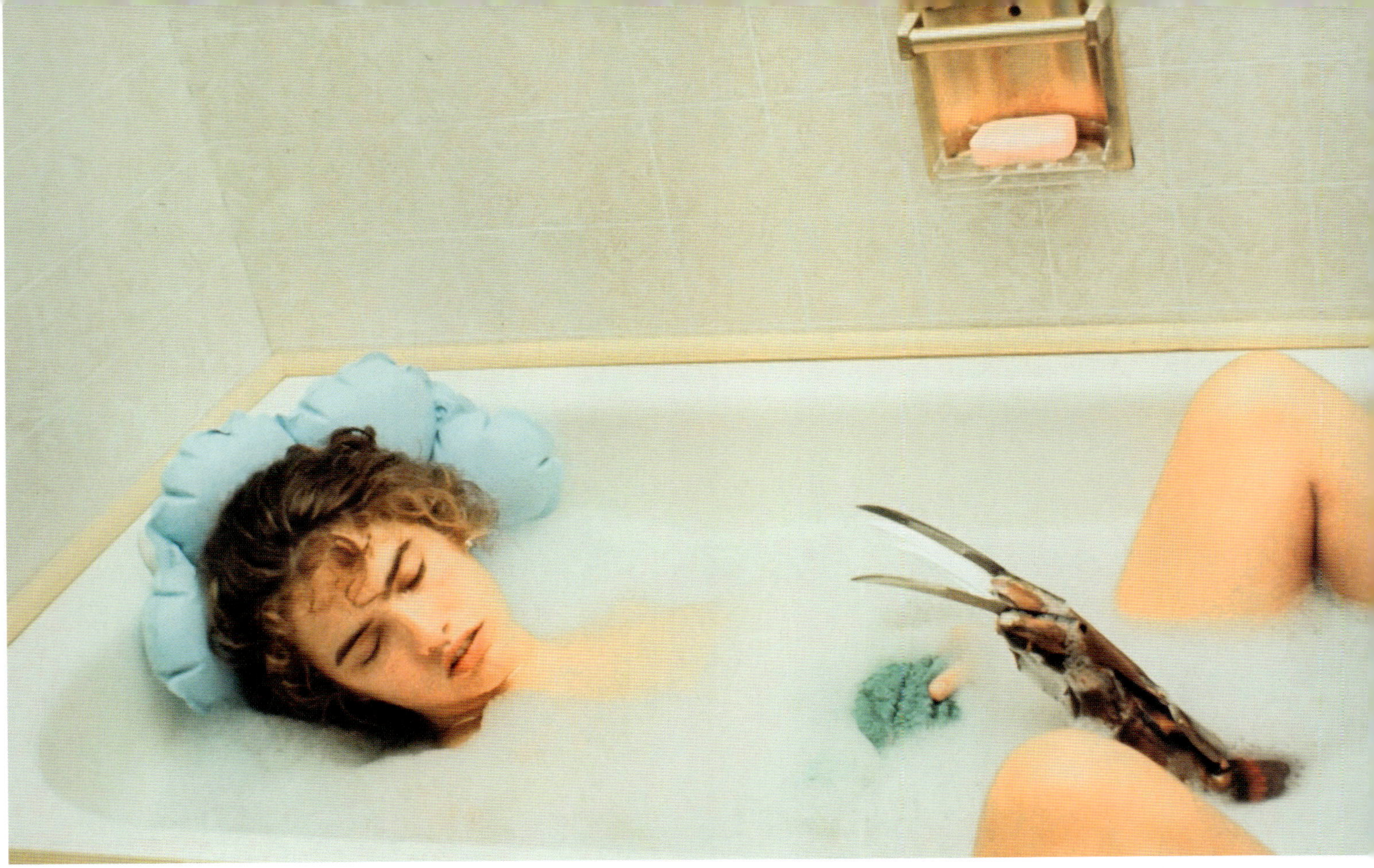

ON FATE, **FREDDY**, AND HAMLET

I always claim that Nancy Thompson (Heather Langenkamp) is really Prince Hamlet for the horror set. Consider that *A Nightmare on Elm Street* serves as a direct thematic counterpoint to John Carpenter's *Halloween* (1978). In *Halloween*, Laurie Strode (Jamie Lee Curtis) sits in high school English class while an unseen adult teacher drones on about "fate" and "destiny." In the midst of the class, Laurie sees Michael Myers's car on the street: *she thus glimpses her fate.* As the teacher explains on the soundtrack that *"you can't escape fate,"* the audience is led, via the film's visuals to understand the connection: *that Laurie cannot escape her impending connection to an escaped serial killer.*

By contrast, *A Nightmare on Elm Street* finds Nancy Thomas in another high school English class as a different teacher discusses the resourcefulness of the melancholy prince in Shakespeare's *Hamlet.* The teacher notes that Hamlet *"stamps out the lies"* of his mother, something which Nancy will do in *Elm Street* as well, and that the prince *"probes and digs"* to find the truth. Again, that's the very task Nancy undertakes: seeking information about the life and death of Freddy Krueger, and her parents' role in his illegal murder. The *Elm Street* philosophy suggests that only by digging beneath the surface, by learning the truth of a thing, can one overcome the sins of one's parents and survive. The key to beating Freddy is to know and understand him: to see that he thrives on the energy of your hate, and then rob him of that energy.

If the *Halloween* movies concern a Monster who is Fate Itself, the Freddy movies revolve around the belief that characters can fight back, and shape their own destiny.

~John Kenneth Muir

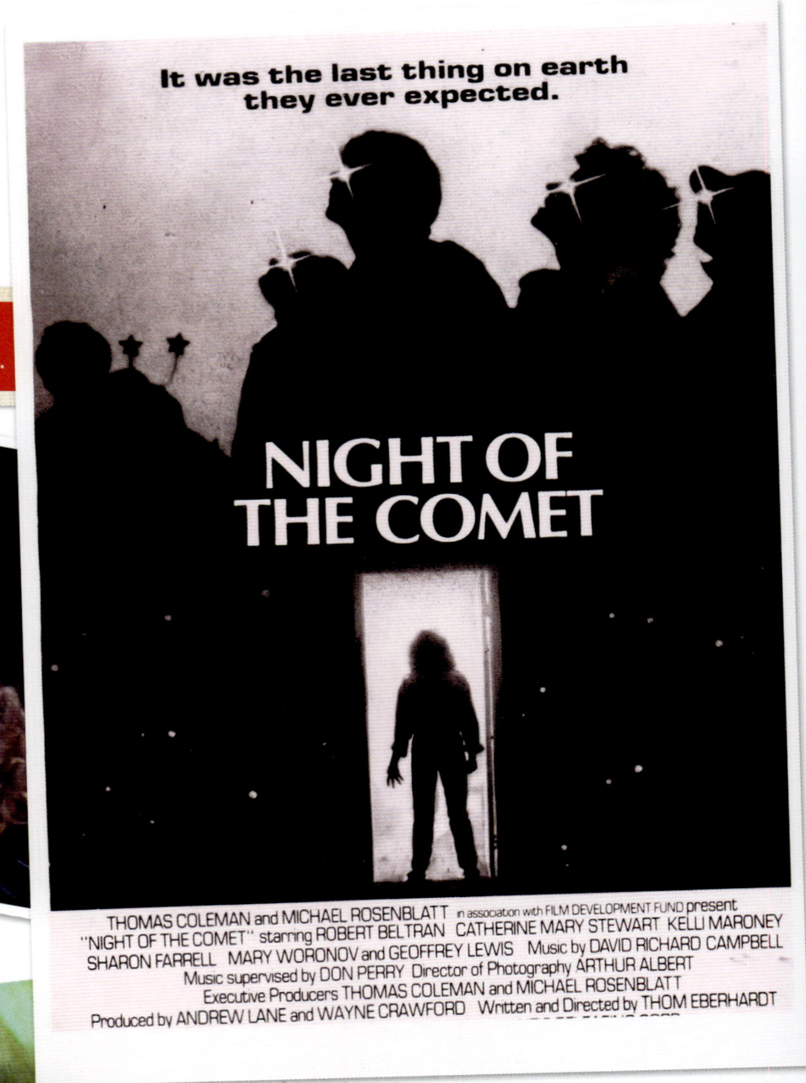

Night of the Comet. Thomas Coleman and Michael Rosenblatt Productions/Film Development Fund (1984).

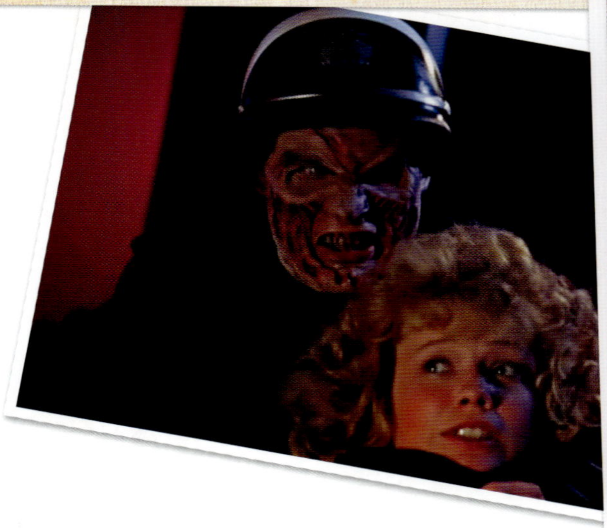

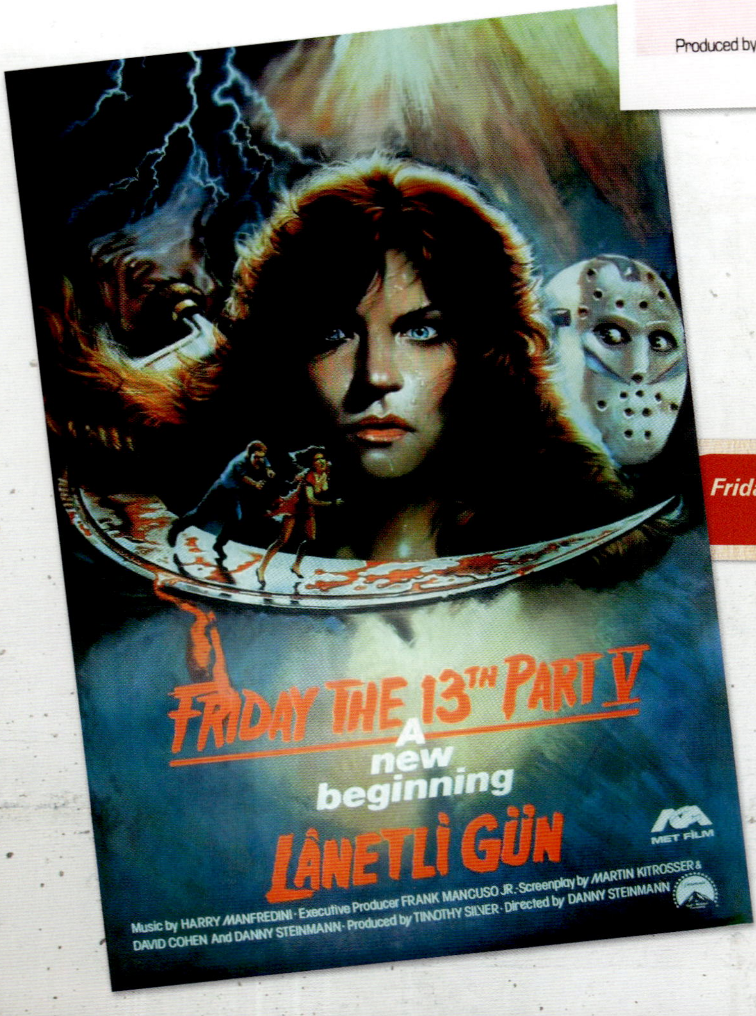

Friday the 13th A New Beginning. Georgetown Productions Inc./ Paramount Pictures/Terror Inc. (1985). Turkey.

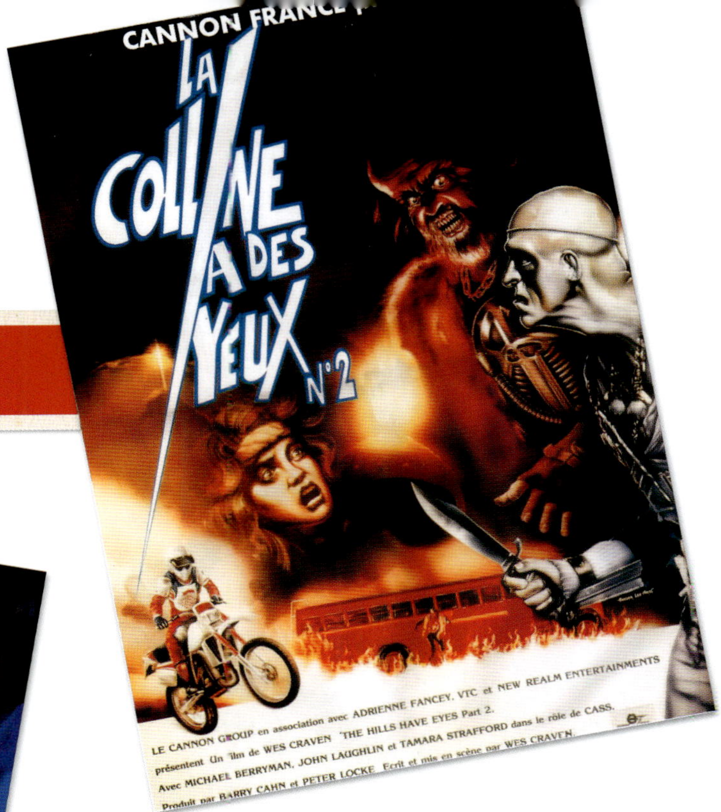

The Hills Have Eyes Part II.
VTC (1985). France.

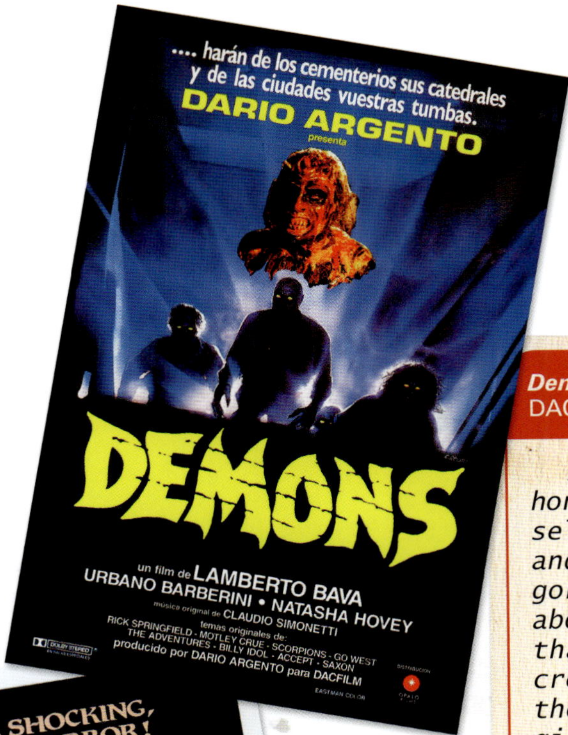

Demons.
DACFILM Rome (1985). Spain.

A decade before Scream made mainstream horror go "meta" (or somewhat pretentiously self-referential), director Lamberto Bava and writer/producer Dario Argento gave gorehounds everywhere a delightful movie about a movie (or is it the theater?) that turns viewers into bloodthirsty creatures more like fast zombies than the intelligent beings that make little girls puke pea soup. I came to this one belatedly, however, right in the thick of the "meta" craze. As I watched people turn into demons while they watched people turn into demons, I was in postmodern heaven (or its demonic equivalent). Stoned film grad students – this one's for you.

L. Andrew Cooper

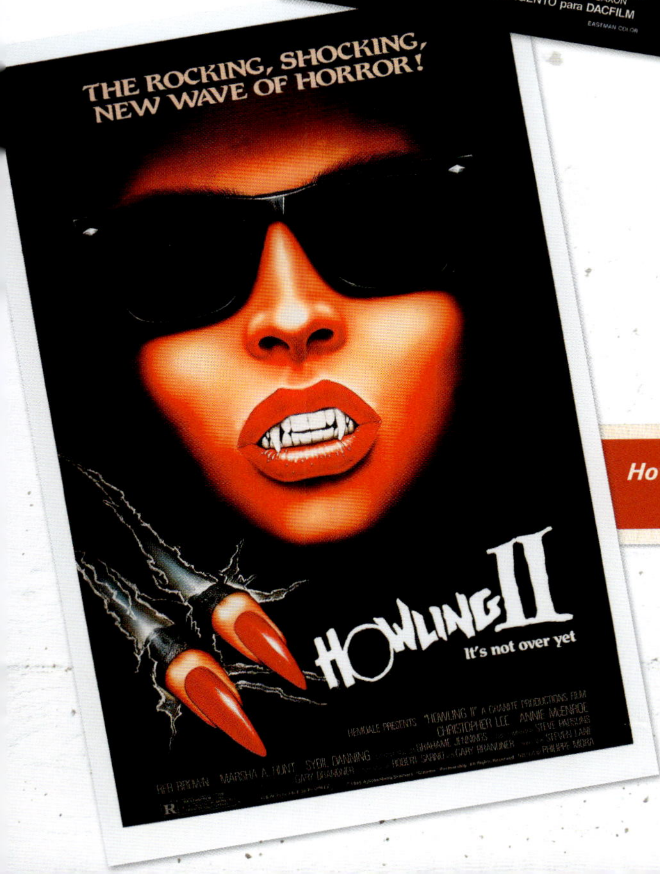

Howling II: ...Your Sister is a Werewolf.
Hemdale Film (1985).

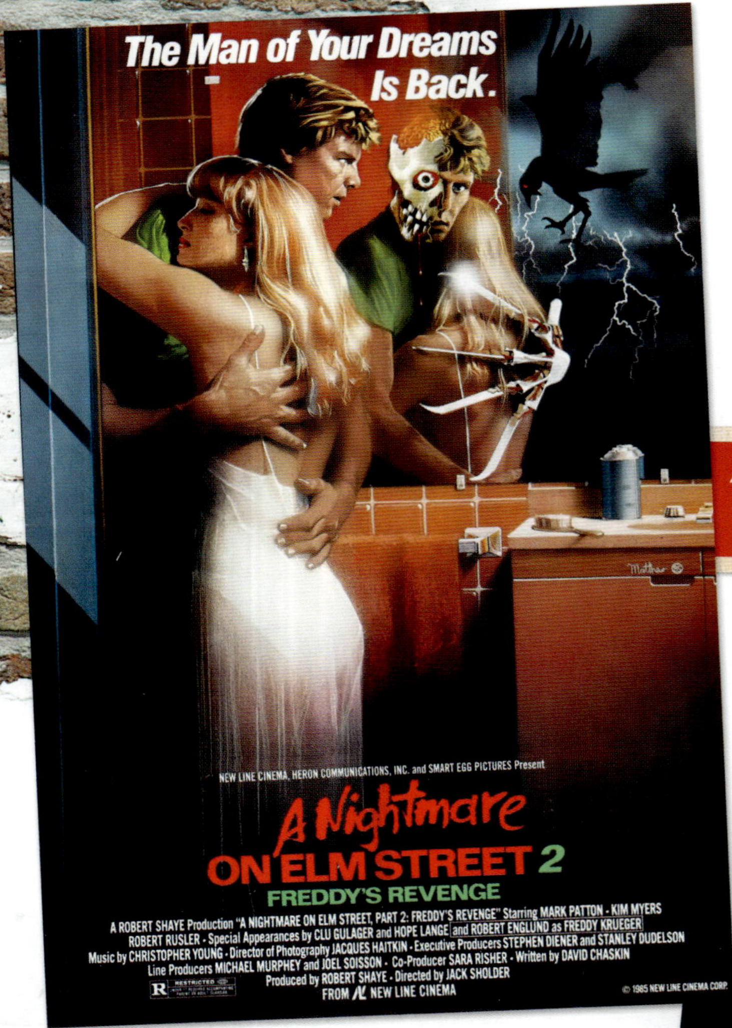

A Nightmare on Elm Street Part 2: Freddy's Revenge.
New Line Cinema/Heron Communications/
Smart Egg Pictures (1985).

Silver Bullet.
Dino De Laurentiis Company/Famous Films (1985). France.

It's hard to adapt what is essentially an illustrate novelette into a full-length picture. Silver Bullet tries hard to be a comedy-horror film, and it does have a moment or two where the dark humor works (I'm thinking primarily of the scene in the fog where you first see a man's arm brandishing a Louisville slugger and then, after a brief and unseen tussle, the next arm that's seen is the hairy arm of the werewolf). Megan Follows, who would go on to play Anne of Green Gables, gives the best performance as Marty's sister, and Gary Busey is not bad as his ne'er-do-well uncle. The character relationships are what make this film worthwhile watching. Its horror elements are derivative and short on true scares.

Bev Vincent

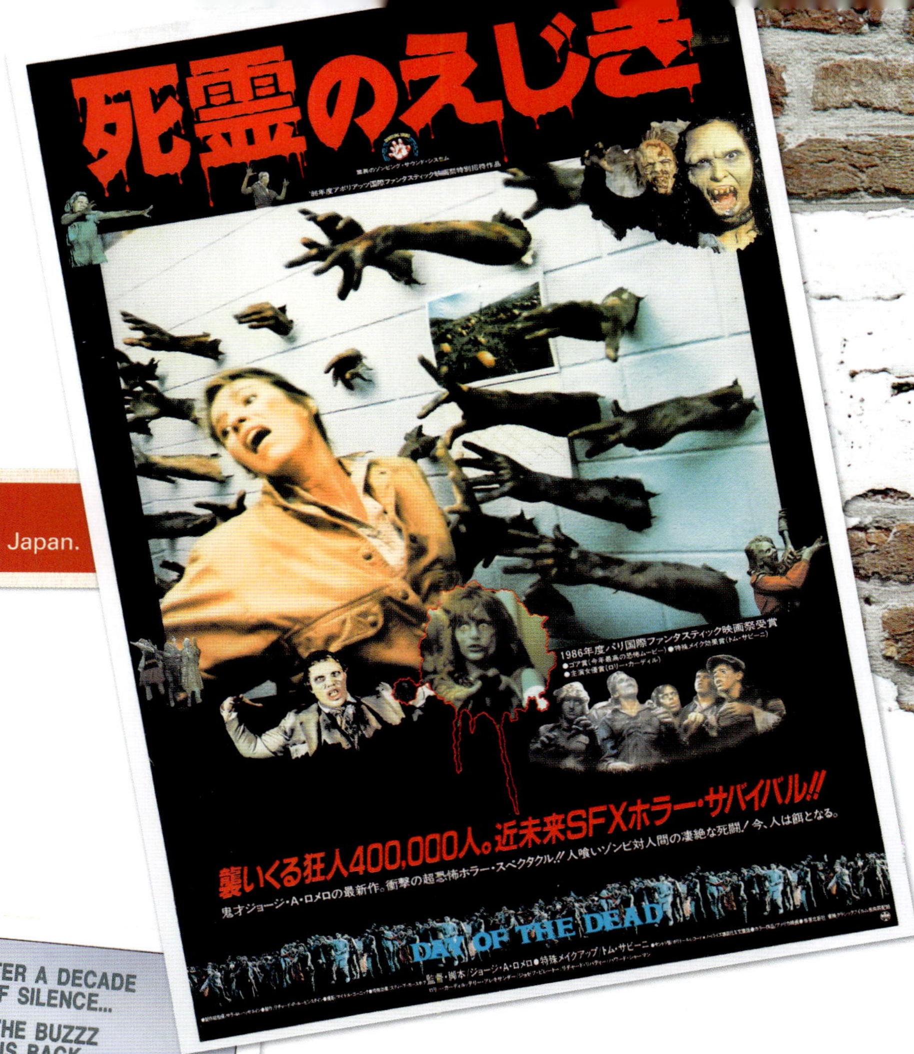

Day of the Dead. Dead Films Inc./
Laurel Entertainment Inc./Laurel-Day Inc. (1985). Japan.

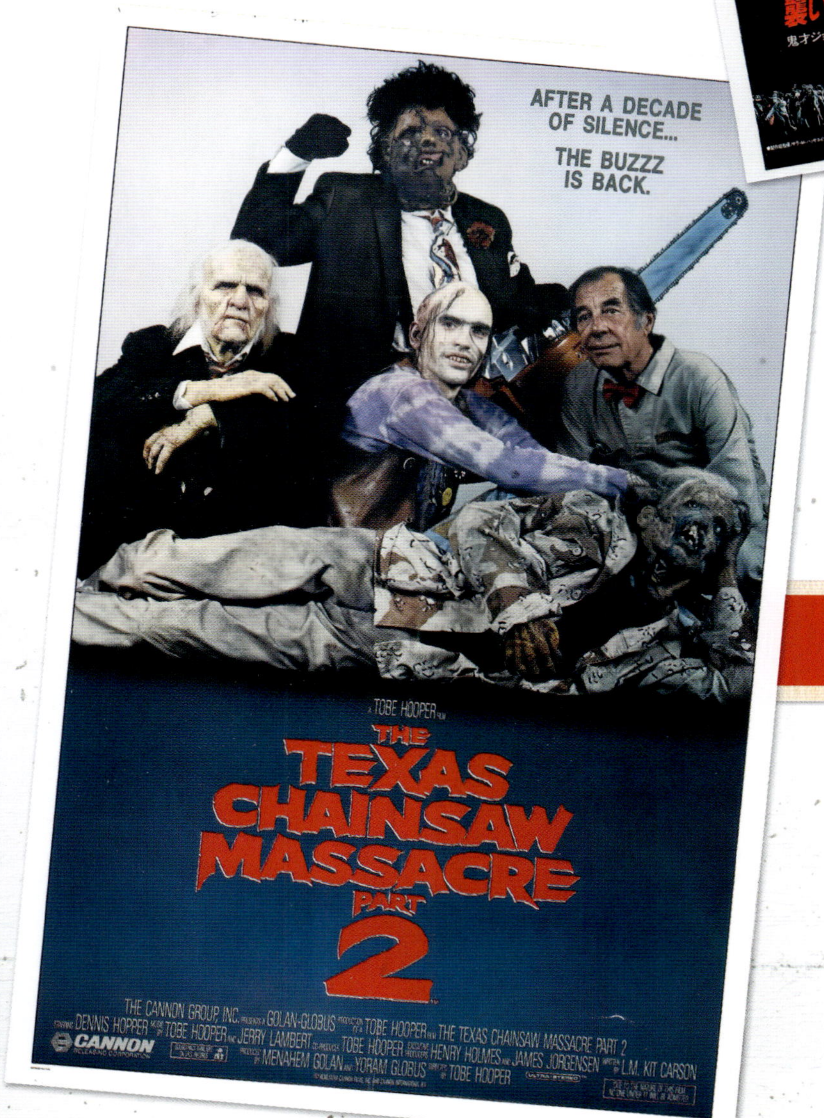

The Texas Chainsaw Massacre 2.
Cannon Films (1986).

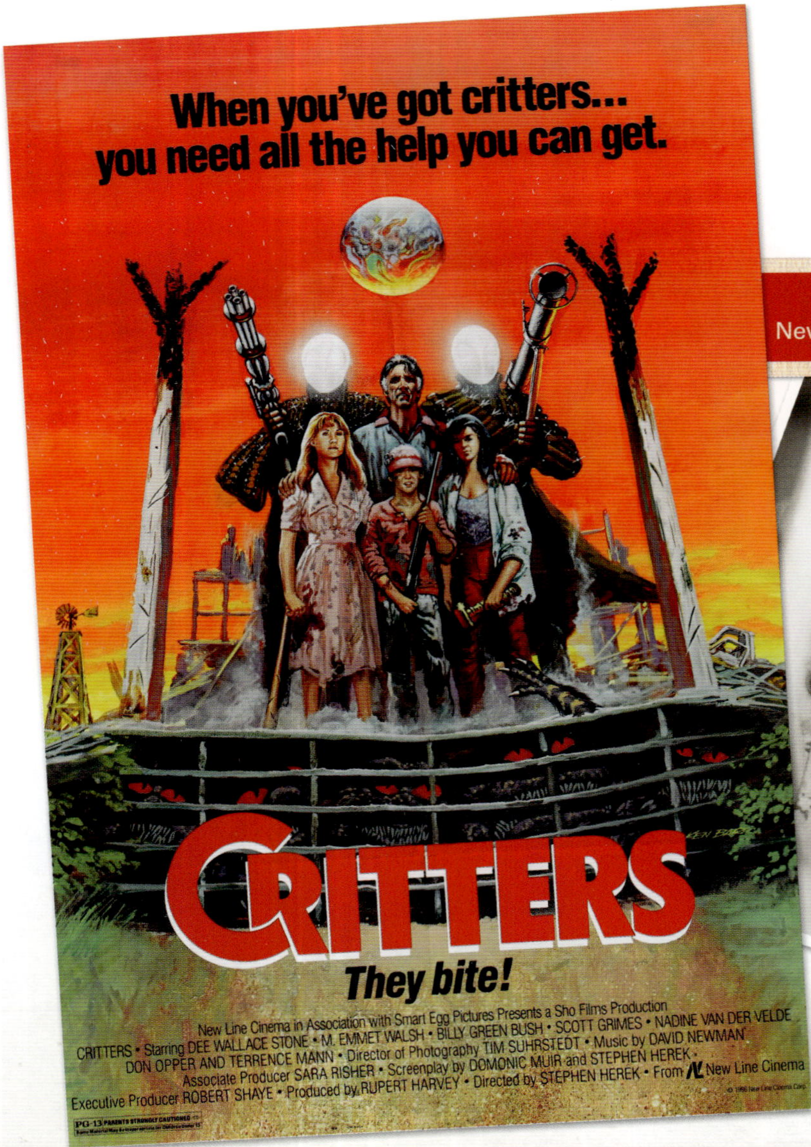

Critters.
New Line Cinema/Sho Films/Smart Egg Pictures (1986).

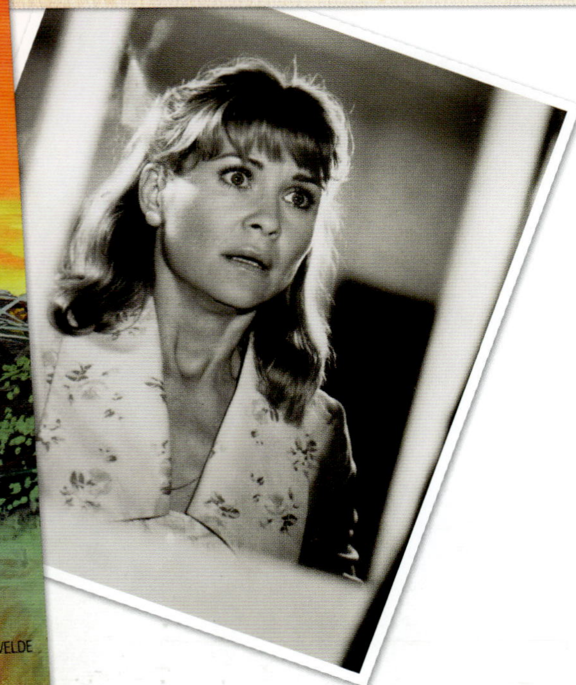

ON SCREAM QUEENS AND **DEE WALLACE**

As the iconic face of 1980s American horror film, Jamie Lee Curtis may deserve all the praise she's received over the years. And yet, to me, that face should be Dee Wallace's. She's hardly ubiquitous, but in the films she made — from Joe Dante's *The Howling* to Spielberg's *E.T.*, Lewis Teague's *Cujo* to Stephen Herek's *Critters* — she has always been the incarnation of wholesome middle-American goodness. Horror films need that character, and need it to be played well. This is what we care about: that which, eventually, gets defiled, threatened, contaminated, and must be redeemed at great cost for a happy ending. Recently, a small part she played in *House of the Devil*, cast with a knowing wink to horror fans by director Ti West, tells me that I'm not alone in my nostalgia for 1980s American horror and my hunch that it had always looked like Dee Wallace.

~Steffen Hantke

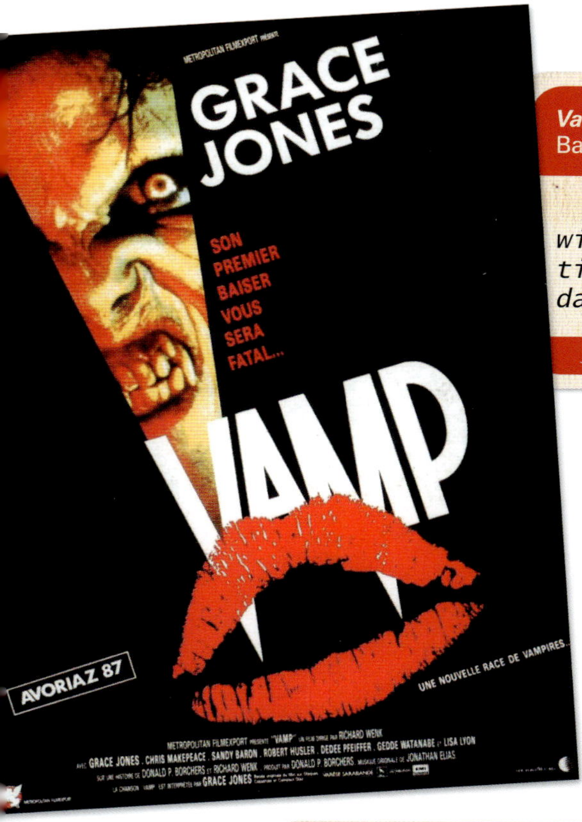

Vamp.
Balcor Film Investors/Planet Productions (1986).

Fun little New World horror comedy, with Grace Jones never better as the titular bloodsucker. Expect a remake any day now...

Tony Timpone

Jason Lives Friday the 13th Part VI.
Paramount Pictures/Terror Films Inc. (1986).

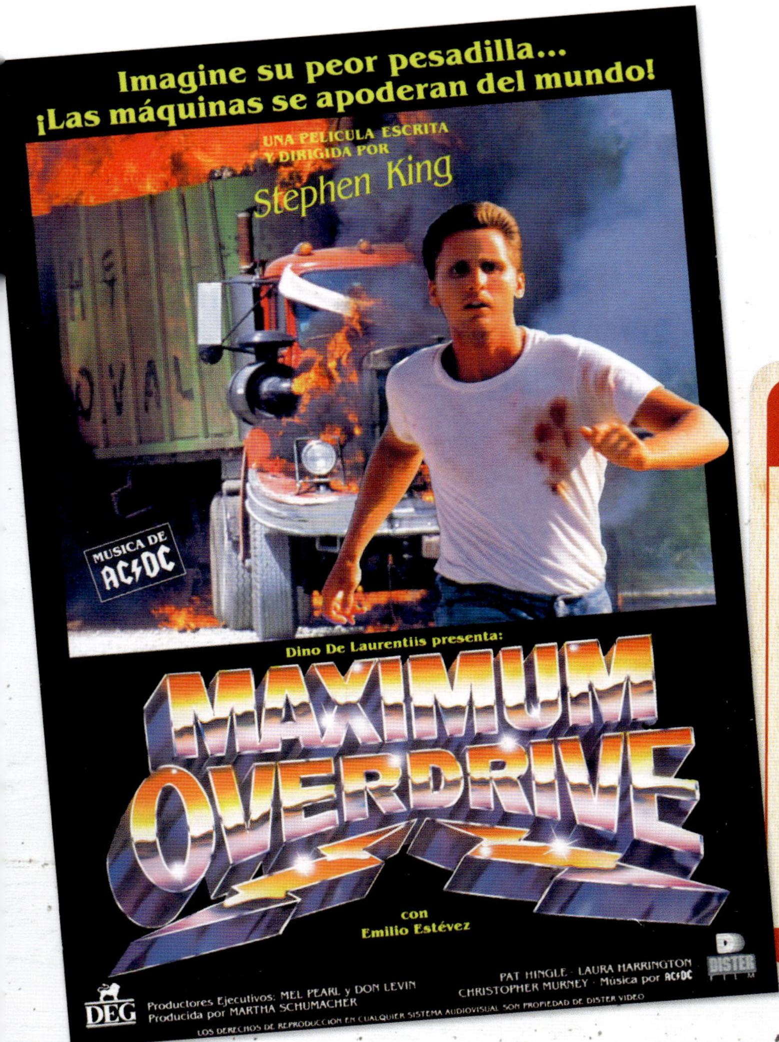

Maximum Overdrive.
De Laurentiis Entertainment Group (1986). Spain.

Give someone enough rope and he will hang himself. Stephen King doesn't quite hang himself with his one and only directing appearance, but there are probably some rope burns around his neck. The basic concept is risible – all the machines on the planet become sentient and they're pissed. The transport with the green goblin face is perhaps the movie's most lingering image, and the AC/DC soundtrack is terrific. King's cameo at the foul-mouthed ATM is funny, and the attack of the soda machine is well executed, too.

Bev Vincent

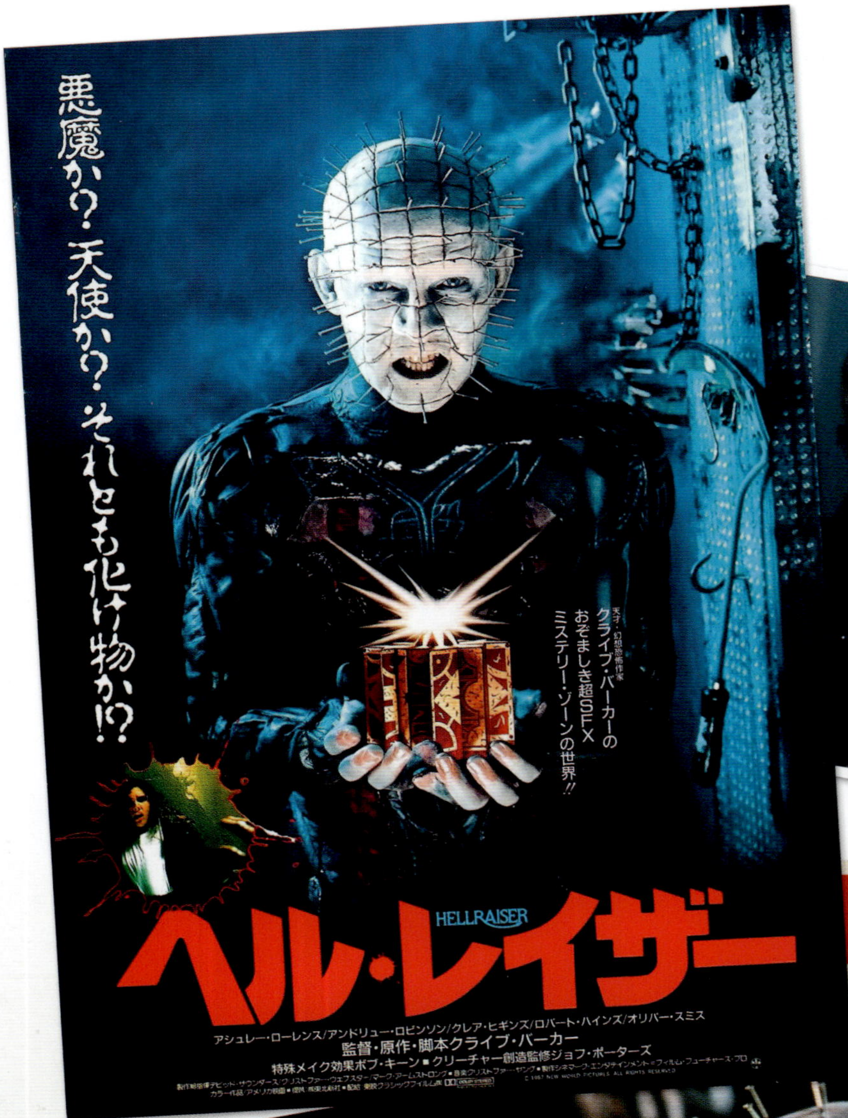

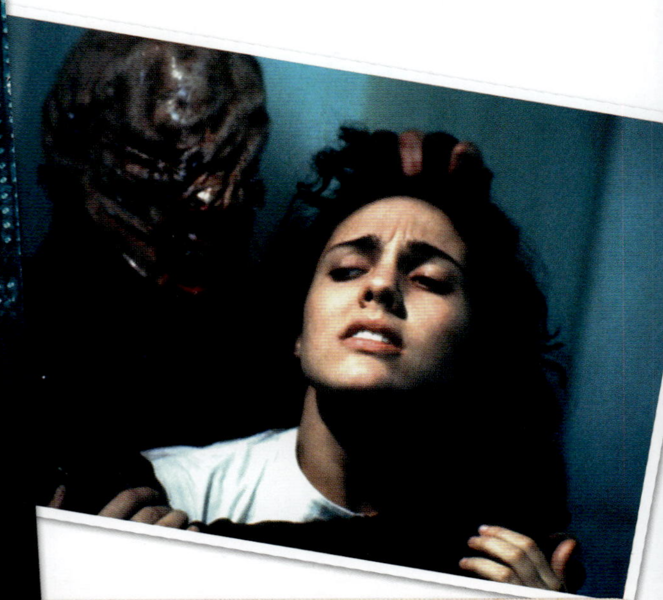

Hellraiser. Cinemarque Entertainment BV/ Film Futures/Rivdel Films (1987). Japan.

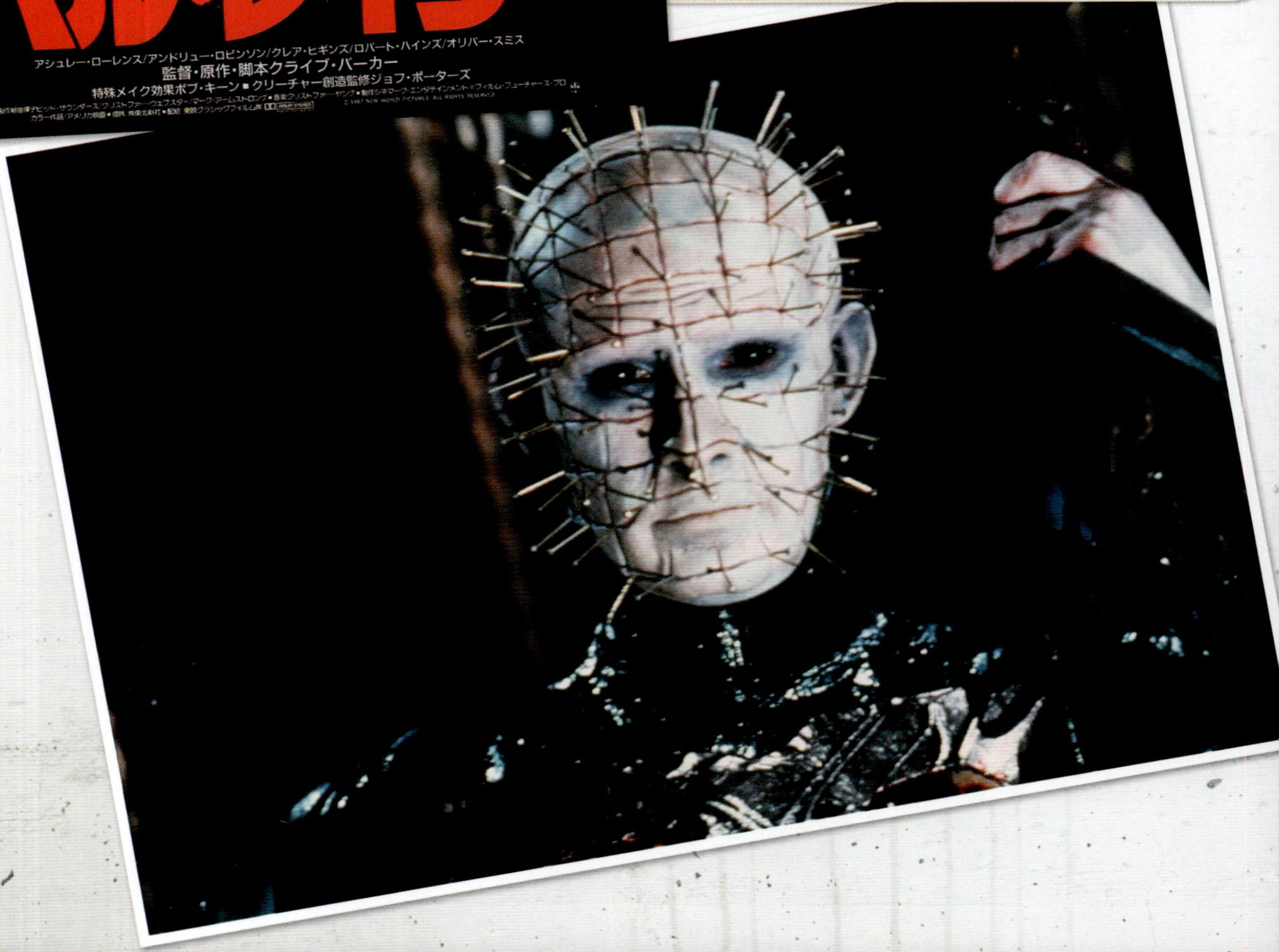

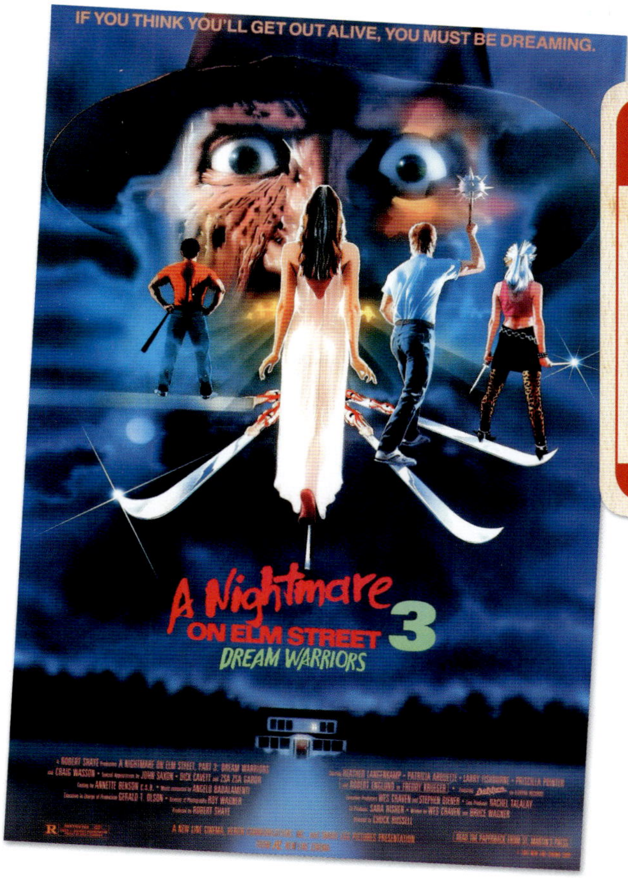

A Nightmare on Elm Street 3: Dream Warriors. New Line Cinema/Heron Communications/Smart Egg Pictures (1987).

At the time, I identified with the Dungeons-and-Dragons-playing kid in a wheelchair who attacks Freddy in a wizard costume. Freddy says, "Sorry, kid, I don't believe in fairytales," and jabs him with his razor glove. A poster of Freddy, a promo for this movie, ended up on my bedroom wall. My hero!

L. Andrew Cooper

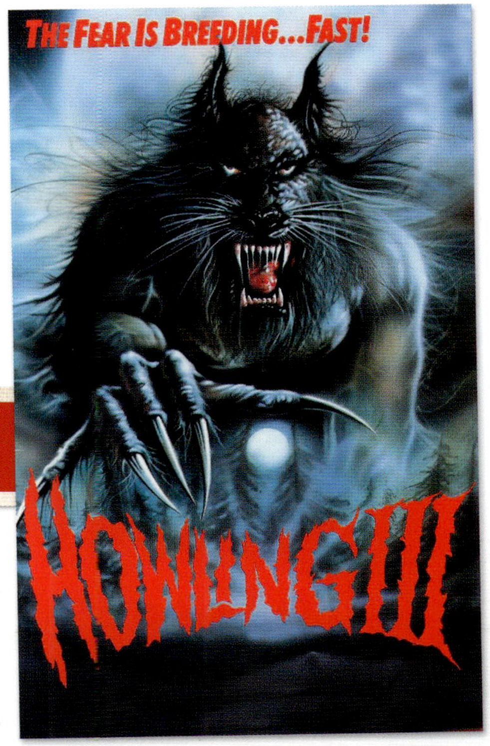

Howling III.
Bancannia Holdings Pty. Ltd. (1987). UK.

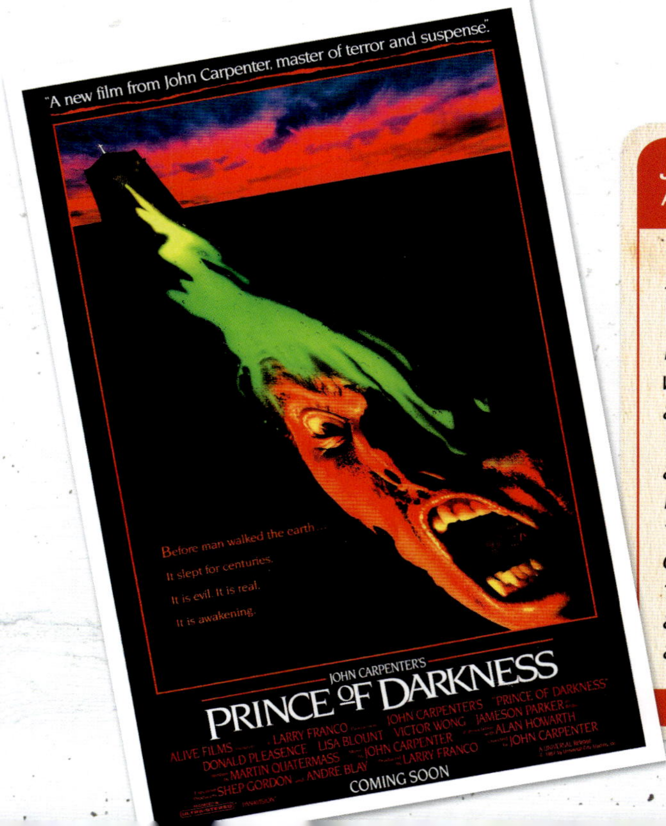

John Carpenter's Prince of Darkness.
Alive Films/Larry Franco Productions (1987).

This is one of my favorite horror films, which builds dread in a torture like the gradual tightening of the rack. It merges the concept of evil with the modern physics of matter and anti-matter. Through a mysterious green liquid swirling in a giant cylinder in an abandoned church, Satan attempts to release the ultimate evil by building an interdimensional portal. Most chilling of all are warning dreams sent from the future to the doomed protagonists. Not a film to watch late at night when you are by yourself!

Rosemary Ellen Guiley

Demons 2.
DACFILM Rome (1987).

A television documentary shows people sneaking into the "forbidden zone" where the first movie took place, and they encounter a demon who crosses into the real world through the television of someone watching the documentary. What's memorable here isn't this sequel's logical leap in media self-referentiality from movie theaters to home viewings, but the way that the everyday world of an apartment building quickly turns into a living nightmare, where with little warning your friends and neighbors grow claws and fangs and try to kill you. It's not without the first one's delightful schlock, but it's also genuinely scary, especially when one little kid runs down a hallway, begging for help, but help doesn't come in time, and when another kid (writer/producer Dario Argento's daughter, Asia, in her debut) watches her father being slaughtered. This film reminded me of being a kid who believed the world could turn out to be much, much scarier than grown-ups would have it be.

L. Andrew Cooper

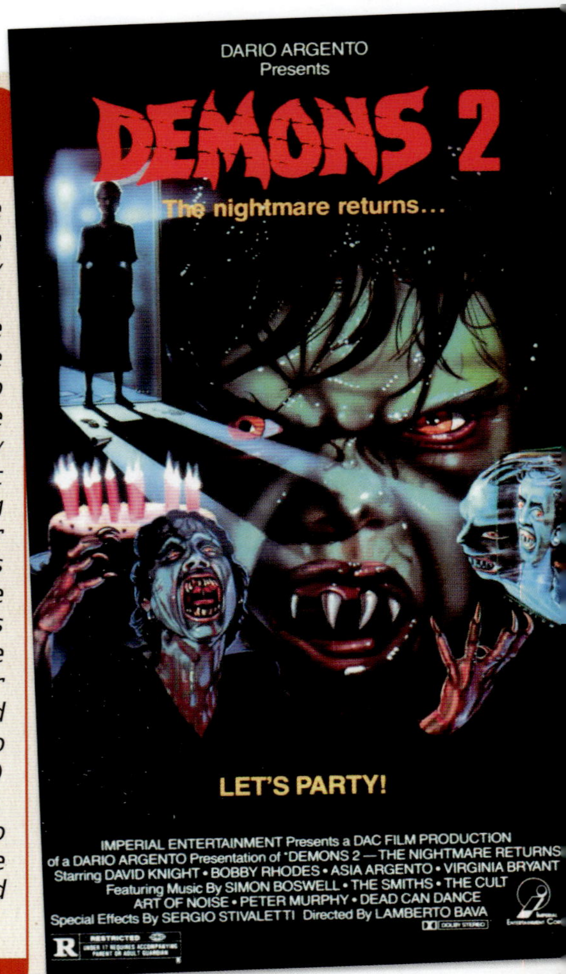

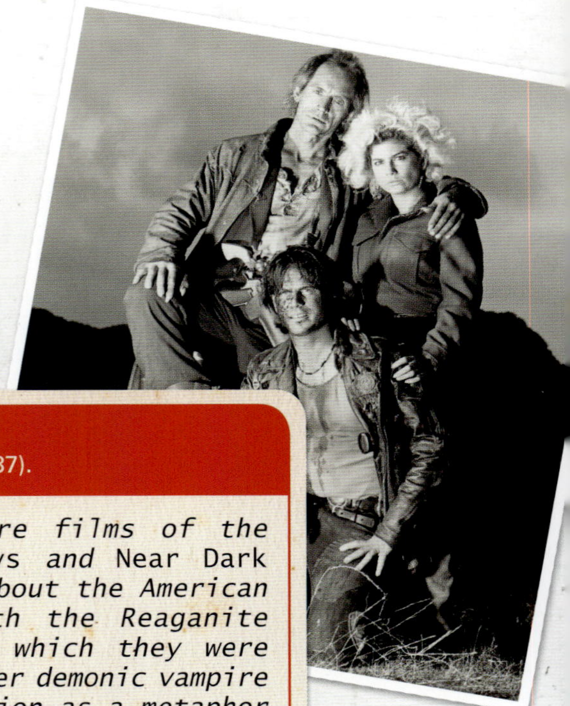

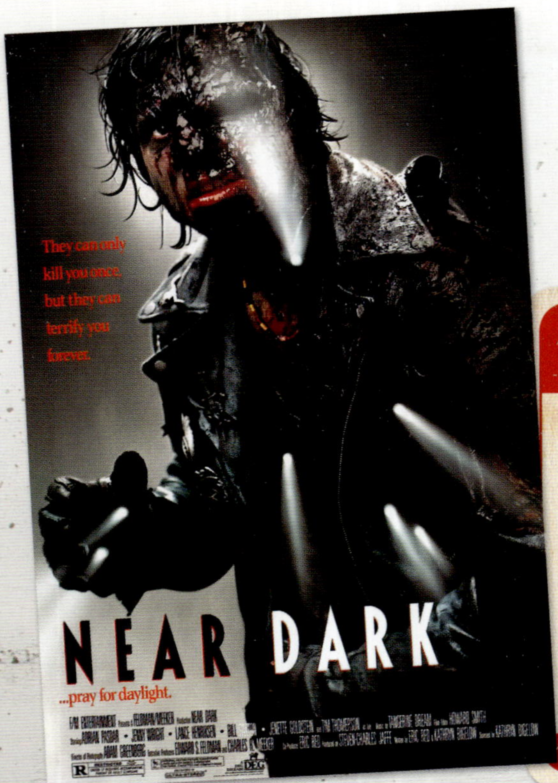

Near Dark.
F/M/Near Dark Joint Venture (1987).

Such popular vampire films of the 1980s as The Lost Boys and Near Dark are, ultimately, all about the American family. Complicit with the Reaganite values of the era in which they were produced, the films offer demonic vampire communities that function as a metaphor for the contemporary dysfunctional family and are set against, and vanquished by, the good human families.

Glennis Byron

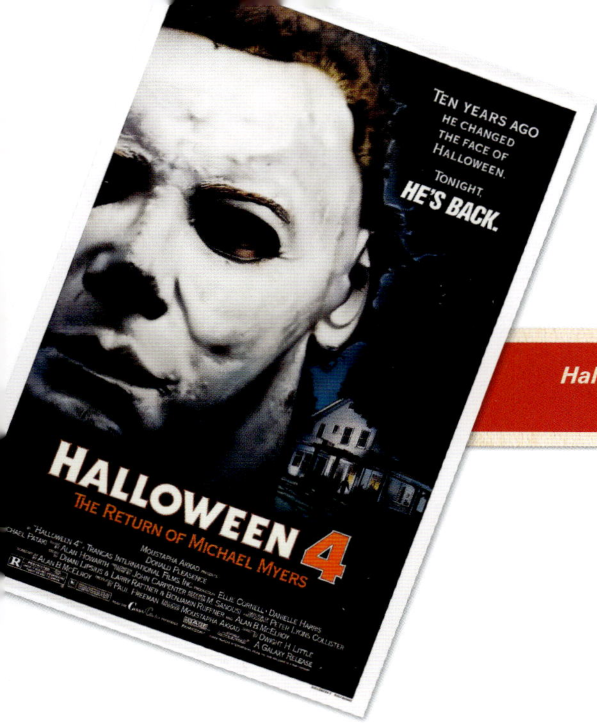

Halloween 4: The Return of Michael Myers.
Trancas International Films (1988). .

Child's Play.
United Artists (1988). France.

A scathing parody of the Cabbage Patch Doll craze of the early 1980s, Tom Holland's Child's Play *is actually a veiled warning about commercialism run awry. Here, a "Good Guys Doll" named Chucky (Brad Dourif) comes to ghoulish life to threaten a small child's very soul. And that child, incidentally, has fallen hook, line, and sinker for the Good Guys "franchise." He eats Good Guys cereal, wears Good Guys fashion, watches Good Guys TV, and has always wanted that wonderful Good Guys Doll...the hot toy this Christmas. In a trenchant, diabolical fashion,* Child's Play *gazes at the ways that children of the mass-media age can become victim to marketers: programmed to want every toy their parents can possibly afford.*

John Kenneth Muir

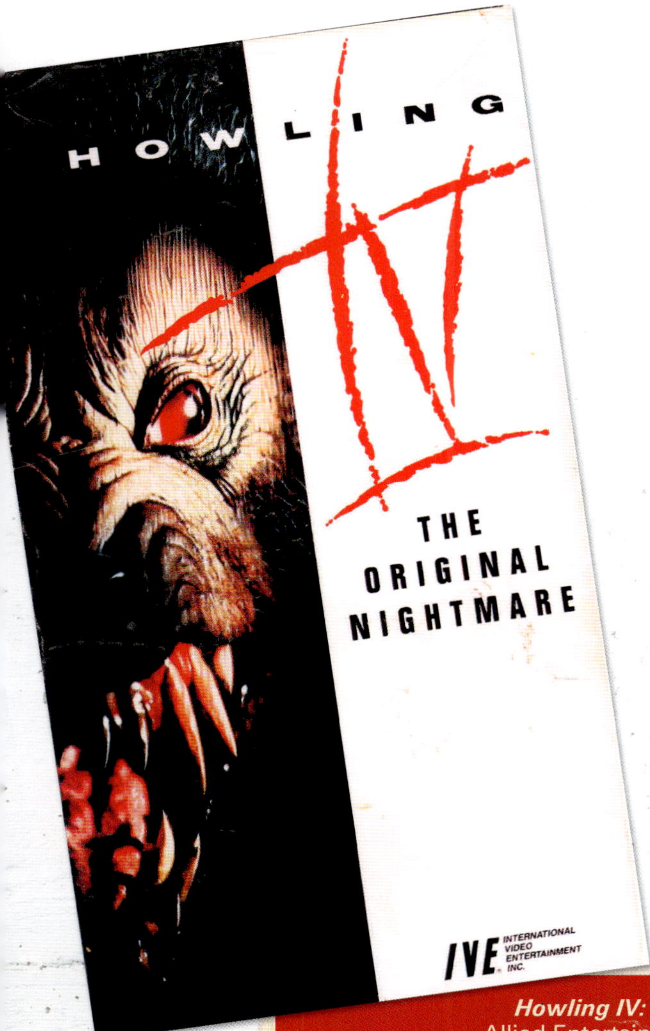

Howling IV: The Original Nightmare.
Allied Entertainments Group PLC (1988).

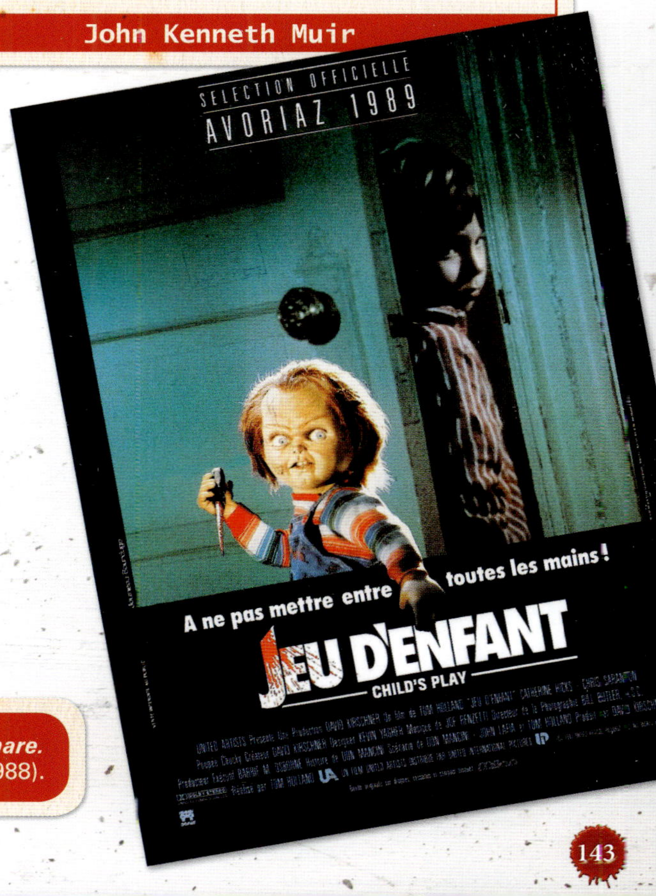

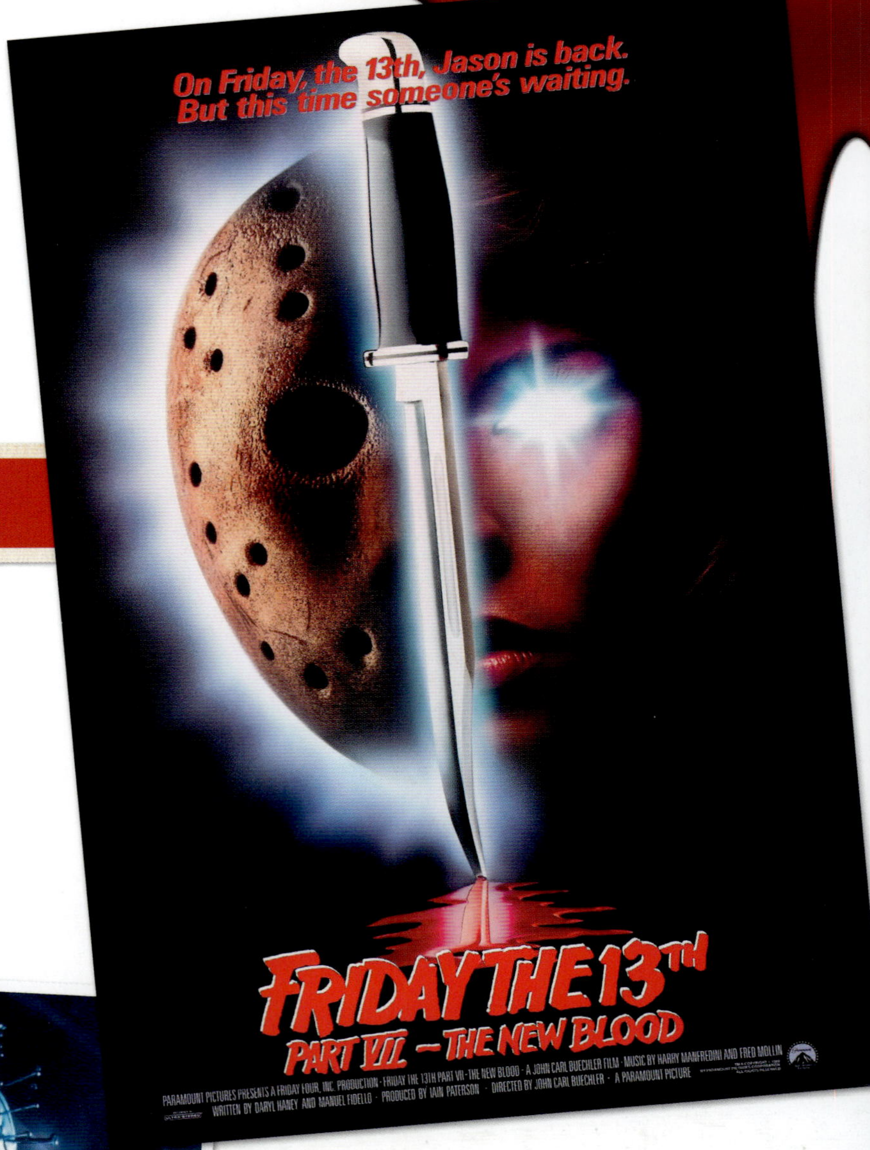

Friday the 13th Part VII: The New Blood. Friday Four Films Inc./Paramount Pictures (1988).

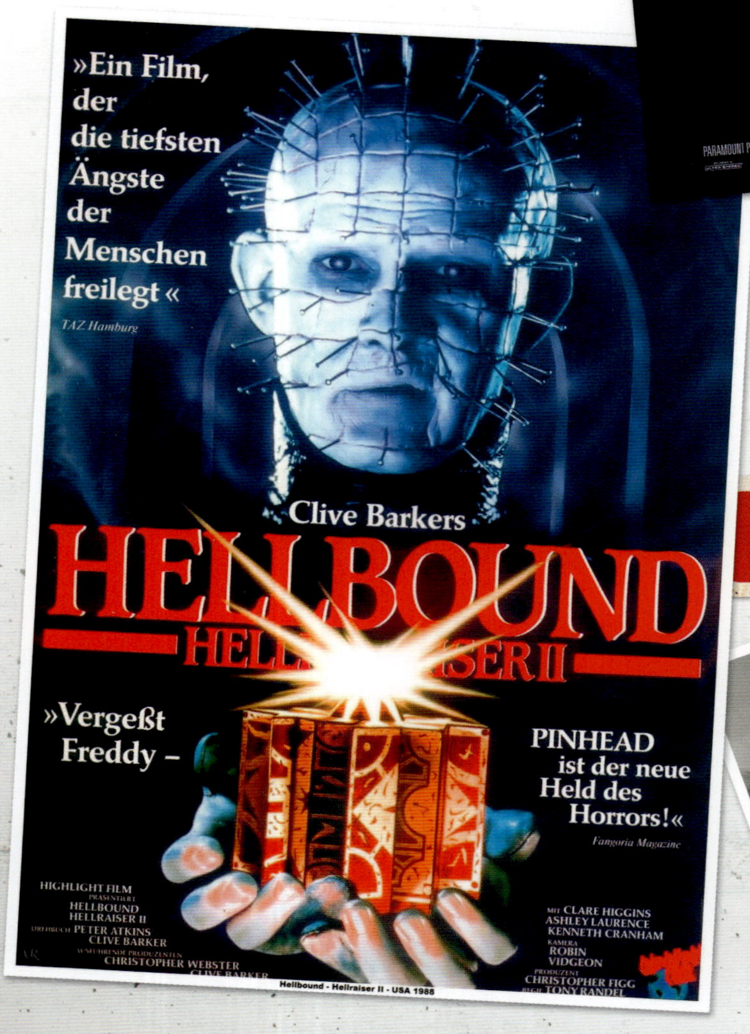

Hellbound: Hellraiser II. Film Futures/ New World Pictures/Troopstar (1988) Germany.

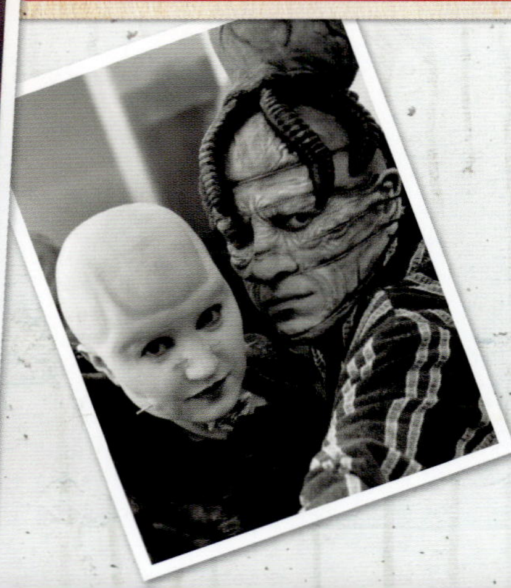

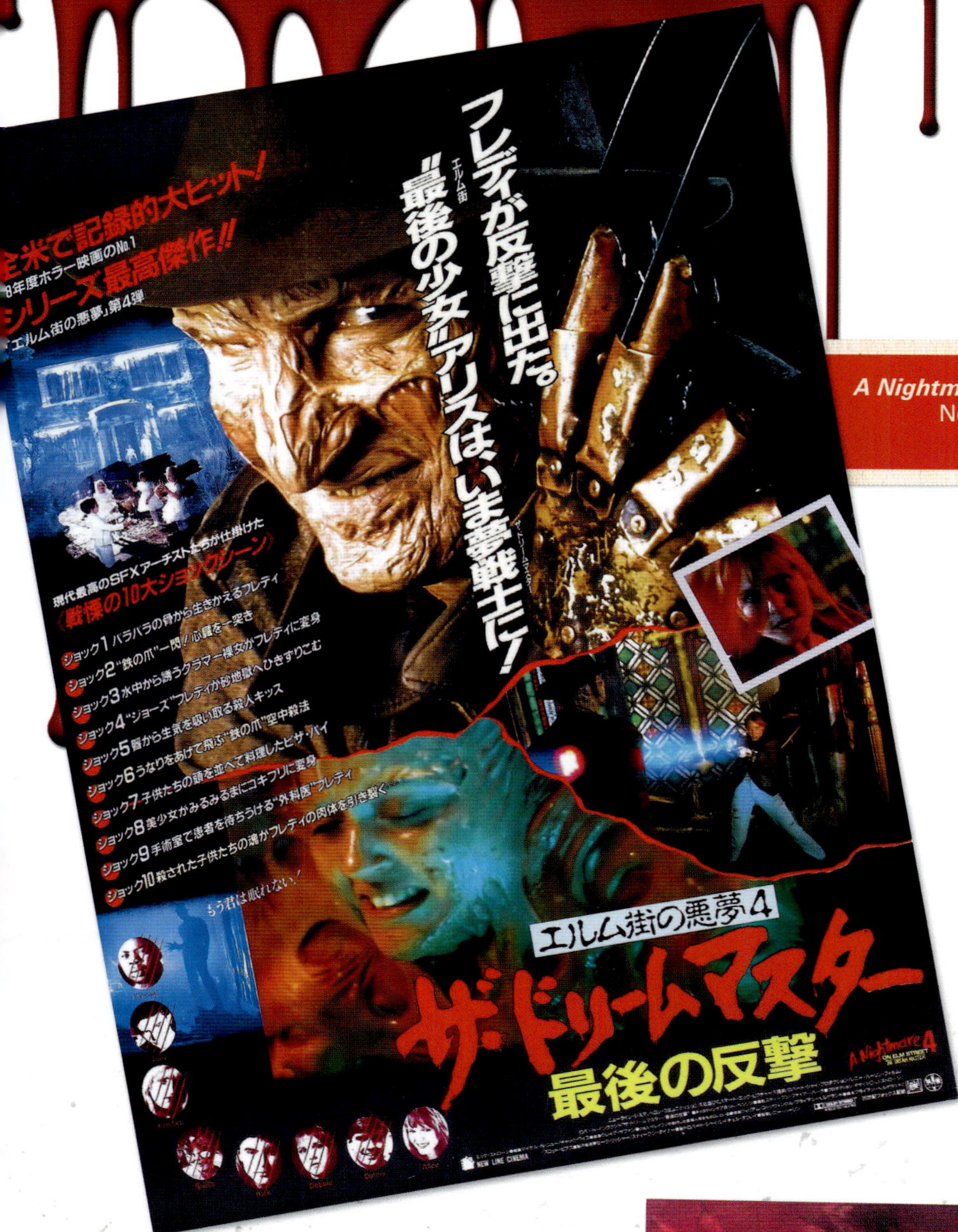

A Nightmare on Elm Street 4: The Dream Master. New Line Cinema/Heron Communications/ Smart Egg Pictures (1988). Japan.

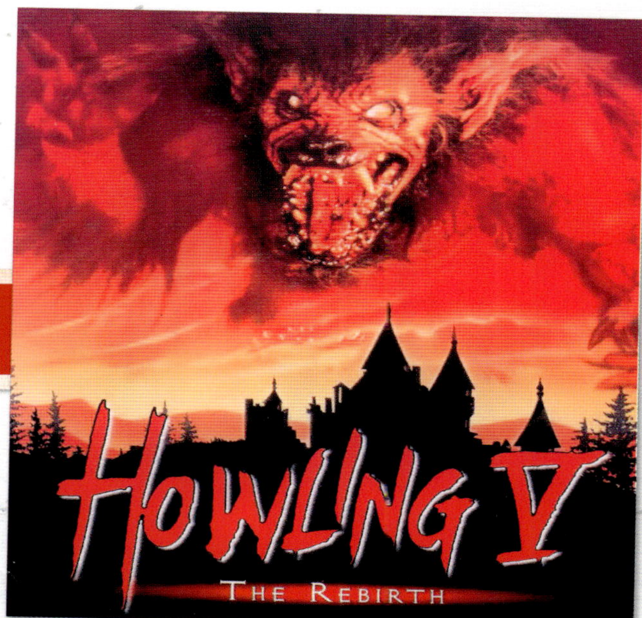

Howling V: The Rebirth. Allied Vision/ Lane Pringle Productions/Mafilm Studios (1989).

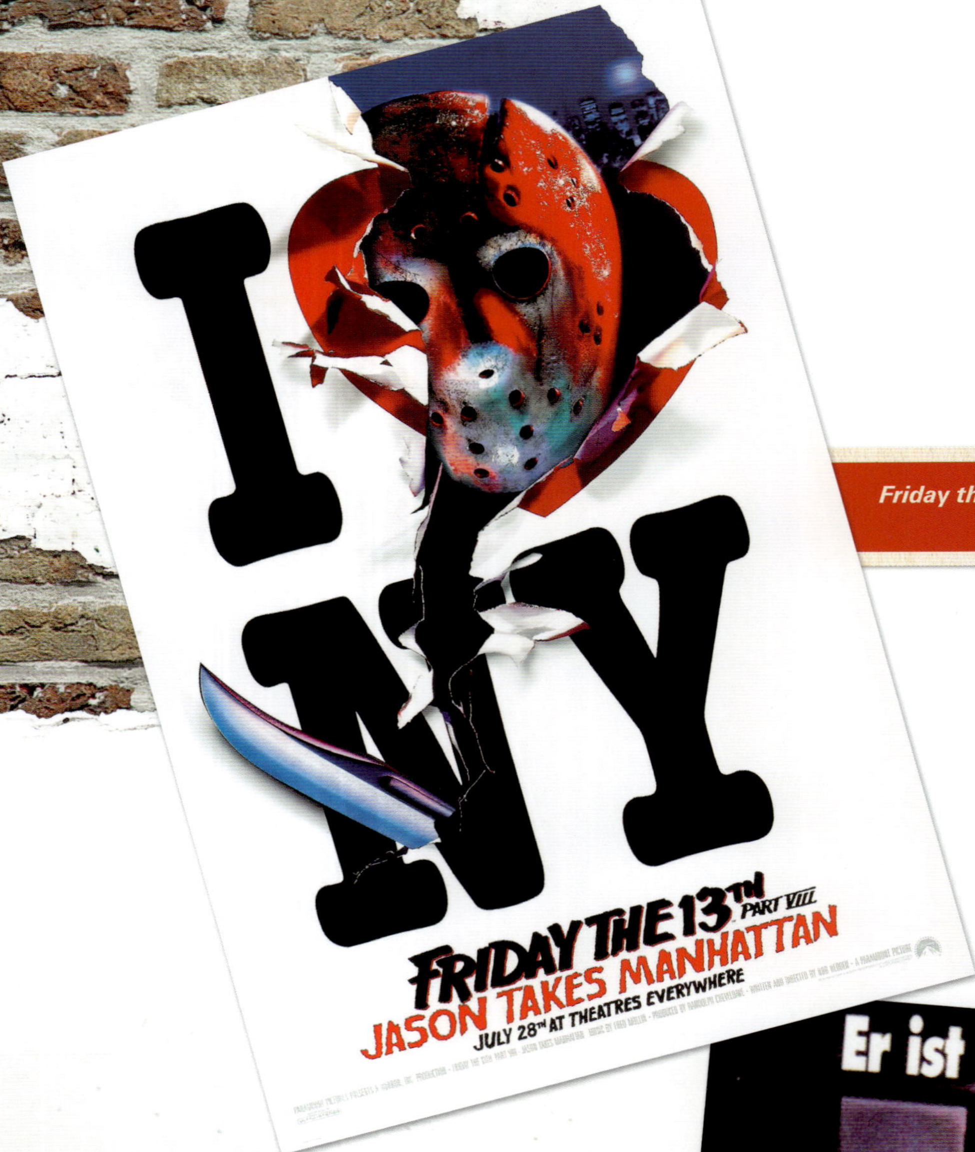

Friday the 13th Part VIII: Jason Takes Manhattan. Paramount Pictures/Horror Inc. (1989).

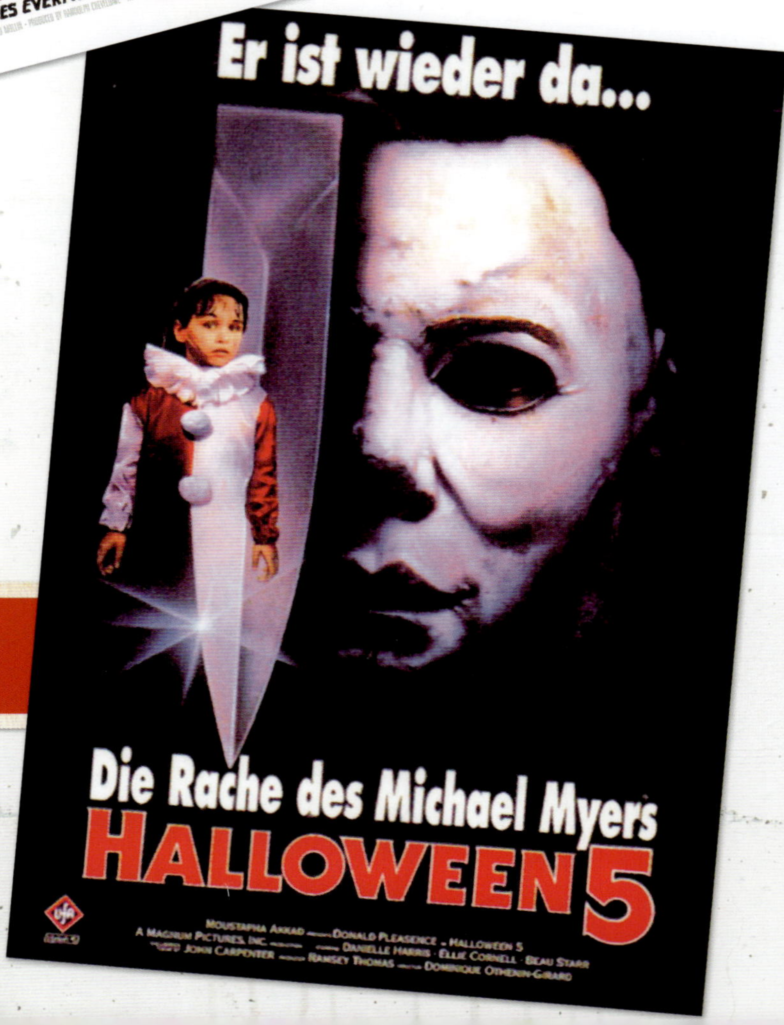

Halloween 5: The Revenge of Michael Myers. Magnum Pictures Inc./The Return of Myers/Trancas International Films (1989). Germany.

A Nightmare on Elm Street 5: The Dream Child. New Line Cinema/Heron Communications/Smart Egg Pictures (1989).

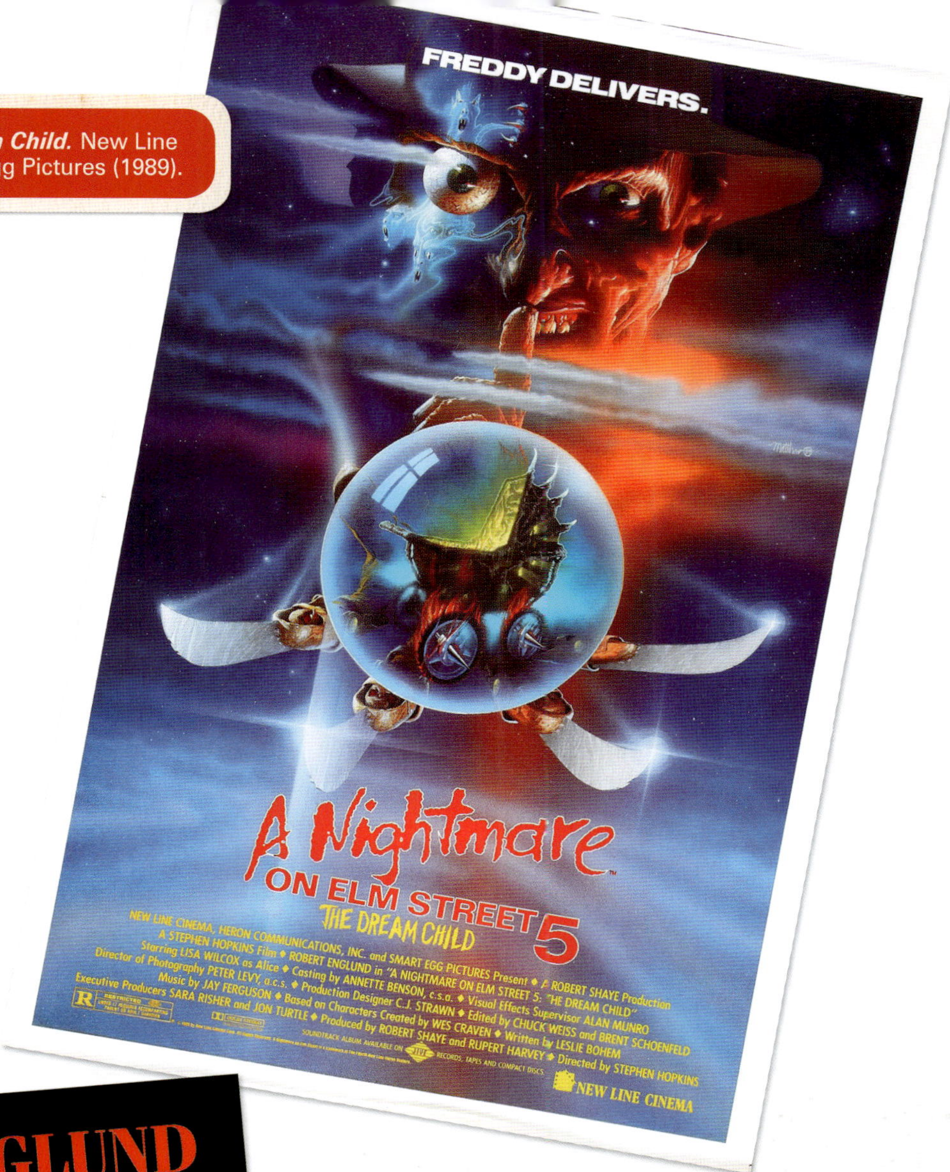

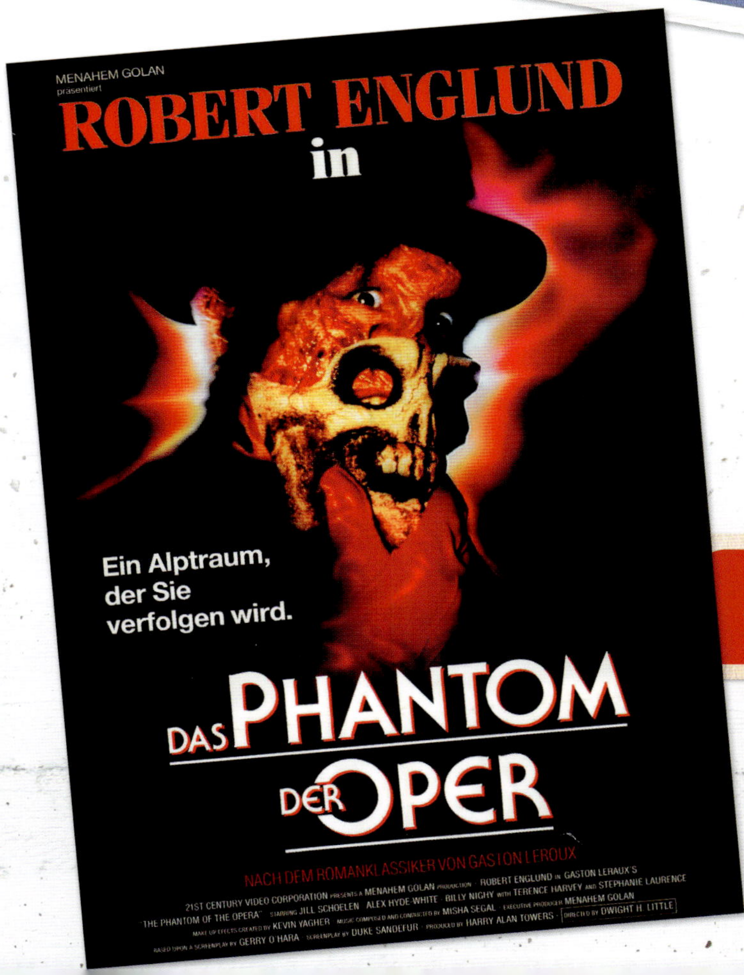

The Phantom of the Opera. 21st Century Film Corporation/Breton Film Productions/ Columbia Pictures Corporation (1989). Germany.

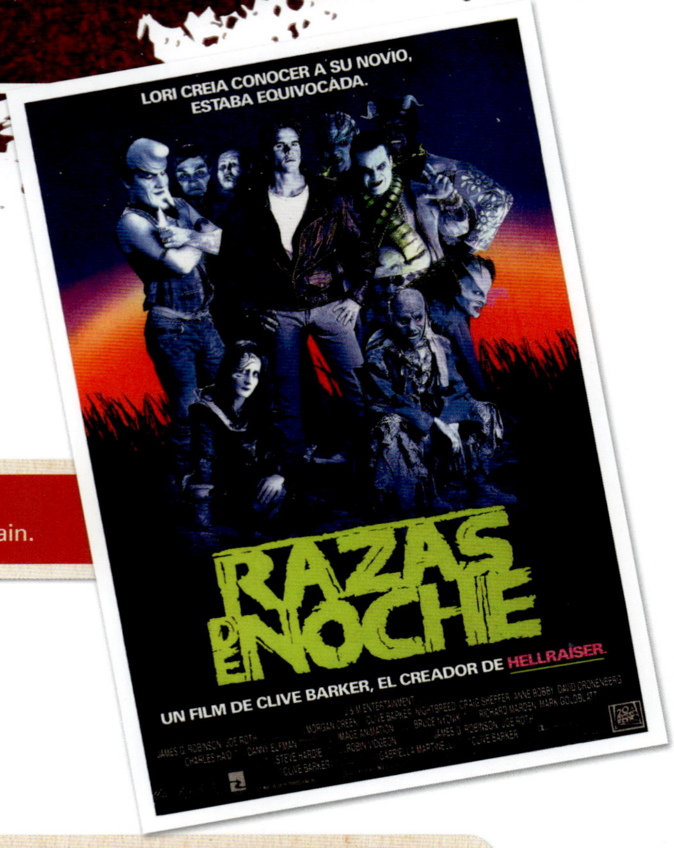

***Nightbreed*.**
Morgan Creek Productions (1990). Spain.

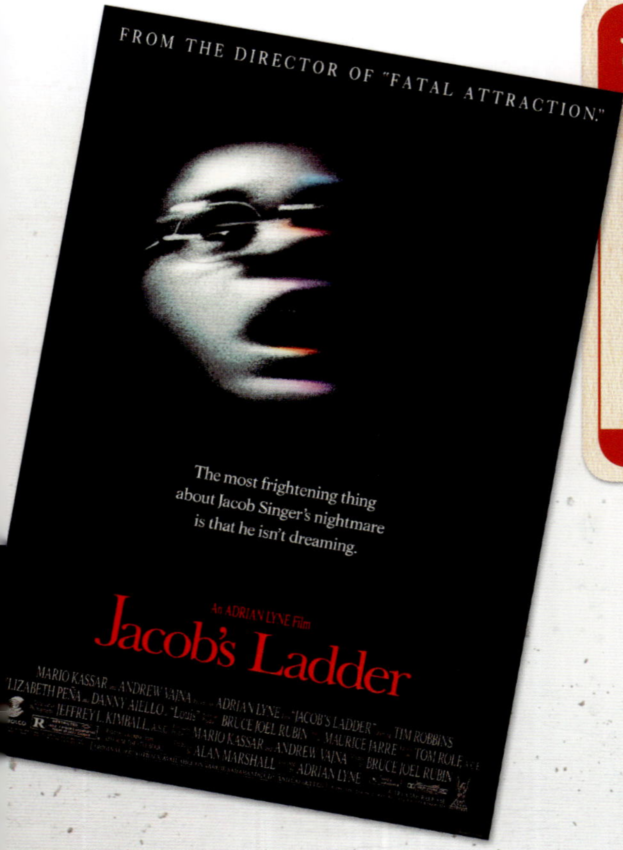

***Jacob's Ladder*.**
Carolco Pictures (1990).

In 1990, I'd become quite jaded regarding horror movies, disappointed by what I perceived to be a steady stream of underwhelming films. Against that backdrop, Jacob's Ladder *seemed like a breath of fresh air – or a gust of chill wind, perhaps. Tim Robbins' portrayal of Vietnam vet Jacob Singer, plagued by flashbacks and hallucinations, is truly harrowing and unforgettable.*

Robert Morrish

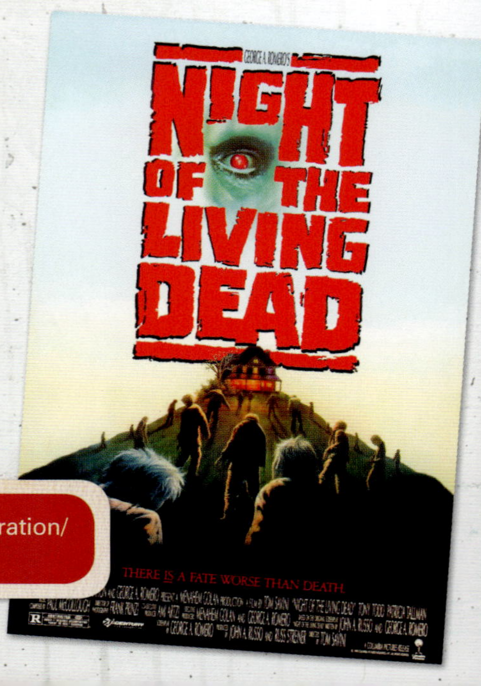

***Night of the Living Dead*.** 21st Century Film Corporation/ Columbia Pictures Corporation (1990).

It.
Green/Epstein Productions/Konigsberg/Sanitsky Company/Lorimar Television/Warner Bros. Television (1990).

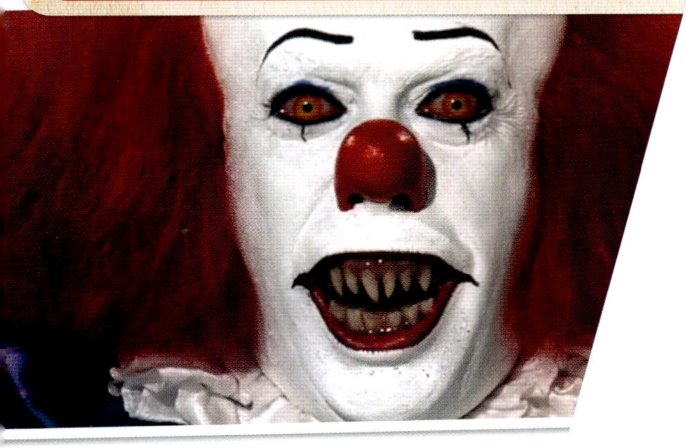

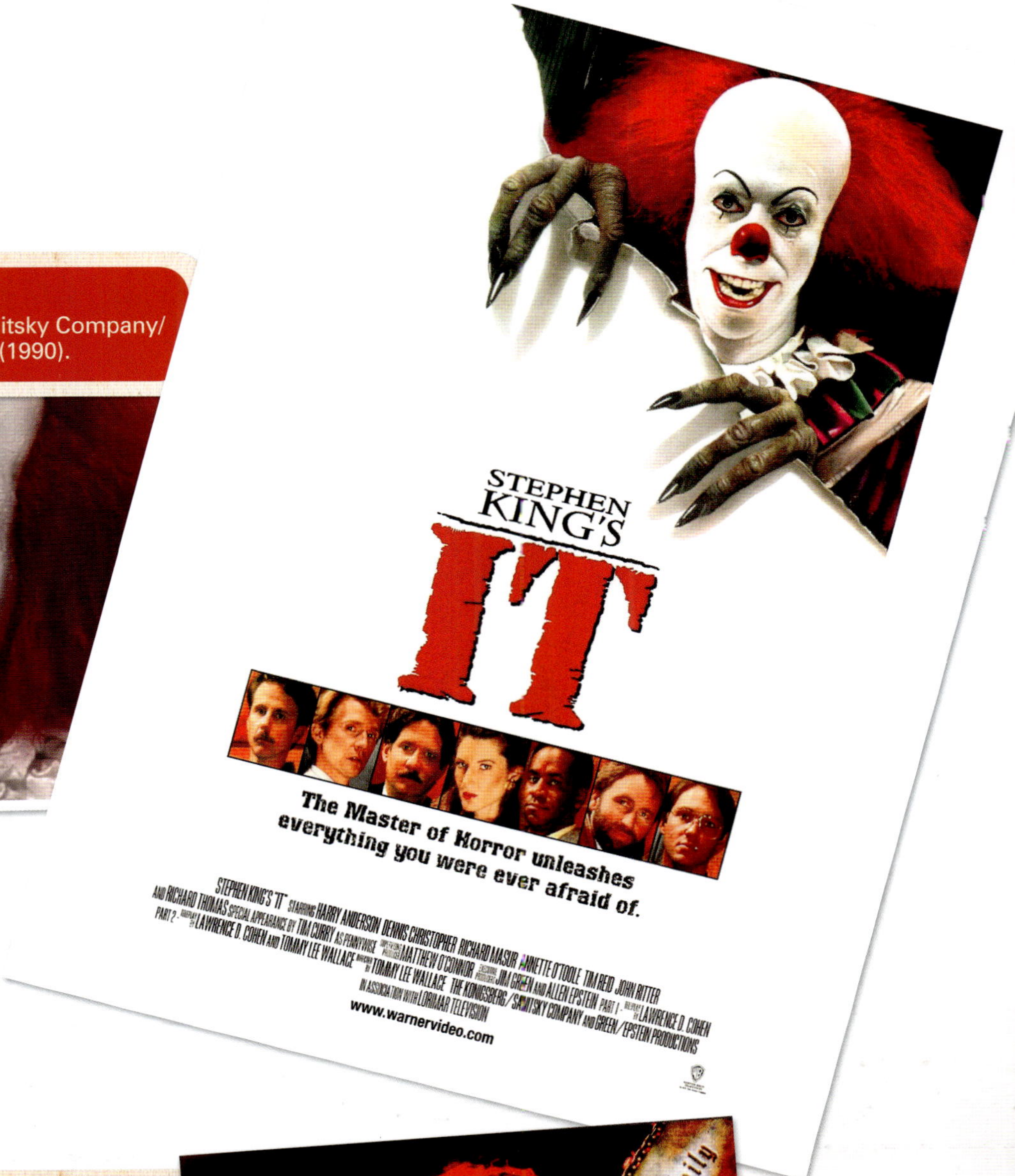

Leatherface: Texas Chainsaw Massacre 3.
New Line Cinema (1990). Argentina.

I own this film. I have a copy of David Schow's script of this film. They have very little to do with each other.

Mort Castle

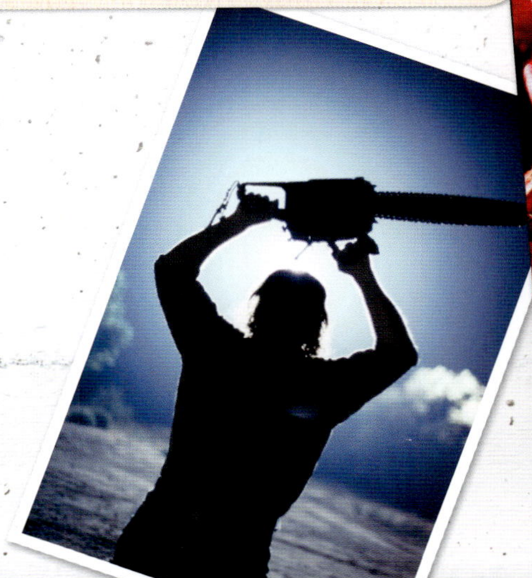

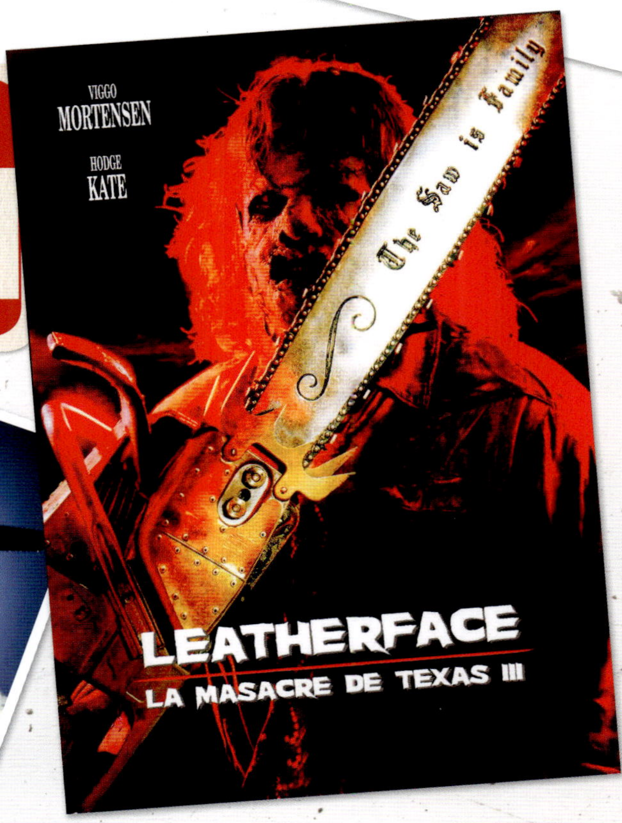

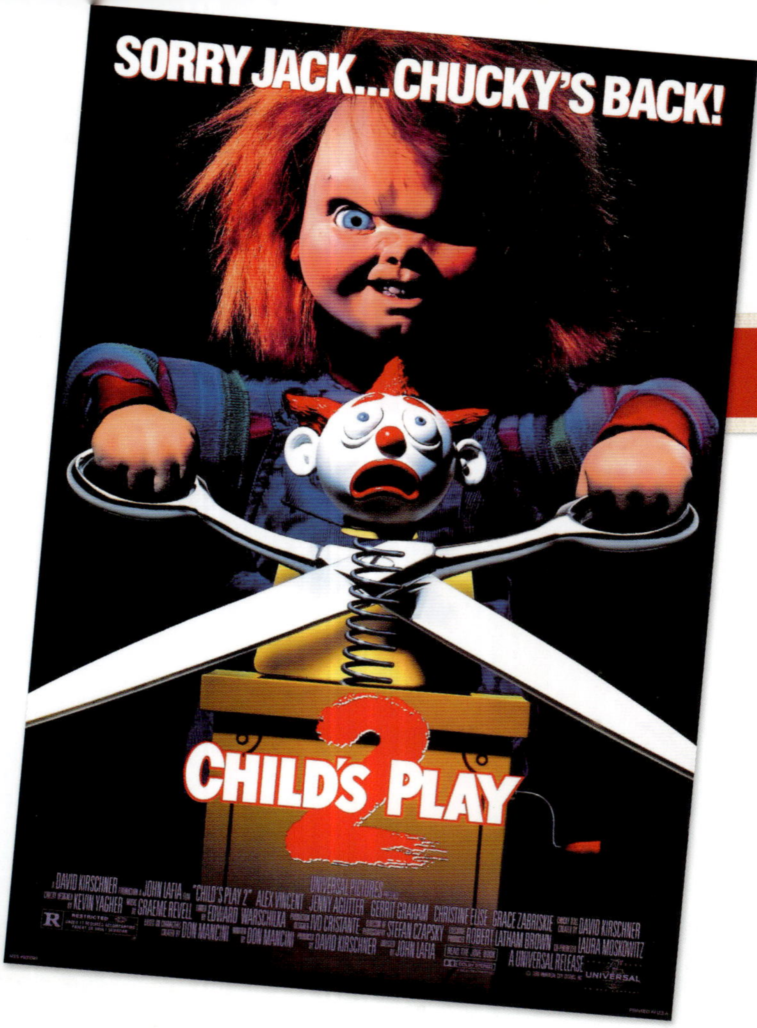

Child's Play 2.
Universal Pictures (1990).

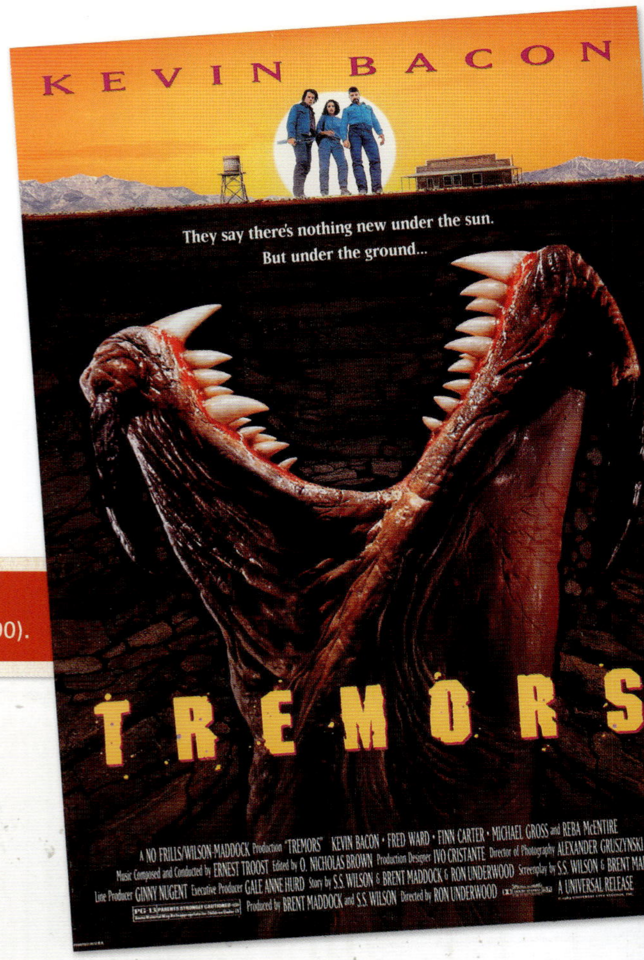

Tremors.
Universal Pictures/No Frills Film Production (1990).

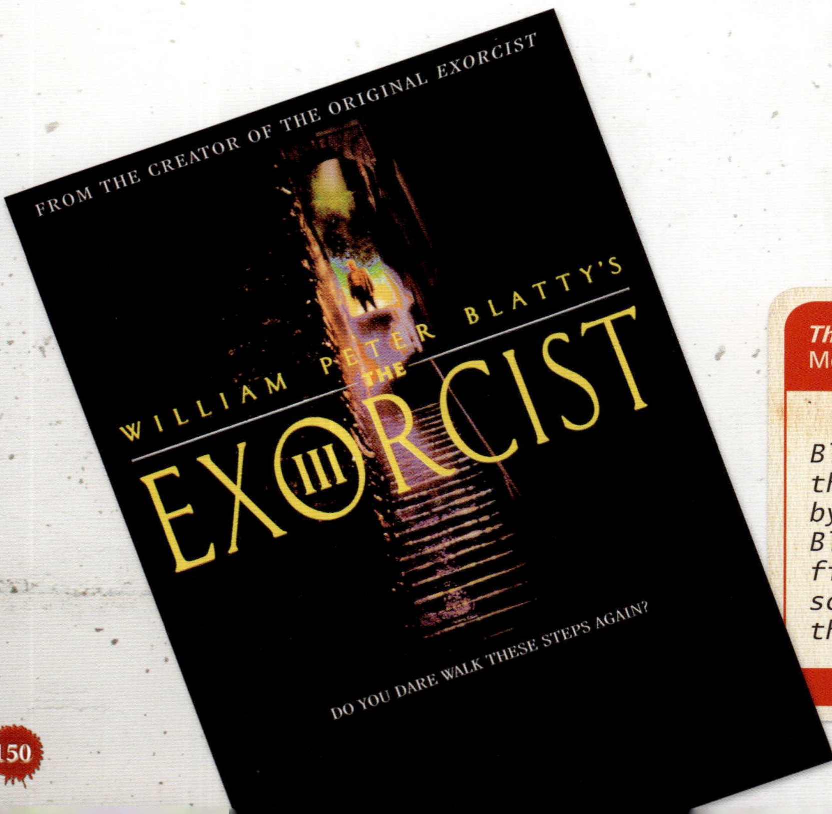

The Exorcist III.
Morgan Creek Productions (1990).

First film's scripter William Peter Blatty directed this semi-sequel, and though the final product was compromised by the studio (there was no exorcism in Blatty's original book, Legion, or the film's initial cut), there are some truly scary moments here. Avoid Exorcist II *and those two prequels at all costs.*

Tony Timpone

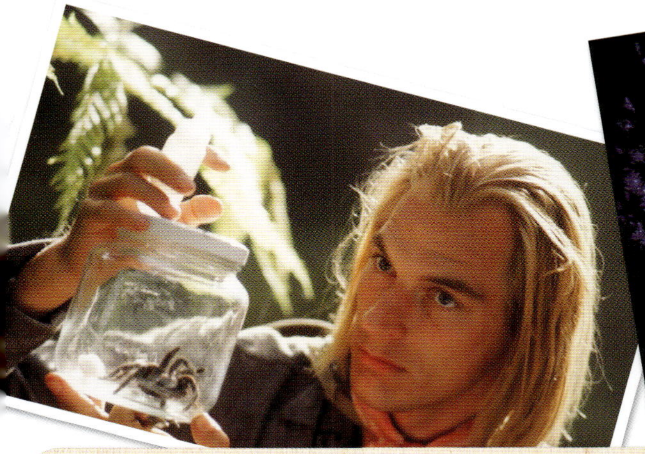

Arachnophobia. Ambiin Entertainment/Hollywood Pictures/Tangled Web Productions (1990). Denmark.

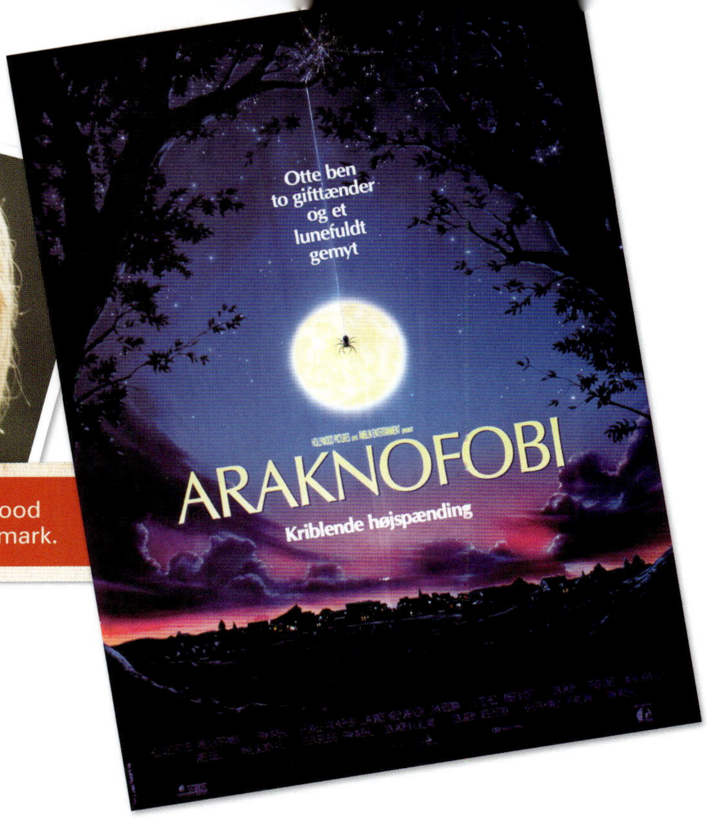

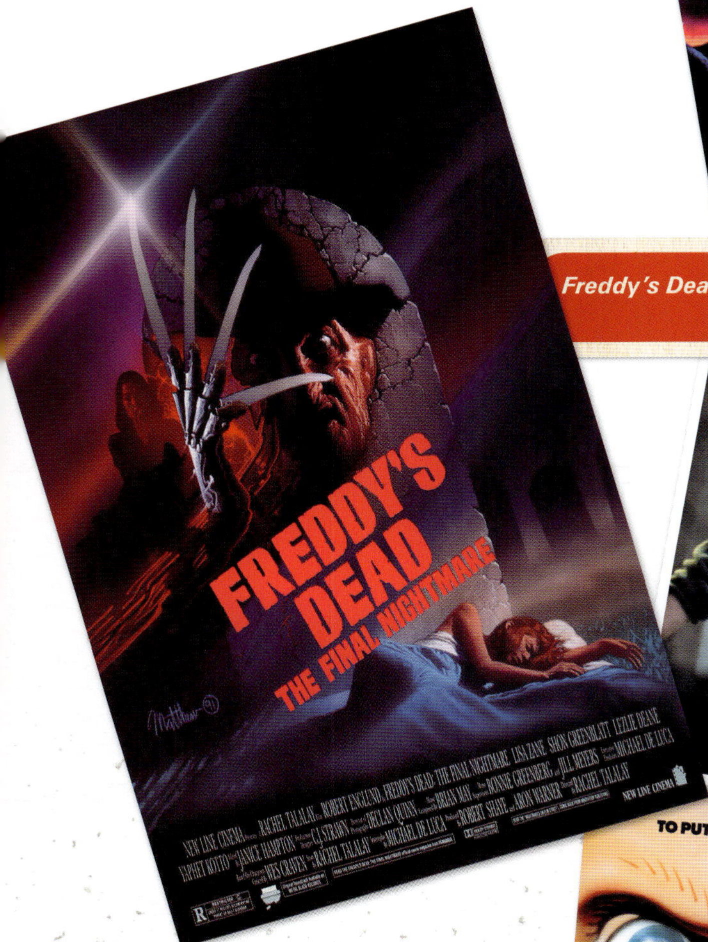

Freddy's Dead: The Final Nightmare. New Line Cinema/ Nicolas Entertainment (1991).

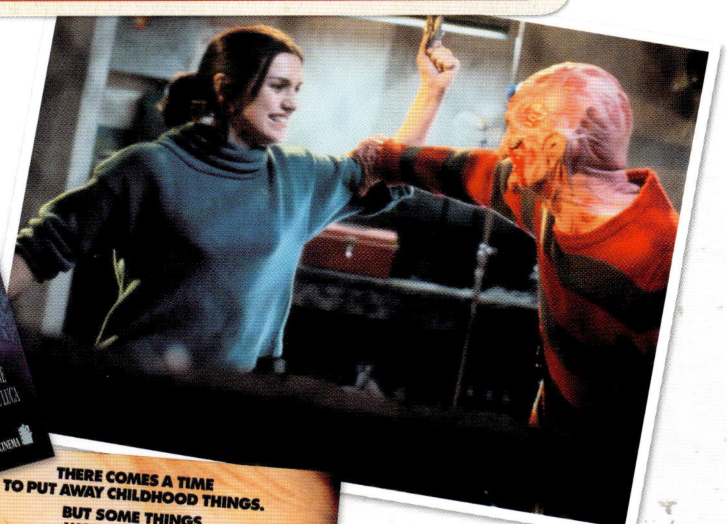

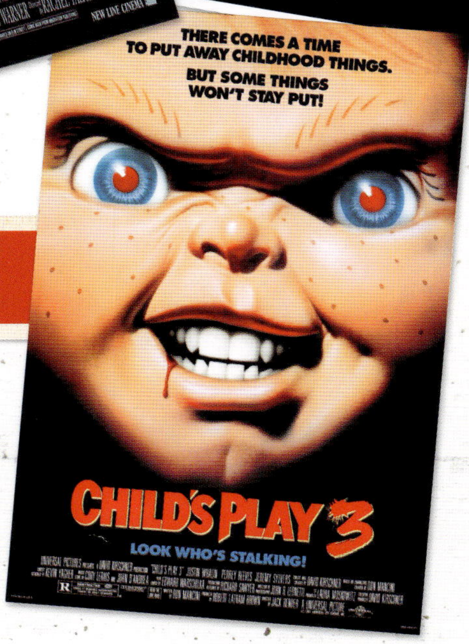

Child's Play 3.
Universal Pictures (1991).

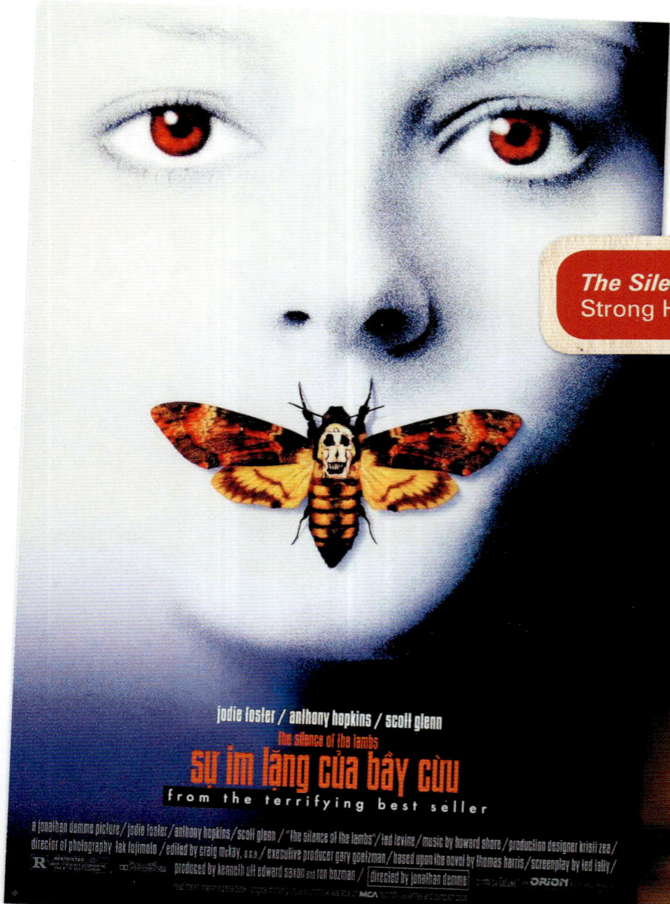

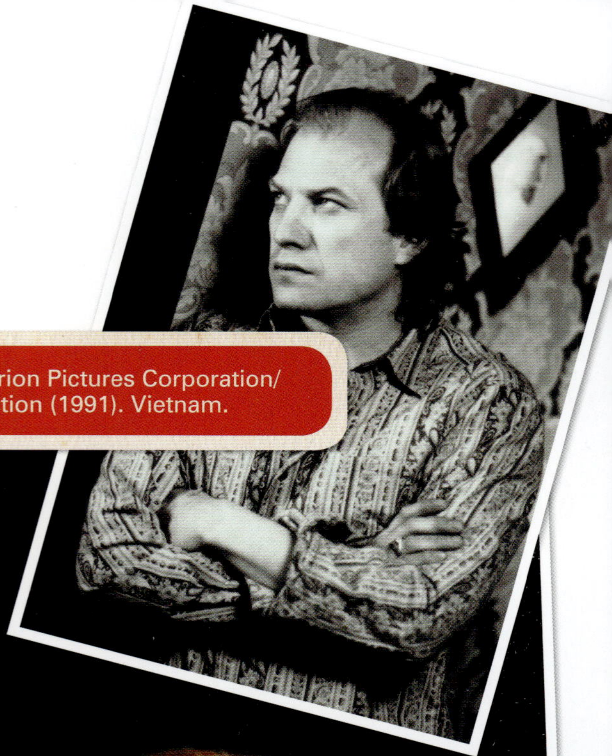

The Silence of the Lambs. Orion Pictures Corporation/ Strong Heart/Demme Production (1991). Vietnam.

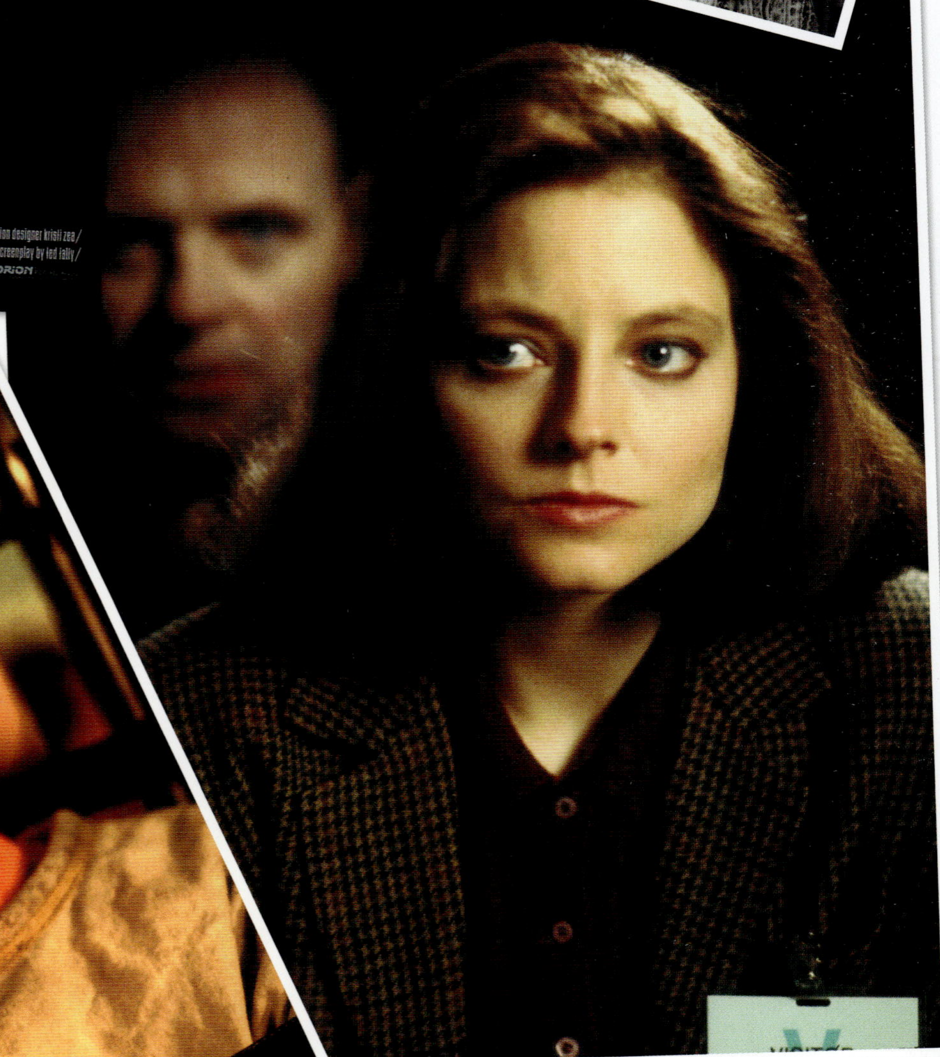

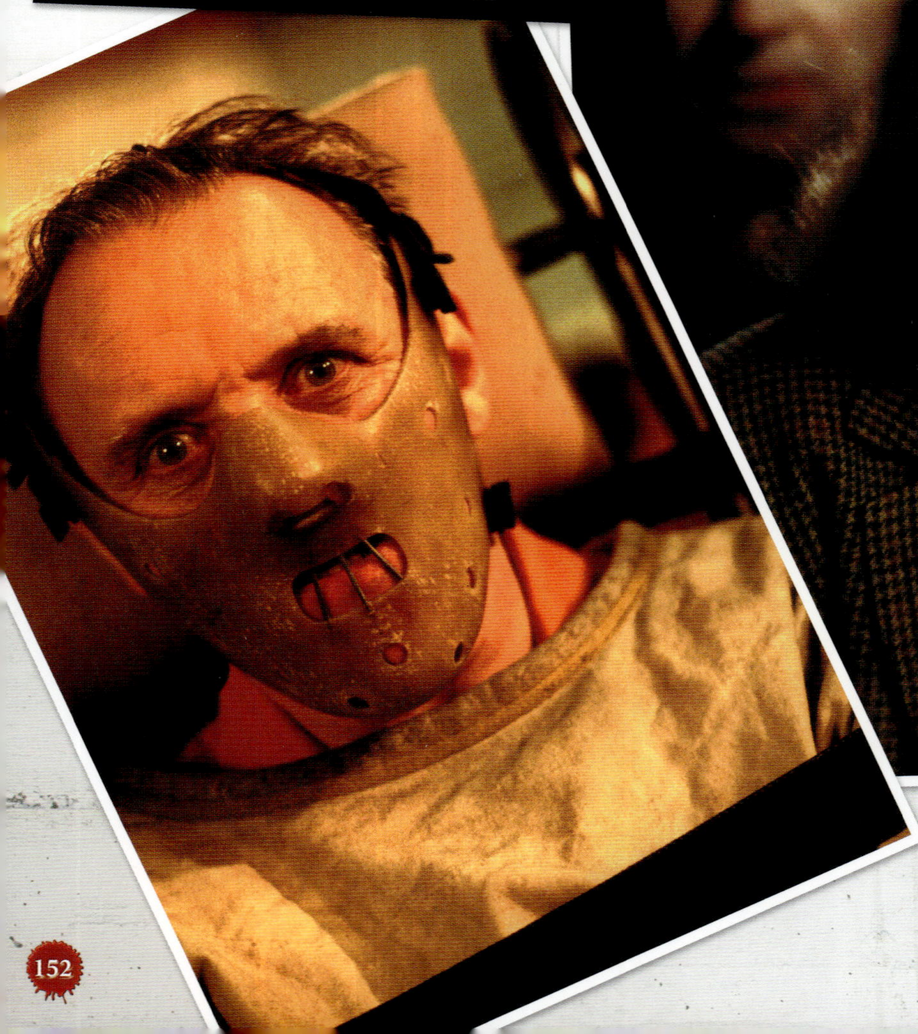

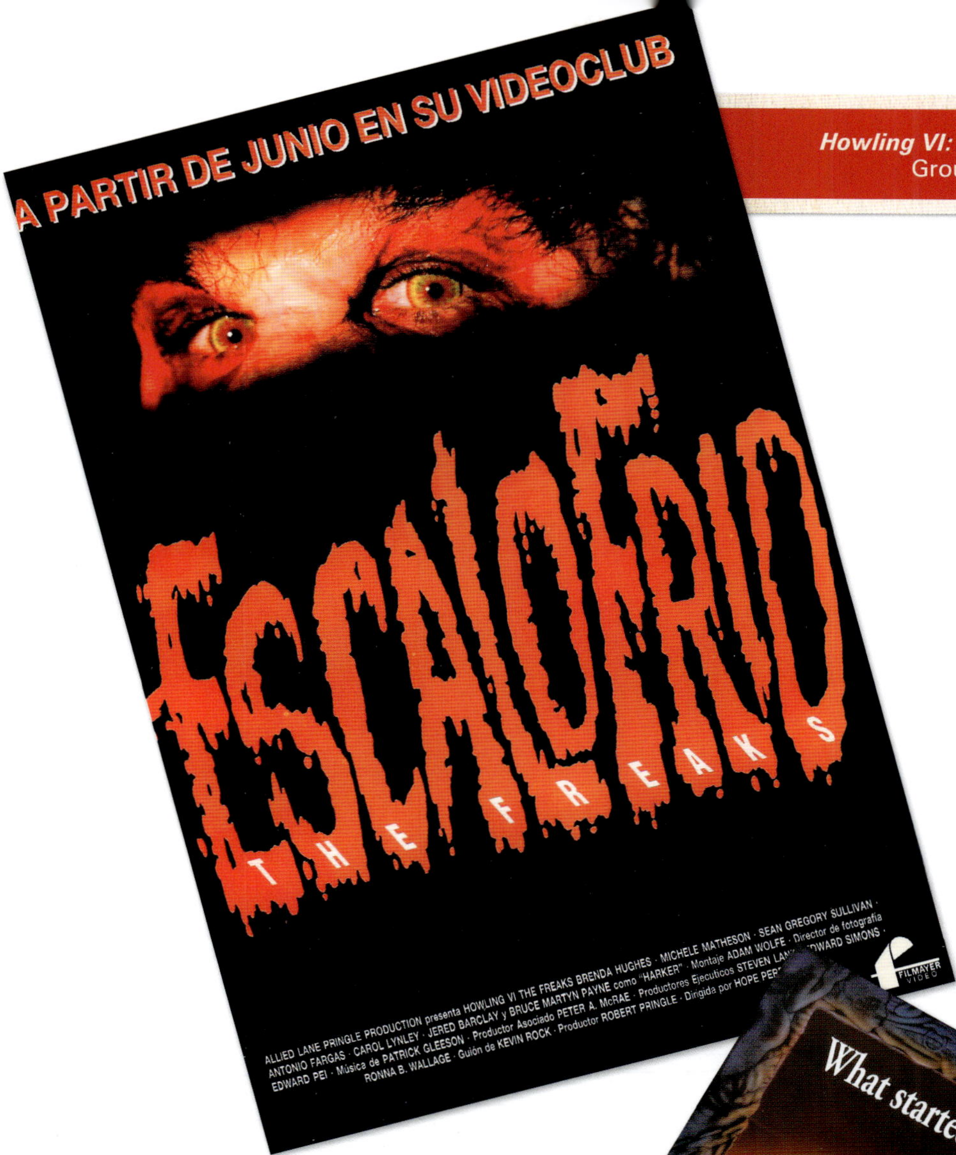

Howling VI: The Freaks. Allied Entertainments Group PLC/Allied Vision (1991). Spain.

Hellraiser III: Hell on Earth. Fifth Avenue Entertainment/ Trans Atlantic Entertainment (1992).

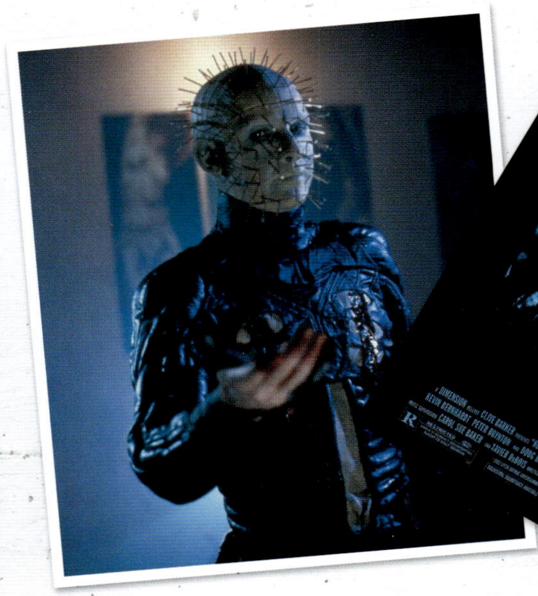

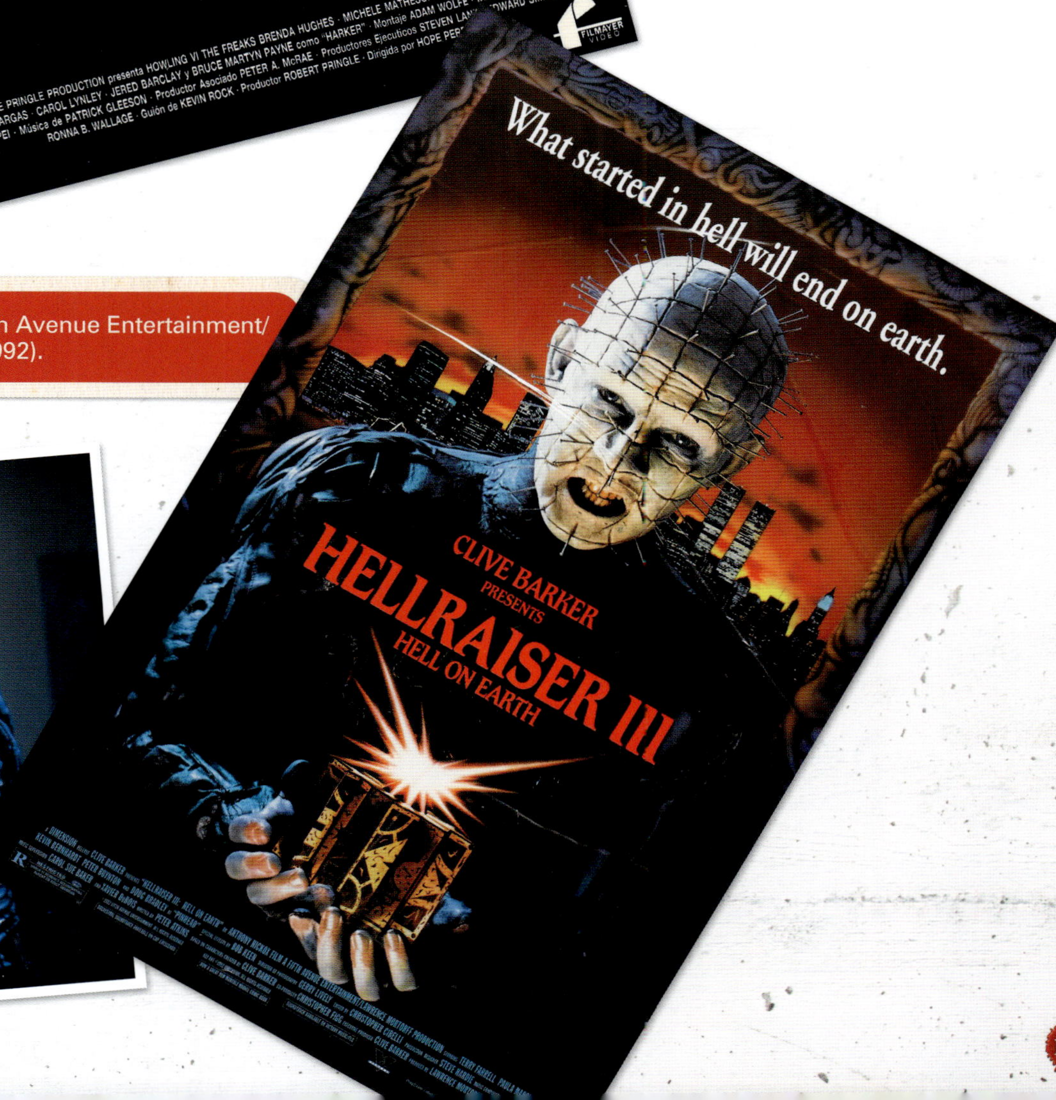

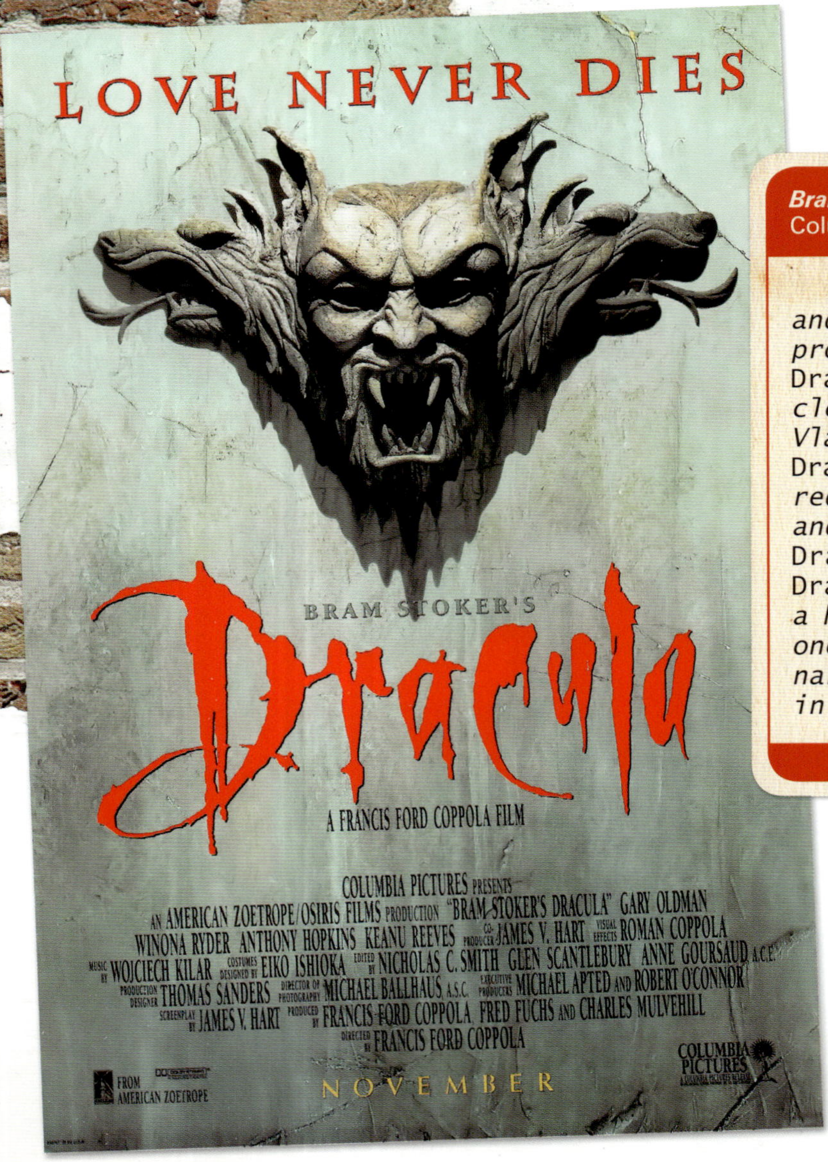

Bram Stoker's Dracula. American Zoetrope/ Columbia Pictures Corporation/Osiris Films (1992).

The forging together of Stoker's Count and Vlad the Impaler became even more pronounced in 1992 with Bram Stoker's Dracula in which Vlad and the Count are clearly the same person, and events in Vlad's life shape the narrative. Coppola's Dracula is essentially a story of love and redemption, far removed from Bram Stoker and his novel. Whatever Bram Stoker's Dracula is, it is not Bram Stoker's Dracula. James Hart's screenplay changes a horror novel into a syrupy love story, one that is so far removed from Stoker's narrative as to make the use of his name in the title close to libelous.

Elizabeth Miller

Bram Stoker's Dracula. American Zoetrope/ Columbia Pictures Corporation/Osiris Films (1992).

I regard this film as more a Gothic romance than a horror film. It takes great liberties with Stoker's original tale. Stoker's Dracula is a manipulative fiend, not a long-lost lover. Gary Oldman is at his best as the weird, blood-licking Count in Transylvania (goofy hairdo notwithstanding), rather than the dapper fellow in Victorian England. I appreciate most the scene where Dracula shape-shifts into a more demonic form before the terrified band of self-appointed vampire hunters. At least we get one glimpse of a vampire more like the horror faced by people long ago. I also like Coppola's depiction of Lucy as a vampire, making her far more terrifying than Stoker's version.

Rosemary Ellen Guiley

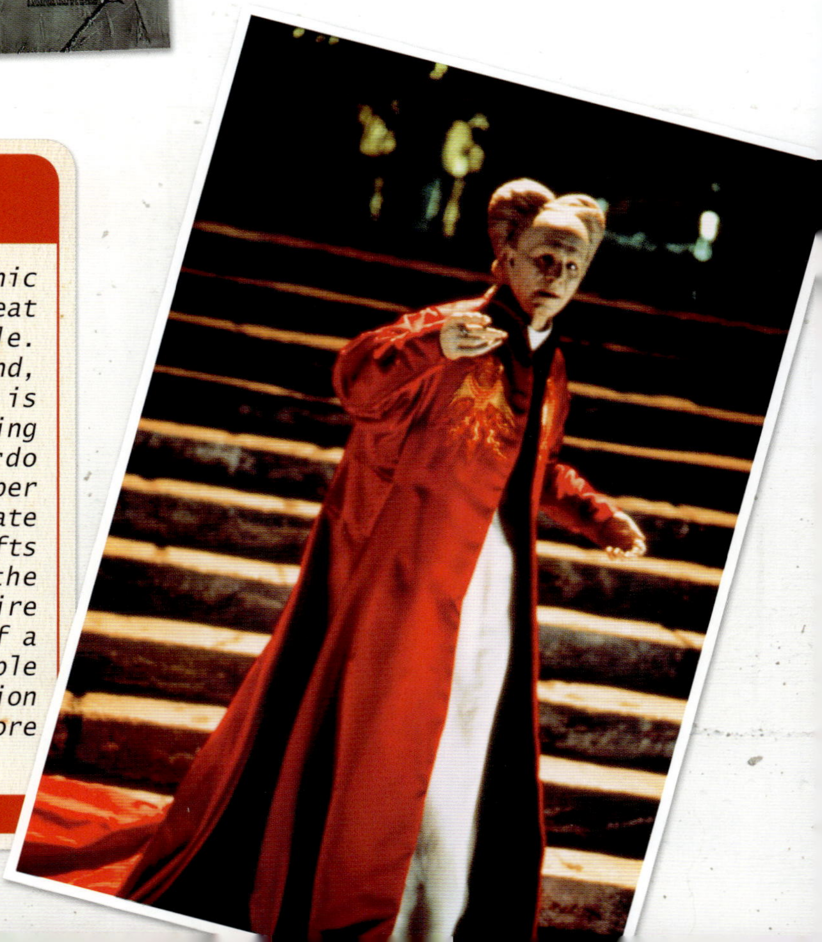

ON *DRACULA* IN THE '90s

When I interviewed Winona Ryder (Mina) at the private New York launch of the film on Halloween night 1992, I asked her what had attracted her enough about James Hart's script to tell F.F. Coppola about it: "It was so *romantic*," she purred. Taken as a whole, she is right about Coppola's movie, which was and still is a *Dracula* for the *fin-de-millenium* '90s, when Romanticism was enjoying one of its many revivals. Despite the "backstory" prologue which Hart dubiously inserts to supply the movie with that romantic thread, and the wooden acting of Keanu Reeves as Jonathan Harker, Coppola follows Stoker's novel more carefully than previous versions, Anthony Hopkins supplying a very convincing Van Helsing. What was then new "in-the-camera" technology also allowed Roman Coppola to create some fantastic special effects. Such as when the figure of Gary Oldman's Dracula as human bat, cornered by the "crew of light," escapes by transforming himself, collapsing into hundreds of scrambling rats. Or the speeded-up pixilating movements of Lucy (Sadie Frost) as the film's most provocative female vampire (although Monica Belluci as one of Dracula's Brides in the opening sequence is undoubtedly the most voluptuous). Gary Oldman's lupine, red-eyed Dracula furtively but vigorously humping away at a swooning Lucy in the garden is another memorable episode of pixilation that also led scores of women to write offering themselves to Gary (he told me later in England for the *South Bank Show TV Dracula* I co-produced). At my first viewing of the film on that Halloween night, I was mostly struck by its physically dark ambience; Oldman was less coy than Ryder or Frances Coppola himself about the "dark" appeal of Dracula when questioned: "It's about sex — it's sexy!" he proclaimed. He should know.

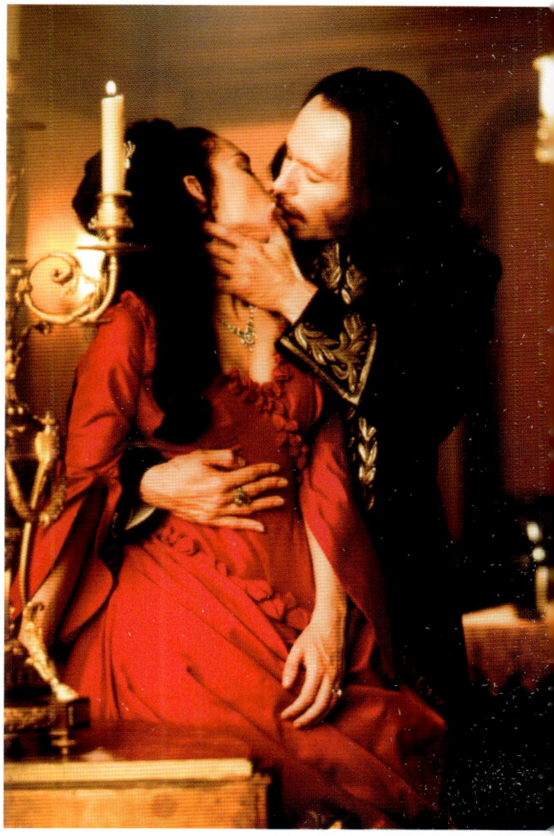

~Maurice Hindle

Candyman.
PolyGram Filmed Entertainment/Propaganda Films (1992).

Is there any smarter or scarier horror film about the racialized city and the failure of white privilege?

Gregory A. Waller

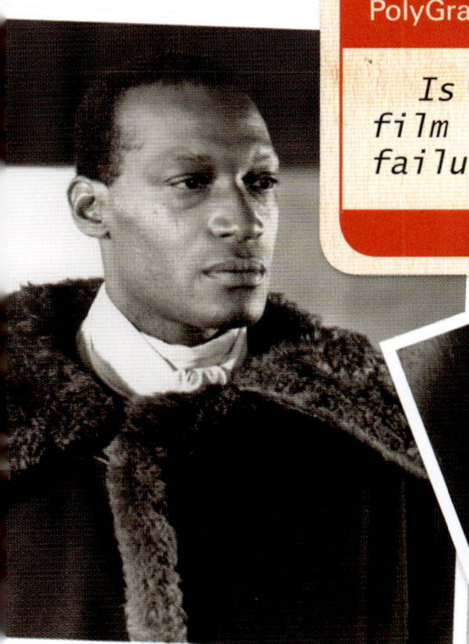

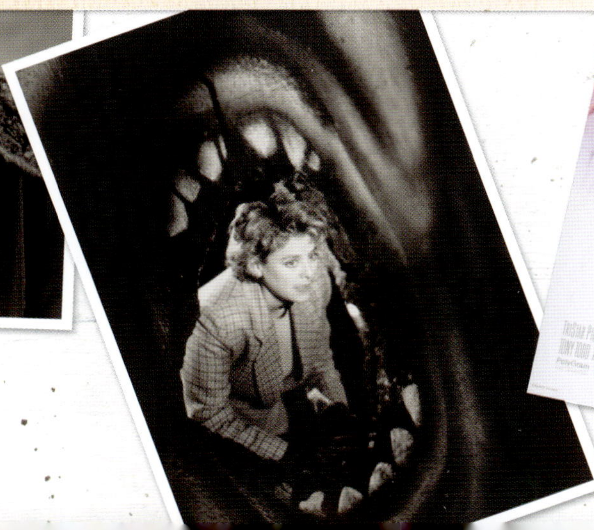

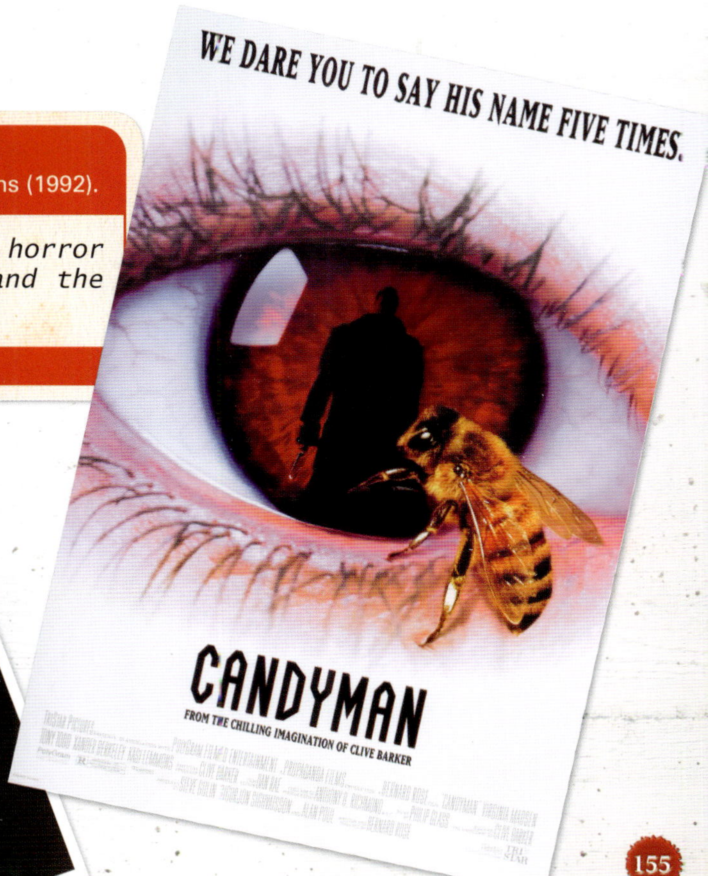

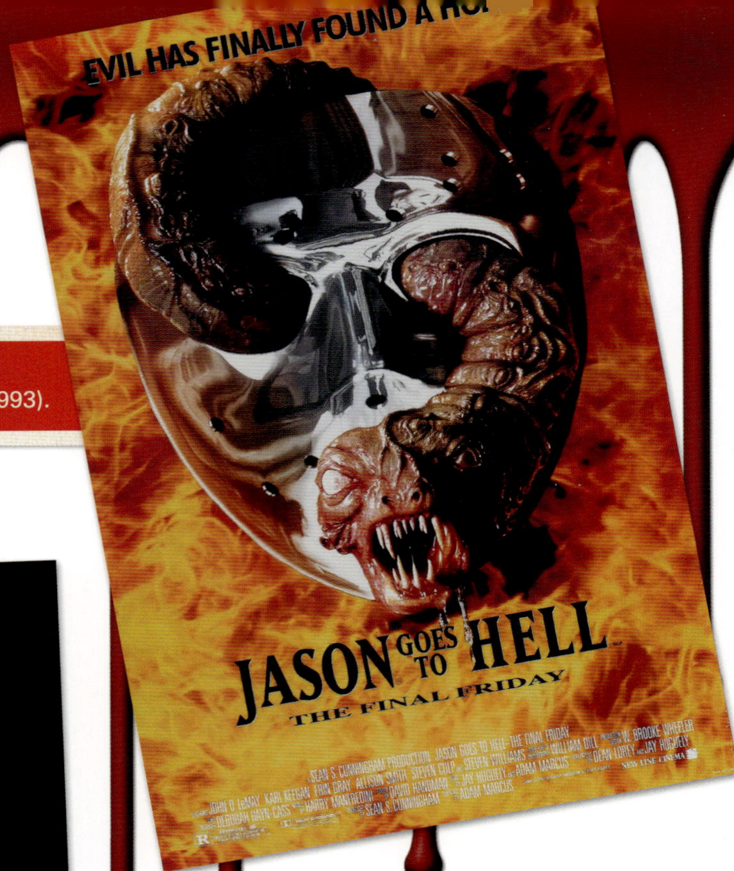

Jason Goes to Hell: The Final Friday.
New Line Cinema/Sean S. Cunningham Films (1993).

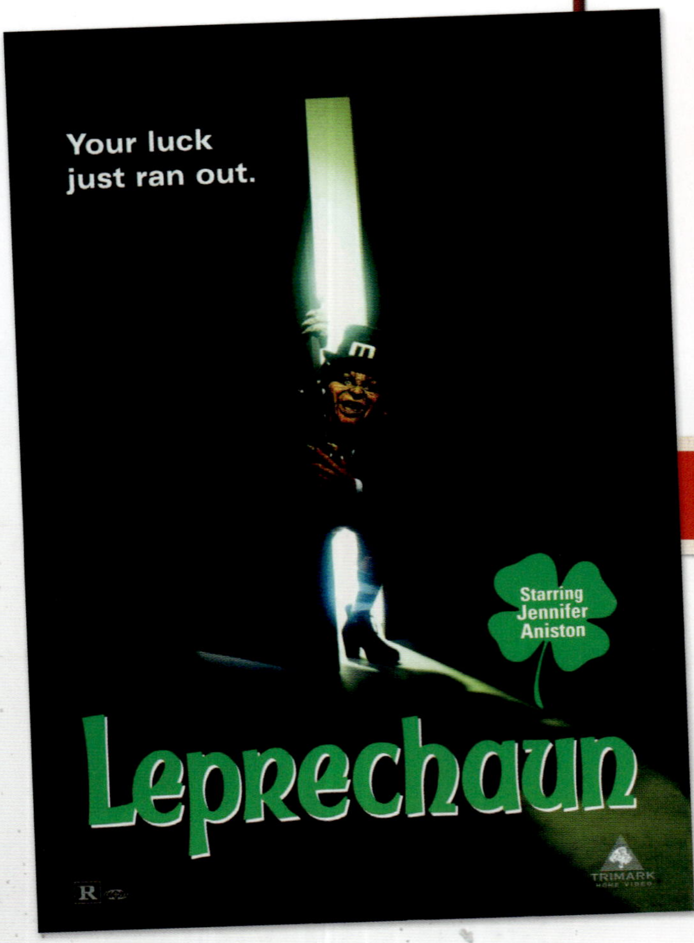

Leprechaun.
Trimark Pictures (1993).

The Texas Chainsaw Massacre: The Next Generation.
Genre Pictures/Return Productions/River City Films/
Ultra Muchos Productions (1994).

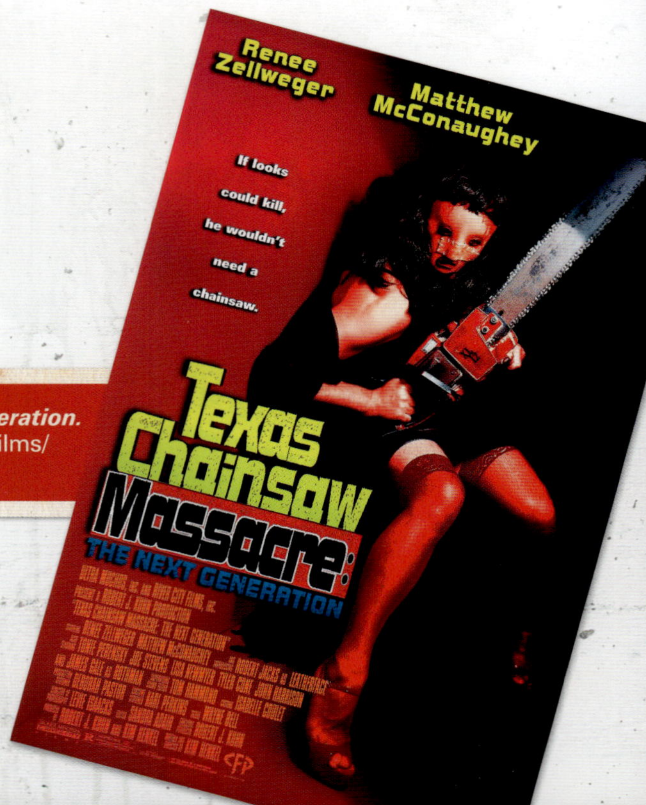

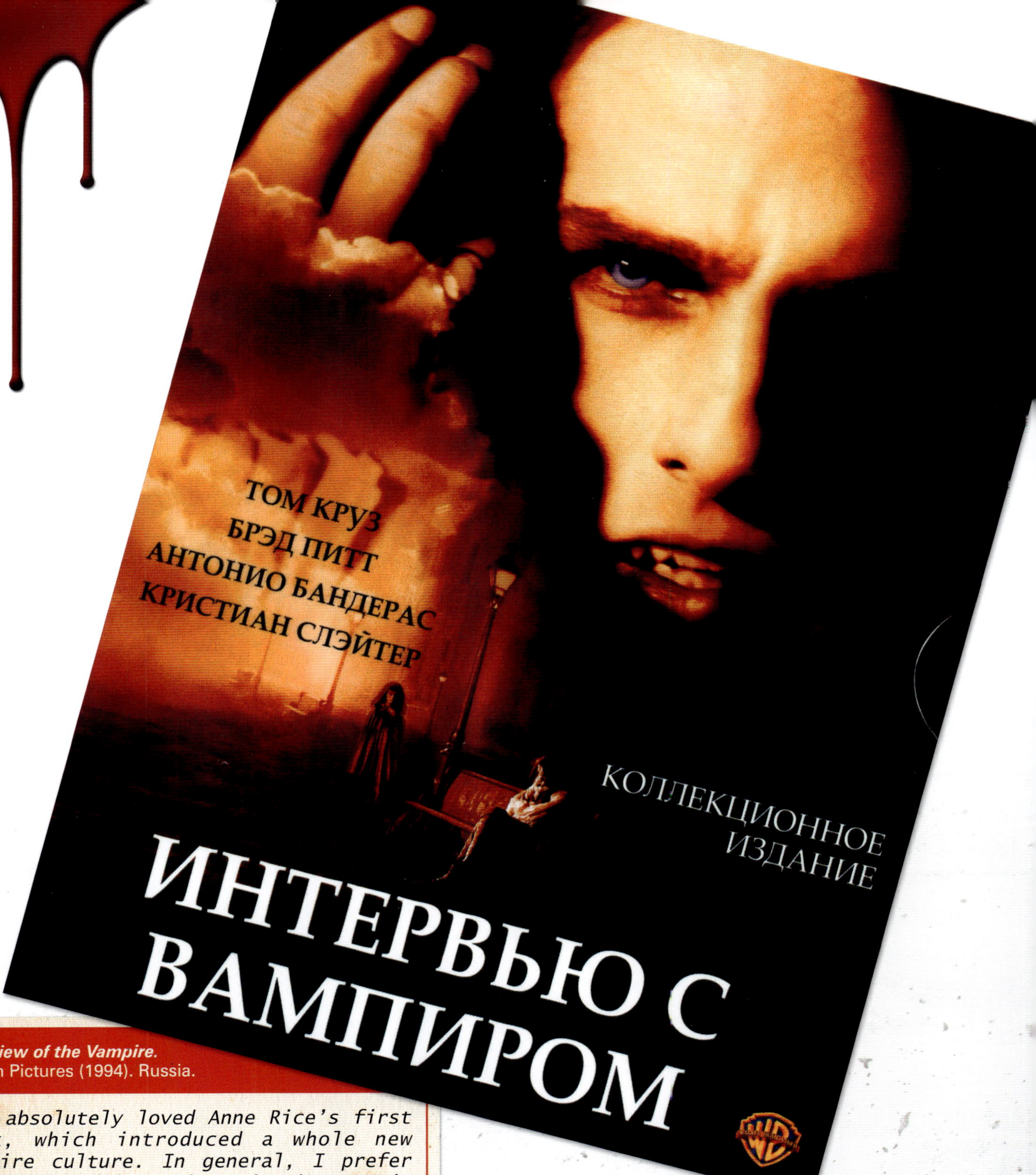

Interview of the Vampire.
Geffen Pictures (1994). Russia.

I absolutely loved Anne Rice's first book, which introduced a whole new vampire culture. In general, I prefer more monsterish vampires, but her exotic creatures are mesmerizing. Even so, I was prepared not to like Tom Cruise as Lestat and Brad Pitt as Louis, because I thought them both too "pretty boy" for even Rice's interpretation of vampires. I was wrong. They fit their roles perfectly, as do Antonio Banderas, Christian Slater – all members of the cast.

Rosemary Ellen Guiley

ON DE NIRO'S "CREATURE" IN *MARY SHELLEY'S FRANKENSTEIN* (1994)

Kenneth Branagh was mainly known for his film adaptations of Shakespeare when this film came out in 1994, appearing hard on the heels of Coppola's 1992 *Bram Stoker's Dracula* — indeed, Coppola was one of its producers. Coppola had needed to regain box office ground with his Gothic movie, whereas Branagh had his eye on shooting Shakespeare's *Hamlet* for the movie theatre, and needed a lot of money to do it. He achieved this over the weekend of the first release *Mary Shelley's Frankenstein* (many people will pay to see a new version of *Frankenstein* around the globe, whatever it's like) — but it was panned by the critics. Having a special interest in Mary Shelley's *Frankenstein* novel (I co-produced a *South Bank Show TV Frankenstein* hooked to the film's release), I felt the movie achieved much that previous versions hadn't, particularly with its injection of the original story's ethical concerns. Unfortunately, because Branagh wanted (as he told me) "to put the audience on the side of a human being, not a hysterical madman — there's an altruistic reason for his experiments," the film almost became a laughing stock with critics and audiences. As with *Bram Stoker's Dracula* — or indeed any other Gothic thriller — what the audience really wants is for its imagination and desires to be *chilled* and *haunted* by what they experience on screen — not a lecture. Gary Oldman supplied these elements amply enough in Coppola's film, and Robert de Niro should have done the same for Branagh's — unfortunately he didn't. In fact, I remember titters rippling through the audience at one point at the film's Odeon Marble Arch London preview. This was in a scene in which the blind man De Lacey (Richard Briers) asks De Niro's "Creature" why people have rejected him, to which he gets the reply, "I am so very ugly." It should have been a very touching moment, but De Niro's New York City pronunciation of "ugly" jarred with the audience's expectations — hence the unforeseen laughter. My view is that while De Niro acted brilliantly in many scenes, Branagh under-directed him in moments like this, the threateningly dark energy that this great actor is capable of communicating not being fully released to us. A memorable film in many ways, but also an opportunity lost.

~Maurice Hindle

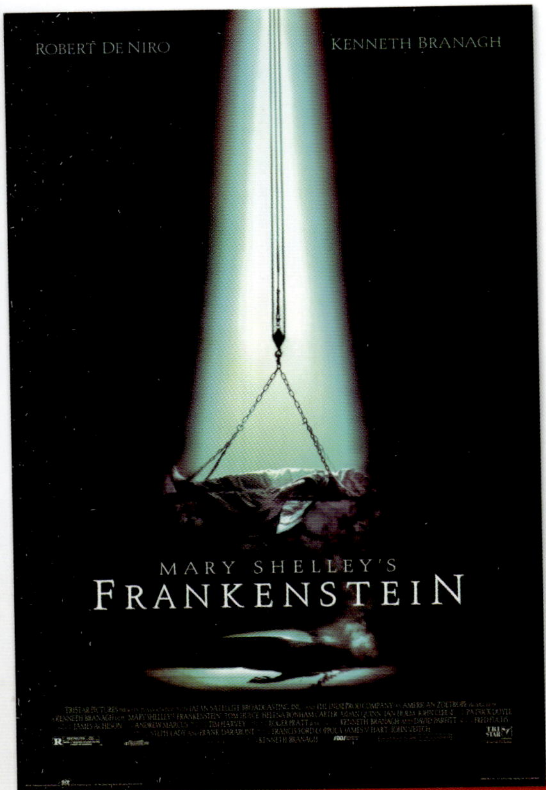

***Mary Shelley's Frankenstein*.**
TriStar Pictures/Japan Satellite Broadcasting/
IndieProd Company Productions/American Zoetrope (1994).

Three of the major innovations of this particular version of the Frankensteinian mytheme were: 1.) the creature's transformation from being a wordless, mindless beast, to being something more complex – gruesome and sensitive, murderous but childlike, chilling but also deserving of sympathy; 2.) an expansion of Elizabeth's role from being either an "angel" or surrogate mother figure to becoming more Victor's equal; 3.) Victor's evolution from being a geeky medical student to being a physically powerful Romantic hero. Yet despite these innovations, its ending remains very similar to Bride of Frankenstein's conclusion: The bride (this time grotesque) is speechless, and in the end, chooses to kill herself.

Caroline Joan (Kay) Picart

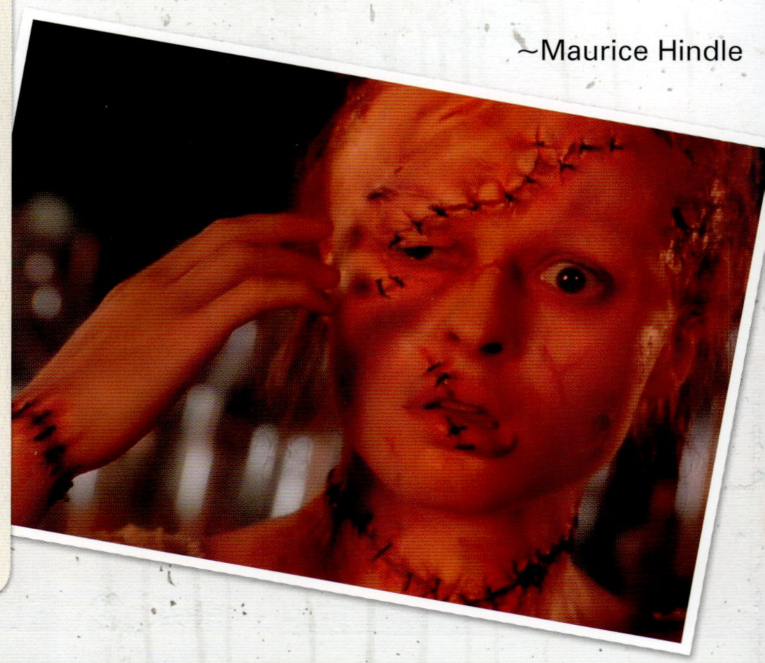

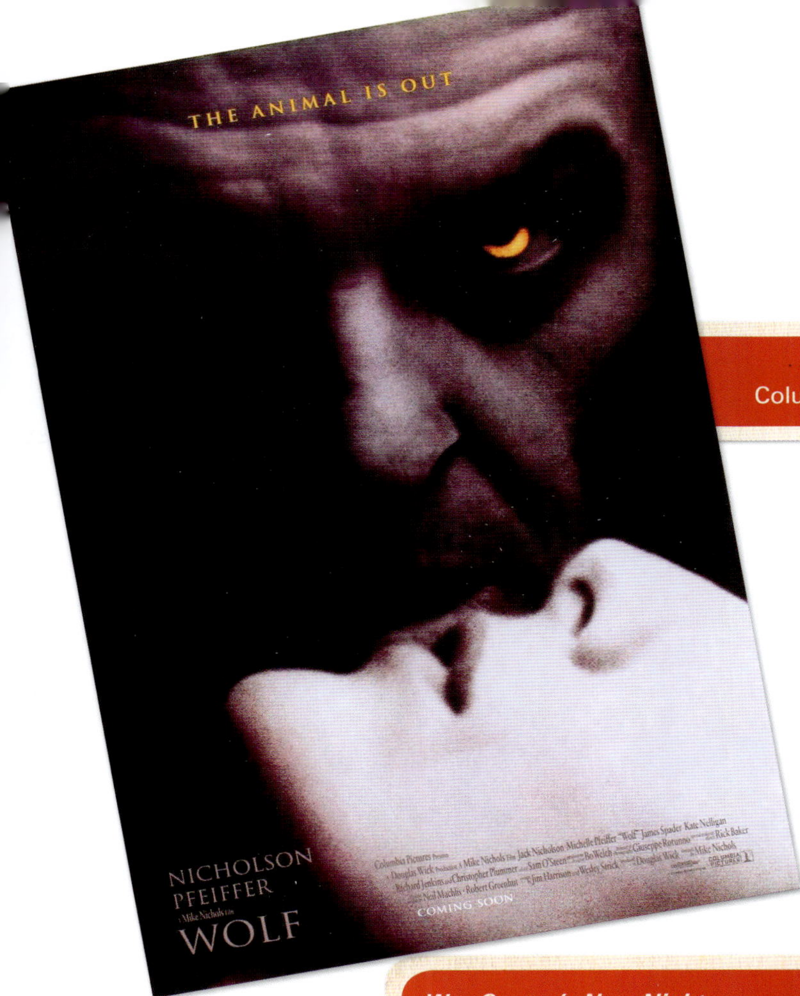

Wolf.
Columbia Pictures Corporation (1994).

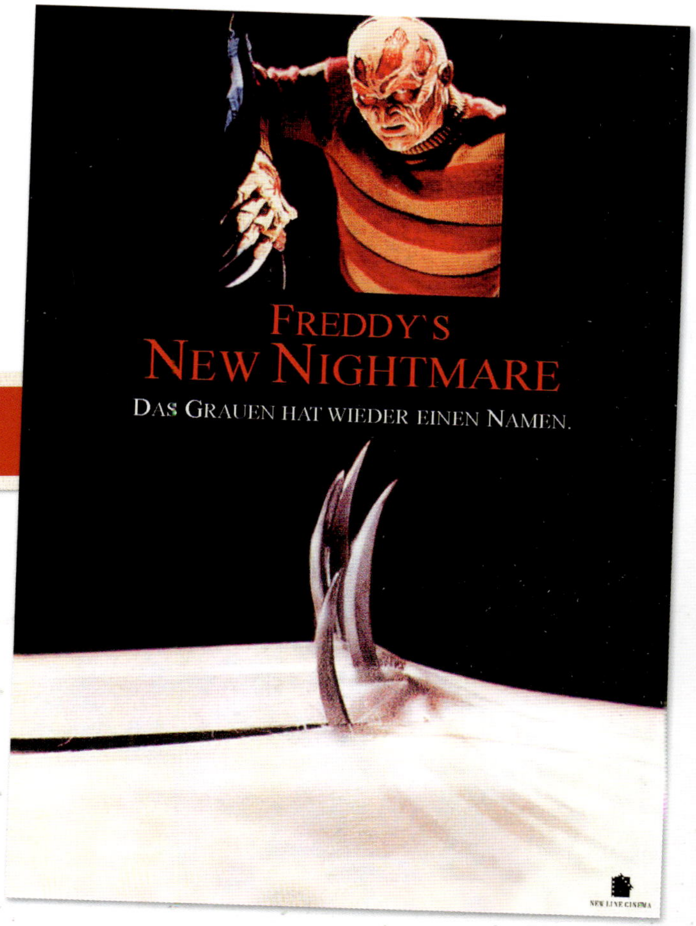

Wes Craven's New Nightmare.
New Line Cinema (1994). Germany.

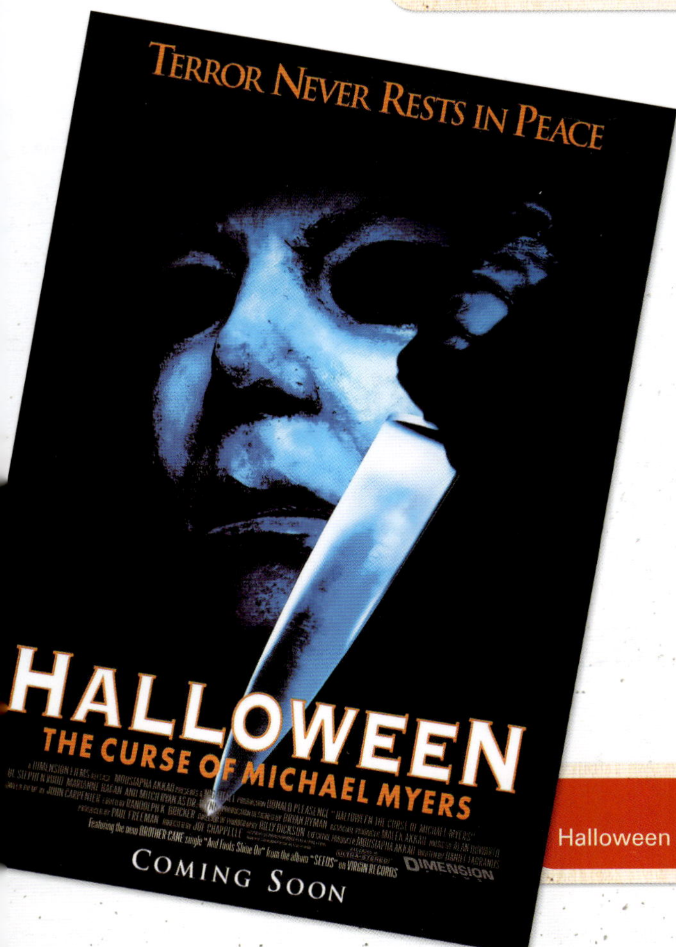

Halloween: The Curse of Michael Myers.
Halloween VI Productions/Miramax Films/Nightfall (1995).

Dracula: Dead and Loving It.
Gaumont/Castle Rock Entertainment/Brooksfilms (1995).

Dracula: Dead and Loving It is my favorite comedic take on vampires. Leslie Nielsen (as the Count) is not the high point here; it's Peter MacNicol as the dopey Renfield and Steven Weber as Jonathan Harker (and Brooks is great too as Van Helsing, with an outrageous accent). Who can resist dialog like this, when Jonathan discovers that Lucy may not be dead:

Jonathan Harker: "She's alive?"
Van Helsing: "She's Nosferatu."
Jonathan Harker: "...She's Italian?"

Leslie Klinger

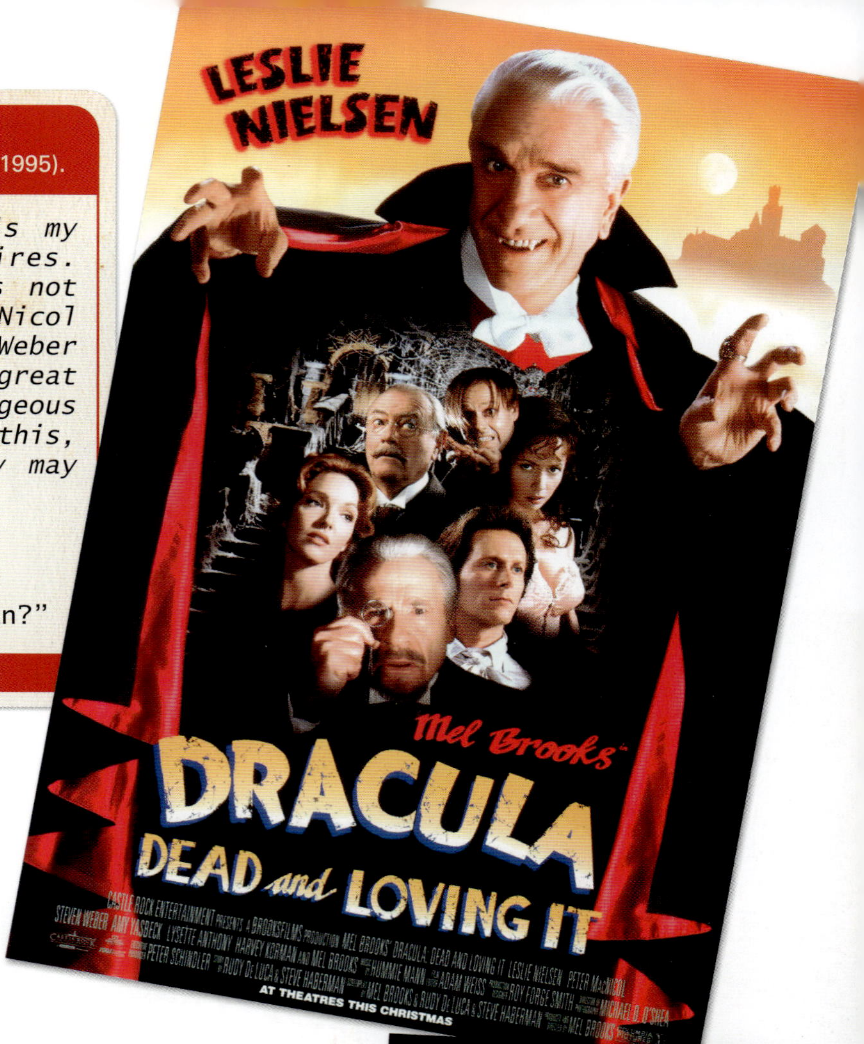

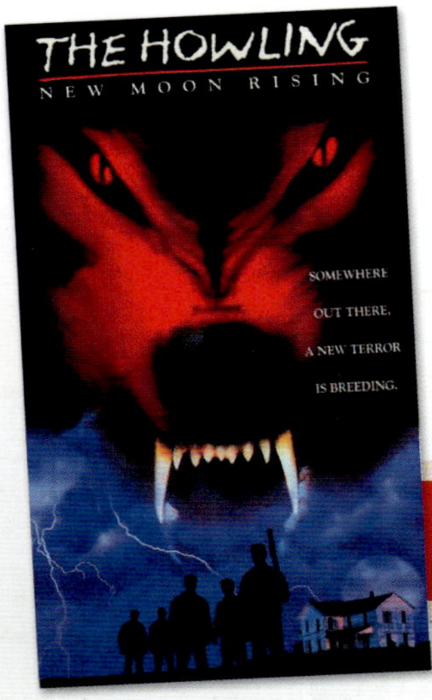

The Howling VII: New Moon Rising.
Allied Entertainments Group PLC/Allied Vision (1995).

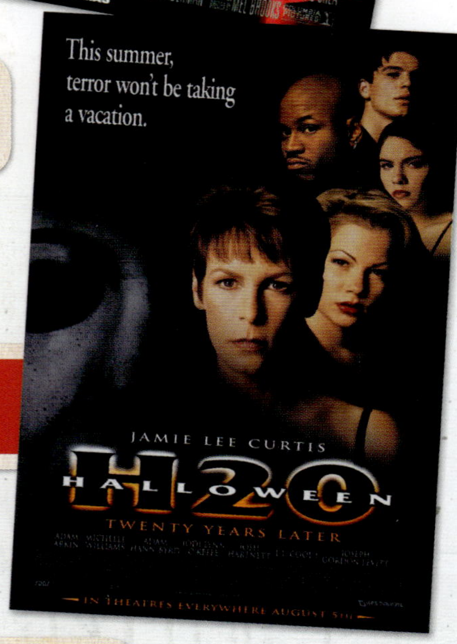

Halloween H20: 20 Years Later.
Dimension Films/Nightfall Productions (1998).

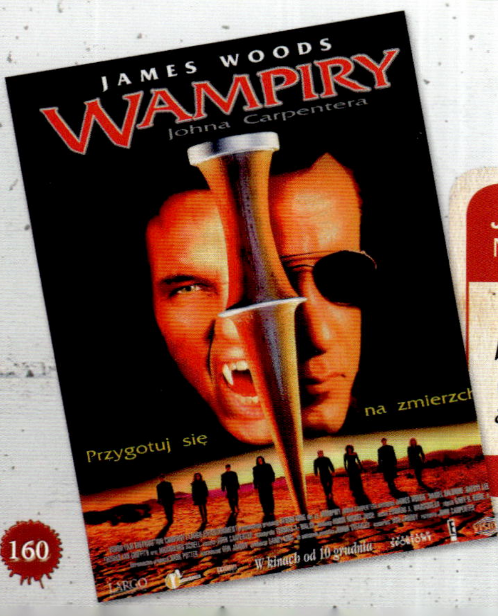

John Carpenter's Vampires. Film Office/JVC Entertainment Networks/Largo Entertainment (1998). Poland.

One of Carpenter's unsung films, this bloodsucker romp boasts solid action (especially the movie's rousing opening), and an improvising James Woods is a hoot.

Tony Timpone

ON **TECHNOSCIENCE** AND VAMPIRISM

Supernatural horror requires from the viewer an investment in the spiritual that modernity and technoscience have undermined, if not altogether destroyed. Unlike her contemporaries working the Gothic, Mary Shelley stands as a harbinger of the fact that, unlike the semi-religious awe, science fiction wants us to experience in the face of science and technology, horror will turn out to be a far more convincing response. Who cares what damage the vampire does to my immortal soul when I can wonder whether, by some heedless sexual encounter, I have let myself become infected with a virus that rewrites my body from the inside out?

Steffen Hantke

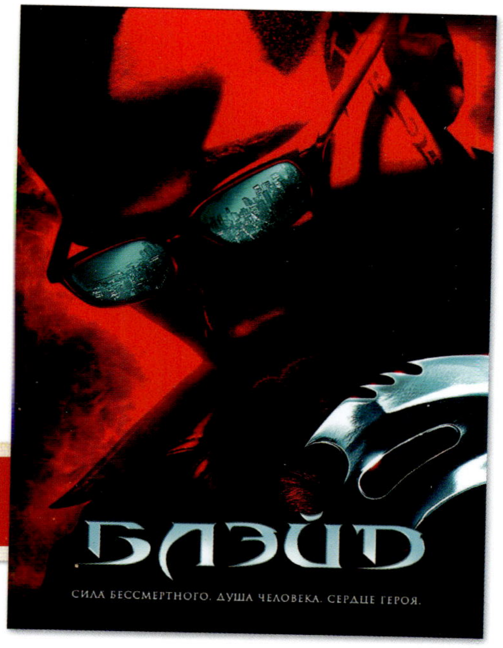

Blade. Amen Ra Films/Imaginary Forces/ Marvel Enterprises/New Line Cinema (1998). Russia

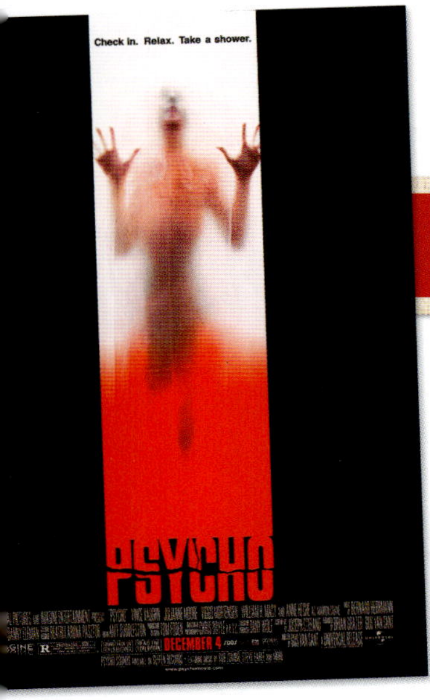

Psycho. Universal Pictures/Imagine Entertainment (1998).

The Haunting of Hill House. DreamWorks SKG/Roth-Arnold Productions (1999).

Panned by the critics for the excessive use of CGI and horror clichés, Jan de Bont's The Haunting of Hill House *may end up being best remembered for attracting 5 Razzie award nominations. For a truly disturbing experience, stick to Shirley Jackson's original novel (1959) or Robert Wise's genuinely creepy film adaptation,* The Haunting *(1963): who can forget the grin given by Rosalie Crutchley as Mrs. Dudley when she tells Eleanor, "there won't be anyone around if you need help . . . No one lives any nearer than town. No one will come any closer than that. In the night . . . In the dark."*

Glennis Byron

ON HORROR'S **HAYDAY**

I'm not a fan of the current rash of "torture porn" one-offs, and franchises...or the endless remakes (what *were* they thinking when they thought they could actually add anything worthwhile to new versions of *Psycho*, *The Haunting*, *House on Haunted Hill*, *Cat People*, *The Fog,* and so on?). If only they would learn that just because one has access to all manner of SFX devices and a budget to accommodate endless hours using them should not mean they have to do so. It seems to me that movie-makers should pay more attention to the old adage that less is more.

~Peter Crowther

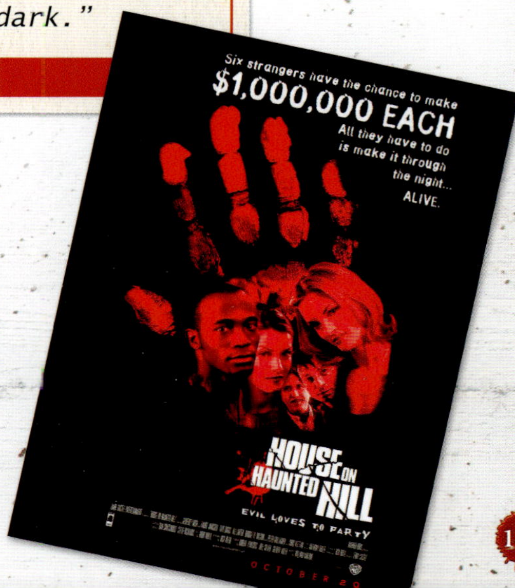

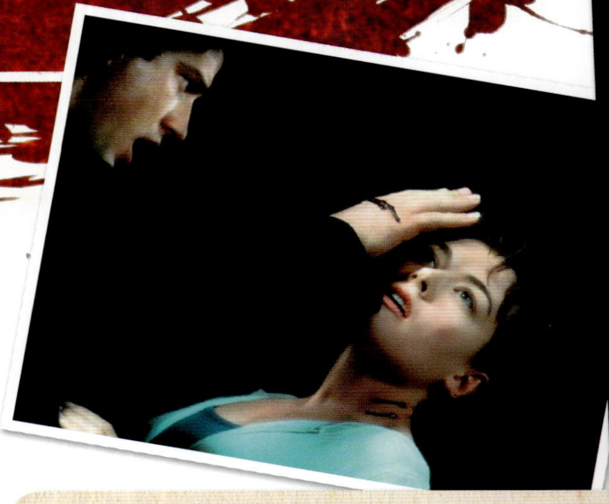

Dracula 2000. Dimension Films, Neo Art & Logic, Wes Craven Films, Carfax Productions Ltd. (2000).

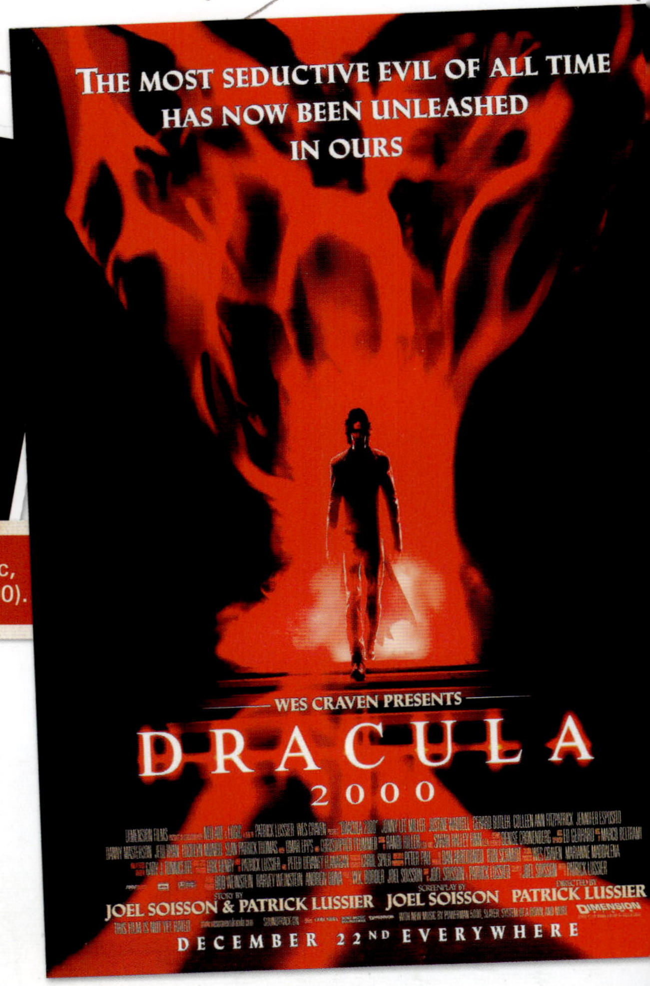

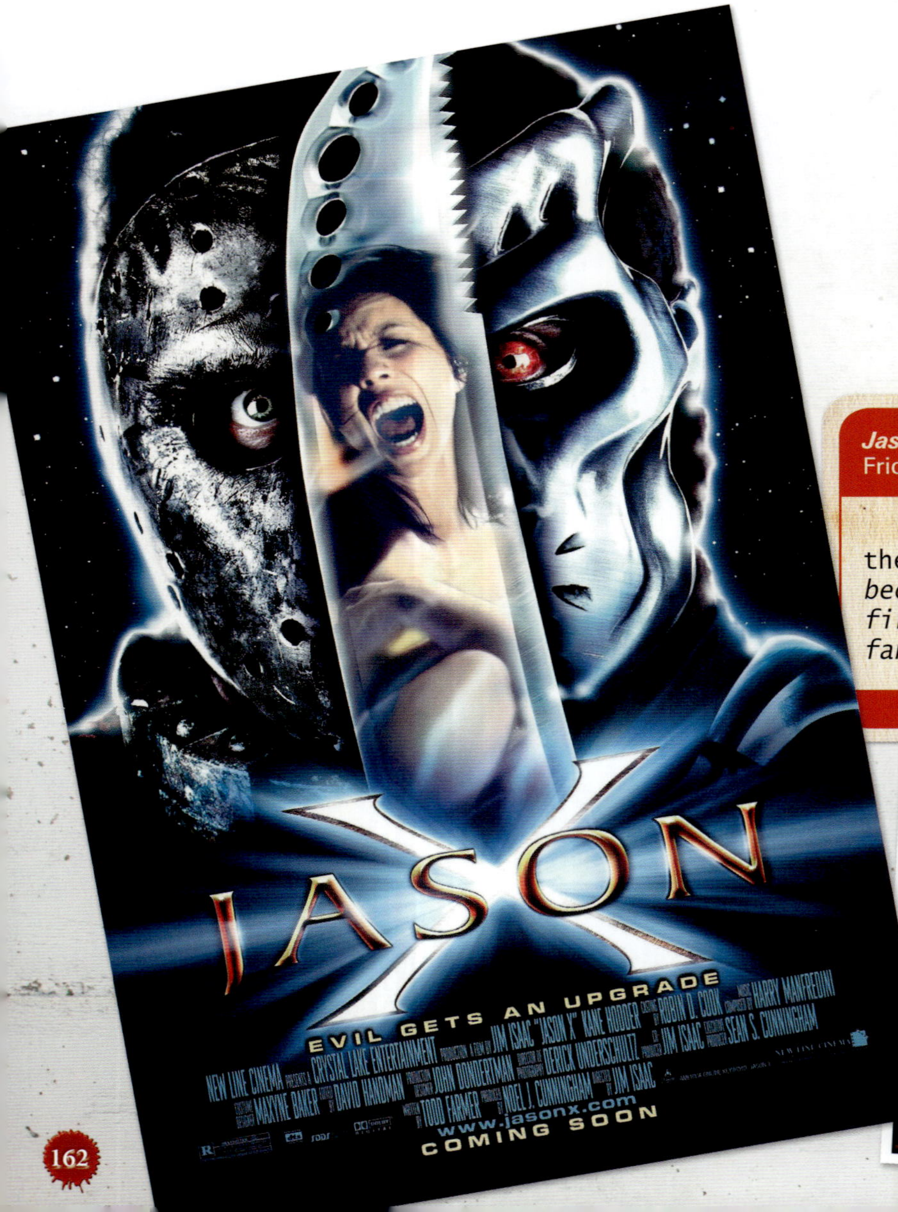

Jason X. Crystal Lake Entertainment/ Friday X Productions/New Line Cinema (2001).

This much-maligned space-set Friday the 13th *movie is better than you'd expect because, thankfully, its (severed) tongue is firmly in cheek. Best bit: Jason's hologram fantasy. A few memorable kills too.*

Tony Timpone

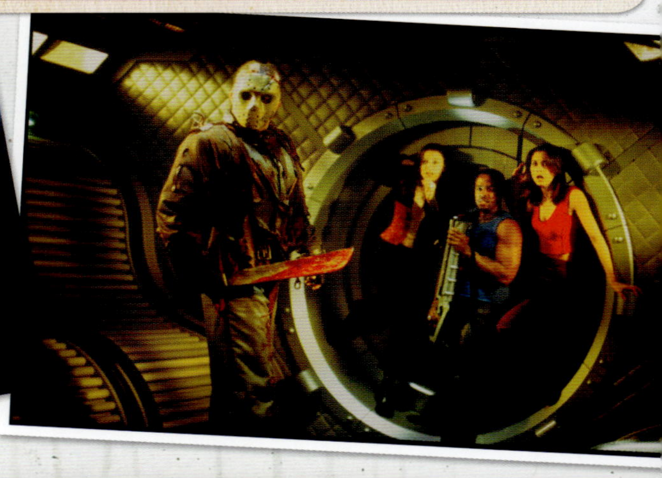

The Others. Cruise/Wagner Productions/ Sociedad General de Cine S.A./Las Producciones del Escorpión S.L. (2001). South Korea.

Like The Haunting, *this film is especially frightening because it suggests, rather than shows, nightmarish things.*

Marvin Kaye

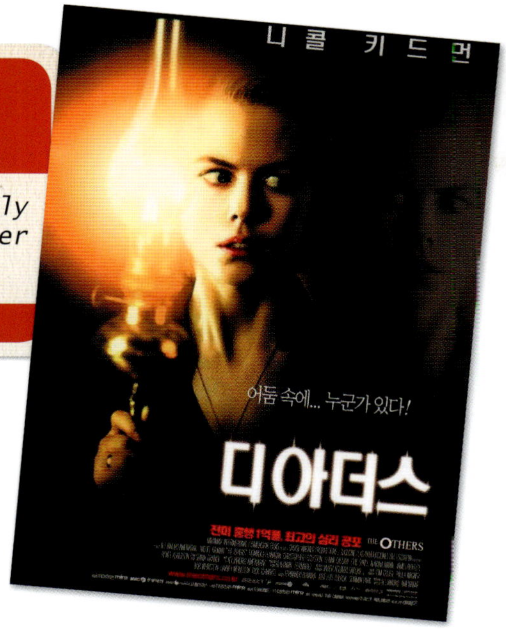

ON THE **BUSH YEARS**

Who made the suggestion that American horror film flourishes every time a Republican is in the White House? While this may be arguable in the case of Nixon (did he give us *The Exorcist*?) or Reagan (did he give us Stephen King?), it rings resoundingly true in the case of George W. Bush. The period roughly between 2001 and 2008 saw, with so-called torture porn, the return of a newly invigorated version of the slasher film; the comparison between stills from Eli Roth's *Hostel* and those infamous photographs from inside Abu Ghraib prison has, by now, become a commonplace of critical discourse. The paranoid xenophobic fantasies of the Bush administration also saw a return of 1950s technohorror: giant creatures wrecking American cities (films like *Cloverfield*), silent and insidious alien invasion (TV series like *Threshold*, *Surface*, and *Invasion*), and a new concern with that central icon of 1950s America — the Bomb (TV series like *Jericho* and *24*). Perhaps it is that schizophrenic mantra of "Be very afraid, keep eyes and ears open — the enemy is everywhere"/"Don't worry — your government, though it can't tell you what it's doing, is protecting you at all times!" that is particularly conducive to horror?

~Steffen Hantke

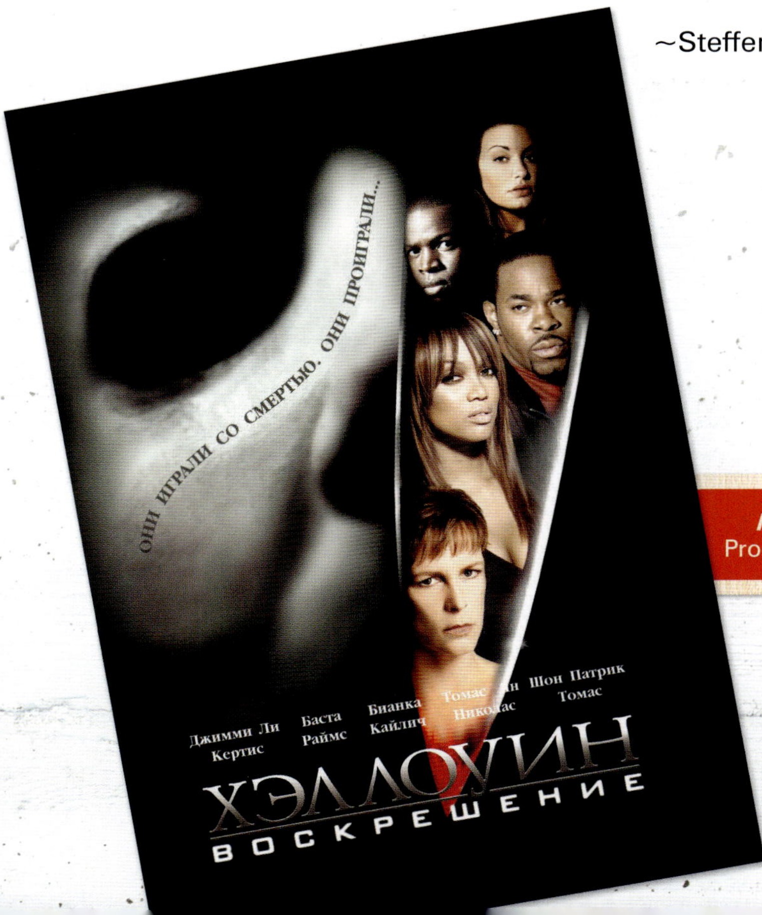

Halloween Resurrection. Dimension Films/Nightfall Productions/Trancas International Films (2002). Russia.

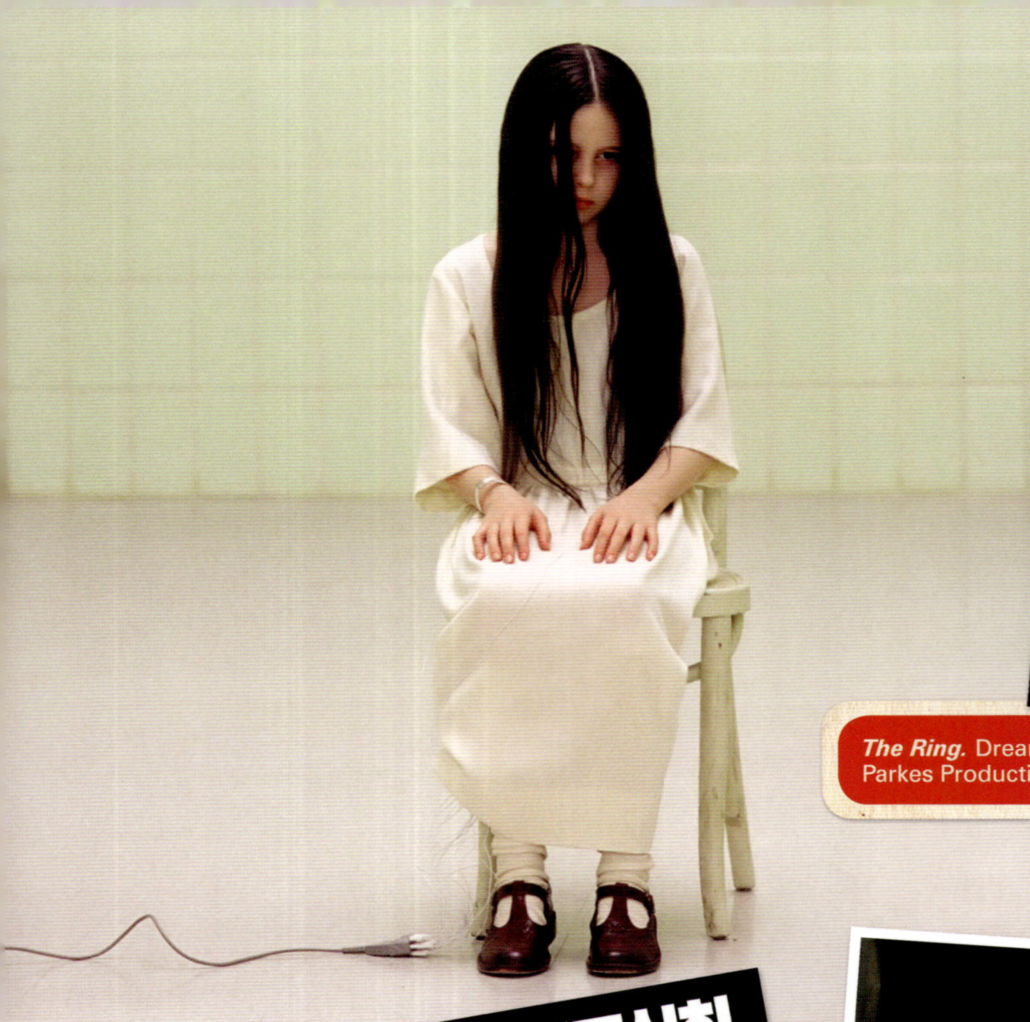

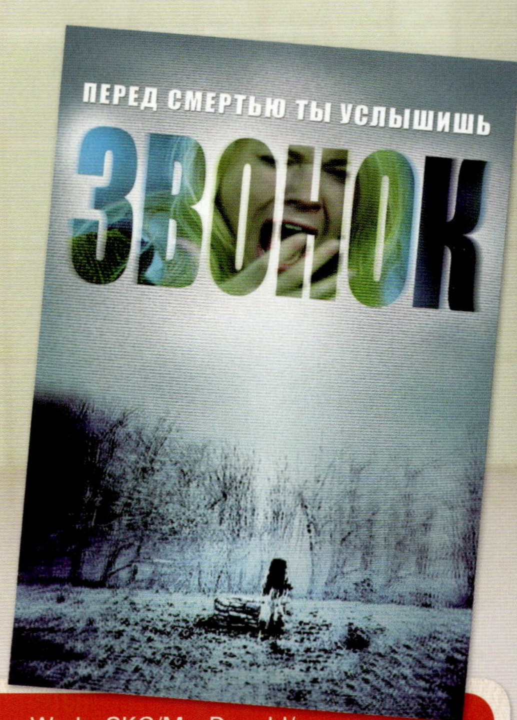

The Ring. DreamWorks SKG/MacDonald/ Parkes Productions/BenderSpink (2002). Russia.

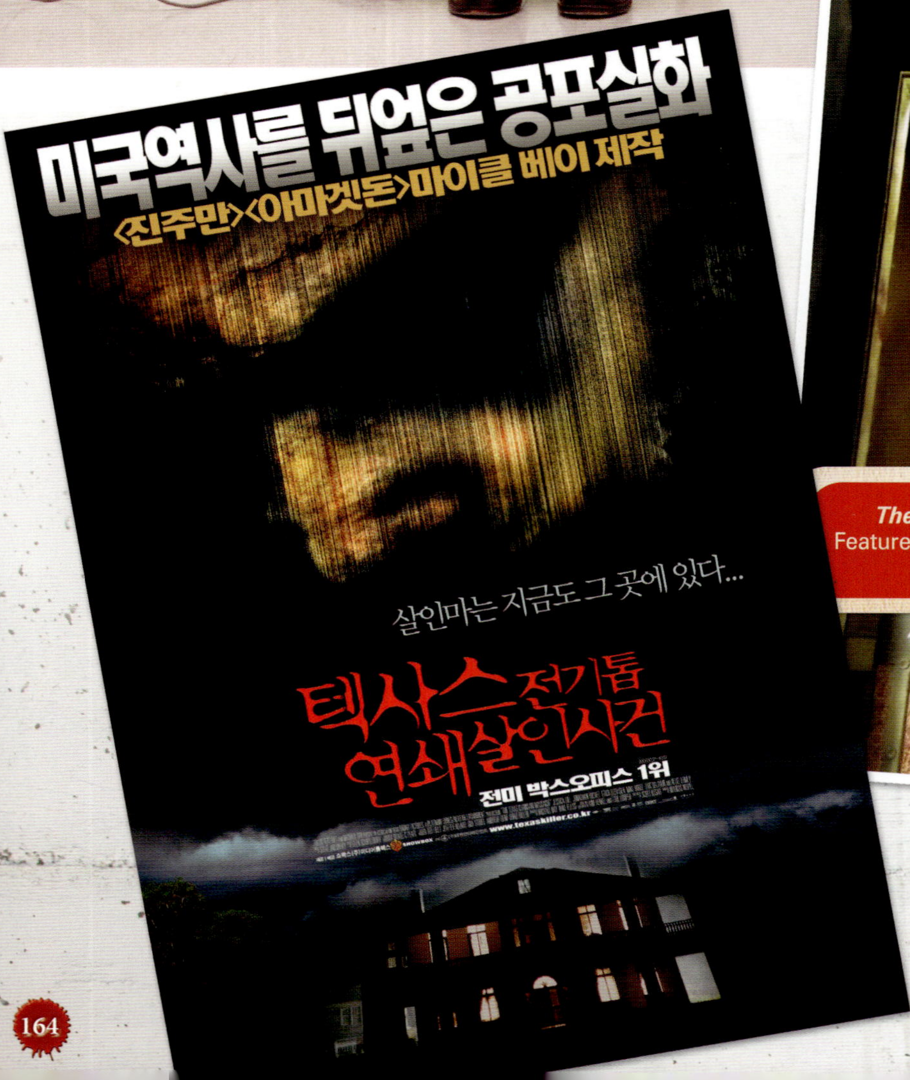

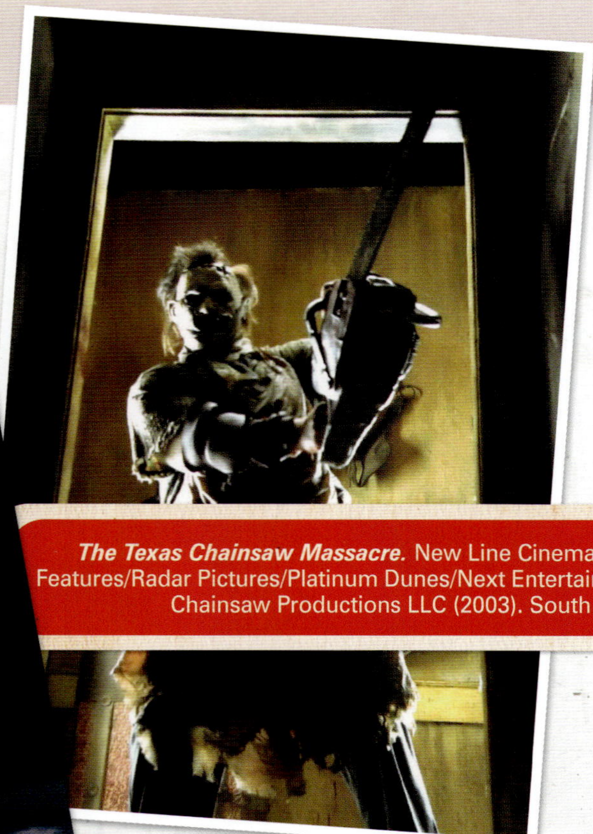

The Texas Chainsaw Massacre. New Line Cinema/Focus Features/Radar Pictures/Platinum Dunes/Next Entertainment/ Chainsaw Productions LLC (2003). South Korea.

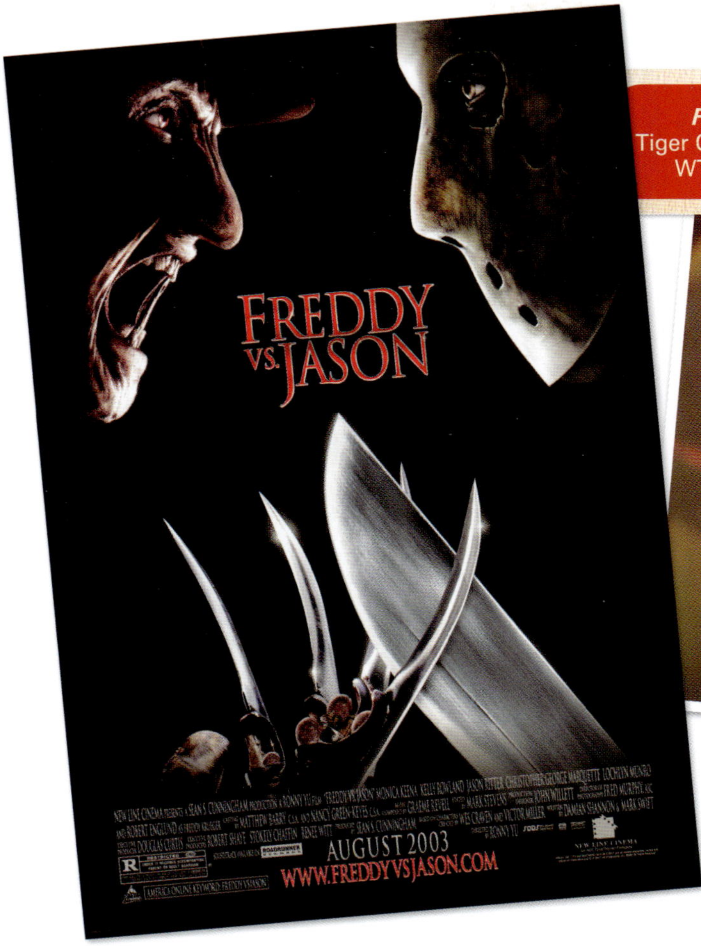

Freddy vs. Jason. New Line Cinema/Cecchi Gori Group Tiger Cinematografica/Avery Pix/Sean S. Cunningham Films/ WTC Productions/Yannix Technology Corporation (2003).

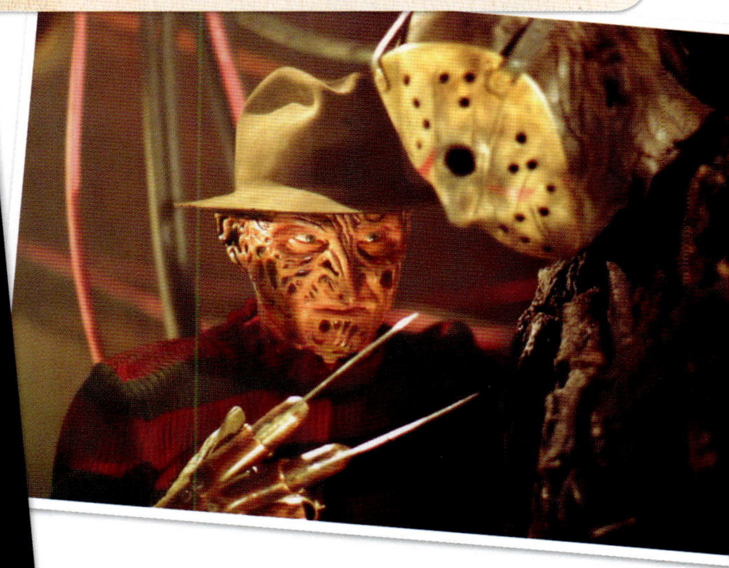

The Machinist. Filmax Group/Castelao Producciones/ Canal+ España/Instituto de la Cinematografía y de las Artes Audiovisuales/ICF (2004). Israel.

Anderson's film brings together two strands of horror: films about characters quietly going insane, with us, the viewers, sharing their experience in all its disorienting visual intensity (especially Polanski's trilogy Repulsion, Rosemary's Baby, *and* The Tenant*); and films which record the fact of something genuinely monstrous having been placed in front of the camera (Tod Browning's* Freaks*) – one intensely subjective and cinematically, stylistically overwrought, the other ostensibly objective reaching out to the viewer with matter-of-fact stylistic sobriety. Hungered down to a body of such dangerous haggardness that it defies credulity, the film's star, Christian Bale, commands absolute visual attention – every flexing of shoulder blades, every stoop and turn, every shot an awful spectacle.*

Steffen Hantke

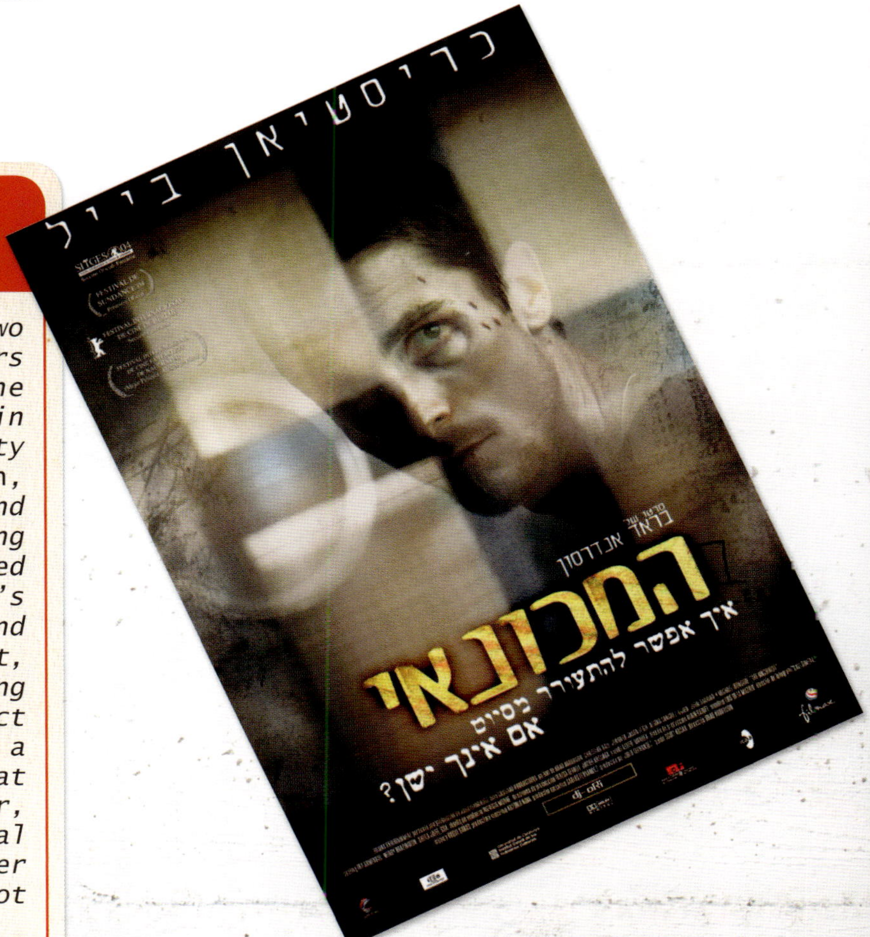

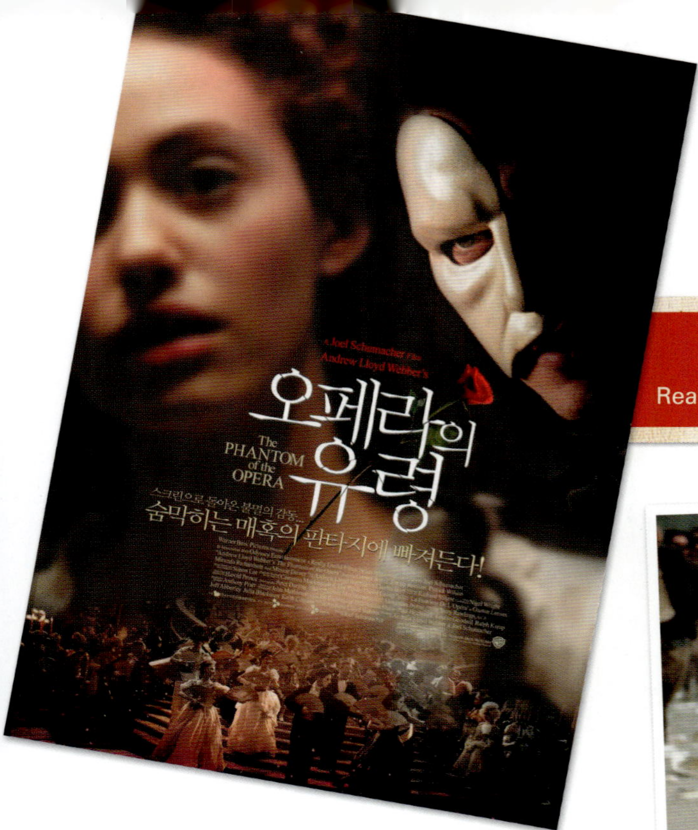

The Phantom of the Opera. Warner Bros. Pictures/Odyssey Entertainment/ Really Useful Films/Scion Films (2004). South Korea.

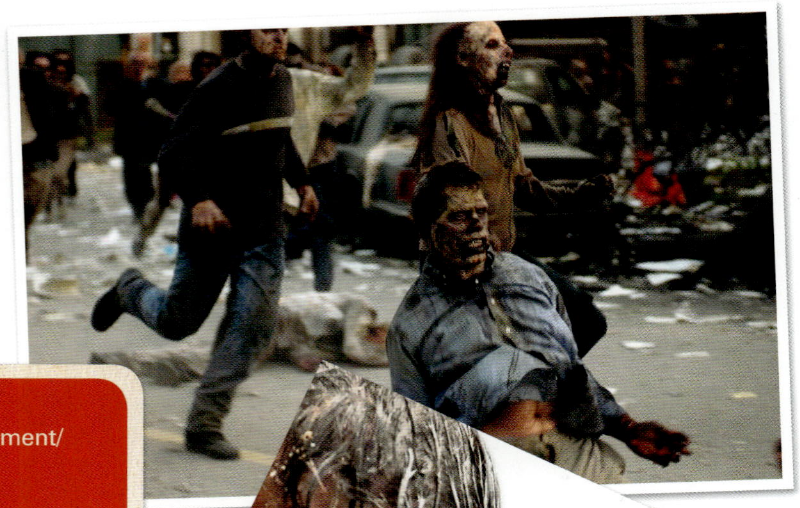

Dawn of the Dead. Universal Pictures/ Strike Entertainment/New Amsterdam Entertainment/ Metropolitan Filmexport/Toho-Towa (2004). Photo by Michael Gibson.

Exactly as with the original, I was hooked as soon as I saw the television ad – this time with a ticker showing the small Wisconsin city's rapidly accelerating descent into undeath. As one of the few zombie films with a name cast, this is one of the best-acted horror films you're going to see, with the most harrowing roller-coaster ride between humorous, poignant, and horrifying moments.

Kim Paffenroth

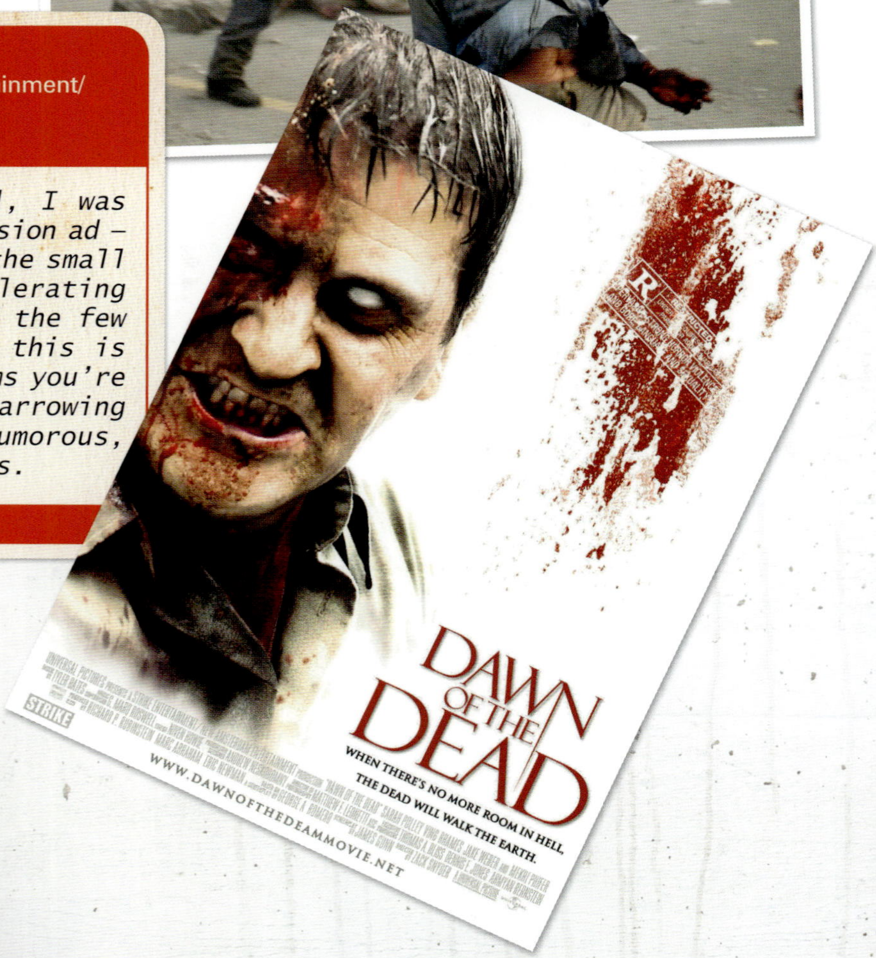

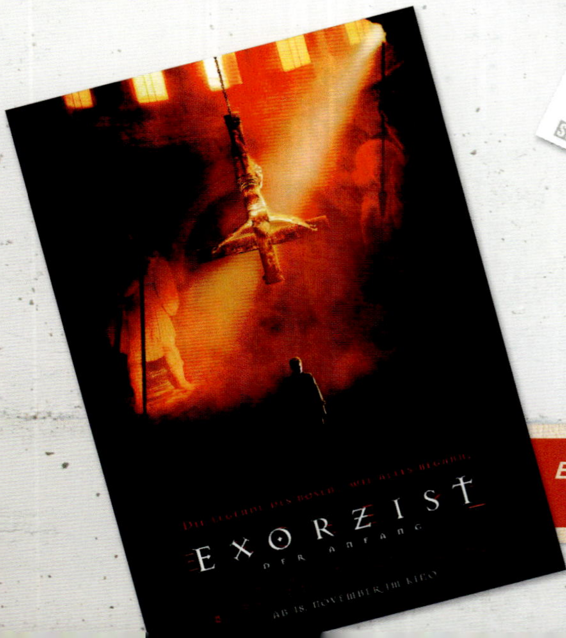

Exorcist: The Beginning. Morgan Creek Productions/ Dominion Productions (2004). Germany.

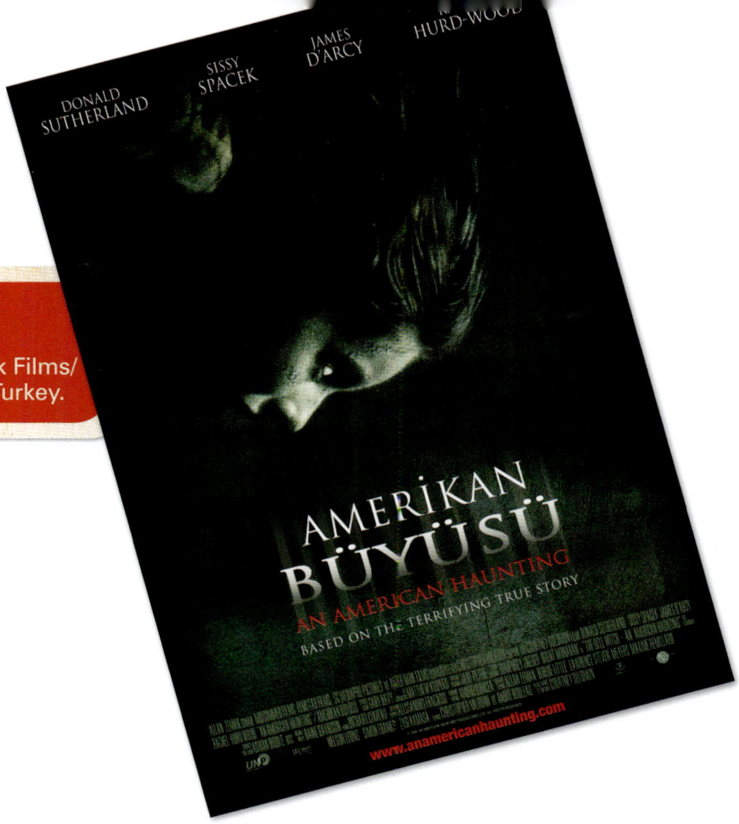

An American Haunting. Allan Zeman Productions/Midsummer Films/Remstar Productions/Media Pro Pictures/After Dark Films/Redbus Pictures/Sweetpea Entertainment (2005). Turkey.

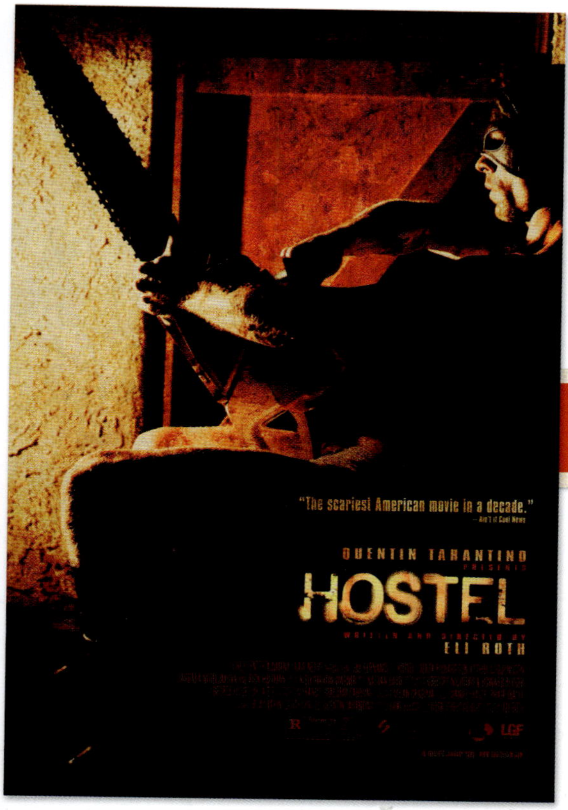

Hostel. Hostel LLC/International Production Company/Next Entertainment/Raw Nerve (2005).

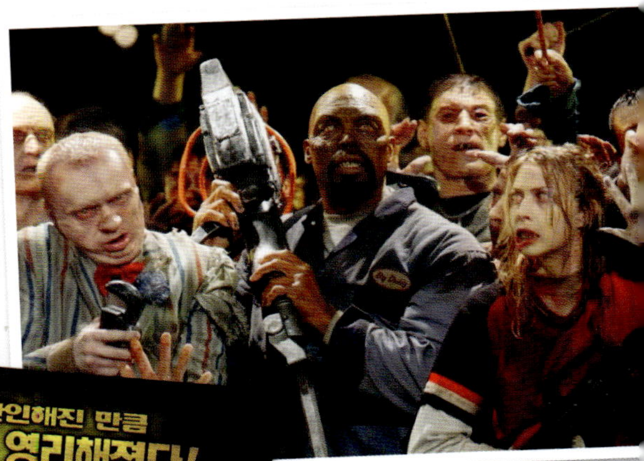

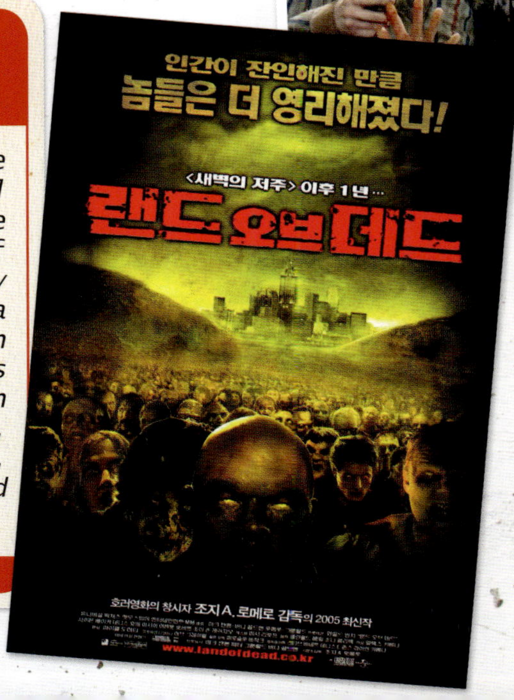

Land of the Dead. Universal Pictures/Atmosphere Entertainment MM/Exception Wild Bunch/Romero-Grunwald Productions (2005). South Korea.

I bought a signed poster of George Romero's Land of the Dead *(2005) well before the film was released. While the film itself, like Romero's own* Dawn of the Dead *(1978), is often exceptionally colorful, the image on the poster is a muted, nearly monochromatic, yellow. In another reversal, the mass of zombies walks away from the city rather than towards it as they do in the film. Here, they march (and stare) at the viewer, acknowledging, implicating, and indeed recognizing us.*

Jesse Stommel

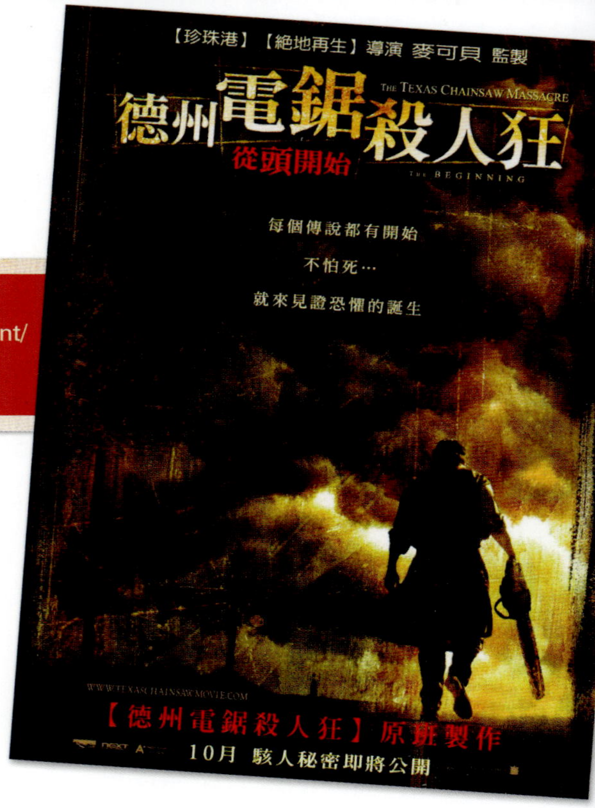

The Texas Chainsaw Massacre: The Beginning. New Line Cinema/Platinum Dunes/Next Entertainment/Vortex/Henkel/Hooper/Texas Chainsaw Productions (2006). Taiwan.

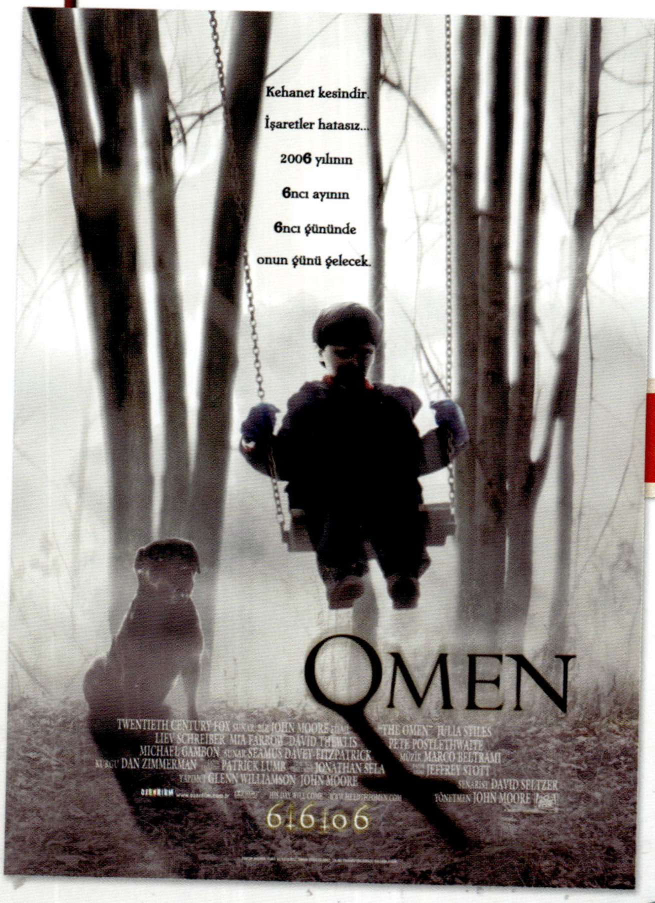

The Omen. Twentieth Century Fox Film Corporation/11:11 Mediaworks (2006). Turkey.

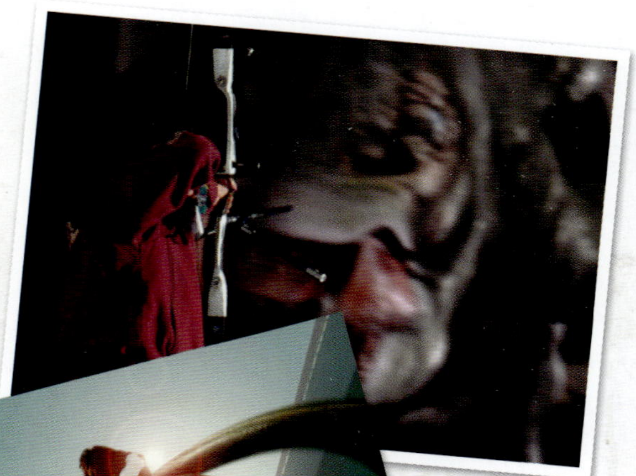

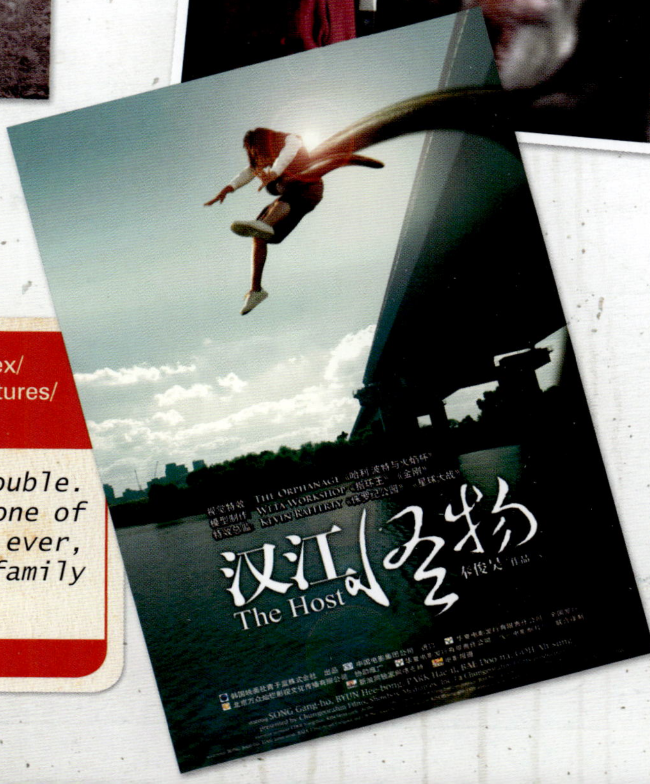

The Host. Chungeorahm Film/Showbox/Mediaplex/Happinet Corporation/Knowledge & Creation Ventures/Sego Entertainment (2006). China.

Big river. Big monster. Big trouble. This South Korean horror drama is one of the best creature feature movies ever, and a touching (and funny) human family drama as well.

Tony Timpone

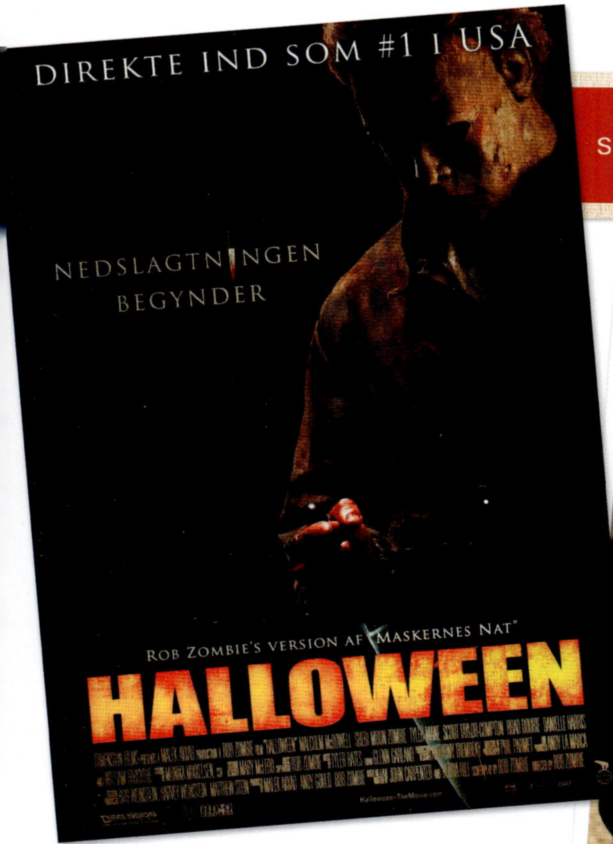

Halloween. Dimension Films/Nightfall Productions/ Spectacle Entertainment Group/Trancas International Films/The Weinstein Company (2007). Norway.

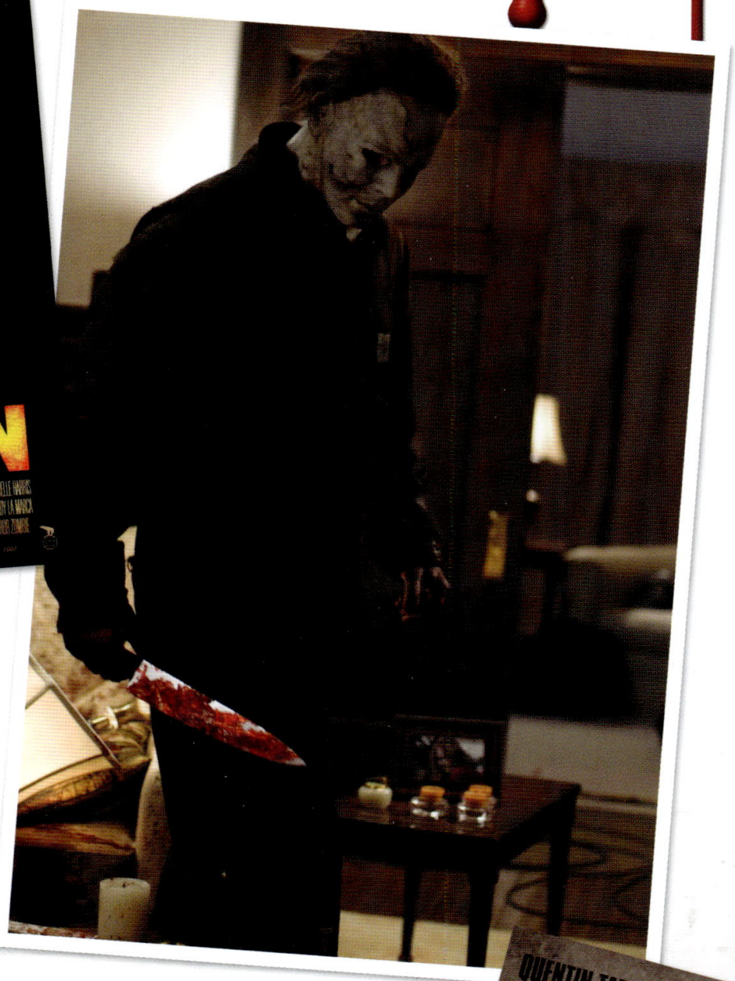

ON ALL THE **GORE**

It's very easy to make me sick: Show me an eviscerated man or woman and I'll probably at least need to look away. But I'm easy prey. Anyone can achieve that. I doubt I'd get off on stepping out into the street to stare at someone who had just been turned into hamburger by a skidding eighteen-wheeler. But now try to make me scared. That's different...and very few have managed it.

~Peter Crowther

Hostel: Part II. Lionsgate/Screen Gems/Next Entertainment/ Raw Nerve/International Production Company (2007).

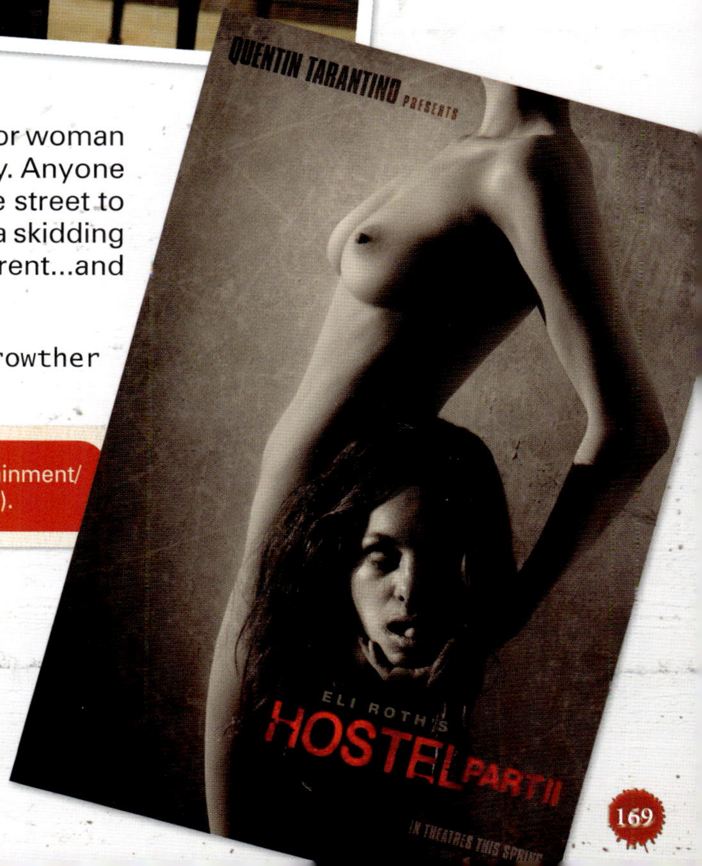

[Rec]. Castelao Producciones/Filmax/Televisión Española/Canal+ España/Instituto de la Cinematografía y de las Artes Audiovisuales/Instituto de Crédito Oficial/ Generalitat de Catalunya, Institut Català de Finances/ Institut Català de les Indústries Culturals (2007).

In the realm of horror films, the following are widely-recognized axioms: 1) the use of "shakey-cam," hand-held video and the concept of "found footage" very rapidly became passé after 1999's Blair Witch Project, and 2) sequels always suck. What, then, to make of 2007's [Rec] and 2009's [Rec] 2, two Spanish films that rely heavily on Blair Witch-style video, and the second of which is a direct sequel to the first? Well, the hand-held approach works marvelously in the sequestered, zombie-infested apartment building that acts as the milieu for both films, and the sequel is not only just as accomplished and frightening as the first film, but it also has the "cojones" to put forth a completely-unexpected cause for the zombie outbreak. All in all, [Rec] and [Rec] 2 are proof that every axiom can have an exception.

Robert Morrish

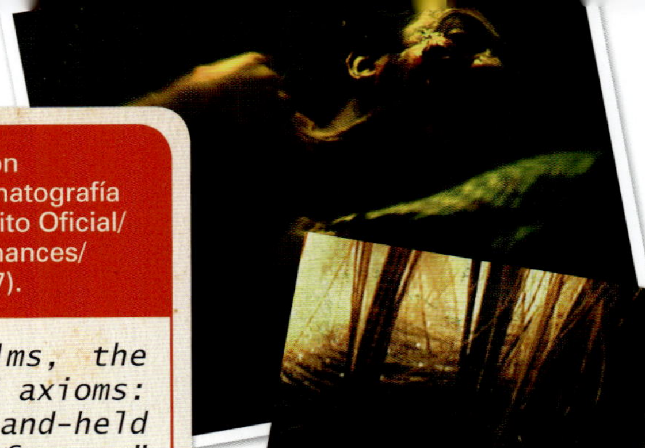

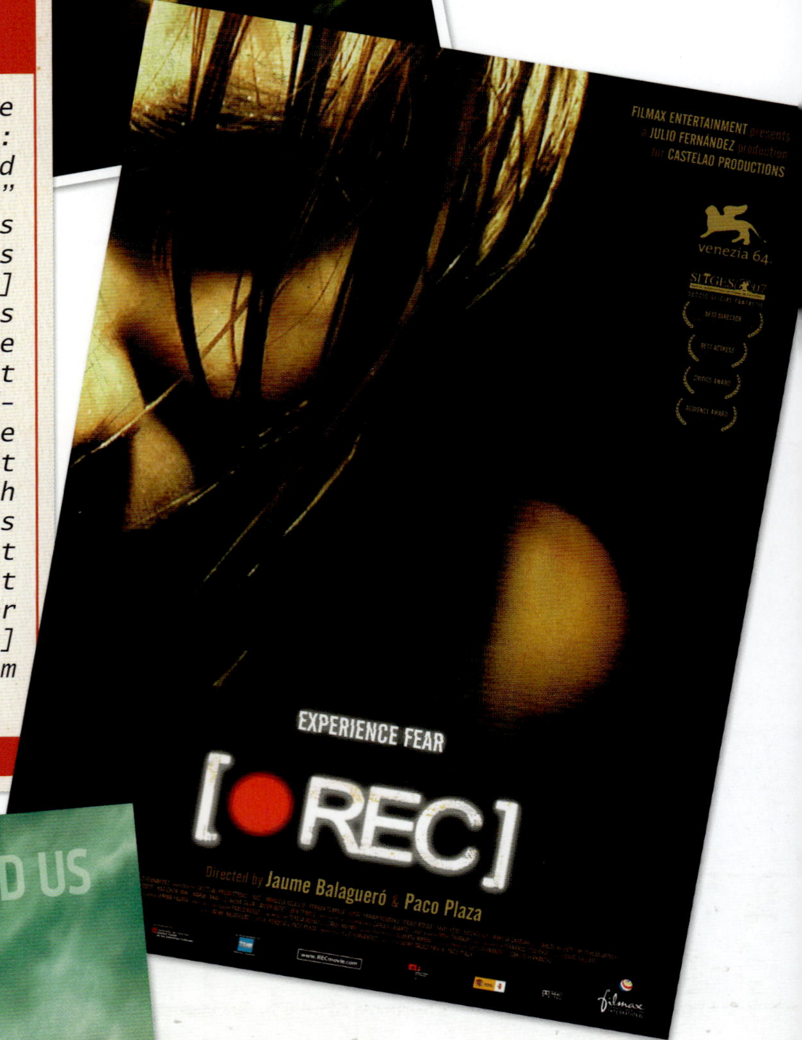

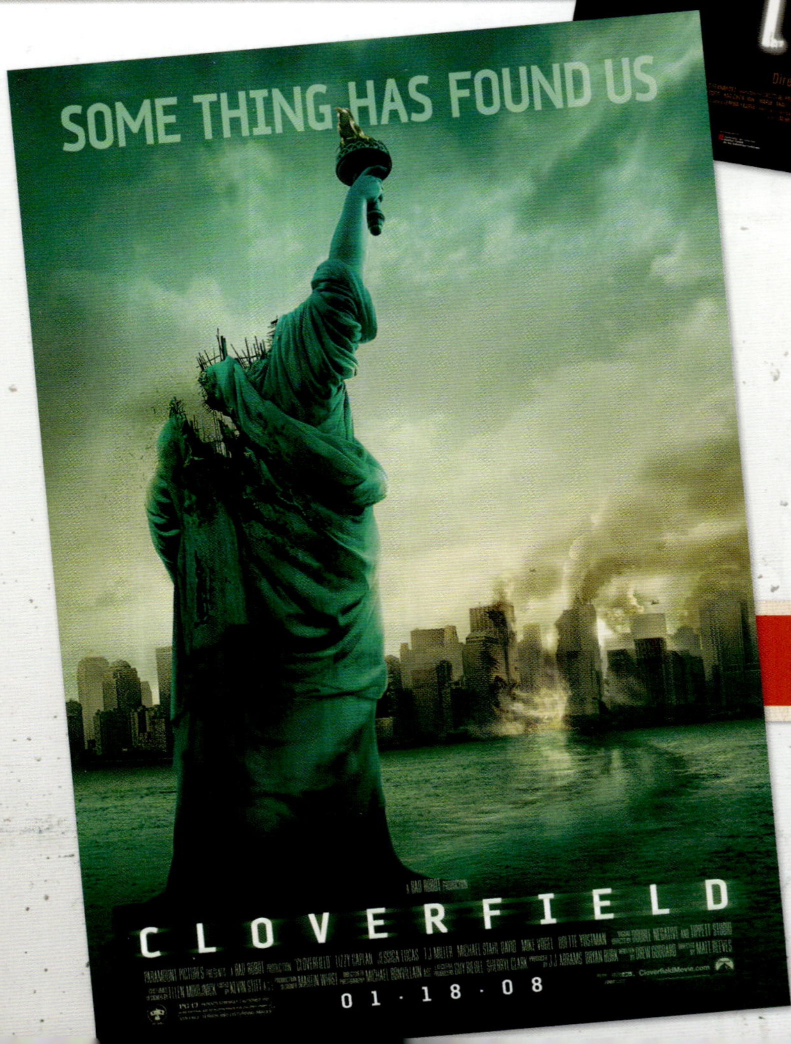

Cloverfield.
Paramount Pictures/Bad Robot (2008).

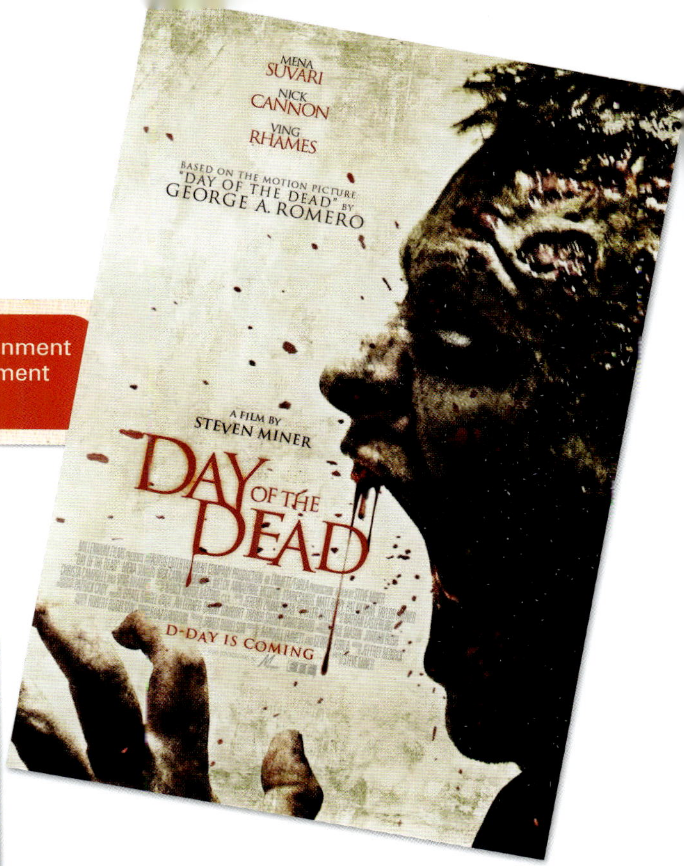

Day of the Dead. Millennium Films/Taurus Entertainment Company/Emmett/Furla Films/Nu Image Entertainment GmbH/D.O.D. Productions (2008).

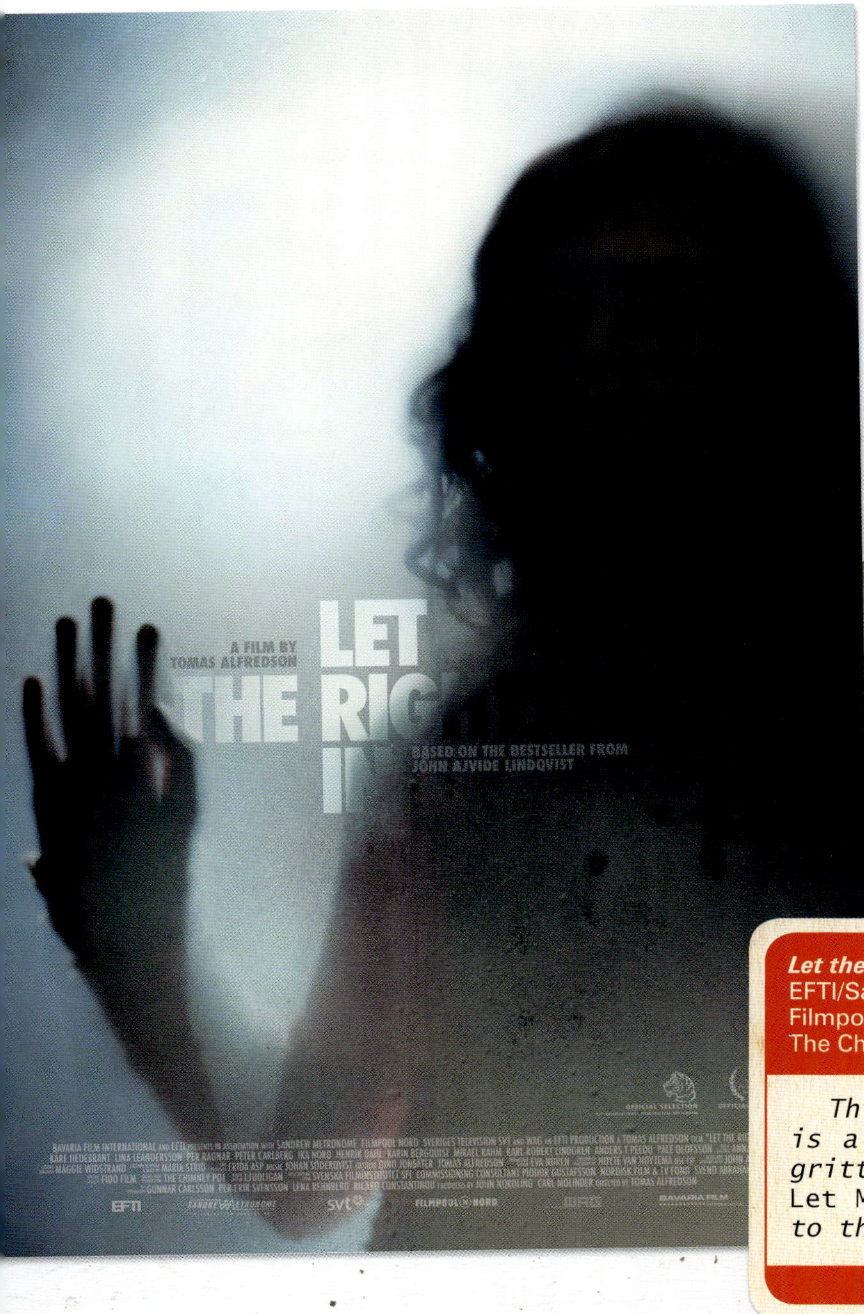

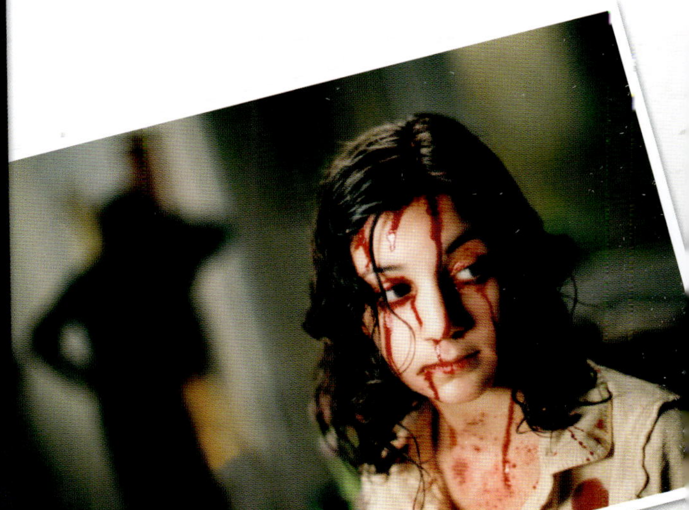

Let the Right One In.
EFTI/Sandrew Metronome Distribution Sverige AB/ Filmpool Nord/Sveriges Television/WAG/Canal+/ The Chimney Pot/Fido Film AB/Ljudligan (2008). UK

This modern horror classic from Sweden is a moving coming of age story and a gritty, unique vampire flick. Remake, Let Me In, *not half bad either, but go to this one first.*

Tony Timpone

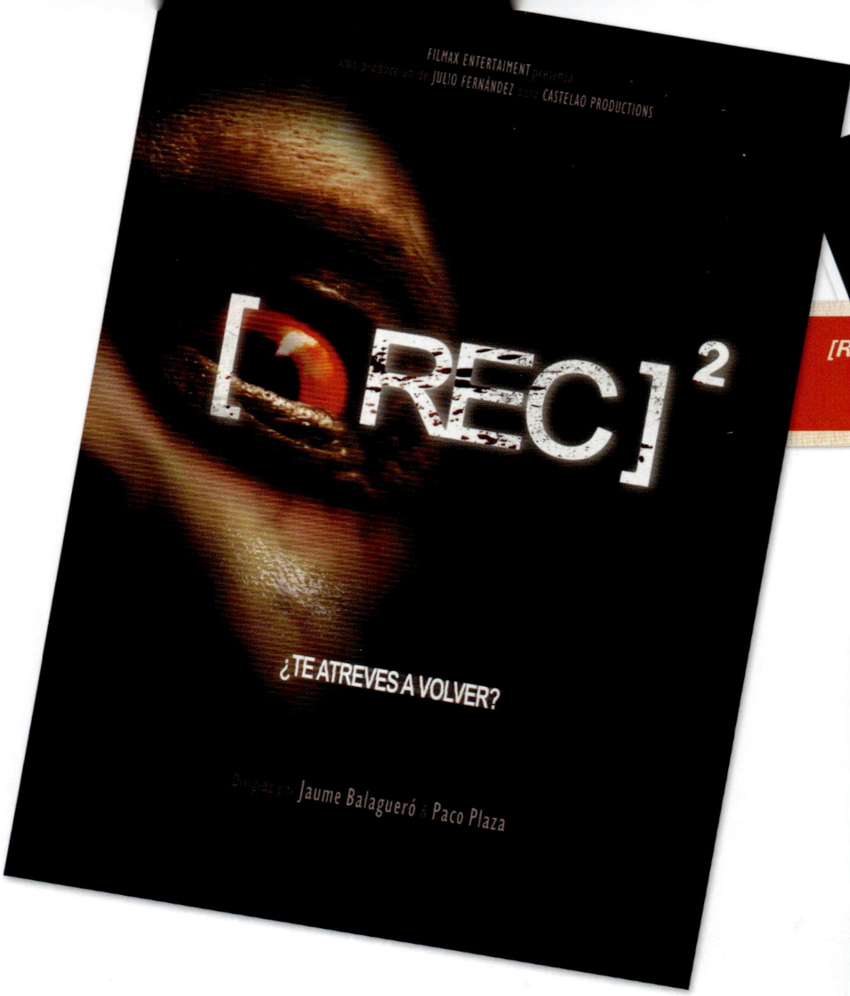

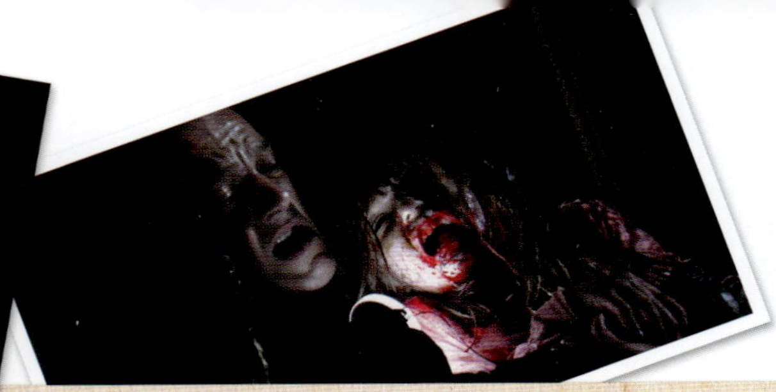

[Rec] 2. Castelao Producciones/Filmax/Generalitat de Catalunya/Instituto de Crédito Oficial/Ministerio de Educación, Cultura y Deportes (2009). Columbia.

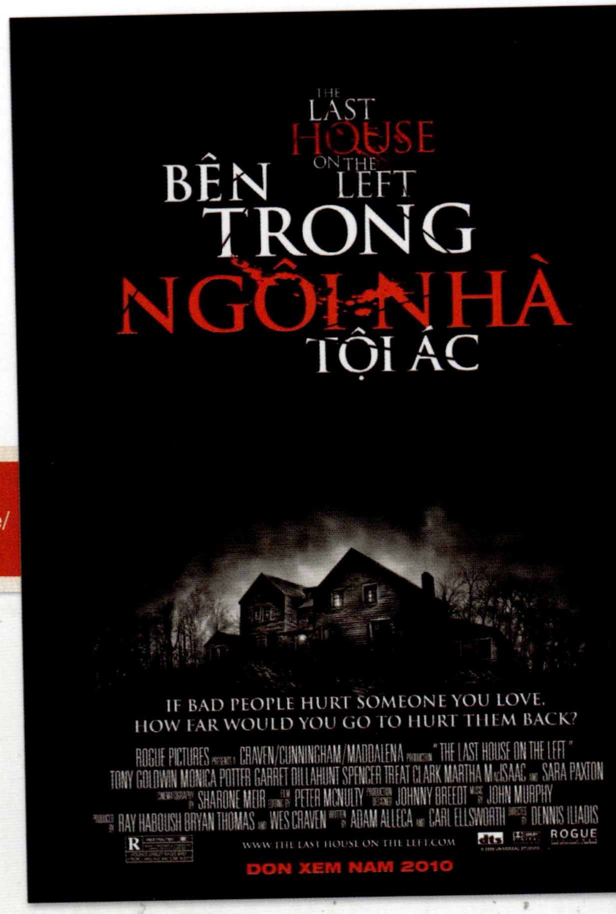

The Last House on the Left.
Rogue Pictures/Scion Films/Film Afrika Worldwide/Midnight Entertainment (2009). Vietnam.

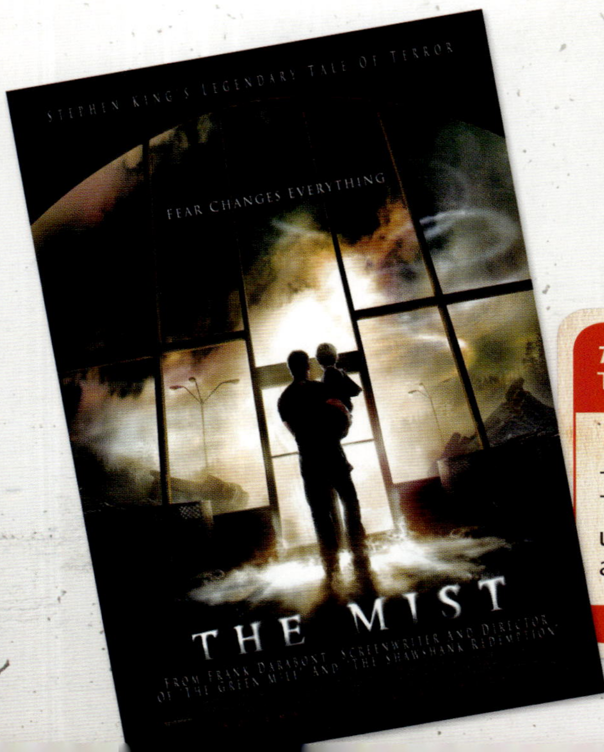

The Mist. Dimension Films/Darkwoods Productions/The Weinstein Company (2009).

We glimpse ever-evolving horrors in the impenetrable mist but come to learn that the deadliest monsters, the ultimate aliens, are our fellow humans and ourselves.

Richard J. Hand

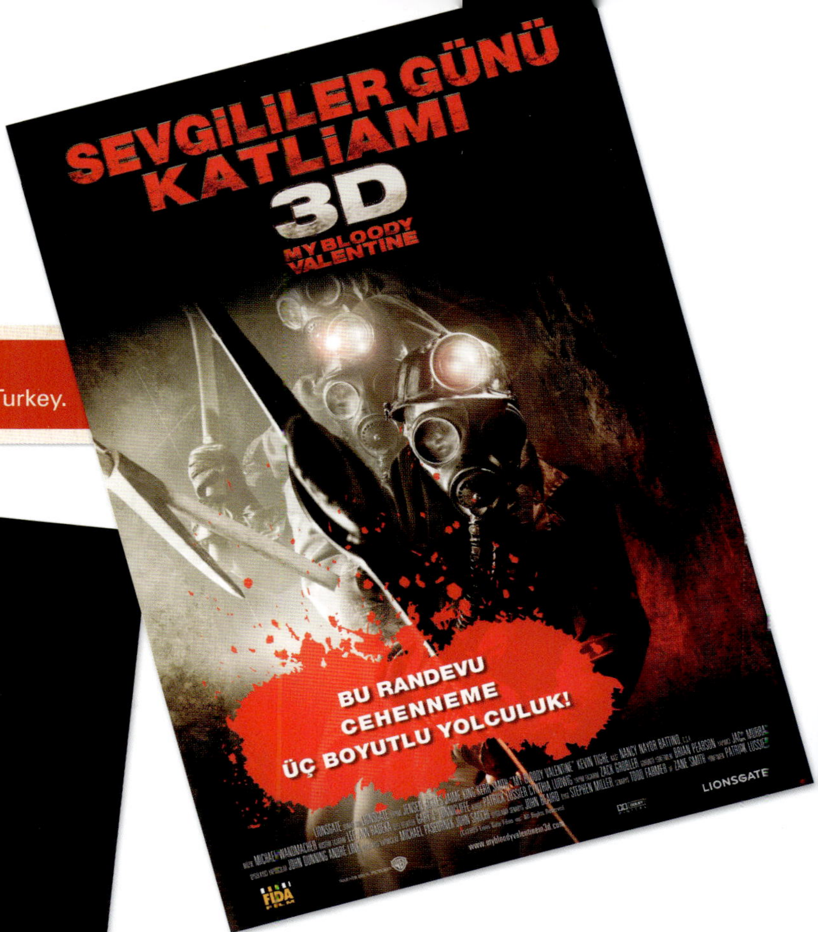

My Bloody Valentine 3-D.
Lionsgate/Paradise F.X. Corp. (2009). Turkey.

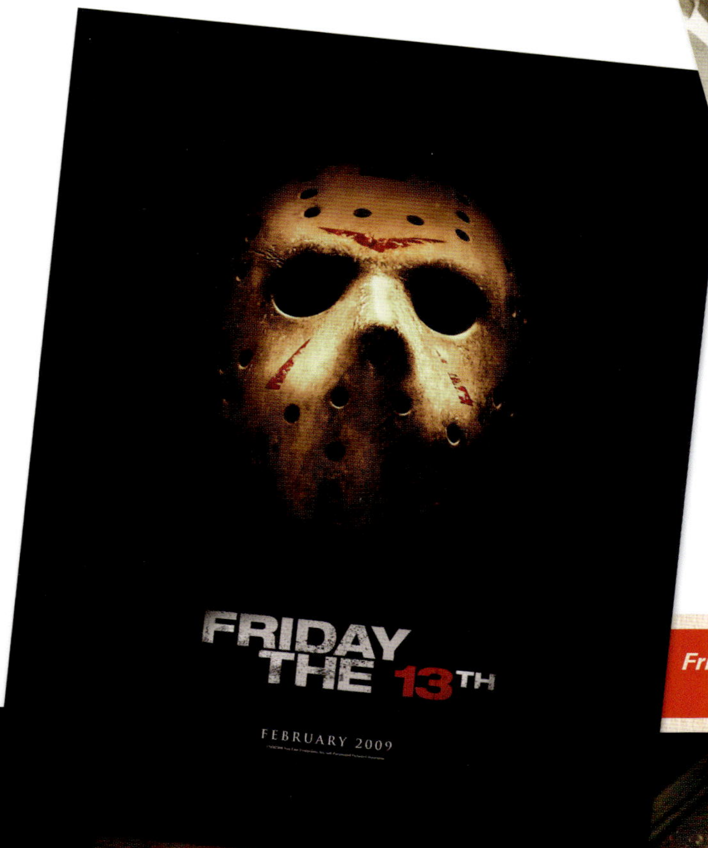

Friday the 13th. New Line Cinema/Paramount Pictures/
Platinum Dunes/Crystal Lake Entertainment (2009).

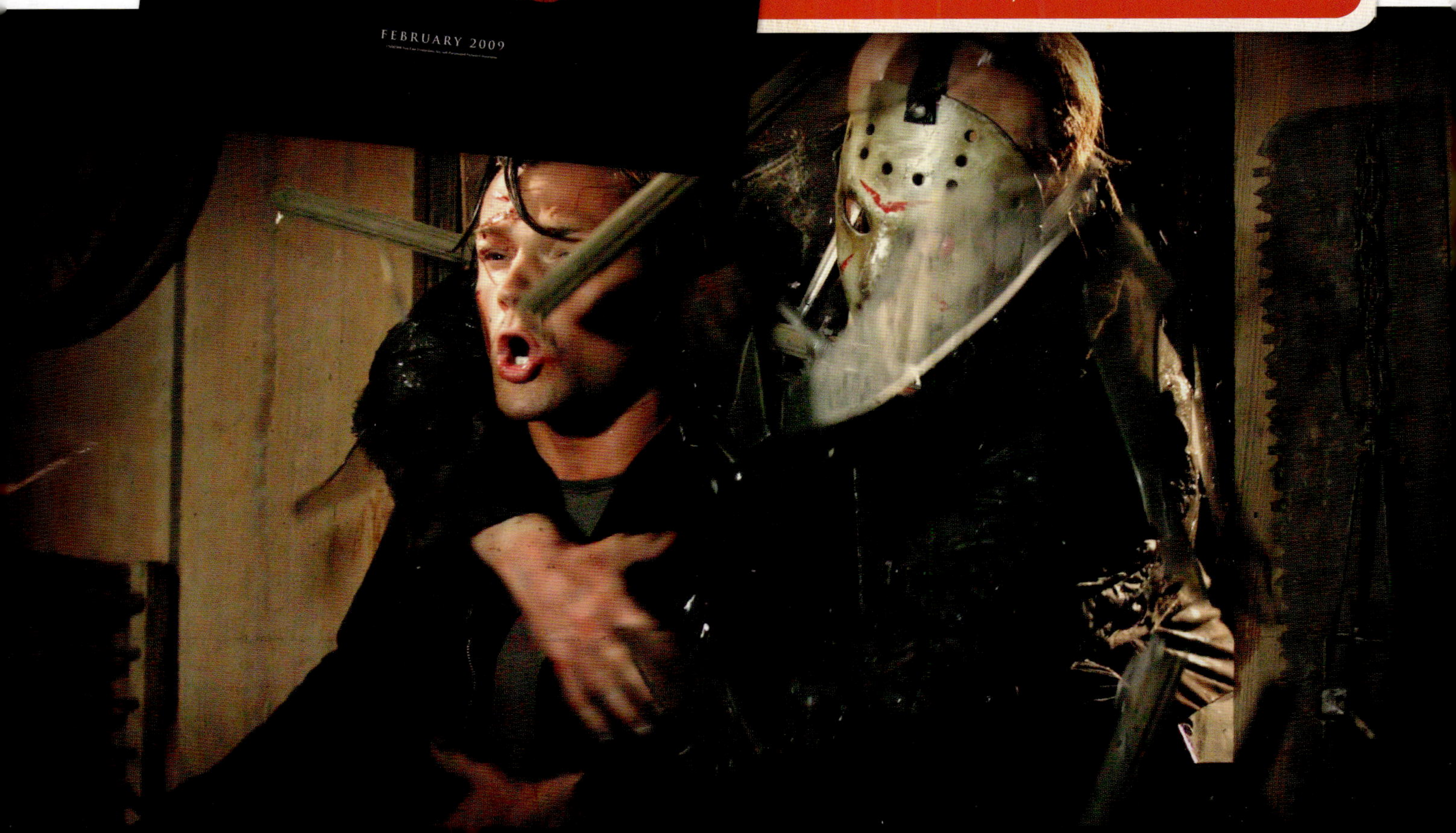

Let Me In. Overture Films/Exclusive Media Group/ Hammer Film Productions/EFTI (2010).

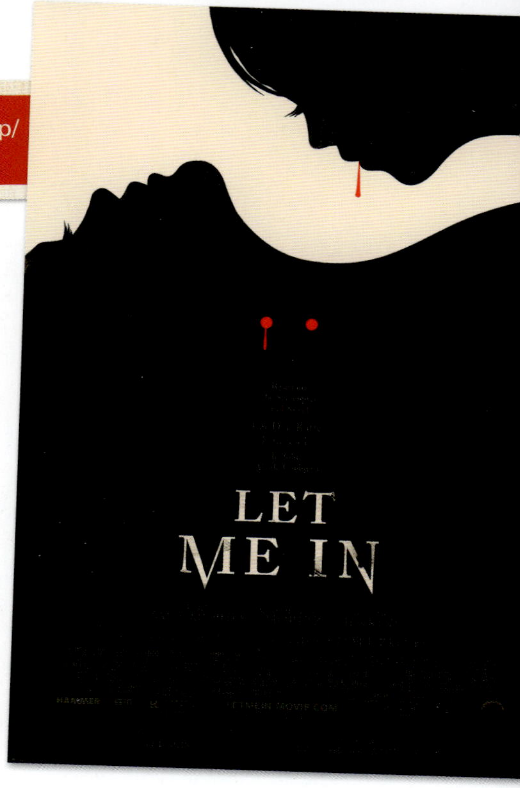

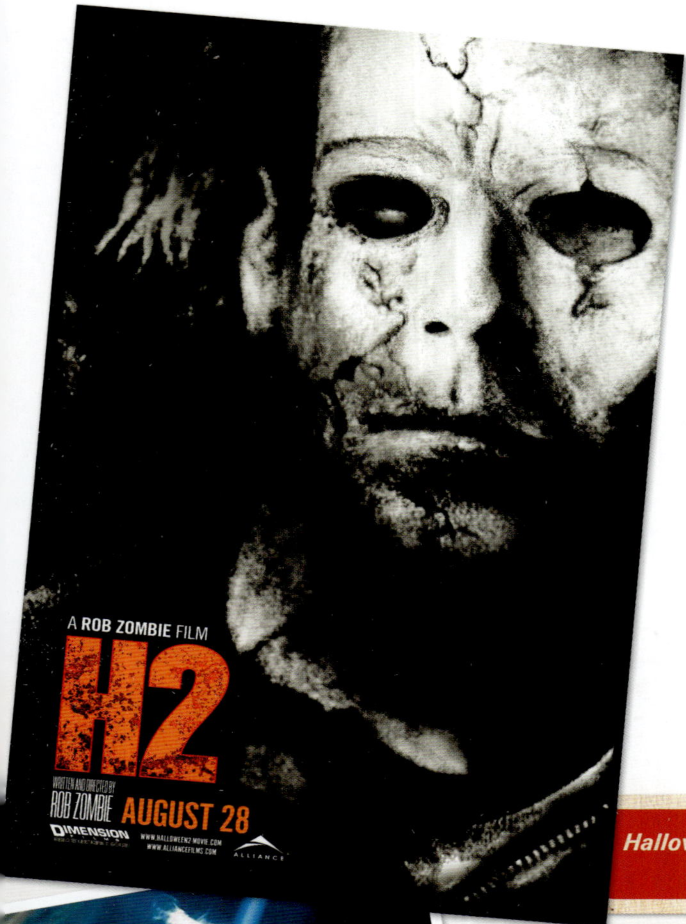

Halloween II. Dimension Films/Spectacle Entertainment Group/Trancas International Films (2009). Canada.

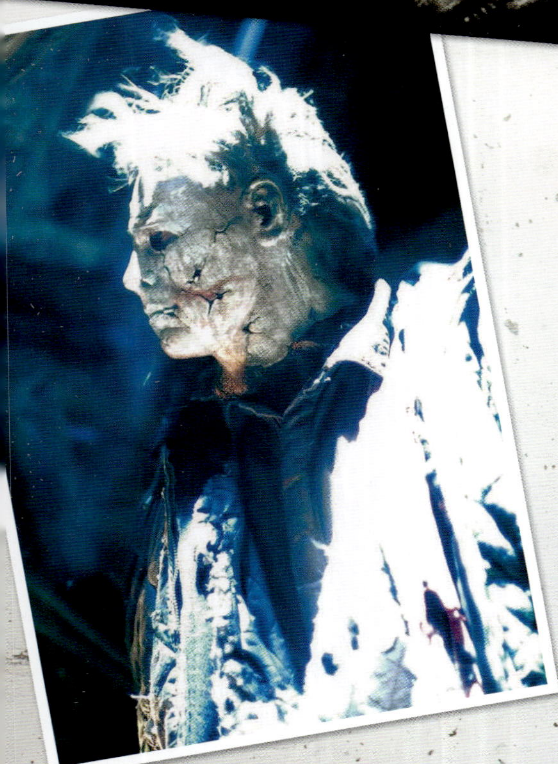

ON ZOMBIE'S VISION OF MICHAEL MYERS

An absolutely unsparing expression of Rob Zombie's personal vision of humanity as irredeemably corrupt and sleazy, *Halloween 2* is the work of mad genius, with not even a small concession granted to long-time franchise fans or general audiences. Zombie ramps up the violence during Michael Myers' rampages to such a degree so that the very film-stock itself seems to convulse and spasm with rage. Some early scenes with Michael Myers traversing beautiful natural landscapes alone or walking through town by moonlight are positively lyrical in presentation, a constant visual reminder of the character's separation from the rest of the human race. Accompanied by the ironic strains of Boudleaux Bryant's "Love Hurts," *Halloween 2's* unforgettable coda synthesizes everything audiences need to know about Zombie's universe and his individual vision: the pain, agony, and psychosis of a life destroyed by violence, and of violence brought on by love and hate within the family unit.

~John Kenneth Muir

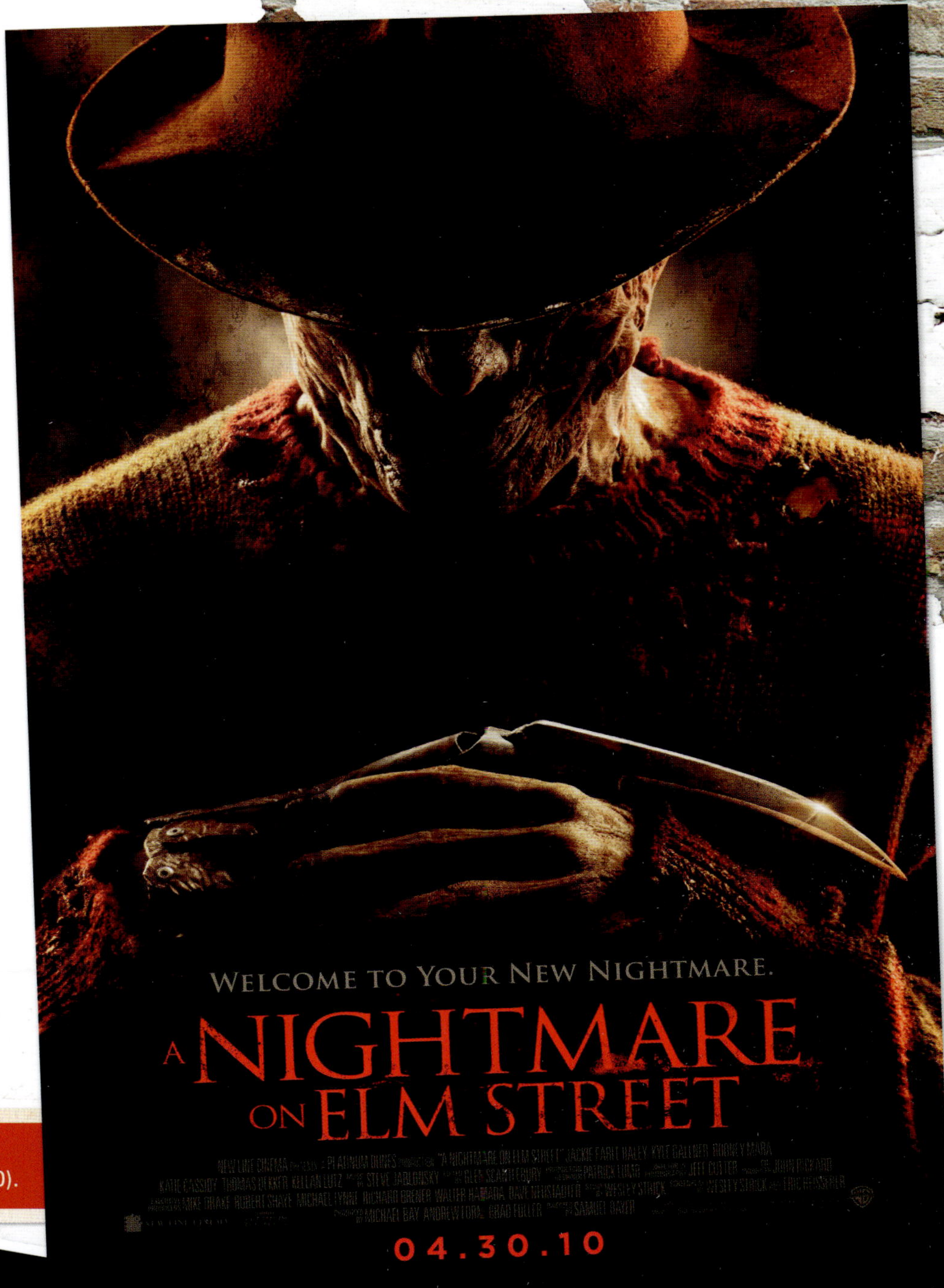

A Nightmare on Elm Street.
New Line Cinema/Platinum Dunes (2010).

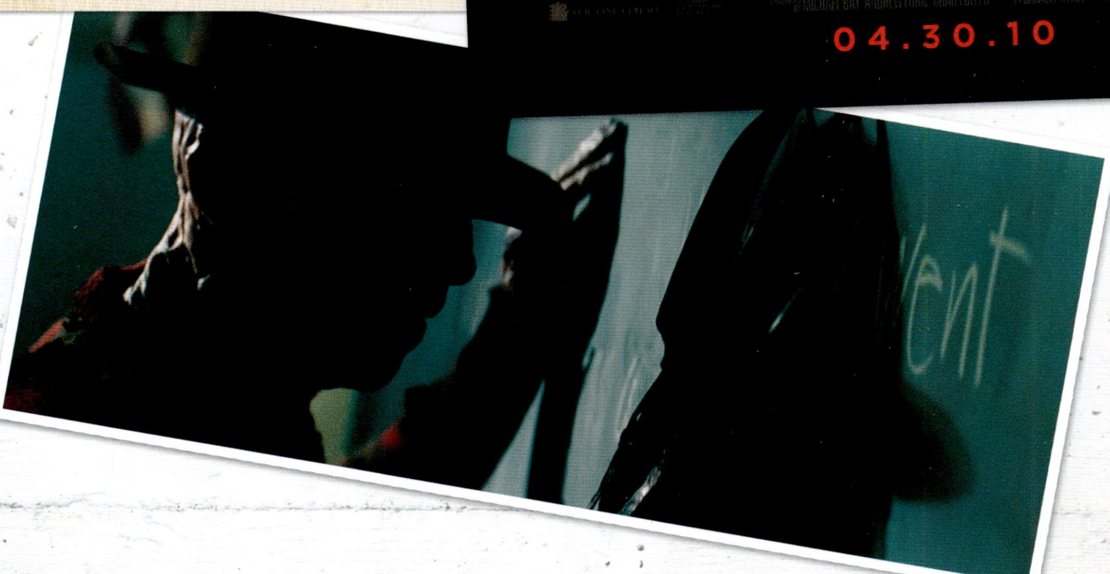

A

AFTERWORD

THE UNDEFINABLE: THE ESSENCE OF HORROR ON THE PAGE AND ON THE SCREEN

Chelsea Quinn Yarbro

Ambiguity, uncertainty, misapprehension, uneasiness, dubiety — each and every one of them has in them the seeds of horror stories in whatever medium they are presented. Whether it is...

- The sounds of footsteps in an empty house
- The shadow-within-a-shadow glimpsed on a wall or the pavement
- The figure in the hooded sweatshirt who might be following you
- The partially destroyed manuscript that implies there is some danger to the reader or the reading and/or viewing audience
- The skulking things you can't quite identify
- An almost-familiar face seen in a window where it is impossible for that face to be
- A passing bus that seems to have no driver, or
- A mirror that does not reflect what is there, or reflects something or someone that isn't...

...all of them evoke horror, that cold finger traveling up or down the spine called a grue, or that quiet gasp, for it is the lack of definition that drives almost all the most memorable horror tales, in all forms of media. There is a very basic reason for this — most people enjoy the frisson of being scared when they are not in actual danger.

It's exciting to be scared if the hazard isn't real. People delight in theme park rides for much the same reason, although there is little of authentic horror in going on one, except where malfunction occurs. Not even the rides that are designed to be scary are part of any real peril.

Adventure fiction and film usually share the fear-without-danger element but are most often at pains to identify the cause of the danger, and put the emphasis on the protagonists' abilities to understand and overcome it, not to leave it unaccounted for, and to be certain that the cause of danger is explained. Consider the difference: A door that opens on its own to reveal a dark and unknown room has far more horror in it than the most shocking explosion. An explosion is a done deal, terrifying and traumatic, but easily defined, and readily comprehended by almost all who experience the event and live to tell the tale. Horror usually saves its blatant shocks — if it has any — for the end, and builds up to them with eeriness, creepiness, mixed messages and motives, and events that might be clues to what is really going on, or might not. Perception, accurate and distorted, is far more important in horror than any other kind of adventure. Often horror provides no reassuring explanation, or the explanation it offers is incomplete or speculative. It is the lack of concrete knowledge that gives the horror story in all its forms its particular hook, and what makes its aficionados keep coming back for more. It is also the reason that horror is deceptively easy-looking when it is well-written or well-presented, and so very disappointing when it is not.

To trace the course of horror on the screen, it is helpful to begin with books and stories, illustrated tales and other forms of publications that have arisen over the last few centuries, and from which many — but not all — of the cinematic images have arisen. As has been observed by others before me, horror stories tend to reflect the anxieties of the times in which they were written, and can be viewed as social commentary of a very metaphorical sort, one that allows the readers to, as the late Robert Bloch put it, "immunize themselves against the dread of the thing the object of horror in the story represents," which can sometimes prove a sticking point for dramatic presentations in all forms of media, for the ambiguity of horror is not always readily maintained in visual forms.

Take the two film versions of Shirley Jackson's *The Haunting* — in the first version, starring Julie Harris, almost everything that is frightening is conveyed by implication or innuendo: the sound of cannon-balls dribbled down a hallway, the carved wood door seeming to breathe, the ornamentation that may or may not be the source of garbled shouts. You do not, as the audience, actually see the cause of any of these very disturbing things, so you, the audience, are free to build in your mind what that cause is, and by building your own horror, you plug into your own fears, making it far more frightening than anything that can be imagined by someone else. Jackson uses that device in her novel, of course, and it packs a wallop for the same reason that the unseen and undefined menaces in the film do. The remake with Katherine Zita-Jones is more of a phantasmagoria of special effects than a true horror film, for far too much is explicit, and the audience has little opportunity to build its own horrors; it is a much of a muchness, impressive to look at, but it has little of the creepiness of what Jackson wrote left in it, and the image of spiritual release at the end seems to me contrived and unconvincing, an excuse for more special effects rather than a story resolution. A horror film that reveals the object of horror at the end is often disappointing for just this reason — that the monster/creature/madman, no matter how dreadful, is not as vivid or as personal as what each individual member of the audience has imagined for him- or herself. I can still shudder at the memory of seeing *Curse of the Demon* (from M. R. James's superb novelette *Casting the Runes)* for the first time: Dana Andrews walking, then running through the woods followed by something invisible that leaves large, taloned, smoking footprints. What I conjured from those footprints pushed almost all my fear buttons because it was based on my own fears. The Medieval demon appearing at the end seemed pretty small potatoes to me after my own imagination had built its own demon. Because so much of horror stories is metaphorical of actual fears and threats, they often are hard to shift from one environment or era to another. That is why some horror stories lose their punch over time. What bothered the readers of Matthew Gregory Lewis — *The Monk* and others — and Mrs. Radcliffe — who wrote a raft of books at the end of the 1700s — does not tend to bother us in the twenty-first century. Lecherous monks, for Lewis, or Italian castles and sinister foreigners for Radcilffe are nowhere near as dangerous to us now as bacteria for deadly diseases, unearthly creatures, or mutations of what humans are supposed to be are in the popular perceptions. As much as those works frightened their audiences in the late eighteenth century, we read them now with a detachment that is the result of not sharing the basic dread their readers had, which defuses and diffuses the stories, leaving them as curiosities more than something that can keep you awake all night. In America, Hawthorne has lost a lot of his capacity to frighten, and present-day adaptations of his work usually have to modify the underlying fear to what bothers us at present rather than what worried people in New England at the onset of the nineteenth century. Poe has a touch of that for present-day readers, and I suspect that may be one of the reasons the works of these highly acclaimed horror writers are particularly difficult to translate to dramatic form now. Some have evolved — for example, our dangerous aliens now tend to come from outer space, not distant lands, with the possible exception in the last decade of foreigners of Middle Eastern origin. Of the classic fear-inducing archetypes only two are still with us largely unaltered: the vampire and the were-creature, and their durability can be seen on shelves and screens throughout the world to this day.

Considering the fluctuations in horror story publication over the years, it would appear on the surface that the field is mercurial by nature, but that would not be truly accurate, for such cycles of popularity are more an artifact of the publishing business — or the film business, or the television business, or the graphic-novel business, or any other form of media business — than the tastes of audiences. Ask any librarian, used book dealer, or DVD, video, or online seller and it will become apparent that the horror genre in all its manifestations has a faithful audience that stays with it through the fads and vagaries that mark the changes in the marketplace. Those who find that horror suits their taste in entertainment are likely to stay with it, in one form or another, for decades.

Recent developments in computer and role-playing games have added another dimension to the horror market, but one that tends more to the adventure genres than the true horror genres. Just as thirty years ago it was assumed that all science fiction was read by fourteen-year-old boys, and mysteries were read by fifty-plus women, the basic approach to computer games tends to be like science fiction used to be — lots of action, explosions, destruction caused by powerful male figures doing testosterone-laden confrontations with machines and/or inhuman creatures, probably addressing the underlying fear of civil violence, war, and the dread of being driven out of the job-market by machines. But there are some back-water computer and role-playing games that deal with horror tropes. These are usually aimed at adolescents and have to do with horror archetypes, a variation on the secret identity modern archetypes like Superman and the Fantastic Four, but reinterpreted in horror context, addressing teenage angst and sexual apprehension, a restructuring that is presently enjoying a great deal of popularity, as reflected in books and film and television series. What troubles me about many of these games and related stories and films is that their horror archetypes are more image than substance, dumbed-down for an audience that for the most part has not yet discerned the difference between image and substance, just as I have trouble with a small, purple T-Rex that dances and sings with kids. Rethinking archetypes can be revealing and engaging if the writer or filmmaker is willing to delve into the history of the archetype, but if it's only a matter of cosmetically enhanced entertainment, whether in print or on the screen, then the results are for the most part superficial, at least for me.

Of course there are a great many subgenres to horror, as there are to all genre-identified stories, and each has its particular flavor. Psychological horror is not the same as what might be called classic or folkloric horror (or fairy tale horror), and although related to folkloric horror, is often used to teach a lesson in a very specific style that is quite unlike, for example, urban horror; splatterpunk works differently than Lovecraftian horror; romantic horror works its horror along more mixed emotions than does devils-and-demons horror; and adventure horror creates its frissons in ways that do not work in that most-difficult-of-all-to-pull-off sub-genre, humorous horror. It is easy to do horror so badly that it's laughable, but funny horror is something different, a skilled storytelling tightrope between the gruesome and the absurd.

The horror genre, as such, is fairly protean, able to encompass other genres in its narratives without so much as a ripple in its tropes. Other genres have more definite boundaries, as well as specific elements that need to be present to be true to its genre. Still, those writers, for the page or all manner of screens, in combining another genre with horror, will have to be mindful of the characteristics and structures of the non-horror genre than they will have to adhere to horror criteria. William Hjortsberg's brilliant *Falling Angel* is both an increasingly surreal mystery and a remarkable horror story, and its translation to the screen, *Angel Heart*, is a spectacular example of successfully externalizing what on the page is largely an introspective story. Henry James's *The Turn of the Screw* is both a classic Gothic romance — a young woman is hired to work in a large, remote house to take care of the young, the old, or the disabled, where she is exposed to unknown and ill-defined dangers — and a particularly haunting horror story, about a figure who literally haunts the place. Another of Shirley Jackson's novels, *We Have Always Lived in the Castle,* proceeds along the usual development of a young adult coming-of-age tale, but with elements that turn this into a spine-curdler of the first water. Jackson was very good at capturing the illusion of normality that helps seduce the audience into the environment of the story, which is among the most successful approaches to contemporary urban horror. By the time the reader or viewer realizes something is very, very wrong with the picture presented, the ordinariness makes it impossible to dismiss, because it is cloaked in the everyday so thoroughly that the horror elements are part of the horror itself. Stephen King uses this "illusion of normality" device in his work, and for the most part, it translates well to the screen.

Like fantasy and science fiction, horror often evokes not only dread, but a sense of wonder. When Belle goes down that long, dark hall with the arms holding torches emerging from the walls in Jean Cocteau's brilliant *Beauty and the Beast*, there is not only fear, but wonder. True, that story is a fairy tale, but as with many fairy tales, there are strong horror elements in its structure, and Cocteau made the most of those images. Unlike a horror story, both Cocteau's story line and the premise of the tale are resolved by the end; in a horror story, there is often the lingering possibility that the Beast will return, his paws smoking from killing the innocent, an image that works much better in film than it does on the page due to its visual impact. Just describing smoking blood is creepy and unpleasant, but seeing it brings about an immediacy that trumps the page every time.

Like all things in art, there is a trade-off: Certain devices work better on the page, and others are stronger for being visual. Adventure fiction often translates well to the screen — by the way, the adventure genre includes both war stories and westerns — and can be tricky in sustaining its pace on the page. In horror, the balance can be more difficult to sustain than in, say, mysteries. Mysteries often have a quality of reportage about them that can move more easily into the high-visibility realms of the screen; horror, with its uncertainty, can easily be ruined by being too visual. On the page, giving the impression of things being not quite right is more easily accomplished than high visuals allow. As a number of contributors to this book have pointed out, the success of horror films is variable. My own least-favorite scenario in what I feel is mislabeled a horror sub-genre instead of that off-shoot of mysteries, suspense stories, involves a group of young people from the city or suburbs on vacation or a study trip in the woods at a remote and ill-reputed house/farm/castle/ruin, where the most sexually active pair in the group gets done in by the monster/ghost/vampire/madman/werewolf/mutant animals first, and the rest try to find a way to get out of the danger zone. There are threats aplenty, but the grue, the frisson, is missing from almost all of them. This is not as true on the page because language can imply, insinuate, and hint at danger better than visuals can.

Anthropology teaches us that all peoples in all times have had horror stories to tell. Some of them remain as cultural archetypes, some have become myths, legends, and folklore, some have changed form but not application, some have lost their punch and become objects of amusement rather than fright, and some have gone from minor threat to major threat as science and technology are interpolated with more ancient dangers. All of these factors in horror tales have been and are being used to power what we read and view in the genre; for those venturing into these depths, respect for the form and its origins is essential to delivering to the audience the full measure of disquiet and the experience of safe danger. Even in pastiches, the frisson is expected and the audience feels cheated if there isn't a hint of whistling-in-a-graveyard humor. Horror needs a delicacy of touch, or it tends to disintegrate into gore and disgust without the fascination that safe danger provides.

Of course, the transfer isn't always from page to screen — occasionally the reverse occurs. I've done the novelization on two horror films — *Dead & Buried* and *Nomads* — and in both instances, working from the screenplay with only sketchy ideas about what the film would look like when it was completed was a challenge. In both instances I had a month in which to complete the novel and I had a meeting early on with the writers. Of the two, *Nomads* posed the greater difficulty, for the five villainous and possibly unnatural characters never spoke. It was a very creepy device on the screen, but truly demanding to pull off. In novelizations there are a number of problems confronting the writer, mostly associated with the things that aren't explained on the screen because the visuals create the immediacy that the page does not. How characters get from one place to another, the manner in which they respond to events, what their thoughts may be, how they identify the nature of the threats they face, all of these must be addressed on the page and convey some of the same excitement that the screen provides. The basic experience for the audience for page and screen is different: The screen reaction is often shared immediately — you watch a film or play a game with someone else, or perhaps a great many someones. Most readers read privately, making the response they have a much more personal one. In taking a work from one medium to another, the way in which the story will be perceived through the nature of the experience itself is crucial to the success of the work. Those novels that are essentially an outline for a film script are all too familiar, and often leave the reader frustrated because of the thinness of the story's environment and characterization. And an overly literal adaptation of book to screen can result in the kind of corrunculation (a word I coined to describe certain opera plots that curl in and around with the complexity of sailors's knots) that renders the film virtually incomprehensible unless the viewer has also read the book.

All art is abstract; some of it is more realistic in appearance or presentation than others, but all of it is based on perceptions, those of the creator and those of the audience. At its best, art reveals something of ourselves to us in our experience of it. For the world of the horror story, the abstraction tends to come from the unknown, the unidentified, the hidden, the ghastly possible. Those writers and filmmakers who embrace this distorted vision can deliver to the audience a remarkable and insightful experience, one that affirms that not everything is as it appears to be, and that not everything experienced can be logically explained. Films of all types, books, illustrated stories, games, the lot of them, can provide thrills and shocks that offer safe insights into the dark side of ourselves, and by doing so, shed light on how we understand ourselves and our world; in recognizing the nature of fears, we can, if only for a moment, banish the grip the reality of dread imposes on our lives and our comprehension of our experiences.

Chelsea Quinn Yarbro is the author of over 70 novels, including the ever-popular Count Saint-Germain vampire series, in addition to numerous works of short fiction. She is the first woman to be named a "Living Legend" by the International Horror Guild (2006). In 2009, she was honored with the Bram Stoker Lifetime Achievement Award by the Horror Writers Association (the third woman, after Joyce Carol Oates and Anne Rice, to be so honored). She is one of only two women ever to be named as "Grand Master" of the World Horror Convention (2003). She is also the recipient of the Fine Foundation Award for Literary Achievement (1993) and (along with Fred Saberhagen) was awarded the Knightly Order of the Brasov Citadel by the Transylvanian Society of Dracula in 1997. In 1995, she was the only novelist guest of the Romanian government for the First World Dracula Congress, sponsored by the Transylvanian Society of Dracula, the Romanian Bureau of Tourism, and the Romanian Ministry of Culture. Her impressive career includes nominations for the Edgar, World Fantasy, and Bram Stoker Awards, in addition to being the first female president of the Horror Writers Association. Yarbro is one of the first women to have made a successful and long career writing modern supernatural fiction.

L

Ghoul School Library

A Selection of Readings in Horror and the Fantastic

Books (fiction) and Short Fiction

Byron, Glennis. *Dracula,* by Bram Stoker (Toronto, ON: Broadview Press, 1998)

Campbell, Ramsey. *The Doll Who Ate His Mother* (Bobbs-Merrill, 1976)

_____. *The Bride of Frankenstein* (as Carl Dreadstone) (Berkley, 1977)

_____. *Dracula's Daughter* (as Carl Dreadstone) (Berkley, 1977)

_____. *The Wolfman* (as Carl Dreadstone) (Berkley, 1977)

_____. *The Face That Must Die* (Star Books, 1979)

_____. *To Wake the Dead* (aka *The Parasite*) (Millington, 1980)

_____. *The Nameless* (Macmillan, 1981)

_____. *Night of the Claw* (writing as Jay Ramsay) (St. Martin's Press, 1983)

_____. *Incarnate* (Macmillan, 1983)

_____. *Obsession* (Macmillan, 1985)

_____. *The Hungry Moon* (Macmillan, 1986)

_____. *The Influence* (Macmillan, 1988)

_____. *Ancient Images* (Scribner, 1989)

_____. *Needing Ghosts* (Century, 1990)

_____. *Midnight Sun* (Macdonald, 1990)

_____. *The Count of Eleven* (Macdonald & Company, 1991)

_____. *The Long Lost* (TOR, 1993)

_____. *The One Safe Place* (Headline, 1995)

_____. *The House on Nazareth Hill* (aka *Nazareth Hill*) (Headline Feature, 1996)

_____. *The Last Voice They Hear* (Forge, 1998)

_____. *Silent Children* (Forge, 2000)

_____. *Pact of the Fathers* (Forge, 2001)

_____. *The Darkest Part of the Woods* (TOR, 2002)

_____. *The Overnight* (PS Publishing, 2004)

_____. *Secret Story* (TOR, 2005)

_____. *The Grin of the Dark* (PS Publishing, 2007)

_____. *Thieving Fear* (PS Publishing, 2008)

_____. *Creatures of the Pool* (Leisure Books, 2009)

_____. *Solomon Kane: Official Movie Novelisation* (Titan, 2010)

_____. *The Seven Days of Cain* (PS Publishing, 2010)

Castle, Mort. *The Deadly Election* (Major, 1976)

_____. *Cursed Be the Child* (Leisure Books, 1990)

_____. *In Memoriam: Papa, Blake and HPL* (DarkTales Publications, 1999)

_____. *The Strangers* (Overlook Connection Press, 2005)

Crowther, Peter. *Escardy Gap* (with James Lovegrove) (TOR, 1996)

_____. *Fugue on a G-String* (Subterranean Press, 1998)

_____. *Gandalph Cohen and the Land at the End of the Working Day* (Subterranean Press, 1999)

_____. *The Hand That Feeds* (Maynard Sims, 1999)

_____. *Darkness, Darkness: Forever Twilight Book One* (Cemetery Dance, 2002)

_____. *Windows of the Soul: Forever Twilight Book Two* (Subterranean Press, 2009)

Drake, David. *Hammer's Slammers* (Ace, 1979)

_____. *The Dragon Lord* (Putnams, 1979)

_____. *Time Safari* (Tor, 1982)

_____. *From the Heart of Darkness* (Tor, 1983)

_____. *Skyripper* (Tor, 1983)

_____. *Cross the Stars* (Tor, 1984)

_____. *Birds of Prey* (Baen, 1984)

_____. *The Forlorn Hope* (Tor, 1984)

_____. *Killer* (with Karl Edward Wagner) (Baen, 1985)

_____. *Active Measures* (with Janet Morris) (Baen, 1985)

_____. *Bridgehead* (Tor, 1986)

_____. *Ranks of Bronze* (Baen, 1986)

_____. *Lacey and His Friends* (Baen, 1986)

_____. *Kill Ratio* (with Janet Morris) (Ace, 1987)

_____. *Fortress* (Tor, 1987)

_____. *Dagger* (Ace, 1988)

_____. *The Sea Hag* (Baen, 1988)

_____. *Target* (with Janet Morris) (Ace, 1989)

_____. *Explorers in Hell* (with Janet Morris) (Baen, 1989)

_____. *Vettiusa and His Friends* (Baen, 1989)

_____. *Rolling Hot* (Baen, 1989)

_____. *Northworld* (Ace, 1990)

_____. *Surface Action* (Ace, 1990)

_____. *The Hunter Returns* (with Jim Kjelgaard) (Baen, 1991)

_____. *Vengeance* (Ace, 1991)

_____. *The Military Dimension* (Baen, 1991)

_____. *Old Nathan* (Baen, 1991)

_____. *The Jungle* (Tor, 1991)

_____. *Justice* (Ace, 1992)

_____. *Starliner* (Baen, 1992)

_____. *The Square Deal* (Tor, 1992)

_____. *The Sharp End* (Hammer Series) (Baen, 1993)

_____. *Igniting the Reaches* (Ace, 1994)

_____. *The Voyage* (Tor, 1994)

_____. *Arc Riders* (with Janet Morris) (Warner, 1995)

_____. *Through the Breach* (Ace, 1995)

_____. *The Fourth Rome* (with Janet Morris) (Warner, 1996)

_____. *All the Way to the Gallows* (Baen, 1996)
_____. *Fireships* (Ace, 1996)
_____. *Redliners* (Baen, 1996)
_____. *Patriots* (Tor, 1996)
_____. *Lord of the Isles* (Tor, 1997)
_____. *The Butcher's Bill* (Baen, 1998)
_____. *Caught in the Crossfire* (Baen, 1998)
_____. *With the Lightnings* (Baen, 1998)
_____. *Queen of Demons* (Tor, 1998)
_____. *Servant of the Dragon* (Tor, 1999)
_____. *Lt Leary, Commanding* (Baen, 2000)
_____. *Mistress of the Catacombs* (Tor, 2001)
_____. *Paying the Piper* (Baen, 2002)
_____. *Grimmer than Hell* (Baen, 2003)
_____. *Goddess of the Ice Realm* (Tor, 2003)
_____. *The Far Side of the Stars* (Baen, 2003)
_____. *Master of the Cauldron* (Tor, 2004)
_____. *The Way to Glory* (Baen, 2005)
_____. *The Fortress of Glass* (Tor, 2006)
_____. *Some Golden Harbor* (Baen, 2006)
_____. *The Mirror of Worlds* (Tor, 2007)
_____. *When the Tide Rises* (Baen, 2008)
_____. *The Gods Return* (Tor, 2008)
_____. *In the Stormy Red* (Baen, 2009)
_____. *The Legions of Fire* (Tor, 2010)
_____. *What Distant Deeps* (Baen, 2010)
_____. *Out of the Waters* (Tor, 2011)
_____. *The Road of Danger* (Baen, 2012)

Hindle, Maurice. *Frankenstein; or, The Modern Prometheus*, by Mary Wollstonecraft Shelley (New York: Penguin Books, 1992/2003)
_____. *Dracula*, by Bram Stoker (New York: Penguin Books, 2003)
_____. *Frankenstein* (Penguin Classics Deluxe Edition), by Mary Mary Wollstonecraft (New York: Penguin, 2007)

Kaye, Marvin. *A Lively Game of Death* (New York: Saturday Review Press, 1972; London: Arthur Barker Ltd., 1974; Munich: Goldmann Verlag, 1974; Rockville, MD: Wildside Press, 2000)
_____. *The Grand Ole Opry Murders* (New York: Dutton, 1974; New York: The Mystery Guild, 1974; New York: Ballantine Books, 1975; Munich: Goldmann Verlag, 1975; as *The Country Music Murders*, Rockville, MD: Wildside Press, 2000)
_____. *Bullets for Macbeth* (New York: Dutton, 1976; New York: The Mystery Guild, 1976; London: Robert Hale, 1978; Rockville, MD: Wildside Press, 2000)
_____. *My Son the Druggist* (New York: Doubleday, 1977; New York: The Mystery Guild, 1977; Rockville, MD: Wildside Press, 2000)
_____. *The Laurel and Hardy Murders* (New York: Dutton, 1977; S. Yarmouth Ma: John Curley, 1979; Rockville, MD: Wildside Press, 2000)
_____. *The Masters of Solitude* (With P. Godwin) (New York: Doubleday, 1978; As Serialization, Boston: Galileo Magazine, 1977-1978; New York: SF Book Club, 1978; New York: Avon Books, 1979; London: Methuen, 1979; Hamburg: Moewig Verlag, 1980; Antwerp: Prisma, 1981; New York: Bantam Books, 1985; London: Futura Books, 1986' Paris: Opta Books, 1986)
_____. *My Brother the Druggist* (New York: Doubleday, 1979; New York: The Mystery Guild, 1979; Rockville, MD: Wildside Press, 2000)
_____. *The Incredible Umbrella* (New York: Doubleday, 1979; as serialization, New York: Fantastic Stories, 1976-1977, 1979; New York: Dell Books, 1980)
_____. *The Amorous Umbrella* (New York: Doubleday, 1981).
_____. *Wintermind* (with Parke Godwin) (New York: Doubleday, 1982; New York: SF Book Club, 1982; New York: Bantam Books, 1984; Paris: Opta, 1986; London: Futura Books, 1987)
_____. *The Soap Opera Slaughters* (New York: Doubleday, 1982; New York: The Mystery Guild, 1982; Rockville, MD: Wildside Press, 2000)
_____. *A Cold Blue Light* (with P. Godwin) (New York: Berkley, 1983; Paris: Editions J'ai Lu, 1986)
_____. *Ghosts of Night and Morning* (New York: Berkley, 1987)
_____. *Fantastique* (New York: St. Martin's Press, 1992.
_____. *The Last Xmas of Ebenezer Scrooge* (Rockville, MD: Wildside Press, 2003)

Kilpatrick, Nancy. *Near Death* (Pocket Books 1994; Pumpkin Books 1998; Mosaic Press 2004)
_____. *As One Dead (with Don Bassingthwaite) (White Wolf Publishing, 1996)*
_____. *Child of the Night* (Robinson Publishing/Raven Imprint 1996; Pumpkin Books 1998; Mosaic Press 2003)
_____. *Dracul: An Eternal Love Story* (Mainstage Productions/Lucard Publishing, 1998)
_____. *Reborn* (Pumpkin Books 1998; Mosaic Press 2007).
_____. *Bloodlover* (Baskerville Books 2000; Mosaic Press 2010)
_____. *Eternal City* (with Michael Kilpatrick) (Five Star Books/Gale Publishing, 2003; Crossroad Publishing, 2011)
_____. *Jason X, No. 3 - Planet of the Beast* (Black Flame Books/New Line Cinema, 2005)
_____. *Jason X, No. 5 - To the Third Power* (Black Flame Books/New Line Cinema, 2006)

Knight, Amarantha. *Dracula* (Masquerade Books, 1993; Masquerade Books, 1995; Circlet Press, 2001; _____. collector's editions MHB, 2010).
_____. *Frankenstein* (Masquerade Books, 1995; Masquerade Books, 1997; Circlet Press, 2003; collector's editions MHB, 2011)
_____. *Dr. Jekyll & Mr. Hyde* (Masquerade Books, 1995; Circlet Press, 2003)
_____. *The Picture of Dorian Gray* (Masquerade Books, 1996)
_____. *The Fall of the House of Usher* (Masquerade Books, 1996)
_____. *Carmilla* (Masquerade Books, 1997)
_____. *The Pit and the Pendulum* (Masquerade Books, 1998)

Knight, Desiree. *Mercedez: Day of the Dead* (Blue Moon Books & Vivid Entertainment 2005)
_____. *Hunted* (Orion Publishing/Neon Imprint, 2007)

Morrish, Robert. "Bug-Eyed Methodists." *The UFO Files*, edited by Ed Gorman, Martin H. Greenberg (DAW Books, 1998; ibook, 2004)
_____. "Simple As a Two Car Funeral." *Subterranean Gallery*, edited by William K. Schafer and Richard T. Chizmar (Subterranean Press, 1999)
_____. "Junkyard of the Damned." *Shivers II*, edited by Richard Chizmar (Cemetery Dance Publications, 2003)
_____. "Mercy to Spare." *Vivisections*, edited by William P. Simmons (Catalyst Press, 2003)
_____. "This House is Not My Home." *Shivers III*, edited by Richard Chizmar (Cemetery Dance Publications, 2004)
_____. "The Bittersweet Deafening Sound of Nothing at All." *Shivers IV*, edited by Richard Chizmar (Cemetery Dance Publications, 2006)
_____. "Looking Glass." *Looking Glass* (Cemetery Dance Publications [Signature Series #1], 2006)
_____. "Recession." *At Ease with the Dead*, edited by Christopher Roden andBarbara Roden (Ash-Tree Press, 2007)
_____. "Each Step I Take is in Darkness." *Shivers V*, edited by Richard Chizmar (Cemetery Dance Publications, 2009)
_____. "Keeping It in the Family." Shivers VI, edited by Richard Chizmar (Cemetery Dance Publications, 2010)

Paffenroth, Kim. *Dying to Live: A Novel of Life among the Undead* (Permuted Press, 2007; German Edition: Festa Verlag, 2010; reissued by Gallery Books, 2010)
_____. *Dying to Live: Life Sentence* (Permuted Press, 2008)

_____. *Orpheus and the Pearl* (Magus Press, 2008; reprinted by Belfire Press, 2010)
_____. *Valley of the Dead (The Truth Behind Dante's Inferno)* (Limited Edition: Cargo Cult Press, 2009; Trade Paperback: Permuted Press, 2010)
_____. *Dying to Live: Last Rites* (Permuted Press, 2011)
Senf, Carol A. *The Mystery of the Sea*, by Bram Stoker (Valancourt Books, 2007)
Stableford, Brian. *Cradle of the Sun* (Ace Double 1969; Sidgwick and Jackson, 1969)
_____. *The Blind Worm* (Ace Double 1970; Sidgwick and Jackson, 1970)
_____. *The Days of Glory* (Ace, 1971)
_____. *In the Kingdom of the Beasts* (Ace, 1971)
_____. *Day of Wrath* (Ace, 1971)
_____. *To Challenge Chaos* (DAW Books, 1972)
_____. *The Halcyon Drift* (DAW Books, 1972; J. M. Dent, 1974)
_____. *Man in a Cage* (John Day, 1975)
_____. *Promised Land* (DAW Books, 1974; J. M. Dent, 1975)
_____. *Rhapsody in Black* (DAW Books, 1973; J. M. Dent, 1975)
_____. *The Face of Heaven* (Quartet Books, 1976)
_____. *The Paradise Game* (DAW Books, 1974; J. M. Dent, 1976)
_____. *The Mind-Riders* (DAW Books, 1976; Fontana, 1977)
_____. *The Realms of Tartarus* (DAW Books, 1977)
_____. *The Fenris Device* (DAW Books, 1974; Pan, 1978)
_____. *The Florians* (DAW Books, 1976; Hamlyn, 1978)
_____. *The Last Days of the Edge of the World* (Hutchinson, 1978; Ace, 1985)
_____. *Swan Song* (DAW Books, 1975; Pan, 1978)
_____. *Critical Threshold* (DAW Books, 1977; Hamlyn, 1979)
_____. *The Walking Shadow* (Fontana, 1979; Carroll and Graf, 1985)
_____. *Wildeblood's Empire* (DAW Books, 1977; Hamlyn, 1979)
_____. *The City of the Sun* (DAW Books, 1978; Hamlyn, 1980)
_____. *Balance of Power* (DAW Books, 1979; Hamlyn, 1984)
_____. *The Paradox of the Sets* (DAW Books, 1979)
_____. *Optiman* (DAW Books, 1980; as *War Games*, Pan UK, 1981)
_____. *The Castaways of Tanagar* (DAW Books, 1981)
_____. *The Gates of Eden* (DAW Books, 1983)
_____. *The Empire of Fear* (Simon and Schuster UK, 1988)
_____. *Zaragoz* (as Brian Craig) (GW Books, 1989)
_____. *Plague Daemon* (as Brian Craig) (GW Books, 1990)
_____. *Storm Warriors* (as Brian Craig) (GW Books, 1991)
_____. *Young Blood* (Simon and Schuster UK, 1992)
_____. *The Werewolves of London* (Simon and Schuster UK, 1990)
_____. *The Angel of Pain* (Simon and Schuster UK, 1991)
_____. *The Carnival of Destruction* (Pocket UK, 1994)
_____. *Ghost Dancers* (as Brian Craig) (GW Books, 1991)
_____. *Serpent's Blood* (Legend, 1995)
_____. *The Hunger and Ecstasy of Vampires* (Mark V. Ziesing 1996)
_____. *Salamander's Fire* (Legend, 1996)
_____. *Chimera's Cradle* (Simon and Schuster UK, 1997)
_____. *Inherit the Earth* (TOR Books, 1998)
_____. *Architects of Emortality* (TOR Books, 1999)
_____. *Fountains of Youth* (TOR Books, 2000)
_____. *The Wine of Dreams* (as Brian Craig) (Black Library, 2000)
_____. *The Cassandra Complex* (TOR Books, 2001)
_____. *The Eleventh Hour* (Cosmos Books 2001)
_____. *Warhammer 40000: Pawns of Chaos* (as Brian Craig) (Black Library, 2001)
_____. *Dark Ararat* (TOR Books, 2002)
_____. *The Omega Expedition* (TOR Books, 2002).
_____. *Year Zero* (Sarob Press, 2000; Five Star, 2003)
_____. *Curse of the Coral Bride* (Immanion Press UK, 2004)
_____. *Kiss the Goat* (Prime Books, 2005)
_____. *The Stones of Camelot* (Black Coat Press, 2006)
_____. *Streaking* (PS Publishing, 2006)
_____. *The New Faust at the Tragicomique* (Black Coat Press, 2007)
_____. *The Shadow of Frankenstein* (Black Coat Press, 2008)
_____. *Alien Abduction: The Wiltshire Revelations* (Borgo Press, 2009)
_____. *The Dragon Man: A Novel of the Future* (Borgo Press, 2009)
_____. *Firefly: A Novel of the Far Future* (Borgo Press 1994; Cosmos Books, 2009)
_____. *Frankenstein and the Vampire Countess* (Black Coat Press, 2009)
_____. *The Moment of Truth* (Borgo Press March 2009)
_____. *Prelude to Eternity: A Romance of the First Time Machine* (Borgo Press, 2009)
_____. *Sherlock Holmes and the Vampires of Eternity* (Black Coat Press, 2009)
_____. *The World Beyond: A Sequel to S. Fowler Wright's The World Below* (Borgo Press, 2009)
_____. *Luscinia: A Romance of Nightingales and Roses* (Borgo Press, 2010)
_____. *The Plurality of Worlds: A Sixteenth-Century Space Opera* (Borgo Press, 2010)
_____. *Frankenstein in London* (Black Coat Press, 2011)
_____. *Xeno's Paradox: A Tale of the Biotech Revolution* (Borgo Press, 2011)
_____. *Zombies Don't Cry: A Tale of the Biotech Revolution* (Borgo Press, 2011)
Wilson, F. Paul. *The Keep* (William Morrow, 1981)
_____. *The Tomb* (Berkley, 1984; as *Rakoshi*, Borderlands Press, 2004)
_____. *The Touch* (G. P. Putnam's Sons, 1986)
_____. *Reborn* (Dark Harvest, 1990; revised ed. TOR Books, 2009)
_____. *Reprisal* (Dark Harvest, 1991; revised ed. TOR Books, 2011)
_____. *Nightworld* (Hodder & Stoughton, 1992; Jove, 1993)
_____. *Midnight Mass* (TOR Books, 2005)
Youngson, Jeanne Keyes. *Dracula Made Easy* (Carlton Press, 1978)
_____. *Count Dracula and the Unicorn* (Adams Press, 1978)
_____. *The Count Dracula Chicken Cookbook* (Adams Press, 1979)
_____. *The Further Perils of Dracula* (Adams Press, 1979)
_____. *The Count Dracula Fan Club Book of Vampire Stories* (Adams Press, 1980)
_____. *A Child's Garden of Vampires* (Adams Press, 1980)
_____. *The Count Dracula Book of Classic Vampire Tales* (Adams Press, 1981)
_____. *Freak Show Vampire*, in *Freak Show Vampire and The Hungry Grass* (with Peter Tremayne) (Adams Press, 1981)

Books (Nonfiction)

Byron, Glennis. *The Gothic (with David Punter)* (Malden, MA: Blackwell Publishers, 2004)
Castle, Mort. *Writing Horror: A Handbook* (Horror Writers Association) (Cincinnati, OH: Writer's Digest Books, 1997)
Cooper, L. Andrew. *Gothic Realities: The Impact of Horror Fiction on Modern Culture* (Jefferson, NC: McFarland and Company, 2010)
_____. *Dario Argento* (Champaign, IL: University of Illinois Press, 2011)
_____. ed. *Dracula: A Norton Critical* Glut, Donald F. *True Vampires of History* (Secaucus, NJ, HC Publishers, 1971)
_____. *The Frankenstein Legend: A Tribute to Mary Shelley and Boris Karloff* (Metuchen, NJ: Scarecrow Press, 1973)
_____. *The Dracula Book* (Metuchen, NJ: Scarecrow Press, 1975)
_____. *Classic Movie Monsters* (Metuchen, NJ: Scarecrow Press, 1978)

_____. *The Dinosaur Scrapbook* (Secaucus, NJ: Citadel Press, 1980)
_____. *The Frankenstein Catalog*. (Jefferson, NC: McFarland and Company, 1984)
_____. *Dinosaur Valley Girls: The Book* (Jefferson, NC: McFarland and Company, 1998)
_____. *True Werewolves of History* (Rockville, MD: Sense of Wonder Press, 2004)
_____. *I Was a Teenage Movie Maker* (Jefferson, NC: McFarland and Company, 2007)
Hand, Richard J. *Grand-Guignol: The French Theatre of Horror* (with Michael Wilson) (Exeter: University of Exeter Press, 2002)
_____. *Terror on the Air: Horror Radio in America, 1931-52* (Jefferson, NC: McFarland and Company, 2006)
_____. *London's Grand-Guignol and the Theatre of Horror* (with Michael Wilson) (Exeter: University of Exeter Press, 2007)
Hutchings, Peter. *Hammer and Beyond: The British Horror Film* (Manchester: Manchester University Press, 1993)
_____. Hutchings, Peter. *Terence Fisher* (Manchester: Manchester University Press, 2002)
_____. *Dracula: British Film Guide* (London: I. B. Tauris, 2003)
_____. *The Horror Film* (London: Pearson, 2004)
_____. *The Historical Dictionary of Horror Cinema* (Lanham, MD: Scarecrow Press, 2008)
Guiley, Rosemary Ellen. *The Vengeful Djinn: Unveiling the Hidden Agendas of Genies* (Woodbury, MN: Llewellyn, 2011)
_____. *Talking to the Dead* (with George Noory) (New York: TOR Books, 2011)
_____. *Haunted Salem* (Mechanicsburg, PA : Stackpole Books, 2011)
_____. *Spirit Communications* (New York: Chelsea House/Facts On File, 2009)
_____. *Ghosthunting Pennsylvania* (Cincinnati, OH: Clerisy Press, 2009)
_____. *The Encyclopedia of Ghosts and Spirits* (New York: Facts On File, 1992; second ed., 2000; third ed., 2007)
_____. *Ghosts and Haunted Places* (New York: Chelsea House/Facts On File, 2008)
_____. *The Encyclopedia of the Strange, Mystical and Unexplained* (New York: Gramercy Books/Random House, 2001)
_____. *The Atlas of the Mysterious in North America* (New York: Facts On File, 1994)
_____. *Harper's Encyclopedia of Mystical and Paranormal Experience* (New York: Harper San Francisco, 1991)
_____. *The Encyclopedia of Demons* (New York: Facts On File, 2009)
_____. *The Encyclopedia of Vampires, Werewolves and Other Monsters* (New York: Facts On File, 2005; second ed., 2011)
_____ *The Monster Show: A Cultural History of Horror* (New York: W.W. Norton, 1993; revised ed. Faber & Faber, 2001)
_____. *Vampires* (New York: Chelsea House/Facts On File, 2008)
_____. *The Complete Vampire Companion* (New York: Macmillan, 1994)
_____. *Vampires Among Us* (New York: Pocket Books, 1991)
_____. *Rosemary Ellen Guiley's Vampires Among Us*, revised ed. (E-book, 2011)
_____. *The Encyclopedia of Magic and Alchemy* (New York: Facts On File, 2006)
_____. *The Encyclopedia of Witches, Witchcraft and Wicca* (New York: Facts On File, 1989; second ed., 1999; third ed., 2008)
_____. *Witches and Witchcraft* (New York: Chelsea House/Facts On File, 2008)
_____. *Fairies* (New York: Chelsea House, 2010)
_____. *Fairy Magic* (London: Thorsons/Element, 2004)
Kaye, Marvin. *Dracula: The Definitive Edition* (New York: Barnes and Noble, 1996)
Kilpatrick, Nancy. *The Goth Bible: A Compendium for the Darkly Inclined* (New York: St. Martin's Press, 2004)
Klinger, Leslie. *The New Annotated Dracula*, by Bram Stoker (New York: W.W. Norton, 2008)
Miller, Elizabeth. Bram Stoker's Dracula: A Documentary Journey into Vampire Country and the Dracula Phenomenon (New York: Pegasus, 2009)
_____. *Bram Stoker's Notes for Dracula: A Facsimile Edition, by Bram Stoker* (with Robert Eighteen-Bisang) (Jefferson, NC: McFarland and Company, 2008)
_____. *Bram Stoker's Dracula: A Documentary Volume*. Dictionary of Literary Biography, vol. 304. (Detroit: Gale, 2005)
_____. *A Dracula Handbook* (Xlibris, 2005)
_____. *Dracula: Sense & Nonsense* (Westcliff-on-Sea, UK: Desert Island Books, 2000; revised ed. 2004)
_____. *Dracula* (New York: Parkstone Press, 2001)
_____. *Dracula: The Shade and the Shadow* (Westcliff-on-Sea, UK: Desert Island Books, 1998)
_____. *Reflections on Dracula* (White Rock, BC: Transylvania Press, 1997)
_____. *Blood Offerings for Dracula: Winning Entries for the Count's Creative Writing Contest* (Los Angeles, CA: TSD Publications, 1997)
Muir, John Kenneth. *The Unseen Force: The Films of Sam Raimi* (Jefferson, NC: McFarland and Company, 2004)
_____. *Wes Craven: The Art of Horror* (Jefferson, NC: McFarland and Company, 2004)
_____. *The Films of John Carpenter* (Jefferson, NC: McFarland and Company, 2005)
_____. *Horror Films of the 1970s*, 2 vols (Jefferson, NC: McFarland and Company, 2007)
_____. *Horror Films of the 1980s* (Jefferson, NC: McFarland and Company, 2007)
_____. *Terror Television: American Series, 1970-1999* (Jefferson, NC: McFarland and Company, 2008)
_____. *Eaten Alive at a Chainsaw Massacre: The Films of Tobe Hooper* (Jefferson, NC: McFarland and Company, 2009)
_____. *Horror Films of the 1990s* (Jefferson, NC: McFarland and Company, 2011)
Paffenroth, Kim. *Gospel of the Living Dead: George Romero's Visions of Hell on Earth.* (Waco, TX: Baylor University Press, 2006)
Picart, Caroline Joan. *Dracula in Visual Media: Film, Television, Comic Book, and Electronic Game Appearances, 1921-2010* (with John Edgar Browning) (Jefferson, NC: McFarland Press and Company, 2010)
_____. Picart, Caroline Joan. *Frames of Evil: Holocaust as Horror in American Film* (with David Frank) (Carbondale, IL: Southern Illinois University Press, 2007)
_____. *Remaking the Frankenstein Myth on Film: Between Laughter and Horror* (Albany, NY: State University of New York Press, 2003)
_____. *The Cinematic Rebirths of Frankenstein: Universal, Hammer and Beyond* (Westport, CT: Praeger Press, 2001)
_____. *The Frankenstein Film Sourcebook* (with Jayne Blodgett and Frank Smoot) (Westport, CT: Greenwood Press, 2001)
Ramsland, Katherine. *The Forensic Psychology of Criminal Minds* (New York: Berkley Trade, 2012)
_____. *The Devil's Dozen: How Cutting-Edge Forensics Took Down 12 Notorious Serial Killers* (New York: Penguin Group, 2009)
_____. *Inside the Minds of Sexual Predator* (with Patrick N. McGrain) (Westport, CT: Praeger, 2009)
_____. *True Stories of C.S.I.: The Real Crimes Behind the Best Episodes of the Popular TV Show* (New York: Penguin Group, 2008)
_____. *Beating the Devil's Game: A History of Forensic Science and Criminal Investigation* (New York: Penguin Group, 2007)

_____. *Bethlehem Ghosts Historical Hauntings In and Around Pennsylvania's Christmas City* (with Dana DeVito) (Gettysburg, PA: Second Chance Publications, 2007)
_____. *Dean Koontz: A Writer's Biography* (New York: HarperCollins Publishers, 2007)
_____. *Inside the Minds of Serial Killers: Why They Kill* (Westport, CT: Praeger Press, 2006)
_____. *The Human Predator: A Historical Chronicle of Serial Murder and Forensic Investigation* (New York: Penguin Group, 2005)
_____. *A Voice for the Dead: A Forensic Investigator's Pursuit of the Truth in the Grave* (with James E. Starrs) (New York: Penguin Group, 2005)
_____ (with). *Unknown Darkness: Profiling the Predators Among Us* (with Gregg O. Mccrary) (New York: HarperCollins Publishers, 2004)
_____. *Ghost: Investigating the Other Side* (New York: St. Martin's Press, 2002)
_____. *The Science of Vampires* (New York: Penguin Group, 2002)
_____. *Cemetery Stories: Haunted Graveyards, Embalming Secrets, and the Life of a Corpse After Death* (New York: HarperCollins Publishers, 2001)
_____. *The Forensic Science of CSI* (New York: Penguin Group, 2001)
_____. *Piercing the Darkness: Undercover with Vampires in America Today* (New York: HarperCollins Publishers, 1998)
_____. *The Anne Rice Reader* (New York: Random House, 1997)
_____. *The Witches' Companion: The Official Guide to Anne Rice's Lives of the Mayfair Witches* (with Anne Rice) (New York: Random House, 1996)
_____. *Vampire Companion: The Official Guide to Anne Rice's The Vampire* Chronicles (with Anne Rice) (New York: Random House, 1995)
_____. *Prism of Night: A Biography of Anne Rice* (New York: Penguin Group, 1994)
Riley, Philip J. *London After Midnight, A Reconstruction* (Duncan, OK: BearManor Media, 2011)
Skal, David J. *Dark Carnival: The Secret World of Tod Browning* (with Elias Savada) (New York: Anchor Books-Doubleday, 1995).
_____. *Death Makes a Holiday: A Cultural History of Halloween* (New York: Bloomsbury, 2002).
_____. *Claude Rains: An Actor's Voice* (with Jessica Rains) (Lexington, KY: University Press of Kentucky, 2008).
_____. ed. *Dracula: A Norton Critical Edition* (with Nina Auerbach) (New York: W.W. Norton, 1997).
_____. ed. *Dracula: The Ultimate, Illustrated Edition of the World-Famous Vampire Play* (New York: St. Martin's Press, 1995).
_____. Hollywood Gothic: The Tangled Web of Dracula from Novel to Stage to Screen (New York: W.W. Norton, 1990; revised ed. Faber & Faber, 2004).
_____. *The Monster Show: A Cultural History of Horror* (New York: W.W. Norton, 1993; revised ed. Faber & Faber, 2001).
_____. *Romancing the Vampire: From Past to Present* (Atlanta, GA: Whitman Publishers, 2009).
_____. *Screams of Reason: Mad Science and Modern Culture* (New York: W.W. Norton, 1997).
_____. ed. *Vampires: Encounters with the Undead* (New York: Black Dog and Leventhal, 2003).
_____. *V is for Vampire: the A-to-Z Guide to Everything Undead* (New York: Plume Books, 1995).
War Eagles (with David Conover) (Duncan, OK: BearManor Media, 2011)
_____. *WAR EAGLES: The Unmaking of an Epic* (Duncan, OK: BearManor Media, 2011)
_____. *Dracula Starring Lon Chaney* (Duncan, OK: BearManor Media, 2010; Kindle ed. 2010)
_____. *Frankenstein, A Play* (Duncan, OK: BearManor Media, 2010)
_____. *James Whale's Dracula's Daughter*, Kindle ed.(Duncan, OK: BearManor Media, 2010)
_____. *Robert Florey's Frankenstein Starring Bela Lugosi* (Duncan, OK: BearManor Media, 2010)
_____. *The Wolf Man vs. Dracula* (Duncan, OK: BearManor Media, 2010)
_____. *Cagliostro* (Duncan, OK: BearManor Media, 2009; Kindle ed. 2010)
_____. *Dracula's Daughter* (Duncan, OK: BearManor Media, 2009)
_____. *The Mummy's Curse: Including the Original Shooting Script* (Chesterfield, NJ: Magicimage Filmbooks, 2000)
_____. *The Phantom of the Opera* (Chesterfield, NJ: Magicimage Filmbooks, 1996)
_____. *House of Dracula* (Chesterfield, NJ: Magicimage Filmbooks, 1993)
_____. *The Wolf Man* (Chesterfield, NJ: Magicimage Filmbooks, 1993)
_____. *Abbott and Costello Meet Frankenstein* (Chesterfield, NJ: Magicimage Filmbooks, 1990)
_____. *Dracula: The Original 1931 Shooting Script* (Chesterfield, NJ: Magicimage Filmbooks, 1990)
_____. *Frankenstein Meets the Wolf Man* (Chesterfield, NJ: Magicimage Filmbooks, 1990)
_____. *House of Frankenstein* (Chesterfield, NJ: Magicimage Filmbooks, 1990)
_____. *The Ghost of Frankenstein* (Chesterfield, NJ: Magicimage Filmbooks, 1990)
_____. *This Island Earth* (Chesterfield, NJ: Magicimage Filmbooks, 1990)
_____. *The Bride of Frankenstein* (Chesterfield, NJ: Magicimage Filmbooks, 1989)
_____. *Frankenstein* (Chesterfield, NJ: Magicimage Filmbooks, 1989)
_____. *Son of Frankenstein* (Chesterfield, NJ: Magicimage Filmbooks, 1989)
_____. *London After Midnight* (New York: Cornwall Books, 1985)
Senf, Carol A. Afterword to *The Vampire, His Kith and Kin: A Critical Edition*, edited by John Edgar Browning (Berkeley, CA: Apocryphile Press, 2011)
_____. *Bram Stoker* (Cardiff, UK: University of Whales Press, 2011)
_____. *Science and Social Science in Bram Stoker's Fiction* (Westport, CT: Praeger Press, 2002)
_____. *Masterwork Studies Series: Dracula* (New York: Twayne Publishers, 1998)
_____. *The Critical Response to Bram Stoker* (Santa Barbara, CA: Greenwood Press, 1993)
_____. *The Vampire in Nineteenth Century English Literature* (Bowling Green, OH: Bowling Green State University Popular Press, 1988)
Stableford, Brian. *The Mysteries of Modern Science* (London: Routledge and Kegan Paul, 1977)
_____. *A Clash of Symbols: The Triumph of James Blish* (San Bernardino, CA: Borgo Press, 1979; 2008)
_____. *Masters of Science Fiction: Essays on Six Science Fiction Authors* (San Bernardino, CA: Borgo Press, 1981)
_____. *The Science in Science Fiction* (with Peter Nicholls and David Langford) (Michael Joseph, 1982; Knopf, 1983)
_____. *Future Man: Brave New World or Genetic Nightmare?* (Crown, 1984).
_____. *The Third Millennium: A History of the World AD 2000-3000* (with David Langford) (Sidgwick and Jackson, 1985; Knopf, 1985)
_____. *Scientific Romance in Britain, 1890-1950* (Fourth Estate Sep. 1985 / St. Martin's Press Nov. 1985)
_____. *The Sociology of Science Fiction* (San Bernardino, CA: Borgo Press, 1987; 2007)
_____. *The Way to Write Science Fiction* (Elm Tree Books, 1989)
_____. *Algebraic Fantasies and Realistic Romances: More Masters of Science Fiction* (San Bernardino, CA: Borgo Press, 1995; 2007)
_____. *Outside the Human Aquarium: Masters of Science Fiction, Second Edition* (San Bernardino, CA: Borgo Press, 1995; 2008)

_____. *Writing Fantasy and Science Fiction and Getting Published* (Teach Yourself Books, 1997)
_____. *Glorious Perversity: The Decline and Fall of Literary Decadence* (San Bernardino, CA: Borgo Press 1998; 2008)
_____. *Yesterday's Bestsellers: A Voyage through Literary History* (San Bernardino, CA: Borgo Press, 1998; 2008)
_____. *The Dictionary of Science Fiction Places* (Fireside Books, 1999)
_____. *Historical Dictionary of Science Fiction Literature* (Lanham, MD: Scarecrow Press, 2004; as *The A to Z of Science Fiction Literature*, Lanham, MD: Scarecrow Press, 2005)
_____. *Historical Dictionary of Fantasy Literature* (Scarecrow Press, 2005; as *The A to Z of Fantasy Literature*, Lanham, MD: Scarecrow Press, 2009)
_____. *Science Fact and Science Fiction: An Encyclopedia* (New York: Routledge, 2006)
_____. *The Devil's Party: A Brief History of Satanic Abuse* (San Bernardino, CA: Borgo Press March 2009)
_____. *News of the Black Feast and Other Random Reviews* (San Bernardino, CA: Borgo Press, 2009)
_____. *Exotic Encounters: Selected Reviews* (San Bernardino, CA: Borgo Press, 2010)
Timpone, Tony. *Fangoria's Best Horror Films* (New York: Crescent Books, 1994)
_____ (as Anthony Timpone) *Fangoria Vampires* (New York: HarperPrism, 1996)
_____. *Men, Makeup and Monsters: Hollywood's Masters of Illusion and FX* (New York: St. Martin's Griffin, 1996)
_____ (as Anthony Timpone). *Fangoria, Masters of the Dark: Stephen King and Clive Barker* (New York: HarperPrism, 1997)
_____ (as editor). *Fangoria's 101 Best Horror Movies You've Never Seen: A Celebration of the World's Most Unheralded Fright Flicks* (with Adam Lukeman as author) (New York: Three Rivers Press, 2003)
Vincent, Bev. *The Road to the Dark Tower* (Forest Hill, Maryland: Cemetery Dance Publications, 2005)
_____. *The Good, The Bad, & The Ugly: Eight Secondary Characters from the Dark Tower Series* (Forest Hill, Maryland: Cemetery Dance Publications, 2005)
_____. *The Illustrated Stephen King Trivia Book* with Brian Freeman (Forest Hill, Maryland: Cemetery Dance Publications, 2005)
_____. *The Stephen King Illustrated Companion* (New York: Fall River Press, 2009)
Waller, Gregory A. *The Living and the Undead: From Stoker's Dracula to Romero's Dawn of the Dead* (Urbana, IL: University of Illinois Press, 1986; as *The Living and the Undead: Slaying Vampires, Exterminating Zombies*, 2010)
Youngson, Jeanne Keyes. *The Count Dracula Chicken Cookbook* (Chicago: Adams Press, 1979)
_____. *Count Dracula's Favorite Christmas Cookie Recipes* (New York: Dracula Press, 1988)
_____. *The World's Best Vampire Jokes* (New York: Dracula Press, 1992)
_____. *The Bizarre World of Vampires* (Chicago: Adams Press, 1996)
_____. *Private Files of a Vampirologist: Case Histories & Letters* (Chicago: Adams Press, 1997)
_____. *Romancing the Vampire: From Past to Present* (Atlanta, GA: Whitman Publishers, 2009)
_____. *Screams of Reason: Mad Science and Modern Culture* (New York: W.W. Norton, 1997)
_____. ed. *Vampires: Encounters with the Undead* (New York: Black Dog and Leventhal, 2003)
_____. *V is for Vampire: the A-to-Z Guide to Everything Undead* (New York: Plume Books, 1995)

Edited Anthologies (Fiction)

Campbell, Ramsey. *The Book of Liverpool: A City in Short Fiction* (with Roger McGough, Margaret Murphy, and Brian Patten) (Comma Press, 2007)
Castle, Mort. *Nukes: Four Horror Writers on the Ultimate Horror: Stories* (Maclay, 1986)
Crowther, Peter. *Narrow Houses* (Little, Brown, and Company, 1992)
_____. *Touch Wood* (Warner Books, 1993)
_____. *Blue Motel* (Little, Brown, and Company, 1994; Warner, 1996)
_____. *Heaven Sent* (Signet, 1995)
_____. *Tombs* (with Edward E. Kramer) (White Wolf Publishing, 1996)
_____. *Dante's Disciples* (with Edward E. Kramer) (White Wolf Publishing, 1997)
_____. *Destination Unknown* (White Wolf Publishing, 1997)
_____. *Tales in Time* (White Wolf Publishing, 1997)
_____. *Tales in Space* (White Wolf Publishing, 1998)
_____. *Moon Shots* (DAW Books, 1999)
_____. *Foursight* (Gollancz, 1999)
_____. *Taps and Sighs* (Subterranean Press, 1999)
_____. *Futures* (Gollancz, 2000)
_____. *Mars Probes* (DAW Books, 2002)
_____. *Infinities* (Gollancz, 2002)
_____. *Cities* (Gollancz, 2003)
_____. *Constellations* (DAW Books, 2005)
_____. *Forbidden Planets* (DAW Books, 2006)
_____. *We Think, Therefore We Are* (DAW Books, 2009)
Kaye, Marvin. *Fiends and Creatures* (Popular Library, 1974; Caralt, 1977)
_____. *Brother Theodore's Chamber of Horrors* (Pinnacle, 1974)
_____. *Ghosts* (Nelson Doubleday Books, 1981; Futura Books, 1993)
_____. *Masterpieces of Terror and the Supernatural* (Doubleday, 1985; Futura Books, 1991)
_____. *Devils and Demons* (Doubleday, 1987; Barnes and Noble Books, 1994)
_____. *Weird Tales: The Magazine That Never Dies* (Doubleday, 1988)
_____. *Witches and Warlocks* (Guild America Books, 1989; as *Penguin Book of Witches and Warlocks*, Penguin, 1991; Barnes & Noble Books, 1994)
_____. *13 Plays of Ghosts and the Supernatural* (Doubleday Book/Music Clubs, 1990)
_____. *Haunted America* (Doubleday Book/Music Clubs, 1991)
_____. *Lovers and Other Monsters* (Doubleday Book/Music Clubs, 1991)
_____. *Sweet Revenge, 10 Plays of Bloody Murder* (The Fireside Theatre, 1992)
_____. *Masterpieces of Terror and the Unknown* (Doubleday Book/Music Clubs, 1993; New York: St. Martin's Press, 1994)
_____. *Angels of Darkness* (Doubleday Book/Music Clubs, 1994)
_____.*The Vampire Sextette* (Doubleday Direct Inc., 2000)
_____. *The Ultimate Halloween* (Byron Preiss, 2001)
Kilpatrick, Nancy. *In the Shadow of the Gargoyle* (with Thomas Roche) (Ace Books, 1999)
_____. *Graven Images: Fifteen Tales of Dark Magic and Ancient Myth* (with Thomas Roche) (Ace Books, 2000)
_____. *Outsiders: 22 All-New Stories from the Edge* (with Nancy Holder) (Roc Publishing, 2005)
_____. *Evolve: Vampire Stories of the New Undead* (EDGE Science Fiction & Fantasy, 2010).
_____. *Evolve Two: Vampire Stories of the Future Undead* (EDGE Science Fiction & Fantasy, 2011
Paffenroth, Kim. *History Is Dead: A Zombie Anthology* (Permuted Press, 2007)
Knight, Amarantha. *Love Bites* (Masquerade Books, 1994)
_____. *Flesh Fantastic* (Masquerade Books, 1995)
_____. *Seductive Spectres* (Masquerade Books, 1996)
_____. *Sex Macabre* (Masquerade Books, 1996)
_____. *Demon Sex* (Masquerade Books, 1998)
_____. *The World Is Dead: A Zombie Anthology* (Permuted Press, 2009)

Edited Anthologies (Nonfiction)

Byron, Glennis. *Dracula: Bram Stoker* (Basingstoke, UK: Macmillan)

_____. *Spectral Readings: Towards a Gothic Geography (with David Punter)* (Macmillan, 1999)

Glut, Donald F. *The Frankenstein Archive: Essays on the Monster, the Myth, the Movies, and More* (Jefferson, NC: McFarland and Company, 2002)

_____. *Jurassic Classics: A Collection of Saurian Essays and Mesozoic Musings* (Jefferson, NC: McFarland and Company, 2001)

Hand, Richard J. *Monstrous Adaptations: Generic and Thematic Transmutations in Horror Film* (with Jay McRoy) (Manchester: Manchester University Press, 2007)

Hantke, Steffen. *American Horror Film: The Genre at the Turn of the Millennium* (Jackson, MS: University Press of Mississippi, 2010)

_____. *Caligari's Heirs: The German Cinema of Fear After 1945* (Lanham, MD: Scarecrow Press, 2007)

_____. *Horror Cinema: Creating and Marketing Fear* (Jackson, MS: University Press of Mississippi, 2004)

_____. *Horror.* Special Topics Issue of *Paradoxa: Studies in World Literary Genres* 17 (Fall 2002)

Picart, Caroline Joan. *Draculas, Vampires, and Other Undead Forms: Essays on Gender, Race and Culture* (John Edgar Browning) (Lanham, MD: Scarecrow Press, 2009)

_____. *Monsters In and Among Us: Towards a Gothic Criminology* (with Cecil Greek) (Fairleigh Dickinson University Press, 2007)

Stableford, Brian. *Opening Minds: Essays on Fantastic Literature* (San Bernardino, CA: Borgo Press, 1995; 2007)

_____. *Slaves of the Death Spiders and Other Essays on Fantastic Literature* (San Bernardino, CA: Borgo Press Nov. 2006)

_____. *Space, Time, and Infinity: Essays on Fantastic Literature* (San Bernardino, CA: Borgo Press, 2006)

_____. *Heterocosms and Other Essays on Fantastic Literature* (San Bernardino, CA: Borgo Press, 2007)

_____. *Gothic Grotesques: Essays on Fantastic Literature* (San Bernardino, CA: Borgo Press, 2009)

_____. *Jaunting on the Scoriac Tempests and Other Essays on Fantastic Literature* (San Bernardino, CA: Borgo Press, 2009)

_____. *Against the New Gods and Other Essays on Writers of Imaginative Fiction* (San Bernardino, CA: Borgo Press, 2009)

_____. *Narrative Strategies in Science Fiction and Other Essays on Imaginative Fiction* (San Bernardino, CA: Borgo Press, 2009)

_____. *Creators of Science Fiction: Essays on Authors, Editors, and Publishers Who Shaped Science Fiction* (San Bernardino, CA: Borgo Press, 2010)

_____. *The Decadent World-View: Selected Essays* (San Bernardino, CA: Borgo Press, 2010)

Waller, Gregory A. *American Horrors: Essays on the Modern American Horror Film* (Urbana, IL: University of Illinois Press, 1987)

Collections

Campbell, Ramsey. *The Inhabitant of the Lake: And Less Welcome Tenants* (Arkham House, 1964)

_____. *Demons by Daylight* (Arkham House, 1973)

_____. *The Height of the Scream* (Arkham House, 1976)

_____. *Dark Companions* (Macmillan Publishing Company, 1982)

_____. *Cold Print* (Scream Press, 1985)

_____. *Black Wine* (with Charles L. Grant) (Dark Harvest, 1986)

_____. *Dark Feasts: The World of Ramsey Campbell* (Robinson, 1987)

_____. *Scared Stiff* (Scream Press, 1987)

_____. *Waking Nightmares* (Tom Doherty Associates, 1991)

_____. *Alone with the Horrors* (Arkham House, 1993)

_____. *Strange Things and Stranger Places* (TOR, 1993)

_____. *Two Obscure Tales* (Necronomicon Press, 1993)

_____. *Far Away and Never* (Necronomicon Press, 1995)

_____. *Ghosts and Grisly Things* (Firebird Distributing, 1997)

_____. *Told by the Dead* (PS Publishing, 2003)

_____. *Inconsequential Tales* (Hippocampus Press, 2008)

_____. *Just Behind You* (PS Publishing, 2009)

Castle, Mort. *So Many Tomorrows: Three Stories About Children* (1986)

_____. *Moon on the Water* (Leisure Books, 2000)

_____. *Nations of the Living, Nations of the Dead* (Prime Books, Inc., 2002)

Crowther, Peter. *The Longest Single Note and Other Strange Compositions* (Cemetery Dance Publications, 1999)

_____. *Lonesome Roads* (RazorBlade, 1999)

_____. *Songs of Leaving* (Subterranean Press, 2004)

_____. *The Spaces Between the Lines* (Subterranean Press, 2007)

_____. *The Land at the End of the Working Day* (Humdrumming, Ltd. 2008)

Drake, David. *At Any Price* (Baen, 1985)

_____. *Counting the Cost* (Baen, 1987)

_____. *The Warrior* (Hammer Series) (Baen, 1991)

_____. *Other Times Than Peace* (Baen, 2006)

_____. *Balefires* (Night Shade, 2007)

Kilpatrick, Nancy. *Vampire Variations* (Edge SF&F Publishing, 2013)

_____. *Cold Comfort* (Dark Tales Publications, 2001)

_____. *The Vampire Stories of Nancy Kilpatrick* (Mosaic Press, 2000)

_____. *Endorphins* (Macabre Ink, 1997)

_____. *Sex & the Single Vampire* (Tal Publications, 1994)

Knight, Amarantha. *The Darker Passions Reader* (Masquerade Books, 1996).

Stableford, Brian. *Sexual Chemistry: Sardonic Tales of the Genetic Revolution* (Simon and Schuster UK, 1991).

_____. *Complications and Other Stories* (Cosmos Books, 2003).

_____. *Designer Genes: Tales of the Biotech Revolution* (Five Star, 2004).

_____. *Salomé and Other Decadent Fantasies* (Cosmos Books, 2004).

_____. *The Wayward Muse* (Black Coat Press, 2005).

_____. *Sheena and Other Gothic Tales* (Immanion Press, 2006).

_____. *The Cure for Love and Other Tales of the Biotech Revolution* (Borgo Press, 2007).

_____. *The Haunted Bookshop and Other Apparitions* (Borgo Press, 2007).

_____. *The Tree of Life and Other Tales of the Biotech Revolution* (Borgo Press, 2007).

_____. *An Oasis of Horror: Decadent Tales and Contes Cruels* (Borgo Press, 2008).

_____. *The Gardens of Tantalus and Other Delusions* (Borgo Press, 2008).

_____. *The Innsmouth Heritage and Other Sequels* (Borgo Press, 2009).

_____. *Changelings and Other Metamorphic Tales* (Borgo Press, 2009).

_____. *In the Flesh and Other Tales of the Biotech Revolution* (Borgo Press, 2009).

_____. *The Cosmic Perspective and Other Black Comedies* (Borgo Press, 2009).

_____. *The Best of Both Worlds and Other Ambiguous Tales* (Borgo Press, 2009).

_____. *The Great Chain of Being and Other Tales of the Biotech Revolution* (Borgo Press, 2009).

_____. *Beyond the Colors of Darkness and Other Exotica* (Borgo Press, 2009).

_____. *The Return of the Djinn and Other Black Melodramas* (Borgo Press, 2009).

_____. *Le Fleurs du Mal/The Undead* (Borgo Press, 2010).

_____. *The Womb of Time* (Perilous Press, 2011).

Chapters and Periodicals

Byron, Glennis. "Gothic in the 1890s." In *A Companion to the Gothic*, edited by David Punter (Malden, MA: Blackwell Publishers, 1999), 132-141

_____. "Bram Stoker's Gothic and the Resources of Science." *Critical Survey* 19, no. 2 (2007): 48-62

_____. "'Where Meaning Collapses': Tunku Halim's *Dark Demon Rising* and the Global Gothic." In *Asian Gothic: Essays on Film, Literature, and Anime*, edited by Andrew Ng Hock Soon (Jefferson, NC: McFarland and Company, 2008): 32-45

Cooper, L. Andrew. "The Indulgence of Critique: Relocating the Sadistic Voyeur in Dario Argento's Opera." *The Quarterly Review of Film and Video* 22, no. 1 (January-March 2005)

_____. "Gothic Threats: The Role of Danger in the Critical Evaluation of *The Monk* and *The Mysteries of Udolpho*." *Gothic Studies* 8, no. 2 (November 2006).

Hand, Richard J. "Dissecting the Gash: Sexual Horror in the 1980s and the Manga of Suehiro Maruo." *M/C: A Journal of Media and Culture* 7, no. 4 (October 2004): <http://www.media-culture.org.au/0410/05_horror.php>

_____. "Proliferating Horrors: Survival Horror and the Resident Evil Franchise." In *Horror Film: Marketing and Creating Fear*, edited by Steffen Hantke (Jackson: University of Mississippi Press, 2004)

_____."Aesthetics of Cruelty: Traditional Japanese Theatre and the Horror Film." In *Japanese Horror Cinema*, edited by Jay McRoy (Edinburgh, UK: University of Edinburgh Press, 2005)

_____. "Horror, History and Homage: Ulli Lommel's *The Tenderness of Wolves*" in *Caligari's Grandchildren: Contemporary German Horror Film*, edited by Steffen Hantke (Lanham, MD: Scarecrow Press, 2007)

_____. "Paradigms of Metamorphosis and Transmutation: Thomas Edison's Frankenstein and John Barrymore's Jekyll and Hyde." In *Monstrous Adaptations: Generic and Thematic Transmutations in Horror Film*, edited by Richard J. Hand and Jay McRoy (Manchester, UK: Manchester University Press, 2007)

_____. "'Stay Tuned for Tricks, Treats and Terror': Halloween and Horror Radio in the Era of American Live Broadcasting." In *Treat or Trick? Halloween in a Globalising World*, edited by Hugh O'Connell and Malcolm Foley (Newcastle upon Tyne, UK: Cambridge Scholars Publishing, 2009)

_____. "Captured Ghosts: Horror Acting in the 1970s in British Television Drama." In *Genre and Performance: Film and Television*, edited by Christine Cornea (Manchester: Manchester University Press, 2010)

Hantke, Steffen. "Historicizing the Bush Years: Politics, Horror Film, and Francis Lawrence's *I Am Legend*." In *Horror After 9/11*, edited by Aviva Briefel and Sam J. Miller (Austin: University of Texas Press, 2011)

_____. "Bush's America and the Return of Cold War Science Fiction: Alien Invasion in *Invasion*, *Threshold*, and *Surface*." *The Journal of Popular Film & Television* 38, no. 3 (Fall 2010): 143-151

_____. "Flirting with Subversion: Mainstream Filmmaking, Transgression, and the Case of Joel Schumacher's *8MM*." In *Cinema Inferno: Celluloid Explosions from the Cultural Margins*, edited by Robert G. Weiner and John Cline (Lanham, MD: Scarecrow Press, 2010)

_____. "The Return of the Giant Creature: Cloverfield and the Political Opposition to the War on Terror." *Extrapolation* 51, no. 2 (Fall 2010): 235-257

_____. "The Military Horror Film: Speculations on a Hybrid Genre." *The Journal of Popular Culture* 43, no. 4 (July 2010): 701-719

_____. "The Aesthetics of Affect in Horror Films and the Shot-by-Shot Remakes of *Psycho* and *Funny Games*." *English Language Notes* 48, no. 1 (Spring/Summer 2010): 113-129

_____. "On the Acceleration of the Undead: Paradigm Change in the American Zombie Film." *Jura Gentium Cinema: Cinema and Globalization*. JGCinema.org. February 18, 2010. <http://www.jgcinema.com/single.php?sl=Horror-Fear-Capitalism-Market>

_____. "Counting Down: The Elimination Plot in Horror Film and Beyond." *StoryTelling: A Critical Journal of Popular Narrative* (Summer 2009): 19-37

_____. "In Plain View: The Body as Site of Detection and Inscription in Serial Killer Narratives." *Caligari: German Journal of Horror Studies* (June 2, 2009): <http://www.caligari-online.de/?p=362>

_____. "The Decline of the Literary Horror Market in the 1990s and Dell's Abyss Series." *The Journal of Popular Culture* 41, no. 1(February 2008): 56-70

_____. "Whistling Past the Graveyard: Academics, Horror Film, and the Price of Scholarship. In *The Frankenstein Set* (Zurich: JRP/Ringier, 2007), 275-293

_____. "Out from the Realist Underground; or, The Baron of Blood Visits Cannes: Recursive and Self-Reflexive Patterns in David Cronenberg's *Videodrome* and *eXistenZ*." In *Monstrous Adaptations: Generic and Thematic Mutations in Horror Film*, edited by Richard J. Hand and Jay McRoy (Manchester: Manchester University Press, 2007), 67-82

_____. "Genre and Authorship in David Cronenberg's Adaptation of William Burroughs' *Naked Lunch*." In *Twentieth Century American Fiction on Screen*, edited by R. Barton Palmer (Cambridge: Cambridge University Press, 2007), 164-79

_____. "Dead Center: Berlin, the Postmodern Gothic, and Norman Ohler's *Mitte*." *Studies in Twentieth and Twenty-First Century Literature* 30, no. 6 (Summer 2007): 306-333

_____. "Consuming the Impossible Body: Horror Film and the Spectacle of Cinematic Special Effects." *Paradoxa: Studies in World Literary Genres* 20 (Fall 2006): 66-80

_____. "The Dialogue with American Popular Culture in Two German Films about the Serial Killer." *Horror International*: *Contemporary Approaches to Film and Television*, Steven Jay Schneider and Tony Williams (Detroit: Wayne State University Press, 2005), 56-83

_____. "Japanese Horror Under Western Eyes: Social Class and Global Culture in Takeshi Miike's *Audition*." In *Japanese Horror Cinema*, edited by Jay McRoy (Edinburgh: Edinburgh University Press, 2005) 54-66

_____. "Spectacular Optics: The Deployment of Special Effects in David Cronenberg's Films." *Film Criticism* 29, no. 2 (Winter 2004-05): 34-53

_____. "Horror Film and the Historical Uncanny: The New Germany in Stefan Ruzowitzky's *Anatomie*." *College Literature* 31, no. 2 (Spring 2004): 117-142

_____. "The Best of Horror: Thoughts on the Formation of a Horror Canon." *Studies in Modern Horror: A Scholarly Journal for the Study of Contemporary Weird Fiction* 2 (Spring 2004): 18-26

_____. "Monstrosity without a Body: Representational Strategies in the Popular Serial Killer Film." *PostScript: Essays in Film and the Humanities* 22, no. 2 (Winter/Spring 2003): 34-55

_____. "In the Belly of the Mechanical Beast: Technological Environments in the *Alien* Films." *Journal of Popular Culture* 36, no. 3 (January 2003): 518-546

_____. "The Origins of Violence in a Peaceful Society." *Kinoeye: A Forthnightly Journal of Film in the NewEurope*. 3, no. 6 (May 26, 2003). <207.68.164.250/cgibin/linkrd?_lang=EN&lah=4592907457dbc20c8a6c2b7b98736110&lat=1054428579&hm___action=http%3a%2f%2fwww%2ekinoeye%2eorg%2f>

Hutchings, Peter. "The Amicus House of Horror." In *British Horror Cinema*, edited by Steve Chibnall and Julian Petley (London: Routledge, 2001)

_____. "The Problem of British Horror." In *The Horror Film Reader*, edited by Mark Jancovich (London: Routledge, 2002)

_____. "The Argento Effect." In *Defining Cult Movies: The Cultural Politics of Oppositional Taste*, edited by Mark Jancovich, Antonio Lázaro Reboll, Julian Stringer, and Andrew Willis (Manchester: Manchester University Press, 2003)

_____. "Uncanny Landscapes in British Film and Television." *Visual Culture in Britain* 5, no. 2 (2004)

_____. "Theatres of Blood: Shakespeare and Horror Cinema." In *Gothic Shakespeare*, edited by *Dale Townsend and John Drakakis* (London: Routledge, 2008)

_____. "Monster Legacies: Memory, Technology and Horror History." In *The Shifting Definitions of Genre: Essays on Labeling Films, Television Shows, and Media*, edited by Lincoln Geraghty and Mark Jancovich (Jefferson, NC: McFarland Press, 2008)

_____. "American Vampires in Britain: Richard Matheson's *I Am Legend* and Hammer's *The Night Creatures*." In *Sights Unseen: Unfinished British Films*, edited by Dan North (Newcastle, UK: Cambridge Scholars Publishing, 2008)

Miller, Elizabeth. "Getting to Know the Un-dead". In *Vampires: Myths and Metaphors of Enduring Evil,* edited by Peter Day (Amsterdam: Rodopi, 2006), 3-19

_____. "(Un)tot auf ewig? Hundert Jahre Dracula und kein Ende." In *Draculas Wiederkehr*, edited by T. LeBlanc, C. Ruthner, and B. Twrsnick (Germany: Wetzlar, 2003) 9-27

_____. "Vampire Hunting in Transylvania." *Newfoundland Quarterly* (December 2002): 33-35

_____. "Shapeshifting *Dracula*: The Abridged Edition of 1901." In *The Fantastic Vampire*, edited by James Craig Holte (Santa Barbara, CA: Greenwood Press, 2002), 3-9

_____. "Back to the Basics: Re-Examining Stoker's Sources for Dracula." *Journal of the Fantastic in the Arts* 10, no. 2 (1999): 187-196

_____. "Bats, Vampires and Dracula." *The Night Flyer: News for the Friends of Florida's Bats* 3, no. 4 (Fall 1998): 1-3

_____. "The Transylvanian Society of Dracula." In *Bram Stoker's Dracula: Sucking Through the Century*, edited by Carol M. Davison (Toronto, ON: Dundurn Press, 1997)

_____. "Dracula: The History of Myth and the Myth of History." *Journal of the Dark,* no. 9 (Spring 1997)

_____. "A Genese do Conde Dracula," translated into Portuguese by Carla C. Periera Gonzales. *Megalon* no. 43 (February 1997)

_____. "Frankenstein and Dracula: A Question of Influence." In *Visions of the Fantastic*, edited by Allienne Becker (Santa Barbara, CA: Greenwood Press, 1996)

_____. Foreword to *Lord of the Vampires,* by Jeanne Kalogridis (New York: Delacorte Press, 1996)

_____. "The Genesis of Count Dracula." *Lumea* (Bucharest, Romania) (September 1996)

_____. "Vampires for the Nineties." *Pro Cinema* (Bucharest, Romania) (August 1996)

_____. "Review of *Gothic Bodies* by Steven Bruhm." *English Studies in Canada* (March 1996)

_____. "The Genesis of Dracula." *Transylvanian Journal: Dracula and Vampire Studies* (October 1995)

_____. "The World Dracula Congress." *Locus* (August 1995)

_____. "Narrative Strategies in *Dracula*." *Udolpho* (September 1995)

Morrish, Robert. Introduction to *Quick Chills II: The Best Horror Fiction from the Specialty Press*, edited by Robert Morrish and Peter Enfantino (Deadline Press, 1992)

_____. "Words from the Editors" (with Richard T. Chizmar). *Cemetery Dance* 35 (2001)

_____. "Words from the Editors" (with Richard T. Chizmar). *Cemetery Dance* 36 (2001)

_____. "Spotlight on Publishing: DarkTales." *Cemetery Dance* 36 (2001)

_____. "Spotlight on Publishing." *Cemetery Dance* 37 (2002)

_____. "Words from the Editors" (with Richard T. Chizmar). *Cemetery Dance* 37 (2002)

_____. "Words from the Editors" (with Richard T. Chizmar). *Cemetery Dance* 39 (2002)

_____. "Words from the Editors" (with Richard T. Chizmar). *Cemetery Dance* 40 (2002)

_____. "Spotlight on Publishing: Wildside Press" (with Richard T. Chizmar). *Cemetery Dance* 40 (2002)

_____. "Words from the Editors" (with Richard T. Chizmar). *Cemetery Dance* 41 (2002)

_____. "Words from the Editors" (with Richard T. Chizmar). *Cemetery Dance* 42 (2003)

_____. "Words from the Editors" (with Richard T. Chizmar). *Cemetery Dance* 43 (2003)

_____. "Words from the Editors" (with Richard T. Chizmar). *Cemetery Dance* 44 (2003)

_____. "Spotline on Publishing." *Cemetery Dance* 44 (2003)

_____. "Words from the Editor" (with Richard T. Chizmar). *Cemetery Dance* 45 (2003)

_____. "Words From the Editors" (with Richard T. Chizmar). *Cemetery Dance* 46 (2003)

_____. "Words from the Editor" (with Richard T. Chizmar). *Cemetery Dance* 47 (2004)

_____. "Words from the Editors" (with Richard T. Chizmar). *Cemetery Dance* 48 (2004)

_____. "Spotlight on Publishing: Marietta Publishing." *Cemetery Dance* 48 (2004)

_____. "Words from the Editors" (with Richard T. Chizmar). *Cemetery Dance* 49 (2004)

_____. "Words from the Editors" (with Richard T. Chizmar). *Cemetery Dance* 50 (2004)

_____. "Words from the Editors" (with Richard T. Chizmar). *Cemetery Dance* 51 (2005)

_____. "Waves of Fear" (with Richard T. Chizmar). *Cemetery Dance* 52 (2005)

_____. "Waves of Fear" (with Richard T. Chizmar). *Cemetery Dance* 53 (2005)

_____. "Words from the Editors" (with Richard T. Chizmar). *Cemetery Dance* 54 (2006)

_____. "Words from the Editors" (with Richard T. Chizmar). *Cemetery Dance* 55 (2006)

_____. "Words from the Editors" (with Richard T. Chizmar). *Cemetery Dance* 56 (2006)

_____. "Words from the Editors" (with Richard T. Chizmar). *Cemetery Dance* 57 (2007)

_____. "Spotlight on Publishing." *Cemetery Dance* 62 (2009)

_____. "Spotlight on Publishing." *Cemetery Dance* 63 (2010)

_____. "Spotlight on Publishing." *Cemetery Dance* 64 (2010)

Picart, Caroline Joan. "General Overview: Documenting Dracula and Global Identities in Film, Anime, and Literature." In *Draculas, Vampires, and Other Undead Forms: Essays on Gender, Race and Culture*, edited by John Edgar Browning and Caroline Joan (Kay) Picart (Lanham, MD: Scarecrow Press, May, 2009)

_____. "When Women Become Serial Killers: Undead Imagery in the Cinematic Portrait of Aileen Wuornos" (with Cecil Greek). In *Draculas, Vampires, and Other Undead Forms: Essays on Gender, Race and Culture*, edited by John Edgar Browning and Caroline Joan (Kay) Picart (Lanham, MD: Scarecrow Press, May, 2009)

_____. "The Compulsions of Real/Reel Serial Killers and Vampires: Toward a Gothic Criminology" (with Cecil Greek). In *Draculas, Vampires, and Other Undead Forms: Essays on Gender, Race and Culture*, edited by John Edgar Browning and Caroline Joan (Kay) Picart (Lanham, MD: Scarecrow Press, May, 2009)

_____. Picart, Caroline J.S. "Crime and the Gothic: Sexualizing Serial Killers." *Journal of Criminal Justice and Popular Culture* 13, no. 1 (Spring 2006): 1-18

_____. "Horror and the Holocaust: Genre Elements in Schindler's List and Psycho" (with David Frank). In *The Horror Film*, edited by Stephen Prince (New Brunswick, NJ: Rutgers University Press, 2004)

_____. "Hammer and Universal Films," *A Frankenstein Film Sourcebook,* eds. Caroline J.S. Picart, Frank Smoot, and Jayne Blodgett Westport, CT and London, England: Greenwood, 2001, 140-172

_____. "Women in Frankenstein Films," *A Frankenstein Film Sourcebook,* eds. Caroline J.S. Picart, Frank Smoot, and Jayne Blodgett Westport, CT and London, England: Greenwood, 2001, 295-308

_____. "Introduction; Frankenstein's Enduring Resurrections," *A Frankenstein Film Sourcebook,* eds. Caroline J.S. Picart, Frank Smoot, and Jayne Blodgett Westport, CT and London, England: Greenwood, 2001, xi-xv

_____. "Media Star and Monster: Imelda Marcos." *Women in Performance* 30, no. 15 (2006): 99-117

_____. "The Holocaust as Horror-Psychological Thriller Film: Working-Through Spielberg's Schindler's List" (with David Frank). *Film and History Annual CD ROM* (2003)

_____. "Humor and Horror in Science Fiction and Comedic Frankenstein Films." *Scope* (May 2004)

_____. "Hybrid Genres and Inverse Parthenogenetic Myths: Horror and Humor in Alien Resurrection." *Communication and Critical/ Cultural Studies* 1, no. 4 (December 2004)

_____. "Ripley as Interstitial Character: White Woman as Monster and Hero in Alien Resurrection." *p.o.v., A Danish Journal of Film Studies*, no. 16 (December 2003): 26-41

_____. "The Compulsions of Serial Killers as Vampires: Toward a Gothic Criminology." *Journal of Criminal Justice and Popular Culture* 10, no. 1 (Winter 2003)

_____. "Sadomasochism, Sexual Torture, and the Holocaust Film: From Misogyny to Homoeroticism and Homophobia in *Apt Pupil*" (with Jason McKahan). *Jump Cut* 45 (September, 2002)

_____. "Visualizing the Monstrous in Frankenstein Films." *Pacific Coast Philology* 35 (September 2000): 17-34

_____. "Remembering Within Remembering in Husserl and Magritte." *Philosophy Today* 41 (1997): 118-126

Senf, Carol A. "'Dracula': Stoker's Response to the New Woman." *Victorian Studies* 26, no. 1 (1982): 33-49

Stommel, Jesse. "'Pity Poor Flesh': Terrible Bodies in the Films of Carpenter, Cronenberg, and Romero." *Bright Lights Film Journal* 56 (May 2007): <www. brightlightsfilm.com/56/>

_____. "The Dead Things We Already Are: Pod People, Body Snatching, and the Horrors of Business as Usual." *Bright Lights Film Journal* 66 (November 2009): <www. brightlightsfilm.com/66/>

_____. "I'm Not a Dead Body; I Just Play One on TV: Buffy the Vampire Slayer and the Performativity of the Corpse." *Slayage: The Journal of the Whedon Studies Association* 8, no. 1 (Spring 2010): <http:// slayageonline.com/Numbers/ slayage29.htm>

_____. "Something that Festers: Silence of the Lambs, Texas Chainsaw Massacre, and the Visual Pleasures of Horror." *Bright Lights Film Journal* 71 (February 2011): <www.brightlightsfilm.com/71/>

_____. "Toward a Zombie Pedagogy: Embodied Teaching and the Student 2.0." *Zombies in the Academy: Living Death in Higher Education,* edited by Andrew Whelan, Chris Moore, and Ruth Walker (Bristol, UK: Intellect Ltd., expected 2012)

Waller, Gregory A. "Seeing It Through: Closure in Four Horror Films." *Proceedings of the Purdue Conference on Film* 7 (1983): 17-24

_____. "The Uses and the Pleasures of Horror." *Quarterly Review of Film Studies* 10 (Summer 1985): 255-260

_____. "Made-for-Television Horror Films." In *American Horrors*, edited by Gregory A. Waller (Urbana, IL: University of Illinois Press, 1987), 145-161

_____. "Tod Browning's *Dracula.*" In *Dracula*, edited by Nina Auerbach and David J. Skal (New York: W.W. Norton, 1997), 382-389

_____. Introduction to *American Horrors*. In *The Horror Reader*, edited by Ken Gelder (New York: Routledge, 2000), 256-264

INDEX

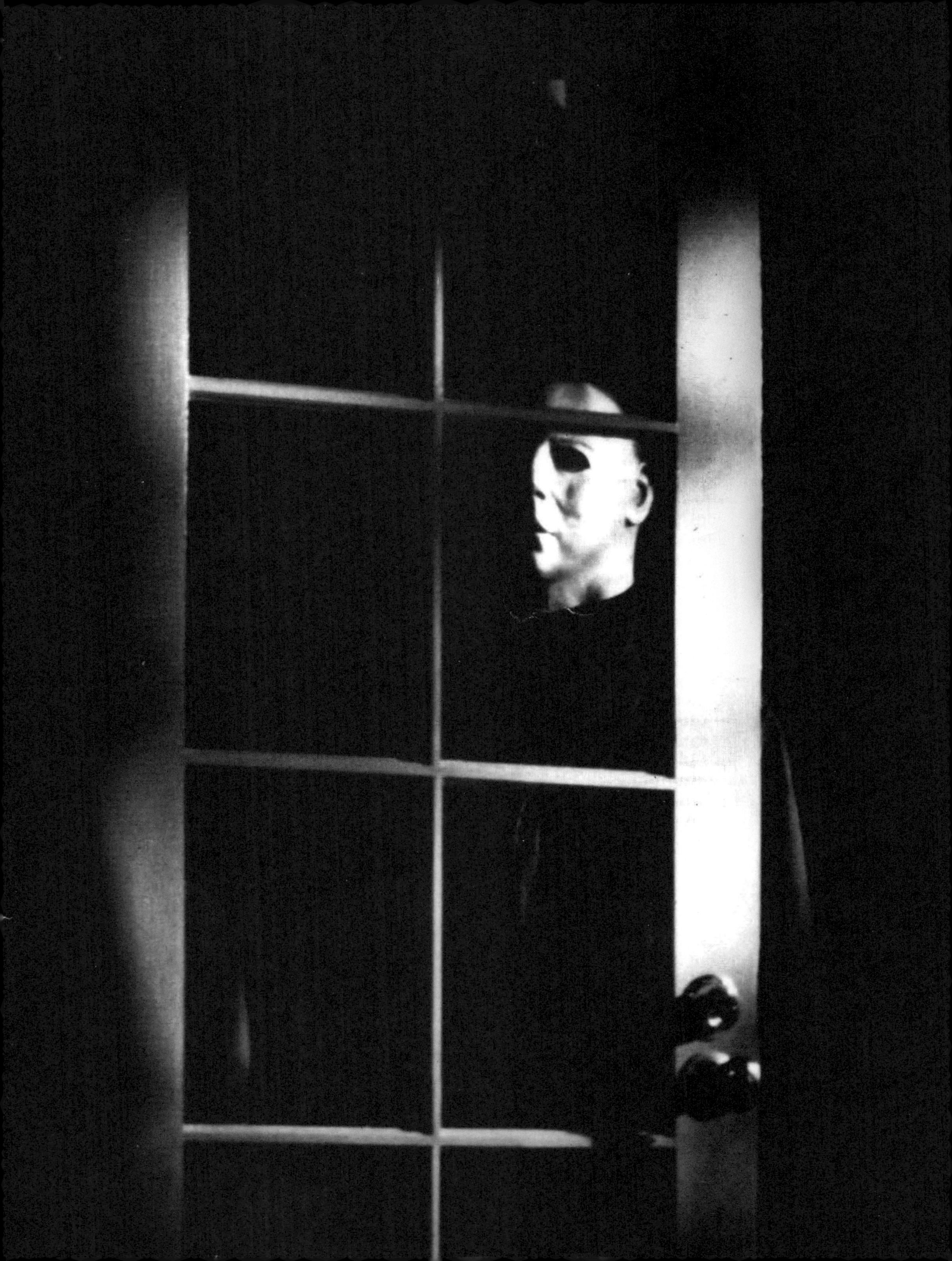